W9-DCH-824

THE HISTORY OF THE
ARMENIAN GENOCIDE

The Armenian genocide, though not given such prominent treatment as the Jewish Holocaust which it precedes, still haunts the Western world and has assumed a new significance in the light of "ethnic cleansing" in Bosnia. This study by the most distinguished scholar of the Armenian tragedy offers an authoritative analysis by presenting it as a case study of genocide and by seeing it as a historical process in which a domestic conflict escalated and was finally consumed by a global war. It also establishes a link between genocide and nationality conflicts in the Balkan peninsula and the Turko-Armenian areas.

This volume contains the results of twenty years of research and analysis and will no doubt be considered the definitive work on the subject for some time to come.

Vahakn N. Dadrian received his PhD from the University of Chicago and was Professor of Sociology at the State University of New York, Geneseo. He is currently director of a large genocide study project supported by the H.F. Guggenheim Foundation.

THE HISTORY OF THE ARMENIAN GENOCIDE

Ethnic Conflict from the Balkans to Anatolia to the Caucasus

Third, Revised Edition

Vahakn N. Dadrian

Berghahn Books
Providence • Oxford

First published in 1995;
revised edition 1996; second revision 1997 by
Berghahn Books
Editorial offices:
165 Taber Avenue, Providence, RI 02906, USA
Bush House, Merewood Avenue, Oxford, OX3 8EF, UK

Library of Congress Cataloging-in-Publication Data
Dadrian, Vahakn N.
   The history of the Armenian genocide : ethnic conflict from the
Balkans to Anatolia to the Caucasus / Vahakn N. Dadrian.
      p.   cm.
   Includes bibliographical references (p.   ) and index.
   ISBN 1-57181-016-1
   1. Armenian massacres. 1915-1923.
IN PROCESS   95-1611
956.6'200491992--dc20   CIP

British Library Cataloguing in Publication Data
A catalogue record for this book is available from
the British Library.

Printed in the United States on acid-free paper.

Acknowledgement
Material from this manuscript has been used for the preparation of an
article which appeared in *Yale Journal of International Law,* vol. 14,
no. 2, (Summer 1989).

CONTENTS

Part IX
A REVIEW OF THE ARMENIAN GENOCIDE IN A COMPARATIVE PERSPECTIVE

ACKNOWLEDGEMENT

Material from this manuscript has been used for the preparation of an article which appeared in *Yale Journal of International Law*, vol. 14, no. 2, (summer 1989).

ABBREVIATIONS

AA	=	*Auswärtiges Amt.* German Foreign Office Archives. Political Department 1A (Bonn).
Am.	=	American
BA/MA	=	*Bundesarchiv/Militärarchiv.* The military archives of the German Federal Republic, Freiburg im Breisgau.
Brit.	=	British
C. J.	=	Chief Justice
Cmd.	=	Command Papers, British Parliament, Session Papers
Cong. Rec.	=	Congressional Record
DAA	=	Diplomatic Archives of Austria, 19th Century
DAF	=	Diplomatic Archives of France, 19th Century
DAG	=	Diplomatic Archives of Germany, 19th Century
Doc.	=	Document
DZA	=	Deutsches Zentralarchiv. The archives of the former German Democratic Republic (East Germany), Potsdam.
ESCOR	=	U.N.'s Economic and Social Council Official Records
Eur. Parl.	=	European Parliament
FO	=	British Foreign Office Archives
For.	=	Foreign
F. R. D.	=	Federal Rules Decisions
G. A. O.	=	General Assembly Official Records (United Nations)
G. A. Res	=	General Assembly Resolutions

Gr. Brit.	=	Great Britain
Int'l	=	International
K. M.	=	*Kriegsministerium.* Ministry of War. Germany, Austria
l.	=	Law
L. N. T. S.	=	League of Nations Treaty Series
M. P.	=	Member of Parliament
N. S.	=	*Nouvelle Série.* French Foreign Ministry Archives (AMAE), Departments Turquie (Arménie) and Jeunes Turcs. Guerre: volumes 887–889, covering events relating to Armenia from August 1914 to May 1918 under the heading Turquie.
RG(L)	=	*Record Group,* U.S. National Archives, Papers Relating to the Foreign Relations of the U.S. 1915 Supplement World War I.
St.	=	State
stat.	=	Statute
Supp.	=	Supplement
T. I. A. S.	=	Treaties and Other International Acts Series
T. V.	=	*Takvimi Vekayi.* Official gazette of the Ottoman government, whose special supplements covering the proceedings of the Extraordinary Turkish Military Tribunal served as a judicial gazette.
U. N. T. S.	=	United Nations Treaty Series
Y.B.	=	Yearbook

A note on the use of dual track dates:

Because of the prevalence in the respective periods of the 20th century of the 13-day differential (12-day for the 19th century) between the Ottoman calendar, otherwise called *rumi,* Julian, or old style (o.s.), and the European-Western calendar, otherwise called *miladi,* Gregorian, or new style (n.s.), both variants have been adduced in connection with the narration of certain specific events for which purpose the slash mark, separating the two, has been used. See, for example, the August 14/26, 1896 date for the Bank Ottoman raid on pp. 36 and 138 and the March 31/April 13, 1909 date for the outbreak of the anti-Ittihadist counter-revolution in the Ottoman capital on p. 181.

PREFACE

The present study has two principal goals: 1) to examine the World War I Armenian genocide through the vast corpus of official Ottoman-Turkish documents, as well as those of Imperial Germany and Imperial Austria, Turkey's wartime political and military allies; 2) to subject that genocide to a critical analysis from a historical perspective. The wartime destruction of the Armenian population of the Ottoman Empire emerges from that perspective as the cataclysmic culmination of a historical process involving the progressive decimation of the Armenians through intermittent and incremental massacres. By thus emphasizing the historical dimensions of the Armenian genocide, the relationship of the genocide to the effects of the history of the Turko-Armenian conflict is cast sharply into relief. This procedure is in line with the main premise of the present study, that the Armenian genocide was but an attempt by Ottoman-Turkish authorities to terminally resolve the corrosive and lingering Turko-Armenian conflict. In the final analysis, it is the genocidal nature of the outcome of that attempt that is the key issue here, superseding all other issues associated with the evolution and escalation of that conflict.

An analysis immersed in such a gruesome subject matter often raises questions as to the motives or reasons of the author involved. I had always been interested in mathematics and its relationship to philosophy, especially epistemology. But a chance exchange with one of my teachers at the University of Vienna, Prof. Friederich Kainz, changed all that. Upon learning that I was an Armenian, he urged me to read *Forty Days of Musa Dagh*, a novel by Franz Werfel, who had been his classmate in school. Werfel had confided to him that the main reason he wrote that novel was to signal to the rest of the world, through the medium of literature, the portentousness for the Jews of the mass murder of the Armenians. The spell of that book, however tragic and macabre in its essence, had an abiding effect on my youthful mind. The asymmetrical configuration in these two volumes of such phenomena as human piety in distress, endurance, and heroism against overwhelming odds on the one hand, and inexorable cruelties, accented by the nonchalance of the rest of the world on the other, ultimately moved me to redirect my interests and concentrate on a new field of inquiry, namely, the victimization of a vulnerable collectivity by a powerful perpetrator group. It appears that under certain circumstances, ideas do still have consequences.

This book is the culmination of decades of labor, involving numerous research trips to Europe, the Middle East, and in North America. Therefore, I would like to take this opportunity to convey my thanks to a number of people who assisted me in this undertaking. The Public Record Office in London and presently at Kew, England, stands out in rendering this assistance. Its vast repositories afforded me access to invaluable documents on the Young Turk Ittihadist regime and its involvement in the organization of the genocide being examined here. My thanks go to Dr. Duncan Chalmers, Director, and G.H. Martin, the Keeper of the Public Records. I wish to thank also Mr. Douglas S. Webb from the British Library-Newspapers at Colindale, London, whose holdings of Turkish Istanbul newspapers from the Armistice period (1918–1920) were most helpful. I am also indebted to Dr. Christine Thomas, Head of the Austrian Foreign Ministry Archives in Vienna, and Dr. Kurt Peball, Head of the Austrian War Ministry Archives; both of them extended special courtesies to me in order to facilitate my research. The assistance which I received from the German Foreign Ministry Archives at Bonn, however, exceeded all other help accorded me. I was able to sift these repositories as thoroughly as I could in the course of 18 separate trips I made to Bonn in the last twenty years. The fact that Germany was the principal ally of Turkey in World War I, and the additional fact of German passion for meticulousness and orderliness in record keeping, combined to enhance my research substantially. I extend my warmest thanks to Dr. Maria Keipert who is in charge of these archives and who went out of her way to assist me in my endeavor.

The preparation of the manuscript was a major effort involving many people. Three of my student-secretaries at SUNY-Geneseo, Mary Standish, Miriam Sabin, and Jennifer Jones, worked on it meticulously over a four-year period. Though full-time undergraduate students, all three applied themselves to the task with dedication, which included typing on weekends. Two individuals were most responsible, however, for the final output. Mr. George Shirinian volunteered to type the first part of the manuscript and subsequently was instrumental in handling many of the administrative details of the production of the manuscript. The main and final typist, Ms. Ann Roach, helped bring the work to completion with great patience and dedication.

Finally, I wish to express my gratitude to two American foundations, each of which twice generously supported my comprehensive and protracted study, including my numerous research trips abroad—namely, The National Science Foundation and The H.F. Guggenheim Foundation. Though they are not responsible for the specifics of my findings and conclusions, I owe the materialization of this book to their decision to grant me the requisite funds to complete my study.

INTRODUCTION

If a man is killed in Paris, it is a murder; the throats of fifty thousand people are cut in the East, and it is a question.

Victor Hugo[1]

During World War I, the authorities of the Turkish Ottoman Empire carried out one of the largest genocides in world history, destroying huge portions of its minority Armenian population. That genocide followed decades of persecution, punctuated by two similar but smaller rounds of massacres in the 1894-96 and 1909 periods that claimed two hundred thousand Armenian deaths. In all, over one million Armenians were put to death during World War I. Adding to this figure are the several hundred thousand Armenians who perished in the course of the Turkish attempt to extend the genocide to Russian Armenia in the Transcausus in the Spring and Summer of 1918 and then again in the Fall of 1920 when Ankara's fledgling government ordered General Karabekir's army to "physically annihilate Armenia." The European Powers, who defeated the Turks time and again on the battlefield, were unable or unwilling to prevent this mass murder. Of even more consequence, they failed to secure punishment of the perpetrators in the aftermath of the war despite the commitment they publicly had made during the war to do so. The events of that time have subsequently slipped into the shadows of world history,[2] thus gaining the title "the forgotten genocide."[3] To this day, Turkey denies the genocidal intent of these massacres.[4] Such a scale of perpetration at the very least warrants a documentary exposure and examination. The results may yet impel the civilized world to show a greater concern for the depth of the anguish that has been tormenting generations of Armenians. It may even move the more enlightened segments of the population of modern Turkey to face the historical fact of the Armenian genocide and try to come to terms with it.

Over the past 80 years, the Armenian nation has struggled to have the history of the Armenian genocide brought to light and examined. Despite

---

Notes for the Introduction begin on page xxv.

the scope of the disaster, however, the international community has only recently officially recognized its genocidal character officially. In April 1984, a group of public figures (including three Nobel Prize laureates, among whom was the late international jurist Sean McBride) conducted, at the Sorbonne in Paris, "People's Tribunal" hearings on the Armenian genocide and adjudged it to be a crime of genocide without statutory limitations.[5] In August 1985, the U.N. Subcommission on Human Rights, which had been deadlocked for over 14 years, took note, by a 14–1 vote (with four abstentions), of the historical fact of the Armenian genocide.[6] Its parent body, the U.N. Commission on Human Rights, followed suit the next year.[7] Finally, in June of 1987, the European Parliament declared the Turkish massacres of World War I to be a crime of genocide under the U.N. Convention on Genocide,[8] and stipulated that Turkey, among other conditions, must recognize the genocide before the Parliament would favorably consider Turkey's application for membership in that body. The European Parliament labeled Turkey's refusal to do so an "insurmountable obstacle to consideration of the possibility of Turkey's accession to the [European] Community."[9] Moreover, on April 24, 1994, the wire services of United Press International and the Associated Press announced that "Israel issued its first official condemnation of the Turkish genocide of the Armenians, ending a tradition of silence to appease its regional ally, Turkey. Deputy Foreign Minister Yossi Beilin told the Israeli Parliament Israel would become part of an effort to ensure the world remembers the Genocide. 'We will always reject any attempt to erase its record, even for some political advantage,' he said. Rejecting Turkish denials of the crime and its claim that the incident was a "civil war," Beilin declared that 'It was not war. It was most certainly massacre and genocide.'"

The relatively low impact of the destruction of one million Armenians on modern public consciousness raises serious questions about the ability of the international community to prevent or punish acts of genocide. Many see the lack of action and reaction following the Armenian genocide as a critical precedent for the ensuing Jewish Holocaust of World War II. Indeed, it has been reported that, in trying to reassure doubters of the morality and viability of his genocidal schemes, Hitler stated, "Who, after all, speaks today of the annihilation of the Armenians?"[10] This precedential connection was raised repeatedly during the U.S. Senate's consideration of the U.N. Convention on Genocide, which the United States ratified on February 19, 1986. A score of Senators, most notably Senators Dole, Boschwitz, Proxmire, Lugar, Levin, Lautenberg, Riegle, Kerry, and Wilson, emphasized the historical precedent of the Armenian case and pointed to the enormous calamity of the Jewish Holocaust that resulted from humanity's disregard of the Armenians' fate.[11]

Nor were, and are, other victim groups in the post-Nuremberg world exempt from the consequences of the obliviousness to which the Armenians were subjected. Foremost among the series of genocidal massacres which stand out in this respect are those that occurred in Bangladesh, Cambodia, and the Kurdish territory in Iraq. In each one of these cases a state system was beset by the pressures of centrifugal movements and revolutions before being engulfed by wars. Thus, given certain conditions of simmering international conflicts, war emerges here as a catalyst for radical methods of conflict resolution. From the standpoint of international law, the central issue is the relationship between the concept of war crimes on the one hand, and that of crimes against humanity on the other.

The recognition of the significance of this relationship for deciding to initiate legal actions against the offenders is evident in the current U.N. efforts to come to grips with the contemporary issues of "ethnic cleansing." In its Resolution 808 (1993), the U.N. Security Council on February 22, 1993 unanimously decided to establish an international tribunal to prosecute and punish the perpetrators associated with the series of wars presently being waged in the territories of the former Yugoslavia, especially in the province of Bosnia.[12] The basis of this initiative was the August 12, 1949, Geneva Civilian Convention relative to the Protection of Civilian Persons in Time of War.[13] The idea is to punish, under international law, the offenders accused of crimes against humanity. However, if the history of the Armenian Case is any guide, the chances of a Nuremberg style outcome appear quite slim.

Even more significant is another, related, fact. As the present study proposes to demonstrate, the Armenian genocide was a by-product of the conflicts in the Balkans which were triggered through contact with Ottoman Turks who, as imperial conquerors, subsequently proceeded to subjugate the many nationalities of the Balkan peninsula. The emergence of the Eastern Question was an expression of the diplomatic quest for reforms in the Balkans, meant to alleviate the plight of the subject nationalities groaning under Turkish misrule. The abortiveness of that quest entailed a series of major conflagrations as a result of which, one by one, these nationalities delivered themselves from the shackles of Ottoman dominion, and the empire shrank considerably. The fear of parallel developments in Asiatic Turkey, where European diplomats were likewise preoccupied with the quest for Armenian reforms, which constituted the kernel of the Armenian Question, catalyzed the Young Turks to seek ways and means to preempt such developments. The emergence of a militant nationalism, bent on resolving the portentous Armenian Question through violent and radical means, was the result. In this sense the Armenian genocide is to be regarded as the manifestation of a historical phenomenon in which the problems of the Eastern Question and the Armenian Question converge and interconnect.

The failures that preceded and followed the Armenian genocide carry important lessons for present-day experts of international law and lawyers seeking to outlaw genocide. While the post-World War II trials in Nuremberg have shaped much of the current thought on the prevention and punishment of genocide, the trials resulted from a set of conditions that will rarely arise. Following World War II, Germany was forced to surrender unconditionally to the Allied forces. The Allies subsequently ran the German government, eliminating any claim of sovereignty that Germany otherwise could have asserted. Furthermore, seeking retributive justice against the Nazis served the Allies' self-interests, since the Nazi persecution was directed also at the Allies' own nationals under German occupation.

Unfortunately, none of these factors was present during or after the extirpation of the Armenians. Although the European Powers did pursue a strategy of "humanitarian intervention" in Ottoman Turkey during the years leading up to World War I, and instituted the concept of "crimes against humanity" in 1915 in response to the unfolding Armenian genocide, the Powers never shared the unity of interests that they had following World War II. Most harmful to the Armenians was the lack of a powerful state to champion their cause; thus, the victors of 1918, one by one and willingly, dropped their humanitarian concerns in exchange for enhanced favor with the insurgent Kemalist regime that was gaining control of Turkey. In addition, the Allies allowed the Turks to maintain their own government following the latter's defeat in the war. As a result, the new Kemalist government blocked efforts by the Allies to punish the perpetrators of the genocide by asserting its sovereign rights. While it is difficult to determine for certain, the recent history of killings in Cambodia, Bangladesh, in certain parts of Africa, such as Rwanda, and Bosnia indicate that the ineffective efforts at genocide prevention preceding World War I and the abortive efforts at punishment following it are more likely to be the norm than are the successes of the Nuremberg trials.

The truth is that the U.N. Convention on Genocide's classification of genocide as a crime under international law, while a positive step, begs the ultimate question of enforcement. Similarly, although the Nuremberg trials stand as a promising example of international cooperation in punishing acts of genocide, one cannot rely on such a complete convergence of interests arising in every case of a multipartite victory.

There are three main lessons that emerge from the events surrounding the Armenian genocide. First, nations generally will not be able, and thus cannot be expected, to effectively police or punish themselves. The post-World War I trials in Turkey, as well as those in Germany, reveal the futility of trusting domestic processes to obtain retribution for state-sanctioned crimes against humanity. The Courts Martial in Turkey are notable in that they documented the crime of organized mass murder against the

Armenians. These trials, however, resulted in only a small number of convictions under Turkish penal law. The political upheaval attending Turkey's response to military defeat impaired, and ultimately destroyed, the judicial proceedings' effectiveness. The Kemalist regime that eventually gained power in postwar Turkey successfully relied on principles of national sovereignty to reject the authority of the European Powers to intervene in the trials. Further, the Kemalists weakened European resolve in this area by manipulating the political tensions that divided the Allies. In Turkey, the rise of nationalist feelings following the Kemalists' victorious emergence conflicted with the purposes behind the prosecution of the accused war criminals. Accordingly, the Turkish government and people were unwilling to accept the stigma of collective guilt that was implied in these trials.

A second lesson, flowing from the first, is that groups of international actors cannot prevent or punish genocidal acts by another state when they do not remain cohesive and unequivocally committed to such ends. In World War I, the Allied Powers decisively defeated the Turkish forces. Further, through their May 24, 1915 declaration expressing their intent to punish the perpetrators of the genocide, England, France, and Russia provided a basis for international jurisdiction over the genocidal acts of the Ittihad government of Turkey. The Allied Powers, however, were nonetheless unable to secure retribution for the genocide. Instead, their efforts were splintered by political divisions, by rival imperial designs and economic interests, and by an inability, or an unwillingness, to invalidate the Ottomans' sovereign right to punish their own people for acts committed against Ottoman subjects on Ottoman soil.[14] This failure is not surprising. The international system, including the United Nations, often countenances acts of sovereign nations that extend to instances of organized violence and mass murder. Noted international law scholar Leo Kuper has explicitly addressed this problem:

> [T]he United Nations remains highly protective of state sovereignty, even where there is overwhelming evidence, not simply of minor violations, but of widespread murder and genocidal massacre. It is no wonder that it may seem to be a conspiracy of governments to deprive their people of their rights.[15]

The final, and perhaps most daunting, lesson of the Armenian genocide is that when international actors intervene in response to persecutions in another state without firm coordination and commitment, any actions they take may actually aggravate rather than alleviate the plight of the victim population. Through their humanitarian intervention in Turkish affairs during the late nineteenth and early twentieth centuries, the European Powers were able to force the Ottoman government to adopt a number of statutory provisions ensuring equal rights for non-Muslim minorities (such as the Armenians). These statutes raised the national consciousness of the Armenian population, who began to press for the actual implementation of these reforms. Unfortunately, the

Ottomans had no intention of enforcing these statutes; they had adopted them merely to appease the Europeans and thereby avert the dangers of a perilous confrontation with any or all of the Powers involved. The European Powers were willing to accept the statutes at face value and never truly attempted to force Ottoman compliance; nor did they offer the Armenians the military or political support that they would need to actually try to secure these statutory rights. The Muslim majority in Ottoman Turkey, who had long viewed the Armenians and other non-Muslims as "tolerated infidels," seized upon the new display of Armenian self-assertiveness, which smacked of defiant nationalism, as an excuse to rid themselves of the "Armenian problem." Thus, the humanitarian intervention of the Europeans, however benign in its original intentions, created the very conditions that ultimately led to the genocide.

By focusing in this study on the relationship between the principle of humanitarian intervention, loosely adopted and diffidently applied by the Powers, and the incidence of the Armenian genocide, certain distinguishing features of that genocide are brought into relief. They may be prefatorily sketched as follows. Unlike other types, the Armenian type of genocide is bound up not only with a history of conflict with the victimizers, the Turks, but more importantly, with a history of conflict punctuated by a series of intermittent massacres committed by the latter. One is dealing here not with an isolated phenomenon, but a palpable legacy of resorting to massacres as a weapon to deal with outbreaks of internal nationality conflicts. In this sense the World War I genocide could hardly be described as "an aberration" in the history of Turko-Armenian relations. The evidence of an established pattern of behavior, logically as well as empirically, precludes the plausibility of such a notion of aberration. It is more pertinent, therefore, to examine it in the context of a cumulative record of lethal violence applied against discordant subject nationalities, so as to determine whether this particular case of genocide was more or less an integral part of this pattern of behavior, amplified in its dimensions only through the opportunities afforded by a global war. In brief, the Armenian genocide has distinct historical dimensions in which, in many respects, it is prefigured.

One of the most abiding features of the series of massacres perpetrated against the Armenians by Ottoman Turks in the decades preceding World War I is the persistence of the impunity accruing to the latter. In itself, impunity in connection with any criminal act is a form of negative reward. However, when such impunity is sustained one way or another over a period of time in the face of recurring massacres, the reward takes on the form of new incentives, as it encourages the perpetrator to be incrementally bolder and more aggressive in crisis situations such as those attending the preceding massacres. Here one may find the nexus, the connecting link, between the relatively limited Abdul Hamit-era massacres and the 1915–18 comprehensive wartime genocide.

The critical significance of the factor of impunity is further explored in this study in relation to another aspect of the exercise of humanitarian intervention by the Powers. Even though punishment by definition is a post-crime undertaking, when projecting into the future, its failure to materialize has pre-crime ramifications. In this scenario, future possibilities of prevention become contingent upon past precedents of punishment. The fact is that one of the primary functions of punishment is, beyond retribution, deterrence through judicial intimidation. In the absence of such punishment, deterrence, at the very least, becomes a dubious task. This raises the question of the relationship between the Powers intervening on the one hand, and the regime being subjected to intervention by the latter on the other. This study will demonstrate that, by the very nature of its structural deficiencies, humanitarian intervention not only failed to discharge its intended functions, but in the course of that failure proved ineffective for nearly everyone concerned, especially the Armenian population of the Ottoman Empire. Two such structural deficiencies are closely examined in the study. One of them involves, on the one hand, ambiguities with which the Powers embraced the ideal of humanitarian intervention, and, on the other, the perfunctoriness with which they tried to execute that ideal in the arena of international relations. The other, closely related to the first, concerns the attempt by these Powers to promote hidden agendas while ostensibly pursuing humanitarian goals. This fact in no small way undermined and even crippled the very unity among the Powers that was a definite prerequisite for effective intervention, as it served to sow seeds of distrust and mutual suspicions among them.

The problem was further compounded by economic factors. Some of the Powers, especially France and England, and subsequently Germany, had enormous investments in Turkey, particularly in the fields of banking, public debts, railways, and import-commerce. By allowing these highly profitable investments to materialize, Sultan Abdul Hamit helped these Powers to become hostage to the grip of vested interests, which they could ill-afford to risk by intervening too effectively or forcefully. In a sense, therefore, these investments had become potential liabilities. Their inaction in the face of ongoing bloodbaths throughout the length and breadth of the Ottoman Empire in the 1894–96 period, and later in Adana in 1909, was to some extent a function of the high premium they placed upon these economic stakes. In the last resort, they had therefore to allow the sultan to survive and prevail, despite the massacres and the attendant decrepitude of his regime.

For all these reasons, the chapter on Manipulative European Diplomacy has been given broad scope. It seeks to examine in some detail the turbulent phases of interaction between the sultan and the diplomatic representatives of the Powers trying to come to grips with the Armenian Question, the associated Turko-Armenian conflict, and its lethal consequences. That chapter is keynoted by the delineation of the important role German Emperor William II played in the evolution and ultimate dispensation of the fate of the Ottoman Armenians at the hands of the Ottoman Turks during the reigns of Abdul Hamit as well as the Ittihadist Young Turks. William II was the only ruler-diplomat whose authority spanned all the periods during which the series of bloodbaths against the Armenians were conceived, organized, and carried out. That role is cast in stark relief by the fact that the culmination of all these episodes of massacre in the World War I cataclysm of genocide coincided with the wartime Turko-German political and military alliance, which was essentially forged by the emperor himself, and within the protective parameters of which the genocide was ultimately consummated. The sweeping compass of the annihilative onslaught is seen here as evidence of an unmistakable genocidal intent yielding this genocidal outcome.[16]

A final note on a specific category of sources and data used in this study may be in order. They originate from within Ottoman Turkey and her allies during World War I, Germany and Austria. Specifically, these sources include:

1. Secret and top secret Ottoman-Turkish state documents, each one of which was authenticated by ministerial officials before being introduced in the Turkish Court Martial Proceedings.

2. The preponderance of German and Austrian documents anticipating and corroborating the findings of the Turkish Military Tribunal. The importance of these documents cannot be overemphasized. As noted above, Germany and Austria were the political and military allies of Turkey during World War I. Their representatives' "confidential," "secret," and "top-secret" reports, mostly composed during the war for internal, in-house purposes only, have an authenticity and immediacy not matched by any other available category of sources and data.

Notes to Introduction

1. Quoted in Peterson, *Catholic World* 61, 43 (1895): 665, 667.

2. A prominent expert on genocide describes these shadows as "the United Nations memory hole." L. Kuper, *Genocide: Its Political Use in the Twentieth Century* (New Haven, CT, 1981), 219.

3. D. Boyajian, *Armenia: The Case of a Forgotten Genocide* (Westwood, N.J., 1972); Housepian, "The Unremembered Genocide," *Commentary* 42, 3 (Sept. 1966): 55–61 (published as a pamphlet).

4. *See, e.g.,* K. Gürün, *Ermeni Dosyası* (1983) (reversing victim-perpetrator roles in the Armenian conflict and denying Turkish genocidal intent); K. Gürün, *The Armenian File: The Myth of Innocence Exposed* (The English translation of the preceding work) (New York, 1985); Ş. Orel and S. Yuca, *Ermenilerce Talât Paşa'ya Atfedilen*

Telegrafların Gerçek Yüzü (The Real Nature of the Telegrams Attributed to Talât Paşa by the Armenians) (Ankara, 1983) (denying authenticity of telegrams reflecting central planning of Armenian massacres); I.C. Özkaya, *Le Peuple Arménien et les Tentatives de Rendre en Servitude le Peuple Turc* (The Armenian People and the Attempts to Subjugate the Turkish People) (Istanbul, 1971) (blaming Armenian revolutionaries for massacres of Armenians preceding and attending genocide).

5. Permanent Peoples' Tribunal, *A Crime of Silence: The Armenian Genocide* (London, 1985).
6. U.N. ESCOR Comm. on Human Rights, Sub-Comm. on Prevention of Discrimination and Protection of Minorities (38th sess.) (Item 57) 7, U.N: Doc. E/CN.4/Sub.2/1985/SR.36 (1985) (summary record of 36th meeting, Aug. 29, 1985).
7. It is significant that Whitaker, author of the report that the Subcommision based its finding on and a British expert-member of the Subcommission renowned for his judiciousness, took eight years to research the matter. See Benjamin Whitaker, *Revised and updated report on the question of the prevention and punishment of the crime of genocide,* 38 U.N. ESCOR Comm. on Human Rights, Subcomm. on Prevention of Discrimination and Protection of Minorities, (Agenda Item 4), 8–9, U.N. Doc. E/CN.4/Sub.2/1985/6 (1985). In a revised and updated report Whitaker made some corrections at the end of the Subcommission's deliberations; *e.g,* in note 13, he changed "1 million" to "40%." U.N. Doc. E/CN.4/Sub.2/1985/6/Corr.1 (1985).
8. Convention on the Prevention and Punishment of Genocide, Dec. 9, 1948, 78 U.N.T.S. 277.
9. *Resolution on a Political Solution to the Armenian Question*, Eur. Parl. Resolution Doc. A2–33/87, No. 10 (Armenian Question), 31 (1987). The resolution was based on a lengthy report prepared by Mr. J. Vandemeulebroucke, as member of the Parliament, who served as Rapporteur of the Political Affairs Committee that was charged by that body to investigate the current status of the Armenian Question and submit a report. After consulting a set of relevant sources and authorities, including Turkish ones, the Committee concluded that "All the acts that can be described as genocide under the [U.N.] Convention on the Prevention and Punishment of the Crime of Genocide (1948) were practiced on the Armenian people ... This accumulation of acts of all kinds and the large scale on which they were carried out strengthen the acquired certainty that there was premeditation." European Communities European Parliament. *Session Documents* English edition 1987–88. Series A, Doc. A2–33/87 (April 15, 1987), 20.
10. K. Bardakjian, *Hitler and the Armenian Genocide*, (Cambridge, MA, 1985), 6.
11. 132 Cong. Rec. S1355–80 (daily ed. Feb. 19, 1986). This historical evidence should be born in mind in considering the recent legislation enacted in the United States that criminalizes genocide under domestic law. In November 1987, a bill was introduced in the Senate by Senators Joseph Biden, William Proxmire, and Howard Metzenbaum, creating a new Federal crime of genocide or attempted genocide. President Reagan signed the bill into law on November 4, 1988. Genocide and attempted genocide is now punishable by imprisonment for not more than twenty years, a fine of not more than $1,000,000, or both. These provisions apply only to nationals of the United States or to an offense committed within U.S. borders.

   J. Griffin, Chairman, Section of International Law and Practice, and J.F. Murphy, Chairman, Committee on United Nations Activities Section of International Law and Practice, American Bar Association, made the following statement on February 19, 1988, before the Senate Judiciary Committee in support of the bill:

   > As familiar as are the historic examples of genocide against the Armenians and the Jews, genocide is a contemporary crime of shocking magnitude, and we must prepare ourselves to fight it— ... What is left to do is, somewhat surprisingly, quite simple: The international crime of genocide must be made part of the criminal law of the United States. In a word, we must formally recognize that which even the few opponents of the treaty must surely concede—that in the United States, as in the world, genocide is a crime ...
   > ... This is good legislation which should have been the law of our land 40 years ago.

13. United Nations Treaty Series, 75 U.N.T.S. 287 (1949).
14. When the Paris Peace Conference convened in January 1919, the first item on the agenda was the matter of punishing war crimes. For this purpose, the Allies created the Commission on the Responsibility of the Authors of the War and the Enforcement of Penalties. Citing Schooner Exchange v. McFadden, 11 U.S.(7 Cranch) 116 (1812)(opinion of Marshall, C.J.), the two American representatives, Secretary of State Robert Lansing (the Commission's chairman) and James Scott, a leading international law scholar, objected to the projected trial of the German Kaiser by the victorious allies. Arguing that such a trial would imply a measure of "responsibility hitherto unknown to municipal or international law, for which no precedents are to be found in the modern practice of nations," Lansing and Scott denied the Allies the right of "legal penalties" while conceding them the right to impose "political sanctions." Carnegie Endowment for International Peace, *Violations of the Laws and Customs of War: Report of the Majority and Dissenting Reports of the American and Japanese Members of the Commission on Responsibilities at the Conference of Paris, 1919*, Pamphlet No. 32 [hereinafter *Violations*]. The dissenting opinions are at pp. 58–79.

By the same token, the genocide perpetrated against the Armenians was excluded from the category of "war crimes" to be prosecuted and punished by the Allies. As Willis put it:

> Not until 1948 would genocide … be clearly defined as an international crime, and in 1919 adherence to time-honored notions of sovereignty placed limitations upon the scope of traditional laws and customs of war. The Hague conventions … [did not deal] with a state's treatment of its own citizens … . From this perspective, Turkish action against Armenians was an internal matter, not subject to the jurisdiction of another government.

J. Willis, *Prologue to Nuremberg: The Politics and Diplomacy of Punishing War Criminals of the First World War*, (Westport, CT, 1982), 157.

Yet as Secretary of State during the war, Lansing did sanction a degree of intervention, which he felt the brutality of the Turkish measures against the Armenians justified. In a Nov. 21, 1916 letter to President Wilson, Lansing granted the "more or less justifiable" right of the Turkish government to deport the Armenians, in so far as they lived "within the zone of military operations." But, he added: "It was not to my mind the deportation which was objectionable but the horrible brutality which attended its execution. It is one of the blackest pages in the history of this war, and I think that we were fully justified in intervening as we did in behalf of the wretched people, even though they were Turkish subjects." RG (L) 59, 763.72115/2631c; *Lansing Papers*, vol. 1, 42–43. As far as it is known, only once did William Jennings Bryan, Lansing's predecessor, issue explicit instructions to Ambassador Morgenthau in Turkey "to secure from Turkish Government order to civil and military officials throughout Palestine and Syria that they will be held personally responsible for lives and property of Jews and Christians in case of massacre and looting. This is required immediately." The occasion for this instruction was the rising tide of anti-Semitism in Syria and Palestine and the concomitant apprehension of organized pogroms during the war. RG (S) 59, 367.116/309a; *Papers Relating to Foreign Relations of the U.S.*, 1915. Supplement. World War I, 979.
15. Kuper, [n. 2], 182.
16. The research findings of this study, based on a detailed scrutiny of pertinent German, Austrian, and American state documents, reinforce this judgment on genocidal intent and genocidal outcome—specifically, when the fate of the Armenian populations of the port city of Smyrna (Izmir) and of Istanbul, then the capital of the Ottoman Empire, are taken into consideration. Contrary to certain assertions, the fate of the Armenian populations of these two cities was not determined by the good will of the Ittihadist perpetrators sparing the destruction of these Armenians through deportation, but rather through a set of exigencies that constrained the Ittihadists. In Smyrna it was the local German military commander who, through his threat of forceful intervention, persuaded the Ittihadist governor-general of the province to cease and desist from resuming "the massive deportation of the Armenians" of the region. As to Istanbul, a whole

German military commander who, through his threat of forceful intervention, persuaded the Ittihadist governor-general of the province to cease and desist from resuming "the massive deportation of the Armenians" of the region. As to Istanbul, a whole range of official and unofficial testimony, including Turkish testimony, clearly indicates that its Armenian population was anything but exempt from deportation and destruction. Official German documents demonstrate, for example, that at least 30,000 Armenians from that city were seized and deported by Turkish security forces. Other sources speak of regular round-ups, often carried out as stealthily as possible, in fulfillment of assigned quotas. These points bear emphasis because some Turkophile scholars, eager to absolve the Turks, both past and present, of any guilt and responsibility on the key issue of genocide are playing up the argument of these puported exemptions. This argument, which is effectively belied by the discoveries of the type of research alluded to above, simply states that since the Armenian populations of these two cities were spared, there could neither have been a genocide, nor a genocidal intent, in the incidence of the anti-Armenian measures launched by the Ottoman authorities; one may therefore speak of regional massacres resulting from a varity of causes, including "Armenian provocations." For a detailed, documentary rebuttal of this line of reasoning, see note 2 of chapter 14 in this volume.

Part I

HUMANITARIAN INTERVENTION BY THE POWERS: A HISTORICAL PERSPECTIVE

Chapter 1

Islamic Sacred Law as a Matrix of Ottoman Legal Order and Nationality Conflicts

As a first step toward a full analysis of the nationality conflicts, it is necessary to examine Islam as a major determinant in the genesis and escalation of these conflicts. The precepts and infallible dogmas of Islam, as interpreted and applied within the framework of a theocratic Ottoman state organization, encompassing a congeries of non-Islamic nationalities, proved to be enduring sources of division in the relationship between the dominant Muslims and the latter. In many ways that conflict was a replica and an extension of conflicts plaguing the relationships of the various nationalities in the Balkans with the Turks who, as conquerors, played the role of overlords towards these subjects over a long period of time. In this sense, it may be observed that Islam not only functioned as a source of unending nationality conflicts both in the Balkans and Turkish Armenia, but it also functioned as a nexus of the correlative Eastern and Armenian questions, through the explosion of which the issues of creed and religious affiliation for decades were catapulted into the forefront of international conflicts.

Although Islam is a religious creed, it is also a way of life for its followers, transcending the boundaries of faith to permeate the social and political fabric of a nation. Islam's bent for divisiveness, exclusivity, and superiority, which overwhelms its nominal tolerance of other religions, is therefore vital to an understanding of a Muslim-dominated, multi-ethnic system such as Ottoman Turkey.

The Islamic character of Ottoman theocracy was a fundamental factor in the Ottoman state's legal organization. The Sultan, who exercised

---

Notes for this chapter begin on page 6.

supreme political power, also carried the title of Khalif (meaning Successor to Mohammed, and a vicar of supreme authority) and thereby served as the supreme protector of Islam. Thus, the Sultan-Khalif was entrusted with the duty of protecting the canon law of Islam, called the *Şeriat*, meaning revelation (of the laws of God as articulated by the prophet Mohammed). The *Şeriat* comprised not only religious precepts, but a fixed and infallible doctrine of duties, including regulations of a juridical and political nature whose prescriptions and proscriptions were restricted to the territorial jurisdiction of the State.

These Islamic doctrines embraced by the Ottoman state circumscribed the status of non-Muslims within its jurisdiction. The Ottoman system was not merely a theocracy but a subjugative political organization based on the principle of fixed superordination and subordination governing the legal relations between Muslims and non-Muslims, and entailing social and political disabilities for the latter.[1] The Koran, the centerpiece of the *Şeriat,* embodies some 260 verses, most of them uttered by Mohammed in Mecca, enjoining the faithful to wage *cihad,* holy war, against the "disbelievers," e.g, those who do not profess the "true faith" *(hakk din),* and to "massacre" *(kıtal)* them.[2] Moreover, the verse "Let there be no coercion in religion"[3] is superseded and thus cancelled *(mensuh)* by Mohammed's command to "wage war against the unbelievers and be severe unto them."[4] The verse that has specific relevance for the religious determination of the legal and political status of non-Muslims whose lands have been conquered by the invading Islamic warriors has this command: "Fight against them who do not follow the religion of truth until they pay tribute [*ciziye*] by right of subjection, and they be reduced low."[5] This stipulation is the fundamental prerequisite to ending warfare and introducing terms of clemency.

The Ottoman Empire's Islamic doctrines and traditions, reinforced by the martial institutions of the State, resulted in the emergence of principles of common law which held sway throughout the history of the Ottoman socio-political system. The Sultan-Khalif's newly incorporated non-Muslim subjects were required to enter into a quasi-legal contract, the *Akdı Zimmet*, whereby the ruler guaranteed the "safeguard" *(ismet)* of their persons, their civil and religious liberties, and, conditionally, their properties, in exchange for the payment of poll and land taxes, and acquiescence to a set of social and legal disabilities. These contracts marked the initiation of a customary law in the Ottoman system that regulated the unequal relations between Muslims and non-Muslims. Ottoman common law thus created the status of "tolerated infidels [relegated to] a caste inferior to that of their fellow Moslem subjects."[6] The Turkish scholar N. Berkes further pointed out that the intractability of this status was a condition of the *Şeriat*, which "could not admit of [non-Muslim] equality in matters over which it ruled. [Even the subsequent secular laws based on] the concept of *Kanun* (law) did not imply legal equality among Muslims and non-Muslims."[7]

This principle of Ottoman common law created a political dichotomy of superordinate and subordinate status. The Muslims, belonging to the *umma*, the politically organized community of believers, were entitled to remain the nation of overlords. Non-Muslims were relegated to the status of tolerated infidels. These twin categories helped perpetuate the divisions between the two religious communities, thereby embedding conflict into the societal structure. Moreover, the split transcended the political power struggle occurring in Ottoman Turkey during this time period. Even when the Young Turk Ittihadists succeeded Sultan Abdul Hamit into power in 1908, they reaffirmed the principle of the ruling nation (*milleti hâkime*). While promising liberty, justice, and equality for all Ottoman subjects, they vowed to preserve the superordinate-subordinate dichotomy. That vow was publicly proclaimed through *Tanin*, the quasi-official publication of the Ittihad party. Hüseyin Cahid, its editor, declared in an editorial that irrespective of the final outcome of the nationality conflict in Turkey, "the Turkish nation is and will remain the ruling nation."[8]

The Ittihad's adherence to the ruling nation principle is particularly noteworthy because the Ittihad were not followers of the tenets of Islam. While the Ittihad continued to run the State largely as a theocracy, its leaders were personally atheists and agnostics. Mardin described this irreligiousness as follows: "Distrust added to disgust was their attitude toward institutional Islam ... [yet they saw fit to develop] a manipulative instrumental attitude toward religion."[9] Moreover, British Ambassador Lowther in a report of June 7, 1909, expressed the opinion that the Young Turk Ittihadist leaders' deprecation of the Koran bordered on "contempt" for it and for what it stood.[10] Morgenthau confirms this view from his personal contacts with these leaders. "I can personally testify that he [Talât] cared nothing for Mohammedanism for, like most of the leaders of his party, he scoffed at all religions. 'I hate all priests, rabbis and *hodjas*,' he once told me.... Practically all of them were atheists."[11]These leaders, however, recognized the pervasive influence of Islam in the country and resolved to exploit it in their plans to eliminate the sources of domestic nationality conflicts. A Turkish sociologist added, "Religion was used [by Ittihad] as a basis of agitation to secure popularity."[12] And the late dean of Turkish political scientists declared that "the Ittihadists had to embrace Islamism as an official and obligatory element of [their] ideology."[13] The Ittihad's actions reveal a central truth of the use of political power within Ottoman Turkey: actual power or influence within the Ottoman Empire could only exist to the extent that it recognized and incorporated the tenets of Islam. The following summary conclusion of the late dean of Turkish historians provides a plausible explanation for this phenomenon: "The Ottomans were unable to separate religion from state affairs, as has been the case in the Western world. Up to its very last years, the Ottoman Empire used religion as a leverage to control state affairs through the medium of *fetvas*" (religious decisions based on the canon law of Islam).[14] These tenets embodied an inherent resistance to change, rendering the specter of innovation threatening, and thus unacceptable, to Muslim subjects.[15]

Notes to Chapter 1

1. Bat Ye'or, *The Dhimmi: Jews and Christians under Islam*, 48, 49, 62, 67, 70, 76, 84, 89, 108, 140–41, 143, 154–56; Doc. No. 52, The Armenians, 281–88; Doc No. 53, Obstacles to Christian Emancipation 289–90, Jacques Ellul's Preface 26–33. D. Maisel, P. Fenon, D. Littman trans. (London, 1985) (Bat Ye'or is the pseudonym of Y. Masriya).
2. *Koran* ch. 47, verse 4; ch. 9, verse 125; ch, 2, verse 211; ch. 3, verses 10, 13, 14, 131; ch. 8, verse 12; ch 9, verses 29, 38, and 41.
3. *Ibid.*, ch. 2, verse 256.
4. *Ibid.*, Ch. 9, verse 73.
5. *Ibid.*, ch. 9, verse 29. See also C.E. Bosworth, "The concept of Dhimma in early Islam." In *Christians and Jews in the Ottoman Empire*, edited by B. Braude and B. Lewis. vol. 1 (New York, 1982), 41.
6. H. Gibb & H. Bowen, *Islamic Society and the West* vol. 1:2 (Oxford, 1962), 208.
7. N. Berkes, *The Development of Secularism in Turkey* (Montreal, 1964), 94. Nelidof, Russian Ambassador to Ottoman Turkey and a contemporary of the episode of the 1895–96 Armenian massacres, on December 24, 1896 diplomatically confided to German ambassador Saurma that "real reforms" for which the Powers were pressuring the Turks, and which fact in no small way had contributed to these massacres, "were simply not feasible." His rationale for this assertion was that, as seen from a Muslim religious point of view, no Christian or Jew could be granted a status equal to that of a Muslim, "even when the former submits to the latter. All references to equality are but appearance intended to deceive the European Powers." *Die Grosse Politik der Europäischen Kabinette 1871–1914*, vol. 12, Part 1, p. 245.
8. *Tanin* (Istanbul), October 25, 1908.
9. Ş. A. Mardin, "Ideology and Religion in the Turkish Revolution," *International Journal of Middle East Studies* 2 (1971): 207–08.
10. FO371/761/22020, folio /83.
11. H. Morgenthau, *Ambassador Morgenthau's Story*, (Garden City, N.Y., 1918), 20, 323.
12. A. Yalman, *The Development of Modern Turkey as Measured by its Press* (New York, 1914), 100.
13. T. Z. Tunaya, *Türkiyede Siyasal Partiler* (Political Parties in Turkey) vol. 3 (Istanbul, 1989), 144.
14. Yusuf H. Bayur, *Türk İnkilâbı Tarihi* (History of the Turkish Revolution) vol. 3, Part 3 (Ankara, 1957), 481.
15. As Leon Festinger stated in his general theory of cognitive dissonance, the existence of an opposing set of beliefs makes the individual less certain of his own beliefs. That individual then acts on his own beliefs more strongly in order to compensate for his uncertainty. L. Festinger, *A Theory of Cognitive Dissonance* (Stanford, California 1957), 263–66.

Chapter 2

Humanitarian Intervention as a Response to Nationality Conflicts in the Balkans

A major difficulty in rendering humanitarian intervention operational was the clash of economic, political, and to some extent religious interests of the Powers, particularly those of Austria, France, England, and Russia. As a result, these Powers at times felt constrained alternately to threaten each other in defense of Ottoman sultans confronting rebellious nationalities in the Balkans and in anticipation of rewards from the former. When Austria marched into Serbia, capturing a number of cities and besieging Belgrade, for example, the French, led by Marquis de Villeneuve, the astute ambassador at Constantinople, did encourage the Turks to respond. At the ensuing 1739 Treaty of Belgrade, Austria was forced to abandon all her territorial acquisitions, including Belgrade, which was retroceded to the Turks. France appears on the diplomatic scene as the first European Power which introduced the idea of publicly pledging to defend the integrity and independence of the Ottoman Empire. For two centuries the Austrians had been fighting the Turks while confronting France as an arch- antagonist in European politics.

Ottoman sultans did not hesitate to exploit these European rivalries; in fact they became unexcelled masters in refining the techniques of such exploitation. France for a long time operated as a singular beneficiary of the associated trade-offs involving a set of extraordinary and even exclusive privileges. As early as 1535 France exacted, for example, a set of concessions under a system of capitulations, granting it privileges in the domains of commerce, law, and religion. These privileges were periodically renewed until the outbreak of World War I when Turkey, allied with

---

Notes for this chapter begin on page 20.

the Central Powers, and thus antagonistic to France and the other Entente Powers, unilaterally cancelled them.[1] These very capitulations proved a bone of contention between France and Russia, precipitating the 1853-56 Crimean War. Barely a quarter of a century later, however, France sought the cooperation of Austria to curb Russian inroads in the Balkans resulting from a succession of Russian military victories over the Turks. The continuous cycle of these Russian victories eventually led to the signing of a treaty with Turkey through which the concept of "humanitarian intervention" was firmly introduced into European diplomacy as a device to mitigate Ottoman-Turkish oppression vis-a-vis subject nationalities.

Humanitarian Intervention and Ottoman Turkish Dominion
The origins of humanitarian intervention in light of rivalries among the Powers

The reign of Catherine the Great in Russia (1762–1796) coincided with the advent of a period of active European concern for the fate of a host of Christian nationalities ruled by the Ottoman State. In the Treaty of Küçük Kaynarca (July 21, 1774),[2] resulting from Catherine the Great's victorious wars against Turkey from 1768 to 1774, article 7 seemingly but not unquestionably (as explained further on in this chapter) conceded to the Russians a right to intercede on behalf of all Russian Orthodox Church members and, by extension, all Orthodox subjects (such as Greeks and Bulgarians). Pursuant to Article 16 of the same treaty, the Principalities of Moldavia and Wallachia, through the granting of a series of privileges became the immediate and direct beneficiaries of this concession.[3] Through Article 4 of the January 9, 1792 Treaty of Yassi and Article 5 of the May 28, 1892 Treaty of Bucharest, these privileges were confirmed, further strengthening Russia's interventionist leverage. Similar privileges were granted the Serbs through Article 8 of the Treaty of Akkerman, and Article 6 of the September 14, 1829 Treaty of Adrianople. Between 1774–1856, "Russia exercised in Turkey a veritable right of *humanitarian intervention*, albeit limited to the protection of Orthodox Christians."[4] Thus began a custom in international law that has been termed *l'intervention d'humanité*. Given the critical significance of this treaty for the rise and crystallization of the Eastern Question in connection with the adoption of the principle of humanitarian intervention, a brief historical review may be in order.

Küçük Kaynarca is a village near Silistria on the Danube (presently it is called Kaynarca, located in the northeast of Bulgaria). The political antecedents of that treaty provide an enlightening background to the future uses and misuses of the principle of humanitarian intervention and may be summarized as follows. With the substitution of the previous

Franco-Austrian conflict by the Franco-Russian conflict, the personalities of two key players, counterposed to each other, dominate the political landscape, namely, Catherine II (the Great) of Russia and Etienne Francois, Duc de Choiseul, France's Minister of Foreign Affairs and War. The latter was anxious to restore the eminent position of Catholic France in the continent, and Russia, the champion of Slavs and Eastern Orthodoxy, was considered an obstacle and a threat. Choiseul instructed Vergennes, his ambassador at Constantinople, to see to it that the Ottomans proceeded to oppose Russia militarily. Russian agents in this period were quite active among the subject peoples of Greece, Bosnia, and Montenegro; these people were led to believe that their deliverance from Ottoman dominion was at hand. In fact, Catherine II in 1770 went out of her way to rouse the populations in the Balkans to insurrection against the Sultan.

Vergennes urged Sultan Mustafa III to counter these incipient signs of rebellion by a preemptive strike for which the Turks soon found a suitable pretext, and on October 6, 1768 they declared war against Russia, accusing it of having intruded into Ottoman territories, i.e., Tartary, having violated Poland's sovereignty, and having imposed Russian policies upon it. The result was a disaster for Turkey, whose army suffered a major defeat on the Dniester in 1769.

At this juncture, England entered the contest on the side of the Russians whose fleet, commanded by the British Admiral Elphinstone, was sweeping down from the Baltic toward the Mediterranean and the Anatolian coast. French Minister Choiseul's efforts to stop this movement were countered by England, whose government served France notice that any act of stopping the Russian fleet would be considered a *casus belli*. Before the Turks suffered a defeat on land and sea, they exacted heavy tolls from the rebellious subject peoples, especially the Greeks, who, along with the Serbs and Romanians, were eagerly waiting to embrace the Russians as liberators. Aided by the British, the Russian naval armada attacked the Turkish fleet at Chios, decimating and forcing them to take refuge in the harbor of Çeşme where the whole fleet was completely annihilated by a fire-ship.

These victories at sea were followed by others on land. The Crimea, Moldavia and Wallachia (Romania) were captured and occupied by Catherine II's army. But once again a European Power, alarmed by the successes of Russia, came to the rescue of Turkey. This time that Power was Austria, which threatened to rush with an army to the aid of Turkey in the event the Russians crossed the Danube. An imminent Austro-Russian war was averted by the intervention of Frederick II (the Great) of Prussia, resulting in the partition of Poland. The Russo-Turkish war, still dragging on, was at last brought to an end with the signing of the Treaty of Küçük Kaynarca in 1774.

The epoch-making significance of this treaty stems from its intimate connection with the rise of the Eastern Question, of which the Armenian Question will later emerge as a by-product. The kernel of that question was the abiding conflict between Ottoman authorities and non-Muslim subject nationalities experiencing continuous oppression of many forms. The introduction of the ideal of humanitarian intervention into European diplomacy, meant to obviate the dangerous consequences of this conflict, served to raise diplomacy to new heights of manipulation. The nationalities, for whose benefit this ideal was embraced by the Powers, often ended up becoming pawns in the unfolding games of diplomatic manipulation. By the same token, Turkey developed its own game of manipulation by playing off the Powers against each other, thereby compounding the difficulties of the Powers in achieving truly humanitarian intervention. In the process, the subject peoples at times paid very high prices. The costly repression, in 1770, of the Greeks in Morea and the Archipelago by the infuriated Turks' severe punishment of the victims for wanting to welcome the Russians as liberators, was possible because in those hours of peril the Greeks were abandoned by the allies to their fate.

This line of conduct by the Powers will recur frequently, establishing a pattern in the handling of the Eastern Question and subsequently the Armenian Question. The broad outlines of the liabilities of the practice of humanitarian intervention were already visible at this juncture.

Serb Insurrection and Russian Intervention

As the conflict between the Turks and their non-Muslim subjects in the Balkans was pushed into religious channels, the Orthodox clergymen in Greece and the Slavic countries assumed a leading role in fomenting, as well as directing, a spirit of anti-Turk rebelliousness among the latter group. For centuries these clergymen had been functioning as the residual apostles of ethnic consciousness aiming at ethnic self-preservation and survival in an environment of domination by Turkish conquerors. The 1804 Serbian insurrection, though prompted by the infectious dynamics of the 1789 French Revolution, was the culmination of this process and, in a sense, the prelude to the subsequent Greek uprising for Hellenic independence. As the first instance of a major national insurgency in the Balkans, that insurrection was also a milestone in the evolution of the Eastern Question.

Nevertheless, there is a paradoxical element in this episode that must be singled out. The Serbs were not rebelling against the government in the Ottoman capital, but rather against the janissaries of the Turkish garrison in Belgrade, who had been terrorizing the indigenous population. Moreover, it was the Turkish chief administrator of the province who encouraged the Serbs to fight against the berserk occupants of that garrison, and whom the Serbs finally drove out in 1806. The independence the Serbs achieved was lost, however, in 1813, again, when the Turks, taking advantage of an opportunity, reconquered the land.

In this major setback, the Serbs experienced a daunting disappointment due to the vagaries of international politics and the attendant unreliability of friendly Powers. Like the Greeks before them, the Serbs were abandoned by their protectors, the Russians, who, through Article 8 of the 1812 Treaty of Bucharest establishing peace between Sultan Mahmud II and Tsar Alexander I, devalued the plight of the Serbs by paying mere lip service to their concern for that plight.

The brutality of the ensuing Ottoman administration triggered, however, a new insurrection in 1815, and in 1819 Turkey had to concede to the inhabitants of the Serbian province limited self-rule circumscribed by the conditions of Ottoman sovereignty. With the outbreak in 1821 of the Greek War of Independence and the successful military intervention of Russia, Turkey, submitting to an ultimatum by Tsar Nicholas I, signed the Convention of Akkerman, on October 7, 1826.[5] In that Convention Turkey made substantial concessions to Serbia which were tantamount to granting it complete autonomy. The terms of the Convention were reconfirmed in the Treaty of Adrianople in 1829,[6] allowing the Turks to garrison eight fortified towns within a district bounded by the rivers Dvina, Save, Danube, and Timok, but forbidding them the right to live anywhere else in the principality of Serbia. The liberties thus attained were quite extensive and were limited only by the tribute the Serbs were to continue to pay to the Ottoman suzerain.

The Greek War of Independence and European Intervention
(to avert a prototype of ethnic cleansing)

Russian initiatives on behalf of Serbia were acts which, in no small way, were influenced by Russian ethnic as well as religious affinities for the Serbs, who were seeking emancipation. In the case of the Greeks, however, different sets of circumstances were prevalent. The common identification with the Orthodox Church served to elevate the religious factor to paramount importance as the Russians advanced claims of protectorship over the Greeks in the Ottoman dominion. These claims were embodied and legitimized in the Treaty of Küçük Kaynarca, described above. But there was a historically lingering legacy surrounding Russia's relations with the Greeks as co-religionists.

The reference is to the ghost of Catherine II's (the Great) so called Greek scheme, forged in 1780 with the concurrence of Emperor Joseph II in the 1781 Austro-Russian Treaty. The Turks were to be evicted from

Europe, the old Greek Empire was to be restored with Catherine II's grandson Constantine (then only 2 years old) acting as emperor, and the Austrians were to be rewarded with the surrender to them of the whole western half of the Balkans. Aware of these Russian designs, the Greeks in 1814 founded in Odessa a secret revolutionary society, the Hetairia Philike, which was in close touch with the Russian government through the contact of two Greeks. One of these was Count Capo d'Istria, a member of that society, and Russia's Foreign Minister at the time. The other was Alexander Hypsilanti, the leader of the Greek insurrectionary movement, and an officer of the Russian army.

The first attempt at rebellion was made in Moldavia in February 1821 and proved abortive, as neither the indigenous Romanians nor the Russian Tsar chose to assist Hypsilanti, who was forced to flee to Hungary, where he was incarcerated and where he died a year later. But within a month the torch of revolution passed to and inflamed Morea and some adjacent Greek islands. With a ferocity betraying accumulated rage against their oppressor, the Greeks, vowing to extirpate them to the last, massacred the local Turks, who were a small minority. The cycle of violence and war that was unleashed in consequence engulfed the entire Balkan peninsula. The Turks retaliated by a series of acts which included the hanging on the dawn of Easter Day on April 22, 1821 of the Greek Patriarch as well as the archbishops of Adrianople (Edirne), Salonica, and Tirnovo. They then proceeded to massacre wholesale the Christians in Thessaly, Macedonia, and Anatolia. The reaction of the Powers, especially Russia, the guardian of the Orthodox Church, was swift. Russia delivered an ultimatum into which several stiff conditions and demands were incorporated and which were not met, prompting the withdrawal of the Russian Ambassador from the Ottoman capital, which signaled the imminence of war.

For their part the Greeks massacred some 10,000 Turks following their capture of Tripolitsa, the main Turkish fortress in the Morea. Having promulgated a constitution, the Greeks then declared their independence. The Turkish retaliation in April 1822 on the island of Chios was likewise swift but it was also massive. Some 30,000 Greeks, the entire population of the island, were punished, most of them having been put to the sword, while several thousand young girls were carried off into slavery. The Turkish fleet, which had captured Chios, was subsequently destroyed by the Greek navy led by Admiral C. Kanaris who, using a Greek device fashioned for maritime warfare, rammed with a fire-ship the Turkish Admiral Kara Ali's flagship, blowing it up with the admiral and 1,000 men on board. The rest of the Turkish navy fled in terror and took refuge in the Dardanelles.

Nevertheless, the Turks struck back by enlisting the support of their Egyptian vassal Muhammed Ali, "the exterminator of infidels," and his son (or stepson according to some sources) Ibrahim, who proceeded to exterminate the inhabitants of Kasos while the Turks themselves did the same in Psara. In his advance to Morea, Ibrahim continued to kill and devastate in all directions. Greece was on the brink of annihilation as the combined Turko-Egyptian armies pressed forward, attacking, besieging, and then capturing first the strategically vital town of Missolonghi and then Athens. In the end, however, the Powers, especially England and Russia, came to the rescue of the Greeks. By utilizing their land and sea forces, they finally defeated and subdued the Turks and their allies, the Egyptian vassals.

The jointly undertaken armed intervention by the two major Powers was a signal event in history in general and the history of the Eastern Question in particular, warranting a brief commentary. There is no doubt that the large-scale massacres enacted by the Turks and their vassals against entire clusters of Greek populations was a determining factor for the decision of England and Russia to align themselves with Greece. These Powers, supported by overwhelming European public opinion, were especially alarmed when rumors began to circulate that Egyptian vassal Ibrahim was planning to carry off into slavery all Greeks of Morea who had escaped destruction, and to repopulate it with Egyptians. The rumors, though repudiated at the time by the Turks, were later given credence by the statements of Stratford Canning, British Ambassador at Constantinople. The British even sent a naval officer to Ibrahim warning him that British naval forces in the Mediterranean would be ordered to interdict in order to prevent the implementation of such a scheme unless Ibrahim was willing to disavow it in writing.

This was a major act of deterrence in modern times, a kind of "humanitarian intervention" against the incidence of a prototype of "ethnic cleansing." The intervention was reflective of the powerful bearings of the then burgeoning Philhellenist movement prevalent in Western Europe, especially in England and France. A foremost exponent of this widespread devotion to—bordering on exaltation of—ancient Greek philosophy, art, and literature, was Lord Byron, who valiantly joined the ranks of the Greek rebels and ultimately sacrificed his life for the cause of Hellas on the battlefield of Missolonghi on April 19, 1824.

An exception to this trend of partisan devotion to the cause of Greece was Prince Metternich, the Austrian Chancellor, a fervent advocate of the principle of stability in Europe at almost any price. He considered the Greeks to be plain rebels endangering peace and tranquillity and spreading insurrectionary ideas in the region. Metternich tried to dissuade Russia from supporting Greece which, he felt, should be left to suffer the fate awaiting her. The predicament of the Greeks was further aggravated by an ailment, which was to persist throughout the modern history of Greece, especially in the episodes in which the Greeks had to confront the Turks militarily, namely, disunity and factionalism. This ailment also severely hampered the Serbs, who, in their struggle against the Turks, often lapsed into dynastic feuds, thereby enfeebling themselves.

The thrust of these observations is to indicate the emergence of a pattern of intervention by the Powers which is intimately connected with the history of humanitarian intervention on behalf of nationalities and minorities suffering various degrees of oppression and at the same time "infected with the virus of nationalism."

During the Greek War of Independence (1821–1830), a series of external attempts to end the war developed this theme of "humanité." England and Russia cooperated to secure limited autonomy for Greece under Turkish suzerainty.[7] This action was followed in 1827 by the Treaty of London,[8] in which France joined England and Russia in a resolution warning Turkey to stop hostilities lest the three Powers proceed to aid Greece militarily. The Preamble of the London Treaty asserted that this effort was intended to serve the interests of peace in Europe, but also to reflect *un sentiment d'humanité.*[9] While article 5 stated that the contracting parties sought no territorial advantages,[10] Turkey's refusal to comply with a subsequent demand for an armistice led to a new war with Russia and to substantial losses of territory in Asiatic and European Turkey. The war ended in 1830 with the complete independence of Greece. The Note of April 8, 1830, in which England, France, and Russia informed the Ottoman government of their decision to grant Greece independence, contained a reiteration of their desire to "fulfill an imperative duty of humanity in putting an end to the troubles which were devastating these unhappy countries … and in even consolidating the existence of the Ottoman Empire."[11] These purportedly "humanitarian interventions" were pivotal in subsequently ushering in Turkey's Charter, comprising the twin *Tanzimat* (reordering) reforms, instituted through the 1839 Act of Gülhane and the 1856 Reform Act.[12] By recognizing for the first time the principle of the equality of non-Muslims, the Act of Gülhane had an almost revolutionary thrust. Yet the decree remained, for all intents and purposes, "a dead letter."[13] This pattern was to be repeated in the future.

The Crimean War: A New Impetus to Humanitarian Intervention

As noted above, the 1856 Reform Act, a sequel to that of 1839, was the high point of a series of diplomatic and military initiatives through which constantly shifting new alignments and rivalries among the Powers pushed the Eastern Question into new directions. The main drive animating these Powers in their dealings with each other was their ever growing ambitions of hegemony in the Near East and of a certain degree of domination over Turkey as a client state. The involvement in the 1824-1828 period of Egyptian vassals on the side of the Turks in the Greek War of Independence complicated the relations of the Powers entangled in the vicissitudes of the Eastern Question; eventually, Egypt herself was to become a bone of contention.

While Russia was primarily absorbed in the core aspects of the Eastern Question, i.e., the ramifications of the minority status of Slavic and Orthodox Christian subjects of the Ottoman Empire, along with corollary territorial ambitions, France injected into the picture a new drive for hegemony in and around Egypt. This was in addition to its traditional concerns for the welfare of the empire's Catholic faithful, including the Latin congregations. It is at this juncture that England made a dramatic entry into Near East diplomacy, with the result that the designs of both France and Russia, described above, were more or less thwarted. It was Canning who, first as Foreign Minister, then as Prime Minister in the 1822-27 period that coincided with the Greek War of Independence, laid the foundation of a policy aimed at denying Russia the right of exclusivity of control in Near Eastern affairs in general, and the fate of the Ottoman Empire in particular. This doctrine was subsequently adopted and firmly pursued by Lord Palmerston, who, as Foreign Minister, established a tradition whereby a single Power, especially Russia, was to be denied a monopoly of this kind. Palmerston substituted for it the method of collective deliberations and actions in the form of some kind of a European coalition.

In this connection, Palmerston rejected proposals for the partition of Turkey, as he did not share the then commonly held view that the Ottoman Empire was moribund or that it was in a state of hopeless decay, a sick organism near death, as maintained by Tsar Nicholas I. The British stance instead aimed at preserving that empire's integrity, territorial and otherwise, and making that stance the cornerstone of the Turkish policy of the Concert of Europe. The adoption of this policy, later resolutely pursued by Disraeli, led to the discarding of some existing agreements, including that of Hunkâr Iskelesi, the terms of which, in 1833, had accorded Russia a privileged right of protectorship over Turkey.[14] This very policy produced, however, a discord between England and France, both of which, up to that point, had acted in controlled harmony in dealing with the problems of the Eastern Question. In supporting Muhammed Ali, Turkey's Egyptian vassal, whose ambitions threatened the integrity of the Ottoman Empire, French Premier Louis Adolphe Thiers found himself confronting Palmerston, who had opposed earlier French ambitions in the Near East, just as he had done in the face of similar Russian ambitions.

In his quest for a new European coalition, Palmerston managed to align on his side Austria, Prussia, and even Russia. Incensed by the double humiliation which England thus ended up inflicting upon France by way of excluding it from this new line-up of a European Concert, and by additionally imposing upon it the collective will of the rest of Europe, Thiers resorted to brinkmanship, risking the outbreak of a major European war. In the end, however, Palmerston's unyielding resoluteness, bordering on defiance, and Citizen King Louis Phillipe's yielding irresoluteness, combined to avert such a war.

This was not the case in a similar confrontation between England and Russia developing a decade later and ultimately erupting in the 1853–56 Crimean War, pitting England, France, and Turkey jointly against Russia. For England the central issue was the same: no Power should succeed in coercing the Ottoman Empire to become a client state; nor should that empire be allowed to break up and disintegrate altogether. The rationale of this policy flowed from a realization, commonly shared by both England and Russia, that the Ottoman Empire was obsolescent socially and politically and, therefore, quite vulnerable to being overrun by powerful states. Unlike France and Russia, England had no religious ties with any of the nationalities of the empire and was, therefore, relatively free from the burdens and temptations these ties engendered; it had no grounds to advance claims of protectorship over co-religionists. In this sense, England was in a more favorable position to befriend Turkey as a more or less disinterested party. That role came into full play in connection with the crisis that produced the Crimean War.

In analyzing the ramifications for the Eastern Question of this very costly and, in retrospect, rather futile European conflagration, one is struck by the confluence of a number of factors influencing the direction of the contests surrounding that Question. First and foremost is the surge of bellicose nationalism, fueled by elements of religion and religious assertiveness. France and Russia were on a collision course in this respect, on account of a conflict between Latin and Greek monks squabbling over guardianship rights of the Holy Places in Bethlehem and Jerusalem. France was pressing for the primacy of the rights of the former, and Russia for that of the latter. The antagonistic interests of Roman Catholicism and Eastern Orthodoxy, propped up by the antagonistic elements of secular nationalism, thus rendered a relatively minor contest both volatile and explosive. As if to underscore the religious dimensions of the escalating conflict, the other Roman Catholic states, namely, Austria, Spain, Sardinia, Portugal, Belgium, and Naples aligned themselves with France in support of the cause of the Latin monks.

Second, the personalities of the principal actors, especially their idiosyncrasies, impinged critically upon the ways and means through which they interacted with one another. This was particularly the case with (Louis) Napoleon III and Tsar Nicholas I, the two arch champions of the national liberation movements of the times and the architects of the disputes surrounding the evolving Eastern Question. The Tsar used his militant ambassador at the Ottoman capital, Prince Alexander Menshikof, to carry out his designs in Turkey. Napoleon III, driven by impulses of autocracy, audacity, and most important, a new brand of French nationalism bent on restoring the ancient "gloire" of France in Europe, but above all in the Near East, set out to reclaim the role of the champion of Roman Catholics. By the stipulations of Articles 33-36 and 82 incorporated in the May 28, 1740 version of the Capitulatory System,[15] France was granted certain privileges in *Les Lieux Saints*, as noted above. At issue was in particular the management of places of pilgrimage at Jerusalem and the Church of Nativity at Bethlehem. Through his ambassador, M. de Lavalette, Napoleon, in 1852, induced Sultan Abdul Mecid to reaffirm these concessions to France, thereby denying the Orthodox Greeks the validity of their counter-claims. Upset by this turn of events, disdainful of the pretensions of Napoleon, and propelled by his own imperial ambitions, Tsar Nicholas decided to force the issue. In 1853 he dispatched his emissary Menshikof to Constantinople, only to suffer a major setback as the mission with which Menshikof was entrusted proved counter-productive, in part because of the manifest arrogance with which the latter, manifesting his military background, conducted himself. He could neither persuade nor prevail upon the Sultan.

This abortive outcome was largely due, however, to the masterful role played in this drama by Sir Stratford Canning, whose cousin, Prime Minister George Canning, had appointed him Ambassador at the Ottoman capital in 1825, and whose diplomatic service in Turkey, with some interruptions, spanned several decades, starting in 1812 and stretching to 1858. Faithful to the established British policy of repudiating the idea of exclusive control over Turkey, Canning outmaneuvered Menshikof in the diplomatic corridors of the Ottoman capital, despite the fact that his original basic goal was to settle the dispute amicably and, if possible, to the satisfaction of the Tsar. But the hidden agenda of the Tsar far exceeded the modest claims he had publicly advanced on behalf of the Greek monks in Palestine. Like his mentor Palmerston before, Canning prevailed because of his unyielding firmness, matched by the pliability of the Sultan, eager to accommodate the British diplomat.

With this success England, paradoxically, albeit temporarily, achieved the kind of monopoly of influence in the Ottoman capital it so eagerly had been repudiating at the expense of first France and then Russia. This result was the more significant when one considers the fact that Canning had resigned in 1852 (after successfully enlisting the support of Russia in the Egyptian-Turkish crisis of 1846, when France had threatened war against England in order to assert her hegemony in the Levant) and was promptly reappointed as Lord Stratford de Redcliffe, with the title of Viscount. He personified the British resolve to prevent Turkey from falling into a state of tutelage to any of the Powers. That tutelage was in fact the principal objective of Tsar Nicholas II, who, in the spring of 1853, attached to his demand on behalf of the Greek monks the additional claim of Russian protectorate over the Christians in the Balkan peninsula. The refusal by the Sultan, inspired by the British, to yield on that additional claim while being accommodating on the former demand, and the rejection by Russia of a rather ambiguous compromise solution worked out by the Powers in Vienna in July 1853, led to the outbreak of the Crimean War in October of that year. That war was joined a year later by France, England and Sardinia on the side of Turkey, while the other Powers, Austria and Prussia, with various excuses, refrained from joining.

The peculiar circumstances of this turn of events call for a brief review so as to underscore the critical import of hidden agendas in certain diplomatic exchanges—specifically, the potent role of semantics in diplomatic parlance. The Russians were adamant about their interpretation of a portion of article 7 of the Küçük Kaynarca Treaty which stipulated "*une protection constante de la religion chrétienne et des églises de cette religion*," without specifying the Power to whose protection the Christian religion and its churches were being committed. In their efforts to hold off the outbreak of what appeared then to be an all but inevitable war between Russia and Turkey, the Powers—England, France, Austria, and Prussia— met in Vienna in July of 1853 and drafted their famous Note. In it they reaffirmed the adherence of Turkey to "the letter and spirit" of the Treaty of Küçük Kaynarca (as well as of Adrianople, 1829) respecting "the protection of the Christian religion." By thus retaining the semantic ambiguity of the terms of article 7, these mediating Powers hoped to pacify, at least for the time being, both Russia and Turkey. Russia accepted the Note within the meaning it attached to these terms, i.e., it was to exercise the right of protection. However, singlemindedly prodded by British Ambassador Sir Stratford Canning, who in this instance apparently was acting against the wishes of his own government, Turkey rejected the Russian interpretation and insisted on its own interpretation: the protection at issue was to be afforded by the Ottoman authorities and not by a foreign Power such as Russia. This was consistent with the Note Turkey sent to the Powers in May 1853 stating that it could never concede to a foreign Power the right to guarantee certain rights and privileges to Greek Orthodox subjects "without compromising gravely her independence and the most fundamental rights of the Sultan over his own subjects."

The stalemate, which amounted to a rejection by Russia of this Turkish interpretation as well as of the companion Turkish proposal to amend accordingly the clause in question, also signaled Turkey's rejection of the Powers' Vienna Note as it stood. Most important, encouraged by Stratford Canning, Turkey resolutely challenged Russia's claims and designs for a general protectorate over Christian subjects of the empire who were identified with the Orthodox faith and Church. That challenge culminated in the Crimean War which Turkey dared to precipitate. This notwithstanding, article 7 of the Küçük Kaynarca Treaty subsequently served as a basis for Russian exertions to compel the Ottoman sultans to yield to the Tsarist claims of a right to humanitarian intervention, if not a protectorate.

The 1856 Reform Act and its Denunciation by Militant Islamists

Toward the end of the Crimean War (1853–1856), which the Turks had precipitated, the Powers informed Turkey that, as one precondition for peace, it had to issue, of its own free will (*proprio motu*), a sequel to the Act of Gülhane.[16] Turkey promptly responded with the second Ottoman Reform Act of February 18, 1856, which not only reaffirmed the provisions of its predecessor, but forbade discrimination against and degradation of non-Muslims.[17] Satisfied with the new legislation, the Powers met at the Congress of Paris in February and March of 1856 and issued the Paris Treaty of March 30, 1856.[18] In this treaty, Russia gave up separate claims to a protectorate over the Christians in Turkey, and the Powers, through Article 9, expressed appreciation for the new Ottoman Reform Act.[19]

Religious fundamentalists and secular nationalists in Turkey, however, rejected the 1856 Reform Act. The Turkish people rejected both the idea of equality for non-Muslims and the influence of European powers intervening on behalf of the Christian nationalities. The success of Islam "in integrating the political life of its adherents" faced a major threat.

As a Turkish historian observed, statutory laws were inimical to "a number of practices derived from the Şeriat and perpetuated through the *millet* system [of religiously defined nationalities]," and the problem was compounded by "the intervention of the powers on behalf of the *millets* ... ."[20] Likewise, as Davison asserted, "large parts of [the 1856 Edict] had been dictated by the British, French and Austrian ambassadors."[21] According to a Turkish historian, the people lamented: "We have lost today our sacred national right which our ancestors had won with their blood. The Islamic nation that was the ruling nation [*milleti hâkime*] has been divested of this right. This is a day for weeping and mourning for the Islamic people."[22] Indeed, the European Powers' "humanitarian intervention" efforts in Ottoman Turkey severely clashed with the fundamental facts of Turkish politics. Derived from entrenched customs of long standing (*adet*), the Islamic common law principle of a ruling nation within the state directly conflicted with the egalitarian principles of European public law. While the European Powers succeeded in imposing their legal principles on formal Turkish law, continued Turkish adherence to the underlying Islamic common law subverted

the Europeans' efforts. Only a unified and forceful effort by the European Powers could have overcome the inherent resistance to change
within the Islamic culture of Ottoman Turkey.

Notes to Chapter 2

1. See E. Mears, ed., "Select Documents," in *Modern Turkey: A Politico-Economic Interpretation, 1908–1923* (New York, 1924), 438–447. For the cancellation of these capitulations see p. 444.
2. The English text of the treaty is in J. Hurewitz, *Diplomacy in the Near and Middle East,
   A Documentary Record: 1535-1914*, vol. 1 (Princeton, N.J., 1956), 54–61. The French
   text is in A. Schopoff, *Les Réformes et la Protection des Chrétiens en Turquie,
   1673-1904*, (Paris, 1904), 12–13.
3. *See* A. Mandelstam, *Das Armenische Problem im Lichte des Völker-und Menschenrechts*, Institut für Internationales Recht an der Univ. Kiel [Lecture Series and Mono-
   graphs] 12 (Berlin, 1931) 12.
4. A. Mandelstam, *La Société des Nations et les Puissances devant le Problème Arménien*
   (Paris, 1926), 6 [Special edition of *Revue Générale de Droit Intnl.* Publ.](emphasis in
   original).
5. See Schopoff, *Réformes* [n. 2], Text no. 10, p. 15.
6. *Ibid.* Text no. 11, p. 16.
7. This objective was accomplished with the St. Petersburg Protocol of 1826. G.
   Noradounghian, *Recueil D'Actes Internationaux de L'Empire Ottoman*, 1789–1856,
   vol. 2 (Paris, 1900), Doc. No. 37.
8. *Ibid.* Doc. No. 42, p. 130-34. This treaty was signed on July 6, 1827.
9. *Ibid.*, p. 131.
10. *Ibid.*, p. 132.
11. *Ibid.*, p. 186 (London Protocol of February 3, 1830).
12. *See* note 17 below.
13. E. Engelhardt, *La Turquie et le Tanzimat ou Histoire des Réformes dans L'Empire
    Ottoman*, vol. 1 (Paris, 1882), 142.
14. See Schopoff, *Réformes* [n. 2], Text 12, 17.
15. See Schopoff, *ibid.* Text 5, p. 5.
16. M. Rolin-Jaequemyns, *Armenia, the Armenians, and the Treaties* (London, 1891), v.
    This work is a revised version of two articles originally published in *Revue de Droit
    International et de Législation Comparée*, the organ of the Belgian Institute of Interna-
    tional Law, dated 1887 and 1889. No translator is indicated.
17. For the English texts of both acts see Hurewitz, *Diplomacy* [n. 2], vol. 1, 113-16 (1839
    Gülhane Act), 149-53 (1856 Act). *See also* F. Bailey, *British Policy and the Turkish
    Reform Movement: A Study in Anglo-Turkish Relations 1826-1853* (New York, 1970),
    277-79 (Act of Gülhane), 287-91 (1856 Reform Act). For the French texts of same see
    Noradounghian, *Recueil*, [n. 7], 288-90 (1839 Act); *ibid.*, 1856–1878, vol. 3 (Paris,
    1902), 83–88.
18. The English text of the Paris Treaty is in Hurewitz, *Diplomacy* [n. 2], 153-56; the
    French text is in Noradounghian, *Recueil* [n. 7], vol. 3, 70-79.
19. Noradounghian, *Recueil* [n. 7], vol. 3, 74.
20. N. Berkes, *The Development of Secularism in Turkey* (Montreal, 1964), 147.
21. R. Davison, "Turkish Attitudes Concerning Christian-Muslim Equality in the Nine-
    teenth Century", *American Historical Review* 59 (1954): 857.
22. A. Cevdet Paşa, *Tezâkir* (Memoirs), vol. 1, C. Baysun, ed. (Ankara, 1953), 68.

Chapter 3

Escalation of the Conflicts and Ottoman Palliatives. The Origins of the Eastern Question Foreshadowing the Armenian Question

Europe's Implausible Legal-Political Embrace of Theocratic Turkey

The discussion in the preceding chapter was intended to expound on in some detail the conditions and processes through which the Eastern Question began to crystallize itself amid criss-crossing trends of imperialism, nationalism, repressive despotism, and Great Power interventionism. Throughout these developments England played a paradoxical role. By insisting on the preservation and protection of the integrity of the Ottoman Empire it inadvertently provided an impetus to the escalation of nationality tensions and conflicts in various parts of the empire. Indeed, the result of that protection was the latitude accruing to Turkey to continue its practice of maladministration and periodic repression. The escalation of the nationality conflicts would, in turn, require types of interventions which at times were the result of a consensus among the Powers and at other times a source of discord and hostility among them.

As will be seen later in this study, the series of violent outbreaks in the Balkans and in Asiatic Turkey in the decades to follow were the by-products of these developments. Even the admission of Turkey, a non-Christian state, into the Concert of Europe and the allied adoption by Turkey of the legal system of European public law right after the end of the Crimean War did not help much. France had already proposed that

Turkey be admitted in 1839 when the first reform act of Gülhane was being promulgated and France was offering to certify the independence and guarantee the territorial integrity of Turkey. Given the fact that the governmental structure of Europe, in terms of public law, was first established by a small group of Christian state entities at the Peace of Westphalia in 1648, the admission of Islam-bound Turkey had already confounded the legal character of the community of nations in Europe. In fact, that European embrace of Turkey as a legally viable partner was reduced to distortions and inevitably to irrelevance by the manner in which a basically theocratic Turkey continued to mistreat its minorities and, in the process, became a caldron of explosive nationality conflicts.

Unless this point is sufficiently appreciated, an understanding of the Eastern Question, and therefore the Armenian Question, will remain inadequate. In the final analysis, these twin questions arose and ultimately engulfed the world in two violent conflagrations because of the clash of two disparate and incompatible legal-political systems. In Westphalia it was decided to subordinate the religious dogmas to the legal principle, thus consecrating secularism as the arch foundation on which to build the system of a family of nations. But the Ottoman Empire, for most of its reign, was, and remained, a theocracy, which, by definition and fact, cannot be secularized; laws that are predicated upon permanently fixed and intractable religious precepts cannot be modified, much less reformed. The late dean of Turkish historians confirmed this observation when he stated that, to its very end the Ottoman Empire basically remained theocratic. (See Chapter 1, n. 14).

Moreover, the issue here is not simply theocracy, but Islamic theocracy which, as explained in chapter 1 and further on in this chapter, is not only intrusive in the conduct of state affairs, as are other forms of theocracy, but it is also pervasive on account of its holistic character. Being a way of life that encompasses and seeks to integrate all principal domains of human existence and endeavor, Islamic theocracy not only permeates the fabric of government, society, and the economy, but also preempts religions and secular encroachments deemed invasive so far as the doctrines of Islam are concerned. Above all Islam constitutes an exigent framework of rules of law as well as laws which are meant to provide justice, as understood within the religious confines of the Koran—notwithstanding the many inconsistencies and incompatibilities among and between its verses. Altogether, Islam is not only a martial religion exalting conquest through war, if not holy war, but it is also a religion based on exclusivity in relation to "disbelievers." When assessed in terms of the core element of European public law, namely, the principle of universal equality, Islam, as portrayed in the Koran, and legally spelled out in the *Şeriat*, recognizes only "the equality of all Muslims," thereby asserting its exclusivity and its right of debarring non-Muslims from the set of rights incorporated in Western public law, especially political rights, and in a certain sense, civil rights as well. In the final analysis the problem is reduced to the implausibility of establishing a parity between two systems—one of which chose to separate the secular from the sacred, the other insisting on keeping them united and forever entwined.

The Massacre of Christian Maronites and a New Protocol for the Protection of the Christians

This mass murder, to which about 40,000 Catholic Maronites fell victim, and in the course of which more than 500 churches and 40 monasteries were destroyed, was the violent eruption of cumulative enmities brewing between the Muslims and Christians of the area now part of Lebanon and Syria. Once more, religious differences and their reflection in political cleavages had served to envenom the relationships of both groups. The religious issue had become a source of simmering trouble with the promulgation of the above cited 1856 Reform Act, which established the equality of Muslims and non-Muslims of the empire. Eager to benefit from the internal feuds and divisions of the disunited Maronites, the Muslim Turks and Druzes joined hands to seize control of the situation and establish their dominion over the former.

Alarmed by the anticipated international repercussions of the carnage, the reformist Turkish Foreign Minister Fuad hurried to the trouble spots in Beirut and Damascus with a contingent of 600 soldiers and a number of civil servants. He instituted at once restorative and punitive measures, as a result of which hundreds of wagons of stolen goods were returned to their former owners; culprits were apprehended, and following a series of special courts martial, 56 condemned men were hanged in the streets of Damascus and 111 were executed by firing squads. Among the latter group were the governor of Damascus, a colonel, two lieutenants-colonels, and three majors.[1] One purpose of this act of swift retribution was to preempt French attempts to secure justice.

Notwithstanding, the Powers, led by British Prime Minister Palmerston, gave France a mandate to intervene militarily. A French expeditionary force of six thousand men, half of the total of the assembled European force, which included a British fleet and a Russian warship, disembarked in Beirut on August 2, 1860 with the mission to secure peace and order. To avert a unilateral French intervention, which could enhance French influence in Lebanon, England had seen to it that its own fleet was on hand to offset such an advantage.

It is most significant that, in an effort to ward off this intervention by the Powers through intimidation, the same Fuad Paşa, prior to his personal intercession had darkly hinted at the possibility of an outbreak of anti-Christian bloodbaths in the region by uncontrollable mobs. French Foreign Minister Thouvenel dismissed this threat as unworthy of attention, arguing that yielding to it would create a precedent for stifling intervention against rampant governmental abuses against minorities. (See Ch. 7, note 16.)

As the Powers continued to admonish and pressure the Porte (the seat of Ottoman government), the incompatibility of Western law and Islamic religion had thus erupted in a major international incident prompting military intervention by the Powers. The Powers intervened, describing their actions as humanitarian in the August 3, 1860 Protocol of Paris. This intervention immediately produced the autonomy of Lebanon as formulated in the *Réglement* of June 9, 1861, and provided for the appointment of a Christian Governor-General.

The Agreement between the European Powers and Turkey outlining the intervention in Lebanon was termed *Protocols pour le rétablissment de la tranquilité en Syrie et la protection des Chrétiens*, thus combining the quest for "order" with that of "protecting the Christians" against massacre.[2] This formula conformed with the first paragraph of article 9 of the Paris Peace Treaty, but it was at odds with the second paragraph of that article, which prohibited interference in the internal affairs of Turkey ("*soit collectivement, soit séparement*") involving the "Sultan's relationships with his subjects" and his provincial administration. The text of article 9 states:

> His Imperial Majesty the Sultan, having in his constant solicitude for the welfare of his subjects, issued a firman which, while ameliorating their condition, without distinction of religion or of race, records his generous intentions towards the Christian populations of his Empire, and wishing to give a further proof of his sentiments in this respect, has resolved to communicate to the contracting parties the said firman, emanating spontaneously from his sovereign will. The contracting Powers recognize the high value of this communication. It is clearly understood that it cannot in any case give the right to the said Powers to interfere, either collectively or separately, in the relations of His Majesty the Sultan with his subjects, nor in the internal administration of his Empire.[3]

The Balkan Insurrections. The Emergence Among Orthodox Slavs of a New Breed of Muslim Overlords

These insurrections were the outcome of a complex process of interethnic and international relations. They evolved in the wake of the above mentioned diplomatic initiatives affecting the direction which the Eastern Question and with it the Armenian Question took. These initiatives had produced the 1856 Paris Peace Treaty on the one hand, and the subsequent corollary of it, the 1856 Ottoman Reform Act, the foundation of a new Turkish domestic or national law, on the other. The ability of the Powers to persuade Turkey, for whom they had sacrificed so much in their victorious pursuit of the anti-Russian Crimean War, to institute this Bill of Rights, the so called *déclaration des droits*, inspired the general hope that Turkey would be successfully integrated in the European system of legalism with a particular emphasis on human rights. Involved was mainly the task of harmonizing Turkish principles of internal legality, civil laws, for example, with external obligations predicated upon the rules of international law. The Balkan insurrections were largely the result of Turkey's failure to adhere to the conditions embodied in the 1856 Reform Act; that failure in turn entailed breaches with respect to the provisions stipulated in the Paris Peace Treaty which was an internationally binding legal document. The Ottoman regime, despite its formal embrace of *Tanzimat* reforms, continued to alternate between its policies of oppression and repression vis a vis the subject nationalities, about which European diplomatic archives are replete with detailed consular and ambassadorial reports.

The obstacles Turkey had to overcome in order to attune itself to a socalled European frame of mind were formidable indeed. As noted above, the deeply entrenched precepts and dogmas of Islam animating its theocratic form of government furnished a special dynamism to the subjugative imperialism the rulers of the Ottoman state pursued and fostered in relation to the non-Muslim subjects of the empire. The realization of this fact had already created at the start of the Crimean War a cleavage among the British political leaders, pitting Lord Palmerston against the royal family and Prime Minister Aberdeen. In expressing doubts about the wisdom of aligning with Turkey in the Crimean War, Prince Consort Albert, the first cousin and at the same time the husband of the reigning Queen Victoria, in a Memorandum on October 21, 1853, had, for example, disputed the claim of some British politicians that England was intervening in the war for the maintenance of "the integrity of the Ottoman Empire." Moreover, he also had voiced his and his Queen's despair about the abiding character of "the ignorant, barbarian and despotic yoke" of the Turks. When Palmerston took issue with this view, Lord Aberdeen retorted with an expression of decrial of the Turkish practice of issuing formal decrees under pressure without the intent or ability to carry them out, adding: "Their whole system is radically vicious and inhuman."

But it would be simplistic to explain the insurrections in question solely, or even mainly, by reference to Ottoman misrule and oppression. As has been noted above, there was the surge of nationalism in Europe and elsewhere, which, in the aftermath of the 1789 French revolution, rendered the Ottoman regime's abusive treatment of the nationalities in the Balkans a triggering mechanism. In its rudimentary stages, indigenous nationalism in the various Balkan provinces consisted of an expression of solidarity with the Eastern Orthodox Church as a bulwark against Muslim domination. That domination set in when the Ottoman Turks in the 14th century had overrun the Balkan peninsula ending the sway of the Serbian Empire and the Greek Empire of Palaeolog.

But the Eastern Orthodox Church, in one respect, was not entirely compatible with the emerging desiderata of modern nationalism. It had a universalistic bearing that transcended ethnic confines and national boundaries. The Balkan nationalities sought, however, a type of identification which was more or less exclusive and which they could call their own. Since most of them were of Slavic stock, Russia spearheaded a movement to bring about a Slavic Patriarch and thereby a new source of religious authority to attend the needs of the Balkan Slavs, mainly Serbs, Macedonians, and Bulgarians. Thus, on March 10, 1870, a compliant Sultan, through an Imperial Rescript, instituted the Exarchate, a new religious authority, separate and independent from the Greek Patriarch in Constantinople, to be headed by a Bulgarian priest.

This Turkish act, ostensibly accommodative on one level, proved most disruptive at another level, confirming subsequent suspicions that this was precisely the higher purpose of the Ottoman government. There soon developed an acute animosity between the Greeks and the Bulgarians, who no longer shared a single religious supreme authority. There ensued the animosity of the Serbs whose aversion to a Bulgar Patriarch was not any less strong than that to a Greek Patriarch. The Serbian church had acknowledged the supremacy of the Greek Patriarch only after the Serbian Patriarchate of Ipek was abolished in 1766—a supremacy Prince Milosh had countermanded by establishing, in 1831, a National Church with a Metropolitan at Belgrade. Nevertheless, the functioning of a Slavic Exarchate provided a significant impetus to the growth of a common bond of Slavic solidarity throughout the Balkan peninsula.

This sense of Slavic solidarity proved quite tenuous, however, when Islam entered the picture. Christianity, under the banner of the spiritual authority of the head of Eastern Orthodoxy, could maintain a modicum of harmony among two diverse ethnic groups, Slavs and Greeks. But Slavism, i.e., the identification with a common ethnic stock, proved not only irrelevant but utterly destructive as well for the Bosnians and Herzegovinians, who were split along Muslim and Christian lines of religious affiliation.

The Balkan insurrections are intimately connected with this feature of the Eastern Question, presaging, as will be seen later on in this work, identical developments in the growth of the Armenian variant of that Question. The immediate and in a sense fundamental source of the outbreak was the simmering conflict between Christian and Muslim Slavs of Bosna and Herzegovina. Following the conquest of these provinces by Ottoman Turks in the 15th century, a portion of the indigenous population involved had converted to Islam as a matter of expediency or convenience. Bosnia in particular was a province of aristocrats—large land-owners whose chief reason for religious conversion was the desire to hold on to their properties instead of running the risk of losing them to the invaders. With remarkable eagerness, these people had embraced the Ottoman system of theocracy that was based on Islam and on the dominant status of the Muslims in relation to non-Muslims. Accordingly, the Tanzimat Reform Edicts of 1839 and 1856, proclaiming the equality of all before the law, were just as hateful to them in Bosnia as to the religious fundamentalists in Turkey proper.

The regime that emerged in Bosnia and Herzegovina under these circumstances was more or less an extension of that prevalent in the other provinces of the Ottoman Empire. Feudal lords subjugating the peasantry, extortionist taxation, and a venal court system were the main features of that regime. As the British Consul in Bosnia, Holmes, stated, that court system was based upon the practice of "open bribery and corruption."[4] The net result of these developments was that the Slavs of Christian faith were reduced to a class of oppressed subjects. The problems became compounded with the financial collapse in 1874 of the Ottoman Empire, due to heavy borrowing abroad and the inordinate extravagance in spending by the reigning Sultan Abdul Aziz. Having defaulted, half the interest on the debt was repudiated. Most important, Turkey once more turned to its subjects for relief by way of imposing new and debilitating taxes on already financially crippled subjects. The cup of outrage was full and the peasants of Bosnia and Herzegovina rose against their twin tormentors: the local Muslim feudal renegades and their cohorts, the Turkish officials who were mostly beyond the pale of control of the central authorities in the Ottoman capital.

The spread of the insurrectionary fervor to the other Slavic peoples in the region, Montenegro, Serbia, and Bulgaria, was evidence of the existence of the fertile soil for such fervor that was capable of exploding into a general conflagration. External triggering mechanisms were also at work. The ideals of panslavism, championed by Russia, were prime movers in this regard. Relying on a network of agents operating in the region, Count Ignatief, Russian ambassador at the Ottoman capital, fanned the flames of nationalism, in the process accentuating existing anti-Turk enmities among the Slavs. The Montenegrins, a small nationality of displaced and warlike Slavs of the purest Serb stock, who rarely hesitated to challenge the Turks from the fastness of their inaccessible mountains, were most responsive to such agitation. But the principal role players in the entire episode were the Serbs, whose overall aspirations, punctuated with some elements of atavism, corresponded to Russian aspirations through the instrumentality of panslavism. Russia's repudiation, in October 1870, of the Black Sea clauses of the Paris Peace Treaty of 1856, to which the Powers had acquiesced with misgivings, had somehow strengthened its prestige in the domain of international posturing. Furthermore, even though that Peace Treaty had implicitly denied Russia any right to exercise protectorate over Serbia, as it had reconfirmed Ottoman sovereignty over it, Serbia for all practical purposes was under Russian protectorate. Also, it was Russia which earlier had forced the Turks to remove their garrisons in Serbia. The arch-prize being pursued by the Russians, was, of course, Constantinople, along with the adjacent Straits providing egress from the Black Sea and ingress into the Aegean.

Encouraged and even reinforced by the Russians, the Serbs were entertaining the idea of reviving the medieval Serbian Empire, encompassing Montenegro, Bosnia, and Herzegovina. The impulse to redress the consequences of the fateful defeat at the Kosovo Polye battle in 1389 at the hands of Ottoman Turks, the urge to extirpate all vestiges of Ottoman occupation of Serb territory and all but terminate Ottoman sovereignty therein had become a national pathos for the Serbs. For three centuries Serbia had endured considerable pain and suffering as a result of Ottoman domination.

When presenting their grievances to the European consuls in Bosnia the insurgents insisted on guarantees for religious freedom, reform of the tax system, or else, they said, access to a corner of some Christian land to which they might emigrate en masse. Unless the country was temporarily occupied by a foreign power, they declared, they would prefer to die rather than suffer continuous subjugation.

In July 1875, the peoples of Bosnia and Herzegovina had risen against Ottoman rule. On December 30, 1875, the Austrian Chancellor Andrassy proposed to the signatories of the Paris Peace Treaty the formation of a Muslim-Christian Commission to enforce the reforms, especially the proviso on the equality before the law of Muslims and Christians alike, and to supervise their implementation.[5] The Sultan again acceded on February 13, 1876. As the bloodshed continued unabated, however, the Powers (with the exception of England, which declined to join due to resentment over not being initially consulted) issued the Berlin Memorandum of May 13, 1876, an extension of the previous Andrassy Note. The memorandum asked Turkey to agree to an armistice, to grant the Christians the right to keep their arms, and to recognize the principle of supervision of the reforms by the consuls of these Powers.

If at the expiration of the armistice the terms stipulated by the Powers had not been met, the option for coercion was to be considered. As England refused to join but instead unilaterally ordered its fleet to Besika Bay, the projected intervention fell through. Despite all counsels for restraint, Montenegro and Serbia in quick succession plunged into war against Turkey on June 30, and July 1, 1876, respectively. The Serbian army consisted largely of Russian volunteers, and was led by a Russian general. Only a Russian ultimatum later in the war prevented the Turks from advancing on Belgrade. Gradually, however, the insurgents gained the upper hand, inflicting a series of defeats upon the Turks. The repetition of a historical pattern throughout this episode is noteworthy. As on the eve of the 1853–56 Crimean War, so in the present case, local disputes involving ethnic rivalries, intensified and expanded as the original issues of dispute gave way to new dimensions of conflict enveloping one or more Powers. Presently, the Balkan insurrections led to a major armed conflict, i.e., the 1877–78 Russo-Turkish war, which nearly became an international war.

The Midhat Constitution

To forestall European control of the implementation of reforms, Ottoman Turkey adopted the Midhat Constitution.[6] The document's liberal provisions improved upon the preceding Reform Acts. Article 8 proclaimed the common citizenship of all Ottoman subjects, irrespective of religion.[7] Article 9 guaranteed their individual liberty.[8] Article 17 proclaimed their equality before the law, and their rights and duties "without prejudice to religion."[9] The Constitution, however, still deferred to the primacy of Islam. Article 4 designated the Sultan as the protector of Islam in his capacity as Khalif.[10] Article 5 declared that "His majesty the Sultan is irresponsible: His person is sacred."[11] Article 11, moreover, while granting "religious privileges" to the other faiths in the Empire, asserted that "Islamism is the religion of the State."[12]

Neither these new constitutionally guaranteed rights, nor "the privileges" of Article 11, purporting to enshrine the Islamic spirit of toleration of other faiths, mitigated the real legal and political disabilities of the non-Muslims, however. The Sultan-Khalif himself obstructed the task of implementation.[13] In addition, one of the high priests of modern Turkish nationalism, Tekin Alp, repudiated the Turkish claim of having granted to the non-Muslim communities, especially the Armenians, privileges of religious autonomy, defining article 11 as "the high separation wall" intended to sustain the segregation to the exclusion of the non-Muslims.[14] French international law scholar Engelhardt, in his renowned study on reforms in nineteenth-century Turkey, similarly rejected the notion of "privilege," substituting for it the entrenched practice of "separation, afforded by reasons of state, religious antagonism," and reinforced by "Muslim disdain" for other religions.[15] This practice derives from the mandate of Verse 51 of Chapter 5 of the Koran exhorting the Muslim faithful as follows: "Take not the Jews and Christians for friends ... . He among you who taketh for friends is [one] of them ... ." As to the claim of "privilege," supposedly accorded the non-Muslim nationalities of the empire, a noted expert on the Middle East, along the lines of the view of

Tekin Alp, cited in note 14, dismissed these Tanzimat era contrivances as "paper privileges."[16] This obstruction was nowhere more manifest than in the administration of justice in the provinces. Particularly instructive among the dozen British Blue Books covering the 1879–1881 period, is Turkey No. 8 (1881), in which the British Foreign Office (in its *Reports on the Administration of Justice in the Civil, Criminal, and Commercial Courts in the Various Provinces of the Ottoman Empire*) described numerous cases involving bribery, "organized perjury," venal judges, and violations of the penal codes of the secular (*Nizamiye*) courts at the expense of non-Muslims.[17] These observations by European diplomats and historians are in accord with the judgment of Turkish historian Bayur, who concedes that the Ottoman legal system, compared to the European, left much to be desired, and that "the courts were in bad shape."[18]

A Belgian jurist specializing in Ottoman legal affairs underscored some of the covert objectives of the new constitution:

> It appears only too clearly from this document that the actual aim of the new charter was to postpone the time when Europe would ask the Porte for something more than fair words and laws made for show. In other words, those who used this fine language intended merely to prevent the interests of the Christian nations still under Turkish rule from being formally and *explicitly* put under the protection of European international law, as they had already been *implicitly* placed by the Treaty of Paris.[19]

Significantly, the new constitution was enacted in the wake of the May 1876 insurrection in Bulgaria, where Turkish irregulars had slaughtered an estimated 15 to 20 thousand Bulgarian women and children. Known as "the Bulgarian horrors"[20]—prompting British Prime Minister Gladstone to write a pamphlet demanding the expulsion of the Turks from Europe—these atrocities set off the wars with the Serbians and the Montenegrins in June and July of 1876. Gladstone's pamphlet stirred English public opinion; within a few days, 40,000 copies were sold. As the French writer Maurois paraphrased the sense of the pamphlet, " ... the Turks, the one great anti-human specimen of humanity ... there was not a criminal in European gaol, nor a cannibal ... whose indignation would not rise at the recital of what had been done."[21] After the Ottoman Turks refused British and French attempts to negotiate an armistice, the Turks yielded to a Russian ultimatum of October 30, 1876.[22] The ensuing Constantinople Conference failed, however, to secure Turkey's consent to reforms to be supervised by Europe. In fact, the Turkish government's proclamation of a new constitution precisely at this time, as noted above, served to preempt this scheme of reforms. In response to this proclamation, the Concert of Europe, led by British Prime Minister Salisbury, warned the Turks of the dire consequences of intransigence.[23] Despite the abortiveness of the Constantinople Conference, England, anxious to preserve peace, persisted in its efforts to secure a settlement, and supported, along with the other Powers, the protocol proposed by Count Shouvalof, the Russian ambassador at London.

From The London Protocol to the Berlin Treaty

The London Protocol of March 31, 1877, was the final manifestation of Europe's relatively harmonious intervention in Ottoman internal affairs on behalf of oppressed nationalities and minorities. Article 9 empowered the six signatories "to watch carefully" (*de veiller avec soin*) the manner in which the Ottoman government carried out its promises. It provided for consultation and joint action in the event that the Powers were "once more disillusioned."[24] Additionally, the quest for general peace (*la paix générale*) was to guide their actions. The Turkish Plenipotentiary rejected the Protocol as

> derogatory to the Sultan's dignity and independence ... . [R]ather than accede to its provisions it would be better for Turkey to face the alternative of war, even if an unsuccessful war, expected to result in the loss of one or two provinces ... [It] was a virtual abrogation of the IXth Article of the Treaty of Paris ... . This foreign intervention ... was a humiliation to which [the] Government would not at any risk submit.[25]

On April 24, exactly two weeks after Turkey formally rejected the London Protocol, the Tsar ordered his armies to cross the frontiers to secure by force what the unanimous efforts of the Powers could not obtain by persuasion. Commenting on this resort to war, a British historian, J. Marriott, declared: "Russia had behaved, in face of prolonged provocation, with commendable patience and restraint, and had shown a genuine desire to maintain the European Concert. The Turk had exhibited throughout his usual mixture of shrewdness and obstinacy."[26]

Defeated on both the Caucasian and the Balkan fronts in less than a year, Turkey sued for peace and had to submit to the humiliating and debilitating terms of the March 3, 1878 San Stefano Treaty dictated by Russia. However, led by England and Austria, the five Concert Powers objected to their exclusion from this treaty, and impelled Russia to reconsider and redraw the terms in a manner consistent with the provisions of articles 9 and 12 of the 1856 Paris Peace Treaty. The result was the July 13, 1878, Treaty of Berlin, through which three Christian nationalities in the Balkans (Serbia, Romania, and Montenegro) were granted the status of independent states, with Bulgaria gaining autonomy under Ottoman suzerainty. The treaty also accorded Eastern Roumelia, south of the Balkan mountains, a special arrangement under the Ottoman government—a Christian governor approved by the Powers—and under Article 23 projected special reforms for Macedonia comprising the provinces of Salonika, Kosovo, and Monastir.[27] Though in 1905 the Powers imposed upon Turkey a clause providing for European control of reforms in Macedonia, they relinquished it following the 1908 Young Turk Revolution as a gesture of faith to the new government.

Marriott characterized the Treaty of Berlin "as a great landmark in the history of the Eastern Question."[28] Mandelstam, a Russian legal scholar, extolled the 1877–1878 Russo-Turkish war producing that treaty as *"une véritable guerre d'humanité,"* describing the clauses of the Berlin Treaty as a punishment of Turkey for violating the terms of the Paris Peace Treaty, and the Treaty itself "as one of the most signal manifestations of *"l'intervention collective d'humanité"* for the sake of the oppressed races of the Ottoman Empire. As to Article 62 guaranteeing "civil and political rights, public employment, free exercise of professions and industrial pursuits," irrespective of "religious differences," Mandelstam called that article "a kind of charter of human rights."[29]

The Lethal Disjunctiveness of Public Law and Common Law in Ottoman Turkey

Although the Great Powers' recourse to humanitarian intervention helped introduce some rules of conduct in international relations,[30] they had little effect on the lives of non-Muslim minorities in Turkey. The Powers' interventions in Ottoman Turkey were designed to obviate domestic conflicts that were threatening peace in the region and thus, indirectly, in all of Europe. Militant Islamic nationalism, however, deflected the political possibilities for introducing successful legal reforms of the Ottoman social system. Insisting on domination as their sovereign right, the Ottoman Turks displaced the Powers' adjudicative politics through an ideology of coercion rooted in the customs and traditions of their society. This response reveals an underlying truth of international law. As Brierly explains: "We must expand our interpretation of the term 'international law.' We must cease to think of it as merely a set of principles to be applied by courts of law, and understand that it includes the whole legal organisation of international life on the basis of peace and order. Such an organisation must provide for the peaceful and orderly use of *political*, as well as judicial, methods of adjustment. The predominant concern of international law with particular concrete problems … seems to carry the corollary … that political methods of adjusting awkward situations will remain … relatively more important than they are in the state."[31]

The public laws for the equality and protection of non-Muslim minorities imposed upon Turkey bore a European-Christian stamp and conflicted with the common law principles of Ottoman society. No one recognized this better than Sultan Abdul Aziz, whose predecessor had allowed the promulgation of these laws through the framework of Tanzimat reforms. This sultan is described by the eminent Turkish jurist Cevdet Paşa as having repeatedly complained that, "It will be impossible to rule as a monarch without doing away with the notion that the administration of the Tanzimat reforms must be arranged in such a way that it is consistent with legal principles."[32] His successor, Abdul Hamit, assumed the same posture as revealed by an admission by his Grand Vizier Said Paşa, who, on December 11, 1882 confided to the British Chargé at Constantinople that the Armenian reforms could not be carried out because of "*un empêchement intérieur*," and which obstacle the Chargé was certain was an allusion to the obstacles erected by the Palace.[33] As a result, Islamic common law principles of supremacy for Muslims invariably preempted them. To the Powers who were wondering why the reforms had not yet materialized, Grand Vizier Fuat Paşa responded, "One wouldn't know how to improvise [methods for] the reforming of customs."[34] Another Grand Vizier, Ali Paşa, a cohort of Fuat, is reported to have offered the following excuse: "but in what country in the world ha[s] it been found practicable to efface in a day the effects of the habits and traditions of ages by a simple change of the law or in the disposition of the Government?"[35] In explaining the reasons why the reforms "failed," Professor Talcot Williams, the former Dean of Columbia University's School of Journalism, who was born and raised in Turkey, wrote, "custom (*adet*) is stronger in the East than codes, courts, and the authority, and the old customs ... [are] still strong over much of the empire."[36]

Excerpts from a Memorandum which longtime Grand Vizier Reşid Paşa addressed to the Sultan in the wake of the 1856 Reform Act proclamation reveal the subversive intent of the Ottoman government. In this Memorandum, he admits that the real intent of the reforms was being concealed (*setr*) from the public by deceptive metaphors. This process was meant to avoid causing alarm and offending the cherished traditions of the Muslim populace. In questioning the wisdom of granting the non-Muslims "complete emancipation" and "perfect equality," Reşid Paşa underscored the complications he anticipated. He wondered whether a six-hundred-year-old empire could transform its inner character into something "entirely repugnant and contrary" (*tamamıyla zıt ve muhalif*). He assured the Sultan that its declared purpose notwithstanding, the text of the Edict relies on "ingenious words" to "deceive" (*iğfal*), through "vague paragraphs," those who insisted on its proclamation.[37] The significance of these statements cannot be overestimated. Reşid is generally identified as a pioneer in the Ottoman reform movement. He not only held the post of Prime Minister six times, but also that of Foreign Minister three times in the 1837–1858 period. The text of the 1839 Reform Charter is attributed to him.[38] Other sources describe him as a manipulator of the Powers, given to double-talk and equivocation, with a firm

commitment to Islam and its precepts. In his famous memorandum, criticizing the abuses of Sultan Mahmud II, who had just died, he chastised
the ruler for "constantly neglecting the law of the Prophet when on each
such occasion he was required to obey it."[39] A French chronicler of the
history of Reşid's tenure in various posts portrays him as conservative,
interested mainly in the status quo while pretending to pursue reforms.[40]
This view is supported by a Turkish legal scholar who refers to Reşid's
general opposition to the idea of granting political rights to the Christians
of the empire.[41] Another Turkish author with multitudinous and ample
experiences in public life is even more unequivocal about this issue. Reference is made to Abdurrahman Şeref who was an official Ottoman historian, prominent in education and the academe, and during the Ittihadist
regime he served as Minister of Education as well as President of the
State Council and in the Kemalist Grand National Assembly he was a
Deputy from Istanbul. He put in a nutshell the pretensions and, therefore,
the misleading claims of the reform initiatives when he stated:

> The reforms of the Tanzimat, i.e., the idea of the organization of the legal state
> is to be framed on paper. Let them deliver speeches, compose advertisements
> and temporize with people inside and outside the country. But they themselves
> [the authors of the Tanzimat] will proceed as they please. This is the meaning
> many people give to the idea of a legal state.[42]

From a European point of view, the matter was placed in a proper perspective by Marquis Salisbury, who was one of the diplomats involved in
the creation and direction of the Eastern Question. On August 8, 1878,
when he was British Foreign Minister, he told Sir Layard, his ambassador
at the Ottoman capital that "the Mahometan races ... are, for the present
at least, unfitted for institutions of this kind, which are alien to their traditions and their habits of thought."[43] Thus, while the European Powers'
humanitarian intervention efforts accomplished some reform of Turkey's
written laws, they were completely ineffectual in eliciting reform of
actual practice.

The Provocative Origin of the Armenian Question.
A French Document

The way they were structured, the international efforts of the European
Powers had the potential for aggravating the plight of the Armenians. By
raising the consciousness and hope of the subject nationalities of the
Ottoman Empire, without concomitantly enhancing their power leverage,
international actors afforded the rulers of that empire both the incentive
and the excuse to inflict greater harm upon these nationalities through an
increase of the level of their oppression. This is how the Armenian Question originated and crystallized itself in the last decades of the nineteenth

century, fueling with greater force the engines of the Turko-Armenian conflict, in which that Question had found its most concrete expression. Encouraged by the promises of the Treaty of Berlin, the Armenians experienced a new sense of national consciousness, which in turn engendered rising expectations. Sporadic displays of assertiveness began to erode their tradition of passively enduring the abuses endemic to the Ottoman system. Additionally, emigré Armenian intellectuals formed committees in the capitals of Europe to protest these abuses and to push for the implementation of the promised reforms. As the Ottoman regime resisted these agitations and refused to execute the reforms in any meaningful way, Armenian revolutionary cells emerged within and without the Empire and prepared for combat. In a report to Paris entitled *Exposé historique de la question arménienne,* long-time French Ambassador Paul Cambon traced the genesis of the "Armenian question" to this period. He wrote:

> A high ranking Turkish official told me, "the Armenian question does not exist but we shall create it." ... Up until 1881 the idea of Armenian independence was non-existent. The masses simply yearned for reforms, dreaming only of a normal administration under Ottoman rule ... The inaction of the Porte served to vitiate the good will of the Armenians. The reforms have not been carried out. The exactions of the officials remained scandalous and justice was not improved ... from one end of the Empire to the other, there is rampant corruption of officials, denial of justice and insecurity of life ... . The Armenian diaspora began denouncing the administrative misdeeds, and in the process managed to transform the condition of simple administrative ineptness into one of racial persecution. It called to the attention of Europe the violation by the Turks of the Treaty of Berlin and thereby summoned up the image of Armenian autonomy in the minds of the Armenian population. France did not respond to the Armenian overtures but the England of Gladstone did: The Armenian revolutionary movement took off from England[44] ... as if it were not enough to provoke Armenian discontent, the Turks were glad to amplify it by the manner in which they handled it. In maintaining that the Armenians were conspiring, the Armenians ended up engaging in conspiracy; in maintaining that there was no Armenia, the Armenians ended up conjuring the reality of her existence ... . The harsh punishment of conspirators, the maintenance in Armenia of a veritable regime of terror, arrests, murders, rapes, all this shows that Turkey is taking pleasure in precipitating the events [in relation to] an inoffensive population. In reality the Armenian Question is nothing but an expression of the antagonism between England and Russia ... . Where does Armenia begin, and where does it end?[45]

Later in the report Cambon prophetically questioned the reasonableness of transporting the Armenians to Mesopotamia, a solution the Ottoman government was reportedly contemplating. Mesopotamia would later, in World War I, serve as the valley of the Armenian genocide.

What stands out in this *exposé* is Cambon's diagnosis of the main problem in the genesis and escalation of the Turko-Armenian conflict, euphemistically described as the Armenian Question: the deliberate aggravation of the underlying issues of that conflict by Ottoman authorities intent on provoking the Armenians to resort to desperate acts of self-defense. His conclusion in this respect that "Turkey is taking pleasure in precipitating events [vis a vis] an inoffensive population," subjected to "a veritable regime of terror, arrests, murders, rapes ... .," deserves particular attention when examining the rise of the Armenian revolutionary movement as a by-product of this "regime of terror."

From Desperation to Desperate Acts: The Advent of Armenian Revolutionaries

The despair of the victims of that regime had undergone a respite when, in 1878, the Powers, through the terms of Article 61 of the Treaty of Berlin, had undertaken to "superintend" the projected reforms and bring relief to the oppressed population. When the respite failed to materialize, a more or less passive endurance turned into desperation, which eventually was infused with some elements of combativeness as Armenian revolutionary cells sprang up within and without Turkey to identify that condition of desperation and to deal with it. As historian Roy Douglas observed, the involvement of the "Armenian revolutionaries" in the escalation of the Turko-Armenian conflict was due to the fact that they "had been driven to desperation by the failure of the Powers to take effective action."[46] Another author, a contemporary of the Hamit era, confirmed, from personal observations, the existence of a state of acute desperation among the Armenians in the Ottoman capital: "If the Armenians were not the most peaceable and submissive people in the world, this city would have been in ashes before this time, for they have had everything to drive them to desperation." He attributes that condition to "the treatment of the Armenians by the Turkish Government," adding "When oppression passes a certain limit and men become desperate, such revolutionary organisation always appears. They are the fruit and not the cause of the existing state of things in Turkey ... ."[47] These views are surprisingly corroborated by German Ambassador Anton von Saurma-Jeltsch whose reluctance to get involved in any plan which might antagonize Hamit was in line with an emerging German policy prescribed by Wilhelm II, the German Kaiser. In an October 4, 1895 report to his Chancellor in Berlin he declared that the entire episode might have been avoided had the Armenians not been driven to hopelessness as a result of the abortiveness of the steps taken on their behalf.[48]

The episode mentioned by the German ambassador refers to the August 13/26, 1896 successful raid which a select group of "freedom fighters" of the Armenian Revolutionary Federation, the Dashnak party, launched against the heavily fortified Ottoman Bank, the foremost bank in the empire, controlled by British and French interests, but enjoying a kind of monopoly in fiscal matters affecting the Treasury of the Ottoman state. The purpose of the armed foray was not robbery but coercion, with a view to pressuring the Powers to finally compel the Sultan to implement the reforms. The result was the three-day bloodbath in the streets of Constantinople to which some 6,000 Armenians fell victim. In commenting on the motivation of the revolutionaries Ambassador Cambon tersely remarked: "Reduced to a state of desperation, these people are willing to risk all to win all" (*Ces gens réduits au désespoir veulent jouer le tout pour le tout*).[49]

In the final analysis, the raid, about which more details are provided in a separate discussion below, proved abortive and the carnage in the Ottoman capital, the second in less than a year, before the very eyes of the countless representatives of the Powers, remained free from the clasps of prosecution and punishment—due largely to what the French ambassador in the above cited report to Paris called "the antagonism between England and Russia."

Notes to Chapter 3

1. Ali Riza-Mehmed Galib, *Geçen Asırda Devlet Adamlarımız* (Our Statesmen of the Past Century), F. Çetin, ed. (Istanbul, 1979), 73–74. For a contemporary in-depth analysis of this episode of nationality conflicts in Syria and Lebanon, see Leila Fawaz, *An Occasion for War. Ethnic Conflict in Lebanon and Damascus* (Berkeley, 1994).
2. G. Noradounghian, *Receuil D'Actes Internationaux de l'Empire Ottoman, 1856–1878*, vol. 3 (Paris, 1902), 144–49 ((Réglement); 125 (French text of Protocol).
3. J. Hurewitz, *Diplomacy in the Near and Middle East, A Documentary Record: 1535–1914*, vol. 1 (Princeton, N. Jersey, 1956), 154. For the original French text of the article see Noradounghian, *Recueil* [n. 2], 74.
4. Great Britain, *Blue Books*. Turkey No. 16 (1877). Doc. No. 21, p. 45.
5. E. Engelhardt, *La Turquie et le Tanzimat ou Histoire des Réformes dans l'"Empire Ottoman*, vol. 2, (Paris, 1882), 145-48. For the full text in French see A. Schopoff, *Les Réformes et la Protection des Chrétiens en Turquie, 1673–1904*, 179-80. For the English text see E. Hertslet, *The Map of Europe by Treaty*, vol. 4, (London, 1875), 2418–29.
6. *Ottoman Constitution.* (Midhat), *reprinted in American Journal of International Law.* 2 (Supp. 1908): 367. The French text of the Constitution is in Schopoff, *Réformes* [n. 5], 192.
7. *Ottoman Constitution*, 367.
8. *Ibid.*
9. *Ibid.,* 369.
10. *Ibid.,* 367.
11. *Ibid.*
12. *Ibid.*, 368.
13. In his book dealing with these obstructions, the son of Midhat Paşa focuses on the Sultan's inveterate aversion to any plan to end segregation, prejudice and discrimination practiced on religious grounds. *See* A. Midhat, *The Life of Midhat Pasha*, (London, 1903), 108, 141–42.
14. T. Alp, *Türkismus und Pantürkismus*, (Weimar, 1915), 89. It should be noted that the word *"imtiyaz"* inserted in article 11 of the Ottoman constitution, while denoting "privilege," also connotes the idea of "separation" or "distinctness" in a more learned diction.

15. Engelhardt, *La Turquie* [n. 5] vol. 2, 299–300.

16. W. Yale, *The Near East. A Modern History.* New and revised. (Ann Arbor, Michigan, 1968), 30.

17. These official publications of the British Foreign Office are British Foreign Office, *Blue Book.* Turkey (hereinafter *Blue Book.* Turkey) No. 10 (1879); *ibid.,* No. 1 (1880); *ibid.,* No. 4 (1880); *ibid.,* No. 7 (1880); *ibid.,* No. 9 (1880); *ibid.,* No. 23 (1880); *ibid.,* No. 5 (1881); *ibid.,* No. 6 (1881); *ibid.,* No. 10 (1881). The Consuls reporting to London were officers of the English Army and included Captain (later Major) Trotter, Captain (later Major) Everett, Captain Clayton, Lieutenant (later Colonel) Chermside, Lieutenant Colonel Wilson, and Captain Steward. See especially No. 8 (1881), 57, 58, 71–72, 109–110. See also the citations in M. Rolin-Jaequemyns, *Armenia, the Armenians, and the Treaties* (London, 1891), 45, 73–76. This work is a revised version of two articles originally published in *Revue de Droit International et de Législation Comparée,* organ of the Belgian Institute of International Law, dated 1887 and 1889. No translator is indicated.

18. Y. H. Bayur, *Türk Inkilâbı Tarihi* (History of the Turkish Revolution) vol. 3, Part 3 (Ankara, 1957), 481–82.

19. Rolin-Jaequemyns, *Armenia,* [n. 17], 33 (emphasis in original). An almost identical view is expressed by the Turkish author Sina Akşin, *100 Soruda Jön Türkler ve Ittihat ve Terakki* (Ittihad ve Terakki in the Context of 100 Questions), (Istanbul, 1980), 12.

20. J. Marriott, *The Eastern Question (An Historical Study in European Diplomacy),* 4th ed. (Glasgow, 1958), 318–34.

21. A. Maurois, *Disraeli,* (Chautaqua, N.Y., 1930), 308.

22. For the ultimatum, see Noradounghian, *Recueil* [n. 2], 399.

23. *Ibid.,* 480. The details of the prolonged Constantinople Conference (Dec. 27, 1876–Jan. 20, 1877), clustered around nine protocols; *Ibid.* 400–93. *See also Das Staatsarchiv,* vol. 32, Nos. 5964–71, 15–33, H. v. Kremer-Auenrode and P. Hirsch eds., (Leipzig, 1877) (compilation of 19th century German archival material) [hereinafter *Das Staatsarchiv*].

24. Engelhardt, *Turquie* [n. 5], 178. For the French text of the Protocol, see Noradounghian, *Recueil* [n. 2], Doc. No. 840, 496, and Schopoff, *Réformes* [n. 5], 3:34, Doc. No. 45, p. 334.

25. The quotation is from British Foreign Minister Earl of Derby's April 9, 1877 communication to his Chargé in Constantinople. *Das Staatsarchiv,* [n. 23], No. 6360, 156–7; *see also* Engelhardt, *Turquie* [n. 5], 179 (April 9, 1877 circular by Ottoman Foreign Minister Safvet, decrying Europe's stance of "humiliating protectorship.")

26. Marriott, *Eastern Question* [n. 20], 333.

27. *Ibid.,* 341–46. For the English text of the Berlin Treaty, ratified in Berlin on August 3, 1878, and the Ottoman ratification on August 28, 1878, see Great Britain, *Parliamentary Papers* 83:690–705 (1878). For the selective reproduction of the minutes of the proceedings involved, see also *Das Staatsarchiv,* [n. 23], vol. 34 (1878) Nos. 6766–73, 226–81. For the text of the Treaty in French, the original language used, see *ibid.* No. 6773, 277–91. For the San Stefano Treaty see *ibid.* No. 6718, 38–48. For the text of articles 58–63 of the Treaty of Berlin, see Hurewitz, *Diplomacy* [n. 3], 189–91. Noradounghian also includes the French text of the San Stefano Treaty. Noradounghian, *Recueil* [n. 2], 509–21.

28. Marriott, *Eastern Question* [n. 20], 345.

29. A. Mandelstam, *La Société des Nations et les Puissances devant le Problème Arménien* (Paris, 1926) [Special edition of Revue Générale de Droit Intnl. Publ.], 17 n. 1, 18.

30. At the Congress of Paris, February 25 to March 30, 1856 for example, four such rules were adopted: 1. the abolition of privateering; 2. a neutral flag covers enemy goods, save contraband; 3. neutral goods, except contraband, are not liable to capture under an enemy flag; 4. blockade, to be binding, must be effective. *See* G. Hackworth, *International Law* 1 (1943): 24–26. When Russia repudiated the Black Sea clauses of the Treaty of Paris in the Protocol of the March 13, 1871 London conference, the plenipotentiaries of Great Britain, Italy, Austria-Hungary, Germany, Russia, and Turkey declared it as "an essential principle of the law of the nations that no power can liberate itself from the engagement of a treaty, nor modify the stipulations thereof, unless with the consent of the contracting powers by means of an amicable agreement." *British and Foreign State Papers, 1870–1871,* 61:1198, cited in J. Scott, *Cases on International Law,* 469 (2nd ed. 1922).

31. J. L. Brierly, "The Rule of Law in the International Society," *Nordisk Tidskrift for International Red, Acta Scandinavica Juris Gentium*, 7 (1936): 3, 15.
32. Prof. Reşat Kaynar, *Türkiyede Hukuk Devleti Kurma Yolundaki Hareketler* (Movements in Turkey for the Creation of a Legal State) (Istanbul, 1960), 55.
33. F0424/132, Doc. No. 147, p. 220. the Chargé was Hugh Wyndham.
34. R. Davison, "Turkish Attitudes Concerning Christian-Muslim Equality in the Nineteenth Century," *American Historical Review* 59 (1954): 853.
35. *Blue Book*. Turkey, Doc. No. 16, (1877); the full text of the statement is in Bat Ye'or, *The Dhimmi: Jews and Christians under Islam* (London, 1985), 289–90.
36. T. Williams, *Turkey: A World Problem of Today* (Garden City, N.Y., 1921), 285.
37. A. Cevdet Paşa, *Tezâkir* (Memoirs), vol. 1 C. Baysun, ed. (Ankara, 1953), 79.
38. F. E. Bailey, *British Policy and the Turkish Reform Movement: A Study in Anglo-Turkish Relations 1826–1853* (New York, 1970), 186, 193, 205.
39. *Ibid.*, 274.
40. M. Destrilhes, *Confidences sur la Turquie* (Paris, 1855), 37–73.
41. Kaynar, *Türkiyede* [n. 32], 38.
42. *Ibid.*, 11.
43. B. Şimşir, *British Documents on Ottoman Armenians* vol. I (1856–1880), Doc. No. 81, (Ankara, 1982), p. 191.
44. In an exchange with his German colleague Saurma, Russian Ambassador Nelidof commented that the Armenians were frustrated not only by the lack of any tangible results from European intervention, but also by the ensuing massacres. *The Diplomatic Archives of the Foreign Ministry of Germany (Die Diplomatischen Akten des Auswärtigen Amtes)*. Die *Grosse Politik der Europäischen Kabinette 1871–1914* (Hereafter cited as DAG). vol. 10. Der Nahe und Ferne Osten. Doc. No. 2426, p. 69. J. Lepsius, A. Bartholdy and F. Thimme eds. 3rd ed. (Berlin, 1927).
45. Diplomatic Archives of Foreign Ministry of France (Documents Diplomatiques Français 1871–1900), vol. 11, Doc. No. 50, pp. 71–74 (1947). *See also Livre Jaune*. Affaires Arméniens. *Projets de réformes dans l'Empire Ottoman 1893-1897*. Doc. No. 6. p. 10-13 (1897).
46. Roy Douglas, "Britain and the Armenian Question 1894–7," *The Historical Journal* 19, 1 (1976): 124.
47. "The Constantinople Massacre" *Contemporary Review* 70 (October 1896): 458, 459. The withholding of the author's name is explained in an editor's note with the words: "for obvious reasons." The article is probably written by a British diplomat at the time on duty in Constantinople, who "may be taken as thoroughly well-informed."
48. *DAG* [n. 44], Doc. No. 2426, cipher No. 138, p. 69.
49. Paul Cambon, *Correspondance 1870–1924* vol. I (1870–1898) (Paris, 1940), 412.

Part II

THE ORIGINS OF THE ARMENIAN QUESTION AND THE TURKO-ARMENIAN CONFLICT

Chapter 4

The Ill-Fated Internationalization of a Domestic Nationality Conflict

The Cleavage Between Armenian and Turkish Revolutionaries Conjointly Seeking the Overthrow of Abdul Hamit

The debacle of the Armenian revolutionary movement,[1] associated with the unhindered enactment of the 1894–96 massacres, did not stop the Armenian revolutionary leaders in Europe, notably those in London, Paris, and Geneva, as they continued their campaign against the Sultan and his regime from outside Turkey. The presence in these European capitals of a small group of Turkish dissidents, equally engaged in a struggle for deliverance from Hamidian despotism, was deemed an opportune moment by these Armenians who sought a rapprochement with them for the purpose of combining the available resources needed to mount a coordinated campaign against the Sultan, with a view to overthrowing him. The leaders of both groups, comprising a wide variety of opposition groups, met twice, i.e., in 1902 and 1907; representatives of other nationalities, i.e., Greeks and Jews, participated in these meetings, which yielded certain memorandums of understanding that were publicized subsequently.

In fact, the origins of the principal Turkish nationalist movement, bent on overthrowing the Abdul Hamit regime, can be traced to the impact upon them of the revolutionary activities of the Armenian political parties challenging the authority of the Sultan in the Ottoman capital. Before these events, the Ittihad ve Terakki Association, secretly formed in 1889 at the Military Medical Academy, was not keen on resorting to violent activities. But the relative success of those Armenian revolutionaries who did not shrink before such tasks and were able to engage the attention of the Powers, thereby unnerving the Sultan, provided these hesitant Turks

Notes for this chapter begin on page 48.

with the impetus to dare and to contest the Sultan's regime, even when some of them still did not want to rely on violence. The thrust of this incipient movement was the broadcasting of the idea that the reforms should not be for the sole benefit of a particular minority, but "for the entire Ottoman community of people." In their first secretly issued manifesto, they berated the Armenians who "dared to assault Babı Ali, which is the highest office of our state and enjoys the respect of the Europeans. We regret these insolent [*küstah*] acts of our Armenian fellow citizens. We Turks too, like the Ottomans in general, demand freedom and reform. [Hence], instead of chastising the Armenians, let us pull down on the edifices of the oppressors, Babı Ali, the center of misrule, despotism and tyranny, Şeyhulislam and Yıldız [palace] ... ." After reproducing this proclamation, Turkish historian Kuran notes, "One can sense from the manner in which it is framed that the Young Turks were spurred by the activities of the Armenian revolutionaries."[2]

Even though the campaign culminated in success as the Sultan was deposed in 1908 as a result of a more or less bloodless military uprising, the fragility of the Turko-Armenian united front against Abdul Hamit portended the erosion of that front and the inevitable onset of a new round of crises fueling the Turko-Armenian conflict. The issue which cast an ominous shadow upon the united front, ever threatening to undermine and eventually to torpedo it, was that of European intervention on behalf of the Armenians, who were seeking reforms in the provinces. Those Turkish leaders who at this time were the opponents of the Hamidian regime, and as such, the ostensible allies of the Armenian revolutionaries, and who most vehemently resisted the inclusion in their program of a commitment to carry out the terms of Article 61 of the Berlin Treaty, subsequently operated as the masterminds of the World War I Armenian genocide. They included Drs. Nazım and Behaeddin Şakir, the preeminent Ittihadist dissidents in Paris, as will be seen later on in this study. As Abdul Hamit himself had demonstrated his vehemence to the same treaty clause by resorting to massacres, the dissident Young Turks on this score identified themselves with the Sultan while opposing him on almost everything else. This type of cleavage between Armenians and Turks persisted, irrespective of change of regimes, becoming a permanent fixture in the evolving stages of the Turko-Armenian conflict.

It is for this reason that practically all Turkish historians and political leaders are prone to trace the modern origin of the Armenian Question to Article 61 of the 1878 Berlin Treaty, the signatories of which were the six Great Powers and Turkey. Foremost among these Turks are Danişmend,[3] Enver Ziya Karal,[4] and Reşad, the Procuror-General of the Turkish Military Tribunal investigating the wartime massacres against the Armenians during the Armistice period; in his closing arguments at the Cabinet ministers' trial, he identified the Berlin Treaty as the source of the Turko-

Armenian conflict.[5] Ahmad Ferid (Tek), Interior Minister in the fledgling Turkish Republic, in the course of a secret session of the Parliament on October 16, 1921, likewise described the Berlin Treaty as the cause of the Turko-Armenian conflict and "the tragedy associated with that conflict,"[6] and Feroz Ahmad, an authority on modern Turkey also singled out Article 61 of the Berlin Treaty, stipulating reforms for the Armenians which, according to him, touched off the Turko-Armenian conflict by internationalizing the Armenian Question.[7]

The Futility of Armenian Efforts for Administrative Remedies

From a strictly chronological point of view, however, the Armenian Question formally arose as a problem of conflict between the Armenian community and the Ottoman central government in one of the sessions of the first Ottoman Parliament, which was sitting during the early phases of the 1877–78 Russo-Turkish War. Several Armenian deputies, supported by Greek and even Turkish colleagues, directed attention to the fact that while the Armenian *millet* was demonstrating its will to defend the Ottoman fatherland, thousands of Armenians were being assaulted and killed in the border regions by marauding regular and irregular Ottoman troops, including Kurds.[8] Apart from this issue of war-related conflict, a more fundamental source of conflict came to the fore and on June 4/16, 1877, which fell on a Saturday, it dominated the debate in the fledgling Ottoman Parliament. It was an issue which, evolving gradually, eventually came to be called Armenian Reforms and as such, it formed the core of the Armenian Question. The issues specifically involved a) the depredations perpetrated against the unarmed Armenian population in the eastern provinces by fully armed Kurdish tribes (*aşirets*); b) the impunity attending and following these depredations; and c) the suspected complicity of the local as well as central authorities. For the first time in Ottoman history, representatives of the *raya*, subject peoples, ventured to publicly and officially raise their voices in protest against inequities endemic in the Ottoman social system.

The first speaker was the Greek deputy Soulides. He compared the plight of the Armenians to that of the Greeks and Bulgarians in the Balkans who, however, were able to sensitize Europe about their suffering and secure remedies. He then added, "Deprived of this vehicle, the Armenians silently endured their bitter hardships. But is it just that the Armenians, the most loyal and obedient subject of the state, be so plagued and persecuted of all people by the Kurds, who are rebels against our state?" He ended his interpellation by demanding "an immediate end to this unbearable state of affairs." He was followed on the podium by Erzurum's Armenian deputy Hamazasp Ballarian. After recounting the litany of abuses committed by a host of Kurdish tribes in Muş, Van, and certain other districts of Erzurum, the Armenian deputy detailed the prevailing procedures of dealing with the offenders caught by the authorities. Upon payment of a bribe, they would be released, "only to resume their crimes with greater ferocity against their accusers. Many of the governors, *valis* and *mutesarrıfs*, were the accomplices of these Kurds and whose names at present I would not care to reveal. Upon my question as to why these Kurds are not being punished when two battalions might be enough to deal with them, the answer which I received was that there lies in this matter high governmental wisdom, a hidden political dispensation [*hikmeti hükümet*]. Only later did I learn what this meant: the Kurds would be needed for the purpose of repressing the Armenians in the event they should rise up in Armenia [eastern provinces of Turkey].

"In addition, these Kurds were envisaged as potential volunteer corps to be engaged in the event of a war against Russia ... . On what grounds did the Kurds manage to inspire such confidence, on the basis of what attributes or what usefulness?" The next speaker was Vasilaki, another Greek deputy, who concurred with the charges and suggestions made by the two previous deputies; he made a motion to authorize the Sublime Porte to initiate concrete steps for the immediate implementation of the remedies proposed. "All Muslim deputies voiced their agreement with the diagnosis of the problem and the proposals for a solution advanced by the three deputies."[9] The Sultan not only ignored these recommendations but subsequently and finally prorogued the Parliament when military setbacks and continuous expressions of discontent against the rule of the Sultan in the winter 1877–78 session by Muslim and non-Muslim deputies proved too unsettling for the monarch. However, the disaffections of the subjects of the Sultan, especially the provincial Armenian populations, were not incidental to the exigencies of the 1877–78 Russo-Turkish war. About a quarter of a century earlier the distinguished British general Sir Fenwick Williams, who heroically had defended the Turkish fortress of Kars against the Russians during the 1853–55 Crimean War as an ally of Turkey, in compelling terms decried the Turkish regime of oppression in the "Armenian provinces" that affected every facet of daily life. In this connection he denounced the Turkish government as "an engine of tyranny perhaps unequalled in the world," adding that "no language can describe the infamy which characterizes the life and character of Turkish police."[10]

In other words, the issue concerned a structural condition handicapping the Armenians vis a vis a subculture of lawlessness and brigandage practiced by marauding Kurdish tribes in cahoots with a stratum of Turkish provincial governors and their subalterns. By denying the Armenians the right to bear arms to defend themselves, the Ottoman system, buttressed by theocratic precepts and dogmas, placed the Armenians in a permanently vulnerable position, providing the nominally Muslim Kurds, who, as a rule, were armed to the teeth, both an advantage and an incentive to target the Armenians. The Turko-Armenian conflict in its inception was essentially a Kurdo-Armenian conflict, which surreptitiously was allowed by the authorities to fester—for a variety of reasons and by a variety of classes and groups of functionaries. It is as a result of this informal permissiveness of abuse at an ever-growing level of marauding operations on the part of the Kurds that the Kurdo-Armenian conflict more and more gravitated towards the tracks of a Turko-Armenian conflict. It became evident that the subcultural aspects of local and regional depredations against the Armenians were, to some extent, reflections of the hidden aspects of the mainstream culture projected from the seat of the central authorities in the Ottoman capital. The realization dawned on many leaders of the Armenian community that the sustained tempo of the depredations was neither happenstance, nor merely an expression of the willfulness of the local perpetrators involved. Rather, there appeared to be a loose structure to these series of assaults against the sedentary Armenian populations, which is aptly subsumed under the label "organized brigandage,"[11] or, in Turkish, *nizam altında haydut*.

The solutions sought by the Armenians with respect to the Kurds remained more or less constant in the rudimentary, as well as advanced, stages of the Turko-Armenian conflict, namely: a quest for administrative remedies against inequities and persecution, and some measure of redress against cumulative wrongs. The idea of separatism or independence was remote, as was the idea of revolutionary struggle and militancy. In contrasting the Armenians with the other nationalities of the empire, Turkish historian Karal sings the praise of the Armenians who "had adopted Turkish culture and were not pursuing independence as was the case with the other Ottoman communities."[12] Yet the fact remains that the latter's recourse to rebellion and combative contest with Ottoman authorities in the end proved more fruitful in terms of enlisting the intervention and support of the Powers than the Armenian reliance for a long time on petitions and supplications to the authorities. This fact came up in a meeting which the Armenian Patriarch Nercess held on December 6, 1876 with British ambassador Sir H. Elliot, for the purpose of presenting to the Ambassador the desiderata of the Armenian National Assembly in the Ottoman capital. The Ambassadors were to convene (The Constantinople Conference of December 1876–January 1877) and try to avert a Russo-Turkish war, for which the Russians were pressing. The conditions of such a war were ripe in the wake of the massacre of the Bulgarians, the ensuing insurrection in Bulgaria, and the outbreak of war between Serbia and Montenegro on the one hand, and Turkey on the other. The Constantinople Conference was to devise arrangements to pacify the region and persuade Turkey to adopt a new reform scheme in order to avoid future troubles. Patriarch Nercess proposed that the Conference also take up the Armenian Reforms issue. When the Ambassador demurred, saying that the agenda of the conference was limited to the disorders in the Balkans beset by insurrection, "the Patriarch replied … if in order to secure the sympathy of the European Powers it was necessary to rise in insurrection, there would be no difficulty in getting such a movement."[13]

Notes to Chapter 4

1. For a survey of the origins and growth of that movement, see Louise Nalbandian, *The Armenian Revolutionary Movement* (Berkeley, 1963).
2. Ahmed Bedevi Kuran, *Osmanlı İmparatorluğunda ve Türkiye Cumhuriyetinde İnkilâp Hareketleri* (Revolutionary Movements in the Ottoman Empire and the Turkish Republic) (Istanbul, 1959), 158–59. For a discussion of the 1902 and 1907 conclaves of Young Turk Ittihadists and Armenians, see *Ibid.*, 344–364, 443–449, and Ernest E. Ramsaur, *The Young Turks. Prelude to the Revolution of 1908* (Beirut, 1965), 14–6, 22–4.
3. Ismail Hami Danişmend, *İzahlı Osmalit Tarihi Kronolojisi* (An Annotated Chronology of Ottoman History) vol. 4 (Istanbul, 1961), 358–59.
4. Enver Ziya Karal, *La Question Arménienne (1878–1923)* transl. by K. Dorsan (Ankara, 1984), 9–10.
5. *L'Entente* (French language Armistice daily in Istanbul), June 26, 1919.
6. *Türkiye Büyük Millet Meclisi Gizli Celse Zabıtları* (The Transcripts of the Secret Sessions of the Grand National Assembly of Turkey) vol. 2 (Ankara, 1985), 343.
7. Feroz Ahmad, "Unionist Relations with the Greek, Armenian and Jewish Communities of the Ottoman Empire, 1908–14," in *Christians and Jews in the Ottoman Empire* vol. 1, B. Braude and B. Lewis, eds. (New York, 1982), 404, 423.
8. A. O. Sarkissian, *History of the Armenian Question to 1885*, reprint, (Urbana, IL, 1938), (*University of Illinois Bulletin*, vol. xxxv, 80 (June 3, 1938): 58–60.
9. These details were culled from the main Armenian newspaper at that time, which appeared in Constantinople., *Massis*, No. 1985, June 7/19, 1877. In a prefatory statement the editors expressed their appreciation for the display of "lofty humanitarian sentiments" of the two Greek deputies and conveyed "the sentiments of gratitude of the entire Armenian nation, upon which they can lay their indisputable claim by virtue of the sublime patriotic statements they made." Two days later the same paper in an editorial declared, "For the first time this important question was raised and a remedy was sought before a great assembly of the state."
10. *Blue Book. Turkey* No. 17 (1877), Doc. No. 6, p. 3.
11. Emile J. Dillon, "The Condition of Armenia," *Contemporary Review* LXVIII (1895): 153–54; James Bryce, *Transcaucasia and Ararat* (London, 1896), 465.
12. Karal, *La question armenienne* [n. 4], 7.
13. FO 424/46, Doc. No. 336, registry No. 1337, Ambassador Elliot's December 7, 1876 report to Foreign Minister Earl of Derby; see also *Blue Book*, Turkey No. 2 (1877), 34.

Chapter 5

The Interactive Dynamics of the Eastern and Armenian Questions

The Common Denominator Undergirding Both Questions

The designation "Question" was a euphemism in diplomatic parlance to convey the idea of abiding nationality conflicts besetting the Ottoman Empire. Essentially these conflicts had a common origin and inevitably affected one another as they evolved and intensified. Indeed, the roots of the Turko-Armenian conflict, which was denoted by the designation "The Armenian Question," were almost identical with those conflicts that the Ottoman Turks continued to have with the Macedonians, Cretans, Greeks, Bulgarians, and Serbs in the Balkans, and which were denoted by the other designation, i.e., "The Eastern Question." To the extent that the underlying issues of both questions overlapped, both questions were at times referred to interchangeably. In fact, the underlying common elements of both questions were internationally recognized and accordingly were made an object of concern in international law through a single legal act, namely, the Treaty of Berlin (1878). Through the insertion in that treaty of two specific articles, the Powers not only elevated two instances of domestic conflict to the plateau of international diplomacy, thereby internationalizing them, but also underscored the identity of the single source of these conflicts, thereby recognizing a common denominator through which the Eastern and Armenian questions can be seen as intersecting and in some ways conditioning one another. That common denominator was the ubiquitousness of Ottoman oppression which continued to exert itself despite the terms of the Treaty of Paris (1856) and the attendant promulgation of an Imperial Edict guaranteeing equality before the law for the non-Muslim subjects of the empire. In consequence, there emerged in the Balkans some revolutionary groups intent on discouraging the continuation of Ottoman oppression by way of the launching of guerilla-style sallies against Ottoman military units and installations. These raids ushered in the period of *komitacis*—small bands of Bulgarian, Greek, and Serbian conspiratorial revolutionaries, or self-styled freedom fighters, taking up arms against Ottoman rulers and, on occasion, against each other.

Through Articles 23 and 61, the Powers were authorized to hold Turkey accountable to them for her future treatment of Macedonian and Armenian minorities respectively, as Turkey, through both articles, undertook to promulgate a new set of reforms in the provinces inhabited by these minorities. The Berlin Treaty thus emerges as the instrument legalizing humanitarian intervention by the six signatory Powers with respect, on the one hand, to Macedonia, which thus became the pivot around which the Eastern Question largely revolved, and, on the other, to the Armenian provincial population in eastern Turkey. It may be argued that the two Questions remained unresolved because the reforms once more proved abortive. The rise of revolutionary groups is directly attributable to this condition. As Marriott points out,

> There is, indeed, a painful monotony in the tale of Turkish misgovernment. Here, as elsewhere, the toiling peasantry were subject to a cross-fire of exactions, and extortions, and persecutions. They suffered at the hands of the Moslems because they were Christians; they were exposed to the lawless depredations of the brigands, frequently of Albanian race, by whom the country was infested; they had to meet the demands, both regular and irregular, of Moslem beys and official tax-farmers; they could obtain no redress in the courts of law; life, property, honour were all at the mercy of the ruling creed.[1]

The analogy to the plight of the Armenian peasants of Sassoun, who ultimately rebelled, is striking. Equally significant is the statement by a student of the history of the Macedonian insurgency that in its formative stages that insurgency was influenced by the example of Sassoun (to be discussed in chapter 8) from which it "took inspiration ... and borrowed from it the idea of ... a revolt."[2] At the very moment (June 1895) the Sultan was stonewalling the May 1895 Reform Project, which the Powers had worked out to redress the inequities that had precipitated the Sassoun outbreak, the Sofia-based Macedonian revolutionaries unleashed their first series of revolutionary forays into Macedonia where for five hundred years the Ottomans had reigned supreme as undisputed overlords, colonizing and at the same time bringing about the conversion of multitudes of indigenous Christians to the Muslim faith.

Armeno-Macedonian Cooperation

The Armenian contribution to the organization of Macedonian guerilla forays against Ottoman rulers was not limited to being a role model, which

Sassoun evidently had been. A number of Armenian experts on explosives were involved in the manufacturing of hand grenades and bombs, all of them operating surreptitiously and under fictitious names. One of them was a chemist and "a prime organizer of terrorist actions against the Ottoman regime"; he belonged to an Armenian revolutionary group. In Constantinople the Macedonians secured the help of "a master bomb maker." The experiments and manufacturing operations were conducted in Sofia, Bulgaria, and the Bulgarian police and other authorities "winked at the activities." In one factory in Sablût, they produced bomb-casing molds, as well as such weapons as knives and daggers. One Armenian expert "taught the revolutionaries how to make gas bombs." The pupils of one of these Armenians "established additional factories elsewhere, even in Sofia, and they in turn served as master bomb makers." The Macedonians received additional help from a number of Armenians from Odessa, Russia, and from two Armenians from the Caucasus who were "excellent pyrotechnicians, casters of bombs, and masters of infernal machines," and who arrived on location to streamline the manufacturing of the explosives.

All this cooperation was achieved on the initiative of the Macedonians, who felt a strong affinity for the Armenian revolutionaries with whom they had established contact in Constantinople. Their biggest plot, which did not materialize, was the assassination of Sultan Abdul Hamit and the simultaneous dynamiting in 1900 of the two Bank Ottoman buildings, namely those in Saloniki and Constantinople, for which purpose two tunnels were dug, without being detected. According to testimony supplied by Macedonian insurgent leaders, "The Armenians were extremely collegial and helpful ... were pleased to assist the Macedonian Revolutionary Organization because both shared a common enemy, the Ottoman Turks, and they were therefore fighting for the same cause."[3] The reciprocal character of this type of help is evidenced by the admission of the Armenian revolutionaries who had captured the Bank Ottoman through a commando-type raid. These revolutionaries revealed in the aftermath of the raid that they had procured their weapons through the channels of the Macedonians.[4] Moreover, they also vowed on board the French steamer which was taking them to Marseille as a measure of banishment from Turkey, that they would return by way of Macedonia to launch new assaults against the Turkish regime.[5]

Greece, Crete and Zeitoun

Another component of the Eastern Question was the lingering Turko-Greek conflict involving the status of the island of Crete. The conditions of Cretan discontent were part of the syndrome of Turkish misrule and oppression as observed by Marriott:

The domestic grievances of the Cretans were practically the same as those with which we have become familiar among other subject peoples in the Ottoman Empire: extortionate and irregular taxation; unequal treatment of Christians and Moslems; denial of justice in the courts; the refusal to carry out the promises contained in the Tanzimat and the Hatti-Humayoun, and so forth.[6]

As a result, the island was beset by a succession of acts of rebellion bent on union with Greece. Through British mediation the Sultan finally made a number of reformist concessions which, on October 25, 1878, were incorporated in the Pact of Halépa.[7] But in 1889, the Sultan's government infringed on the terms of that pact, provoking an insurrection on the island which was put down when the Powers showed no interest in intervening. One of the by-products of this regime of repression was the rise, among others, of the revolutionary secret society, *Ethniké Hetaireia*, whose aims included the defense of Greek interests in Macedonia, and above all, the union of Crete with mainland Greece. When the Sultan in 1895 again violated the terms of the Pact of Halépa by removing from his post the Christian Governor-General of the island, social unrest, fueled by the spread of nationalism in Greece and the island, helped precipitate the outbreak of the 1896-97 Cretan insurrection. This time the Powers intervened, forcing the Sultan to restore the terms of the Pact of Halépa and eventually accept, on August 25, 1896, on the eve of the Dashnak raid on Bank Ottoman in Constantinople (to be discussed in chapter 8), a new reform scheme for the island of Crete.

Thereafter, Crete, in the space of two years, managed to emancipate itself, and the triggering mechanism for this development was massacre. On September 18, 1898, the Muslims in Candia, a coastal town, burned the British Vice-Consul in his own house and proceeded to slaughter all the Christians they could lay their hands on. This was the last straw for the Powers and, by November, the last of the Turkish troops and civil servants had vacated the island in compliance with the demand of the Powers. The latter appointed Prince George of Greece to the post of High Commissioner of Crete, which was a transparent move to bring about in stages and indirectly the island's union with Greece.

The thread interlinking insurrectionary outbreaks involving Greek and Armenian revolutionaries is discernible, for instance, in the case of Zeitoun. The willingness of the Sultan to come to terms with Zeitoun's rebellious Armenians was not entirely due to the military setbacks the Ottoman troops suffered at the hands of the former. There was a new round of trouble brewing in both the island of Crete and mainland Greece involving Greek and Cretan insurgents. The Cretans launched their insurrection at the very moment the Sultan was negotiating peace with the Zeitounlis, i.e., February 1896. The sovereign and his advisers felt constrained to welcome an opportunity to stop military operations against the Zeitounlis, a kind of insurgent minority which had no parent-state to rely on for support and which was hopelessly isolated in the interior of Turkey.

The interconnections of insurgencies in the Balkans and in Asia Minor became even more evident when Zeitoun is assessed in relation to Montenegro, and even to Lebanon; one may thereby discern a commonly generated impact upon the rulers of the Ottoman Empire. During the 1861-62 insurrection, for example, the Zeitoun highlanders had dispatched two emissaries to Napoleon III to solicit his intervention; he responded by arranging the sending of one of the dragomans of the French Embassy at Constantinople to investigate the conditions in Zeitoun and prepare a report, which he did.[8] Thereupon, an official note by the French government informed the Sublime Porte that France "always recognized Zeitoun as independent and exempt from taxes." This event was coincidental with the period of the massacre of the Maronites in Lebanon and the military intervention of France. That intervention had led to the autonomy of Lebanon and to the signing of a protocol by the Powers and Turkey which was intended to restore order and "protect the Christians." Mindful of this setback, Grand Vizier Ali Paşa yielded to Napoleon III in order to avoid confronting another Montenegro in that part of Asia Minor.[9] Commenting on this episode, a Turkish chronicler identifies two such Armenians, one of them a priest, who persuaded the French monarch to intercede on behalf of the Armenians, and as a result, the military attack against Zeitoun was cancelled, and the governor of the district of nearby Maraş who had prepared the plan of the attack, was relieved of his post.[10] This event has been described in France as an act of humanitarian intervention. According to French Academician Albert Vandal, "France adopted the cause of Zeitoun, whose deliverance it obtained. When eight years later, in 1870, it became known in the distant Orient that France herself was besieged, invaded and in mortal danger, some habitants of Zeitoun, led by one of their priests, left their country ... they came to enroll in our ranks and to fight with us. At a time when the great nations had abandoned us and turned away from us, these humble men, these ignorant men, these rough mountaineers, remembered the favor they had received and came to pay their debt with their blood."[11]

This rudimentary form of humanitarian intervention was applied in 1878 again when, in yet another episode of insurrection, England had sent Colonel Chermside to Zeitoun to conduct his own investigation and submit recommendations in his report. The significance of Zeitoun lies not so much in the valor with which the Armenian highlanders fought against, and for all practical purposes defeated, the large regular and irregular contingents of the Turkish army, but in the fact that the insurrection was to a large degree a by-product of a general insurrectionary movement sweeping the various sectors of the Ottoman dominion. Montenegro, Bosnia, and Herzegovina were enveloped with revolutionary fervor in 1861. As noted above, the Powers had intervened with military force in Lebanon the year before, forcing the Turkish authorities to punish the authors of the massacre of Christian Maronites and to grant Lebanon limited autonomy. Already at that time Zeitoun had become an incipient emblem of the Armenian Question which was shaping up as an extension of the emerging Eastern Question.

Nor can one minimize the contagious effects of the 1848 revolution; one of the pillars of which, Mikhail Bakunin, in May 1862, proposed in a letter to Garibaldi, the champion of the principle of national liberation, to coopt the Armenians, along with the Greeks, for his campaign of *Risorgimento*. At the same time, he also wrote to Michael Nalbandian, the 19th-century apostle of Armenian revolutionism, identified with the ideals of Bakunin and his cohort Alexander Herzen, to organize insurrectionary actions, especially among the people in the region of Cilicia, including Zeitoun.[12] Thus, the ideals of the French Revolution, Russian panslavism and anarchism, and Italian national emancipation combined to yield a type of interactive dynamism through which Turkish dominance and subjugation became issues of contest for a certain group of Armenian leaders exposed to these ideals and mindful of their tangible consequences elsewhere. The meaning of submission to abusive authority was not only reexamined but also redefined as unwarranted and unacceptable. Yet the end result of such a new orientation markedly differed from that obtained by the other nationalities mentioned above. Zeitoun over a period of time scored a series of daunting triumphs against the dominant Turks but in the end was wiped off the face of the earth. Clearly, in order to succeed, insurrectionary movements need to rely on factors other than mere adoptive ideologies. As asserted by a prominent Armenian historian, Zeitoun was not accorded the same help as Lebanon because the Armenian Gregorian Church leadership obstinately rebuffed the French stipulation requiring conversion to Catholicism, as was the case with the Maronites of Lebanon; this was then traditional French policy for the Orient, and Napoleon III left the Zeitounlis in the lurch.[13]

Returning to the success of the other nationalities, the mainland Greeks, through the agitation of two revolutionary bands, the Cretan Committee and the Ethniké Hetairia, effectively backed a second Cretan insurrection in 1896 which, one way or another, paved the way for the Turko-Greek war that followed. It is no coincidence that in the ensuing Turkish victory in 1897, the Fifth Army Corps, which was so battered in its campaign against the insurgents of Zeitoun in the 1895-96 insurrectionary war, played a major role in this victory. Equally significant, that Corps was led by the same general, who, having replaced the unsuccessful previous commander, negotiated the peace terms with the Zeitounlis, namely, Edhem Paşa.

The employ of the same army corps against Armenians and Greeks in a span of 15 months epitomizes the type of nationality conflicts the authorities of the empire faced, namely, as interconnected problems. The interconnection was evident on two fronts, internal and external. Internally, the Ottoman authorities were cognizant of the fact that the struggle of one nationality group through revolutionary activities was influencing that of another group. From the point of view of these authorities, the outcome of these challenges were, therefore, critical for controlling the spread of insurrections, which virtually threatened the survival of the empire. Repression was chosen as the only viable option, and it was applied accordingly. But then the external factor entered the picture. Depending on the circumstances, repression of the Ottoman brand more often than not tended to invite some kind of intervention by the Powers. Such interventions in turn tended to counteract and reduce the impact of Turkish repressive measures and served to inspire hope among the victims prone to purposefully escalate the level of the conflict with a view to triggering more drastic steps of intervention by the Powers.

Convergence in Origin But Divergence in Outcome

This interconnective process is succinctly described by a prominent Ottoman-Turkish statesman, who, in the 1885-1913 period, four times occupied the post of Grand Vizier and was an active player in the evolving stages of the Turko-Armenian conflict. Most important, he held various administrative posts in Syria and Lebanon, and in the critical 1877-79 period was Governor-General of the province of Aleppo in which Zeitoun was a county (*kaza*) and at that time had once more rebelled. When commenting on the proneness of the inhabitants of Zeitoun to rise up and rebel, Kâmil Paşa, the Governor-General, in his memoirs declares, "Seeing that the Bulgarians and Greeks were gaining independence, the Armenians became desirous of emulating them and began to pursue the goal of an Armenian kingdom" for which purpose they were banking on British support. He goes on to say that compared with the Russians, the British were at a disadvantage as far as the task of influencing the Armenians in the interior of Turkey was concerned.[14]

What the Grand Vizier was not saying, however, was that compared to the Greeks and Bulgarians, the Armenians themselves were at a greater disadvantage insofar as their chances of securing at that time effective intervention by the Powers was concerned. During the February 1897 Cretan insurrection, which set the stage for the eventual union of the island with Greece, Russia was actively engaged in efforts to facilitate that union, with her new Foreign Minister, Muravief, playing a leading role in the organization of the concerted action of the Powers. As French Ambassador Cambon at the time reflected, "The Russians are not indifferent there, as they are towards the Armenians; the issue is the welfare of the Orthodox Greeks, her special clients. In this case they, the Russians, are insisting on imposing on the Turks serious reforms."[15] Almost simultaneously, the Russians restored their old fraternal ties with Bulgaria when Boris, the crown prince, through conversion, embraced the Orthodox faith. Henceforth, Bulgaria was no longer anathema, as it had been before when a host of Russian diplomats, especially Lobanof, were invoking the specter of a foreboding "second Bulgaria," which, they avowed, would materialize as a result of reforms in Turkish Armenia and then eventually grow into a greater Armenia, combining Turkish and Russian Armenia in its realm. Based on these assertions, the Russian government at that time opposed the idea of coercive measures against the Sultan as a means to compel the Turks to implement the promised reforms.

This differential treatment of the Armenian Question by the Powers, especially Russia, most assuredly contributed to its differential outcome as compared to that of the Eastern Question. In his assessment of the reasons why the Sultan was amenable to the settlement of the Cretan conflict but not so of a similar conflict in the Armenian case, French Ambassador Cambon, in his "confidential" cipher to his Foreign Minister, Hanotaux, offered a simple but cogent formula:

> The Cretan problem has been settled because the Sultan was able to persuade himself that the prolongation of the [Cretan] insurrection would invite a forceful European intervention. The Armenian problem [on the other hand] drags on and becomes aggravated because the Sultan thinks he is safe [*à l'abri*] from such intervention.[16]

Unable to repress Macedonia with intimidating force, or with equal severity, the Turkish authorities targeted instead the vulnerable Armenian population. This kind of relationship between the two issues in international diplomacy is acknowledged by Turkish chronicler Hocaoğlu, who describes the Armenian Question as a product of manipulative diplomacy fostered by the Powers who were more interested in the solution of the Eastern Question.[17]

Notes to Chapter 5

1. J. Marriott, *The Eastern Question: An Historical Study in European Diplomacy* 4th ed. Reprinted (Glasgow, 1958), 415.
2. Duncan M. Perry, "The Macedonian Revolutionary Organization's Armenian Connection," *Armenian Review* 42, 1/165 (Spring 1989): 63.
3. *Ibid.*, 62, 63, 64, 65, 66.
4. *Houshabadoum Hai Heghapokhagan Dashnaktzoutian* (Commemorative Tome of the Armenian Revolutionary Federation) (1890-1950), (Boston, 1950), 282.
5. *Blue Book*. Turkey No. 1 (1897) enclosure 4 in Doc. No. 25, p. 17, Chargé Herbert's August 24, 1896 report.

6. Marriott, *The Eastern Question* [n. 1], 376.
7. E. Hertslet, *The Map of Europe by Treaty*, vol. 4, 1875 to 1891 (London, 1891) Doc. No. 35, p. 2810.
8. *Diplomatic Archives of the Foreign Ministry of France (Documents Diplomatiques. Affaires Arméniennes.* (Hereafter cited as DAF.) Supplément. 1895-1896 (Paris, 1897) Doc. No. 81, p. 67. Cambon's January 12, 1896, report to Foreign Minister Berthelot.
9. Victor Bérard, *La politique du Sultan* (Paris, 1897), 128-29, 302.
10. Esat Uras, *Tarihte Ermeniler ve Ermeni Meselesi* (Armenians and the Armenian Question in History) (Istanbul, 1976), 489-90.
11. A. Vidâl, *Les Arméniens et la réforme de la Turquie* (Paris, 1897), 41-2.
12. Leo, (Arakel Babakhanian), *Turkahai Heghopokhutian Kaghaparapanoutiunu* (The Ideology of the Revolution of Turkish Armenian) vol. 1, (Paris, 1934), 25-31.
13. *Ibid.*, 31.
14. Hilmi K. Bayur, *Sadrazam Kâmil Paşa. Siyasi Hayatı* (Grand Vizier Kâmil Paşa. His Political Life) (Ankara, 1954), 73.
15. Paul Cambon, *Correspondance* 1870-1924. vol. 1 (Paris, 1940), 409.
16. *DAF* [n. 8] 1871-1914 1ʳᵉ Série (1871-1900) vol. 12 (May 8, 1895-October 14, 1896) (Paris, 1951) Doc. No. 461, registry No. 353, pp. 757-58, September 30, 1896.
17. Mehmed Hocaoğlu, *Arşiv Vesikalarıyla Tarihte Ermeni Mezâlimi ve Ermeniler* (Armenians and Armenian Atrocities in History Through Archive Documents) (Istanbul, 1976), 661.

Part III

THE DYSFUNCTIONS OF HUMANITARIAN INTERVENTION IN THE RISE AND TREATMENT OF THE ARMENIAN QUESTION

Chapter 6

Manipulative Diplomacy Supplanting the Ideals of Humanitarian Intervention

The European interventions historically hinged upon a modicum of consensus among the Great Powers. Until the 1878 Berlin Treaty, the unified pressure of England and Russia, the dominant Powers in the Concert of Europe, could induce, if not compel, Turkey to submit to some degree of intervention by the Powers.[1] However, this line of cooperation was not exclusive of rivalries on many other levels; nor were these interventions purely "humanitarian."[2] But the Treaty of Berlin ushered in a period of increasingly acute distrust between Russia and England, thus ensuring the gradual collapse of the Concert of Europe. The necessity of cooperation among the Powers, and the ever-present suspicion of ulterior motives, are limitations inherent in the principle of multilateral intervention, whether humanitarian or not.

The Armenian Question as a Pawn in British Party Politics. The Sway of a Moral Dilemma

These limitations became distinct liabilities for the Armenians, as European concern for Turkey's implementation of Article 61 of the Berlin Treaty lessened and eventually evaporated in the face of the Anglo-Russian rivalry and mutual suspicion. The rivalries found expression in the British challenge to the provisions of Article 16 of the San Stefano Treaty, in which Russia had acquired the right to continue to occupy the eastern provinces of Turkey, which they had conquered through the

---

1877–1878 Russo-Turkish War, until Turkey had carried out the reforms it had promised. Considering the presence of Russian troops in that region a threat to British colonial interests in India, Disraeli went through the motions of preliminary mobilization to signal to Russia his intent to wage war, if necessary, to force Russian withdrawal. This British manoeuvre directly affected Armenia. The public manifestation of a sense of compunction by British statesmen associated with the British war effort and the victory achieved in 1918 is described in the two passages below; the sentiments contained in these passages are an indirect indictment of the Armenian policy of their forebears. First, the statement of wartime Prime Minister Lloyd George:

> Had it not been for our sinister intervention, the great majority of the Armenians would have been placed, by the Treaty of San Stefano in 1878, under the protection of the Russian flag.
>
> The Treaty of San Stefano provided that Russian troops should remain in occupation of the Armenian provinces until satisfactory reforms were carried out. By the Treaty of Berlin (1878)—which was entirely due to our minatory pressure and which was acclaimed by us as a great British triumph which brought "Peace with honour"—that article was superseded. Armenia was sacrificed on the triumphal altar we had erected. The Russians were forced to withdraw; the wretched Armenians were once more placed under the heel of their old masters, subject to a pledge to "introduce ameliorations and reforms into the provinces inhabited by Armenians." We all know how these pledges were broken for forty years, in spite of repeated protests from the country that was primarily responsible for restoring Armenia to Turkish rule. The action of the British Government led inevitably to the terrible massacres of 1895–97, 1909, and worst of all to the holocausts of 1915. By these atrocities, almost unparalleled in the black record of Turkish misrule, the Armenian population was reduced in numbers by well over a million.
>
> Having regard to the part we had taken in making these outrages possible, we were morally bound to take the first opportunity that came our way to redress the wrong we had perpetrated, and in so far as it was in our power, to make it impossible to repeat the horrors for which history will always hold us culpable.
>
> When therefore in the Great War, the Turks forced us into this quarrel, and deliberately challenged the British Empire to a life and death struggle, we realised that at last an opportunity had been given us to rectify the cruel wrong for which we were responsible.[3]

During the Nov. 18, 1918, Parliamentary debates in the House of Commons, Aneurin Williams raised the same question, declaring,

> This country owes a debt to Armenia, because, after all, we more than forty years ago prevented Armenia from being released by Russia from Turkish tyranny. If we had not done that, the awful sufferings which have occurred since would not have occurred. We, therefore, owe them a debt. We owe them a further debt because they have fought valiantly for us in this War.[4]

In the years following the 1878 Berlin Congress, England was not entirely aloof regarding the plight of the Ottoman Armenians. This was in part due to the Cyprus Convention signed on June 4, 1878, i.e., just before the convening of the Berlin Congress, by England and Turkey. Article 1 of that Convention committed England to pursue the matter of Armenian reforms ("the Sultan promises to England to introduce necessary reforms ... for the protection of the Christian and other subjects ... in these territories."). In return for its willingness to protect "by force of arms" Turkey against Russian territorial encroachments, beyond Kars, Ardahan and Batum, England was allowed to occupy the island of Cyprus.[5] This provision, together with the stipulations of Article 61 of the Berlin Treaty, somehow entitled England the option of considering intervention and a willingness to use force for that purpose.

The tenuous character of this willingness bordered on deception. Diplomatic records highlight the incidence of frivolous party politics carried out under the guise of "humanitarian intervention." The British handling of the Armenian Question exemplified the influence of domestic party squabbles on foreign policy, pitting the Gladstonian liberals against the conservatives represented by Disraeli, and subsequently by Salisbury. In dismissing Gladstone's fervent pronouncements in support of efforts to extricate subject races from the Ottoman yoke, for example, Disraeli denounced Gladstone as "an unprincipled maniac, extraordinary mixture of envy, vindictiveness, hypocrisy ... never a gentleman."[6] These views may deserve some attention in light of the statement of William Summers, a liberal Member of Parliament (and a colleague of Gladstone) who, during a brief visit in Constantinople in 1890, met with some diplomats. In his September 28, 1890 report to his Chancellor in Berlin, German Ambassador Radowitz, after describing Summers as "the most energetic supporter of the Armenian cause in England," quoted Summers as follows: "Gladstone and I are involved in the Armenian Question for the sole purpose of causing difficulties to the Salisbury Cabinet."[7] This was the period when Conservatives and Liberals often went out of their way to introduce motions in the Parliament "in order to embarrass their opponents."[8]

The pattern of exploitation of the Armenian Question as an extension of party politics continued all the way to the eve of the outbreak of the 1895–96 empire-wide series of massacres. In a report to his Chancellor in Berlin, Count von Hatzfeldt, the German Ambassador to Turkey, disclosed that Lord Salisbury, whose Cabinet on June 26, 1895 had replaced that of the Liberals, had "confidentially" revealed to him that he, Salisbury, was aware of the game the latter were playing and that he would respond in kind. Lord Rosebery in a major speech in Albert Hall on July 5, 1895 had challenged Salisbury to follow in the footsteps of the Liberals. He suggested that in cooperation with France and Russia, Salisbury should exert pressure in Constantinople in order to "protect the Armenians against unbearable oppression, unbearable cruelties and unbearable acts of barbarism" in the Ottoman realm. Salisbury told Hatzfeldt that he would "outflank" Rosebery by publicly maintaining that England was interested in the fate of the Armenians and that it in no way would shrink from this interest insofar as he could thereby avoid setting off a confrontation.[9]

But as complex a problem as the Armenian Question was becoming at the time, the description of British policies in this regard cannot be reduced to simplistic frames of reference. Armenia and Armenian interests were, perhaps necessarily, and only in part, treated by the British as subsidiary matters; these interests lent themselves to manipulative handling in the same way that one may handle a pawn in a chess game. Not infrequently, British statesmen, including the royalty, were sufficiently outraged at chronic Turkish misrule and its frequent degeneration into massacres to consider the adoption of drastic remedies, including the liquidation through partition of the Ottoman Empire, of the regime itself. The Conservative leader Salisbury stood out in this regard. His political career ran parallel to the unfolding of the turmoils besetting the Ottoman Empire in the second half of the nineteenth century. As early as 1858 Salisbury, then known only as Lord Robert Cecil, in a speech he delivered in the House of Commons, had denounced the Turkish government as "the most oppressive and rapacious of all governments." Thus, on July 30, 1895, i.e., 24 days after he had expressed his intention to "outflank" the leaders of the Liberal opposition and feign solicitousness for the plight of the Armenians, he "confidentially" (*unter Voraussetzung voller Diskretion*), told German Ambassador Hatzfeldt in London in a conversation dealing with the Armenian Question that "the Turkish Empire was rotting and that its eventual partition was a compelling necessity." Ambassador Hatzfeldt then added in his "very confidential" report to Berlin that Salisbury made a "very significant" statement, namely: it was a very big mistake for England to rebuff Tsar Nicholas I's proposal for the partition of Turkey, which the Tsar had made in January and February 1853 (months before the outbreak of the Crimean War) to British Ambassador Sir George Hamilton Seymour. "He, Lord Salisbury, would have certainly accepted the proposal, he said." Salisbury then exacted a promise from the German ambassador not to report officially this exchange.[10]

But Salisbury's solution was not shared by others capable of pushing it through. As early as 1876 when he and the other Powers failed to induce the Turks at the Constantinople Conference to adopt a European scheme of reforms, he had proposed to the British Cabinet that it abandon the traditional British policy towards Turkey and press instead for partition. Disraeli, the Prime Minister, decried the proposal as "immoral" and prevailed upon the Cabinet to reject the proposal.[11] And, one month after his confidential exchange with German Ambassador Hatzfeldt, described above, Salisbury one more time attempted to coopt Germany into a plan for partitioning Turkey. The German Emperor was visiting at Cowes and, upon his request on August 8, 1895, he had an audience with

Salisbury on board the Hohenzollern. Salisbury once more reiterated his view that the Armenian massacres had demonstrated the imperviousness of Turkey to liberal reforms, that the empire was in a state of decay, was not worth preserving, and that, therefore, it should be dismembered. Mentally prepared in advance by Holstein, a highly suspicious, but nevertheless influential Anglophobe councillor in the German Foreign Office, as well as by the German ambassador himself, the Emperor disputed the accuracy of Salisbury's diagnosis of Turkey's afflictions, at the same time belittling the import of the atrocities committed against the Armenians. Salisbury's failure to persuade the Emperor was largely the result of major policy differences but nevertheless it also bore the effects of the Emperor's displeasure caused by the tardiness of the British Prime Minister; due to an unfortunate accident he had arrived one hour later than the appointed time.

Such are the quirks of posturing in international diplomacy, allowing as they do some scope for assertive egos to exert themselves and, in the process, impinge upon the direction and outcome of the negotiations involved. One hurt ego helped produce in the course of the interaction another deflated ego, with the result that, according to the interpretation of German Undersecretary Rotenhan, Salisbury himself was "annoyed" enough to avoid a second meeting which the German Emperor had requested.[12]

There is no doubt that in the final analysis, the most decisive factor in foreign policy is the relationship between national interests and national values. When the weight of the priority of a given national interest significantly exceeds that of a given national value, then resourceful and clever politicians, often by resort to disingenuousness, will be able to justify, or at least try to justify, a policy inimical to a certain national value. Disraeli in a way rescued Turkey from disintegration by rejecting as "immoral" a plan for partitioning Turkey, which was proposed first by Russia and subsequently supported by his subaltern Salisbury. In the process, he conveniently dismissed or discounted the cumulative evidence of atrocities committed by the regime he was determined to preserve, thereby supplying a new twist to the idea of morality, as then understood and fostered in British public life. It is most significant to note in this respect that two decades later the German Emperor turned down Salisbury's proposal on almost identical grounds; he belittled the scope and significance of the atrocities, and favored the idea of preserving the Ottoman Empire. As will be seen in the section dealing with German attitudes on the Armenian Question, the public statements in this regard of the highest policy makers in Germany carried the concept of morality in national and international politics to new levels of amorality, i.e., a value-free stance, by invoking superordinate national interests. In doing so, Germany eventually displaced and replaced overall British influence in Turkey in conjunction with the turmoil that the Abdul Hamit era Armenian massacres had entailed throughout the Near East, the Balkans, and the rest of Europe.

It is this fact that the British statesman Grey of Fallodon most laments in his memoirs. One of the architects of the Triple Entente through which England, Russia, and France aligned themselves against Germany seven years before the outbreak of World War I, this Foreign Secretary, a Liberal, concurred with Salisbury, the Conservative, in decrying Turkey as a country where "misgovernment and ill-treatment of Christian minorities … was endemic, outrage and massacre was epidemic."[13]

In a lengthy discussion on this subject, Grey argued that Abdul Hamit was very adept at playing off one government against another, ever ready to grant influence and concessions at a price. That price was the willingness to shield the Sultan and allow him to carry on the "Armenian massacres," in spite of the constraints imposed upon him by the Concert of Europe. Here are some portions of Grey's commentary:

> The German Government and the German Emperor paid the price and got the position that Great Britain had once held at Constantinople. No British Government could pay this price. Lord Salisbury could not have done it, if he would, and he made it evident, after the horrors of 1895, that he would not, if he could. The German Government and the German Emperor paid the price and got the position that Great Britain had once held at Constantinople … British representations about Armenian massacres made us hated, but not feared … . Public opinion in Britain demanded that we should make representations; we did so, to the cost of British material interests in Turkey. The irony of it all was that little or no good was done … Germany at Constantinople exploited the situation steadily to her own advantage … we did indeed keep our hands clean and acquit the national conscience, but to do this without effectively helping the objects of our efforts and our sympathy … German policy seems to have been based upon a deliberate belief that moral scruples and altruistic motives do not count in international affairs … . It was this mistaken view of human affairs between nations that lost her the war."[14]

These comments could not possibly suggest the idea that England was a paragon of virtue in the formulation of foreign policy in general, and with respect to the handling of the Armenian Question in particular. After all, Palmerston's legacy of disavowing the need of permanent friends and foes, and advocating instead the need to cultivate permanent British interests in the design of British foreign policy remained a guiding principle throughout. But Britain differed from Germany as well as Russia in one major respect. Britain's highly developed democratic institutions afforded a public debate of foreign policy issues out of which there emerged the factor of public opinion, a factor which undoubtedly constrained, modified, and even to some extent channelled British foreign policy, especially in times of crisis. Observers may, therefore, argue that British intervention on behalf of the Ottoman Armenians was exactly that, no more, no less, i.e., initiatives to merely mollify British public opinion by recourse to a series of remonstrances which allegorically have been equated with the act of "firing paper pellets at Abdul Hamit," the vehement manifestation of public outrage and official consternation at the perpetration of a series of massacres against the Armenians notwithstanding.

In the overall appraisal of the historical role of British diplomacy confronting the Armenian Question, the overriding fact engaging one's attention concerns the manipulative skill with which that diplomacy derailed the original Russian plan to solve that question effectively and, in all likelihood, permanently. British avowals of humanitarian concerns for the plight of the wretched Armenian subjects of the Sultan were here expediently supplanted by the mandate of the Palmerstonian legacy, which, as noted above, enjoins British statesmen to safeguard first and foremost British national interests. As described elsewhere in this study, Russia was willing to maintain its occupation of Turkey's eastern provinces, which they had conquered in the course of the 1877–78 Russo-Turkish War, until such time as Turkey would introduce and in fact implement the requisite reforms "in the Armenian provinces," i.e., in the eastern provinces of Turkey. Defeated and prostrate Turkey had accepted this stipulation, which then was incorporated in the Treaty of San Stefano as Article 16. But England interceded promptly, and under threat of resisting Russia through war, for the preparation of which, including the act of mobilization, the government in a very brief span of time had spent six million pounds sterling, it compelled Russia to agree to substituting for that treaty the Berlin Treaty of 1878, in which Article 16 was modified and emasculated to become Article 61. The Russian troops had to withdraw forthwith, and the matter of implementation of the reforms was left to the good will of the Sultan. By successfully protecting what it considered to be one of the strategic inland gateways to India, England ended up creating another gateway, of a kind that ushered in the protracted ordeals of Armenia, and ultimately led to the destruction of the Ottoman Armenian population, as noted by such British statesmen as Lloyd George and Aneurin Williams (see notes 3 and 4 in this chapter).

Equally significant is the legal, or more precisely, international law aspect of this derailment. In order to justify it, England had invoked the 1856 Paris Treaty, Article 9 of which in its 2nd paragraph forbade the Powers, individually, or collectively, to get involved in the internal affairs of Turkey, and the 7th Article of which likewise forbade tampering with "the independence and territorial integrity of the Ottoman Empire," adding that any violation of this clause will have to be dealt with as a problem affecting all the Powers. But nine days before the Congress of Berlin convened, England, on June 4, 1878, secretly signed the Cyprus Convention with Turkey, Article I of which involved a Defensive Alliance with the latter. By engineering this deal, however, England itself violated the very same Paris Peace Treaty with the violation of which Russia was

charged in the first place, and which charge was the reason for the convening of the Berlin Congress. In exchange for the privilege of occupying the island of Cyprus, England was to undertake the responsibility to
defend by force of arms Turkish territories should they be seized by Russia in the future. "In return," the Sultan "promises to England to introduce
necessary reforms" in these territories inhabited by the Armenians. All
these conditions and clauses were breaches of the terms of Articles 7 and
9 of the Paris Treaty mentioned above. No Power was to make, singlehandedly, not to speak of secretly, arrangements affecting Turkish territorial integrity and domestic relations. Moreover, the first part of Article
7 of that Treaty states that the European signatories involved "declare the
Sublime Porte admitted to participate in the advantages of the public law
and system (*concert*) of Europe." In this sense, the Cyprus Convention
was even more an abrogation of the public law of Europe; it withheld
from the Powers the right to exercise the supreme jurisdiction to which
they were entitled by treaty law.

In brief, when the dictates of supreme national interests were
involved, England was not immune from the temptation to extort the ces-
sion of an island from a client state and in the process vitiate the provisions of a treaty it simultaneously pretended to uphold in a contest
involving a rival Power.

The Austrian Policy of Acquiescence to the Massacres

The significance of discontinuities in the exercise of foreign policy by the
Powers is exceeded only by the significance of the incidence of about-
faces and reversals in the design of such policy. As in the case of the other
Powers, especially Russia and England, such a reversal characterized the
vacillations in Austria's stance on Turkey, and on reforms in Ottoman
Turkey. The Concert of Europe had functioned, despite minor and intermittent frictions, reasonably well throughout the decades preceding and
following the Crimean War. During that war it had prevailed upon Turkey
and induced it to promulgate laws more or less consistent with the public laws of Europe. These interventions were for the benefit of the Christian subjects of the empire in general. Consistent with this general policy,
Count Friedrich Beust, Austria's Prime Minister and Chancellor, who
was instrumental in ushering in the regime of the Austro-Hungarian
Monarchy, in 1867 openly advocated a system of autonomy for the
Christian nationalities of the Ottoman Empire, to which they would have
a loose tie of vassalage. Beust considered that empire sick and moribund,
and pressed for "a medical consultation" to devise "heroic remedies,"
including a plan for the partition of the empire. Ironically, Russia, which
also would reverse its policy a quarter of a century later, at the very same

time advocated the same policy through Prince Alexander Gorchakof, its Chancellor and Foreign Minister, who nevertheless was antagonistic to Austria on account of the latter's role in the Paris Peace Treaty, signed in the wake of the Crimean War. Now Beust was conceding that the Treaty of Paris had failed to secure improvements in the treatment of the Christian subjects of Turkey and was proposing a new arrangement whereby these subjects would be placed under the protective wings of Europe. But this stance during the period of the massacres gave way to a new policy.

There is no doubt that on the matter of the Armenian Question Austria more or less echoed German views and postures on that question. In fact, Prince Philipp 3rd Eulenburg, German Ambassador to Austria, in an exchange with Marchand, French Chargé at Vienna, expressed a hope that Austria would emulate Germany in this respect, while declaring that the Armenian Question doesn't exist "for us." In another exchange with Welsersheimb, Section Chief of the Austrian Ministry of Foreign Affairs, Marchand was told by the latter that the Armenian massacres, which were then running their full course, were such as to demand from Austria the exercise of "reserve and utmost circumspection." He dismissed British efforts to introduce reforms in Turkey as proof of "their total ignorance of that country's state of affairs." Referring to the reforms stipulated by the Treaty of Berlin, Welsersheimb rejected them as treaty engagements which have "hidden complications for the Powers. We would like to accord the Sultan his freedom of action. He must be freed from the restraints and constraints imposed upon his authority." In registering this piece of communication from Marchand, officials of the French Foreign Ministry appended this note: "this is almost the language of the Russian government."[15] The state organization in the Austro-Hungarian Empire was akin to that of the Ottoman Empire; both were multi-ethnic systems and both were beset by interminable nationality conflicts. Thus, if one disregards other considerations, from this vantage point alone, Austria had a stake in the preservation of the Ottoman system, for the defense of which it would engage diplomatically, lest the perils involved in the disintegration of the Ottoman Empire might become contagious and reach into the Austrian realm. But beyond this, being an imperial power, and bent on aggrandizement, Austria was not free from a propensity to entertain designs on Ottoman territories. Solving the Armenian Question through the effective promulgation of reforms was viewed as a remedy inimical with such colonial aspirations—inasmuch as the reforms were likely to strengthen Turkey and prolong its viability as an empire, at the same time improving the condition of the Armenians. The solution to the underlying ambivalence of this posture was to see to it that the Turko-Armenian conflict continued its pace of escalation to the point of exhaustion for Turks and Armenians alike. Only then would the opportunity possibly present itself to substitute imperial ambitions for dubious initiatives of humanitarian intervention. As one British author averred, "Austria, more than Russia, has been opposed to the coercion of the Sultan, and that she too is waiting for the opportune moment to snatch Ottoman lands."[16]

This may have been true of the attitude of Count Agenor Goluchowski, Austrian Foreign Minister 1895–1906, who, during his summer 1896 meeting in Vienna with Russian Foreign Minister Prince Lobanof, agreed to a joint declaration in which the two ministers mutually pledged each other to preserve the Turkish Empire to the limit of their ability. During the 1894–96 massacres the Austrian minister opposed the mounting of any coercive action against the Sultan, irrespective of the tragic dimensions of the mass murder involved. Here are some of his comments as reproduced on December 17, 1895 in a report to London by Sir Edmund Monson, British Ambassador at Vienna 1893–96:

> Intervention of any other kind must inevitably result in the further disaggregation of the Ottoman Empire … beyond making representations [to the Sultan] the Powers can do nothing for the Armenians.[17]

In a January 14, 1896 statement, when the massacres were continuing unabated, the same Austrian Foreign Minister declared:

> In the presence of this heartrending prospect, it is intelligible that numbers of humane people are revolted at the idea that Europe is powerless, and regardless of consequences, would wish that *action should be taken by some, or even one of the Powers, to put a stop to the extermination of the miserable Armenians. But practical statesmen are bound to consider the situation from another standpoint.*[18] [Italics added]

The Role-Reversal of Russia: the Crux of the Armenian Disaster

The Armenian policy of Tsarist Russia gradually stiffened, assuming a harsh and uncompromising stance in the last two decades of the 19th century. Having given a major impetus to the process of adoption of the principle of humanitarian intervention by the Great Powers in the course of the preceding five decades, the assumption of this posture by Russia was a singular instance of role reversal, with disastrous consequences for the Armenians of the Ottoman Empire. Several considerations impinged upon the adoption of this new policy. The Russian Romanof dynasty, facing "nihilistic" challenges from within, developed a measure of apprehension that variably was shared by the other imperial dynasties of Europe, such as the German Hohenzollern and the Austrian Hapsburg-Lorraine dynasties. They all became wary of the possibilities of internal disaffections exploding into insurgency, with the potential to cause the overthrow of their regimes.

The emergence of Armenian revolutionary movements in Transcaucasia, and their designs to deliver their kinsmen in the Ottoman Empire from Turkish bondage, were viewed by Tsarist authorities as portentous. The specter of a future consolidated Armenia bestriding eastern Turkey and western Caucasus and asserting itself against Russian domination was part of this apprehension. Armenian reforms in Turkey, it was thought, may abet this process and conversely, the averting of these reforms may continue to fuel the Turko-Armenian conflict, thereby enfeebling not only the Armenians but Turkey also. This latter prospect was compatible with long-standing Russian aspirations on certain parts of Turkish territory. As a result, Russia embarked upon a series of diplomatic manoeuvres and machinations, and in the process thwarted the efforts of the other Powers, especially those of Great Britain. It is therefore warranted to review briefly the conditions of the rise and exercise of this drift of Russian policy.

The foremost exponent of that policy was Prince Alexis Borisovich Lobanof-Rostowksi. His rise to power coincided with the turbulent period during which the Turko-Armenian conflict intensified, mainly as a result of its ever-widening compass and eventual internationalization. Lobanof was Russian Ambassador at Vienna (1882–1894) and was promoted to the post of Foreign Minister in 1895, at which post he served until his death (August 30, 1896). Equally important, he was Russia's Ambassador to Turkey during the 1878 Berlin Congress. As is often the case, however, he inherited a legacy, forged by his predecessors, in which one finds Lobanof's Armenian policy more or less foreshadowed.

What is so salient in this legacy is the impact of Russian disillusionment in the Balkans upon their subsequent Armenian policy. The ingredients of the nationality conflicts in the Balkans in many ways were comparable to those of the Turko-Armenian conflict. Hence the Russians began to draw some inferences, and accordingly extrapolated. The disillusionment issued from what they considered the dismal outcome of their many deeds of "humanitarian intervention" in the Balkan peninsula. Indeed, ever since Russia began to intervene on behalf of the Balkan nationalities and substantially helped them emancipate themselves from Turkish domination, its expectations were consistently nullified or degraded by the spell of an intoxicating nationalism that animated these nationalities in the aftermath of their emancipation. Consequently, a number of Russian statesmen and diplomats proceeded to disparage these manifestations of nationalism, defining them as nefarious manifestations of ingratitude. The following excerpt from a communication to Tsar Nicholas I (1825–1855) by Baron von Brunnow, Russia's ambassador to Great Britain, epitomized the problem; he is advising his sovereign not to get involved in a war with Turkey (the 1853–56 Crimea War) that, in his opinion, may lead to the break-up of that country and to new problems for Russia. Putting the problem in a nutshell, he stated:

The war in its results would cause to spring out of the ruins of Turkey all kinds of new states, as ungrateful to us as Greece has been, as troublesome as the Danubian Principalities have been, and an order of things where our influence will be more sharply combated, resisted, restrained, by the rivalries of France, England, Austria, than it has ever been under the Ottoman.... The Ottoman empire may be transformed into independent states, which for us will only become either burdensome clients or hostile neighbours.[19]

This attitude became even more entrenched in the decade following the signing of the 1878 Berlin Treaty when Bulgaria, which was decisively helped by Russia in its struggle for autonomy, actually a stepping-stone for independence, began to assert itself against the latter, refusing to be treated as a colony. During that period Russian officers and officials descended on Bulgaria's capital in a swarm and reduced the country to a Russian province. Any complaint was branded as "ingratitude." Growing discontent, attended by anti-Russian sentiments, led to the 1881 overthrow of the regime. Russia responded by appointing Russian generals, who took their orders directly from the Tsar, and "Russian generals were appointed to the Ministries of Interior, War, and Justice." Nationalists in Bulgaria subsequently coined the phrase "Bulgaria for the Bulgarians." These are the conditions under which Bulgarian "ingratitude" arose and crystallized.[20]

It was primarily in response to this development that Russia abandoned its active participation in the collective exercise of the principle of humanitarian intervention and, through a role reversal, assumed the posture of a contrarian in the pursuit of the goal of the Powers to impose "Armenian" reforms upon Turkey. The original architect of this policy was Nikolaus Giers, who, in the 1882–95 period was Foreign Minister of Russia, thus Lobanof's immediate predecessor. Moreover, in the 1876–82 period, Giers was the Assistant of Prince Michael Gorchakof, Russian Chancellor (1870–72) and Foreign Minister (1856–82). Giers granted that the Armenians were "exposed to terrible abuses on the part of the Muslim populations; from the point of view of humanity one cannot be indifferent towards that condition, the truth of which is impossible to deny." Nevertheless Russia is "far from being ready to raise [*soulever*] the Armenian Question," even though the provisions of the Berlin Treaty still remain unimplemented. "Russia however has no interest in it, and will, therefore, do nothing to expedite a solution." Russia's interest in the cities of Kars and Batum are purely strategic, but Russia is "absolutely averse to increasing the sizes of its Armenian and Muslim populations." Giers then outlined in succinct terms Russia's Armenian policy:

Russia has no reason at all to desire the formation of a second Bulgaria. The emergence of an autonomous Armenian principality would then entail the danger for Russia that the Russian Armenians will aspire to become part of it.[21]

Lobanof, who at the time of Giers' appointment as Foreign Minister was himself a candidate for that post, but told the Tsar that Giers would be a better minister on account of his range of experiences, was quite familiar with conditions of Turkish politics. He had replaced General Ignatief for the post of Russian Ambassador to Turkey in 1878, a post which he had already occupied in the 1860s. In the aftermath of the 1878 Berlin Treaty, he went out of his way to befriend, through many visitations, Sultan Abdul Hamit, with the intent to dissuade him from adopting the reforms under the provisions of that treaty, and to sensitize him regarding what he considered the sinister, imperial designs of England. At that time, British military consuls were being deployed in the Asiatic provinces of Turkey to serve as consuls but were suspected by the Russians of being charged with missions of military intelligence directed against Russia. This view was personally conveyed to the German Emperor, William I, on September 4, 1879, by Russia's Minister of War Milyutin who, with Russian Foreign Minister Giers and General Adlerberg, the Tsar's Aide de Camp, had an audience with the Emperor on the occasion of the latter's meeting in Alexandrovo with Tsar Alexander II.

These Russian efforts of agitation against England and rapprochement with Turkey culminated in the concluding in Constantinople of a formal and secret agreement between Russia and Turkey, or more specifically, between the Tsar and the Sultan. Arranged by Ambassador Lobanof, Sultan Abdul Hamit in the fall of 1879 received in audience General Obruchef, the Chief of Russia's General Staff, and the representative of Russian War Minister Milyutin. He had come to the Ottoman capital on a confidential mission from the Tsar. Neither the Turkish Foreign Minister, nor the First Imperial Interpreter were present at this private meeting. Against some Turkish concessions and military positions involving the ceding of the Passes of the Balkans, the Tsar is reported to have committed himself to defend the Sultan and his throne against all aggression from within and without Turkey, including internal insurgencies.[22]

Lobanof was not only Giers' successor but was also a close friend of his. Whether genuine, pretended, or only partly credible, Russia's projective concern about a new Bulgaria on its southern borders came into full play during the tenure of Lobanof as Russia's Foreign Minister. It was during this time, 1895–96, that the viability of the principle of humanitarian intervention as a normative rule in international relations was sorely tested and, due to Lobanof's studied intransigence, was subverted through manipulative diplomacy. As a result, Abdul Hamit was more or less left free to initiate in this very same period the empire-wide massacres to be described below. During the protracted negotiations on Armenian Reforms in the critical March-October 1895 period, for example, Lobanof twice declared to Sir Frank Cavendish Lascelles, British Ambassador to Russia, that his government could not tolerate "another Bulgaria" in Russia's southern border region.[23] Moreover, Lobanof in several exchanges emphatically rejected the British suggestion to apply "coercion" against

the Sultan.[24] He subsequently instructed Nelidof, his ambassador to
Turkey, to extend his support to the Sultan and refuse participation in any
scheme that provided for hostile action against the latter.[25]

German and French diplomats became cognizant of the real meaning
of these steps which they defined as an obstruction of a collective plan of
forceful intervention by the Powers, and so they reported it to their governments. Count Henckel von Donnersmarck, the German Chargé in the
Ottoman capital, informed his Chancellor in Berlin that "Russia is undermining the effects of British warnings to Turkey" by way of "secretly
spurring the latter [*geheime Ermunterung*] to resist the warnings."[26]
Prince von Radolin, the German Ambassador at St. Petersburg, informed
Berlin likewise that "the Russians are ostensibly cooperating with the
British but underhandedly [*unter der Hand*] are supporting the Sultan."[27]
A contemporary Turkish historian expressed an identical view when
declaring that "Abdul Hamit was able to push forth his Armenian policy
thanks to the underhanded [*el altından*] support of the Tsar."[28] The Sultan
at that very moment had rejected the 1895 May Reform project proposed
by the Powers. Four months later, Radolin reported again to Berlin:
"While the Russian government externally and officially cooperated with
England, it secretly has been winking to the Sultan with all kinds of reassuring signals, admonishing him not to take seriously the Armenian
Reforms."[29] For his part Saurma, the German Ambassador to Turkey,
directed attention to Russia's secret designs on Turkey as an ancillary reason for its "conspicuous indifference to the present atrocities in Asiatic
Turkey." Saurma suggested in this "very confidential" report that "Russia
is actually lying in wait to launch a surprise attack against Turkey when
she reckons the moment to be propitious and to be such as to warrant a
swift success. For this reason Russia wants Turkey's atrophy and destruction rather than the amelioration of her conditions through reforms."[30]

The massacre of August 1896 was the last link in the chain of massacres occurring in the 1894–96 period. In covering these massacres in
their contemporary reports to their governments in Berlin, London, and
France, German, British, and French diplomats unequivocally placed the
onus of blame at the doorstep of Lobanof. His Armenian policy is
depicted as a stratagem, the sinister character of which is portrayed as a
reflection of the personal callousness of Lobanof himself. The entire
episode has an element of irony, however, that calls for singling out. By
a melancholy twist of fate Lobanof had become the ultimate victim of the
callousness alluded to. French Ambassador Cambon was told by Nelidof,
Lobanof's ambassador at Constantinople, that "Lobanof has been killed
in consequence of the last occurrences [the August 1896 massacre] just
like an ordinary Armenian [who was a typical victim of that massacre].
He never believed that the peril [of mass murder] was real. Only recently
he took lightly the gravity of the state of affairs, about which affairs I had

forewarned him. Upon hearing in Vienna the news of the massacre, he suddenly became alive [to the grimness of the situation], realizing that I had told him the truth, and he must have sensed his responsibility, and must have felt a profound sense of remorse. I am sure that the stroke which extirpated him had no other cause."[31]

This revelation about the cause of Lobanof's demise is borne out by additional details provided by the French political scientist Victor Bérard, who covered that particular massacre in his major work on the subject following his on-the-spot investigation of the atrocities. According to him, Lobanof had callously dismissed the tragic nature of the ongoing massacres on the very eve of the stroke that felled him. He was approached by the kindly Austrian Emperor Francis Joseph I, who reportedly tried to "soften" him (*attendrir*) with a view to inducing him to agree to "an intervention" on behalf of the Armenians. "But he died suddenly in the train carrying him from Vienna. All the chancelleries recount that this unexpected death occurred upon his opening of a telegraphic dispatch announcing the outbreak of the slaughters on August 26, 1896." In interpreting the concurrence of Lobanof and Hanotaux on the Armenian Question, Bérard maintains that both diplomats acted as if they had a personal stake in protecting Abdul Hamit and preserving his regime. They were more or less successful in this regard, argues Bérard, because neither in France nor in Russia was public opinion a factor to reckon with, as was the case in England. Equally significant, according to the same author, both men shared a deep sense of disappointment with some nationalities which through Russian and French assistance had become free, and afterwards proved ungrateful.[32]

The diplomatic correspondence ensuing in the wake of the passing of Lobanof sheds light on the underlying causes of the failure of the Powers to prevent and to punish the crime of mass murder committed against the Armenians, at the same time underscoring the critical role in this failure of Russia's implacable posture. Within hours after the demise of Lobanof, Tsar Nicholas II (1894–1917) went out of his way to express his sympathy with the Sultan and told the Turkish Ambassador in Vienna that he had no sympathy with the Armenians "who had attempted similar deeds in the Caucasus."[33] In a second and more detailed report, filed the same day by British Ambassador to Russia, Sir N.R. O'Conor, the critical importance of an Anglo-Russian accord for the application of humanitarian intervention comes once more to the forefront of attention. In a mood "more outspoken than usual in regard to political affairs," Russia's Deputy Foreign Minister Chichkine disclosed to him that in meetings in Vienna and Breslau the Emperors of Russia, Austria, and Germany had agreed upon the need "to maintain as long as possible the existing regime" in Turkey lest "serious political complications" may develop through resort to "any violent alteration." O'Conor appealed to him not to distrust Great Britain, and in the name of "humanity and civilization" to cooperate with her for "unless the two countries" coordinated their efforts "these atrocities would probably go on"; besides, he added, "the Sultan could not withstand the joint energetic pressure of Russia and England." Chichkine demurred, arguing that in the past England herself had frustrated Russian efforts to solve the Armenian Question; "whenever Russia attempted to move forward she found England stopping her way ... ."[34]

France's Adhesion to Russia and the Tension Between Humanitarianism and Opportunism in French Foreign Policy

Long before the other Powers were occasioned to involve themselves in the problems of the Ottoman Empire, France had already established itself as a privileged Power in the realm of the Ottoman Empire which, as noted above, had granted it, as early as 1535, a set of concessions in the fields of commerce, law, and religious prerogatives. As a result, French culture and influence in due course of time became predominant throughout the Ottoman-Turkish dominion. The most important French contribution to the career of the Ottoman Empire came during the incipient stages of the reign of Napoleon III, who, in defense of Turkish national interests, entered into a coalition arrayed against Russia, and subsequently, i.e., in the 1853–55 Crimean War period, sacrificed considerable human, material, and fiscal resources to come to the rescue of Turkey. More important, Napoleon III played a major role in the framing of the terms drafted for the ensuing Paris Peace Treaty (March 30, 1856). Foremost among these terms was the engagement of the Powers to protect the integrity of the Ottoman Empire, to restore its boundaries to the prewar limits (to the detriment of Russia), and the commitment through a promulgation by the Sultan to grant the non-Muslim subjects equality of status before the law. Superseding in importance all this, however, was the admission of Turkey to the Concert of Europe, afforded largely by the drive and exertions of Napoleon III.

During the turbulence of the reign of Abdul Hamit, the position of France in the affairs of the Ottoman Empire had become even more predominant. Thanks to large and extensive investments in the national economy of that empire, France had gained ascendancy, eclipsing in that respect the other Powers. According to French Ambassador Cambon, at the time of the 1894–96 massacres, 70% of Ottoman securities assets belonged to France.[35] In fact four years after the last massacre was perpetrated in connection with the Bank Ottoman raid (September 1896), the French holdings of Ottoman debts and investments in Ottoman commerce and industry had surpassed those of any other country, i.e., two billion French francs. On the eve of World War I that figure had risen to over three billion.[36] Thus, for France in particular the stakes were very high, as far as the fate of the Sultan and his regime were concerned. For this reason alone, if for no other reason, it was imperative for France to do everything possible to maintain the status quo in this regard and to resist as adamantly as possible attempts to change or even modify the existing Ottoman system. Such a stance implied an aversion, if not outright opposition, to reforms. As the French historian René Pinon observed, "A reformed, strengthened Turkey, capable of achieving self-sufficiency … that would mean the end of profitable concessions, of fatty arrangements. A tutor who draws great benefits by administering the goods of his pupil wishes neither his death nor his adulthood and, if he is a little scrupulous, he tries to keep him in good health, but in a state of infancy."[37] Another French author, Victor Bérard, more familiar with the details of the massacres, further elaborated these points declaring that "Abdul Hamit enabled France, her financiers, her engineers and her contractors to make money. He gave money and decorations to her journalists. It was, therefore, necessary not only to avert all possibility of the diminution of his empire, but also of his absolutism." Bérard went so far as to berate his country for its "conspiracy of silence" in face of the tragedy of these massacres, scorning especially the French press.

> However grave, however improbable, however odious it may sound, this country, which in 1860 rose up against the murderers in Syria, and which for a century has been boasting of having endured [on behalf of oppressed peoples] the pain borne out of all the crimes against humanity, this country has ignored the Armenian problem. The conspiracy of silence was undoubtedly paid for by the Turkish Embassy—17 French newspapers received subsidies—but the French government tolerated it … . For two years the politicians could labor in the midst of the blood of an entire people without being troubled by the cries of suffering and the splash of mud.[38]

The question then arises as to what did the French government do or, more specifically, the French Ministry of Foreign Affairs. There were two occupants of this post in the 1894–96 period of massacres. The less consequential of the two was Marcellin Berthelot, a chemist and a professor by occupation, as well as a member of the Academy of Sciences. In the November 1895–April 1896 period, coinciding with the outbreak of the series of massacres, he served as France's Foreign Affairs Minister. He more or less followed in the footsteps of Gabriel Hanotaux (1853–1944), who preceded and followed him in that office, namely, 1894–October 30, 1895, and April 22, 1896–1898. Twenty-six years younger in age than Berthelot, Hanotaux, in terms of diplomatic experience, knowledge of Ottoman affairs, and political acumen, was more competent than the latter. He was not only a member of the Académie Française but was also a prolific historian, producing significant historical works, including the volumes on Richelieu, Jeanne d'Arc, and on contemporary France.

Hanotaux's policy on Turkey and the Armenians of Turkey was based on an amalgam of national interests and priorities on the one hand, and personal sentiments for and loyalty to Abdul Hamit on the other. His diplomatic career went through a meteoric rise while as a very young man, barely in his twenties, he served first as Councillor and later as Chargé in the French Embassy in Constantinople. His success was "undoubtedly due to his very real intelligence but also to the very special benevolence which Abdul Hamit for ten years continued to show toward him." In return, Hanotaux was appreciative of and grateful toward the Sultan, and remained under the spell of his charm. Hanotaux could not bring himself to admit that something or somebody could have changed in the course of ten years.[39] In the words of one of the advisers of the Sultan, Hanotaux "had preserved a feeling of respect and admiration for Abdul Hamit."[40] This is one reason why Hanotaux practically ignored his ambassador to Turkey, Cambon, and for all practical purposes directed a highly personalized Turkey policy from Quai d'Orsay in distant Paris. Russian Foreign Minister Lobanof was doing exactly the same thing in the same period towards Nelidof, his ambassador in Constantinople; he too had previously served in the Ottoman capital and had come to know the Sultan previously.

Hanotaux's frame of mind in this entire episode came to light when, barely a month out of power, he anonymously published an article in *Revue de Paris* in which he articulated his views and his position. Referring to the massacres which were then running their course in the interior of Turkey, he declared, "Let me be frank. I cannot bring myself to consider this spectacle as a tragedy [*à prendre cet spectacle au tragique*]. Abdul Hamit is too attentive and too prudent to allow himself to be surprised…. He has shown towards his subjects true qualities of tenderness, generosity and impartiality…. In the final analysis, we are dealing here with one of those thousand incidents of struggle between Christians and Muslims…. May the crisis remain solely an internal one; this is what the entire world should wish for…. The entire world should wish that the authority of the Sultan should exert itself, and exert by itself, alone."[41] Even though at the time Hanotaux composed this article the full scope and intensity of the empire-wide massacres were not known, the nature and thrust of those of the Sassoun episode, as well as those of the first Constantinople pogrom, were fairly ascertained and disseminated throughout the world. It may be that Victor Bérard had correctly diagnosed the problem. Hanotaux was not only removed from the scenes of the slaughters but was fixated on his image of the Sultan he had formed nearly ten years earlier, thus precluding the need to consider the onset of new circumstances, and by the same token disregarding the possibility of change in the Sultan's attitudes relative to the Armenians and the allied Armenian Question.

The other occasion for Hanotaux to articulate and defend his policy was a public one, forced upon him by a group of parliamentarians of the French Chamber of Deputies led by Denys Cochin who, thanks to his personal ties to French Ambassador Cambon, was fully apprised of the character of the ongoing massacres. Assisted by two other deputies, Albert de Mun, the mouth-piece of the Catholic Right, and Jean Jaurés, representing the Socialist party, Cochin on November 3, 1896, launched an interpellation in the Chamber, demanding from Hanotaux an explanation of the rationale of the French policy on the Armenian issue.[42] In his speech Cochin appealed to the duties of France, "the first and most sacred ones being to know how to defend the weak, to take the part of the oppressed, and to make sacrifices on behalf of justice and liberty." In response, Hanotaux reiterated the argument that the Concert of Europe should work with the Ottoman government in order to ensure the well-being of the Ottoman Empire, and that "no direct interference" (*immixtion directe*) will be allowed. He too insisted that the proposed reforms should be extended to the entire population of the empire and not be limited to the areas largely inhabited by the Armenians. As to the threat of coercion, he declared that he might consider the option when the situation warrants such a recourse. Supported mainly by the deputies of the Center, Hanotaux carried the day by winning the vote of confidence with 402 voting for and 90 against.[43]

The exertions of these dissident deputies resulted, among other things, in the French Foreign Affairs Ministry's commitment to publish the French *Livre Jaune* encompassing, however deficiently, the documents of French diplomatic correspondence dealing with the Armenian massacres. More significantly, they managed to mobilize public opinion through a second round of interpellation on February 2, 1897, which was supported by Alexandre Millerand, who during the following decades rose to several ministerial positions, including Minister of War 1914–15, Prime Minister 1920, and President of the Republic 1920–25. In the course of that second interpellation, Socialist Deputy Jaurés declared, "These were the massacres which caused the Eastern question to be revived. The massacres took place because the Armenian reforms issue was not pursued with sufficient energy. For three years, from 1894 to 1897, the French government indulged in a theatrical display of hollow promises, hollow manifestations, hollow words, hollow threats, and behind this theatricality, [there was] the reality of oppression, the reality of massacre."[44] As Ternon points out, thanks to a series of public lectures, conferences, books, articles and pamphlets, there emerged a movement championing the cause of the Armenians in France. The pillars of that movement were part of the pantheon of French idealists, men of letters, historians and publicists, whose intellectual courage was matched by their pathos for what they considered to be supreme issues of truth and justice. They included such luminaries as Pierre Quillard, Anatole France, Francis de Pressensé, Henri Rochefort, Albert Vandal, Victor Bérard, Bernard Lazare, Charmatant, de Mun, Jean Jaurès, Jules Lemaitre and future Premier Georges Clemenceau. Through them "France discovered the woes of Armenia."[45] But their assumption that through such discovery France might be prompted to change her course of politics and thereby help improve the lot of the Armenian subjects of the Sultan proved ill-conceived. The series of public lectures launched by many of the figures listed above helped expose the inequities and atrocities inflicted upon the Armenians. But public opinion in France at that time was not as effective a factor in the molding of French foreign policy as it was in England. The limitations of such undertakings of exposure were further accented by the operative sway of the standards of French *Realpolitik* applied vis a vis Turkey where French special interests, and particularly economic stakes, were preponderant, if not supreme. Thus, the tension between the expository idealism of French intellectuals and the reticent pragmatism of the architects of French foreign policy persisted to the end of the reign of Abdul Hamit.

The Saga of a Dissident French Ambassador

And yet there was another Frenchmen whose first-hand knowledge of the ordeals of Armenia could be measured in terms of its breadth and depth. His role in the overall effort to put an effective end to these ordeals stands out as a monument to the triumph of human decency in an atmosphere of pervasive callousness and opportunism. As a veteran diplomat, representing France in Turkey during the fateful 1891–98 period, Paul Cambon (1843–1924) vainly but valiantly tried to change the course of France's Turkish policy regarding the issue of Armenian reforms. Risking the displeasure of his superiors at Quai d'Orsay and a possible removal from his post in the Ottoman capital, Cambon persisted in his endeavors to persuade his Foreign Affairs Ministry that the exterminatory massacres against the Armenians was an enormous crime which should not be tolerated by the Powers, much less allowed by France. His dealings with the Sultan, which included several private audiences lasting 2–3 hours, were animated with the same spirit of vexation and weariness. Pushing his ambassadorial authority to the limit, he warned Abdul Hamit of the dire consequences of the mass murder which, he said, might imperil his throne and regime. He went out of his way to arrange meetings and consultations among the other ambassadors with a view to forging an agreement that was required for initiating a concerted action against the Sultan.

Given the significance of this uncommon dedication to the principle of humanitarian intervention by an ambassador operating under stringent constraints, a discussion of the notable features of Cambon's dissentience may be in order. Subsumed under several categories, these features are presented below. Cambon felt that the absence of coverage in the French press of the grim facts surrounding the massacres and the allied silence of the editors of French newspapers were instrumental in keeping the French public in the dark in this respect. Like Bérard and others, he denounced this condition as a conspiracy of silence which, he said, permitted the government to continue its business-as-usual attitude vis a vis the Ottoman government, thereby indirectly encouraging it in its Armenian policy of massacre. In letters to his mother on February 15, October 3 and 10, 1895, he castigated "the continuous indifference of the French press" which is content with "publishing the communiqués released by the Ottoman Embassy in Paris," and "extolling the [good] intentions of the Sultan."[46] In another letter, Cambon forecasts for the year 1896 new acts of "killing, burning and pillaging, and the French newspapers will be pitying the poor Turks."[47] In this spirit of bitterness, Cambon on December 12, 1895, directed his ire at the *Journal de Débats*, and more specifically its editors Jules Dietz and Francis Charmes, who "can close their eyes to the daily horrors of which we are the witnesses." They may believe that "the death of 50,000 and even 100,000 Armenians, whose corpses are strewn all over Asia Minor, is not worth the life of a single French soldier. But at least one should be cognizant of the reality of the facts. Gabriel Charmes should shudder in his grave in face of the silence of the *Débats*."[48] At exactly the same time, however, Hanotaux in his article, mentioned above, was enjoining the French editors and other newspaper men "To be vigilant lest the press propagates alarmist news [on the episode of the massacres]."[49] Cambon's final salvo against the French press was his following indictments: "It follows from all this that the press is the world's most ignoble press."[50] In a cynical vein, Cambon suggested that when the time comes and "the small French stockholders see their Ottoman dividends threatened, we will then undoubtedly see philanthropy sprout in their hearts."[51]

Cambon's broader sweep of criticism was directed against his own government and, more specifically, against the designers of its foreign policy. "It makes me furious to see that at a time when the opportunity presents itself to play a decisive role, our government appears to be without any ideas over foreign policy."[52] Having identified the source of this indecisiveness, Cambon in a series of communications inveighs against it as a source of pernicious influence upon French foreign policy, distorting it and derailing it from a path more consonant with French national interests. That source was Russia and, in particular, Lobanof, the architect of its foreign policy. In a rather lengthy brief composed in the form of a letter to his son Henri, Cambon on December 16, 1896, outlined his main objections to contemporary current French foreign policy, severely criticizing its domination by Russia. The occasion for this exposé was a lecture which French Academician Albert Vandal was intending to give with a view to "enlightening French public opinion on the Armenian massacres." Henri, Cambon's son, was a student of Professor Vandal who, aware of the delicate issue of advocating the resort to coercion in Turkey against the wishes of the Russian ally, wanted to consult the father of his student, the Ambassador.

Before offering his advice, Cambon proceeded to diagnose what he considered to be the ills of the alliance with Russia in terms of both its origins and current application. The French officials involved in these tasks "unfortunately have never understood that in order to be taken seriously [by one's ally] one has to remain true to oneself...." He explained that an alliance is a two-sided business and that in the case of France, equipped with an imposing army and a cumulative historical experience, one had every right to deal with the Tsar as an equal partner. He complained that from the very inception of the alliance "our men have assumed the role of subalterns. They believed that in order to get something it was necessary for them to surrender themselves." He then cited the example of Mohrenheim, the Russian ambassador at Paris, who is reported to have reminded French diplomats that "you have offered us everything but we have promised you nothing." Cambon considered this attitude the kernel of the trouble of the alliance with Russia. In explaining the conditions under which France undertook to seek an alliance with Russia, Cambon pointed out the reason for the inveterate urge of French diplomats to be subservient to Russia. According to him, it was Napoleon III, who was highly appreciative of the Tsar's antipathies against Germany, a Germany which Napoleon resented, and who alone initiated the alliance. Turning to the issue at hand, i.e., the vexations of the Armenian Question, Cambon underscored "the very distinctness" of French interests in this matter as compared to those of Russia. He argued that the French government was the first government which was put in a position to anticipate the massacres and should have, therefore, warned friends, should have forced them to see where things were headed and to engage them in a dialogue with a view to impressing them on the existence of reciprocal interests. "But, as the Russians shut their eyes [to the massacres], we too shut our eyes, thinking that by maintaining a silence it would be possible to fend off questions which may pose themselves. These questions pose themselves today more gravely and urgently than ever before, and we no longer have our freedom of movement."

He preferred another course of action, "which I tried and to some extent succeeded in initiating, but which has not been followed, and which to resume it is too late." That course involved, he said, a policy of rapprochement among the Powers, mediated by France. France was in an ideal position "to inspire confidence in everybody and thereby to exercise a superior brand of arbitration." But, ignorant of all the options available, "our ministers proceeded to place themselves behind rather than beside or even in front of the Russians." Considering the extreme sensibilities of the Russians, Professor Vandal should inform French public opinion in a judicious manner, without appearing hostile to the alliance with Russia and without startling the public. He should "impress the Russians without displeasing them. This last point is the most delicate one for the Russian is full of imagination and nerves ... he is animated with a national egoism that is more ferocious than that of England. One should handle it with rubber gloves as if it were dynamite."[53] In more specific terms, Cambon places the onus of blame in the matter of Armenian massacres on the dominant and uncompromising role of Russian Foreign Minister Lobanof, who is viewed by him as an autocrat virtually dictating the terms of France's policy. "He exercised over Hanotaux *'une attraction dominante,'* and more than anyone else, is responsible for the present state of affairs in Turkey." Referring to the news of Lobanof's death, he wrote to his mother. "I don't regret him."[54]

In discussing "the Armenian question" in one of his communications to Hanotaux, Cambon explicitly stated that "... it has been transformed and presently involves the application of the Treaty of Berlin, and Europe will be obligated to enter the picture." He added that the assumption by Salisbury, "and especially Lobanof," of the responsibility to directly negotiate with the Sultan compounded the problems at hand. Had these men allowed their ambassadors to handle the matter, "we would have been able to make the Sultan accept an adequate plan of reforms."[55] The hint contained in this remark is a message to Hanotaux himself to let Cambon handle the problem of Armenian reforms in relation to the other Powers and to the Sultan, inasmuch as Hanotaux, like Lobanof and Salisbury, at that time had assumed full and exclusive control in this regard.[56] In yet another letter, he appealed to Hanotaux to shake off Lobanof's influence on French policy on the matter of Armenian reforms. "If the Powers last year had carried out their duties as civilized nations, and if Prince Lobanof had lent credence to the reality of the occurrences on which he was apprised by his ambassador," said Cambon, there would be none of the massacres taking place at that very moment in the streets of the Ottoman capital. Elsewhere in the same private letter to his Foreign Minister, Cambon added: "At present the Sultan is certain of our impotence. I have never seen him more calm, more in control of himself ... he now knows that he can do everything, and he did everything."[57]

Lobanof's influence upon, if not control, of, Hanotaux in this respect is somewhat documented in British diplomatic correspondence. On July 3, 1895, Marquess of Dufferin, England's ambassador to France, informed London that Hanotaux, anxious to defuse the grave situation surrounding the Armenian issue, was bent on seeking an agreement among the three Powers—England, France, and Russia—to induce the Sultan to make concessions.[58] But Lobanof in response raised his voice and forbade going too far, forcing the French government to beat a retreat.[59] In two private letters written to Hanotaux in the wake of Lobanof's demise, Cambon took issue with the reputation of Lobanof as a statesman. "He was a diplomat, that is all, a clever man who knew how to disentangle himself from a current embarrassing situation, but without foresight, without a spirit of generosity ... his Armenian policy has been compromised, creating for us inextricable impediments. Therefore, don't be impressed with the legacy of Lobanof's proposals respecting the questions of the Orient." The new, young Tsar, Nicholas II, was to visit Paris in October 1896 and Cambon appealed to Hanotaux to seize the opportunity to convince him, and the new Acting Foreign Minister Chechkine, that unless a remedy was found, a disaster of major proportions was in the offing. "If the Emperor [Tsar] wants to avoid adventures and surprises, he shouldn't fold his arms; it is necessary to act for which the only vehicle is an accord." Cambon then spells out the terms of such an accord:

> The Sultan will be notified that the Powers have agreed to eventually intervene without telling him when and how. At the same time, the cruisers will be sent to Besika Bay for a few days in order to give authority to this declaration. This act will suffice to make Abdul Hamit wiser.[60]

In one of these letters Cambon underscored once more the importance of the Sultan relying on his presentiment, which allowed him to anticipate Europe's inaction. On October 29, he elaborated that point:

> I have always maintained that our difficulties stemmed from the fact that the Sultan was not convinced of the reality of the European Concert. Let us concede that he was right. Our accord was a purely fictional thing, and all our démarches were, at the very outset, doomed to sterility.... Refusing to grant the fact that all the evils were due to the misrule of the Sultan, the Russian government for more than a year has been steadily encouraging the latter in his stonewalling the councils of Europe.[61]

In his analysis of the problems of French policy towards Turkey Cambon finally focused on two underlying, historical issues. First, he stressed the matter of basic cultural differences. As far as he was concerned "the Turks are as fanatical as they are cruel; they are a people as apart from us as they were when they made their entrance into Constantinople [1453]. They have committed horrors against the Armenians." Within this perspective, he assailed the historical initiative of France in ushering in Turkey's admission into the Concert of Europe and particularly inveighed against Napoleon III as the driving force behind this initiative which was launched in the aftermath of the Crimean War. A similar line of criticism is encapsulated in Lord Salisbury's lament that "we put our money on the wrong horse." Salisbury was ventilating his life-long disappointments with Turkish governments whose interests were defended against the encroachments of Russia by England in the battles of the Crimean War, just like France, and in the Congress of Berlin. Cambon too felt that Napoleon III had misjudged the situation: "Of all the errors he committed, the least of them has not been his muddling the situation after the Crimean War when he admitted Turkey in the Concert of Europe." Cambon nevertheless sub-scribed to the policy of France, in "whose interest it is to preserve Turkey, but one doesn't have to be a dupe in the process; one can be friends with-out entertaining illusions."[62] Despite his sustained efforts, Cambon undoubtedly failed in his quest for a solution to the Armenian Question. Abdul Hamit continued to rule unhampered. Instead of reform, the Arme-nians were dealt a major blow through a series of massacres. Moreover, there was no retribution in any form and on any scale. The failure was in part due to his inability to prevail upon the French Foreign Affairs Ministry with a view to recasting French foreign policy vis a vis Turkey and the other Powers, the signatories to the Berlin Treaty. Despite the constraints imposed upon him by Paris, however, he had appreciable latitudes to manoeuvre in the Ottoman capital, using his ambassadorial position as a tool and as leverage, and he amply utilized it. With the exception perhaps of British ambassadorial colleagues, especially Currie and his Deputy Her-bert, Cambon displayed unusual candor in relaying to his government in Paris the "frightful" (*épouvantable*) realities of the mass murder that was being enacted in the 1894–96 period. In fact, he went out of his way to obviate the suffering of the Armenians when instead he could have blandly pursued his government's policy of permissiveness towards Sultan Abdul Hamit, as did many other ambassadors. Eschewing the option of an out-right opposition to that policy and a consequent resignation, he elected to remain in his post to explore alternative policies through what might be called dissuasive persuasion. It was an exercise in the marginal diplomacy that avoids total identification with prevalent polar policies or postures, adapted by the other Powers, and focuses instead on proposals or schemes that are interposed between them. The idea was to persuade his government and the other Powers, more or less inclined to be in agreement, of the via-bility of new and intermediary remedies to the crisis at hand. A success at this level was likely to dissuade the Sultan regarding the pursuit of his pol-icy of decimation of the victim population. This was in tune with the spirit of the emerging principle of humanitarian intervention in the context of which Cambon's saga of dissident diplomacy needs to be appraised.

The German Policy of Rejecting Both Humanitarianism and Intervention

The conditions under which the other Powers, especially France, Russia, and England, developed the idea of humanitarian intervention and eventually became identified with it did not apply to Germany. Protracted internal turmoils had encumbered the process of German unification and delayed the formation and advent of a unitary German state. A congeries of princes, especially the dukes of the great duchies of Bavaria, Saxony, Swabia, Franconia, and Thuringia, continued to assert themselves at the expense of a centrally authoritative ruler, such as Rudolf I, the count of Habsburg who, after 1273, served as German king. The Reformation movement of the 15th century in no small way contributed to the growth of schisms along Protestant and Catholic lines. These cleavages debilitated Germany during the Thirty Years War (1618–1648), which was aggravated by the involvement in it of such countries as Spain, France, Denmark, Sweden, and England. The ensuing Peace of Westphalia in 1648 helped create a new Germany which, nevertheless, remained fragmented through a system of constituent states, with Prussia, Saxony, and Bavaria emerging as principal centers of a loose German confederation. This system was formalized at the Congress of Vienna (1815), giving rise to 39 states of which 35 were monarchies and four were free cities. The Austrian-Prussian War in 1866 led to its dissolution and replacement by the North German Confederation, dominated by Prussia. In brief, Germany was lagging behind the other Powers in terms of achieving the status of a major colonial power prone to entertain the kind of imperial designs which, in the case of the other Powers, were more often than not intertwined with the espousal of the principle of humanitarian intervention.

The emergence of the Armenian Question more or less coincides with the emergence of German unification. Significantly, the architect of German unification is also the architect of the rudiments of a more or less sustained German policy relative to that question. Indeed, it was Bismarck who, imbued with the traditions of a Prussian Junker, rose to the rank of Premier in the government of the German Confederation and relentlessly pushed for the unification of Germany under the aegis of Prussia. After precipitating in 1866 the war with Austria and emerging victorious after seven weeks of fighting, Bismarck took the first decisive step toward the act of unification by reorganizing it under Prussian leadership. By subsequently precipitating the 1870–71 Franco-Prussian War, Bismarck managed to draw the states of Southern Germany into the orbit of a Prussian-led German Confederation, whose military incursion into France led to the latter's defeat, and in 1871, the year of victory, the first German Reich was ushered in, with Bismarck becoming its first Chancellor.

In the process of forging a German eastern policy, Bismarck left the indelible imprint of his personality upon the foundations and direction of that policy. The thrust of that incipient policy was the avoidance of any and all entanglements in conflicts dealing with the East, especially the Balkans and the Armenians in Turkey, since he had determined that at the time Germany had no interest whatsoever in those areas and the people involved. He thus had concluded that Germany could neither see a necessity to intervene nor have the motivation to entertain the ideal of humanitarianism. What stands out in this articulation of policy is the manifestation of brutal frankness. Commenting on the insurrectionary wars against the Turkish occupiers in Bosnia and Herzegovina, Bismarck in a speech in 1875 took exception to the general tendency of the Concert of Europe to intervene. His argument was that "there was nothing in the whole thing in which Germany could have an interest...." Continuing on, he pronounced his famous maxim (which subsequently served as a guidepost and rationale for many German statesmen and diplomats, including Emperor William II) namely, that these things "excuse, please, the bluntness of the expression, were not worth the healthy bones of a single musketeer from Pomerania [a historic Prussian province]. I meant to say that we should be more sparing with the blood of our countrymen and not waste it for the benefit of a willful policy to [the framing and adoption of] which no German interest compels us."[63] On January 11, 1877, he repeated the gist of this credo as he complained that the original statement was often misused and abused. "The entire Eastern Question is for us no [sufficient] ground warranting [involvement in] a war."[64]

In due course of time Bismarck unhesitatingly applied this maxim to the German method of handling the emerging Armenian Question, at the same time urging the other Powers to adopt the same stance. The occasion arose when Turkey's failure to carry out the terms of Article 61 of the 1878 Berlin Peace treaty, providing for Armenian reforms, created a diplomatic crisis. Bismarck was proud of the fact that he had presided over that Congress as he performed the role of what he called "an honest broker" (*eines ehrlichen Maklers*).[65] Yet, on May 17, 1883 he saw fit to deprecate the significance of that article and its terms, the intent of which was to effectively introduce:

> the so-called "Armenian Reforms" [which to Bismarck's mind were] idealistic and theoretical efforts constituting the ornamental part of the [Berlin] Congress. Their practical significance is of very doubtful value and for the Armenians means [a] double-edged [sword] ... I cannot join Lord Dufferin [British Ambassador to Turkey] in a policy which sacrifices its practical goals to a temporary philanthropic halo.[66]

A day before, on May 16, Bismarck had told Lord Ampthill (Odo Russell), British Ambassador at Berlin, that the concern of the Powers for the welfare of the subjects of the Sultan "was philanthropy, and that he [Bismarck] hated philanthropy in politics." Bismarck then stated that his main concern was "the new danger looming in the distance, in the shape of an alliance between Bulgaria, Serbia, Montenegro and Greece" against Turkey. He should, therefore, prefer helping the Sultan prepare for self-defense.[67]

Apprised of Bismarck's policy, which amounted to a deliberate derogation of Article 61, British Foreign Affairs Minister Granville two years earlier had ordered Ambassador Goschen at Constantinople to cease to pursue the Armenian Question "in consequence of the objections raised by the German Government."[68] After Bismarck had thus preempted the further pursuit by the Powers of the Armenian Question for more than a decade, Kaiser Wilhelm II ratified the Bismarckian attitude regarding the Armenian reforms when he declared, on November 22, 1895, that "the Berlin Congress was a mistake and that it entailed grave consequences. I will never agree to the convening of a second one."[69] A day earlier, the Kaiser in a dialogue with his wife, the Queen, had declared that "The Berlin Congress offers no protection at all to the Christians and doesn't prevent the Turks from cutting off their necks."[70]

The internationalization in Berlin of the Turko-Armenian conflict continued to have ramifications for the allied Armenian Question, which began to impinge upon the evolving diplomatic relations in Europe. Like the other statesmen and diplomats, Bismarck proceeded to view the Armenian Question in the context of existing and anticipated broader problems affecting German national interests as he envisaged and defined them. In the decade following the inauguration of a united Germany, Bismarck's main concern was the security and preservation of the first *das Deutsche Reich* he had forged. This concern mainly issued from the anticipation of a French initiative, meant to avenge the defeat of 1871. Léon Gambetta, who gallantly had fought against the Prussian forces and was organizing a government of national defense to expel the Germans from occupied territories, kept urging his countrymen to contemplate with resolve the conditions under which France in the future would stage a counter-blow against Germany without openly speaking about it. (*N'en parler jamais, y penser toujours*).

Accordingly, Bismarck proceeded to weave a web of security alliances largely predicated upon the principle of an abiding accord between and among the Emperors of Russia, Austria, and Germany. Among the resulting deals were Russia's acquiescence to Austria's desire to annex at an opportune moment Bosnia and Herzegovina (January 15, 1877 Reichstadt). In return, Austria agreed to remain neutral in the anticipated 1877–78 Russo-Turkish war. Furthermore, Germany in 1870 had supported Russia's abrogation of the Black Sea clauses of the Paris Treaty, (1856) describing them as "unduly restrictive and unnatural" and even "humiliating" for a maritime Black Sea power such as Russia. Russia, which, for her part, had maintained neutrality during the Franco-Prussian War, tacitly supporting Germany, needed some protection against Austrian policy in the Balkans through an alliance with Germany.

Despite these accords, Russian resentment against Bismarck, which was ventilated through the Russian press, lingered for a long time to come. For all practical purposes the Berlin Congress had denied Russia the fruits of her victory over Turkey in the Russo-Turkish War. Even though England, and to some extent Austria, were mainly responsible for this outcome, the Russians continued to blame Bismarck for not having safeguarded Russian interests in that Congress and accordingly accused him of ungratefulness in view of the past record of Russian support for Germany. In response, Bismarck on December 14, 1886 bitterly complained that "the anti-German mood in Russia in the aftermath of the Berlin Congress was hostile to an extent never encountered at any time during the last 100 years."[71] Yet in the same document Bismarck contended that at the Congress he couldn't conceive of any request or wish which might have been presented to him by the Russians for which he would have not "interceded" (*eingetreten*), and which he would have not "pushed through successfully" (*siegreich durchgeführt*).[72] In his great Reichstag speech, delivered about a year later, he went on to state that at the Congress he felt thrust in the role of an adjunct Russian delegate, serving Russian interests, so much so that he thought at the end of the Congress he would have been rewarded with the act of bestowing upon him the highest Russian medal, adorned with brilliants. In the same vein, he disclosed that Prince Gorchakof, the top Russian plenipotentiary at the Congress, and Russia's Foreign Minister at the same time, was, throughout the proceedings, very inept and ineffective, and that "no Russian wish" was presented to him which Bismarck gladly "would have endorsed and pushed through." Bismarck concluded saying that Gorchakof failed to adequately protect the interests of Russia, to a degree that his deputy, Shuvalof, Russian Ambassador at Berlin, did.[73]

To the extent that these descriptions by Bismarck are accurate, the facts they convey may be considered as consequential for the further evolution of the Armenian Question—in terms of a steady deterioration of the fate of the Armenian people that ultimately led to its cataclysmic demise in Turkey. The principal reason for this was the Russian failure in Berlin to insist on the retention of the terms of Article 16 of the Treaty of San Stefano (March 3, 1878), which stipulated that the departure of Russian occupation forces from the eastern provinces of Turkey would depend on a single fact: the actual implementation, rather than the mere formal promulgation of the reforms Turkey had undertaken under Article 16 of the San Stefano Treaty to introduce in "Armenia." By substituting Article 61 for Article 16, the Powers in Berlin not only compelled the Russians to vacate prematurely the provinces they had conquered in the course of the war, but, for all practical purposes, left the implementation of the reforms to the good will of the Turkish authorities. That act cast a deep shadow on the future fate of the Armenians in Turkey, as it allowed the intransigent and defiant monarch, Abdul Hamit, to try to supplant the goal of reforming the provincial administration with that of deforming the population, for whose benefit the reforms were projected in the first place. Despite sustained Russian hostility to him, Bismarck for a while continued to support Russian aspirations and at one time deplored the fact that Russia, at the end of its military victory over Turkey in February 1878, "let slip (*versäumt*) the opportunity to occupy Constantinople and the Straits."[74]

As a result of some differences with him on subsequent policy toward Russia—when Bismarck in 1888 defiantly was proclaiming in the Reichstag that "We Germans fear God and nothing else in the world," meaning primarily Russia—and as a result of other discords, Emperor William II, who was then only 30 years old, forced Bismarck's resignation on March 18, 1890. Eager to rule as an autocrat and to personally direct the foreign affairs of Germany involving the twin Eastern and Armenian Questions, the young Emperor gradually discarded the Bismarckian legacy of disinterestedness in these regards; in the last decade of the 19th century he fostered a focused interest in Turkish affairs. This new orientation in German foreign policy was in part due to the emperor's stratagem to exploit Sultan Abdul Hamit's alienation from most of the other Powers of the Concert of Europe, whose representatives were pressuring Turkey to adopt a scheme of provincial reforms, within the purview of a concept of humanitarian intervention, and to which concept the emperor himself was basically averse. Not being a colonial power on a scale comparable to that of the other Powers, which were identified with a tradition of imperial conquest and new appetites for further aggrandizement, Germany was not suspect in the eyes of Turkish authorities.[75] As a result, William II gave impetus to the proliferation of German economic designs on Turkey with a view to penetrating it commercially and industrially. Partly out of spite against France and England in particular, the Sultan went often out of his way to facilitate this penetration. The Baghdad Railway Construction project is a case in point. The entire process was decisively accelerated by the two trips the emperor made to Turkey in 1889 and 1898.

These were the circumstances against the background of which Germany's response to the Armenian massacres of the Abdul Hamit era should be examined and assessed. In one major respect that response has a saliency deserving attention. The response was such as to augment the chances of impunity accruing to the Sultan and his coterie of perpetrators. The massacres thus proved affordable, as far as these authors were concerned. Equally important, the uniform attitude of German diplomats, controlled as that attitude was by the emperor, presaged an almost identical German response in connection with the World War I enactment of the Armenian genocide. Here, the German monarch emerges as the functional nexus, interconnecting the two episodes of organized mass murder. Paul Rohrbach, one of the notable advocates of German colonial expansionism in Turkey and the Near East, imputed the vast scope of the massacres of the 1894–96 period to "the steepness of Germany's turkophile attitudes."[76] Even though there were certain groups in Germany voicing

their revulsion and protest against the massacres and against the policy of
the German government, the latter almost imperturbably continued to
pamper the Sultan through its ambassador Marschall von Bieberstein,
who, at the time, together with the emperor, was recasting the new German policy towards Turkey, in the process eliciting profuse thanks from
Sultan Abdul Hamit. The relish of the Germans in the pomp and cere-
mony attending William II's second visit to Turkey in 1898, i.e., barely
two years after the end of the series of the empire-wide massacres, when
a benumbed Europe was still abhorring them, anathematizing its author,
"the Red Sultan," was a kind of indulgence that signaled a German proclivity to condone the butchery of a subject nationality. For this indulgence the emperor was amply rewarded by his host. In the language of
French ambassador Cambon, the Sultan proved a veritable "milch cow,"
dispensing a string of most valuable gifts to his guest.[77] The net result of
all these endeavors was the emergence of Germany as the dominant economic factor in the development of Turkish commerce, industry, and military procurement, at the same time displacing France's privileged
position in the Near East in general and in Turkey in particular.[78]

The Germans were neither apologetic nor anxious to relent in their
efforts to accommodate the Turks in pursuit of their drive to penetrate
Turkey still further—both economically and politically. In doing so they
did not conceal their disdain for England and France, who continued to
press for reforms as part of their mission to pacify Turkey by seeking
remedies for the lingering nationality conflicts in that land. The roots of
that disdain were planted by Bismarck. Months before the start of the
Congress of Berlin, when the Russian army was still battling against the
Turkish army, Paul von Oubril, Russian ambassador to Germany, told
Prince Bernhard von Bülow, the German Foreign Minister at the time,
that Russia was not fighting with any ulterior motivation but in the name
of "humanity" as well as "for the sake of the Christians" of the Ottoman
Empire. In responding, Bismarck inserted on the margin of Bülow's
report the words: "Why such hypocrisy in the course of a confidential
exchange."[79] Emperor William II was even more vehement in his decrial
of what he regarded as British resort to hypocrisy in such matters. On the
eve of World War I he enjoined his diplomatic and consular representatives to "tear off England's mask of Christian" pretence, denouncing the
British as a whole as "a hated, mendacious, unscrupulous nation of hag-
glers" (*dieses verhasste, verlogene, gewissenlose Krämervolk*).[80]

The most dominant thesis in the annals of German public debate on
the Armenian Question, and the massacres of the era of Abdul Hamit, is
articulated by Friedrich Naumann, a theologian by training but, by profession, a "political pastor," to use his own description of himself. He had
accompanied the emperor on his 1898 trip, thereby spending a month in
Turkey. Faithful to the legacy of Bismarck's brand of nationalism, but at

the same time completely identified with William II's posture on Turkey, Naumann, with brutal frankness, declared that Germany's higher interests require the maintaining of "our political indifference to the sufferings of Christians in the Turkish Empire, painful as these must be to our private feelings." Describing this position as one based "on deep moral grounds," he went on to provide a rationale for the Armenian massacres of the 1894–96 period.

> Diminishing in numbers, constantly in retreat, the Turk acquired a characteristic which he probably did not possess before. He acquired the cunning of people who at their core are broken people but who want to continue existing as far as the outside world is concerned. Like a small animal which instinctively knows how in all its weakness it can still use its teeth and claws, so knows the Turk also as to when he may once more act as a barbarian and shed blood. The genocide of the Armenians [*Armeniermord*] was the last opportunity affording the act of Turkish barbarism.

In the final analysis this act of "Armenocide" was, according to Naumann, a political event marking Turkey's method of handling "internal affairs" and as such was "a piece of political history, expressing itself in asiatic form."[81]

The import of the publication of this thesis is exceeded only by the articulation of the respective official German position, mirroring more or less an identical thesis. It was framed in the wake of the last phase of the Abdul Hamit era massacres, i.e., November 1896, by Alfons Mumm von Schwarzenstein, chief adviser for Near East Affairs in the Political Issues Section of the German Foreign Office. The German stance is expounded in a brief, comprising 12 pages, which are written in a succinct and rather blunt style. Three main lines of argument keynote the contents of this document. 1) The Armenians, a crafty and seditious race, provoked the Turks, who became enveloped with a sense of peril to their national existence; 2) Germany has no reason to intervene on behalf of a race in which she has absolutely no interest; nor can it be the duty of German politics to embark upon a crusade against the Crescent for the sake of a Christian people, for the benefit of whom the interventionist Powers last year interceded only to aggravate the plight of that people; 3) given the dangers which are otherwise threatening the integrity of Turkey and the business interests of numerous Germans in Turkey, the bloodbaths in "Armenia," as regrettable as they are, should be regarded as being the lesser of evils in the overall picture. This policy declaration ends with the conclusion that Germany can but only remain an observer of the scene, avoiding any and all action "which might precipitate matters." After approving it, Foreign Minister Marshall, on the very same day, November 26, 1896, forwarded the position paper to Chancellor Chlodwig Prince von Hohenlohe-Schillingsfürst.[82] The Chancellor was actually in agreement with the basic thrust of the paper. He told his sister that the German Parliament, the Reichstag, mindful of Bismarck's famous maxim on the priceless value of the bones of a German musketeer, would resolutely oppose any proposal to move against Turkey for the sake of the Armenians. He then posed the rhetorical question: why then alienate the Sultan and by the same token forfeit German influence in Turkey?[83]

These postures, adopted in the name of higher German national interests, did not always square, however, with the personal sentiments and persuasions of both Bismarck and William II, as revealed in certain pieces of German diplomatic correspondence. Nor did Bismarck and the monarch absolutely reject principles of humanitarianism. At times both rulers reacted rather vehemently to tales of unspeakable Turkish atrocities. Even Bismarck, the Iron Chancellor, could not contain his indignation in face of "the heinous atrocities perpetrated by the Turks against the wounded and the defenseless. It is difficult to maintain diplomatic quiet in view of such barbarities, and I believe that the sense of indignation is common among all Christian Powers." Bismarck directed these words to his Emperor William I at the time of the 1877–78 Russo-Turkish war, urging the dispatch, together with the other Powers, of a protest note to Turkey.[84]

More revealing are the frequent outbursts of William II, reacting to the ferocity with which the Armenians were being slaughtered in that period. Twice on these occasions he exclaimed "shame on us all" for allowing the perpetration of such horrors.[85] On two other occasions he noted that the only solution to the problem of the massacres was "the deposing" of the Turkish monarch (*Man setze ihn ab*).[86] On another occasion he called the latter "a nauseating human being" (*ekelhaft*).[87] In the same vein, he declared that bombarding the Yıldız Palace with cannon-balls was the only effective way to get rid of him;[88] he even suggested that the Sultan could be eliminated in the same way as was his predecessor Sultan Aziz,[89] whose ostensible suicide was considered by many a ploy to disguise his murder. At one point William II went even so far as to concede that British Prime Minister Salisbury's proposal to end by force Sultan Abdul Hamit's regime, which at the time he had rebuffed, was an appropriate one.[90]

Nevertheless, Emperor William II weighed his options and in reality decided to stick with the man he in privately circulated documents so repeatedly had castigated and condemned. His government did all it could to suppress efforts of disseminating news and details about the massacres; any expression of criticism of the Turkish government in Germany at the time was considered an expression of hostility to the Reich.[91] The German emperor even called the Sultan and his regime "a blessing for his subjects—except for a handful of Armenians," believing as he did that, as a ruler, Abdul Hamit could serve as "a model for other countries."[92] When the Young Turk revolutionaries in 1908 did in fact depose the Sultan, William II, by way of a delayed reaction, four years later called for the expulsion from Europe of these revolutionaries for "they dethroned my friend, the sultan."[93]

These mutually incompatible and often out and out contradictory utterances are, beyond the level of an indulgence in royal vagaries, indicative of the range of his idiosyncracies, signaling at the same time the probability of their intrusion into his political thinking and decision making. Given to fluctuations of moods, often impulsive, and prone to being influenced by fleeting and deceptive impressions, William II was often hostage to the exertions of a steady stream of inner conflicts encumbering his ability to chart a steady course of action. More often than not he relied on his imperial ego to resolve his inner conflicts. As Admiral Alfred von Tirpitz, Marine Minister (until 1916) in wartime Germany and the architect of the buildup of German naval power, in his memoirs pointed out, William II more often than not waivered, recoiling before situations requiring resolve and decisiveness.[94] Part of his modus operandi was based on his penchant for utmost secrecy in transactions of dubious character, requiring autonomous decisions and actions. One of the two of Abdul Hamit's most trusted advisors disclosed in his memoirs, for instance, that "on the emperor's initiative and technical assistance he supplied" there was installed in the Yıldız Palace a highly secret equipment for wireless communication; the two monarchs were thus enabled to consult one another, personally and informally. "Neither their Cabinet members, nor their ambassadors knew of this arrangement, and the code key for the exchange of ciphers was kept locked in the office in which his [Abdul Hamit's] most important documents were kept."[95]

Given the nature and implications of this type of interaction between the two monarchs, it becomes evident that there are limits to the task of exploring completely the conditions of political decisions and actions emanating from the regimes these monarchs represented. Official records are part of this problem of limitation and restriction; they do not always tell the whole story. Even Bismarck was not entirely free from this resort to informal and conceivably surreptitious transmission of advice. In the summer of 1896, i.e., six years after his retirement from office, and amidst ongoing massacres against the Armenians, Bismarck in a private letter to the Sultan advised him to "not be afraid of England whose power is dissipated all over the world," and to "rely on Russia" in opposing the scheme of Armenian reforms as well as other similar projects.[96]

In fact, Bismarck, in one of his explanations on the value of communicating secret material, stressed the critical importance of using informal channels as a vehicle of communication; he dismissed official documents as material which is "nothing unusual." As he stated, "the most important [*das Wichtigste*] material consists of private letters and confidentially relayed verbal communications, which do not become part of archival documents."[97]

Wangenheim, the wartime German ambassador to Turkey, in April 1915 expressed himself in the same vein. In a report to German Chancellor Bethmann Hollweg he admitted to "often" (*öfters*) using such an informal channel for conveying "material, the transmission of which by me, i.e., through the official avenue, is inappropriate." He was referring to Marine Attaché Hans Humann, a bosom friend of War Minister Enver, as the vehicle for unofficial communications. Wangenheim added that Enver reciprocated by using the same method, through the same intermediary, and for the same purpose.[98]

Despite all these impediments, however, certain essential facts which are not in dispute do allow a final assessment of the German policy as it related to the problems posed by the Armenian Question during the reign of Abdul Hamit. After all, one of the most telling methods to gauge the main thrust of a policy, apart from the conditions of its genesis, is to examine it in relation to certain outcomes reflecting, one way or another, the bearings of that policy in operation; the policy is seen here as entwined with certain consequences directly or indirectly attached to the implementation phase of that policy. First, despite the incidence of Berlin's patent indifference to the tragic fate of the Armenians, German diplomatic, consular and military representatives on duty in Turkey during the massacres, recorded and officially reported these massacres, thereby authenticating their occurrence and confirming the complicity of the central authorities in sanctioning and organizing them. Second, the supportive attitude of Berlin was duly appreciated and rewarded by the Sultan, at the expense of the other Powers who had been intervening on behalf of the Armenians to secure relief for them from oppression. Third, defying all manner of public opinion and dismissing the resentment of some of the other Powers still chafing from their knowledge of the horrors of the massacres, William II set out to cultivate the kind of amicable relations with the Sultan which served to strengthen the latter's regime, buttress his policies, and ultimately make him, the emperor, appear to be approving, however reluctantly, of the massacres—as a necessity to safeguard the perceived higher interests of the state and the monarchy. When transposed to the level of a broader perspective, this supportive role of the German monarch assumes even greater significance, bringing into relief the part Germany played, whether willingly or unintentionally, in the materialization of the tragic fate of Ottoman Armenians. That perspective encompasses two periods of Turkish history, marking the sway of two distinct and separate regimes, in the careers of which the fact of the continuity of the imperial rule of William II parallels the fact of the continuity of the processes of the ultimate obliteration of the Armenians. Given the sustained character of the partnership of Germany with Turkey throughout these periods, William II, with all his pronounced predilections for Turkey, emerges as the functional connecting link between the eras of Sultan

Abdul Hamit and the Young Turk Ittihadists (who succeeded him to power), in which eras these processes of destruction unfolded.

That element of continuity is authoritatively revealed in two separate German official documents from these two periods, attesting to the constancy of the German policy at issue here, namely, acquiescence, under plea of rather spurious arguments, to the Turkish resolve to eliminate the Armenians. In the formulation of German policy concerning the Abdul Hamit era massacres, prepared in 1896 by the German Foreign Office, and approved by both the Foreign Affairs Minister and the Chancellor, for example, the most striking point is the conclusion reached that Germany should not intercede on behalf of the Armenians lest German interests may thereby be compromised and the plight of the Armenians further aggravated.[99] Or, in the view of Naumann, cited above, Christian Germans should let the massacres "run their own course" (*eigenen Weg gehen lassen*), and limit themselves to the task of "binding the wounds of the victims."[100] The second document is of World War I vintage; it was drawn up by the German Ambassador to Turkey ten days before the ostentatious launching of the genocide by the mass arrest of the leaders of the Armenian community of Turkey. The ambassador in that document declared that Germany must be "especially careful not to antagonize the Turkish government. Otherwise we run the risk of jeopardizing more important, and for us more crucial, interests by intervening in a perhaps hopeless matter."[101]

Germany's acquiescence in World War I calls for an additional comment since it was effected within the purview of an alliance affording Germany such leeways for preventive or inhibitory intervention, which did not exist in the 1894–96 period when there was neither a war, nor an alliance. Nor can the evidence of perfunctory official protests by the German government, lodged with the clear intent of creating a record to serve as a basis for postwar efforts of exculpation, be remotely considered as a persuasive form of intervention. What renders this instance of acquiescence much more grave and consequential is its inconsistency with the leverage of influence and control Imperial Germany had established in wartime Turkey. Turkey at that time was not only dependent upon Germany in broad and general terms, but was specifically dependent upon Germany to maintain its capacity to wage war in the first place. Without the steady infusion of massive German material help, involving military, economic, and fiscal resources, Turkey's ability to survive, let alone to wage a comprehensive war, was practically nil. As if to accentuate the decision for acquiescence, William II issued strict orders to his high ranking military officers on duty in Turkey "not to interfere in Turkey's internal affairs," including those pertaining to "the Armenian Question."[102] He also instructed the authorities in charge of the Office of Censorship of the Wartime Press to remain reticent about the treatment of the Armenians.[103]

This line of support of Turkish policy of exterminatory massacres against the Armenians was an extension of an identical support which Emperor William II covertly extended to Sultan Abdul Hamit in the 1894–96 period of "the Armenocide" (*Armeniermord*).[104] According to material gathered at the time by Russian intelligence Emperor William II's government: 1) allowed Abdul Hamit to send his secret service agents to Germany who, consorting with German authorities, helped suppress the news of Armenian massacres; 2) instructed its ambassadors in Russia, England, and France to collect information on Armenian nationalists in these countries. "The results of this investigation, contained in voluminous reports, were handed over to Abdul Hamit in Constantinople"; 3) ordered the German consuls, operating in the provinces of Turkey, "to acquaint Abdul Hamit with everything concerning the Armenians living in their districts"; 4) authorized through a 1898 circular its ambassador in Turkey to exhort the German consuls throughout Turkey not to intercede on behalf of the Armenians; not to be concerned with the manner local authorities have been dealing with the Armenians; to prepare a complete list of Armenian merchants, artisans, etc., who live in their districts. Moreover, there were 32 German and Austrian agents who spied on Armenians in Turkey, reporting not only to Abdul Hamit but also to the German Embassy. Equally significant, Abdul Hamit invested huge amounts of money in subventions thereby indirectly, and sometimes directly, bribing such foremost German newspapers as *Berliner Tageblatt, Frankfurter Zeitung, Vossische Zeitung, NordDeutsche Allgemeine Zeitung, Berliner Lokal-Anzeiger,* as well as their correspondents in Constantinople through separate monthly allotments ranging from 50 to 100 Turkish pounds.[105]

For all these reasons, the conclusion becomes inescapable that the wartime German act of acquiescence in the final analysis was tantamount to an act of endorsing the genocide consummated in the course of the war, and that the German legacy of such acquiescence dating back to the period of Abdul Hamit was functional and consequential in this regard.

Notes to Chapter 6

1. The cooperation of these two Powers started with the April 4, 1826 St. Petersburg Protocol, in which they agreed to mediate between the Turks and Greeks on the basis of complete autonomy for Greece under Turkish suzerainty. See J. Marriott, *The Eastern Question (An Historical Study in European Diplomacy)* 4th ed. (Glasgow 1958), 214. The July 6, 1827 Treaty of London, which, under the name of "humanitarian intervention" threatened Turkey with military support for Greece, was likewise initiated jointly by Britain and Russia. *Ibid.,* 218. The December 1876 Constantinople Conference, at which the Powers insisted on European control and supervision of Ottoman reforms,

was the consequence of Anglo-Russian agreement as to the terms of the projected peace between Salisbury and Ignatief, the respective plenipotentiaries. British Foreign Office, *Blue Book*, Turkey, No. 1, (1877), Doc. No. 1053, p. 719. The July 13, 1878 Berlin Treaty followed a secret Anglo-Russian Agreement (May 30, 1878), engineered by Shuvalof, the Russian ambassador to Britain. *Encyclopedia of World History*, 735–36 (W. Langer rev. ed. Boston, 1948) The Anglo-Russian accords on major issues were thus crucial to the Concert of Europe's united action bringing pressure upon the Ottoman authorities.

2. In the Gentlemen's Agreement of 1844, Tsar Nicholas I proposed a joint action for the disposition of the Ottoman Empire in the event of its collapse, which was then anticipated. Nine years later, during discussions with Lord Seymour, the Tsar described the Ottoman Empire as "the sick man," and bid for its partition. *Das Staatsarchiv*, Vol. 62, Doc. No. 5612, p. 167 and Doc. No. 5613, p. 169. In the July 8, 1876 Reichstadt Agreement, Russia and Austria laid out contingency plans involving territorial acquisitions in the event the Turks should suffer defeat at the hands of the Serbs and Montenegrins. DAG [n. 7] vol. 3. Doc. No. 605, p. 293 (1926); *Encyclopedia of World History*, [n. 1], 734. In the January 15, 1877 Budapest Convention between Russia and Austria, similar plans were devised for disposing of Turkish territories, *Ibid.*, 735. Most important, Austria was given a mandate to occupy Bosnia and Herzegovina and to garrison the district of Novi Bazar, a strip between Serbia and Montenegro; similarly, in a secret Anglo-Turkish agreement, Great Britain took Cyprus from Ottoman dominion. For the French text of the agreement see G. Noradounghian, *Recueil D'Actes Internationaux de L'Empire Ottoman*, vol. 3 (Paris, 1902), 522–25. For the English text see E. Hertslet, *The Map of Europe by Treaty*, v. 4, (London, 1875), 2721–22. All these events were directly connected to the Treaty of Berlin. To the Russians, the benefits of victory in the 1877–1878 conflict were minimal enough to plant in their minds the seeds of bitterness toward Great Britain that lasted for decades.

3. D. Lloyd George, *Memoirs of the Peace Conference*, vol. 2 (London, 1939), 811.

4. *Armenia, Parliamentary Debates* (House of Lords, November 13, 1918), House of Commons October 23, 24, 30, 31, November 6, 7, 12, 14, 18, 1918) 16–17 (A. Raffi, ed. 1918).

5. J. C. Hurewitz, *Diplomacy in the Near and Middle East A Documentary Record: 1535–1914*, vol. 1 (Princeton, New Jersey, 1956), 188.

6. A. Maurois, *Disraeli* (New York, 1930), 310.

7. *The Diplomatic Archives of the Foreign Ministry of Germany (Die Diplomatischen Akten des Auswärtigen Amtes)* Die Grosse Politik der Europäischen Kabinette. 1871–1914. (Hereafter cited as *DAG*) vol. 9, Doc. No. 2178, p. 194.

8. G.P. Gooch, *History of Modern Europe 1878–1919* (New York, 1923), 244–45.

9. *DAG* [n. 7] vol. 10, Doc. No. 2394, p. 39, July 6, 1895 report.

10. *Ibid.*, Doc. No. 2371, July 30, 1895 report, p. 10 and a more detailed "private letter" on the same subject in Doc. No. 2372, July 31, 1895 report, p. 12. Salisbury's diagnosis of the ills of Turkey is borne out by the descriptions of a prominent Turkish author who portrayed these ills in terms of an "Ottoman system, which was then in a state of corruption and disorganization." He called the regime "corrupt" and the empire "decadent." Niyazi Berkes, *Turkish Nationalism and Western Civilization. Selected Essays of Ziya Gökalp* (London, 1959), 16, 21.

11. Lady Gwendolen Cecil, (Salisbury's daughter) *Life of Robert, Marquis of Salisbury* 4 vols. (London, 1921–1931), vol 2, 134.

12. Gooch [n. 8], 213–214. For German sources and data on this incident see *DAG* [n. 7], vol. 10, Doc. No. 2385, No. 2 "secret" report of Hatzfeldt, pp. 25–26, August 7, 1895; Doc. No. 2388, Holstein's private communication, p. 29, August 14, 1895; Doc. No. 2389, Undersecretary Rotenhan's cipher No. 244, p. 29, August 15, 1895.

13. Viscount Grey of Fallodon, *Twenty-Five Years. 1892–1916.* vol. 1 (New York, 1925), 126.

14. *Ibid.*, 127, 128, 129.

15. *The Diplomatic Archives of the Foreign Ministry of France (Documents Diplomatiques Français 1871–1900)* (Hereafter cited as *DAF*) vol. 12, Doc. No. 248, p. 371, Marchand's December 24, 1895, report to Berthelot, the French Foreign Minister. The French note regarding Austria adopting the Russian view that there is no Armenian

Question is a reference to a remark attributed to a secretary of the Russian Embassy in Paris, who reportedly declared in 1888 that "there should not, should not be an Armenian Question." Bérard, *La politique* [n. 32], 284.

16. Malcolm MacColl, *The Sultan and the Powers* (London, 1896), 56, 63. Austria's secret diplomacy demonstrates the presence in Austrian dealings with Sultan Hamit of covert designs which were used as trump cards in connection with Hamit's difficulties during the period of the Armenian massacres. In a report to Count Goluchowski, Austria's Foreign Minister, Ambassador Baron von Calice, gives an account of his audience with the Sultan, "which lasted more than an hour." He speaks of the praises he lavished on the Sultan, and of the assurances of his Emperor and the Austrian government regarding "the friendly sentiments they entertained towards the Sultan and his empire." Calice evidently reminded the Sultan of the difficulties his country experienced as a result of the Austrian goverment's "Turkophile" activities in the councils of the European Powers, and of Austria's support of Turkey "during the grave crisis which the Turkish empire had to overcome," which however, he argued, deserved to be appreciated and rewarded. The issue was railway concessions for Austria which Hamit had promised but subsequently "a communication to the Porte countermanded this concession." Calice felt that the Sultan had tricked and double-crossed Austria and that he, therefore, let him know that unless the Sultan, through concrete acts, redressed the situation, Austria might not be able to continue her pro-Turkish policy. *The Diplomatic Archives of the Foreign Ministry of Austria* (Die Akten des k. u. k. Ministeriums des Äussern) 1848–1918 (hereafter cited as *DAA*). *DAA* P. A. XII/168, No. 43, A. K., folios 1024–1030, October 21, 1897.

17. *Blue Book*, Turkey No. 2 (1896), Doc. No. 458, p. 252.

18. *Ibid.*, Doc. No. 526, p. 290.

19. John Morley, *The Life of Gladstone* vol. 1 (New York, 1909), 479, 480.

20. G. P. Gooch [n. 8], 3–6.

21. *DAG* [n. 7], vol. 9. Doc. No. 2177, pp. 193–94. The statement is from a September 15, 1890, No. 238 report sent by Count von Pourtalés, Germany's Ambassador at St. Petersburg, to Count Leo von Caprici, Chancellor of Germany and Prussian General.

22. Regarding Lobanof's personal visits at the Palace of the Sultan and his anti-English agitations there see Boris Nolde, *L'Alliance franco-russe* (Paris, 1936), 228; Regarding the meetings at Alexandrovo, see *DAG* [n. 7] vol. 3, Doc. No. 460, p. 49, Councillor Otto von Bülow's September 7, 1879 report to German Foreign Minister Bernhard Ernst von Bülow and Doc. No. 465, p. 64, Emperor William I's undated Memoradum (Berlin, 1926); the details of the secret understanding between the Sultan and the Tsar are in *The Memoirs of Ismail Kemal Bey*, Sommerville Story, ed. (London, 1920), 257, and in Ismail Kemal Bey, "Armenia and the Armenians" *Fortnightly Review* DCX, New Series (October 1, 1917): 497. As noted elsewhere, the author was a veteran Ottoman statesman of Albanian origin. In the critical period of negotiations on Armenian reforms between the Sultan and the Powers in 1895, he was deputized by Abdul Hamit to negotiate terms with British Chargé Herbert and in that capacity he offered his counsels to the monarch only to be rebuffed by the latter.

23. *Blue Book*. Turkey No. 1 (1896), Doc. No. 83, p. 83; Doc. No. 94, p. 87.

24. *Ibid.*, These exchanges are reported to and by British Ambassador at St. Petersburg, Lascelles, as follows. Doc. No. 65, p. 71 (May 30); Doc. No. 71, p. 73 (June 4); Doc. No. 83, p. 83 (June 13); Doc. No. 91, p. 86 (June 21); Doc. No. 110, p. 93 (July 3); Doc. No. 120, p. 97 (July 25); Doc. No. 238, p. 120 (August 16); Doc. No. 139, p. 121 (August 9, 1895).

25. *DAG* [n. 7], Doc. No. 2479, cipher No. 233, p. 127.

26. *Ibid.*, vol. 9, Doc. No. 2206, cipher No. 62, p. 232.

27. *Ibid.*, Doc. No. 2208, cipher No. 215, p. 233.

28. Doğan Avcıoğlu, *Milli Kurtuluş Tarihi*, (History of National Liberation) vol. 1 (Istanbul, 1974), 41.

29. *DAG* [n. 7], Doc. No. 2446, cipher No. 408, p. 92.

30. *Ibid.*, Doc. No. 2448, cipher No. 168, p. 94.

31. Paul Cambon, *Correspondance* 1870–1924 vol. I (1870–1898) (Paris, 1940), 412, 414–15.

32. Victor Bérard, *La politique du Sultan* 3d ed. (Paris, 1897), 280–90, 346–47.

33. FO424/188, Doc. No. 160, "secret" cipher No. 373, British Chargé in Constantinople Herbert's August 31, 1896 report to Prime Minister Salisbury.

34. *Ibid.*, Doc. No. 258, "confidential" cipher No. 208, O'Conor's September 17, 1896 dispatch to Salisbury.

35. Cambon, *Correspondance* [n. 31], 422.

36. Herbert Feis, *Europe, the World's Banker 1870–1914* (New Haven, 1930), 51, 320. See also Kurt Ziemke, *Die Neue Türkei. Politische Entwicklung 1914–1929* (Berlin, 1930), 9.

37. René Pinon, *L'Europe et L'Empire Ottoman* (Paris, 1917), 311.

38. Bérard, *La politique* [n. 32], 282, 290. In an earlier work Bérard asserted that Sultan Hamit spent considerable parts of the revenues of the state for direct and indirect bribery. His pool of foreign candidates for this purpose included "purchasing agents, governmental functionaries, stock market traders, newspaper men, financiers, embassy personnel, a whole slew of corrupt parliamentarians and politicians of all countries." *La Mort de Stamboul* (Paris, 1913), 218. A Turkish political leader with a rich background of political party affiliation, publishing experience, and ministerial posts in the Turkish government, conveyed his nation's sense of shame when acknowledging Hamit's resort to the practice of "giving gifts, bribes and decorations to emperors and political figures with the intent to forestall an incident resulting from the massacre he committed against the Armenian … he trampled upon the dignity and honor of the country and in the end he acquired the epithet of 'the Red Sultan'." Hüseyin Kâzım Kadri, *Balkanlardan Hicaz'a Imparatorluğun Tasfiyesi. 10 Temmuz Inkilâbı ve Netayici* (The Liquidation of the Empire from the Balkans to Hejaz. The July 10 Revolution and its Results) K. Büyükcoşkun ed. (Istanbul, 1992), 133. In the original Ottoman-script text, published in 1920, it is on p. 123. Hamit's First Secretary in his memoirs discloses that in order to win over the Russian Tsar at the time of the massacres the Sultan sent "a number of gifts" to the Russian monarch who was then visiting in Yalta. Tahsin Paşa, *Abdülhamit Yıldız Hatıraları* (Abdul Hamit's *Yıldız* [Palace] Memoirs) (Istanbul, 1931), 46. Another Turkish author, Mehmed Murad (originally from Dağistan), who vainly tried to influence the Sultan to change his ways of ruling and in the end escaped to England, in a letter in the London *Times*, October 13, 1896, accused Hamit of raiding the Treasury to bribe European luminaries and politicians with a view to "purchasing public opinion in Europe." An official French document confirms another episode of gift-giving by the Sultan. To express his appreciation for the support he received from him in the period of the Armenian massacres, Hamit sent Arif Paşa as a bearer of his gifts to Tsar Nicholas II. *DAF* [n. 15], Doc. No. 270, p. 402, Cambon's January 14, 1896 report to Foreign Minister Berthelot. During the period of intense pressures brought to bear upon the Sultan by the British in conjunction with the draft of the May 1895 Reform project, Sultan Abdul Hamit, in a period of less than one week, bestowed upon a large group of Rusian generals, high ranking officers of the Foreign Afffairs Ministry, and palace functionaries, a number of decorations. In the first round, on May 7/19, 1895, the Chief of General Staff of the Russian Army, General Obruchef, received the Osmaniye Order, "enriched with diamonds", and General Vorontsof-Dashkof, the Mecidiye Order, "enriched with diamonds." Several Princesses and wives of diplomats received Şefakat orders of 2d and 3d class. FO 195/1877, folio 115. In the Second round, on May 15/27, Deputy and later Acting Minister of Foreign Affairs, Chichkine, General Stolifin, the Tsar's Aide-de-Camp, and Prince Alexandre Dolgaurouki, a Palace functionary, received The Grand Cordon of Osmaniye, whereas Baron de Frederiks, the Adjudant to the palace's Grand Marshal, received the Grand Cordon of Mecidiye. *Ibid.*

39. Bérard, *La politique* [n. 38], 285.

40. Kemal, "Armenia and the Armenians" [n. 22], 500.

41. (G. Hanotaux), "En Orient" *Revue de Paris* 6 (December 1, 1895): 459.

42. Yves Ternon, *Les Arméniens, histoire d'un génocide* (Paris, 1977), 132.

43. *DAF* [Doc. No. 15] Affaires Arméniennes. Livre Jaune. Doc. No. 284, pp. 312–19, and *Blue Book*, Turkey No. 2 (1897) Doc. No. 7, pp. 6–7.

44. Official parliamentary records. *Journal Officiel*, February 23, 1897, covering the debates of the preceeding day. Quoted in Ternon, *Les Arméniens* [n. 42], 132, n. 1.

45. Ternon, *Les Arméniens* [n. 42], 132.

46. Cambon, *Correspondance* [n. 31], 385, 393, 395.

47. *Ibid.*, 398, December 23, 1895 letter.

48. *Ibid.*, 397.

49. Hanotaux [n. 41], 459.

50. Cambon, *Correspondance* [n. 31], 399, January 20, 1896 letter to his mother.

51. *Ibid.*, 398.

52. *Ibid.*, 397, 399.

53. *Ibid.*, 421–23. The lecture by Vandal was delivered on February 2, 1897 before an audience of 1,500 Frenchmen that included such luminaries as deputy Count de Mun who presided, deputies D. Cochin, Delafosse and J. Reinach, former ambassadors Marquis de Vogüe (Turkey) and Count Benedetti (Germany), members of the *Académie Française* Marquis, Costa de Beauregard, Count d'Haussonville, Lavisse, Gaston Paris, and Grand Rabbi of France, Zadoc-Khan.

54. *Ibid.*, 411, September 1, 1896 letter.

55. *Ibid.*, 391, 392.

56. For a description of the ways of this control see P. Quillard and L. Margery, *La Question d'Orient et la politque personelle de Monsieur Hanotaux* (Paris, 1879).

57. Cambon, *Correspondance* [n. 31], 415.

58. *Blue Book* [n. 23], Doc. No. 103, p. 91.

59. *Ibid.*, Doc. No. 120, p. 97, the July 25, 1895 cipher of Sir F. Lascelles, British Ambassador to Russia. See for reference to these accounts Bérard, *La politique* [n. 32], 309.

60. Cambon, *Correspondance* [n. 31], 415–16.

61. *Ibid.*, 420.

62. *Ibid.*, 394, 395.

63. Bismarck, *Denkwürdigkeiten* (Memoirs) P. Liman, ed. (Culled from his letters, speeches, and personal recollections) (Berlin, 1899), p. 478.

64. *DAG* [n. 7], vol. 5, Doc. No. 1006, January 24, 1887 report No. 52. "secret" communication to Count von Werthern, edit. note, p. 117.

65. Bismarck, *Denkwürdigkeiten* [n. 63], p. 479.

66. *DAG* [n. 7], vol. 9, Doc. No. 2183, p. 200 n.*(starred).

67. *British Documents on Ottoman Armenians* vol. II 1880–1890. B. Şimşir ed. (Ankara, 1983), Doc. No. 204, cipher No. 165A, p. 462.

68. *Blue Book*. Turkey No. 6 (1881), Report No. 170, p. 322 (February 10, 1881); see also pp. 290, 311, 313.

69. *DAG* [n. 7], Doc. No. 2464, Emperor's marginalia on p. 114, n. 5.

70. *Ibid.*, Doc. No. 2463, p. 109.

71. *DAG* [n. 7], vol. 5, Doc. No. 1001, p. 98.

72. *Ibid.*, 97. The same view is expressed in a document dated February 2, 1878. *Ibid.*, vol. 2, Doc. No. 310, p. 181.

73. Bismarck, *Denkwürdigkeiten* [n. 63] 479; the speech was delivered on February 6, 1888.

74. *DAG* [n. 7], vol. 5, Doc. No. 1001, p. 97.

75. *Anhang zu den Gedanken und Erinnerungen* (Supplementary volume to Bismarck's Thoughts and Memoirs) (Stuttgart, 1901), August 13, 1875 letter to the monarch Emperor William I, 260. For additional German sources and data on this point see Norbert Saupp, *Das Deutsche Reich und die Armenische Frage* (The German Empire and the Armenian Question) (Cologne or Köln, doctoral thesis at the University of Köln, 1990), 25–32.

76. Quoted in Wilhelm von Kampen, *Studien zur Deutschen Türkeipolitik in der Zeit Wilhelms II* (Studies on Germany's Policy on Turkey in William II's Time) (Kiel, doctoral thesis at the University of Kiel, 1968), 418, n. 322.

77. Cambon, *Correspondance* [n. 31], 443. Among the "innumerable gifts" the Emperor and the Empress collected were, the rugs which he got by "cleaning up the entire factory of rugs, and by pocketing a necklace studded with old diamonds worth 5–600,000 francs. In return, he left as souvenir to his host two small busts of his grandfather and grandmother, made of cheap bronze material, along with another bronze object representing an Arab on horseback; the three objects are worth 7 or 800 francs." *Ibid.*, moreover, William II was so intoxicated with the "gift" of the Baghdad Railway construction project, extracted from the sultan, that he called it "my railway" (*meine Bahn*). Emil Ludwig, *Wilhelm der Zweite* (Berlin, 1926), 391–92.

78. *DAG* [n. 7], vol. 12, part 2, p. 558; see also *ibid.*, Appendix. Doc. Nos. 3357, 3361, 3362. Commenting on the Emperor's trip, the French writer François Coppé declared, "After the Armenian massacres Sultan Abdul Hamit had become odious in the eyes of all mankind. Now that he became the vassal of the German Emperor, he has become even more odious in the eyes of the Frenchman." Doc. No. 3370, p. 613.

79. *DAG* [n. 7], vol. 2, Doc. No. 308, February 2, 1878 report by Bülow, p. 179, n. 15.

80. *Die deutschen Dokumente zum Kriegsausbruch 1914* (The German Documents on the Outbreak of the War 1914), compiled by K. Kautsky, ed. by Max Graf von Montgelas and Walter Schückling, 2d expanded ed., vol. 1, Doc. No. 401 (Berlin, 1922), 130 ff.

81. Friedrich Naumann, *Asia*, 8th ed. (Berlin, 1911), 2, 134, 137, 139, 145.

82. A. A. Orientalia Generalia. No. 5, vol. 30. The Mumm *Konzept*.

83. Chlodwig Hohenlohe-Schillingshurst, *Denkwürdigkeiten der Reichskanzlerzeit* (Memoirs from the Time of Service as Chancellor) (Stuttgart, 1931), 264.

84. Anhang [n. 75], August 11, 1877 letter, p. 273.

85. *DAG* [n. 7], vol. 10, Doc. No. 2457, Ambassador Saurma's November 11, 1895 report that Armenians in Diyarbekir are being slaughtered like sheep. "And, as Christians and Europeans ... we have to watch these things quietly." The Emperor's marginalia, p. 102; *ibid.*, vol. 12, part 1, Doc. No. 2893, cipher No. 176, Saurma's July 29, 1896 report, in which he was informing Berlin that the Turkish plan was the terminal liquidation of the Armenians as Christians (*für alle Zeiten unschädlich gemacht werden müssen*) William II's marginalia, p. 18. "This means that all Christians are to be slayed."

86. *Ibid.*, Doc. No. 2898. August 28, 1896 cipher. Marginalia. p. 20; Doc. No. 2901. August 29, 1896. Marginalia. p. 22.

87. *DAG* [n. 7], vol. 10, Doc. No. 2482. December 19, 1895. Marginalia. p. 133.

88. *Ibid.*, Doc. No. 2484, cipher No. 177. December 23, 1895. Marginalia. p. 134.

89. *DAG* [n. 7], vol. 12, Doc. No. 2893. July 29, 1896 report. Marginalia. p. 18.

90. *Ibid.*, vol. 10, Doc. No. 2416, cipher No. 117. August 22, 1895. Marginalia. p. 61.

91. Bernhard Guttmann, *Schattenriss einer Generation* (The Silhouette of a Generation) (Stuttgart , 1950), 262.

92. Alfred Graf von Waldersee, *Denkwürdigkeiten* (Memoirs) H. O. Meisner ed., vol. 1 (Stuttgart, 1923), 269.

93. Georg Alexander von Müller, *Der Kaiser ... Aufzeichnungen des Chefs des Marinekabinetts Admiral G. A. V. Müller über die Ära Wilhelms II.* (Navy Cabinet Chef Admiral Müller's Notes on William II's Era of Rule) W. Görlitz ed., (Göttingen, 1965), 122.

94. Alfred von Tirpitz, *Erinnerungen* (Memoirs) (Leipzig, 1919), 435.

95. Tahsin Paşa, *Abdülhamit* [n. 38], 285.

96. The excerpts from Bismarck's letter to the Sultan are from the diaries of Theodor Herzl. The entire letter was read to Herzl by Philip Michael de Newlinski, a Polish-Austrian journalist and political agent, who had managed to befriend Sultan Abdul Hamit and his foremost confidant and adviser Izzet (Arab). Newlinski was very eager to assist Herzl, who was trying to gain fundamental concessions from the Sultan for a Palestinian homeland for the Jews. Newlinski, the publisher of *Correspondance de l'Est*, had also befriended two Armenians for this purpose, both of them occupying high positions in the offices of the Ottoman Ministry of Foreign Affairs. Herzl describes Artin Dadian, the Undersecretary, as "a new helper" for the success of his enterprise, and Gabriel Noradounghian, Councillor in the Legal Department of the Foreign Affairs Ministry (whose identity is concealed by the use of the letter N.), as a man who is "fire and flame" for the proposal made by Herzl, and who is "completely for us" (*ganz für uns*); he "promised greatest help." *Theodor Herzl's Tagebücher 1895–1904* 3 vols., vol. 1 (1922), vols. 2 and 3 (Berlin, 1923). The excerpts from Bismarck's letter are in vol. 1, p. 502, July 22, 1896 diary entry. The comments on Noradounghian are in vol. I, pp. 153, 440–41, 449, and on Artin Paşa, vol. 2, 271–72, 312–13. In vol. 1, pp. 396, 464 Newlinski is described as stating that the Sultan gave him a confidential mission involving contact with Armenian revolutionary groups in Brussels and as asking Herzl to act as a mediator between the Sultan and the Armenians in exchange for concessions from the former for the cause of Zionism which was being pursued by Herzl. On p. 427 in the same volume Newlinski is likewise quoted as saying that Russia gained the upper hand in the counsels of the Palace, where "First

Secretary Izzet favors Russia." June 18, 1896 entry. Equally significant, the May 7, 1896 entry in vol. 1 discloses the fact that already at that time the Palace knew of the assault and expected the Armenians to strike (*losschlagen*), probably a reference to the capture of Bank Ottoman. Newlinski, therefore, proposed to Herzl to try to get the Armenians "to wait for a month" so that he could "usefully drag the Armenian issue" in order to benefit "the Jewish issue" (p. 396).

97. Ernst Jäckh, *Der Goldene Pflug* (The Golden Ploughshare) (Stuttgart, 1954), 9.
98. A. A. *Grosses Hauptquartier* vol. 187, file Türkei 18/3 and 4, Registry no. AS1705, April 13, 1915.
99. See note 82.
100. Naumann, *Asia* [n. 81], 140.
101. *German Foreign Ministry Archives* (Bonn). A. A. Türkei, 183/36, No. 228, April 15, 1915 report. The portion cited in this note is deleted from the volume compiled by Lepsius, *Deutschland und Armenien* (Potsdam-Berlin, 1919), Doc. No. 26, p. 49.
102. Vahakn N. Dadrian, "Documentation of the Armenian Genocide in German and Austrian Sources" in *The Widening Circle of Genocide* I. Charny, ed. (New Brunswick, N.J., 1994), p. 87, n. 8.
103. *Ibid.*
104. See note 81 for the Term Armenocide, coined by Friedrich Naumann, one of the ardent supporters of the Kaiser and his policy on Turkey and the Armenians.
105. FO 96/211, part VII, 5 pp. report adapted from the Russian newspaper *Petrograd Bourse Gazette* of World War I vintage.

Chapter 7

The Impotence of Discordant Diplomacy: The Disconnective Vulnerabilities of the Armenians

Factors Handicapping the Armenian Quest for Relief

Indeed, there was no problem for securing the means needed for the creation of an Armenian movement of insurrection as suggested by the Armenian Patriarch (ch. 4, n. 13) but plenty of problems in terms of its outcome. This is the area by which the Eastern and Armenian Questions differ from one another. It reflects the difference between the experience of ultimate national redemption at the end of a series of national disasters on the one hand, and a series of incremental disasters in the absence of a redemptive end result on the other. In trying to explain this difference in the fates of the Balkan nationalities and the Armenians, the following considerations deserve attention.

The Armenians' failure to achieve the goal of national emancipation attained by other non-Muslim nationalities under Ottoman rule was a direct result of their lack of tutelage and active sponsorship by any of the European Powers. The Slavic nationalities—the Serbs, the Bulgars, and the Montenegrins—enjoyed Russian guardianship because of their ties of racial and ethnic kinship. Religious ties through the Eastern Orthodox Church account for the Russian guardianship of the Greeks and the Rumanians of Wallachia. The French, for their part, virtually rescued the

Catholic Maronites of Lebanon by invading Lebanon and compelling the Turks to give the Maronites limited autonomy. The Armenians, however, did not enjoy sufficient religious or ethnic bonds with any European power to warrant similar treatment—despite their identification with them within the broad category of Christianity.

Another factor separating the Armenians from other Ottoman subject nationalities involved geo-political considerations. All the other nationalities for whom the European powers intervened were located on the periphery of the Ottoman Empire, whereas Armenia's historical location caused it to be regarded as a threat to the Turkish heartland. Logistical difficulties involved in providing assistance, such as Armenia's lack of ports for British vessels, further compounded the problem.

Russia was the only power capable of overcoming these logistical difficulties, irrespective of the issue of sovereignty. Early Russian policy on the matter of conflict between claims of the territorial sovereignty of the state and the moral dictates of the principle of humanitarian intervention was articulated by Russian Foreign Minister Alexander Gorchakof. In a November 7, 1876 dispatch to Count Paul Shuvalof, Russian Ambassador to Berlin, he stated, "if the Great Powers wish to accomplish a real work ... it is necessary ... to recognize that the independence and integrity of Turkey must be subordinated to the guarantees demanded by humanity, the sentiment of Christian Europe and the general peace."[1] And British author Pears noted, "Armenians were to be protected if they would abandon their national Church and become formally united with the Russian faith, but not otherwise."[2]

The Armenians were also hindered because they lacked the advantage of a geographic concentration enjoyed by the Balkan nationalities. The Turks, through a series of acts of redistricting in the aftermath of the Berlin Congress, had brought about critical changes in the statistical distribution of the provincial Armenian population.[3] As a result, demographic imbalances between the category of Muslims, which included several ethnic groups besides the Turks, and that of the Armenians, were further augmented in favor of the Muslims, especially in such regions of historic Armenia as the provinces of Erzurum, Van, and Bitlis. Additionally, a significant portion of the Armenian population seeking relief from depredations (as well as in a quest for economic opportunities) resorted to internal migration. The resulting geographic dispersion diluted any idea of a concrete future Armenian state analogous, perhaps, to Greece or Bulgaria.

For all these reasons the Armenian Question was reduced to a self-defeating issue and as such it imperiled the fate of the very people for whose benefit it was introduced into the arena of international diplomacy. This fact warrants refocusing attention on the ramifications of the relevant clauses of the 1878 Berlin Treaty and the consequences of their abortiveness.

Abortive Treaty Engagements

Although the European powers had repeatedly forced Turkey to publicly proclaim equality for its non-Muslim subjects, they were unwilling or unable to force the Ottomans to honor such promises. As seen above, Turkey had many opportunities to make good on its agreements, but ultimately failed to do so. By 1878, when the Treaty of Berlin was signed, the Armenian Question had ceased to be a merely domestic problem for the Ottoman Empire. That treaty calls, therefore, for reconsideration as the crux of the problem examined in this segment of the chapter. Article 61 of that treaty read:

> The Sublime Porte undertakes to carry out, without further delay, the amelio-rations and reforms demanded by local requirements in the provinces inhab-ited by the Armenians, and to guarantee their security against the Circassians and the Kurds ... . It will make known periodically the steps taken to this effect to the Powers, who will superintend their application.

Commenting on the significance of this clause and Article 62 of the treaty—which provided for religious liberty, civil, and political rights, as well as admission to the public employments, functions, and honors—Rolin-Jaequemyns asserted that the Armenians were placed *"under the express protection of international law of contract, and under the control of the Great Powers.* The natural obligations of the Turkish Government have become ... as regards the Armenians, *strict engagements* with the States which are parties to the Treaty ... ."[4]

As in the case of the previous reform acts of 1839 and 1856, and the 1876 Constitution, the Berlin Treaty clauses regarding the treatment of nationalities and minorities thus remained dead letters also. Their formal enactment was a measure of expediency, intended to forestall more dras-tic initiatives on the part of the Powers. Noted British historian Gooch aptly summed up the entire process as follows:

> The [European] Concert was dead ... it became clear that pressure without the intention of resorting to force stiffened rather than weakened the resistance of the Sultan, who had no intention of allowing Armenia to go the way of Bul-garia ... . The lamentable result of the fitful interest shown by the Powers was to awaken the hopes in the Armenian highlands which could not be fulfilled, and to arouse suspicions in the breast of the Sultan which were to bear fruit in organized massacre and outrage in the days to come.[5]

For a variety of reasons, however, the Powers abdicated the responsibili-ties they had assumed as signatories to the Treaty of Berlin.

The vague and imprecise terms of the Treaties of Paris and Berlin also allowed the Powers to hedge and, when convenient, to disclaim responsi-bility. For example, Article 9 of the Paris Treaty stipulated reforms while prohibiting any intervention, "either collectively or separately," in the internal affairs of Turkey. The imprecision of the word "superintend,"

inserted into the last paragraph of Article 61 of the Berlin Treaty, compounded the treaty's ambivalence. The specific functions of superinten-
dence were left undefined, allowing any signatory to argue that the Powers
were contractually responsible only to each other and to no one else. Thus,
in practice, the reforms were left unmonitored. Moreover, Article 61
implicitly proscribed unilateral action by any of the signatory Powers
through the introduction in that clause of the corporate term "the Powers."

As England's Duke of Argyll noted, "What was everybody's business
was nobody's business."[6] British scholar Dawson reasserted this point
nearly 30 years later: "No solemn international covenant has been so
systematically and openly infringed and ignored, in part by the Signatory
Powers themselves, as the Treaty which was concluded in Berlin in July,
1878, 'in the name of Almighty God.'"[7] In a speech in the British Parliament, Lord Salisbury, later Foreign and Prime Minister of England, noted
skeptically, "[w]hether it ever will be possible to induce the six Powers to
agree together to use, not diplomatic pressure, but naval and military
force, I very much doubt ... I am sure nothing can be gained by a compromise between the two ... ."[8]

An additional factor in this failure was the disparity in the degree to
which the six Powers were involved in the series of diplomatic démarches
and remonstrances against Turkey in the decades following the signing of
the Berlin Treaty, for the Powers were not all equally or consistently
engaged. The May 1895 Reform Project, which was elaborated in the
wake of the 1894 Sassoun massacre, for example, was proposed to the
Sultan solely by the Entente Powers. Germany and Austria likewise
detached themselves from the Concert of Europe which was grappling
with the crisis on Crete; only England, France, Russia, and Italy endeavored and succeeded in securing in 1899 the island's autonomy.

The Factor of Hedging Through Diplomatic Semantics

That is precisely what happened when Salisbury, in his dual capacity of
Foreign and Prime Minister of England, in the wake of the massacres of
August 1896 in Constantinople, sent a long memorandum to the capitals
of the five other Great Powers. It was the last attempt by England to compel the Sultan to comply with the conditions stipulated in Article 61 of
the Berlin Treaty.

After outlining the history of humanitarian intervention by the Powers
in connection with the unfolding of the Armenian Question and the respective contractual obligations which Turkey had undertaken through a series
of treaties, Salisbury reminded the other Powers that the time had come to
confront Turkey resolutely. Without wavering on the commitment of the
Powers "to maintain the territorial status quo of the Empire," Salisbury

stressed the point that this external protection may not save Turkey "from the effect of misgovernment and decay" and that "the forbearance of the Powers of Europe will be unable to protract the existence of a dominion which by its own vices is crumbling into ruin." He once more reiterated "the primary importance" of the need for preserving the Concert of Europe and of adherence to the treaty provision that the Powers can only intervene through unanimity and in the form of a coalition. He then came to his main point: once the Powers unanimously reach a resolution, it "should be carried into operation ... it must not be admitted, at the point which we have at present reached, that the objections of the Turkish Government can be an obstacle to their being carried into effect." He appealed to his colleagues to "come to a definitive understanding that their unanimous decision in these matters is to be final, and will be executed up to the measure of such force as the Powers have at their command."[9]

While Austria[10] and Italy[11] promptly agreed, with Italy invoking "the principles of civilization and humanity" and emphasizing the need to maintain "the moral authority of the Concert of Europe" for the effective implementation of the reforms, the other three Powers were in less than complete agreement. Germany too agreed, but suggested that the reforms should have the objective "of improving the condition, not only of the Armenian, but of all the subjects of the Sultan, to whatever race or religion they might belong."[12]

Though ostensibly agreeing in principle, the French and Russian governments relented on the issue of coercive measures to be applied against the Sultan, if and when necessary. Salisbury had indicated in his circular that irrespective of any course of action the Powers may agree on, their long-standing treaty engagements to refrain from unilateral action, to preserve the integrity of the Ottoman Empire, and to avoid establishing a condominium, were still in force. Ignoring these qualifiers, however, Hanotaux, the French Foreign Minister, predicated his response to the circular upon a recitation of these stipulations, presenting them as his terms for considering collective action. One can only surmise that he either did not read carefully the circular, or he was just being evasive or nonchalant. Moreover, Salisbury had underscored a very important condition: the Powers should agree beforehand on the steps by which to compel Turkey to comply with their demands in case of Turkish objections, inasmuch as "their unanimous decision ... is to be final." In complete disregard of this emphasis, Hanotaux, much like the Russians, expressed willingness "to examine them [coercive measures] ... at the proper moment."[13] In brief, the Turkish model of temporizing and evasiveness was now being emulated by those Powers tacitly supporting the Sultan while pretending to contest him.

The Russian response was somewhat more convoluted. First, it conveyed agreement.[14] Then the Russian government expressed its "repugnance" at the suggestion of coercion against the country of "an independent sovereign." Then followed a clarification to the effect that repugnance was not coterminous with rejection.[15] Finally, that government explicitly endorsed the idea of coercion.[16]

The standard Turkish reaction to threats of the use of force was the raising of the specter of general massacre against the entire nationality in the given provinces. In the 1860 French intervention in Lebanon, French Foreign Minister M. Thouvenel dismissed this threat stating, "[i]f such reasoning were once to be admitted, it would be put forward on every occasion when an abuse was to be corrected in Turkey."[17]

Notwithstanding, in the case of the Armenians, the Turks, a quarter of a century later demonstrated their unmitigated capacity to carry out such threats. Sultan Abdul Hamit, whose name and regime are associated with the nineteenth-century Armenian massacres, understood the reluctance of the Powers to intervene actively on behalf of the Armenians and appreciated their proclivity to take refuge in the imperfections of the Treaty clauses involved. In the final analysis, the Powers' main reaction to the massacres was to remonstrate with Turkey and issue ambiguous threats. But what was most consequential for the Armenians was the Turkish reaction to these remonstrances and threats as manifested in the attitudes of the authorities directly implicated in the organization of the massacres. Henry Barnham, the veteran British Consul at Aleppo, in his detailed report on the string of massacres in his consular district, especially in Ayıntab, Urfa, and Maraş, dismissed the notion that the perpetrators might be fearful of apprehension. On the contrary, he argued as follows:

> I ... fail to see anything in the behaviour of the authorities but the utmost contempt and defiance of European interference.[18]

Notes to Chapter 7

1. *Blue Book.* Turkey, No.1 (1877), Doc. No.1053, p. 90.
2. Sir Edwin Pears, "Turkey, Islam, and Turanianism," *Contemporary Review* 14, (1918): 373.
3. "The Armenian Question" *The Contemporary Review* xxxvii (1880): 545. (The author is described as an Eastern Statesman with twenty-five years of experience in Turkey.) When redistricting in the eastern provinces was all but complete, a German expert on the Near East, who travelled through these districts, wrote: "The question in Turkey actually revolves around the Armenian population. Soon after the Berlin Congress when Turkey was expected to introduce reforms in her Armenian provinces, it carried out a very transparent act of manipulation ... it entailed the rearrangement of the regions inhabited by the Armenians. When this program was completed, strangely no Armenian majority could be found in any of these *vilayets.* Thereupon the Turkish statesman concluded that no reforms could be imposed on non-Armenian majorities for the sake of Armenian minorities which were at odd with the latter. The matter was thereby settled ...." Paul Rohrbach, *In Turan und Armenien* (Berlin, 1898), 231. *See*

also FO40170/19208/13/44, the "very confidential" No. 747 report of British diplomat Sir Charles Marling. Included in that report of August 27, 1913 is the extensive brief of Fitzmaurice, the Chief Dragoman of the British Embassy in the Ottoman capital. Fitzmaurice stated that "the Armenian provinces were in 1878 designedly broken up into exceptionally small units to enable the Ottoman Government to deal more effectually with the Armenian population by process of elimination ...." Reproduced in *British Documents,* vol. 21, p. 508. *See also* André Mandelstam, *Das armenische Problem im Lichte des Völker-und Menschenrechts* (Kiel, 1931), 125.

4. M. Rolin-Jaequemyns, *Armenia, the Armenians, and the Treaties* (London, 1891), 38.

5. G.P. Gooch, *History of Modern Europe 1878-1919,* (New York, 1923), 22-23.

6. G. Campbell (Duke of Argyll), *Our Responsibilities for Turkey* (London, 1896), 74.

7. W. H. Dawson, *The Cambridge History of British Foreign Policy,* vol. 3 (Cambridge, 1923), 143.

8. London *Times,* Oct. 24, 1890. Quoted in M. MacColl, *The Sultan and the Powers* (London, 1896), 291.

9. *Blue Book.* Turkey No. 2 (1897), Doc. No. 2, pp. 1–5. The circular is dated October 20, 1896. The French translation of the circular-memorandum, along with the original English, is in *Documents Diplomatiques.* Affaires Arméniennes. Livre Jaune. 1893–1897. (Hereafter cited as *DAF*). Enclosure in Doc. No. 277, pp. 304–309. English original is on pp. 298–303.

10. *Blue Book* [n. 8], Doc. No. 4, p. 5, October 23, 1896 and Doc. No. 26, p. 17, December 21, 1896.

11. *Ibid.,* Doc. No. 30, pp. 21, Salisbury's January 2, 1897 report to Sir Clare Ford, Ambassador to Italy.

12. *Ibid.,* Doc. No. 5, p. 5, England's Ambassador to Germany Sir F. Lascelles' October 23, 1896 report to Salisbury.

13. *Blue Book* [n. 8], Doc. No. 28, French original on p. 18, English translation on p. 19; they are included in the December 23, 1896 report to Salisbury from Baron de Courcel, France's Ambassador to England. See also *DAF* [n. 8], Doc. No. 322, p. 336.

14. *Ibid.,* Doc. No. 22, p. 15, British Ambassador to Russia Sir N. O'Conor's November 25, 1896 report to Salisbury.

15. *Ibid.,* Doc. No. 24, pp. 15–6, Salisbury's November 25, 1896 report to O'Conor.

16. *Ibid.,* Doc. No. 25, pp. 16–7, O'Conor's November 25, 1896 report to Salisbury.

17. MacColl, *The Sultan* [n. 7], 34.

18. *Blue Book,* Turkey No. 8 (1896), enclosure 1 in Doc. No. 52, p. 47, Ambassador Currie's February 19, 1896 report to Salisbury.

Part IV

THE INAUGURATION OF A PROTO-GENOCIDAL POLICY

Chapter 8

The Era of the
Abdul Hamit Massacres

The European drive to force reforms and the Turkish resistance to legal-political change set the stage for an internal Turkish response to the escalation of the Turko-Armenian conflict. In this clash, the disjunctiveness of public law and customary law described above deteriorated into a sharp conflict between the two legal domains. Taking the series of enacted reforms seriously, the Armenians pressed for their actual implementation as a matter of legal entitlement. The Turks, however, relied on their common law claims of traditional superordination. The result was that a new emphasis was placed on superordination, the dynamics of which were such as to bring into acute relief the forces of oppression implicit in such superordination. In response to Armenian clamors for equality and other ancillary rights, the dominant group set out to exercise its institutionalized power by applying that power as force. Massacres are, however, byproducts of the application of a level of force that has crossed the thresholds of oppression and entered into the fulcrum of repression. The crossing of such thresholds are, as a rule, contingent upon the onset of acute crises in the relationships between the superordinate and subordinate parties. The eruption of such a contest is often symptomatic of the undercurrent operation of latent tensions pressing for outlets or vehicles to surface and to exert themselves. In the context of violent international conflicts, this social psychological mechanism is described as a precipitating factor. The examination below of a series of episodes of massacres in the era of Sultan Abdul Hamit, often portrayed by historians as "the Armenian massacres," highlights the incidence of such precipitating factors, at the same time demonstrating the ease with which a regime of oppression can abruptly turn into one of repression.

Notes for this chapter begin on page 163.

The Sassoun Uprising

The series of Abdul Hamit era massacres was launched with the 1894 Sassoun massacres under circumstances not unlike those surrounding the 1876 Balkan insurrections and the Turkish response to them. The indigenous Armenian peasantry had long endured the kind of oppression which, in the case of the Slavs in the Balkans, had triggered their uprising, namely, a host of inequities imposed upon them, but chiefly a system of double taxation. The Armenians were forced to pay taxes not only to government officials, ostensibly representing the central government, but also to local Kurdish chieftains. The resulting uprising of the mountaineers of Sassoun, often compared with the mountaineers of Montenegro, was thus analogous to that of the peasants of Bosnia and Herzegovina. Like the Armenians in eastern Turkey, these too were subjected to a system of double taxation facing two separate classes of oppressors: on the one hand, local Muslim landowners and tribal chiefs who were themselves Slavs but had converted to Islam, and on the other, extortionist Turkish officials. Nor does the parallel end here. Both victim groups were exposed to external agitation, including some tacit encouragements from Russia. As one Turkish author conceded, the Sassoun uprising was set off by the imposition of incremental taxes, "The Sassoun Armenians refused to submit to double taxation … . Enraged [by this insubordination] the ignorant and obstinate governor thereupon began to incite the local Muslims against the Armenians."[1]

British historian Lord Kinross, at the end of his analysis of the Sassoun massacre, declared that Armenian refusal "to submit to this double exaction" of taxes "served as a pretext in 1894 for an atrocious campaign of massacres launched by the Sultan's orders." Kinross described the plight of Sassoun Armenians by referring to "the exactions of the Kurdish chieftains [which] had evolved into an organized system of tribute by blackmail, paid for their protection by the Armenian population."[2] The French chronicler of the Abdul Hamit era massacres, Victor Bérard, explained the Sassoun massacre in the same vein. According to him, as early as 1892, the governor of Muş district in Bitlis province, of which Sassoun was a *kaza* (county) (administratively connected, however, with Siirt district in the same province), encountered resistance from the area's three Armenian mountain villages which protested, saying that they "couldn't serve two masters at the same time." They added, however, that they "certainly would prefer serving the Turks" but that they "already are paying the Kurds heavy taxes."[3]

There is no doubt that the Hunchakists, one of the Armenian revolutionary parties, exacerbated the situation by their intervention in the conflict when two of their leaders, through agitation, tried to organize an armed insurrection. Commenting on this issue the British Vice Consul at

Van who, because of his proximity to the site of the atrocities, was closely monitoring the events there, two months later stated in his report to his Ambassador in Constantinople, "I do not believe that the agitation amounted to much, or had much effect on the villagers."[4] The effort proved fruitless indeed, as evidenced in the conclusion reached by the three European Delegates (French, Russian, British), who were attached to the Turkish Commission of Inquiry, and which reluctantly was formed by the Sultan to conduct an investigation on the outbreak. In their separate report, embracing some 60 pages, they declared that "the refusal of seven or eight wards, consisting of seventy or eighty houses" of a village, "to pay taxes ... affords no proof of revolutionary spirit among the inhabitants who paid tribute to the Kurds." They further stated that "some isolated acts of brigandage" by an Armenian band, or some "resistance to the troops" likewise did not constitute "an open revolt," as claimed by the authorities.[5]

The reports by contemporary European diplomats uniformly attest to the complicity of the central authorities, more specifically, of the Palace and Sultan Abdul Hamit, in the launching of the massacres "without distinction of age or sex ... of old people, the sick and the children" who were unable to flee.[6] These reports indicate that the tax issue was utilized by the authorities as a pretext to decimate the Armenians. In a December 19, 1894 report, marked "*très confidentiel*," French Ambassador Cambon wrote to his Foreign Minister in Paris, Hanotaux, that he has "definite" information about the Sultan issuing orders to the Commander of the Fourth Army Corps, (which handled the massacres) "without the knowledge of the Porte[7] (*à l'insu de la Porte*)," the Porte being the seat of the Ottoman government. Hallward, English Consul at nearby Van, told his ambassador in Constantinople that "there seems no reasonable doubt ... that the orders emanated from Yıldız [Palace]."[8] In the wake of the massacres, that Commander, Zeki Paşa, was decorated by the Sultan with the insignia of the Order of *Imtiyaz* "for his faithful and laudable services and excellent and able efforts." Upon his return from the site of the massacres, the General, later Marshal, was further decorated with the Order of *Liyakat*, a golden medallion bearing the Imperial monogram and the inscription "for loyalty and valor."[9] The complicity of the Sultan was certified by British Foreign Minister Earl of Kimberley, who told his Prime Minister, Archibald Earl of Rosebery, that the Sultan himself was the author of the merciless measures against the Armenians, and that the signal honors conferred upon Zeki Paşa "are a deliberate affront to us and the other Powers. I did not think this at first, but recent information leaves, I fear, no doubt of this."

Turkish historians less identified with national politics and state interest have not hesitated to expose the ploy to implicate the Kurds as the authors of the Sassoun massacre. Historian Osman Nuri, in the second volume of his three-volume biography of Abdul Hamit, directs attention to this fact. He indicates that the purpose was to shift the blame from the authorities to the Kurds regarding the massacres, "the enormous dimensions" of which were a reflection of the introduction in the conflict of regular army units following the failure of the Kurds to subdue and massacre the Armenians. These military contingents devastated the region, "torching villages and killing many people."[10] In his memoirs, four-time occupant of the office of Grand Vizier, Kâmil Paşa, referred to "the burning and killing" of Sassoun Armenians.[11] Another Turkish historian emphasizes with reference to Sassoun, the Turkish application of a strategic design in the creation and employ of the Kurdish Hamidiye regiments, namely, their use as instruments of "bloody" violence against the Armenians.[12] As British historian Marriott observed, "Kurds were encouraged to extort more and more taxes from the Armenian highlanders. Supported by Turkish regulars, the Kurds were then bidden to stamp out the insurrection in blood."[13] This type of recourse to proxies has the characteristics of a stratagem involving an attempt to conceal the authorship of the mass murder. Nevertheless, as noted above, evidence from many sources demonstrates that the decisive blows of destruction were delivered not by the Kurdish irregulars but by the regular units of the Fourth Army Corps "150 [soldiers of which] were killed while fighting in disguise in company with Kurds."[14] German General von der Goltz, relying on information supplied to him by Turkish Divisional General Abdullah Paşa, the Aide de Camp of the Sultan, cites the units involving several regiments, infantry and cavalry, as well as numbers of rifles, swords and mountain cannons used against the Armenians[15]—exclusive of the thousands of the irregulars, most of whom were Kurds. A French historian enumerates these units as follows: 12 infantry battalions, four Hamidiye cavalry regiments, and several batteries of artillery.[16]

The Sterility of the European Response to the Sassoun Massacre

The armed resistance to double taxation by the highlanders of Sassoun, often characterized as "The Sassoun Uprising," has a degree of significance that transcends the boundaries of the massacre it precipitated. The very outcome of that massacre proved portentous for developments through which new and different forms of opposition to the Ottoman regime emerged, eventually precipitating massacres of much greater magnitude. The outlines of an incremental chain reaction are unmistakably observable here. In order to understand these developments it is, therefore, necessary to examine and dissect that outcome. This may be undertaken at two levels: the nature and scope of the destruction at Sassoun, and the subsequent impunity that was accorded the perpetrators.

The Sassoun massacre was the first instance of organized mass murder of Armenians in modern Ottoman history that was carried out in peace time and had no connection with any foreign war. It lasted 24 days (August 18–September 10, 1894). The details are provided by British Vice Consul Cecil M. Hallward, who was able to conduct an investigation in the area of the atrocities within weeks after the occurrence of these atrocities. According to his report, "a large majority of the population of some twenty-five villages perished, and some of the villages were unusually large for this country." The contingent of soldiers from Bitlis alone "took eighty tins of petroleum ... [which] was utilized for burning the houses, together with the inhabitants inside them." At one particular village, Geligüzan, "a number of young men were bound hand and foot, laid out in a row, had brushwood piled on them, and were burnt alive." Otherwise, "the bayonet ... was the weapon principally employed throughout." But, "many other disgusting barbarities are said to have been committed, such as ripping open pregnant women, tearing children to pieces by main force ... ." In another place, "some sixty young women and girls were driven into a church, where the soldiers were ordered to do as they liked with them and afterwards kill them, which order was carried out." He adds in that report, "the details given above were principally collected from soldiers who took part in the massacre, and I have heard the main facts substantiated from various different quarters, among others by a Turkish *zaptieh* [military police], who was there and saw the whole affair."[17]

The scale of destruction, in terms of both human and material losses, is an essential part of the outcome of a mass murder; but it does not cover the entire picture. There are two additional components requiring depiction and review. One of them is the post-crime attitude of the perpetrators, and the other, which is closely related to the first, is the response, or the lack of it, of the outside world. Turkish official communiques at the time not only denied the incidence of atrocities against the Armenians, but they branded the latter as the perpetrators of crimes against the local Muslims. To this day the Sassoun outbreak is portrayed by nearly all Turkish historians and their cohorts in the academes of the West as "a major coup," as an Armenian outburst of violence against Turkish authority and against innocent Muslim populations, as a result of which "the entire population [of these Muslim villages] had been wiped out."[18] To support and document this attribution of guilt to the Armenians, a group of Turkish authors, identified with a Research Center, has come up recently with a tome, comprising 85 Ottoman documents, along with English translations, annotations, and large historical introduction.[19]

The legacy of the denial of the Sassoun massacre was established immediately after the consummation of the act. Yielding to the combined pressures of the Powers, the Sultan had appointed the Anatolian Investigation Commission to ascertain facts and to make appropriate recommendations. But through threats and intimidation the Commission suppressed those facts which were capable of revealing the complicity of the authorities, and after an orchestrated effort of marshaling evidence which, by design was limited to the testimony obtained from officials and agents of the government, it indicted the Armenians as the responsible party.

Refusing to be part of this, what British historian Gooch called "sham inquiry,"[20] the European Commissioners, attached to the Turkish Commission, compiled their own report in which, in detail, they exposed the tactics of obstruction and "intimidation, and bribery"[21] used by the Turkish authorities in the course of the investigation. These even included "the violation by the Turkish police of the Delegates' domicile."[22] In addition to the Joint Report, Shipley, the British Delegate, prepared his own separate report, in which he dismissed the Turkish charge against the Armenians as "the pseudo-revolt, or the pretended outrages."[23] In his "Secret Report" Russian delegate M. Prjewalski one by one enumerated the methods the Turkish police used to subvert the rules of an impartial investigation, making a mockery of the goals of justice being pursued.[24] Finally, there is the summary judgement of British Vice Consul Hallward who, as noted above, conducted his own on-the-spot investigation, independently from the Commission. He framed it as follows:

> There was no insurrection, as was reported in Constantinople; the villagers simply took up arms to defend themselves against the Kurds. The statement made to me by an official here of their having killed soldiers and zaptiehs, I found after careful inquiry to be false. Before arriving in Moush, I naturally supposed that something of the sort must have occurred to call for such a display of military force, but neither the Mutessarif nor the Military Commandant with whom I spoke on the subject hinted at anything of the sort, nor did I learn elsewhere that the Armenians had been guilty of any act of rebellion against the Government.[25]

The disparity of levels of approach to the task of what British Ambassador Currie in his report to Prime Minister Earl of Kimberley called "a just and impartial manner [of] inquiry [so] the guilty would be punished"[26] was insurmountable. The Turks tried to preempt the exercise of impartiality and justice by formally declaring in their announcement of the appointment of the Anatolian Investigation Commission, otherwise called the Sassoun Inquiry Commission, that the purpose of the inquiry was to deal with "the criminal acts committed by a body of Armenian insurgents … ."[27] Lord Kimberley, reacting to the overall attitude of the Turkish authorities in this matter, felt constrained to abandon the rules of diplomatic decorum and in a communication to Ambassador Currie branded the Turkish government as "vicious" and "corrupt."[28] European standards of fact-finding and justice were still on a collision course with established Turkish traditions consecrating the age old Ottoman principle of "by the right of my sword" (*kılıcımın hakkı ile*).

The question arises as to what was the response, if any, of the Powers to the entire episode. At one point British Ambassador Currie stated that England might "claim a right under the Article 61 of the Treaty of Berlin" to intervene by sending a colonel "to inquire into the treatment of the Armenians."[29] It is presumed that this threat was crucial in compelling the Sultan to agree to the need for an official inquiry, the commissioning of which he had first implacably resisted. But the findings of the Turkish Inquiry Commission were a foregone conclusion, largely prescribed by the Sultan himself,[30] and categorically rejected by the other Powers. As a British statesman declared, "[the] Inquiry was a farce from beginning to end; and the Italian Government was so impressed by its evidently fraudulent character, that they would not submit to the indignity of taking even a nominal part in connection with it."[31]

Despite the intransigence of the Sultan who, in his own tested ways, was practically defying them, the Powers refrained from invoking any of the treaties through which they had engaged themselves to assume some responsibility for the protection of the Armenians. Thus, they turned their attention to the next best thing they could do, namely, to come up with yet another new reform design, which has been labeled The May Reform project, and the details of which were hammered out mostly in May 1895. For months thereafter the Sultan used various techniques of stalling, temporizing, equivocation and even rejection in order to evade a final, binding commitment. Supported by Russia, Abdul Hamit dismissed England's repeated warnings of grave consequences, and even ignored the advice of the Austrian Ambassador,[32] and twice the admonition of the German Emperor, to accommodate the Powers, with the Germans issuing the exhortation that Germany was not prepared to intervene on behalf of Turkey.[33]

The Hunchakist Demonstration: the Sequela to the Sassoun Massacre

It is against this background that another phase in the cycle of precipitating acts needs to be examined. That was the September 19/October 1, 1895 demonstration in the Ottoman capital, which was organized by the Hunchak party leadership, with the help of the members of another political party, the Armenakan. Originally scheduled for the preceding day, the demonstration consisted of a march to the Sublime Porte, the seat of the Ottoman government, by some 4,000 Armenians who wanted to deliver a protest-petition regarding the Sassoun massacre, the imperiled conditions of the provincial Armenian population and the inaction of the central authorities. Accordingly, they spelled out their demands on civil rights, equitable taxation, guarantees for life, property, and honor, deliverance from the depredations of the Kurds, including the abolition of extortionist taxes paid to the latter, and permission to bear arms if the Kurds could not be disarmed. It was the first time in Ottoman history that a non-Muslim, subject minority had dared to confront the central authorities in the very capital of the empire with a large protest that amounted to a challenge. (The July 15/27, 1890 protest attempt against the Yıldız Palace was aborted by the police, which prevented the procession from leaving the area of the Armenian Cathedral at Kumkapu, its point of collection and departure). In any event, most of the participants were humble provincials, consisting of porters, laborers, and servants, who had come to the capital to eke out a living and save enough money to support their needy families in the interior. Before the petition could be handed out, however, Major Servet, the adjutant to the Minister of Police, barred the act of delivery, at the same time using pejorative language against the Armenians. Following an altercation, an exchange of shots took place, and the massacre began.

Several aspects of it evince the premeditated and organized character of the bloodbath that ensued in the streets of the Ottoman capital, in broad daylight, and before the very eyes of scores of European diplomats and many other foreigners. It was clear that the authorities, instead of preventing the demonstration, about which they and the representatives of the Powers were informed beforehand by the organizers, welcomed the opportunity of a confrontation to effect a sanguinary repression. The ferocity with which the Armenians were randomly killed is indicated by the widespread and uniform use of cudgels. These implements are described by the Austrian Military Attaché, who, in 1896, was an eyewitness, as sticks fitted with a piece of iron (*eisenbeschlagen*). At a signal, the mobs, who were equipped with these cudgels, were "to start killing Armenians, irrespective of age and gender ... the method of killing involved bludgeoning the victims with blows on their heads. These horrible scenes repeated themselves before my eyes interminably."[34] German Ambassador Saurma on October 4, 1895 informed Chancellor Hohnlohe in a "confidential" report that "the Turkish authorities are responsible for the bloody excesses of Istanbul's Muslim population. Instead of simply preventing through troops the intended Armenian demonstration, about which they were apprised, these authorities [deliberately] allowed it to take place while the police equipped the mob with secret weapons, especially thick cudgels [*dicke Knüttel*] ... ."[35] The same Ambassador on November 10, 1895 informed his Foreign Minister in Berlin, that "there is a consensus among the most diverse sources that the Armenian massacres are largely attributable to secret orders [*geheime Befehle*] emanating from the Palace."[36]

Nor were all murderous acts limited to the use of cudgels. A military policeman (*zaptiye*) described to Professor A. Moriz how during the massacres he placed Armenian infants on his leather-apron and slaughtered them, relishing on their ensuing convulsions; "they were jerking and twitching like chickens."[37] The sentiments of animosity energizing this enterprise appeared to be pervasive, enveloping the highest echelons of the Ottoman government. In a letter which he wrote under the spell of the ongoing carnage, French Ambassador Cambon expressed his shock to his mother when relating the following incident. "On Monday these fine gentlemen of the Foreign Ministry have themselves trampled to death with their kicks an expiring Armenian who was cast into the court-yard of the ministry after the demonstration. Can you imagine our young people at Quai d'Orsay [French Foreign Minister] kicking after a dis-turbance a wounded person for pleasure." In his memoirs, on the same page, Cambon wrote on November 4, 1895, "Asia Minor is truly ablaze. The massacres are occurring almost everywhere." The astute French diplomat for three years has been forecasting the inevitability of exactly such massacres.[38]

The Formative Elements of a Subculture of Massacre Against the Armenians

The depiction of the October 1895 Constantinople massacre as a sequel to that of Sassoun, which preceded it by almost a year, is only a partial description of the event. The large issue to be addressed is the sequel of the Constantinople massacre itself. In doing so, one gains insight into the subtle processes through which a pattern of behavior emerges and crys-tallizes itself. When, however, that pattern endures and reaches a point where the actors involved take it for granted, a culture takes shape, ren-dering that pattern as an acceptable and/or a desirable form of behavior or, presently, a culture of massacre. However, counterposed to this there is also an equally prevalent culture of denial. Throughout modern history Turkish authorities have consistently denied the existence of anything resembling a culture of massacre, or any policy related to it. All episodes involving the massacre of the Armenians have been described as situa-tional "disorders" and outbreaks of violence, pitting Muslim populations against provocative, rebellious Armenians. This fact, in addition to the use of proxies by the government, who were more often than not recruited from the substrata of Ottoman society, and who often were criminals released from the prisons, is significant enough to warrant the substitution of the term subculture of massacre for that of a culture of massacre. The Ottoman-Turkish propensity to resolve acute conflicts with subject nationalities, especially non-Muslim nationalities, by resort to violence, and the allied proclivity to rely on massacre as the most effective means of violence, was successfully tested, with minimum adverse consequences, on the Armenians of the empire. This is the story of the genesis of the Turkish legacy of massacre as a cardinal weapon against the Armenian. As a British author explained:

> The Turk had never had much aptitude for business; his military valour had always been matched by his indolence in commerce and industry. The decay of the Empire must to a great extent be ascribed to the Turk's utter inability to comprehend the principles of sound administration and colonisation. Squeezing the last piastre from subject populations and overcoming their understandable reluctance by means of massacre had been the only method understood by countless Pashas in charge of Turkish or foreign provinces.[39]

It was largely this practice of effecting conquest-and-booty that led to the rise of a culture of violence against subject peoples throughout the Ottoman realm. A pattern of success in military incursions and conquests helped generate the mentality of "by the right of my conquest," by virtue of which the need for governance was supplanted by the impulse for expropriation and subjugation. Resistance under the exigencies of such a regime could not be understood, much less allowed. The result almost everywhere in the Ottoman dominion was the onset of a cycle of violence punctuated by massacres against those organizing resistance against the oppressors. When in some instances the victims dared to retaliate by some measure of counter-violence, the oppressors escalated the conflict to a level of repression that bore no proportion to the scale of that act of retaliation. Inept in the art of government, but adept in the administration of violence in amplified form, Ottoman authorities developed a mode of procedure which targeted an entire collectivity, one way or another identified with those either known or suspected of having resorted to retaliation.

This penchant for recklessly transfering guilt to a mass of inoffensive people, which thus are assaulted to be destroyed, is the alpha and omega of the culture of massacre. In his study on the rise of a tradition of torture and massacre in Ottoman-Turkish history, a Turkish author traces the beginnings of that tradition to Turkish acts of murder and mass murder in retaliation to atrocities perpetrated in the Balkans and in the Caucasus. In one particular instance a Grand Vizier is depicted in the act of personally ordering the killing at random of several Greeks in the streets of Constantinople and having still others hanged the next day—in retaliation for the massacre by the Greeks of Muslims in Greece. Spurred by these random killings, several gangs from various parts of the city proceed to attack the Christian wards of that city, targeting not only Greeks but Armenians as well. As the author points out in this connection, one may discern here "something akin to the excuse for or rationale of the [legacy of] Ottoman and Turkish massacres. The issue here transcends the presence of a state policy and requires speaking of a condition of a spirit dominating the mind-set of the Muslim-Turk peoples" (*Müslüman-Türk halkına egemen olan bir ruh hali*).[40]

The succession of mass murders committed against the Armenians in the 1894–96 period offers a pertinent frame of reference for analysis of the conditions involved, especially the circumstances linking the series of the massacres with one another. Inasmuch as the 1894 Sassoun massacre and its outcome facilitated that of October 1895 Constantinople massacre, the latter most assuredly paved the ground for the outbreak of the empire-wide massacres that lasted months, engulfing large portions of the empire's Armenian population.

French Ambassador Cambon's forecasting of the massacres, noted above, was to a large extent based on his perception of Sultan Abdul Hamit's propensities in this regard and the predictability of a course of action that involved a customary reliance on massacres. By any definition culture, after all, is predictable behavior. However, in one sense such predictability is a by-product of the behavior of others responding to an act that involves culpability of one kind or other. When the response, for all practical purposes, is inaction, the predictability of such violent behavior becomes a function of the predictability of the ensuing inaction. The interdependence at work here constitutes the core mechanism in the genesis of a culture favoring the resort to massacre as an instrument of state policy.[41] The Sassoun massacre was allowed to go unpunished through the void of inaction. When recurrent, such inaction allows leeways to the perpetrators to amplify the force of their lethal strikes in the future. The progressive escalation of the level of massacres in the period under review in many respects was bound up with the anticipated inactions of the Powers. This is the factor of consequence through which cumulative indulgences in inaction acquire a certain attribute of permissiveness in default. From Sassoun to Constantinople, and then from Constantinople to the provinces, there is observable a steady increase in the scope of destruction in terms of both human and material damages. This point bears underscoring, for the subsequent World War I genocide of the Armenians all but proved to be the apogee of a process of incremental massacres, a process the central mechanism of which was and remained the appreciation by the perpetrators of a measure of post-massacre impunity accruing to them.

But there was also a retroactive component to this episode of massacres interconnecting the dynamics of the Eastern to the Armenian Question. The Ottoman-Turks were painfully aware of the outcome of the massacres they committed in the Balkans and seemed to be determined to thwart a similar outcome in eastern Turkey, capitalizing on the demographic dispersion of the Armenians. This was the thrust of the message the Sultan sent to the German Emperor in the course of an audience he granted German Ambassador Radolin on November 16, 1894. Abdul Hamit specifically cited the success of the Bulgarians in achieving a certain degree of independence through "stories of Bulgarian atrocities" which, he said, the Armenians were trying to emulate. To his request that the German Emperor assist him in dispelling the stories of Armenian massacres the emperor responded with derisive comments he put as marginalia to the Ambassador's report he was reading, including the retort, "I'll do nothing of the kind" (*Ich werde den Teufel thun*).[42]

It is clear that the Armenian genocide has historical dimensions, revolving around the factor of consequence outlined above. This principle of consequentialness was explained in terms of the concept of impunity. But impunity is part of a larger syndrome in which three other elements configure and which may be described as follows. Given the ramifications of the crime of mass murder, organized by a state, impunity in the present case was neither direct, nor absolute. There were always risks to reckon with. The Powers could unexpectedly compose their differences and intervene forcibly; or they could retaliate afterwards by a variety of punitive measures. A certain element of uncertainty as to the possible reaction of the Powers encumbered, therefore, the proneness of the decision makers authorizing the massacres. The sporadic expressions of implicit or explicit threats by the former served well this purpose. Yet, when probing into the ancillary features of the phenomenon of such impunity, one can discern a companion phenomenon operating as a kind of safety valve for the impunity sought. This is the state of testing. Incipient acts, presaging atrocities on a larger scale, are committed for the purpose of probing the reaction of the outside world. In this respect, the Sassoun massacre was a ground-breaking precedent. Unlike in the many other previous cases in the Balkan peninsula and Lebanon, where atrocities were of very short durations, in Sassoun the Turks were allowed for more than three weeks to decimate the victim population and, what is more, no repairs and remedies were granted the Armenians afterwards. The October 1895 massacre in the wake of the Babı Ali demonstration was not only a logical sequence to that of Sassoun but, more important, it was a miniature onslaught that probed the suitability of the projected empire-wide, large-scale massacres that followed.

Another element alluded to above refers to a core part of the culture of massacre that is being currently examined. It is the practice of exacerbating a crisis by acts that are intended to aggravate it; the Armenians are driven to some kinds of counter-actions in face of deliberately engineered excesses. This is the stage of provocation; the potential victim is artfully pushed into acts of desperation by the potential perpetrator in order to create a temporary expedient for unleashing the assault. The operative significance of this ploy is underscored by the fact that even the foreknowledge of the imminence of the act of desperation by the targeted group is utilized by the perpetrator group for its own ends; instead of resorting to preventive measures, it deliberately allows that act to materialize. The massacres committed in connection with the October 1895

Babı Ali demonstration epitomize the viability of this tactic of expediency as an integral part of the design of provocation. The following excerpt from the memoirs of one of Sultan Abdul Hamit's high ranking officials encapsulates the picture; months later that official was to serve as the Sultan's emissary, negotiating the thorny issue of Armenian reforms with the British Chargé Michael Herbert:

> The Porte, which had the right, and whose duty even it was, having learned of their intention of a pacific demonstration, to send for the Armenian leaders, to ask them to present their desiderata in another form, and to forbid the demonstration, not only did nothing at all in the matter, but by its attitude rather provoked the demonstration, with the evident object of profiting by it in order to take repressive measures against the demonstrators. Soldiers were posted in position, and people armed with cudgels took up positions hidden behind them.[43]

A third element is intimately connected with the level of provocation described above. But it has a novel aspect. In issuing statements, orders, denials or any other commentary on the violent aspects of the Turko-Armenian conflict, the Ottoman authorities consistently depicted the Armenians as the antagonists of the Muslims. Even though the Armenophiles in Europe likewise portrayed the Armenians in religious terms by appending the label "Christian" when voicing their concern over the plight of the Armenians, the Ottoman practice was of a different nature. The concept of a Turkish nation was largely absent in the perception and treatment of conflicts with non-Muslim nationalities. Instead, the theocratic principle of *ümmet* (which denotes the idea of a grouping of peoples sharing the same religion, and connotes the idea of religion as the principal force coalescing these peoples), was the operative term of identification. Thus, whatever transgressions were attributed to the Armenians by the authorities, the victims associated with these transgressions were always described as "Muslims." Such a definition of the conflict promised twin benefits for the authorities. It accentuated the existing religious cleavages by pitting against the Armenians all other Muslim ethnic groups, especially Lazes, Kurds, and Circassians. Religion was thus used to enlist diverse ethnic groups, cement cohesiveness among them by way of instigation, and create a united front against a subject nationality, which happened to be Christian. The provocative thrust implicit in governmental endeavors to press for violent confrontations with the Armenians did, through this mechanism, engender a new level of provocation affecting the Muslim populace, whose support the authorities needed for the execution of their designs. That support involved the active participation of that populace in the massacres. In two successive reports from Adana, British Vice Consul P.H. Massy describes the application of this tactic of two-track provocation:

> On perfectly reliable authority, I regret to have to inform your Excellency that the state of Féké district of Kozan could not be much worse. Oppression and

terror reign, and the prisons are full to overflowing with innocent Armenians. The people are being goaded apparently into open rebellion. All direct remonstrance with the Governor-General of Adana proves useless. A disaster is to be feared at any moment if the present Kaïmakam of Féké be not removed ... .

With reference to my recent journey in the Provinces of Adana and Aleppo, I have the honour to submit to your Excellency the following brief summary of the present state of the parts visited.

The Armenian population is everywhere oppressed by a system of government which takes from them the means of circulating freely, of earning a livelihood, and of enjoying a feeling of security to life and property, even on the most frequented highway. Taxes are levied without mercy, even from the poorest. The prisons are filled with innocent men, who lie there for months without trial.

While the Armenians threaten to lose patience and to break out into some act of rebellion, the Government officials have everywhere informed me that their orders are "to be ready" and to exterminate the Armenian wherever he may lift his head. The Moslem populace is everywhere armed in readiness for the unarmed Armenian, and we may expect disturbances whenever and wherever a spark may kindle.

I have everywhere warned the Armenians to give no cause for massacre or disturbance, but their patience is waning; they have waited so long without any result, they say, that they are losing hope, and they prefer death to enduring their present sufferings.[44]

The benefit flowing from this active engagement of the populace consisted not only of the relative ease with which the victim population was destroyed but, far more important, a plausible excuse was afforded in order to shift the onus of the blame to unruly outlaws, portrayed as being beyond the control of the central authorities. In his article dealing with the provocation thesis, Robert Melson touches on this point, arguing that "massacre may ... have been attractive to the regime because it was a subterfuge [allowing] local authorities and peasants to participate [to ensure] the desired results without clearly implicating the central government."[45]

In the overall analysis of the functions of impunity in the formation of a culture of massacre, this dual track mechanism of provocation merits due attention for it has a bearing on the processes through which the attainment of impunity is facilitated. Indeed, to the extent that the victim, which was provoked in the first place, can be portrayed as the instigator and the matter of guilt can be deflected by blaming the Muslim populace, to that extent the outside world may be confounded and the task of punishment may thereby be encumbered, if not entirely undermined. Thus, impunity is not always or entirely the result of indifference on the part of those capable of administering punishment but of conditions of obfuscation purposefully created by the perpetrator. When transposed to the domain of politics and international relations, the issue is reduced to a simple formula: unless acute "national interests" are involved, no Power, or combination of Powers, is likely to seriously consider forceful intervention. In the evolving phases of the Turko-Armenian conflict, the

Armenians were not only of marginal significance to the Powers, but awareness of the value of huge investments in the economy of the Ottoman Empire—aside from other imperial and colonial aspirations—inhibited some of these Powers. In the final analysis, they decided in favor of non-intervention in order to protect those investments.

These are the circumstances under which impunity became the most consequential factor in the formation of a Turkish subculture of massacre as a principal weapon to deal with the Turko-Armenian conflict. This consequentialness is once more highlighted in the discussion below, examining another phase in the chain of massacres in the 1894–96 period.

The 1895–96 Zeitoun Uprising

Parallel to the insurgencies mounted by bands of Greek, Bulgarian, and Macedonian revolutionaries, the Armenians launched their own forays in the interior as well as the capital of the empire. However defensive in its thrust, Sassoun was the first major Armenian attempt to challenge Ottoman authority. Its bloody outcome and the losses the Armenians thereby sustained did not deter the Hunchaks from organizing a "pacific" demonstration in the Ottoman capital one year later, only to suffer another bloodbath there, as described above. But the third Hunchakist attempt against the Ottoman regime was crowned with a relative success. It involved the organization of the Zeitoun rebellion (October 24, 1895–February 2, 1896). Like Sassoun, Zeitoun at a distance of 40 miles northwest of Maraş, offered all the advantages of armed resistance from the perch of a mountain fastness. Like the highlanders of Sassoun, those from Zeitoun were bent on ending the abuses of a regime which, coincidental with the empire-wide massacres of that period, was using every available method to provoke the mountaineers. Some Turkish participants of secret meetings, at which the impending massacre of the Armenians was discussed, confidentially alerted their Armenian friends. The influx of new contingents of military units, the erection of new barracks and munitions depots, and the mistreatment of the local population by these new arrivals were ominous signals. The soldiers would bellow to the Armenian clergyman such calls as "osh, osh," which in that area are calls shouted at dogs. They would buy goods but refuse to pay for them; they would molest young people sexually, and swear at the mountaineers, with the government itself resorting to tax-related acts of confiscation. Some impatient Turks began to shout: "You infidel dogs, your time is running out; we shall massacre you."

When the government deposed the governor of the county of Zeitoun and replaced him with a certain Avni Bey, reportedly a sworn enemy of the Armenians, the deposed man disclosed to his close Armenian friend, a certain Artin Agha Gulvanessian, that Zeitoun was doomed as preparations to destroy its population were under way. He then reportedly added: "in the entire area of Cilicia, Zeitoun, and Hacın, are two eminently Armenian towns, and as such they are thorns in our flesh. The threat coming from you, Armenians, is greater than that posed by Bulgaria. The Sultan is set to deliver a formidable blow against the entire Armenian nation. Beware, and be careful." Finally, military units began to deploy nightly and proceeded to burn down selected Armenian villages in the area. The Zeitounlis promptly retaliated, and this is what the authorities were waiting for. The military commander informed the Sultan by wire that the Zeitounlis were in rebellion and were mercilessly massacring the Muslims.[46] Having the benefit of a long-standing status of semi-autonomy and the cumulative experience of a series of limited uprisings in the second half of the nineteenth century, the Zeitounlis, inspired and directed by a few Hunchak leaders, launched an open rebellion declaring, "This time, our mountains are going to be our prisons."

The Zeitoun insurrection is notable in several respects. It involved a string of ferocious battles, in the course of which the Ottoman army, more specifically the 5th Army Corps, stationed at nearby Maraş, repeatedly failed to break through the Armenian defense perimeter, while sustaining heavy losses. In the end, Remzi Paşa, the Commander-in-Chief, was dismissed and was replaced by Edhem Paşa. Altogether 24 battalions, 12 cannons, reinforced by the 8,000 men of a Zeibek division from Smyrna (Izmir), and about 30–35,000 Kurdish, Turkish and Circassian irregulars, could not subdue by force of arms the 1,500 insurgents, equipped with only flintlock and 400 martin rifles. Thousands of the Turkish soldiers froze to death in the subzero winter temperatures, other thousands died from their wounds in the hospitals of Maraş. The larger losses involved battlefield casualties. Notwithstanding, the condition of the Armenian defenders deteriorated gradually due to the processes of depletion of resources and attrition, aggravated by a steadily tightening ring of encirclement effected by the Ottoman troops, which were being constantly replenished.

It was under these circumstances that the six Powers took the initiative, offering both the insurgents and the Sultan their good offices for mediation. The significance of the swiftness with which the Armenians accepted the offer was exceeded only by the urgency with which the Sultan himself responded to the offer, thereby surprising the Ambassadors of the Powers. After ten days of "laborious" negotiations, an accord was reached and was put into effect on February 12, 1896. The Sultan agreed to grant tax relief to the Zeitounlis, agreed to allow that, except for the judge, all governmental employees and law enforcement agents be appointed from among indigenous Zeitounlis, and again promised to introduce specific reforms which were recommended by the representatives of the intervening Powers; the centerpiece of the accord was the Turkish commitment to appoint a Christian governor (*kaymakam*) for Zeitoun county (*kaza*). After much stalling in face of the pressures brought to bear upon the Sultan by the Powers, that *kaymakam* was finally appointed on July 7, 1896, but arrived at his post on September 9. In return, the insurgents surrendered their combat weapons; under the terms of a general amnesty the four top leaders were to be expelled from the territories of the empire. On February 13, 1896 they were escorted from Zeitoun to the Turkish port of Mersin for their trip on March 12 to Marseille, France. To save face, however, the entire accord was made to appear as a Sultan's pardon to rebels willing to submit.

Zeitoun, but especially nearby Adana with its huge concentration of Armenians in and around the city, escaped the massacres, which at that time were engulfing the rest of the empire's Armenian population. The military defeats suffered by the Ottoman troops were severe enough to restrain in this respect potential perpetrators in the entire region. Whether justified or not, there was fear that the Zeitounlis may break through the military cordon of encirclement and rush down to the plane of Adana to exact, in a burst of vengeance, heavy tolls from the area's Turkish-Muslim population. The news of the military setbacks of the Ottoman armed forces, which had stunned that population, were no idle rumors or fantasies. All the European consuls of the region dutifully reported these news after ascertaining their factualness. The British Consul, Barnham, in his January 6, 1896 report, stated that "the Turkish troops had met with a serious defeat at Zeitoun ... at least 5,000 have been killed though common report swells the number to 10,000 ... ." He conceded that the Zeitounlis "always fought with great bravery, and their rifle shooting from behind hastily provided stockades was admitted by the Turks to be excellent ... their rifle practice was so good that the troops did not care to face it, and kept themselves as much as possible under cover." As to the losses sustained by both sides, Barnham estimated the total number of "Armenians who perished during the revolt from war, disease or want was probably about 6,000." According to him, the city of Zeitoun, whose population before the revolt was 7,500, was burdened by the influx of 12,000 refugees, escaping massacre and destruction from the environs of the city.[47] Austria's Aleppo Consul, J. Bertrand, relayed to the Austrian Consul General of Syria, Chevalier de Rémy-Berzenovich, "confidentially" received information that "the Zeytounlis, fighting like real heros, killed 1,300 Turkish soldiers in the last battle. Of the four battalions sent from Aleppo and Cebel Samaan, more than half have been killed." The Italian Consul at Aleppo, i.e., the Italian consular representative conducting negotiations on behalf of the Powers in Zeitoun, E. Vitto, in a February 16, 1896 letter to his Austrian colleague Bertrand, stated that "The Sublime Porte has accepted the terms formulated by the insurgents."[48] As

related by French Ambassador Cambon, the offer of the Powers to mediate for an accord "was first received coldly" by the Sultan, who apparently was sanguine about his ability to crush the Armenians through a
new offensive. The day he "thanked us for offering our good offices, the
very same day the Turkish commander received his order to finish off the
Armenians." However, after a few futile onslaughts, launched for this
purpose, the request for mediation ensued "with a very significant tone of
insistence ... the Ottoman troops are in quite a bad situation." Cambon
described the terrible plight of the 17,000-man Ottoman Corps which
was being "decimated," forecasting "terrible consequences" in the event
"the mediation of the Powers does not promptly materialize."

In assessing this type of outcome, uncommon in the annals of
Ottoman imperial history, a French military expert, Colonel de Vialar,
French military attaché to Turkey, offered the following comments:

> The Zeitounli combatants numbered about 1,500 and were equipped but with
> old flintlock guns, including 400 guns they took from the soldiers of the bar-
> racks. The Turkish troops, 24 battalions, numbered about 20,000 men,
> equipped with good weapons and ample ammunition; add to these 30,000
> *başıbozuks* (irregulars) Kurds and Circassians. At the end, the Zeytounlis,
> having exhausted their ammunition had prepared a plan of attack to be carried
> out with cold steel. It involved a nightly assault, to be launched simultane-
> ously at many points, against the 10,000 soldiers of Ali Bey, [one of the com-
> manders of the brigades comprising the Fifth Army Corps]. Despite their
> numerical inferiority, they might have succeeded in routing the Turks.
> Besides, the Zeytounlis consider every war they wage as a crusade. They han-
> dle the dagger with a dexterity that is incredible. Furthermore, they knew that
> had the Ottoman troops entered the city, they wouldn't have spared even the
> infants and the women. That is why they would have sold dear their lives.

The comment of the French Chargé at Constantinople, M. de la
Boulinière, is telling in this regard. "Ever since the troubles began, this is
the second time that the Powers rendered a great service to the Sultan by
extricating him from a difficult and alarming situation ... he was much
happy to see the Powers intervene" (*Il a été trés heureux de l'intervention
des Puissances*).[49] In yet two other reports Ambassador Cambon first
informed Paris that the Sultan's "recourse to the Powers [to secure their
intervention] was due to military failure" (*échec*),[50] and then described
the Sultan's supplication of the Powers in the sense that they should hurry
up to secure cessation of hostilities in order to spare his troops the ordeals
of war in severe winter weather.[51] During the negotiations with the Armenians to end hostilities, the Turkish Commander of the western front
forces in the battle for Zeitoun, Ali Bey, is reported to have told Aghassi,
the leader of the insurgents, that in addition to the intrepidity, the quality
he admired most in the Zeitounlis was "their incredible marksmanship."[52]
On the other hand, French author Pierre Quillard estimates Turkish losses
at 20,000.[53] Generally speaking, there are no reliable, concise statistics on

any of the categories relative to losses directly associated with the insurrection, and the Turkish military campaign to repress it. It is worth noting in this respect that the British statesman and a student of the histories of the Eastern and Armenian questions, James Bryce, discerned an analogy in the fate of both Montenegrins and the Zeitounlis in terms of their struggle against Turkish oppression. Zeitoun "was a sort of Asiatic Montenegro, and the gallantry with which these Zeitounlis defended themselves against vastly superior forces in the winter of 1895–96 proved these isolated Christians to be worthy compeers of the men of Tsernagora, whose dauntless valor has been commemorated by the greatest poet of this generation."[54] Finally, an agreement was reached and a press release spelled out the conditions of the accords; they have been published in Armenian[55] as well as French.[56] The entire episode has been narrated, from an Armenian point of view, in English also.[57]

The Conflagration of Van

Unlike in all the previous cases of revolutionary activity against the Ottoman regime, in the case of Van the Hunchaks and the Dashnaks were not only united but, more significant, they were substantially aided by a third party, the Armenakans. An indigenous party which antedated the other two in terms of origin and organization, but not necessarily in terms of ideology and purpose, the Armenakans were less "revolutionary" in the sense that they limited their activities strictly to local defense purposes; their targets were local government officials and marauding Kurds oppressing the Armenian population of Van. More important, the leadership almost entirely consisted of native Armenians, whereas the other two parties were essentially led and directed by Armenians from Russia, Europe, and to some extent even the U.S.A. Van is located about one mile from the shores of Lake Van in eastern Turkey. The city and its environs contained one of the largest concentrations of Armenians of the Ottoman Empire. Whether taken separately or together, both the Turks and the Kurds were numerically inferior to the Armenians.[58] The entire region was considered by the Armenians as hallowed territory, a landmark of Armenian culture and civilization, steeped in the traditions of the ancient Armenian church. Its contiguity to Russia was a factor that only served to aggravate the Ottoman authorities facing Armenian revolutionaries in that area. To counteract Russian influence, generated in the area by the Russian consulate, France, and Great Britain had likewise established consulates in Van city.

The Armenians of Van had a somewhat modest legacy of rebellion, such as the one that took place in 1862. Its significance lay in the fact that it was undertaken in alliance with the Kurds of the surrounding areas. This was one of the very rare instances in which Armenians and Kurds had combined their resources in contesting the Ottoman regime. But in 1879, in the wake of the signing of the Treaty of Berlin, Article 61 of which stipulated governmental remedies against anti-Armenian Kurdish depredations, the Sultan had dispatched Marshal Sami to Van with the mission to stimulate the intensification of the level of these depredations, at the same time pretending to champion the ethnocentric aspirations of the Kurds. Sami proceeded to settle large groups of Kurds in the outlying zones of Van city as a counterweight to the overall sway of the Armenians of Van.

Next to the Armenakans, the party most effectively organized and influential were the Hunchaks, who, in several respects, differed from the former. The tenets of their nationalist ideology were often confounded with those of international socialism. This fact helped them foster overt and covert ties with foreign support groups sharing similar ideological dogmas. Unlike the Armenakans, the Hunchaks believed in and occasionally resorted to bravado as a tactical device to arouse the apolitical Armenian masses, at the same time challenging the authorities as instruments of oppression. They were led by a 25-year-old University student from the neighbouring Transcaucasus, who boasted of having under his command several hundred squads, each squad consisting of 8–15 men, but with very little training, or combat experience, and possessing altogether no more than two rifles. This leader's credo was summed up as follows: "We would be content if out of a total of four million Armenians a mere 100,000 survive, but end up living in freedom in a socialist regime. It makes no difference to me whether that regime is headed by a sultan or by the Armenian King Tigranes." An Armenian author, a contemporary, described him as a typical "ivory tower utopist, kind, truly sincere, forthright, a strict disciplinarian, impeccably honest in his dealings with others, and a very noble young man."[59] The Hunchaks tried to compensate for their limited resources of power by their proclivity to resort to terror, assassinating those Kurds and Turks whom they branded as the tormentors of the Armenian people; nor did they spare those Armenians whom they labeled as collaborators of the regime, or whom they considered as serious obstacles to the fulfilment of their designs. Three months before the June 1896 conflagration, the Hunchaks tried but failed to assassinate a Kurdish brigand chief, Şakir, who, in an act of revenge, exacted a heavy toll by sword and fire in the areas of Nordouz and Hayotz Tzor.

The Dashnaks were rather latecomers to the scene. Nevertheless, they quickly gained a foothold in the region through the organization of a network of revolutionary cells. Among the three factions, they were the most disciplined and the least handicapped in terms of resources. The Dashnaks, too, developed, and relished in, a taste for bravado, and availed themselves of the methods of terror to punish those whom they considered as guilty of crimes against the Armenian people—be they Turks, Kurds, or even Armenians.

Prior to the June 1896 conflagration, Armenian life in and around Van was beset with a history of a factionalism among the three parties that virtually crippled the general movement launched to alleviate the plight of the Armenian population. Many of the leaders involved mistook their dedication to a cause for proof of their competence in leadership or polit-ical acumen; the attributes of daring and intrepidity were confounded with qualifications that, as a rule, are prerequisites for effective leader-ship and were needed at that time to successfully deal with the antago-nistic Turks and Kurds of the area. Perhaps the greatest handicap was the alien origin of most of the leaders of the Hunchak and Dashnak parties, who were rather "imported" leaders. Some of them were products of European education, others of Russian culture. As such, they lacked familiarity with regional and local conditions. Armenians from the Tran-scaucasus, notably from Tbilisi and Baku, for example, didn't know and understand much about the Ottoman Empire, Turks and Kurds, and by the same token, the intricate nature of the problems of the Ottoman Armenians. These were the conditions against the background of which the conflagration of Van needs to be examined.

Of all the material available from official European sources, the reports of Major W. H. Williams, British Vice Consul at Van at the time, are the most detailed, even when they have a pro-Ottoman slant. He had arrived on the scene five months before the outbreak. While most other centers of Armenian community life in the rest of Turkey were attacked and devastated during the fall 1895 empire-wide massacres, Van was spared on account of several factors. The governor and the military com-mander were opposed to violence and disorder, and could exercise con-trol in this regard. Also, the Armenians of Van, unlike those in many other Armenian-populated cities in the interior of Turkey, could not be treated by the Turks as an easy prey for slaughter. Due to their proximity to Russia and Iran, they had managed to smuggle arms for stockpiling. Moreover, the Armenakans, then the dominant party in Van were, unlike the other two parties, most cautious and circumspect in their defense-ori-ented preparations—in anticipation of a major assault by the Turks and Kurds. In October 1895, at the height of the inferno engulfing many Armenian communities elsewhere, Van Armenians had sustained very limited casualties, which largely resulted from an accidental skirmish between Armenakan arms smugglers and Kurds.

In his January 14, 1896 report to his ambassador at Constantinople, British Vice Consul Major Williams speaks of a large number of Armen-ian villages "which have been looted ... these poor people are suffering considerable hardship ... . Generally speaking the situation is very bad; the Armenians are everywhere in a state bordering on panic, afraid lest the spring will bring still further disasters ... ."[60] On February 19, Williams wrote to Ambassador Currie: "Eight Armenians were killed in a village near here ... . Two other Armenians are reported to have been killed in villages ... unless steps are taken in the near future to obtain some hold over the Kurds, I am afraid the coming summer will see very grave events in this vilayet." Williams then made the following diagnosis to explain his prognosis, which, in the light of the June outbreak, proved prophetic and has reference to

> ... the method by which the Government deals with the Kurdish question. Instead of arresting one or two or more of such [Kurdish] Chiefs as they could easily catch, the Mushir [Marshal Zeki, the Commander of the Fourth Army Corps] at Erzincan telegraphs the [Kurdish] Hamidiye Commanders to "keep quiet." Such an order practically condones past offences.[61]

This fact of indulging, if not encouraging, the Kurds in their assaults against the Armenians was confirmed by P. Defrance, the French representative, who called attention to "the armed Kurds enjoying [the benefits of] impunity."[62] To restrain these Kurds, Armenian revolutionary bands began to organize retaliatory surprise raids in some cases, engaged in open combat in other cases, and still in other cases resorted to terror acts to intimidate actual and potential perpetrators among the Kurds and their Turkish supporters. In the course of these operations scores of Turks, but mostly Kurds, were killed.[63]

In this state of affairs Sultan Abdul Hamit used one of his standard devices to decimate and subdue the Armenians of Van. He sent his Aide de Camp, General Saadeddin, to Van, ostensibly to superintend the reforms which he had promulgated through an Imperial Rescript on October 17, 1895, and had informed the Powers of it three days later. However, the general not only did not pursue reforms but held a series of secret meetings with Kurdish chieftains, who reportedly richly rewarded him. He also engineered the resignation of the Governor-General of the province, Nazım Paşa, who had been trying to mollify the Sultan while actually opposing massacres, a fact the Armenians had acknowledged with gratitude.[64] But, as French Ambassador Cambon reported to his Foreign Minister in Paris, Saadeddin, disagreeing with the policy of the Governor General "wants to indulge the Kurds in order to use them against the Armenians, whereas the Governor-General is in favor of measures of conciliation."[65] This method of organizing massacres while pretending to carry out the promulgated reforms insisted on by the Powers was used throughout the six Armenian-populated provinces in the 1895–96 period by High Commissioner Şakir Paşa; he too was an Aide de Camp of Sultan Hamit, and with great fanfare was dispatched to the provinces avowedly to supervise the implementation of the reforms. But almost everywhere he went to "inspect," massacres, instead of reforms, became the by-products of his visits, especially in Erzurum. Describing him as "one of the Sultan's more sinister advisors," Kinross explains his lethal mission as follows:

> His ostensible post was that of "inspector of certain localities in the provinces of Asiatic Turkey" in connection with the Sultan's own pretended reform plans. Under this cover his actual role was the planning and execution of massacres in each specified locality.[66]

Encouraged by the success of this ploy, the Sultan had now engaged General Saadeddin. In order to deflect from his clandestine activities and to give legitimacy to the massacres which, according to the French Chargé at Constantinople, M. de la Boulinière, "were long in preparation by the Kurds," Saadeddin framed a Report on the conditions of the province of Van. Upon receipt of a copy of it, and after checking with Vice Consul Williams at Van, the British Chargé Michael H. Herbert in a dispatch to his Prime Minister Salisbury, denounced that report for "the numerous inaccuracies contained therein."[67] A skirmish between a Turkish patrol and an unknown group of assailants, suspected to be either Armenian revolutionaries, or "a party of Turks smuggling salt,"[68] and resulting in the death of a Turkish gendarme and a soldier, triggered the eruption of what the Armenians dubbed "The Great Event of Van." After describing this occurrence as an engineered incident providing "the awaited pretext" for the Turks to unleash their onslaught, Cambon points out to another stratagem. According to the information that was then available to him, part of the effort of the authorities to handle the situation consisted in the cynical issuance of an order "forbidding to fire at Muslims, thus making it possible for the troops to impassively look on as the Armenians were being killed by the Turks pursuing them."[69] According to British Vice Consul Williams, "the disturbances were begun by a mob of Turks, gipsies and zaptiehs [military police], the latter being out of hand during the whole week, and responsible for much that has happened."[70]

The conflagration lasted nine days (old style: June 3–11; new style following the Ottoman calendar: June 15–23). The leaders of the three Armenian parties established a Joint Directorate of Defense, which, on the basis of prepared lists, deployed 500 young men at 33 strategic positions in and around Aikesdan (Garden City), where the bulk of Van's Armenian population lived, and where villas and other homes stood, enveloped by flower and vegetable gardens and orchards. More important, here were also located the consulates of France, Russia, Persia, England, and the American Mission compound. Four miles west of the Garden City was located the twin part of Van, the walled city, containing the shops, the public buildings; the City Hall, the Military School, the Central Police Station, the Central Prison, and Post and Telegraph offices. The central authorities sent "four battalions and some cavalry" to Van to deal with the Armenians; of these, one battalion and two squadrons were from Erzurum, two battalions from Harput, and one battalion came from Muş.[71]

On the third day of the conflagration, the Muslims gathered in the mosques from which they dashed to launch their assault. The Armenians of four exposed quarters with mixed populations were the first victims; without distinction of age or gender, men, women and children were killed with axes, sticks, hammers, and daggers, as some others were burned alive.[72] As a result, the rest of the Armenian population tried to escape to the Armenian quarters. Throughout five days and nights the intense and unequal combats raged. The defenders, whose "total number amounted to 600 or 700,"[73] not only maintained their positions, but were able to repulse the attackers several times. Saadeddin, the Inspector of Reforms, called in the Kurdish cavalry, who likewise were repulsed with heavy losses. The defenders cut scores of giant willows to use them as roadblocks. They inundated all the roads linking the Armenian and Turkish sections by obstructing the flow of the streams running through these sections. Many residents had converted their houses and gardens into individual small fortresses. Vice Consul Major Williams who, as a potential mediator, was allowed access to the front lines by both parties to the conflict, observed that "the revolutionists had fortified in a very skilful manner certain houses ... I visited two of the fortified positions. I was astonished to find how intelligently their affairs were conducted."[74] The Armenians even managed to capture two cannons during an assault.

It was at this juncture that Sultan Abdul Hamit sought, as he had done in the case of Zeitoun few months before, the mediation of the Powers, especially France and England, while promising to the French Ambassador that he "will guarantee the lives and safety of all the other Armenians in the town of Van."[75] However, when his plenipotentiary, General Saadeddin, stipulated two conditions, the Armenians rejected the offer. He wanted the surrender of the top ten leaders directing the Armenians' defense, and the surrender to the consular officials of all the weapons. The Armenians were arguing that they were not rebelling but exercising their right of self-defense inasmuch as the government had failed to prevent the massacre of hundreds of Armenians and that their fight was essentially directed against the mob and rabble among which were select gendarmes and soldiers acting in disguise. The Turks thereupon introduced several new cannons and began a massive bombardment. With ammunition running out, and unable to cope with the effects of this new weapon of devastation, the defenders agreed to a second proposal— insisted upon by the British who considered it more fair[76]—to leave the country under the supervision of the consuls. Splitting in three groups, the Armenian combatants and their adherents set out to remove themselves from Ottoman territories. The Armenakan group comprised 200 armed and about 700 unarmed men; of the Dashnak contingent of 125, only 58 joined the exodus, as did 25 Hunchaks. In spite of solemn Turkish pledges of safety to be provided for the exodus all the way to the Iran-ian borders, the three detachments were surrounded and engaged at Karahisar mountain by regular Turkish troops and Kurdish irregulars. After a hopeless and last-ditch combat, the Armenians were annihilated, with only 35 of them managing to survive. Thus, "the cream of the Armenian youth of Van," along with a group of intellectuals, altogether some 1,000 men, perished as a result of a governmental act of perfidy. "Through this loss Van practically was deprived of its valuable youth. The sorrow and overall impact of this occurrence was indescribable. The tragic news of this massacre stupefied the entire population of Van, plunging it in deep mourning."[77] Nevertheless, the defense of Van, however costly for the defenders in terms of their post-battle entrapment and destruction, ultimately served its purpose in that the rest of the Armenian population escaped massacre—save for the approximately 400 victims residing in quarters with mixed, i.e. Turkish and Kurdish, populations. As one went further away from Van city, in the direction of outlying villages, however, the Armenian losses grew exponentially. These losses are estimated to be in the vicinity of 20,000.[78] A British "eye-witness" reported the destruction of 350 hamlets and villages.[79] Major Williams confirms the "great destruction of villages by Kurds," adding that "150 of the best Armenian houses in Van have been burnt, and many more pillaged … The reports from the villages are heartrending … ."[80] At the same time he acknowledged that among Turkish fatalities were "a considerable number of soldiers and some officers."[81] Williams underscores the fact that "about twelve or fifteen" of the Armenian leaders were "outsiders," among whom there were "a Russian and a Bulgarian … together with Armenians [who were] naturalized subjects of Russia and America."[82]

Even though Williams was instrumental in the cessation of combat activities and the expulsion of the leaders from Van, Armenian sources accuse him of supporting Ottoman authorities covertly, if not conspiratorially. He is portrayed as a military expert who, wearing a *fez*, Turkish headgear, inspected the Armenian positions, spied on them, and even helped the Turks adjust their cannons for better aiming. These sources further claim that Williams was not so much interested in ending the massacre but the resistance of the Armenians.[83] Another Armenian author attributes this performance by Williams to British wariness that Russia, exploiting the opportunity presented by the Van conflagration, may invade Turkey and annex captured territory.[84] As if to give credence to these speculations, Williams then collected some 60 Armenian notables among the survivors, along with the *locum tenens*, and literally ordered them to sign a telegram, swearing loyalty to the Sultan, expressing gratitude to him, and denouncing the Armenian revolutionaries for the disaster that befell Van Armenians. Williams confirms[85] this act of producing the collective confessional and the allied loyalty conjuration, otherwise a *mazbata* (protocol), which was often used by the Turks to extort from

Armenians such testimonies. Shocked by the threats and intimidations of Vice Consul Major Williams, one of the notables reportedly became demented, suffered a stroke, and died shortly thereafter.[86]

The Capture of Bank Ottoman

As if eager to follow the example set by the other two political parties, who had played a major role in the organization of the Sassoun outbreak in August 1894 and the Babı Ali demonstration in September 1895, namely the Armenakans and Hunchaks, respectively, the Dashnaks embarked upon a most daring assault in the capital of the Ottoman Empire. After weeks of preparations, they raided and captured, on August 14/26, 1896, the Ottoman Bank, a bastion of European finance where British, but especially French, investments predominated and accordingly the bank was managed and controlled by those interest groups. Actually the Dashnaks had approached the Hunchaks a year before for a major demonstration to be undertaken jointly in Constantinople, but no agreement could be reached.[87] Other and more forceful initiatives, which the Dashnaks had considered in a preliminary fashion in the months preceding the bank raid, were relinquished in the light of the widespread massacres of that period and the post-Van debacle, as a result of which the party had lost several of its leaders. Among the initiatives being contemplated was a plot to assassinate Sultan Abdul Hamit, but the fear of a massive and more devastating assault on the unarmed and most vulnerable provincial Armenian population by the Muslim populace and mobs deterred the revolutionaries.[88]

The plan was to force the entrance of the bank through a surprise attack by six avant-guard commandos. After a brief skirmish with the four guards, three of whom fell and one managed to flee, the bank was seized by the remaining 19 commandos when four of the latter brought in a stockpile of hand grenades, dynamite, and ammunition, which they carried on their backs and which resembled those used there for transporting silver. All of the members of the band were equipped with at least two pistols and other hand guns, along with several cartridge clips and cartridge belts. Prior to the incursion, the leaders of the raiding group had prepared fliers in order to explain, in the name of the Dashnak Central Committee of Constantinople, the reasons for the assault; one of the fliers was directed to the Turkish, another to the Armenian people, and still two more to the Powers, i.e., the ambassadors in the Ottoman capital, which included the post-capture demands of the Armenian revolutionaries. They were dictated in French to six bank employees by Armen Karo, who had taken charge of the command of the operations after the original leader, Papken Siuni, was killed during the initial skirmish. By sheer coincidence, Ibrahim Hakkı, the palace interpreter (*mabeyn mütercim*), was in the bank when it was seized. Trembling with fear, he in French portrayed himself to Karo as a liberal Turk, always opposed to massacres against the Armenians. (In the 1910–1911 period he rose to the highest rank in the Ottoman government, i.e., Grand Vizier). Hakkı was allowed to leave the bank in order to present the same demands to the Ottoman authorities, including the Sultan and Grand Vizier Halil Rifat, both of whom were adamantly opposed to negotiating with the Armenians and were inclined to retaliate with force. In fact, Sultan Abdul Hamit reportedly had already issued orders to the ministers of War and Marine to direct artillery fire to the bank to end "this scandal."[89]

The appeal to the Turkish people contained the following declaration:

> For centuries our forbears have been living with you in peace and harmony ... but recently your government, conceived in crimes, began to sow discords among us in order to strangle us and you with greater ease. You, people, did not understand this diabolical scheme of politics and, socking yourself in the blood of our brothers, you became an accomplice in the perpetration of the heinous crime. Nevertheless, know well that our fight is not against you, but your government, against which your own best sons are fighting also.[90]

One of the flyers, directed to the Powers, refers to the Turkish government's "unpunished crimes," adding, "The Powers, by their attitude, make themselves the accomplices of the Porte ... . But the patience of down-trodden nations has its limits." The second flyer contained statements despairing of the sustained plight of the Armenians in the provinces, and berating the Powers for tolerating "Turkish tyranny ... Sultan Hamit's murderous vengeance. Europe has beheld this fearful crime and has kept silence. Not only has Europe not stayed the hand of the executioner, but she has insolently imposed upon us [her solution, i.e.] resignation ... . The time of diplomatic play is passed. The blood shed by our 100,000 martyrs gives us the right to demand liberty." After enumerating other conditions, the flyer demanded the enactment of "judicial reforms according to the European system," and "The nomination for Armenia of a High Commissioner, of European origin and nationality, elected by the Six Great Powers."[91]

Before the terrified employees of the bank could be collected together and held as prisoners, Sir Edgar Vincent, the Director General of the bank, managed to escape from his office on the top story of the building through a skylight on the roof and into the adjoining building of the Tobacco Régie. He negotiated a deal with the Ottoman Council of Ministers which was in session at the Palace. He was aided in this respect by M. Maximoff, the First Dragoman of the Russian Embassy, who had rushed to the Palace as soon as he had heard of the capture. The deal, agreed to by the Sultan himself, was that the revolutionaries were to be offered a free pardon and permission to leave the country unmolested;

these terms were to be guaranteed by Maximof on behalf of the Russian Embassy. The deputy of Vincent, M. Auboyneau, a Frenchman, was allowed to leave the bank for the purpose of presenting the conditions of the insurgents to the Powers.

One of the demands included in the letter which, as noted above, was composed on the premises of the bank, was the immediate cessation of the massacre then in progress in the streets of Constantinople and of the armed assaults from the outside against the bank that was being defended by the Armenians, who in the meantime had fortified it. "Otherwise, after exhausting our supply of ammunition, we will be forced to blow up the building."[92] This letter had all the trappings of an ultimatum. There were three hours of tortuous negotiations during which the Armenians several times had turned down the pending Turko-European offer because it contained no written guarantees and commitments regarding the understanding that the massacres will not be resumed, and regarding the fulfilment of the specific conditions of reform insisted upon in the flyers and the letter. In still another letter, addressed to the French Chargé at Constantinople, five leaders of the bank had insisted on the need for "securing of peace throughout the entire country by international intervention," at the same time explaining that "It is the criminal indifference of humanity which has pushed us to this extreme." They then assured everyone concerned that the manifold riches of the treasury, stored at the bank, will not be touched by the revolutionaries who stressed the fact that they were not interested in money or assets but in the securing of simple human rights.[93]

Four factors finally impelled the two leaders of the occupants of the bank, who had trouble in agreeing among themselves, to reluctantly agree to the terms proposed to them. 1) They were running low in ammunition and through stock-taking realized that not enough dynamite was left to blast the bank; for several hours after the capture, they had fought bloody battles from the various windows, the roof and other positions of the bank-edifice to repulse the series of onslaughts of regular army troops and streams of mobs, led by large numbers of turbaned *softas*, Muslim theology students, exacting heavy tolls in the process. 2) Moreover, in the course of these engagements, of the original 25 men, six had been wounded and four had died, including the principal leader; the resulting lack of immediate clear direction, and lack of a display of leadership resolve had adversely affected the overall moral of the group. 3) The gripping apprehension that should they proceed to destroy the bank with all of its European employees inside it, not only would the Turks wreak yet a new round of vengeance of gigantic proportions against the vulnerable Armenian population of the provinces, but Europe might abandon Armenia to its fate, thus giving license to the Turks to deal with the Armenians in their customary way, and without much inhibition. 4) The persuasive skills of Maximof and Auboyneau in their role as mediators.

When Maximof learned of the initial and angry reaction of the Sultan, of his wanting to smash the Armenian revolutionaries by an armed attack on the bank that included the order to bombard and reduce the building, he reportedly threatened on behalf of all the Powers to batter the Palace through cannon fire from the battleships[94] stationed in the Bosphorus, thereby dissuading the Sultan. On the other hand, Maximof pleaded with the Armenians, who claim that he implored them with these words: "I beg you, I go down on my knees, please hurray up and leave the premises. I obtained Sultan's permission with great difficulty. Tomorrow he may change his mind. Think of the enormous responsibility falling on your shoulders, should new waves of massacre further decimate your people."[95] French Ambassador Cambon credits both Auboyneau and Maximof, specially the latter's "clever eloquence," for skilfully mediating between the Sultan, the Armenians, and Grand Vizier Halil Rifat, whose "lack of interest in the fate of the great financial establishment was matched by his desire to allow things to develop to a point where the atrocities resulting from the anger of the Muslims against the Armenians could be justified."[96] The 15 surviving insurgents finally evacuated the bank at 3:30 a.m. and under protective guard were taken on board of Director General Vincent's yacht for transfer to the French steamer Gironde, which a day later took them to Marseille, and into temporary exile in France. The five wounded men were taken to the Russian hospital of the city, and upon full recovery, were transported to Egypt under Russian protection, as promised by Maximof. The authorities were surprised to find out that only 25 insurgents had seized the bank, whereas they mistakenly had believed their number to be at least 200. In his summary report on the entire episode, British Chargé Herbert informed Prime Minister Salisbury that the insurgents had left behind "forty-five gunpowder bombs, twenty-five dynamite cartridges, and eleven kilogram dynamite." He then added "no attempt was made to take any money. Thus ended somewhat tamely a most daring outrage … ."[97]

Some publicists and many diplomats denounced the bank seizure as a foolish act of terrorism. British historian Kinross thought that "As young men of ideals inexperienced in the wiles of political agitation, they had failed to benefit their friends and had played into the hands of their enemies."[98] A number of European newspapers, such as *Freie Presse* of Vienna, *Berliner Tageblatt* of Berlin, and *Étoile Belge* of Bruxelles, praised, however, the Dashnak revolutionaries for their scrupulous honesty with which they comported themselves in face of the enormous riches they left untouched, and the singular courage with which they attacked and seized the nerve center of international finance in the Ottoman capital. The staff physician of the steamer Gironde, who spent six days with the insurgents on their trip to Marseille, sent a correspondence to *Étoile Belge* in which, among others, he offered the following comments.

These dauntless men with a sense of complete self-sacrifice, captured in broad daylight the most important institution of the Ottoman Empire … . They were neither thieves nor robbers … not a penny was lifted. On one of the counters of the bank was lying a case containing 10,000 Turkish gold pounds and a large number of bank notes which their leader personally handed over to one of the directors of the bank. In the panic created by the armed assault, the main vault of the bank was left open and, upon the request of the same director, was immediately shut by the raiders. After holding it for 13 hours, they withdrew in the most honorable way. We were for six days in the company of these young heroes and thus were in a position to scrutinize and assess them. The officers and other personnel, all of us, we all admire, honor and love them.[99]

The seizure of the bank was but the main part of the overall plan to create chaos and confusion in the Ottoman capital and provoke military intervention by the Powers. In a limited way they had succeeded in this respect, as small contingents of British and Russian marines and sailors had landed at various spots of the Straits of Bosphorus to protect their nationals. To augment and intensify the terror in the city several major police stations were selected by the insurgent Armenians as targets for hand grenades and bombs, especially those of Samatia in the Istanbul part of the city, and of Galatasaray in the Beyoğlu part. Additionally, the carriage of the Grand Vizier, who was expected to pass through the Galata bridge on his way to his office, the Sublime Porte, was designated as a prime target for bomb throwing. These sallies were synchronized in order to amplify their overall impact. They all had to start at exactly 6 p.m. However the attack on the Grand Vizier did not materialize and none of the undertakings proved effective. The authorities one way or another were apprised of the imminence of an Armenian revolutionary onslaught, in Samatia in particular, where the bloodiest battles took place. Fortified in a number of buildings as their last bastion of combat, a small group of Dashnak insurgents, including some young women for fourteen hours fought an unequal and desperate battle against a combined force of police and military stormtroopers. Many of these insurgents used their last bullet to end their lives to avoid being captured alive.

The Unleashing by the Authorities of the Predesigned Massacres

Under certain circumstances of human conflict, the leap from a condition of despair to the compulsion to assume the role of a desperado is just a matter of subliminal catharsis. The inveterate urge for self-sacrifice for a cause tends to eclipse the need to consider the probable consequences of desperado-specific behavior. The glaring aspects of the impunity accruing to the perpetrators of the massacre of the Sassoun episode and that of the Babı Ali demonstration in the preceding two years had shaken and at the same time stirred many Armenians to the point that they were eager to counteract in some spectacular way. Of the four leaders responsible for organizing the bank seizure, two, Armen Karo and Huratch Tiryakian, had interrupted their higher education in France spontaneously upon hearing the news of the massacres; they immediately involved themselves in revolutionary activity. The third, the supreme leader of the entire band, Papken Siunee (Bedros Parian), a 23-year-old scion of old aristocratic lineage, who was killed at the very start of the raid, was described by all who knew him as a young man of impeccable character, and as "an archetypical Armenian" by the dean of the college he attended.[100]

One may assume that the nature of revolutionary idealism is such that it creates its own norms and that in this sense terror is a means of making a statement for which other channels are long denied. Thus, the resort to terror becomes a kind of normative behavior for the revolutionary actor bent on overcoming barriers in his drive to deal with oppression. His acts committed in this connection are not only spectacular in nature but are expected also to jolt the oppressors. Closely linked to this objective is the hope that the violent outburst will serve as a triggering mechanism for precipitating developments that may result in a drastic change of the oppressive status quo. The idea is to force the hands of outside powers, capable of effective intervention but, through a lapse into a protracted hesitation or ambivalence, incapable of resolute action. In other words, one has to probe into the world of the expectations of the conspirators in order to more fully understand their motivations and agenda. The more acute and visceral these expectations are, the greater the dynamism of the aggression propelling the act of terror. The narrative of the leader directing the operations of the seizure of the bank is quite instructive in this respect. When describing their last hours together on the eve of the raid, he states that "should our operations proceed as planned, Constantinople could be seized and occupied by European military forces. The Armenian Question could then find the desired solution."[101] This expectation was based on the mistaken belief that the Powers, during the May Reform Plan exchanges in 1895, had formally warned the Ottoman government with a threat to land sailors and marines from their 12 warships, available for this purpose, to restore order, in the event new disorders erupted in Constantinople.[102] "Precisely for this reason we opted for the seizure of Bank Ottoman; we wanted to force the hands of the Powers in this regard."[103]

Since expectations are not to be confused with air-tight assurances or guarantees, revolutionary actors, by necessity, have to bank on contingencies that have elements of uncertainty; accordingly, they have to reckon with and take risks. In the final analysis, the initiative being contemplated is, as a rule, reduced to a balancing act; potential gains and liabilities are weighed and whichever of them tip the scales may become the factor determining the outcome of the deliberations. But revolutionaries have a temperament, and a rationale to go with it, which allows them to substitute brinkmanship for restrictive deliberations. They must often rely on the animus of daring, as advocated by the French revolutionary leader Danton, who enjoined his cohorts as follows: *Il nous faut de l'audace, et encore de l'audace, et toujours de l'audace."* (We need audacity, and more audacity, and always audacity). Presently, the rationale was that the massacres of 1894 and 1895 had reached a certain apex of cataclysm and that new major attempts at massacre either might not be ventured by the perpetrators or might not be tolerated by the Powers. This approach to hazardousness and the procilivity for risk-taking is akin to what might be called a "threshold mentality," which often permeates revolutionary subcultures. The goals are never in doubt and the will to contest the established authority is resolute. But an awareness of the disparity in resources, handicapping a revolutionary movement vis a vis the established authorities, is a consideration that influences the timing and shaping of the particular revolutionary act. The targeted party must not be cornered hopelessly and the terror act must not be structured in a way that preempts or precludes negotiation. In such situations, the outcome is almost always contingent on two possible developments; 1) the degree to which outside powers are in fact drawn in the conflict by way of intervention or 2) the nature of the response of the party targeted by the revolutionaries, in the absence of such an intervention. It is this zone of uncertainty that is responsible for the emergence of a threshold mentality alluded to above.

The capture of the bank was a stark challenge to the authority of the Sultan's government in the very capital of the empire; it was prepared in a spirit of uncommon revolutionary dedication and was executed with intrepidity. Notwithstanding, it proved cataclysmic for the rest of the unarmed and innocent Armenian population of the city. For two days the streets of Constantinople ran with blood as thousands of inoffensive Armenians were bludgeoned to death. The British Chargé identified the perpetrators as consisting of "the Turkish mob [assisted by] a large number of *softas* and other fanatics … individuals wearing turbans and long linen robes rarely seen in this part of the town. They mostly carried clubs which had evidently been carefully shaped after a uniform pattern; some had, instead of these, iron bars … there is nothing improbable in the stories current that the clubs and bars … were furnished by the municipal authorities."[104] The French Ambassador scorned the direct complicity of the Sultan on account of "the interminable series of events which exhaustively prove that it is the Sultan himself who arms these bludgeoners, exhorting them to go out and extirpate all that is Armenian. It is maintained that the police had given advance notice to all these rascals, distributing to them the cudgels, and deploying them at convenient spots … ."[105]

The Austrian Military Attaché, an eyewitness of the carnage, as noted above, confirmed these reports. According to him, the central authorities, through their agents, had learned of the impending Armenian assault and proceeded to distribute to the mobs cudgels and sticks "fitted with a piece of iron" (*einbeschlagene*), with the instruction that at the signal given, they were "to start killing Armenians, irrespective of age and gender, for the duration of 48 hours ... the method of killing involved the bludgeoning of the victims with blows on their heads. These horrible scenes repeated themselves before my eyes interminably."[106] French political scientist Bérard, who conducted a post-massacre study at the sites of the bloodbaths, concluded that "all was prepared in advance, the slaughterers, the sticks, the police informers, and the carts [to remove and dispose of the corpses of the victims] ... . Prior to the Bank Ottoman raid, the palace authorities had arranged for the transport from the eastern provinces to Constantinople of a Hamidiye regimental unit consisting of about 500 Kurds who upon arrival were quartered in the Selimiye barracks."[107] England's Consul at Erzurum, R.W. Graves,[108] and French Ambassador Cambon,[109] both confirm this engagement of the Kurds from the provinces. On September 2, 1896, Herbert, in a report to Prime Minister Salisbury in London, stated that "There is evidence that the authorities organized and armed the mob which committed all the massacres on Wednesday and Thursday. It was only on Thursday evening that the Sultan sent orders to stop the mob,when they were instantly obeyed."[110]

In their first Collective Note to the Porte, the Powers openly accused the Turkish government of allowing the participation in the massacre and pillage of "the police, ... zaptiyes [rural police], armed soldiers, and even officers ... ."[111] In a follow-up Note the Powers expressed their indignation at the evidence of the engagement of "savage gangs who massacred the Armenians and [who appeared to belong to] a special organization ... ." As if to confirm British Chargé Herbert's finding that "the authorities certainly knew"[112] in advance, the Powers in this Note underscored the following facts as "proving" that there was both advance knowledge of an Armenian plot and preparation for mass murder against the Armenian population of the Ottoman capital. The killer gangs appeared simultaneously in different parts of the city on the first news of the occupation of the bank; "even before the police and military had arrived on the scene ... . A large proportion of the persons forming these gangs were dressed and armed alike ... . They were allowed to circulate freely, and execute their crimes with impunity before the eyes of the troops and their officers ... . These facts need no comment."[113] According to the findings of British Embassy investigators, the Armenian victims were of the lower classes who had come to Constantinople in great numbers to eke out a living as porters, dock laborers, caretakers in offices, custodians in buildings, etc. "As in the case of the provincial massacres, the mob were most methodical in their proceedings, and evidently wished to spare all but Gregorian Armenians."[114] According to the First Secretary of Sultan Hamit, it was one of these cudgels with which Russian Embassy Dragoman Maximof, who negotiated the deal between the Sultan and the insurgents, had rushed to the Palace, complaining out loud, "The Turks are killing in the streets the poor Armenians with these cudgels ... ."[115]

A Special Case of Collective Punishment Through Mass Murder

Frustrated that under European pressure they were forced to allow the insurgents to leave the country under protective escort, and not satisfied with the extent of the carnage in Constantinople, the Turkish authorities undertook to organize a new massacre in the distant city of Egin (Agn), in Harput province, in the interior of Turkey. They did this after establishing that the original leader of the raiding party of insurgents, Papken Siuni, who was killed at the very start of the raid, was a native of Egin. In one brief period on September 15, 1896, i.e., three weeks after the bank raid, "a terrible massacre" was enacted during which "troops" killed "upwards of 2,000 Armenians," including "many women and children," according to a report of the French Ambassador. Of the 1,500 houses located in the Armenian quarter of the city, 980 were pillaged and burned.[116] According to the Acting British Consul at Harput " ... an indirect order was sent from the Palace for the massacre in question to be carried out ... ." The cipher from the Palace issued the coded signal for the slaughter by stating that the Armenians of Egin were set to cause trouble and that the authorities should "take the necessary action." Therefore the Military Governor mobilized the requisite contingents of "the Imperial troops" with the order "to surround the Armenian quarter ... . Shortly afterwards a gun was fired and the massacre began."[117]

In a subsequent November 8, 1896 report, the same consul relayed to his government the findings of a Turkish "official who investigated" the massacre. According to this report, the Armenians were trying to secure protection at the military barracks, where they sought shelter. "They were summoned from there to the Government House and on their way they were attacked by troops assisted by Musselmans. Fifteen hundred in all were killed of whom two hundred were women and children. They gave no offence. There was no revolutionary movement whatever and no powder magazine exploded. A few pistols and revolvers were found in the ruins of burnt houses."[118] The city of Egin or Agn was initially founded by Armenians who had migrated there from Iran. With its suburbs it encompassed in 1896 some 4,000 houses, about evenly divided between Armenians and Muslims, i.e., Turks and Kurds. Recognized for its relative wealth, the city had escaped the earlier 1895–96 massacres and destruction through a ransom payment by the city's Armenians of 1,500 Turkish gold pounds.

The Religious Dimensions of the Massacres

One cardinal common law principle, discussed in chapter 1, refers to a rule in the *Akdı Zimmet* (contract with the ruled nationality) which stipulates cessation of hostility against non-Muslim subjects following their conquest and submission in the wake of a conquest; once conquered, these subjects are granted refuge and protection, or *dehalet*. By attempting to influence Turkish nationality policy in their favor through the intercession of foreign Powers, the Ottoman Turks argued, the Armenians had violated this fundamental treaty provision, and thus, under the prevailing common laws, had forfeited the grant of exemption (*Berat*) i.e., their right to clemency.

The legal consequences of the disjunction between public and common laws in the Ottoman system had already been predicted by Grand Vizier Reşid. In the above cited Memorandum of 1856, Reşid foresaw the possibility of "a great slaughter" (*bir mukateleyi azîme*) in connection with efforts to establish equality through the enactment of public laws. (See ch. 3, note 37.)

The cycle of massacres preceding the World War I genocide was rationalized essentially in this fashion. In describing the scenes of the 1895 Urfa massacre and the entire 1894–1896 era of Abdul Hamit massacres, the Chief Dragoman of the British Embassy, who was fluent in Turkish and based his report on evidence supplied to him by local Muslims during his inspection of the sites of the atrocities, wrote the following:

> [The perpetrators] are guided in their general action by the prescriptions of the Sheri Law. That law prescribes that if the "rayah" [subject] Christian attempts, by having recourse to foreign powers, to overstep the limits of privileges allowed to them by their Mussulman masters, and free themselves from their bondage, their lives and property are to be forfeited, and are at the mercy of the Mussulmans. To the Turkish mind the Armenians had tried to overstep those limits by appealing to foreign powers, especially England. They, therefore, considered it their religious duty and a righteous thing to destroy and seize the lives and property of the Armenians ... . [119]

This reasoning is confirmed by the contemporary Israeli historian, Bat Ye'or, as follows: the Armenian quest for reforms invalidated their "legal status," which involved a "contract." This "breach ... restored to the *umma* [the Muslim community] its initial right to kill the subjugated minority [the *dhimmis*], [and] seize their property ... ."[120]

In the recourse to massacre as a method of conflict resolution, the religious tenets of the preeminent common law destroyed the public law's efficacy. To emphasize the religious thrust of the laws, the perpetrators performed, whenever suitable, Muslim rites while killing their victims. In reference to Urfa, Lord Kinross, the British historian, provides the following example:

> When a large group of young Armenians were brought before a sheikh, he had them thrown down on their backs and held by their hands and feet. Then, in the words of an observer, he recited verses of the Koran and "cut their throats after the Mecca rite of sacrificing sheep."[121]

The British Consul Barnham, whose district's consular jurisdiction included the cities of Ayıntab and Birecik in Aleppo province, in his report to his government underscored the religious avowals of the gangs and mobs perpetrating the massacre in Ayıntab.

> The butchers and the tanners, with sleeves tucked up to the shoulders, armed with clubs and cleavers, cut down the Christians, with cries of "Allahu Akbar!" broke down the doors of the houses with pickaxes and levers, or scaled the walls with ladders. Then when mid-day came they knelt down and said their prayers, and then jumped up and resumed the dreadful work, carrying it on far into the night. Whenever they were unable to break down the doors they fired the houses with petroleum, and the fact that at the end of November petroleum was almost unpurchasable in Aleppo suggests that enormous quantities were brought up and sent north for this purpose ... . Much of this has been told before, but it is evidence which must be emphasized in order to refute the accusations so wantonly hurled against these poor Armenians of Aintab.

Speaking of similar atrocities in nearby Birecik, the consul provided these details:

> On the 1st January, about two hours after sunrise, the massacre began without apparent cause, and continued until night. The soldiers and Moslems of the city generally participated in the work ... . Profession of Islamism or death was the alternative ... . Many of the victims were dragged to the Euphrates, and with weights tied to their feet thrown in ... . [122]

One of the methods to pave the ground for a planned massacre was the warning, issued from the Palace, that the Armenians in a given city or town were about to attack the mosque and that, therefore, the local authorities should take preventive measures. This is clearly documented in a dispatch of March 18, 1896 by Vice Consul Hallward from Harput. He told the provincial governor that the Armenians "live in daily terror of the local Kurds" and that "there is a general and increasing apprehension throughout the vilayet, caused by threats of massacre for Bairam [religious holiday] and the inaction of the Government." The governor's response was that he "had received instructions from Constantinople to take steps to prevent an attack by Armenians on the mosques during the Bairam festival. This remark is of a most disquieting nature, as it seems to imply the Government intend to use the same pretext as before for making further attacks on the Armenians."[123]

The locus where task-oriented religious fanaticism was whipped up through excitatory harangues by agitators, often disguised as religious notables or dignitaries (Islam does not have a sacerdotal clerical system), was the mosque. The most frightful episodes of carnage often coincided with Friday religious services immediately following which the assaults were unleashed. The following graphic description of a particular such episode by Kinross is punctuated by his attendant remark that "often the massacres were timed for a Friday, when the Moslems were in their mosques."

[The massacre's] objective, based on the convenient consideration that Armenians were now tentatively starting to question their inferior status, was the ruthless reduction, with a view to elimination of the Armenian Christians, and the expropriation of their lands for the Moslem Turks. Each operation, between the bugle calls, followed a similar pattern. First the Turkish troops came into a town for the purpose of massacre; then came the Kurdish irregulars and tribesmen for the purpose of plunder. Finally came the holocaust, by fire and destruction, which spread, with the pursuit of the fugitives and mopping-up operations, throughout the lands and villages of the surrounding province. This murderous winter of 1895 thus saw the decimation of much of the Armenian population and the devastation of their property in some twenty districts of eastern Turkey ... . Cruellest and most ruinous of all were the massacres of Urfa, where the Armenian Christians numbered a third of the total population ... . When the bugle blast ended the day's operations, some three thousand refugees poured into the cathedral, hoping for sanctuary. But the next morning—a Sunday—a fanatic mob swarmed into the church in an orgy of slaughter, rifling its shrines with cries of "Call upon Christ to prove Himself a greater prophet than Mohammed." Then they amassed a large pile of straw matting, which they spread over the litter of corpses and set alight with thirty cans of petroleum. The woodwork of the gallery where a crowd of women and children crouched, wailing with terror, caught fire, and all perished in the flames. Punctiliously at three-thirty in the afternoon the bugle blew once more, and the Moslem officials proceeded around the Armenian quarter to proclaim that the massacres were over ... the total casualties in the town, including those slaughtered in the cathedral, amounted to eight thousand dead.[124]

The ability to mobilize so swiftly large multitudes for purposes of massacre and pillage is a phenomenon deserving special attention. It cannot be explained solely in terms of the authority of the Sultan, or the Khalif, or the Sultan-Khalif recognized by the faithful as the supreme ruler of the land. Authority emanating from a distant seat of power may be suitable for issuing orders but it is not equipped to handle the implementation aspects of the orders; local instruments are needed for this task, which requires a measure of what sociologists call social control: the ability to persuade a group to respond to certain suggestions or exhortations for certain ends, deemed as desirable and/or legitimate. The orders for massacre were often framed in such covert language as to be needing interpretation before being restated in clear and simple forms; they were mostly put in implicit phrases and their conversion into explicit injunctions called for mediation by agents of local social control. The religious leaders comprising the theocratic strata of the Ottoman social system were these agents of social control. In this sense they were also authority figures—beyond the compass of their social influence. One way or another they had to certify that the massacres against the Armenians in given situations were in accord with the *Şeriat*, the canon law of Islam.

Notable among this class of religious influentials were the *müftis*, the so called jurisconsults serving as Muslim jurists and senior religious authorities dispensing formal legal opinions, a kind of Supreme Court justice, and *kadis*, as Muslim judges who, as the guardians of law and order, as magistrates, represented "by far the most important category in the Turkish system."[125] In the domain of education there were the *ulemas*, doctors of Muslim theology, a powerful vested interest group that steadily fought against secularization, modernism and "infidel" inroads in the fabric of Ottoman theocracy. Their paramountcy derived from the fact that their authority superseded the will of the Khalif in matters involving the dogmas, the rituals and the canon law of Islam; in the strictest sense of the word, they were the sole protectors of the religious unity of Sunnite Islamism, since they had the status of "the heirs of the prophets." The *mollas* (or *mullahs*) were devotees of Islam with some level of literacy in religious culture and education. The *softas* were the Muslim theology students, the standard bearers of the ideology of the ulemas, who were often in the forefront of the campaign of massacre against the Armenians.

These men of religion, with very few exceptions, played a pivotal role in motivating and legitimizing the massacres. Speaking of these exceptions, Pears describes them as being "lamentably rare."[126] In his account of the frightful features of the massacre of Palu (Diyarbekir province), for example, British Vice Consul Hallward stated in his report that "One of the worst men in Palou is the Mufti, who was very active in the massacre and killed the principal Protestant, Manoog Aga, with his own hand."[127] The British Chargé, in his report to Salisbury on the August 1896 massacre in Constantinople, included information on the role of "imams" and "softas," by whom "the mob was led in certain places." In another report filed the same day, i.e., September 3, 1896, by the same Chargé, the testimony of "an official of the British Consulate, who had seen the attacks," is adduced. According to it, "a Mollah came out of the neighbouring mosque and encouraged the mob by chanting a prayer, which was taken up by the fanatical crowd."[128]

The mosques, as pointed out above, played a signal role in the mobilization of the faithful through a variety of techniques of incitement, notably during the large scale massacres in Bitlis and Diyarbekir. "They gathered the Moslems in the largest mosque, harangued them as to their duty to their sovereign and religion and urged them on … ."[129] Conversely, Armenian churches, the symbols of the Christian faith of the hated infidels, were reduced to slaughterhouses. Here is a description by one of the survivors of an assault of this type, involving two Armenian churches in Severek (Diyarbekir province), a Gregorian, and subsequently, a Protestant one.

> The mob had plundered the Gregorian church, desecrated it, murdered all who had sought shelter there, and as a sacrifice, beheaded the sexton on the stone

threshold. Now it filled our yard. The blows of an axe crashed in the church doors. The attacker rushed in, tore the Bibles and hymnbooks to pieces, broke and shattered whatever they could, blasphemed the cross and, as a sign of victory, chanted the Mohammedan prayer "La ilaha ill-Allah, Muhammedin Rasula-Ilah" (There is no other God but one God, and Mohammed is his prophet). We could see and hear all these things from the room in which we huddled ... They were coming up the stairs ... now butchers and victims were face to face. The leader of the mob cried: "Muhammede salavat" (Believe in Mohammed and deny your religion). [Disregarding our supplications to be spared] squinting horribly, he repeated his words in a terrifying voice. [when no one responded] the leader repeated again and gave orders to massacre. The first attack was on our pastor. The blow of an axe decapitated him. His blood, spurting in all directions, spattered the walls and ceiling with red. Then I was in the midst of the butchers. One of them drew his dagger and stabbed my left arm ... . Another second, I lost consciousness ... .[130]

Here one can discern evidence of a dual-track religious fanaticism and its culmination in massacre. There is contempt for the religion of the potential victim, which is attended by a coercive demand for abjuration; at the same time the victim is likewise coerced for conjuration of Islam. Murder follows upon refusal to yield to coercion.

This discussion may be ended with a comment by Pears on the relationship between a general trend of Armenian stubbornness in clinging to their faith on the one hand, and the high price they paid for that stubbornness, i.e., massacre, on the other hand. He is referring to the burning alive of 2,500 Armenians in the cathedral of Urfa.

This was the deliberate sacrifice of a cathedral full of people. The hideous holocaust will not and ought not to be forgotten. The ugly barn-like Cathedral, like the mountain of sacrifice of Mexico, like the Bridge of Sighs of Venice and the other monuments of man's inhumanity to man, ought to be religiously preserved as a memorial of the stiff-necked determination of the Armenians to die rather than change their religion, and of the infernal brutality which can be practiced in the name of religion.[131]

The Demography of the Empire-Wide Massacres and of Destruction: the Nature and Sweep of Armenian Losses

The main purpose of this entire chapter is to correlate the evolution of the Turko-Armenian conflict to the Abdul Hamit-era massacres, the resort to which is seen as a radical means of resolving that conflict. The emphasis here is on sequential developments, not on the overall panorama of the empire-wide massacres. Moreover, these massacres of the 1894–96 period are depicted as a test case for the political feasibility, if not acceptability by the rest of the world, of the enactment by central authorities of the organized mass murder of a discordant nationality. Within this perspective, the World War I Armenian genocide is considered to be grim evi-

dence of the persistence of that correlation. As the Turko-Armenian conflict continued to escalate in the decades preceding World War I, the massacres grew in intensity and scale, eventually culminating in the genocide.

Even though this series of massacres in its totality was a national
calamity of the first magnitude for the victim population, substantially decimating it in its ancestral territories, crippling its community institutions,
and debilitating its collective psyche, a narrative of these massacres is not
the focus of this volume. This series of bloodbaths involved hundreds of
small and large massacres throughout the length and breadth of the Ottoman Empire. The atrocities were not limited to the method of killing the
victims with a variety of blunt instruments but included such operations as
burning them alive and drowning them in large groups. The scale of these
exterminations is such that the subject deserves the kind of separate treatment and detailed analysis for which there is no space in this volume.

Nevertheless, a brief review of these massacres is in order at this juncture of the present study. Any review must be predicated in the main
upon the pioneering work of German Protestant historian Lepsius. In it,
Lepsius compiled, however incompletely, the various data and figures in
several categories of Armenian losses following his on-the-spot investigations which were undertaken immediately after the end of the massacres.
These data and figures are referenced in note 146 of this chapter. Since
some of these massacres have already been dealt with earlier in this chapter, viz., the 1894 Sassoun, the 1895 and 1896 twin Constantinople, and
the 1896 Van and Egin massacres, the discussion below will consist of a
sketch of the rest of the series of massacres. These were enacted in the six
"Armenian inhabited" provinces in central and eastern Turkey, namely,
Sıvas, Harput, Diyarbekir, Erzurum, Bitlis, and Van, as well as in the
provinces of Ankara (Kayseri and environs), Aleppo, Trabzon, and the
independent district (*sancak*) Izmit, east of Istanbul. Except for the coun-
ties of Payas and Çokmarzban (Dörtyöl), the province of Adana escaped
the sweep of the massacres when one disregards the string of acts of
plunder and pillage the Armenians of that province were subjected to.
The military successes of the Armenian highlanders of Zeitoun (discussed earlier in this chapter) were a major factor in deterring the perpetrators and preventing the slaughter of Adana Armenians at that time.

As indicated elsewhere in this work, the enactment of these massacres
was an initiative which was intimately connected with the explosive issue
of Armenian Reforms, the kernel of the Turko-Armenian conflict. Following the August-September 1894 Sassoun massacre, the six Powers
elaborated the May 11, 1895 Armenian Reform scheme which, after
much temporizing and haggling, the Sultan finally accepted and signed
on October 17, 1895. This notwithstanding, the series of massacres,
which had already been predesigned by the Palace, were allowed to
erupt, engulfing in fire and blood the very population for the supposed

benefit of whom the reforms were formally intended. In rapid succession a network of major centers of Armenian national life were suddenly and ferociously attacked. The carnage started in Trabzon on October 8, 1895, i.e., precisely five days after the end of the October 1–3, 1895 bloodbath in Constantinople.

The chainlike unfolding of the cataclysm is evident in the following constellation of the sequelae of these massacres interlinked together through the dynamics of that cataclysm. October 8, 1895, Trabzon, Akhisar (in the independent district of Izmit); October 11, Gümüşhane (Trabzon province); October 13, Bayburt (Erzurum province); October 21, Erzincan (Erzurum province); October 25, Diyarbekir, Palu (Diyarbekir province); October 28, Tomarza (Kayseri district, Ankara province), Urfa (Aleppo province); October 30, Erzurum, Khnus (Erzurum province), Muş (Bitlis province); November 6, Arabkir (Harput province); November 8, Tomarza (Kayseri district, Ankara province); November 11, Harput; November 10, Gürün (Sıvas province); November 12, Sıvas; November 15, Muş (Bitlis province), Ayıntab (Aleppo province); November 26, Zile (Sıvas province); November 30, Kayseri (Ankara province); December 28–29, Urfa (Aleppo province); January 1, 1896, Birecik (Aleppo province); June 1896, Niksar (Sıvas province).

It is in the nature of things that the penchant of a victim of crime for exaggeration is more often than not commensurate to a similar penchant by the victimizer for minimizing the losses involved. The former seeks redemption through the optimal punishment of the perpetrator, including ample indemnities, and the latter is anxious to diminish the scope of culpability, if and when denial is rendered impossible. Thus, both Armenian sources and Turkish sources are inherently suspect in this regard. Owing to the fact, however, that Turkish sources have the attribute of officialness involving the availability of state archives as repositories of "primary sources," and therefore can be deemed to be of a higher value, a problem of discrepancies has been created. The reliance in recent times by some scholars, identified with the "Turkish viewpoint," on these "primary sources" and their attendant works belittling the scope of the Armenian massacres, warrants a comment on the reliability of these sources as far as the number of Armenian victims of the 1894–96 massacres is concerned.

To the extent that European consuls and vice consuls were able to investigate these massacres in different parts of Turkey, often through the assistance of Turkish informers immediately following the enactment of the atrocities, to that extent they tried to assemble reliable facts to quantify the Armenian losses, both human and material. In the course of these inquiries, they consistently observed significant discrepancies between the figures they themselves arrived at, and the figures supplied by the Turkish authorities. The following examples will illustrate the point; they may allow extrapolations in terms of large-scale deficiencies in official

Turkish figures. In his long report accounting for the massacre in one day of the Armenian population of the port city of Trabzon on the Black Sea, the French Consul Cillière compares the figure 180 supplied by "the authorities" as representing the number of Armenians killed, with his own data indicating "more than 500" killed.[132] In the same vein, Carlier, the French Vice Consul at Sıvas, comes up with a 2–300 to 500 comparison.[133] Harput's British Vice Consul Hallward's compilations reveal a much higher level of discrepancy, yielding a 1:7 ratio, i.e., his figure of 350 Armenian dead is placed in significant contrast with that of 50 furnished by the Turkish Governor-General.[134] A 1:5.5 ratio results in the case of Kilis (in Aleppo province), where Armenians were suddenly and briefly attacked. British Ambassador Currie, as well as Aleppo's Austrian Consul J. Bertrand, refers to 100 Armenians killed and wounded; they contrast that figure in their reports with that of 18 which represents "the official version."[135] When reporting on the number of Armenian victims in the massacre in Trabzon, German Ambassador Saurma advised the Foreign Office in Berlin that "official data" (*offizielle Angaben*), released by the Turkish government "fall short of the truth" (*hinter der Wahrheit zurück bleiben*).[136]

This pattern of official misrepresentation is extended to the act of displaying victims wounded during the August 1896 massacre in Constantinople; the attempt at misrepresentation is exposed by the British as an act of outright deceit. Here are excerpts from the account of that act, prepared by Ambassador Currie for Prime Minister Salisbury:

> The Sultan lately sent to me, in common with my colleagues, an urgent message inviting the six Representatives to visit the military and municipal hospitals in order to see for themselves the number of Turkish soldiers and civilians who had been wounded during the recent disturbances.
>
> I accordingly requested Surgeon Tomlinson, of Her Majesty's ship "Imogene," to make the round of the hospitals in company with Mr. Blech, of Her Majesty's Embassy … .
>
> The hospital authorities made attempts to pass off wounded Christians as Mussulmans. Thus, the 112 in the Stamboul prison were represented as being Turks, and it was only discovered by accident that 109 were Christians.[137]

Given these conditions of deliberately arranged misrepresentations and miscounting, it is futile to expect such reliable data on the extent of Armenian losses as might be compiled by Turkish authorities, unless one is willing to roughly factor in estimated ratios of misrepresentation of the kind described above. On the other hand, as a victim nation, decimated and dislocated, the Armenians were in an even less suitable position to assess the extent of damage and produce fairly reliable figures. One is thus forced to fall back on sources which, under the present circumstances, are relatively impartial and, therefore, more trustworthy than anything else available, namely, European diplomatic and consular representatives at the time stationed in Turkey. In this connection it is worth noting that most of these representatives had very little sympathy for the Armenians, as they were pursuing the higher interests of their governments; the idea was to maintain the integrity of the Ottoman Empire, and they were eager to avert the conflagrations at issue here in order to prevent the outbreak of a war which they feared might ensnarl the Powers in a contest against each other. In fact, in a draft "confidential" report to Salisbury, British Chargé in the Ottoman capital Herbert, commenting on the issue of the disinterestedness on the part of British Consuls in Turkey, especially with respect to the Turko-Armenian conflict, stated that these consuls "are generally Turkophil and dislike the Armenians."[138] Moreover, the reports they filed at the time were strictly for internal purposes and, therefore, were not for publicity or propaganda purposes. The picture emerging from their accounts is as follows. According to German Emperor William II, up to December 20, 1895, 80,000 Armenians were slain (*umgebracht*) in the course of the massacres then in progress; he personally conveyed this information to Colonel Swaine, the British Military Chargé in Berlin.[139] British Ambassador White on the other hand estimated, on the basis of data sent to him by the British consuls, 100,000 victims for the period up to early December 1895.[140] As is known, however, the period of massacres extended to October 1896, including the August 26–28 Constantinople massacre, claiming 5–6,000 victims.[141] German Foreign Ministry operative and Turkophile author, E. Jäckh, estimates the total Armenian victims as follows: 200,000 killed, 50,000 expelled and one million pillaged and plundered.[142] On the other hand, the eminent late French historian, Pierre Renouvin, the President of the Commission in charge of assembling and classifying French diplomatic documents, in a postwar volume, based on authenticated documents, provided the 250,000 figure representing the sum total of the Armenian victims of the massacres in question.[143]

In any episode as cataclysmic as that of the 1894–96 massacres, the balance sheet of victims is likely to be flawed if it embraces only those who were immediately killed during the slaughter. There are two more categories of victims to be considered as candidates of death, the inclusion of which is temporarily delayed. One of them concerns the severely wounded or crippled; the other involves those rendered acutely vulnerable to the effects of privation, exposure, and debilitating trauma. After consulting with German General Kolmar von der Goltz, who, in the 1883–1895 period was entrusted with the task of modernizing and reorganizing the Turkish army, and at one point also served as Sultan Abdul Hamit's political advisor, Germany's Ambassador at Vienna, Prince Philipp zu Eulenburg, revealed to France's Ambassador in the same Austrian capital, Lozé, that the combined figure of Armenian victims was 200,000. Declaring the situation to be "frightful" (*épouvantable*), Lozé on January 2, 1896 estimated that 150,000 children, old men, and women were doomed to die during the winter from hunger and cold.[144] As if to confirm this assessment, the French Vice Consul at Ankara reckoned that of the 2–3,000 wounded Armenian survivors of the massacre at Kayseri, "more than half will succumb to their injuries."[145]

Such scales of losses of human lives cannot be separated, however, from the collateral material damage they entail. The real test of the success of exterminatory assaults is the extent to which the social fabric and cultural institutions undergirding the victim population as a national or ethnic entity are devastated in the process. Following his two-month (May-June, 1896) inspection trip to the sites of the massacres, Lepsius compiled the following data. Two thousand five hundred towns and villages were desolated and 645 churches and monasteries destroyed. The survivors of 559 villages and hundreds of families in cities were forcibly (*zwangsweise*) converted to Islam. Included in this are fifteen thousand Armenians each from the provinces of Erzurum and Harput, who under threat of death thus converted. Moreover, 328 churches were recast into mosques and 546,000 people were reduced to a state of destitution (*Not*). In addition, 508 churches and monasteries were completely plundered and twenty-one Protestant and 170 Gregorian-Apostolic priests were done to death.[146] Lepsius' data on forcible religious conversions match the data on similar large-scale conversions elsewhere in the interior of Turkey, as documented by European consuls. In a March 31, 1896 report to Salisbury, British Ambassador Currie stated that as a result of "forced conversions … there are absolutely no Christians left" in Birecik (Aleppo province). He based this conclusion on the findings of the First Dragoman of the British Embassy whom he had sent to the provinces for an inquiry into the massacres. "His investigations established [this] fact."[147] Charles S. Hampson, British Vice Consul at Muş (Bitlis province), reported to his ambassador that "no Christians remained in the district of Siart (Sıırt, Bitlis province). About 15,000 had been killed, 19,000 converted to Mahommedanism, and 2,500 women carried off."[148] Diyarbekir's Vice Consul, Cecil M. Hallward, in a report on March 17, 1896, declared that in the county of Silvan (Diyarbekir province), 7,000 Armenians were "forcibly made Moslem," and "upwards of 500 women and girls have been abducted."[149] For the entire province, Hallward estimated that "25,000 turned Moslem." In a breakdown of that figure, he adduced the following specific numbers for forcible conversions in certain towns: Palu, 3,000; Severek, including the villages of the district, 2,500; "At the village of Uzun Ova, which is largely Protestant in that district, eight men were shot in cold blood for refusing to turn Moslem; thirty-two women and children then seeing what was in store for them drowned themselves in the Euphrates, and the rest of the villagers declared themselves Moslem. A Turkish 'hoca' has been assigned to them with a salary which they have to pay."[150] The number of converted in the entire province of Bitlis is 22,000, according to Vice Consul Hampson.[151] It should be noted that in some instances of forcible conversions, a number of apostates, circumstances permitting, returned to their original faith following the termination of the massacres and the restoration of a semblance of order and peace.[152]

In assessing the matter of accuracy of these figures, furnished by the European diplomats and consuls, one has to recognize that they are mostly, but not entirely, rough estimates, especially in cases involving victims in large districts and provinces; given the overall prevailing conditions, they couldn't be otherwise. But in two respects, the figures in question have a saliency affording a large measure of validity for them, without disregarding the incidence of various margins of error. They come from disinterested parties and they are in stark contrast with those supplied by the Turkish authorities in terms of essential disparities. One has to take into account the fact that Turkey is not only an interested party, but she is also the accused party in a dispute involving mass murder and ancillary crimes. Equally important, the sway of cultural traditions in the matter of training for accurate reporting, respect for facts, and the observation of established codes for discharging consular duties, are crucial factors in evaluating the worth of European data submitted. Conversely, the principle of veracity, when not entirely relinquished, is often compromised in cases where state secrets are involved and the stakes are, therefore, high, as far as the perpetrator camp is concerned.

Superseding all these considerations, which essentially deal with a recurrent policy of massacre and its material consequences, there is another aspect of the problem of the demography of destruction meriting due attention. It concerns the set of values underlying that policy.

The Issue of Cultural and Subcultural Components of Massacre Revisited

At issue are the particulars providing for a culture of massacre, the formation of which was briefly commented upon in a section of this chapter. At the core of any culture is an array of beliefs which condition the people identified with them to consider certain lines of conduct as socially desirable, preferable, praiseworthy or expected, to the point that they may be taken for granted as variations of a standard of normal behavior. Of all the scholars who hitherto dealt with the Armenian massacres of the era of Abdul Hamit and tried to explain them, the British ethnographer William M. Ramsay stands out for the incisiveness with which he attempted to provide a frame of analysis. He had spent more than a decade intermittently conducting research in Turkey in a period covering the last two decades of the 19th century. Sufficiently fluent in

Turkish, he was able to mingle with Turks and interact with them. Given the importance of his observations in this regard, two lengthy excerpts from a text containing these observations are adduced below. First, Ramsay describes entrenched Turkish attitudes towards the Armenians, thereby indicating the cultural character of the beliefs associated with these attitudes.

> Turkish rule ... meant unutterable contempt ... . The Armenians (and the Greek) were dogs and pigs ... to be spat upon, if their shadow darkened a Turk, to be outraged, to be the mats on which he wiped the mud from his feet. Conceive the inevitable result of centuries of slavery, of subjection to insult and scorn, centuries in which nothing that belonged to the Armenian, neither his property, his house, his life, his person, nor his family, was sacred or safe from violence—capricious, unprovoked violence—to resist which by violence meant death! I do not mean that every Armenian suffered so; but that every one lived in conscious danger from any chance disturbance or riot.[153]

These observations are further accented by the fact that, far from being an Armenophil, Ramsay in several pages explains his personal dislike of the Armenians he dealt with.[154] Yet, his account of certain features of a culture allowing the perpetration of massacre against the Armenians is as salient as penetrating; it casts in stark relief "the darker side of Turkish massacre."

> [Such a massacre] does not mean merely that thousands are killed in a few days by the sword, the torture, or the fire. It does not mean merely that everything they possess is stolen, their houses and shops looted and often burned, every article worth a halfpenny taken, the corpses stripped. It does not mean merely that the survivors are left penniless—without food, sometimes literally stark naked. That is only the beginning, the brighter and lighter side of a massacre in Turkey. Sometimes, when the Turks have been specially merciful, they have offered their victims an escape from death by accepting Mohammedanism. But as to the darker side of Turkish massacre—personal outrage and shame—take what the more freespoken historians of former times have told; gather together the details of the most horrible and indescribable outrages that occasional criminals of half-lunatic character commit in this country; imagine those criminals collected in thousands, heated with the hard work of murder, inciting each other and vying with each other, encouraged by the government officials with promises of impunity and hope of plunder—imagine the result if you can, and you will have some faint idea of the massacres in the eastern parts of Turkey.
>
> There has been no exaggeration in the worst accounts of the horrors of Armenia. A writer with the vivid imagination of Dumas and the knowledge of evil that Zola possesses could not attain, by any description, the effect that the sight of one massacre in the Kurdish part of Armenia would produce on any spectator. The Kurdish part of Armenia is the "black country." It has become a charnel house. One dare not enter it. One cannot think about it. One knows not how many maimed, mutilated, outraged Armenians are still starving there ... .
>
> But it is not the case that all Turks in any city took part in massacre. The better class disapproved; many regretted; some even tried to save Armenian friends. It must be remembered that it needs an extraordinary strength of emotion to rouse a Turk to actual interference with what he regards as the will of God; and their natural view was that the massacre had been willed by God and

the Padishah (monarch), and the fact must be accepted; and yet some did interfere. But the city mob, after it was once roused by priests and officials, revelled in the work ... . But, it may be said, the Armenians have been craven to accept this lot, and should have preferred death. Let those who have proved that they could themselves choose death in preference to a slave's life, cast reproach at them; and those who reproach the Armenians that have lived are all the more bound to approve the Armenians that have rebelled.[155]

Compressed in this succinct account is a portrayal of the anatomy of a typical, traditional Turkish massacre, in which configure the interactive effects of a web of such factors as motivation, methods, implements, victim vulnerability, the sanctions of sacred and secular law, and the incentive to indulge in lethal cupidity. Superseding all this is the arch factor warranting the unimpeded consummation of the holocaust: a legacy of impunity. But it is necessary to refocus attention on the strictly cultural and subcultural aspects of these episodes of mass murder. The atrocities are acts which are entwined with collateral attitudes affording these acts. The centerpiece of these attitudes is a level of contempt for the victim that allows the perpetrator to dehumanize it, reducing it to the imagery of a dog. The European diplomatic and consular reports are replete with descriptions bearing out the assertion of the existence of such relationships obtaining between the attitudes and the acts of the perpetrators engaged in massacres. The material adduced below merits singling out because it is emblematic in this regard. In a report marked "confidential," a British Consul enclosed two letters in their original Turkish (and translated into English by the Consulate), which either fell into British hands or were somehow intercepted by British agents. They were written by a Turkish soldier (identified by name and surname) from the 4th Company, 2d Battalion, 25th Regiment on duty in Erzurum, and were addressed to his parents and brother in Harput. Here are excerpts.

First letter, dated November 23, 1895:
My brother, if you want news from here we have killed 1,200 Armenians, *all of them as food for the dogs* ... Mother, I am safe and sound. Father, 20 days ago we made war on the Armenian unbelievers. Through God's grace no harm befell us ... . There is a rumour afoot that our Battalion will be ordered to your part of the world —if so, we will kill all the Armenians there. Besides, 511 Armenians were wounded, one or two perish every day. If you ask after the soldiers and Bashi Bozouks [wild irregulars], not one of their noses has bled ... May God bless you ... . [italics added].

Second letter, dated December 23, 1895:
I killed [the Armenians] like dogs ... . If you ask news in this matter, we slew 2,500 Armenians and looted their goods.[156]

The nonchalant tone of these family letters is matched by the total abandon with which participation in a mass murder is being openly broadcast, and it is exceeded only by the relish expressed about the hideous manner of disposal of the remains of the victims. One is dealing here not only with the manifestation of attitudes affording gruesome forms of massacre as a commonplace phenomenon, but with the evidence of a state system identified with these attitudes. Here is a regimental unit of the standing army engaged in broad daylight in peace-time killing operations against unarmed civilian populations.

Massacre as an Instrument of a Radical Policy

In order to understand the relationship, however furtive or covert, between a state system and cultural attitudes favoring massacre against a largely inoffensive population, it is important to reconsider the operative links between state authority and state policy on the one hand, and the mechanisms of the enactment of the massacres, on the other. The corpus of diplomatic correspondence dealing with the massacres has been amply utilized in this study to demonstrate the critical significance of these operative links. That significance is epitomized by the expression "an official crime" which, in the language of Harput district's British consul, "the better-disposed" Turks of that district have coined; the occasion for the contrivance of this sarcastic term was the November 1895 Harput massacre and the collateral acts of destruction in that city.[157] One is dealing here not with the judgment of the victims, the Armenians, or that of neutral observers, the Europeans, but with that of Turks, eyewitnesses of the carnage and, by the same token, impotent dissidents vis a vis a state policy responsible for that carnage.

In this connection one of the most revealing items from the data emerging since the times of the conflagration is that which is provided by a Turkish intelligence officer with a record of service to both Ittihadist and Kemalist regimes. According to his account Hamit, annoyed by the incessant remonstrances of the Powers, invited a group of the European ambassadors to a room in the Palace, stacked with the cudgels, which were described above as having been employed against the Armenians. Hamit then reportedly ordered his interpreter to tell them that his subjects "defended themselves against the Armenians with these sticks," adding, "These sticks were manufactured from wood harvested from our timber woods."[158] The total absence of regret, not to speak of compunction, in this episode of exhibitionism indulged in by the Sultan, is essentially identical to the spirit of the Turkish soldier boasting to his family of the number of Armenians his regimental unit killed "as food for the dogs." When a deed is taken for granted by the actor, the issue of compunction is reduced to irrelevance. More than that, the resort to exterminatory massacres was viewed by the whole array of perpetrators as a problem-solving behavior. The Turko-Armenian conflict required a solution to be devised by the central authorities. Since that conflict basically revolved around a system of reforms which, to these authorities, especially to the monarch, were anathema, and since the pressure of the Powers to adopt these reforms was becoming intense and portentous, the option for a radical solution was considered and decided upon. The result was the design of a policy of massacre.[159] By substantially decimating the Armenian population in the provinces, the issue of Armenian reforms would erode, and, by the same token, through such punishment and terror, the Armenians would be reduced to an impoverished, cowed and even more submissive entity. More important, Abdul Hamit sought to achieve this goal by ruining the Armenians economically. This is what his private First Secretary asserted in his memoirs. According to him, the actions of the Armenian revolutionaries in the 1894–96 period so irked him that he "decided to pursue a policy of severity and terror against the Armenians, and in order to succeed in this respect he elected the method of dealing them an economic blow ... he ordered to absolutely avoid negotiating or discussing anything with the Armenians and to inflict upon them a decisive strike to settle scores." (*Kendilerile kat'ı hesap olunmasını sureti kat'iyede emretti*).[160] This propensity to penalize an entire community for the transgressions of a few is punctuated by an assessment Hamit had made six years earlier. In a conversation with British Ambassador White on the topic of the Armenian Question, Hamit divided the Ottoman Armenians in three categories: 1) independence seekers; 2) annexation seekers; 3) those who were perfectly loyal, adding that there were very few of the first, more of the second, and that "the large mass" belonged to the third category.[161]

Apart from considerations of culture or subculture, the propensity to reduce a collectivity for the presumed or demonstrated culpability of a few was largely motivated by demographic considerations, as noted above. Sultan Abdul Hamit was apprehensive that, if and when granted the reforms they were seeking, the Armenians were likely to gain the upper hand and control the overall direction of provincial life. In a Memorandum addressed to the office of the Grand Vizier, he articulated his apprehensions in this respect. He was afraid that some reform-minded, high-ranking Turkish officials were "drifting towards European ideals of administration and governance, and away from the idea of loyalty to the Sultan, and away from adherence to Islam," mentioning the names of Foreign Minister Said Paşa and Abidin Paşa. He stated further that "service to him, the Khalif, is service to the Muslim people. Any other course of action is bound to lead to the establishment of an Armenian principality. The Powers are delimiting boundaries for Armenia in connection with the plan of reforms for the six provinces. Yet, unlike in the case of Bulgaria, the Armenians don't reach even a 30% population ratio in Erzurum province where they have a large population." Hamit then inveighed against Grand Vizier Ahmed Cevad Paşa (1891–1895) who "gave impetus to this trend in order to be praised in Europe and ingratiate himself with the ambassadors, all the while forgetting that he bears a Muslim name and is the son of a Muslim."[162]

The redundant emphasis and overemphasis in these communications on Islam, the Khalifate and the idea of ultimate authority, is indicative of the high premium placed by the monarch and absolute ruler upon the theocratic destiny of the Ottoman state. Though this attitude was in part an expediency, a desire to protect his throne by taking refuge in the auspices of Islam, to a greater degree it also reflected an expedient response to the weariness of the Muslims in the provinces. Like their ruler, they too were apprehensive about the possibility of the ascendancy of the Armenians in the event the reforms were in fact implemented, irrespective of the latter's numerical inferiority. This posture of the Sultan often cast him in the role of opposing the policy designs of his own government, i.e., the Sublime Porte, its occupants, the Grand Vizier, and the Foreign Minister. With a view to countering and overcoming the influence of the Porte, Sultan Hamit, in the same Memorandum, resorted to an unusual step; he outlined a ploy to sabotage the authority of the Porte in the matter of the Armenian reforms. Here is the prescription by Hamit:

> The Porte (Babı Ali) may give the appointed official [in this case it was Raif Paşa] such oral and written instructions which may run counter to the thinking of the monarch. However, since he has confidence in [the appointed Inspectors'] loyalty and competence, it is required that this official casts aside with little risk such solutions to problems, which are impossible to attain, by adducing persuasive proofs (*delâil-i muknia irâdı ile geçiştirilmesi*) in order to justify the necessity of his act of shelving [such solutions]. One should be concerned not only with this, but the other world as well. One should be mindful of the gravity of such behavior as such behavior might cause the ruination of Islam … . The only remedy is the loyalty of the appointed Inspector, namely, the willingness to protect the Islamic faith and the legal prerogatives of the Royal Highness. In such a case it is certain that he will be rewarded by him.[163]

In the end Hamit, determined as he was, prevailed. Whether as a result of coercion, persuasion, or independent thinking on his part, Kâmil came around to Hamit's stance. Sharing his monarchs resolve to sabotage by all means the scheme of Armenian reforms, Grand Vizier Kâmil, in October 1895, sent a circular memo to provincial governors denying[164] the validity of the very reform concessions Hamit had finally made to the Armenians on October 17, 1895 under intense European pressure.[165] Kâmil continued this stance even after he was deposed by the Young Turk Ittihadists in January 1913 through a coup; at that time, the Armenian Reforms issue had been resuscitated and was being negotiated between Turkey and the Powers. In a reception in May in Beirut, he expressed his opposition to European intervention in the matter.[166]

This mind-set of the Sultan, to oppose by all means available any and all efforts of Armenian reforms, was revealed in the course of one of his private meetings with an ambassador. In a dispatch to Berlin, Prince Radolin, the German Ambassador, informed his Chancellor in Berlin of an audience he had had with the Sultan on November 16, 1894, i.e., in the wake of the Sassoun massacre, during which Abdul Hamit "solemnly swore that under no circumstances would he yield to the unjust Armenian pressure, and that he would rather die than introduce far-reaching reforms in Armenia."[167] Thus, the die was cast, internally and externally. Armenian Reforms, as envisaged both by the Armenians and the Powers, were out of the question as far as the monarch and his regime were concerned. And, when the cycle of the 1894–96 massacres was completed, Sultan Abdul Hamit in 1897 declared that "the Armenian question was closed."[168] The late eminent Harvard historian, William Langer, summarized the emerging views on this episode of a historical process of genocide by declaring conclusively, "It was perfectly obvious that the Sultan was determined to end the Armenian question by exterminating the Armenians."[169] The issue of Armenian Reform, the kernel of the Armenian Question, proved a lethal experiment for a policy of humanitarian intervention conducted by the Powers on behalf of the Armenians; the experiment lacked the requisite control mechanisms, namely, safeguards for the Armenians. As Turkish historian Osman Nuri observed, "The mere mention of the word 'reform' irritated him [Abdul Hamit], inciting his criminal instincts."[170]

Notes to Chapter 8

1. Mithat Sertoğlu, "Türkiyede Ermeni Meselesi" (The Armenian Question in Turkey) *Belgelerle Türk Tarih Dergisi* 2 (November 1967): 48.
2. Lord Kinross, *The Ottoman Centuries* (New York 1977), 557–58.
3. Victor Bérard, *La Politique du Sultan* 3d ed. (Paris, 1897), 883 passim.
4. *Blue Book.* Turkey No. 1 (1895) Part I, enclosure 2 in Doc. No. 60, p. 369 November 6, 1894 report which Ambassador Philip Currie forwarded to London on November 26, 1894 under "Confidential" Doc. No. 754, cipher No. 539.
5. *Ibid.*, Doc. No. 252, Joint Report No. 255, written on July 20, submitted on August 15, 1895, pp. 133–193. The quotations are from pp. 170, 171, 173. The French Text is in *The Diplomatic Archives of the Foreign Ministry of France* (*Documents Diplomatiques 1871–1900*) (Hereafter cited as *DAF*) Affaires Arméniennes. Livre Jaune (1897) Doc. No. 86 (August 16, 1895) of which Annex No. is the Joint Report, pp. 96–111, and Annex No. 2 is the supplement to Doc. No. 1, pp. 111–136.
6. *Ibid.*, 173.
7. *Ibid.*, vol. 11, Doc. No. 318, p. 493 (1947).
8. FO 881/6645 enclosure No. 3 containing the report of A. Block.
9. *Blue Book* [n. 4], Doc. No. 49, p. 27, Doc., No. 68, p. 42, and Doc. No. 82, p. 45; for the *Liyakat* decoration see *DAF* [n. 5], Doc. No. 13, p. 19, Erzurum's French Consul Bergeron's November 24, 1895 report.
10. Osman Nuri, *Abdulhamid Sani ve Devri Saltanatı. Hayatı Hususiye ve Siyasiyesi.* (Abdulhamit the Second and His Period of Rule. His Private and Political Life).

Ottoman script. Vol. 2 (Istanbul, 1328/1912), 372. The work, interrupted by the death of the author, was completed by historian Ahmed Refik (Altınay).

11. Kâmil Paşa, *Hatıratı Sadrı Esbak Kâmil Paşa* (The Memoirs of former Grand Vizier Kâmil Paşa) Ottoman Script, (Istanbul, [1913]), 180–81, 187.

12. Doğan Avcıoğlu, *Milli Kurtuluş Tarihi* (The History of National Liberation) vol. 3 (Istanbul, 1974), 1088.

13. J. Marriott, *The Eastern Question: An Historical Study in European Diplomacy* 4th ed. Reprinted. (Glasgow, 1958), 399.

14. *The Times* (London), March 30, 1895. C.M. Hallward, British Vice Consul at Van, in a November 6, 1894 report confirms that Turkish troops "assumed Kurdish custom and joined in an attack which was more successful" after the Kurds were repulsed by the Armenians and "refused to return to the attack unless they were helped by the [Turkish] soldier." See note 17 below, p. 1 of the report.

15. From an article in the influential German newspaper *Kölnische Zeitung*, February 24, 1895.

16. Le Vte. de la Jonquière, *Histoire de l'Empire Ottoman depuis les origines jusqu'a nos jours* vol. II, new, enlarged edition (Paris, 1914), 134.

17. *Blue Book* [n. 4], 36, 37, 38. In a privately published pamphlet, titled *Extracts from Letters of C. M. H.*, Hallward in a letter to his mother on October 29, 1894, sent from Bitlis, describes these "frightful atrocities" which "have been reported by the soldiers themselves, such as burning people alive, including women and children … ." p. 12.

18. Stanford J. Shaw and Ezel Kural Shaw, *History of the Ottoman Empire and Modern Turkey* vol. 2. *Reform, Revolution and Republic: The Rise of Modern Turkey 1808–1975* (Cambridge, 1977), 203–04.

19. Ottoman Archives. Yıldız Collection. *The Armenian Question,* vol. 1 *Tailori Incidents* (Istanbul Research Center, 1989), 371.

20. G. P. Gooch, *History of Modern Europe 1878–1919* (New York, 1923), 234.

21. *Blue Book* [n. 4], Doc. No. 197, p. 109, British Ambassador Currie's May 2, 1895 report.

22. *Ibid.*, Currie's three reports: Doc. No. 214, p. 119, May 30; Doc. No. 218, p. 121, June 1; Doc. No. 222, p. 122, June 3, 1895.

23. *Ibid.*, Doc. no. 267, pp. 206–07.

24. The English translation is in FO 881/6645, pp. 28–9, enclosure in Doc. No. 4 in Ambassador Currie's April 20, 1895 report to London. The date of Prjewalski' secret report is March 20, 1895.

25. *Blue Book* [n. 4], 38.

26. *Ibid.*, Doc. No. 66, p. 41, November 26, 1894.

27. *Ibid.*, Doc. No. 63, p. 39, from London to Currie, November 30; Doc. No. 66, p. 40, November 26, 1894.

28. *Ibid.*, Doc. No. 29, p. 13, November 7, 1894.

29. *Ibid.*, Doc. No. 66, p. 41, November 26, 1894 report to Kimberley.

30. Mehmet Hocaoğlu, *Abdulhamit Han'ın Muhtıraları. Belgeler* (Abdul Hamit's Memoranda. Documents) (Istanbul, 1989), 239–240.

31. Duke of Argyll (George John Douglas Campbell, formerly Secretary of State for India and Lord Privy Seal), *Our Responsibilities for Turkey* (London, 1896), 92.

32. *Blue Book.* Turkey No. 1 (1896), Doc. No. 38, p. 33, May 6, 1895.

33. *Ibid.*, Doc. No. 49, p. 65, May 18, Doc. No. 147, p. 123, August 24, 1895. See also *DAG* [n. 35], Doc. No. 2407, pp. 48–9, German Ambassador Saurma's August 10, 1895 report to Berlin and Emperor Williams' marginalia on p. 49.

34. Wladimir Giesl, *Zwei Jahrzehnte im Nahen Orient* (Two Decades in the Near East. The Notes of General Of Cavalry) Major-General R. V. Steinitz ed. (Berlin, 1927), 118.

35. The Diplomatic Archives of the Foreign Ministry of Germany (*Die Diplomatischen Akten des Auswärtigen Amtes*) Die Grosse Politik (Hereafter cited as *DAG*) vol. 10, Doc. No. 2425, registry No. 136, p. 68.

36. *Ibid.*, Doc. No. 2456, registry No. 118, p. 101.

37. Joseph Marquart, *Die Entstehung und Wiederherstellung der armenischen Nation* (Berlin-Schöneberg, 1919), 74, note 26. Both professors, Moriz and Marquart, the author, were prominent Orientalists, i.e., specialists in Turkish, Kurdish, and Armenian studies.

38. Paul Cambon, *Correspondance 1870–1924*, vol. I (1870–1898) (Paris, 1940). 393, 395, October 10, 1895 letter.

39. Philip Paneth, *Turkey. Decadence and Rebirth* (London, 1943), 52.

40. Taner Akçam, *Siyasi Kültürümüzde Zulüm ve İşkence* (Atrocity and Torture in Our Political Culture) (Istanbul, 1992), 140–41. In pp. 229–305 the author discusses, under the title The Armenian Massacres, the specifics of the Sultan Abdul Hamit-era massacres, indicating that they all were centrally organized. "Drawing from the lessons of conflicts with other Christian nationalities, the measures against the Armenians involved [endeavors of] extremely centralized planning. The slightest pretext was used as a necessity to act" (*en küçük bir vesile dahi gerekçe olarak kullanılarak*). He concludes that the assaults against the Armenians were, therefore, different (*farklı*) from those launched against the other minorities. (p. 303).

41. Roy Douglas, "Britain and the Armenian Question 1894–7," *The Historical Journal*, 19, 1 (1976): 132. This author termed these massacres "as deliberate acts of policy." Another British author traces the origins of this attitude to the rule of Mohamed II (1451–1481), the founder of the Ottoman Empire, when discussing the theories of Paul Wittek, a specialist of Ottoman history. He speaks of Mohamed's "recourse to cruelty as an instrument of state policy." Colin Heywood, "Boundless Dreams of the Levant: Paul Wittek, the George-Kreis, and the Writing of Ottoman History," *Journal of the Royal Asiatic Society*, 1 (1989): 44.

42. *DAG* [n. 35], vol. 9, Doc. No. 2184, cipher No. 157, pp. 202, 204. In a message to the British Ambassador, Currie, the Sultan conveyed the same assertion, and linked the Armenian Question to the Eastern Question, citing the case of the Bulgarian massacres, which he called a "concocted" story, and ruling out for the Armenians the granting of autonomy through "separate provinces." *Blue Book* [n. 4], Doc. No. 35, enclosure, p. 18, November 4, 1895.

43. *The Memoirs of Ismail Kemal Bey* (London, 1920), 264. The description of his negotiations with Herbert are in pp. 267–8. His nomination as Governor of Tripoli and its cancellation in order to carry out his duties as an emissary are described on pp. 259–260.

44. *Blue Book*. Turkey, No. 3 (1897) Doc. No. 105, enclosure, October 1; Doc. No. 104, October 3, 1896, pp. 91–2.

45. Robert Melson, "A Theoretical Inquiry into the Armenian Massacres 1894–96," *Comparative Studies in Society and History* 24, 3 (July, 1982): 506–07. Melson in his latest work reiterates and expands his argument. *See his Revolution and Genocide—On the Origins of the Armenian Genocide and the Holocaust*. (Chicago, 1992), 49–53. In this latter study Melson also calls into question "the provocation thesis [which] rests on a simple action-reaction model of human events without making either action or reaction credible." Focusing on the arch exponents of this thesis, the Shaws, he points out that in their zeal to shift all the blame to the Armenians, especially Armenian revolutionaries, the Shaws make assertions without "any citations or qualifying remarks" and without evidence of corroboration by "other historians." *Ibid.*, 50, 51. The reason for this approach is clear, however. The Shaws chose to rely almost completely on Ottoman archives as the undisputable repository of truth, completely disregarding the fraudulent character of many of the governmental documents contained in them on the subject of the Sassoun massacre episode. This fact was brought out and underscored by the three European (French, Russian, British) Commissioners (who were attached to the Turkish Inquiry Commission) in their separately filed Joint Report, and it was reiterated with detail by the British and Russian Commissioners who felt constrained to file their own supplementary reports to drive home the issue of falsehoods permeating the ensemble of documents collected by the Turkish authorities. One of the ramifications for historical scholarship of this type of revisionism is that the Shaws and some other cohorts, operating as the advocates of the "Turkish point of view," are attempting to rewrite history. When trying to belittle the scope of the destruction caused by the Sassoun massacre, the Shaws invoke the findings of the "mixed Ottoman and foreign commission," conveying the impression that the commission functioned in harmony and reached a consensus. As indicated above, this is not only untrue in general, but the assertion that the commission agreed that the reports on the scope of destruction were "exaggerated" is specifically belied by the following British document. When he prepared an account, Shipley, the

British Commissioner, alerted his Ambassador at Constantinople of the gap between what the Turkish members of the Commission were finding and what the European members were establishing as facts. Currie then reported to London as follows:

> "From the evidence now before the Commission it is becoming evident that the magnitude of the Sassoun affair was not in the least exaggerated in the early reports received at Constantinople and elsewhere … no semblance of evidence being brought forward on the other side to show they are merely Armenian inventions devised for the purpose of discrediting the Turkish government … the Turkish Commissioners appear to be endeavouring to substantiate the theory of Armenian rebellion … but this theory was not borne out by the facts which have come before them."

Blue Book [n. 4], Doc. No. 206, p. 122, Curries' dispatch of May 16, 1895. Shipley's report was prepared on May 3, 1895. Despite the thrust of all conclusions incorporated in the Joint Report of the European members of the Turkish Inquiry Commission, the Shaws chose to insist that the Armenians were "rebels," had launched "a major coup at Sasun," that all that the police and the troops were instructed to do was "to restore order," and that the Armenian campaign for justice and redress was in essence a "terrorist cause," only to conclude that it was inevitable that the other Armenians, not identified with terrorism, would suffer, "and suffer they did." Shaw, *History* [n. 18], 203–04. The uncritical reliance on the documents of a government identified with a legacy of massacres may be a dubious form of scholarship. But to go beyond reliance and to ardently defend the government involved while displaying a scorn for the multitudes of the victims of that government's lethal policies is scholarship subverted by truculent partisanship—a condition which is rendered even more acute by the fact that a publishing house as venerable as Cambridge University Press saw fit to endorse it by publishing the book highlighting that discussion.

46. Aghassi (Garabed Tour-Sarkissian), *Zeitoun yev eer Shurtchanakneru* (Zeitoun and its Environs) (Paris, 1968), 154–57.
47. The reference to Turkish losses involving number of troops is in *Blue Book* Turkey No. 8 (1896), Doc. No. 10, enclosure, p. 13; the other referring to the military prowess of the Zeitounlis is in *ibid.*, Doc. No. 265, p. 218. This latter document represents England's Aleppo Consul Henry Barnham's lengthy report, pp. 212–222 on the conditions of the Zeitoun insurrection.
48. *The Diplomatic Archives of the Foreign Ministry of Austria* (Die Akten des k. u. k. Ministeriums des Äussern) 1848–1918. (Hereafter cited as *DAA*) *DAA*. P. A. Konsulate A. G. XXXVIII/303. Bertrand's February 26, 1896 communication to Austria's Consul General of Syria, Remy, and Vitto's February 16, 1896 letter to Bertrand, written in Italian. This fact of the acceptance is confirmed by Burnham *Blue Book* [n. 47], enclosure in Doc. No. 265, p. 212.
49. *DAF* [n. 5], Affaires Arméniennes. Supplément. 1895–96 (Paris, 1897). Cambon's first set of quotations is from Doc. No. 81, January 12, 1896, pp. 64, 65, 66. Colonel de Vialar's figures on the force structure of the Zeitounlis is in *ibid.*, Doc. No. 117, April 1896, p. 85. French Chargé de la Boulinière's comment is in *ibid*, Livre Jaune, Doc. No. 174, January 3, 1896, p. 194.
50. Cambon's second set of comments is from *ibid.*, Livre Jaune, Doc. No. 174, January 3, 1896, p. 194.
51. *Ibid.*, Doc. No. 175, January 10, 1896, pp. 194–95.
52. Aghassi, *Zeitoun* [n. 46], 301, 344.
53. Pierre Quillard, "Pour l'Arménie," *Memoire et Dossier* (19th issue of the series) (Paris, 1902), 40.
54. James Bryce, *Transcaucasia and Ararat* (London, 1896), 464, 501.
55. Aghassi, *Zeitoun* [n. 46], 354–356.
56. *L'Époque*, February 18, 1896.
57. Avetis Nazarbek, "Zeitoun", *The Contemporary Review* LXIX, 364 (April, 1896): 513–528.
58. Kemal Karpat, *Ottoman Population 1830–1914* (Madison, WI, 1985), 146. Karpat's respective tables extend to and include the year 1893; this holds true for both categories, i.e., whether Van is treated as a *sancak* (district) or as a *vilayet* (province), the Armenians are shown to exceed in numbers by a small margin the combined Turko-Kurdish,

i.e., the Muslim, population. The British author Lynch adduces, on the other hand, a much larger margin. Out of a total of a population of 64,000 for Van and its environs, he apportions 17,000 to the Muslims, and 47, 000 to the Armenians. H. F. B. Lynch, *Armenia* vol. 2 (1965, Beirut), 79.

59. Hamparzoum Yeramian, *Houshartzan Van-Vaspourakanee* (Memorial for Van-Vaspourakan) vol. 1 (Alexandria, Egypt, 1929), 352, 353.

60. *Blue Book* [n. 47], enclosure in Doc. No. 25, p. 23.

61. *Ibid.*, enclosure in Doc. No. 104, pp. 91–92. R. W. Graves, British Consul at Erzurum, on May 29, 1896, stated that Marshal Zeki "exerted his influence" in preventing the chastising of the Kurdish Chiefs who are his "protégés." *Ibid.*, enclosure 2 in Doc. No. 241, p. 200.

62. *DAF* [n. 5], Doc. No. 210, p. 235.

63. *Ibid.*, *Blue Book* [n. 47], enclosure No. 2 in Doc. No. 104, p. 92 February 19, 1896; enclosure in No. 117, p. 108, March 1, 1896; Doc. No. 256, pp. 207–08, June 21, 1896.

64. *Ibid.*, British Vice Consul Williams' April 22, 1895 report, Doc. No. 161, p. 150; on the induced resignation of Nazım Paşa see *Ibid.*, Doc. No. p. 242, British Chargé Herbert's July 2, 1896 report. For the matter of Armenian gratitude to Governor General Nazım see Yeramian, *Houshartzan* [n. 59], 351. One of the organizers of the Armenian defense in his memoirs emphatically denies Armenian responsibility for the outbreak,stating that all Armenians exercised utmost caution in order not to provoke the Turks and deny them any excuse to inveigh against the Armenians. Armenag Yegarian, *Housher* (Memoirs), H. Adjemian ed. (Cairo, 1947), 98.

65. *DAF* [n. 5], Doc. No. 210, p. 235, June 10, 1896.

66. Kinross, *Ottoman Centuries* [n. 2], 559.

67. *Blue Book* [n. 47], Doc. No.351, p. 281, July 30, 1896; see also Doc. No. 262, p. 210.

68. *Ibid.*, enclosure in Doc. No. 337, p. 271, through the medium of Consul Williams' June 28, 1896 report.

69. *DAF* [n. 5], Doc. No.227, p. 247, July 9, 1896.

70. *Blue Book* [n. 47], enclosure in Doc. No.337, p. 271, June 28, 1896 report.

71. *Ibid.*, Doc. No. 257, p. 208, Chargé Herbert's June 21, 1896 report to Salisbury; and Doc. No. 270, p. 223, Williams' June 25, 1896 report.

72. According to the British Vice Consul, 400 Armenians were killed in the town. *Ibid.*, Doc. No. 266, Chargé Herbert's June 23, 1896 report to Salisbury, p. 222.

73. *Ibid.*, enclosure in Doc. No.337, p. 272, Van's British Vice Consul's June 28, 1896 report.

74. *Ibid.*, enclosure in Doc. No. 337, p. 272, his June 28, 1896 report.

75. *Ibid.*, Doc. No. 250, p. 205, Chargé Herbert's June 19, 1896 report to Salisbury. *DAF* [n. 5], Doc. No. 215, p. 240, Cambon's June 20, 1896 report to Hanotaux.

76. *Blue Book* [n. 47], Doc. No. 256, pp. 207–08, Chargé Herbert's June 21, 1896 report to Salisbury.

77. Yeramian, *Houshartzan* [n. 59], 108.

78. *Ibid.*, 373.

79. William W. Howard, "Horrors of Armenia" *Armenian Review* XVIII, 4 (Winter, 1965): 71.

80. *Blue Book* [n. 47], enclosure in Doc. No. 337, p 272, his June 28, 1896 report.

81. *Ibid.*, Doc. No. 266, p. 222, Chargé Herbert's June 23, 1896 report to Salisbury.

82. *Ibid.*, p. 273.

83. Yeramian, *Houshartzan* [n. 59], 363, Yegarian, *Housher* [n. 64], 101.

84. Rafik Hovannissian, "Vanee 1896 Tuwee Eenknabashdbanoutiunu" (The Self-Defense of Van in 1896) *Lraper* (July, 1976): 63.

85. *Blue Book* [n. 47], enclosure in Doc. No. 337, p. 273.

86. Yeramian, *Houshartzan* [n. 59], 369; Yegarian, *Housher* [n. 64], 105.

87. *Houshabadoum Hai Heghapokhagan Dashnakzoutian. 1890–1950* (Commemorative Tome on the Armenian Revolutionary Federation. 1890–1950) (Boston, 1950), 283.

88. *Ibid.*, 284–85.

89. Armen Karo, *Abruadz Orer* (Days That Have Been Lived) (Boston, 1948), 158–59. According to the author, Maximof had confided this information to Georges Gaulis, the correspondent of *Le Journal de Débats*, who at the time of the incident was in Constantinople.

90. Mikayel Varantian, *Hai Heghapokhagan Dashnakzoutian Badmoutiun* (History of the Armenian Revolutionary Federation) vol. 1, (Paris, 1932), 159.

91. *Blue Book.* Turkey No. 1 (1897), enclosure Nos. 1 and 2 in Doc. No. 25, pp. 13,15.

92. *Houshabadoum* [n. 87], 294–95.

93. *Blue Book* [n. 91], enclosure No. 3 in Doc. No. 25, p. 16.

94. Karo, *Abruadz Orer* [n. 89], 158. Maximof is quoted as saying that had he arrived half an hour later at the Palace, the order in all likelihood would have been carried out.

95. Varantyan, *Hai* [n. 90], 168–69.

96. *DAF* [n. 5] Doc. No. 254, p. 275, September 3, 1896 report.

97. *Blue Book* [n. 91] Doc. No. 25, p. 12, his August 27, 1896 report.

98. Kinross, *Ottoman Centuries* [n. 2], 561.

99. Quoted in Varantyan *Hai* [n. 90], 174.

100. *Ibid.*, 174–75.

101. Karo, *Abruadz* [n. 89], 108.

102. There is no diplomatic record to confirm the existence of such a threat, other than the general feeling that the maritime Powers might have been expected to land such forces in order to mainly, if not only, protect their nationals, should the bloodbaths go out of control in the Ottoman capital. General and vague threats against the Sultan, his throne and regime were recurrent phenomena throughout the 1894–96 period, but not in terms of a direct forcible intervention by the Powers. Rather, they were in terms of the consequences of an anticipated chaos and anarchy which were deemed capable of overwhelming the Sultan's authority and government. The only initiative in this respect came on November 15, 1895, from German Foreign Minister Marschall, who, rather than threatening Turkey, admonished the latter's Chargé in Berlin to let the Sultan know that Europe's patience is nearing its end and that "Europe today is mightier than the Sultan" who should mend his ways. When reporting this to his Ambassador in the Ottoman capital, Marschall described his step as "our last warning to the Sultan." *DAG* [n. 35] Doc. No. 2510, p. 176. Evidently shaken by that castigation, or in the words of the German ambassador, Saurma, "deeply dismayed" (*tiefste Bestürzung*) by it, the Sultan immediately let it be known that "from here on forward he is ready to do anything and everything required of him. He asked me to indicate the kind of policy he will have to follow in order to gain the confidence of Europe." *Ibid.*, Doc. No. 2517, pp. 182–83, November 17, 1895.

103. Karo, *Abruadz* [n. 89], 108.

104. *Blue Book* [n. 91], Doc. No. 26, p. 18, August 31, 1896.

105. *DAF* [n. 96].

106. Giesl, *Zwei Jahrzehnte* [n. 34], 117.

107. Bérard, *La politique* [n. 3], 5, 15, 17.

108. *Blue Book* [n. 47], enclosure in Doc. No. 243, p. 202, May 28, 1896.

109. Cambon, *Correspondance* [n. 38], 417.18.

110. *Blue Book* [n. 91] Doc. No. 21, p. 9.

111. *Ibid.*, enclosure No. 1 in Doc. No. 26, p. 21, August 27, 1896.

112. *Ibid.*, Doc.No. 26, p. 18, Herbert's August 31, 1896 report.

113. *Ibid.*, enclosure in Doc. No. 28, p. 29, August 31, 1896.

114. *Ibid.*, Doc. No. 33, p. 34, Chargé Herbert's September 3, 1896 report.

115. Tahsin Paşa, *Abdülhmait Yıldız Hatıraları* (Yıldız Palace Memoirs of Abdul Hamit) (Istanbul, 1931), 44.

116. *DAF* [n. 5], Doc. No. 273, p. 296, October 18, 1896 report.

117. FO 195/1944, Doc. No. 46, folios 253–54, September 29, 1896 report. The Consul identified his source as "a Turk connected with the Telegraph Office here." The massacre in Trabzon likewise was triggered off by a report that "the Armenians were in a state of latent revolt, ready by a sudden assault to reduce the number of Moslems ... " *Blue Book* [n. 47], Doc. No. 61, p. 62, British Consul H. Z. Longworth's February 8, 1896 reports.

118. *Ibid.*, FO, 195/1944, folio 303.

119. FO 195/1930, folio 34/187.

120. Bat Ye'or, *The Dhimmi: Jews and Christians under Islam*, Transl. by D. Maisel, P. Fentoni), Littman (London, 1985), 48, 67, 101.

121. Kinross, *Ottoman* [n. 2], 560. In his long report of August 28, 1896, filed from Harput, Vice Consul Fontana describes a similar scene of throat-cutting performed as a religious rite in Malatya. At the home of a Turk, Harici Oğlu Abdullah, "over 100 Armenians had gathered for safety. They were circumcised, and afterwards killed as 'kurban', i.e. thrown upon their backs and their throats cut, after the manner in which sheep are sacrificed." *Blue Book* Turkey, No. 3 (1897) enclosure 1 in Doc. No. 80, p. 64, Currie's September 28, 1896 report to Salisbury.

122. *Blue Book* [n. 47], enclosure 1 in Doc. No. 52, pp. 47, 48, Ambassador Currie's February 19, 1896 report.

123. *Blue Book* [n. 47], Doc. No. 107, p. 93, Currie's March 18, 1896 report to Salisbury.

124. Kinross, *Ottoman* [n. 2], 559–60. The full account of the Urfa holocaust as personally investigated and reported on March 16, 1896, by Gerald H. Fitzmaurice, British Consul and Dragoman, is in FO 195/1930, pp. 30–72 (folios 185–206).

125. Niyazi Berkes, *The Development of Secularism in Turkey* (Montreal, 1964), 15. Their importance is evidenced in the practice to appoint them acting district-, or acting county governors in situations involving temporary vacancies in these posts. One such appointment involved the *kadı* of Zeitoun who became the *kaymakam* of that city on the eve of the Zeitoun uprising. According to the memorandum prepared by British Consul Barnham regarding the circumstances surrounding the Zeitoun uprising, he was "a notorious fanatic, made the situation intolerable." He "commonly addressed the Zeitounlis as 'dogs' or 'giaours', saying that if they did not pay [arrears of taxes] he would have the guns fired on them from the barracks, and they should fare as others had done in Sasun." *Blue Book* [n. 47], enclosure in Doc. No. 265, p. 213.

126. Sir Edwin Pears, *Forty Years in Constantinople. The Recollections of Sir Edwin Pears 1873–1915* (New York, 1916), 157. Among these rare instances is the behavior of the *müfti* and *kadı* in Hacın, a town in Adana province. According to the French Consul's official report both religious leaders opposed the local Turkish governor, the *kaymakam*, who had ordered the massacre of the Armenians. Upon their complaint, that governor was replaced. *DAF* [n. 49], Doc. No. 132, p. 97, Consul Summaripa's November 19, 1895 report. The same Consul in his December 14, 1895 report states that the old *müfti* of Tarsus, assisted by the *kaymakam*, blocked the way of the local mob which was about to launch the assault for the planned massacre. *Ibid.*, Doc. No. 135, p. 98. In yet another instance, involving Ayıntab (in Aleppo province), the *müfti* with twenty soldiers prevented the resumption of the massacre there on the second day, "because it was feared" that "the enormous throng" involved "would plunder Moslems as well as Christians." *Blue Book* [n. 47] enclosure in Doc. No. 52, p. 47, British Consul Barnham's report February 19, 1896.

127. *Ibid.*, enclosure in Doc. No. 140, p. 128, March 17, 1896.

128. The first citation is in *Blue Book*, [n. 91] enclosure in Doc. No. 32, p. 33, September 3, 1896; the second is in *Ibid.*, enclosure in Doc. No. 31, p. 32.

129. Sir Edwin Pears, *Turkey and its People* (London, 1912), 278.

130. Abraham H. Hartunian, *Neither to Laugh Nor to Weep. A Memoir of the Armenian Genocide* (Transl. by Vartan Hartunian) (Boston, 1968), 12–14. A similar scene of inferno is provided by France's Vice Consul at Ankara, Guillois. In his narration of the massacre in Kayseri he describes how the perpetrators slaughtered first the men, women and children, and burned alive the old men in the houses after pillaging their contents. Subsequently, "the more fanatical ones among them proceeded to try to impose conversion to Islam upon those women whom they had just reduced to widowhood, and children whom they had made orphans. Many of these people accepted the conversion to escape death but those who refused were cast alive into the flames." *DAF* [n. 5], Supplément, Doc. No. 161, p. 114, December 18, 1895 report.

131. Pears, *Turkey* [n. 129], 287.

132. *DAF* [n. 49], Doc. No. 10, p. 13, October 15, 1895.

133. *DAF* [n. 49], Doc. No. 53, p. 40, November 12, 1895.

134. *Blue Book* (n. 47], Doc. No. 107, p. 96, Currie's March 18, 1896 report.

135. *Ibid.*, Doc. No. 128, p. 118, April 2, 1896 report to Salisbury; the Austrian report is in *DAA*, P. A. XXXVIII/303, Doc. No. 90, March 26, 1896.

136. *DAG* [n. 35], Doc. No. 2434, p. 74, footnote. October 18, 1895 report.

137. *Blue Book* [n. 91], Doc. No. 46, p. 46, September 16, 1896; see also FO 424/188, Doc. No. 226, folio 204.

138. FO 195/1870, Doc. No. 794 or 799 (difficulty in legibility), 3d page of report, November 13, 1895.

139. From the transcripts of a report on his conversation with the colonel, dictated by the Emperor himself. *DAG* [n. 35], Doc. No. 2572, p.251, December 20, 1895.

140. *Ibid.*, Doc. No. 2479, report No. 233, p. 127, German Ambassador Saurma's December 16, 1895 communication to the German Chancellor in Berlin, Prince von Hohenlohe.

141. *Blue Book* [n. 91], Doc. No.33, p. 33, Chargé Herbert's September 3, 1896 report.

142. Ernest Jäckh, *Der Aufsteigende Halbmond*, 6th ed. (Berlin, 1916), 139.

143. P. Renouvin, E. Preclin, G. Hardy, *L'Epoque contemporaine. La paix armée et la Grande Guerre.* 2d ed. (Paris, 1947), 176, quoted in A. Beylerian, *Les Grandes Puissances, L'Empire Ottoman, et les Arméniens dans les Archives Françaises (1914–1918).* (Paris, 1983), XXIII.

144. *DAF* [n. 5], Vol. 12, Doc. No. 265, p. 384, Lozé to Foreign Minister Berthelot.

145. *Ibid.*, Doc. No. 161, p. 114, December 18, 1895 report.

146. J. Lepsius, *Armenien und Europa* (Berlin, 1897), 34, 35.

147. *Blue Book* [n. 47], Doc.No. 123, p. 112, March 31, 1896.

148. *Ibid.*, p. 113. It appears that the figure on conversions in Sıırt is a revised one, for Hampson on March 5 had provided the 17,080 number. *Ibid.* Doc. No. 146, p. 132.

149. *Ibid.*, enclosure in Doc. No. 140, p. 127. In the same report Hallward states that in the city of Diyarbekir 1,100, in the outlying villages 800 or 900 Armenians were killed, 155 women and girls were carried off by Kurds. In Silvan which, along with Palu, has "the largest Armenian population in this vilayet ... 7,500 are reduced to destitution and 4,000 disappeared: killed, died of cold, etc., or escaped elsewhere."

150. *Ibid.*, p. 128.

151. *Ibid.*, Doc. No. 146, p. 132, March 5, 1896.

152. Fitzmaurice, the First Dragoman of the British Embassy, cites such a case in Urfa where 600 Armenians had embraced Islam "Subsequent to the massacre here in December last ... in the hope of preserving their lives in the event of a repetition of that massacre, but during the last eight months the majority have either reverted to their old religion here, or quitted Urfa to do so elsewhere, there remaining over 200, who still keep up an outward profession of Islam." *Blue Book* [n. 91], enclosure in Doc. No. 113, p. 103, September 10, 1896 report to Ambassador Currie.

153. William M. Ramsay, *Impressions of Turkey During Twelve Years' Wanderings* (New York, 1897) 206–07.

154. *Ibid.*, 190–202. On p. 216 the author states, " ... of all the races with whom I have mixed in Turkey, there is none that I have personally liked less than the Armenians ... ."

155. *Ibid.*, 211–214. Ramsay's account on the nature of a Turkish massacre is replicated in a rather compressed form by the following statement which is excerpted from a private correspondence of British Ambassador White who deliberately excluded it from his official correspondence: "The last few days have enabled me to realize what St. Bartholomew's Day was like, and the sights I have witnessed have made a profound impression upon me ... The awful cold-blooded barbarity of the mob, which was deliberately organized and armed by the Turkish Government ... ." Douglas, "Britain and the Armenian Question." [n. 41], 127, 132.

156. FO 195/1944, Doc. No. 14, folios 66–67, "confidential" report by Harput's Vice Consul Raphael A. Fontana. May 18, 1896.

157. *Ibid.*, folio 11, Fontana's April 25, 1896 report to Ambassador Currie.

158. Hüsamettin Ertürk, *Iki Devrin Perde Arkası* (Behind the Scenes in Two Eras) (Istanbul, 1957), 41.

159. Douglas, "Britain and the Armenian Question" [n. 41], 132.

160. Tahsin Paşa, *Yıldız Hatıraları* [n. 115], 133.

161. *British Documents on Ottoman Armenians*, vol. 2 (1880–1890) B. Simşir, ed. (Ankara, 1983) Doc. No. 278, registry No. 182, p. 554, Ambassador White's April 30, 1888 report to Salisbury.

162. Sultan II Abdülhamid Han, *Devlet ve Memleket Görüşlerim* (My Views on State and Country) A. A. Çetin and R. Yıldız eds. (Istanbul, 1976), 198–99. See *Başbakanlık Arşivi*, Yıldız Esâs Evrakı: Kısım 9, Evrak 2610, Zarf 72, Karton 4.

163. *Ibid.*, 199–200. Sultan Abdul Hamit's complaint about Foreign Minister Said stems from the fact that the latter recognized the sources of the Turko-Armenian conflict and recommended appropriate remedies. In an exchange with German Ambassador Radolin on November 28, 1894, he "confidentially" told the Ambassador that "the mismanagement of the Turkish officials was responsible for the situation in Armenia," that he "repeatedly gave the Sultan to understand that unless there was improvement in this respect, Russia alone, or under a European mandate, would occupy the Armenian provinces in order to establish there law and order in the interest of her own security needs ..." The Foreign Minister then continued, "unfortunately, in *Yıldız* [Palace] they prefer to listen to the advice of miserable creatures than to the proposal of the Porte." Continuing further, Said stated that he got "no support (*kein Rückhalt*) from the Grand Vizier who was more concerned with ingratiating himself with the Sultan than with the interests of the empire." *DAG* [n. 35], v. 9, Doc. No. 2186, pp. 206–07, Radolin's November 28, 1894 report No. 160. Another Turkish Foreign Minister, Ahmed Tevfik Paşa, Said's successor in office, likewise had the audacity to acknowledge to French Ambassador Cambon the complicity of the authorities in the massacres. He is quoted as saying "If we don't punish all the instigators and the authorities who allowed all these atrocities, it will soon become impossible to restore order to have a government functioning in Asia Minor. I shall request from his Majesty the dispatch to the sites of judicial inquiry commissions, competent to hang or execute by fire squads those who are principally guilty. It is necessary to act fast, otherwise worse disasters may come." Commented Cambon, "I believe in his sincerity, but I can anticipate the fate of his proposals. Sultan will never issue orders against guilty Muslims, and even less so against guilty authorities." *DAF* [n. 5], vol. 12, Doc. No. 265, pp. 364–65, Cambon to Foreign Minister Berthelot, January 8, 1896.

164. *DAF* [n. 5] Supplément, Doc. No.65, p. 52, the October 26, 1895 report of Barthélemy, the Gerent of France's Aleppo Consulate, to Ambassador Cambon.

165. *Blue Book*. Turkey No. 1 (1896). Armenian Provinces in Asiatic Turkey. Doc. No. 200, p. 159, Ambassador Currie's, October 17, 1895 report.

166. FO 195/2452, Turkey, cipher No. 2526, the May 27, 1913 report of Cumberbatch, England's Consul General at Aleppo.

167. *DAG* [n. 35], Doc. No. 2184, p. 203, report No. 157.

168. Douglas, "Britain and the Armenian Question" [n. 41], 132, Ambassador Currie's October 28, 1897 report to Salisbury.

169. William L. Langer, *The Diplomacy of Imperialism 1890–1902* Vol. 1 (New York, 1935), 203.

170. Nuri, *Abdulhamid Sani* [n. 10], Vol. 1 (Istanbul, 1327 [1911–12]), 838.

Chapter 9

The Portentousness of the Abdul Hamit Era Massacres

The significance of any given historical period is best measured by its degree of relevance to the unfolding of subsequent events. From the perspective of nationality conflicts besetting the Ottoman Empire in the later stages of its career, the most signal aspect of the era of Sultan Abdul Hamit is the series of massacres unleashed against the Armenians.

The question which arises in this regard is whether these massacres can be viewed merely as an episodic occurrence or whether they were consequential beyond the span of their occurrence, especially with respect to the subsequent fate of the victim population in relation to the subsequent conduct of the victimizers. Given the historical fact of the World War I Armenian genocide, the answer to this question necessarily must revolve around the fundamental issue of the portentousness of these massacres. To what extent and in what respect does the enactment of that genocide actually prefigure in the enactment of these massacres? Implied in the framing of these questions is the view that one is dealing here with the reality of a historical continuum in which the lethal character of a perpetrator-victim relationship is not only sustained but its level is escalated and its dimensions are amplified to the point of the termination of the existence of the victim, i.e., the vast Armenian population of the Ottoman Empire.

The continuity is further accented by the fact that in two respects the two episodes at issue here differed markedly from each other. First of all, there was no external war during the 1894–96 massacres, as was the case with the subsequent genocide. Second, there was a change in regimes. The 1894–96 massacres were engineered by and during the reign of Abdul Hamit, who was denounced as a tyrant and toppled by the leaders of the successor regime, the Ittihadist Young Turks who, nevertheless, are identified as the architects of the subsequent genocide. The constancy of the trend to decimate and obliterate a targeted population group, despite such major differences incidental to the structure and the circumstances of the two regimes involved, suggests the operativeness of factors superseding in importance the significance of these differences. One of these factors was the persistence of a tradition, in part rooted in the dogmas of Islam, that more or less sanctioned the resort to lethal violence in the handling of acute conflicts with non-Muslim subject nationalities of the empire.

The festering Turko-Armenian conflict was not only treated as a strictly internal Turkish affair by the leaders of these regimes, but was also defined as a fundamental dispute challenging the idea of the supremacy of Islam. To them, and the multitudes of their followers, Islam was a religious creed which, however, dispensed politically inspired mandates, including the assignment to the empire's non-Muslim subjects the status of a permanent inferiority, irrespective of the issuance of certain decrees and legislative promulgations. The series of confidential memoranda (referred to in chapter 8 above), in which Abdul Hamit outlined his basic policy relative to the Armenian Question, and the policy declarations of Talât, the Ittihadist party boss and Interior Minister, made in August 1910 in a secret conclave of party leaders (to be discussed in the next chapter), attest to this fact. The imperial and theocratic bearings of the Ottoman state system combined to create the prerequisites for the formation of certain general attitudes which tended to allow, if not to legitimize, under certain circumstances, the application of lethal violence against discordant minorities. There emerged a mentality which had elements of a cryptic culture sanctioning massacres as an instrument of state policy.

But state policies with ramifications extending beyond the realm of a state, as a rule, cannot be taken for granted by the perpetrators as far as the problem of viability is concerned. They must be determined upon in relation to contingencies with a potential to affect the outcome of such policies. If one should consider the established mentality, favoring massacres, as a dependent variable in the scheme of an imaginary quantitative analysis, one has to account then for the function of an independent variable impinging upon it and influencing its operativeness. Here, one comes face to face with a crucial aspect of the problem: the historical continuum of the policy at issue. The pursuit by the Powers of the goal of humanitarian intervention, however ineffective in its major thrust, was such as to always inject an element of uncertainty, and even some apprehension, in the calculations of the organizers of the massacres as to the thresholds beyond which the extent and forms of atrocities may not be tolerated by one or several Powers; there was always a chance that a forceful intervention could be touched off. However, the consistency with which such thresholds failed to materialize, or remained imperceptible, irrespective of the incremental tempo of the atrocities, i.e., the inaction of the Powers, emerges here as the most salient independent variable in the sense described above. It became the most overarching factor in the episodic reprise by a state of a policy providing for the decimation and extirpation of a minority population. In brief, that policy is seen as a by-product of the absence of deterrence from without.

Deterrence basically refers to prevention, but here it is inextricably interwoven with its twin component, punishment. The constancy of the absence of deterrence was attended by a parallel constancy of an absence of punishment of any kind after each and every episode of massacre. (This issue will be discussed with greater detail in the chapters to follow.) The persistence of the lack of external deterrence, despite occasional pronouncements of threats which were fashioned in such a way as to be ill-conceived for the purpose of dissuasion, and the corollary factor, impunity, proved the twin warrants for the destruction of Ottoman Armenians by rendering that destruction affordable for the perpetrators. It may be argued that the Abdul Hamit-era massacres were a testing ground, an opportunity, to probe the limits, if any, of the scope and methods of destruction one may dare launch against a targeted population. In this sense that era emerges as the experimental prelude to the World War I holocaust, presaging its occurrence as a logical extension of the ethos of that era, as well as a function of the established legacy of the twin indulgences of the Powers: lack of credible deterrence prior to and predictable impunity after the fact.

These reflections on the issue of portentousness may furnish the rationale for a meaningful transition to the rest of this study highlighting the role of the Ittihadist Young Turks in a new era of massacres. The discussion may be ended with some excerpts from the writings of two authors, an Englishman and an American, who closely examined the Abdul Hamit era massacres and with a cogent premonition forecast the inevitability of the ultimate destruction of the bulk of the Armenian population of Turkey.

When James G. Bennett, American newspaper man and publisher of the *New York Herald*, became skeptical of the veracity of reports on the 1894–96 massacres, described as examples of unparalleled savagery, he prevailed upon Sultan Hamit to obtain a permission to have the story of the massacres impartially investigated by a team. Hopeful that such a team could be influenced to favor him in a final report, Hamit consented. A member of that team was American author and Civil War observer George Hepworth, who described himself as having a "rather keen appetite for facts." With a retinue of Turkish military officials, including a colonel, a lieutenant colonel, a secretary, and a bodyguard, the team proceeded to the sites of the atrocities and conducted a two-month investigation. In 1898 Hepworth summed up his findings as follows. "Now to summarize. When I say that the Armenian massacres were caused by Armenian revolutionists, I tell a truth, and a very important truth, but it is not the whole truth. It would be more correct to say that the presence of the revolutionists gave occasion and excuse for the massacres. That the Turks were looking for an occasion and an excuse, no one can doubt who has traversed that country. Way down in the bottom of his heart, the Turk hates the Armenian. He will swear to the contrary, but I am convinced that the statement is true nevertheless. The reasons for this are abundant, as I have tried to show in other chapters of this book. The Turk is extremely jealous of the Armenian, jealous of his mental superiority, of his thrift, and business enterprise. He has, therefore, resorted to oppression, and his steady purpose has been and is now, to keep his victims poor. Equal opportunities for all are a delusion and a snare. They do not exist ... ."[1] "I am afraid that the reforms which are needed in Turkey can never be instituted ... ."[2] By way of extrapolation, Hepworth made a prognostication, anticipating the World War I genocide fully two decades before its incidence. "During my travels in Armenia I have been more and more deeply convinced that the future of the Armenians is extremely clouded. It may be that the hand of the Turk will be held back through fear of Europe but I am sure that the object of the Turk is extermination, and that he will pursue that end if the opportunity offers. He has already come very near to its accomplishment ... ."[3]

The other prediction comes from the pen of the astute British ethnographer William Ramsay, whose studies took him to Turkey several times in the last two decades of the nineteenth century. (See a detailed review of his observations in chapter 8, notes 153–55.) When extrapolating the portents of the 1894–97 massacres, the number of victims of which he placed at "about 200,000," he declared in 1897, "The Armenians will in all probability be exterminated except the remnant that escapes to other lands."[4]

Even more significant, the Powers themselves had, in a September 7, 1880 Collective Note addressed to the Ottoman central authorities, anticipated a similar fate for the Armenians. They were expressing their displeasure at Turkish tactics of stalling the introduction of reforms in those provinces whose "peculiar characteristic ... is the predominance of the Christian population over large areas of the territory in question; if this predominance is not taken into account no real reform would be effected." In the same vein the Powers berated the Turkish government for "delaying" the arrangements needed to carry out "the proposed census" of the populations, especially the Armenians. They suggested, by the same token, that "the present geographical limits of the various vilayets will have to be recast" in order to render the reforms viable and effective. They thus touched a very sensitive nerve, and the Ottoman response was swift. Immediately thereafter the authorities embarked upon a series of administrative initiatives whereby the provincial boundaries were recast through redistricting with the result that in virtually every province, and even in the district of a province, the Armenians were reduced to absolute numerical minorities—not in relation to the Turks as such but to "Muslims" in general, a category that comprised an assortment of non-Turkish nationalities such as Kurds, Circassians, Lases, and Kızılbaş.

The six Powers, whose representatives had signed this Note, had officially linked the brewing Turko-Armenian conflict at this stage to Article 61 of the Berlin Treaty of 1878, whose stipulations, they argued, were treaty engagements and, therefore, binding for Turkey. They thus injected in that Note their premonition that failure to execute the terms of that article "would in all probability lead to the destruction of the Christian [i.e., Armenian] population of vast districts."[5]

Notes to Chapter 9

1. George H. Hepworth, *Through Armenia on Horseback*, (N.Y.: Dutton, 1898), 339–40.
2. *Ibid.*, 263.
3. *Ibid.*, 146–7. In several passages of his work Hepworth describes the structural vulnerability of the Armenians, the ensuing development of submissiveness and the resulting ease with which they were slaughtered. Here are some examples: "I ... found that every Turk and every Kurd I met in the streets had either a pistol or a long dagger, but I do not remember a single instance in which an Armenian was armed in the same way." The author then explains the dangers for an Armenian daring to want to acquire a weapon, 249–51. The Turks and Kurds "are fighting men, each one armed to the teeth," the Armenians "are not only unarmed, but unacquainted with the use of arms," 161. To illustrate the fatal consequences of this line of disparity, Hepworth relates an incident his companion had witnessed during the 1896 Constantinople massacre. After stating that during the carnage, of which "he witnessed a large part ... not in a single instance did the Armenians make a resistance ... I saw an Armenian come out of his house to see what was going on. A Turk caught sight of him, and raised his stick. The Armenian was perhaps dazed, I cannot tell, but he made no motion,—stood still as a marble statue. The fatal blow was struck, and the poor fellow dropped to the ground." *Ibid.*, 165.
4. William M. Ramsay, *Impressions of Turkey During Twelve Years' Wanderings* (New York: Putnam's, 1897), 156–57.
5. British Foreign Office Records. Turkey No. 23 (1880), Doc. No. 154, p. 275–78.

Part V

THE WARS AND MASSACRES OF THE NEW YOUNG TURK REGIME AND THE DEMISE OF HUMANITARIAN INTERVENTIONISM

Chapter 10

The 1909 Twin Adana Massacres

The Hidden Agenda of the Young Turks Seizing Power

The transition in July, 1908, to a new regime in Turkey through a blood-less revolution that deposed Sultan Abdul Hamit and installed the Itti-hadists (also known as the Young Turks) only compounded the problems of domestic conflict in general and the Turko-Armenian conflict in par-ticular. Though their regime (1908–1918) was dubbed the Second Era of the Constitution, the Young Turk Ittihad leaders, like their predecessor, Abdul Hamit ("the Red Sultan"), embraced violent measures against the minorities on whose behalf the Powers had again begun to intercede. Their policy of repression helped spark the 1912 Balkan war and later played a role in the adoption of nationalist policies that plunged Turkey into World War I. As Marriott stated,

> The Young Turk revolution brought matters to a head. [That undertaking] was in fact a last effort of the Moslem minority to retain its ascendancy in the face of growing resistance on the part of subject races and impending European intervention. The revival of the constitution was little more than an ingenious device for appeasing Liberal sentiment abroad while furnishing a pretext for the abrogation of the historic rights of the Christian nationalities at home.[1]

At the 1910 annual Ittihadist Congress at Saloniki, the secret discus-sions outside the formal sittings revolved around the plan for the coercive homogenization of Turkey, euphemistically called "the complete Ottoman-ization of all Turkish subjects."[2] British Ambassador Lowther observed that "[t]o them 'Ottoman' evidently means 'Turk' and their present policy of 'Ottomanization' is one of pounding the non-Turkish elements in a Turk-ish mortar."[3] Surveying the thrust of these decisions, the British Foreign Office in a report employed the words "to level," with the forecast that "the

---

Young Turks will endeavor to extend the 'levelling' system to the Kurds and the Arabs."[4] In a series of reports based on "authentic documents" furnished by confidential sources, the French Consul at Saloniki informed his Foreign Ministry in Paris that the Young Turks decided to employ force and violence, including massacres, as a last resort for the resolution of nationality conflicts.[5] All these disclosures are confirmed by the Dean of Turkish historians who stated that, weary of the protracted Turko-Armenian conflict, Ittihad would turn to the army to resolve the conflict by force of arms.[6]

A final clue to understanding this repudiation of social and political reform and the opting instead for the fretful alternative of "levelling," i.e., homogenizing Ottoman society, is found in a secret speech by Talât, who was the preeminent Young Turk leader and Interior Minister. He delivered the speech to a conclave of Ittihad leaders assembled in Saloniki in August, 1910 for a pre-Congress strategy meeting. Austrian, French, and British intelligence sources in that city confirmed the occurrence of this meeting and the authenticity of the speech. The British Vice Consul at Monastir, Arthur Geary, vouched for "the accurate reproduction of the gist of Talât's discourse" as it was obtained from "an unimpeachable source." The relevant portion reads:

> You are aware that by the terms of the Constitution equality of Mussulman and Ghiaur [infidel, a derogatory label applied to non-Muslims] was affirmed but you one and all know and feel that this is an unrealizable ideal. The Sheriat [the religious laws of Islam], our whole past history and the sentiments of hundreds of thousands of Mussulmans and even the sentiments of the Ghiaurs themselves ... present an impenetrable barrier to the establishment of real equality.... There can therefore be no question of equality until we have succeeded in our task of Ottomanizing the Empire.[7]

The homogeneous Ottoman society Talât envisioned as a precondition for real equality thus required the liquidation in one form or another of the existing heterogeneous elements. In confirming the authenticity of that speech, a fourth source, a French diplomat, spoke of the Ittihad resolve to "deracinate" (*déraciner*) the bases of nationalistic tendencies and to "deform" the nationalities themselves.[8] Two prominent Turkish sociologists both confirm and explain the inevitability of this decision of Ittihad to resort to the violent elimination of non-Turkic nationalities. One concluded that Ittihad meant to "assimilate them through coercive methods, if necessary."[9] The other, the high priest of Ittihadist ideology, traced the lingering nationality conflicts to the introduction of statutory public laws, equating Muslims with non-Muslims. In a rarely publicized internal party document written during the World War I genocide against the Armenians, bearing the title: "The Two Mistakes of Tanzimat," ideologue Ziya Gökalp lambasted the 1839 and 1856 reform edicts. Declaring them serious mistakes, he reasserted the concept of the nation of overlords (*milleti hakime*) with the watchword: "Islam mandates domination." According to the author of the book in which this document was published for the first time in 1949, the document was in the possession of Ittihad party Secretary-General Midhat Şükrü Bleda.[10] Another author has revealed that Gökalp wrote this essay for the benefit of the Ittihadist leaders to whom they were then distributed at the party's 1916 convention.[11] In explaining the ideological grounds for adopting this new policy, an American expert on modern Turkey states that Ittihad "soon turned from equality and Ottomanization to Turkification."[12]

Within a year of seizing power, the Young Turks introduced a number of constitutional changes and laws purporting to liberalize the regime. Although promulgated through the Parliament, these changes brought no relief to the minorities. In the Balkans (particularly Macedonia and Albania), in the eastern provinces with large concentrations of Armenians, and even in distant Yemen, Ottoman misrule deteriorated into bloody oppression. With the exception of the Armenians, the subject nationalities resorted to open rebellion. Many of these rebellions were successful, and the empire, as a result, suffered further shrinkage of its territories.

That the commitment to constitutionalism was both tenuous and less than uniform, as far as all the ethnic elements of the empire were concerned, was a fact which came into full relief in April 1909. It is a fact that the March 31/April 13, 1909 counter-revolution, staged by an assortment of Islamic fundamentalists, opponents of Ittihad, and Abdul Hamit loyalists, was crushed when contingents of the Ottoman IIIrd Army marched into Istanbul from Saloniki and restored both the Ittihadist regime and the principle of constitutionality which was identified with that regime. But a signally contributing factor to that outbreak was the assassination of the chief editor of a Turkish newspaper who, defying all threats to his life, was severely criticizing Ittihadist measures of autocracy and coerciveness. The failure of the authorities to track down and apprehend the assassin or assassins aroused the ire of many people, precipitating the counter-revolution. What is even more significant, this act of plain murder heralded a series of subsequent murders to which other prominent editors, equally critical of the regime, fell victim, and the culprits of which crimes likewise managed to escape and remained free. As time progressed and the problems mounted, the Young Turk revolutionaries gradually relinquished their adherence to constitutional principles and adopted severe measures of repression, thereby surpassing, in many respects, the notoriety of the preceding Abdul Hamit regime.

The Reenactment of Massacres as Rehearsal for the Genocide

The illusory character of the Ittihadist Young Turk constitutionalist revolution came into full view with the launching of the two-tiered Adana massacre in the April 1/14–April 14/27, 1909, period, to which some 25,000 Armenians fell victim. In contrast to the multitudes in the Ottoman capital which had unleashed the counter-revolution, the Armenians in Adana were recognized as the manifest and at times demonstrative champions of the Ittihadist principles of constitutional liberties. Intoxicated with their new found freedoms they flaunted it, to the point of provoking many Turks, some of whom were Abdul Hamit loyalists who resented the new leadership of the Young Turks, some others were residual bureaucrats apprehensive about their jobs, and most of them were aroused and angry at the idea of considering their former *rayas*, the "infidel" subjects, their equals. Moreover, Adana and its environs were those rare spots which had escaped the massacres and devastations of the 1894-1896 Abdul Hamit-era. This fact, plus the relative affluence of the indigenous Armenian population, served to render them a suitable target for annihilation at a propitious moment.

Thus, cupidity, a drive by many officials to maintain their positions and jobs, religious dogmas and occasional displays of victim bravados, were factors converging at a level of conflict which produced the pogroms. But superseding in importance all these factors was the fact of the secrecy of the organization of the bloodbath which consisted mainly in the cooperation of the governmental functionaries with Ottoman military authorities, who made ample use of the arsenals of the local garrisons. The Ottoman government publicly and officially exonerated the Armenians, thereby implicitly recognizing their victim-fate. Moreover, during an interpellation in the Ottoman Chamber of Deputies, i.e., the Lower House of Ottoman Parliament, Grand Vizier Hilmi Paşa scorned "the reactionary, criminal scoundrels who were bent on massacring and plundering the Armenians through a surprise attack." Local tribunals and military courts-martial altogether convicted and executed on the gallows 124 Turks in the period of May 28/June 10, 1909–November 30/December 13, 1910. To mollify Muslim sentiment, altogether seven Armenians were also hanged.

Two salient points about this episode merit depiction. First of all the matter of the vulnerability, or more precisely, the degree of the vulnerability of the Armenians as the victim group. As stated above, the 1909 Holocaust had two stages. The first one proved more or less abortive for the assaulting forces. Anticipating the eventuality of the onslaught, several hundred young Armenians had secured arms and devised strategy for self-defense. As a result, they not only warded off the attacks and protected the larger populations residing in the Armenian wards of the city of Adana, but in the process exacted heavy tolls from the assaulting forces. This fact demonstrated the viability of deterrence or mitigation through organized self-defense for groups targeted for destruction by inexorable foes.

However, there are also limits to the possibilities of success for such undertakings. Having experienced a depletion of their resources of armed resistance, and in a condition of utmost exhaustion, the Armenians wearily consented to disarm for a truce arranged by the British Consul at nearby Mersin. In the meantime, new contingents of the Turkish army had arrived ostensibly to restore "peace and order." What followed was one of the most gruesome and savage bloodbaths ever recorded in human history. Enraged by the magnitude of the losses they sustained during the first round of the conflagration, the Turks, directly supported by the newly arrived army contingents, descended upon the totally disarmed and defenseless Armenians, butchering and burning them alive by the thousands. Schools, hospitals, and churches were especially selected for this purpose. The overwhelming majority of the twenty-five thousand Armenian victims of the Adana Holocaust in fact died at this second stage of the perpetration of mass murder.

Second, the internal vulnerability of the victim population was compounded by the external vulnerability factor. The warships of seven nations, England, France, Italy, Austria, Russia, Germany, and the United States, had steamed into the waters near Adana's port city Mersin; these consisted mostly of cruisers and frigates, with their regular complements of combat sailors ready for action. But none of them was ordered to intervene, inasmuch as the victims were Ottoman subjects and, therefore, outside the pale of their protective duties. The non-materialization of the anticipated and at the same time feared intervention was not only a great relief to the perpetrators but an incentive to renew the carnage with even greater ferocity. This failure of external deterrence only served to amplify the vulnerability of the targeted group as it emboldened the perpetrator group considerably. This critical fact underscores the dysfunctional aspects of the principle of humanitarian intervention. The naval forces of the Powers failed to intervene for a variety of reasons, chief among which were the following:

1)   There was no concrete agreement to act jointly.
2)   Each Power was anxious to protect its own nationals trapped in the conflagration, including consular personnel.
3)   Mutual suspicions of imperial and/or colonial designs on a decaying empire stifled the will for unilateral initiative on the part of any of the Powers.
4)   The abruptness of the outbreak of the bloodbath astounded the governments of these Powers, denying them the possibility to clearly define the situation and work out a response; they were, in a sense, paralyzed by confusion and uncertainty.

The net result of all this was that the commanders and the naval forces at their disposal comprising this formidable, international armada were reduced to the ignominious role of spectators of the 1909 Adana holocaust.

Notes to Chapter 10

1. J. Marriott, *The Eastern Question: An Historical Study in European Diplomacy* 4th ed. (reprinted Glasgow, 1958), 443-44.

2. FO 195/2359, folio 276.

3. *British Documents on the Origins of the War 1889–1914,* part 1, vol. 9, Doc. No. 181, Sept. 6, 1910 report, p. 207 (Gooch and Temperley eds., 1926).

4. FO 424/250, Annual Report 1910, p. 4.

5. M. Choublier, *La Question D'Orient Depuis le Traité de Berlin* (1889). In his Nov. 15, 1910 report, quoting Halil, the head of the parliamentary branch of the party comprising Ittihadist deputies, Consul Choublier mentions the proposal of relying "solely on military might" in order to deal with the nationalities. N.S. Turquie. Politique Interieure, Jeunes Turcs, 7:149. In his November 16 report, the Consul revealed a divergence of opinion as to the choice between "deportation" and "massacre" in handling the problem of Macedonia and the Bulgarians in Adrianople (Edirne). *Ibid.,* p. 150. According to the highly confidential information supplied to him (Nov. 16, 1910 report), the Monastir branch opted for the deportation to Asiatic Turkey of parts of the Christian population of Macedonia to be supplanted by Muslim refugees, whereas the Adrianople branch opted for the massacre of the resident Christian population *(l'extermination de tous les chrétiens hostiles à la jeune Turquie),* should the implanting of large bodies of Muslim immigrants fail to attain the desired results. In the Nov. 17 report he speaks of the resolve of Ittihad to resort to "la force des armes" if efforts "to achieve peacefully the unity of Turkey should fail ... for which purpose we should develop the patriotism of the Turks." *Ibid.,* p. 151.

6. Y. Bayur, *Turk Inkilâbı Tarihi* (The History of the Turkish Revolution) vol. 2, Part 4 (Ankara, 1952), 13.

7. *British Documents on the Origins of the War 1889-1914,* [n. 3], 208. Confirmation of the speech is in Austrian Vice Consul von Zitkovsky's No. 69 "secret" report of October 14, 1910. in A.A. Türkei 159 No. 2, Bd. 12, A18643. French confirmation is in N.S. Turquie, 7:92–97. A particular additional phrase in this French version, not found in the British report, is Talât's proposal to lull the potential victims of the Ottomanization program to complacency: "il faut que nous tranquillisions nos voisins." This report is stamped "received" by the Direction Politique et Commerciale of the French Foreign Ministry, bearing the symbols D, Carton 391, and the date August 6, 1910, thus indicating that it was wired on the very same day on which the speech was delivered.

8. This source was the French Chargé at distant Hidjaz in Arabia, who was reporting to Pichon, the French Foreign Minister. N.S. Turquie, 7, January 26, 1911.

9. A. Yalman, *The Development of Modern Turkey as Measured by its Press* (New York, 1914), 101.

10. K. Duru, *Ziya Gökalp* (Istanbul, 1949), 60–69.

11. Ziya Gökalp, *Turkish Nationalism and Western Civilization,* Niyazi Berkes, trans., ed.,(London, 1959), 319, n. 6.

12. Roderic Davison, "The Armenian Crisis, 1912-1914" *American Historical Review* 53, 3 (1948): 482-83.

Chapter 11

The Eviction of the Turks from the Balkan Peninsula: A New Sense of Peril for Anatolia

Turkish Military Defeats in the 1912 Balkan War
The historical background of the Balkan War

In terms of its origin and outcome, this war had a profound effect upon the Young Turk Ittihadist leadership grappling with the task of maintaining the integrity of an Ottoman Empire in danger of disintegration through centrifugal forces. The Balkan peninsula emerged as the main theater on which these forces exerted themselves, effectively challenging the sovereign authority of the Ottoman state. In other words, the nationality question or, more specifically, the Eastern Question, became a crucible for the survival of the empire. Equally important, to the extent that the Armenian Question had become an extension of the Eastern Question, the Turko-Armenian conflict functioned as an integral part of that crucible, i.e., a test case for the preservation of the empire.

The disastrous outcome of the 1912 Balkan war left the very survival of that empire hanging in the balance, however. The attempt of the Armenians to revive at this critical juncture of Ottoman history the thorny Armenian reform question, with all that it portended for the Turks, served to arouse the ire and fury of the despondent Ittihadists, thereby further intensifying the already simmering Turko-Armenian conflict. The ground was prepared for the Turks to redefine the Armenian Question as an ominous variant of the Eastern Question warranting drastic and preemptive measures to avert a total disaster. In order to understand these developments more fully, a brief historical review of the events surrounding the 1912 Balkan war may be in order.

Notes for this chapter begin on page 199.

The rising tide of nationalism in Europe and elsewhere had certain roots which were independent from any experience of foreign or colonial domination but were nevertheless susceptible to being reinforced by such experiences. The nationalism that was beginning to blossom in the Balkans was substantially influenced by the legacy of the French Revolution which consecrated the twin ideas of liberty and nationality. Nor can one disregard the impetus which the Great Powers inadvertently provided in this regard in their pursuit of aggrandizement, riches, and hegemony. The efforts of Napoleon III stand out in this connection. As a measure of spite against the Habsburg Empire, he encouraged among the Balkan nationalities, for example, the spread of nationalism. With England, and later Germany merely playing the role of more or less disinterested and benevolent mediators, Russia in due course of time assumed a predominant role. Ethnic and religious affinities on the one hand, and an eye on the big prize, Constantinople, on the other, energized that role.

Notwithstanding, Russia had some grounds for bitterness motivating it to engage in behavior that somehow was offsetting. Its spectacular victories in the 1877–78 Russo-Turkish war were reduced to insignificance at the July 1878 Berlin Congress through the manoeuvres of Austria and Germany, but especially England. The ensuing Berlin Treaty contained many of the seeds of discontent animating the Serbian, Bulgarian, and Macedonian nationalists who were to play a major role in the precipitation of the subsequent 1912 Balkan war.

At that Congress Bosnia and Herzegovina were handed over to Austria, thereby angering the Serbs, who, as a result, lost Nish and Mitrovitza and additionally were cut off from their kinsmen, the Montenegrins, through the loss of Novibazar, the military occupation of which by Austria was sanctioned by the Congress. Furthermore, the Three Emperor's League, involving Germany, Austria, and Russia, established in 1881 and renewed in 1884 for three years, granted Austria the right to annex the dual provinces of Bosnia and Herzegovina whenever it, Austria, deemed it opportune. The terms of the Berlin Treaty were considered even more damaging to Bulgarian interests and aspirations, as the territories granted Bulgaria by the March 1878 San Stefano Treaty, the forerunner of the Berlin Treaty, were reduced by two-thirds. Moreover, it had lost Macedonia and was cut off from the Aegean Sea. Pro-Russian Montenegro likewise sustained territorial losses, such as a strip of Bosnia. Perhaps most important, Russia in the Berlin Congress had to acquiesce to the imposition by the other Powers of all these terms under a very real threat of war against it by Austria and England.

In substituting the Berlin Treaty for that of San Stefano, the Powers were once more outlining and solidifying their notion of humanitarian intervention, while jealously guarding their own national interests. At issue were the nationality conflicts subsumed under both the Eastern Question and the Armenian Question. The San Stefano Treaty was virtually dictated by victorious Russia to the defeated Turks who had sued for peace; thus, it had a bilateral character. However, the terms of both the 1856 Paris Peace Treaty and the 1871 London agreement stipulated that any change in the terms involved respecting the status of Turkey, including its borders, could not be valid without the collective assent of the Powers.

In 1870 Russia had repudiated the Black Sea clauses of the Treaty of Paris and the Powers, while grudgingly accepting this Russian *fait accompli*, declared there and then against unilateral breaches of international agreements. The same San Stefano Treaty's article 16 had made the departure of Russian troops from "the Armenian provinces" in eastern Turkey contingent on the actual implementation of the reforms provided in that article. In the substitute Berlin Treaty, that article was sufficiently diluted to render it inoperative. This was done by acceding to the Turkish demand to let it assume responsibility for the implementation of the reforms it had committed itself to undertake—without the presence of Russian occupation troops, which eventually left as a result.

The reforms not only failed to materialize but the Ottoman authorities embarked upon a deliberate campaign of massacre and repression to reduce the issue of reform to irrelevance. Consequently, Macedonia, which under article 23 of the Berlin Treaty was guaranteed similar reforms, together with Armenia, became a testing ground for Turkish defiance of treaty obligations and Turkish resolve to obviate, if not eliminate, the Macedonian and Armenian Questions by a new wave of persecutions, decimation of the native populations involved through a series of massacres, and through compulsory demographic changes, including the importation for resettlement of large numbers of Muslim refugees.

Through articles 23 and 61 the Berlin Treaty thus emerges as the immediate nexus, the acute connecting link, between the Eastern Question and the Armenian Question, highlighting their convergence in the processes through which, as noted above, the notion of humanitarian intervention gradually emerged and crystallized itself. Russian insistence and persistence on wanting to protect in the Ottoman Empire Eastern Orthodox subjects, had led to two major wars, the 1853–56 Crimean War, and the 1877–78 Russo-Turkish war, producing the Paris Peace Treaty and the Berlin Treaty respectively. In order to stymie this Russian penchant for unilateral protectionism, the Powers, led by England, supplanted it by an insistence on the need for collective engagement on the part of the Concert of Europe. The objection of the Powers rested on the argument that they all had a stake in the improvement of the conditions of the nationalities seeking reform and even deliverance from Ottoman dominion, if not yoke. Therefore, they maintained, no single Power was entitled to monopolize this overall humanitarian concern for remedies.

When one examines the relationship between the terms of the settlement incorporated in the Berlin Treaty on the one hand, and the 1912 Balkan war on the other, one cannot but help to observe again the ineffective, if not counter-productive, aspects of the principle of humanitarian intervention. The Powers could agree among themselves, reach a modicum of consensus, but in the process generated a treaty which was pregnant with an inevitable future conflict among the peoples on which its terms were imposed as a humanitarian service. Macedonia was a major source of such a conflict. Serbia, Bulgaria, and Greece had conflicting claims inasmuch as that province was almost entirely populated by Greeks, Serbs, and mostly Bulgarians. The severity with which the Young Turk Ittihadist regime began to forcibly denude Macedonia of its indigenous Christian population and repopulate it with Muslim immigrants was such as to alarm and agitate these three nationalities, who began exploring the possibility of an alliance against Turkey primarily. As described in note 7 of Chapter 10, already during the secret meetings of their 1910 annual congress the Ittihadists had resolved to resort to massacre, if necessary, in order to cleanse Macedonia of Christians.

The first initiative for an alliance came from the Serbs approaching the Bulgarians, with whom they had fought and lost a war in 1885. The Serbs were angry about the loss of Bosnia which Austria finally had incorporated [as allowed in the Three Emperor's League agreement] in the wake of the 1908 Young Turk revolution; at the same time, almost simultaneously, Bulgaria had proclaimed its complete independence, repudiating the existing arrangement of Ottoman suzerainty. Likewise angry at the Turkish policy of extermination in Macedonia, the Russophil Bulgarian Premier, after some hesitation, not only responded favorably to the Serbian overture, but proposed even a wider Balkan alliance.

The outbreak and outcome of the war

Within the space of two months in 1912, there was first forged the Serbo-Bulgar pact under the guidance and sponsorship of Russia, with a secret annex providing for a common action, subject to Russian approval, against Turkey, in the event of a threat of war or an outbreak, such as a massacre. This pact was followed by a Greco-Bulgar alliance, supplemented by a military convention, and joined by Montenegro. The resulting Balkan League, disguised as a defensive alliance, was an instrument designed to pounce at an opportune moment on a foe who for centuries had oppressed the subject peoples in the Balkan peninsula and whose expulsion from Europe, once and for all, was presently held to be warranted.[1]

The Serbo-Bulgar pact also provided for the rearrangement of the boundaries of the two countries by an eventual partition of Macedonia on which, as noted above, both countries had respective claims. To enhance the significance of the treaty, not only the ministers, but also the sovereigns of the two states signed it. Apart from aspirations which it entertained with respect to Macedonia, Serbia, which, compared to a relatively aggrandized Bulgaria was a tiny, land-locked state, had high hopes of creating the nucleus of a future Yugoslav Empire.

As if to accommodate the zeal of the partners of the new Balkan coalition, the Ottoman regime was not long in providing the opportunity for these partners to go collectively into offensive action, preceded by the dispatch to Turkey of unacceptable ultimatums. As usual, the opportunity involved the instance of twin massacres the Turks perpetrated in the summer of 1912. One massacre took place in the town of Ishtib, east of Skopje, and the other and major one, in Koçani, southeast of Skopje, the capital city of Kosovo province, in Macedonia. The bloodbaths aroused the people of Bulgaria and galvanized the governments of the Balkan Alliance which, led by tiny Montenegro, one by one proceeded to carry out the projected war against Turkey.

The intercession by the Powers, first through persuasion and subsequently through a warning that no territorial conquest by any of the partners of the coalition would be recognized, was of no avail. For their part, Turkish masses, led by Ittihadist leaders and university students, launched a series of noisy and militant demonstrations in the streets of Istanbul, defiantly insulting their former subjects, chanting in unison, "We want war, war, war." They also shouted such battle cries as "To Sofia, to Sofia," "Down with Greece! Greeks, bow your heads," and some other unprintable epithets at both Greeks and Bulgarians. Equally significant, the university students kept screaming, "Down with Article 23, down with it" when confronting Grand Vizier and veteran army commander Ahmed Muhtar Paşa, in whose presence some of the students even went so far as to cry out the words, "Down with equality ... we don't want equality," referring to the central provision of article 23 of the Berlin Treaty stipulating reforms to benefit the downtrodden Christian subjects. With an inclination to underscore the religious dimensions of the escalating conflicts, other demonstrators shouted out, "The Balkan dogs are trampling on Islam," "They are insulting an empire which is adorned with the laurels of victories amassed in the course of six centuries, and which can crush that pack of dog lice with a single blow of the heel."

As if to publicly confirm the interconnectedness of articles 23 (Macedonia) and 61 (Armenia) of the Berlin Treaty, and their similar, if not identical, ramifications for Turkey, *Tanin*, the semi-official mouthpiece of Ittihad, declared in an editorial:

> Who can guarantee that Article 61 will not follow Article 23, which Article they presently want to resuscitate. Europe's intervention and Europe's desire to control our internal affairs is a warning to us to ponder the fate not only of Rumelia [Macedonia], but also eastern Turkey for it will be impossible to spare eastern Turkey the fate awaiting Rumelia.[2]

Similar meetings and demonstrations were taking place in Sofia, Belgrade, and Athens where bellicosity and clamors for war were no less pronounced. But there was a sense of self-righteousness in these gatherings which Bulgarian Premier I.E. Geshof articulated as follows: "The present war in which the Greeks, Bulgarians, Serbians, Catholic Albanians and Orthodox Montenegrins will fight hand in hand, is not a product of panslavist agitation. It is a crusade against unbearable Turkish tyranny that is exploiting and martyrizing the Christians of the Balkan peninsula."[3]

In less than three weeks that crusade harnessed a series of spectacular military victories, with each of the three major partners of the coalition displaying inordinate martial prowess on the battlefields involved. The redoubtable Ottoman army suffered humiliating defeats which were as unexpected as devastating. The Bulgarians under General Savof scored a series of victories in the battles of Kırkkilise in Thrace, and Luleburgaz, forcing the Turks to full retreat and in the process reaching on the one hand the outskirts of Adrianople (Edirne), and on the other, the gates of Istanbul at Çatalca.

Equally, if not more, successful were the Serbs. On October 18 the Serb King, Peter, issued a proclamation to his troops declaring that the object of the Balkan League was to liberate Macedonia and bring liberty, fraternity, and equality to the Christian and Muslim Serbs as well as Albanians with whom, he added, Serbs had coexisted for 13 centuries. The 150,000 men strong Serbian army was victorious first at Novibazar, out of which district the Turks were cleared. A portion of that army subsequently occupied Pristina. The main part of that army began to march towards Üsküb (Skopje) in Macedonia, the ancient capital of the Serbs. The Turks blocked the way by occupying Kumanovo. There, the two armies met and after three days of fierce fighting (October 22–24, 1912), the Serbs scored a complete victory. Two days later the Turks were forced to yield Üsküb. The triumphant entry in that ancient Serbian capital marked a historical milestone for the Serbs, who, for 500 years, had waited to avenge their defeat at the hands of the Turks in the battle of Kossovo Polye on June 15, 1389. It was a defeat which, for five centuries, had sealed the fate of the Serbs, many of whom afterwards had sought refuge in the mountains of Montenegro to wage war against the Turks throughout the ages, and many more had migrated to Bosnia. In quick succession the Serbs had become the masters of Novibazar, Old Serbia, western Macedonia, and the Albanian coast of Durazzo on the Adriatic.

Similar victories were scored by the Greeks, who, after three days of combat at Yenice, entered Saloniki on November 3, 1912. In the second round of the Balkan war, which started on February 3, 1913, the Bulgarians, aided by the Serbs, finally captured Adrianople, the ancient Ottoman capital. On March 6, the Greeks won a phenomenal victory at Janine;

with the fall of this almost impregnable fortress, 200 guns and the 33,000 soldiers of the garrison there were captured by the Greeks.

The conduct of the Powers in face of these victories of the coalition was significant in several respects, but was critical in one respect, namely, the rise of acute dissension in its ranks and the formation of two types of alignments more or less counterpoised to each other. This splitting fore-shadowed, in a sense, the establishment of the two enemy camps preva-lent at the outbreak of the war, i.e., the Entente Powers, consisting of England, France, and Russia, on the one hand, and the Central Powers, consisting of Germany, Austria, and Italy, on the other. Even though these Powers, especially Austria and Russia, had warned Serbia, Montenegro, Bulgaria, and Greece that they would be denied the right to appropriate the lands they might conquer in the war, they now were in disagreement about this issue. Sympathetic from the very start with the cause of the coalition, Russia already on November 2, 1912, i.e., in the midst of the war, suggested that the conquered territories belonged to the victors by right of occupation and should be partitioned by way of friendly agree-ment among them. British opinion was almost unanimous on the side of the allies of the coalition. Prime Minister Herbert Asquith on November 9 declared that the Powers would recognize accomplished facts and would not oppose the recognition of the territorial changes achieved through military victory.

The Central Powers, on the other hand, demurred and resisted such accommodation. A particular bone of contention was Serbia's retention of Durazzo, which afforded it access to the Adriatic. The Entente Powers were willing to support Serbia's stance but it was opposed by Italy and especially Austria, which considered the Adriatic its sole preserve and was willing to wage war for it. In the interest of an autonomous Albania, not only Serbia but Montenegro was also pressured by Austria to surren-der Scutari (Işkodra), which it had captured during the war.

The Balkan League was formed under the auspices of the Russian Tsar. It essentially revolved around Serbia, which had become Russia's outpost in the Balkans. The League did not last long, however, as the Serbs and Greeks were forced to reunite, this time against Bulgaria which, by twin surprise attacks against Serbia and Greece, had made a mockery of the coalition. Reportedly engineered by Savof, the Bulgarian Commander in Chief, without the knowledge of the Cabinet and Premier Geshof, the initiative backfired at great cost to Bulgaria. This war of par-tition among the former allies lasted one month, June-July 29, 1913.

In the meantime Austria and Russia had resorted to partial mobiliza-tion, with Russia massing troops on the Caucasian frontier and informing Turkey that if the war in the Balkans started again, it could not promise neutrality. Germany sternly let it be known thereupon that an attack on Turkey might trigger an all out European war. One of the consequences of the military defeats sustained by Turkey was that the Central Powers, especially Germany, became most apprehensive about the designs of Russia and its slavic client states in the Balkans.

This is the context in which the Powers, after much haggling, in 1913–1914 combined their influences to persuade Turkey to agree to a set of Armenian reforms for which the Armenians had been clamoring for decades. There were three elements in this undertaking which rendered the ensuing February 8, 1914 Reform Agreement ill-fated. It was initiated by the Russians, the mortal enemies of the Turks. It coincided with one of the worst moments of Turkish-Ottoman history. And finally, the Turks were impelled, if not compelled, by the Powers to accede to it.

The Dissolution of the Eastern Question into the Armenian Question
The accentuation of Armenian vulnerability

As one student of the Young Turks observed, the Albanians, Greeks, and the different Slavic nationalities in the Balkans one by one emancipated themselves from Ottoman dominion, and by 1913 "only the Armenians and Arabs remained" as subject nationalities.[4] In one particular respect the Armenians stood out among all the subject nationalities, such as the Albanians and various Arab groups, the Yemenis, the Syrians, Lebanese, and Jordanians. The Armenians avoided militancy and confrontation, consistently seeking remedies through appeals and pleas, which were always suffused with pledges of unswerving loyalty, while the Balkan nationalities and the Arabs resorted to rebellion to end Ottoman subjugation and attendant repression. For this display of fidelity the Armenians were characterized by Sultan Mahmud II, and subsequently, by Sultan Abdul Hamit, as "the loyal nation" (*milleti sadıka*).[5] Their subsequent transformation from loyal servants of the State into its militant opponents is, however, an example of the futility of entreaties and pleas applied to regimes thriving on oppression and tyranny. The exchange between the Patriarch and the British Ambassador to Turkey in this respect is instructive. It has been described in note 13 of chapter 4, but it bears reintroducing here. In a meeting with British Ambassador Sir Henry Elliot on December 6, 1876, Patriarch Varjabedian, the duly recognized religious head of the Armenians, expressed the hope that the impending Constantinople Conference would not urge the Porte to accord certain privileges to the rebel provinces (Serbs, Bulgars, Montenegrins) and to deny the same to the loyal ones (the Armenians). The Ambassador demurred, saying that the purpose of the Conference was not to scrutinize the entire Administration of Turkey but to secure peace and tranquility in those provinces whose revolts were threatening the general peace. The Patriarch retorted that if rebellion were a prerequisite for enlisting the support of European Powers, there would be no difficulty whatsoever in organizing a movement of that nature.[6] Since the Arabs were far more numerous, inhabited areas which were peripheral to the heartland of the empire, and perhaps most significant, were of Muslim faith, the Turks turned their attention to the Armenians as a residual minority of primary importance. Their catastrophic experiences in the first Balkan war in 1912 not only shocked but also informed them of the potential perils mistreated nationalities could bring about on the empire. As a result of that Balkan war catastrophe, Turkey had lost nearly 70% of its European population, and about 85% of its European territory. The streets, mosques, and other communal places of abode in Istanbul were full of destitute and emaciated Muslims who had fled the war zones, or were dislocated as a result of Greek, Serb, and Bulgar territorial conquests in the former Ottoman provinces in the Balkans. It was against this overall backdrop that the Armenian leadership once more chose to launch inside and outside Turkey its campaign for Armenian reforms, mobilizing prominent diplomats, clergymen, and public figures in Russia and Europe. But, from a Turkish point of view, this was a time of deep mourning, reflection, taking stock and new initiatives for remedies and national redemption.

Halil (Menteşe), the President of the Ottoman Chamber of Deputies (and Foreign Minister in World War I), openly lamented the losses in the Balkans, and in 1914 declared in the Parliament: "I exhort my nation from this eminent podium that it should not forget [the tragedy in the Balkans] (shouts of 'we won't forget').... We have on the other side of our borders brothers to be freed.... Only thus can we protect our future from the dangers of repeating the mistakes which led to our defeats and tragedies."[7]

One major conclusion the Ittihadists derived from this state of affairs was that the renewal of the Armenian pursuit of reforms, if successful, had all the potential of becoming an extension of the Balkan disaster to eastern Turkey, with far graver consequences for the future of Turkey. Abdullah Cevdet, one of the original pillars of Ittihadist ideology, a military physician, a veteran publicist, and an exponent of the drive for Westernization in Turkey, in a statement linked his lamentations for the losses in the Balkans to his apprehensions of greater potential dangers in Asiatic Turkey: "Will these thunderous roars on our European borders, these blows, awaken us?... Don't kid yourself that because of our preoccupations in European Turkey, we should not worry about Anatolia. Anatolia is the well spring of every fibre of our life. It is our heart, head, and the air we breathe."[8]

However implicit, the message contained in this statement is clear: beware of the Armenians and their clamors for reform to be introduced in the heart of our fatherland. For the Turks it was not easy to forget that the Balkan nationalities' attainment of complete freedom and independence was traceable to the rudimentary demands for reform which eventually entailed some form of autonomy. By projecting into future possibilities and probabilities, any kind of autonomy in any scheme of reforms for the Armenians was thus defined by the Ittihadist leaders as a *non plus ultra* for Turkey.

As if to exacerbate the situation, several other factors entered the picture. The resumption of the campaign for Armenian reforms occurred during the critical months in the fall of 1912 when Turkey was suffering setbacks externally, i.e., the Balkan war military defeats, and internally when Ittihad temporarily was forced out of power. Moreover, a number of non-Turkish members of the Ottoman Chamber of Deputies, including Greeks and Armenians, were becoming more vocal about their criticism of Turkish nationality policies in Europe and in Asiatic Turkey. In the meantime, the deposed Sultan Abdul Hamit was chiding the Ittihadist leaders as misguided patriots for allowing non-Muslims such scope for dissidence and opposition in the Ottoman Parliament, thereby critically undermining Turkish national interests. Turkish exacerbation reached its apex through the most crucial factor at work in the entire episode. The Armenian reform movement was spearheaded by the Russians who, reversing their policy of tacit support of the anti-Armenian campaign of Sultan Abdul Hamit at the time of the 1894–96 Armenian massacres, now had become the defenders, if not champions, of the Armenian cause. Through their persistence, and willingness to address the concerns of the Turks, and through the reluctant cooperation of the latter's advocates, the Germans, the Russians finally succeeded in overcoming the obstacles created by Turkish methods of stalling and temporizing. On February 8, 1914, the Armenian Reform Agreement, reflecting a hard won consensus by the Powers, and grudgingly approved by Turkey, was signed in Istanbul as a document of international law, akin to a treaty. The most critical and consequential feature of the Agreement was a provision for foreign Inspectors-General to administer and superintend the reforms, a provision which as much alarmed and offended the Turks as it inspired and relieved the Armenians.[9] But the Turkish intent to derail the implementation of the Agreement was evident in the resentment of many Ittihadist leaders about the collective pressure they felt the Powers brought to bear upon Turkey to sign the Agreement. These Powers had once more succeeded in ironing out and composing their differences through the forging of a more or less united front, mainly through the active engagement of Russia and Germany, and in impelling Turkey to accommodate. The lasting effects of this resentment were manifest at the outbreak of World War I when several Ittihadist leaders, including party boss Talât, openly berated and vilified the Armenian leaders for resuscitating the reform issue at the most painful and vulnerable moment of Turkish history; the resentment gave way to rage when these same Ittihadists made reference to the fact that the Armenians had dared to seek and obtain foreign intervention on their behalf. The more blunt of these Ittihadists are reported to have gleefully reminded some of the Armenian leaders on their way to liquidation during the World War I genocide that "This is our moment of settling scores" (*Şimdi intikam zamanıdır*).[10]

The adoption of a radical Turkish ideology

Parallel to the projections of a potential Armenian threat to the integrity of the Turkish state, the Young Turk Ittihadists embarked upon a comprehensive program of national renewal and political reorientation. One aspect of this undertaking was the vehemence with which Ittihad proceeded to deal with dissidents from within and opponents from without the party. There was a prevailing sense among the party leaders that the recent misfortunes befalling Turkey were largely due to their "mistake" of having allowed their political and military antagonists to challenge the party and its leaders. Several prominent party members, bitterly opposed to the party, had resigned from it to form the Freedom and Accord party (*Hürriyet ve Itilâf*) in November 1911, and were agitating for the downfall of Ittihad. This new party of liberals included in its ranks non-Muslims, especially Armenians, whose essential common objective was the overthrow of the Ittihadist regime.

In addition, there was the active opposition of the Savior Officers (*Halâskar*) group, which had close ties to the above mentioned Freedom and Accord party. Their objective was the demolition of the Ittihadist power structure, the disengagement of military officers from the fetters of politics, and the restoration of a "legal government." Through a variety of pressures, which culminated in an ultimatum demanding the dissolution of the Ottoman Parliament, they managed to oust Ittihad from power in July 1912. These initiatives coincided with the re-eruption of the Macedonian crisis and the subsequent outbreak of the Balkan war, giving rise to a general conviction that the rift among the Turkish military, pitting Ittihadist against anti-Ittihadist officers, in no small way contributed to the defeats the Ottoman army suffered in that war.

The Ittihadist program of national renewal essentially aimed at discarding as useless, and even as pernicious, the traditional concept of multi-ethnic Ottomanism based on the premise of harmony among the various nationalities. This concept was predicated upon the dual assumptions that the Turks would be first among the equals, thus maintaining their predominance, and that the other ethnic elements would in due course of time integrate themselves in the Ottoman system, relinquishing most of their ethnic ties, with the temporary exception of their bonds to various religions. These assumptions proved not only illusory but ill-advised inasmuch as they implied eventual assimilation—a condition that was anathema to these nationalities, including the Armenians. Ottomanism was therefore to be dismantled and replaced by a narrowly conceived nationalism, glorifying Turkism and seeking the Turkification of the entire fabric of Ottoman society. With this turn of events the liberal ideals of the Young Turk Ittihadist revolution were doomed to being relinquished, if not repudiated.

The main instrument for this radical change was the Ittihadist party, relying on its organization and hierarchy of leadership, including its covert structures. Top priority was given to the task of creating a vast network of party branches in the provinces to be directed by trusted party loyalists. They were to be entrusted with party secrets and the execution of related party directives—independent from and sometimes in contradiction of officially stated policies. These measures of party penetration and expansion were applied most resolutely in those provinces of Anatolia and eastern Turkey in which there were large clusters of Armenian populations. As it turned out, the principal aim of the entire undertaking was to gradually gain control over these populations, emasculate them further through legal-political confinements, and create a general atmosphere of anti-Armenianism among the Muslim multitudes of these provinces. In the secret August 6, 1910 speech of Talât, alluded to above, there was already a provision made for this type of party build-up and secrecy of certain party designs about which even regular civilian functionaries in the Ottoman provincial administration were to be kept incognito.[11]

Consistent with the thrust of these administrative initiatives Ittihad, in the very midst of Turkish military reverses in the 1912 Balkan war, launched a comprehensive program of indoctrination and para-military training of Turkish youth. There was a new mood of nationalism and militancy, which Ittihad tried to inculcate in the young generation committed to its care. The Association for the Promotion of Turkish Strength (*Türk Gücu Cemiyeti*), established in 1913, in its No. 1 statute speaks of the need for "military training [of the youth] to enable the nation to become again a warrior (*silahşor*) nation," in order to avert "the decay of the Turkish race" (*Türk ırkı inhitata*). There were additionally a number of Ottoman youth groups which, under the direction of the War Ministry, were to be prepared "for the defense of the fatherland" and for which purpose "the ministry is to supply, free of charge, rifles, bullets, and ammunition."[12]

These activities were directed by Ittihadist War Minister Enver and chief Ittihadist idealogue Ziya Gökalp. Both leaders were indicted by the postwar Turkish Military Tribunal investigating the wartime Armenian massacres, with Enver having been sentenced to death. The League for National Defense (*Müdafaa-i Milliye Cemiyeti*), likewise established in the midst of the Balkan war, had the mission to prepare the Turks for combat despite its profession of such other ancillary ends as peace, prosperity, and happiness, and a lack of interest in political and party involvements. These professions were belied by the subsequent activities of the League. Equally important, the founders of the League included the top leadership stratum of Ittihad, who at the same time were Cabinet Ministers, namely, Interior Minister Talât, War Minister Enver, Foreign Minister Said Halim, Marine Minister Cemal and Justice Minister Ibrahim.[13]

The preparatory military initiatives

Given the preeminent role of military officers in the outbreak of the Ittihadist revolution and the general sway of militarism in the unfolding of the career of the Ottoman Empire, the military, in launching these initiatives, functioned as the backbone of the party organization. As a first step, the officer corps of the armed forces were purged inexorably. Ittihadist War Minister Enver abruptly dismissed altogether 1,100 officers of all ranks, including generals, many of whom were considered less than loyal to or outright opponents of Ittihad.[14] Concomitantly, the same War Minister promoted trusted young Ittihadist officers, including himself, to much higher ranks than normal procedure would allow. The net result of these undertakings was the optimal politicization of the officer corps and the swift ascendancy in it of Ittihadist zealots of all ranks.

Under the auspices of still the same War Minister, and in close cooperation with the Supreme Directorate of the party, led by party boss Talât, the Turks reactivated and enlarged the Special Organization. A quasi-military outfit, led by regular army officers, this organization in its nuclear form was already active in the 1913 second Balkan War, conducting guerilla operations, mainly against the Bulgarians. As publicly stated, a vital part of its assigned task was surveillance and "neutralization" of internal foes. But its secret mission was to liquidate at the first opportunity the discordant and "alien" minorities, defined as a major threat to Turkish national security, as evidenced later in the war with respect to the treatment of the Armenians, who proved to be the prime target heading the list of such minorities.

The party directorate, in close cooperation with the Security Office (*Emniyeti Umumiye*) of the Interior Ministry, set up in the General Directorate of Turkish Police a special department of surveillance and intelligence where secret files were compiled on Armenian clerical, political, and educational leaders as well as journalists and intellectuals as warrants for future action against them.

A number of members of the League of National Defense enrolled in the ranks of the Special Organization which, as noted above, served as the principal instrument in the implementation of the Armenian genocide. These Special Organization contingents were led by such highly committed and prominent Ittihadist officers as Yakub Cemil, Halil (Kut) and Yenibahçeli Nail, who were heavily implicated in the direction of the massacres against the Armenians. They simply transferred the skills they had acquired as guerilla leaders in the Balkans[15] to their new field of operations involving the extermination of the bulk of the Armenian population in Turkey during World War I.

The successful achievement of that objective was in tune with the objectives of the new nationalism of the Ittihadists, which centered on the goal of radically restructuring Ottoman society by way of converting a heterogeneous social system into a more or less homogeneous one, i.e., optimal Turkification of a residual empire.

In brief, the ejection from the Balkan peninsula, attended by enormous human and material losses, not only jolted the Turks, shaking their faith in their long cherished martial prowess, but also stunned the Ittihadist leadership. The Armenian attempt to capitalize on this debilitating debacle by reviving the dormant Armenian Reforms issue, from a Turkish point of view was nothing but a provocative act which could serve no other purpose than further aggravate the plight of the state. The radical wing of the Ittihadist party, led by the two seemingly all-powerful physician-politicians, Drs. Nazım and Şakir, furtively supported by Ziya Gökalp, the party's ideological guru, proceeded to exploit this new development to gain control of the Central Committee that later, during World War I, operated as a supreme directorate, a kind of party *politburo*. It was this body that set the standards of a new Armenian policy, which was geared to the objective of achieving a radical solution to the lingering and troublesome Armenian Question. The discussion below will attempt to demonstrate that this objective was achieved, as that solution proved to be the Turkish variant of a Final Solution.

Two episodes of large scale massacres emerge here as consequences of abortive reform acts: 1) the 1878 Berlin Treaty (article 61) and the Abdul Hamit-era massacres; 2) the February 1914 Agreement and the 1915 genocide. In his massive volume, dealing with the latter, Toynbee recognized these interconnections. He wrote:

> The deportations of 1915 followed as inexorably from the Balkan War and the Project [Agreement] of 1914 as the massacres of 1895–6 had followed from the Russian War and the Project of 1878 [Berlin Treaty].[16]

In both instances the reform projects, elaborated in the wake of major Turkish military defeats, were more or less imposed upon the Turks by the same Powers one way or other identified with the genesis of the ideals of humanitarian intervention. Thus, humanitarian intervention in the last analysis paradoxically emerges as a catalyst for the eruption of types and scales of violence manifesting "man's inhumanity to man."

Notes to Chapter 11

1. On the formation of the Balkan League and the associated wars see G.P. Gooch, *History of Modern Europe, 1878–1919* (New York, 1923), 500–510; A.J. Grant and H. Temper-

ley, *Europe in the Nineteenth and Twentieth Centuries (1789–1950)*, 6th ed., (London, 1962), 375–380; C. Seymour, *The Diplomatic Background of the War 1870–1914*, (New Haven, 1927), 221–239; R. Sontag, *European Diplomatic History 1871–1932*, (New York, 1933), 176–182; W.S. Davis, *The Roots of the War*, (New York, 1918), 426–443.

2. A. Andonian, *Untartzag Badmoutiun Balkanian Baderazmeen* (Comprehensive History of the Balkan War) vol. 3 (Istanbul, 1912), 499. There was bitter irony in these humiliating defeats despite confidence implicit in the discharge of invectives and diatribes the Ittihadists and their followers displayed in the streets of Istanbul prior to the outbreak of the war. In commenting on this irony, the Turkish commander of the 2nd Eastern Army participating in the 1912 Balkan War remarked: "God punished us for our haughtiness and arrogance." Mahmud Muhtar Paşa, *Meine Führung im Balkankrieg 1912*. 5th ed,., Imhoff Pascha trans. (Berlin, 1913), 184.

3. *Ibid.*, Andonian, 503.

4. F. Ahmad, *The Young Turks*, (Oxford, 1969), 154.

5. Cemal Kutay, *Talât Paşanın Gurbet Hatıraları* (The Memoirs of Talât Paşa in Exile). According to an account, provided by Talât, the term was coined by Sultan Mahmud II (1808–1839), vol. 3, 115–6. The adoption of the term, for a while at least, by Sultan Abdul Hamit (1876–1909), is indicated in vol. 2, 587. Both volumes published in (Istanbul, 1983).

6. FO 424/46, Doc. No. 336, December 7, 1876 (Elliot's communication to British Foreign Minister Lord Derby).

7. T. Z. Tunaya, *Türkiyede Siyasal Partiler* (The Political Parties in Turkey), 2nd enlarged edition, vol. 3 (Istanbul, 1984), 465.

8. *Ibid.*, 463.

9. W. J. van der Dussen, "The Westenenk File. The Question of Armenian Reforms in 1913–1914," *Armenian Review* 39, 1 (1986): 1–89.

10. The testimony of Ottoman Civil Inspector Mihran Boyadjian, the French version of which is in *Renaissance*, June 25, 1919. In his memoirs Ittihadist leader Halil Menteşe discloses that before the Powers began to pressure Turkey to revive and reconsider the Armenian Reforms issue, he himself urged Grand Vizier Mahmud Şevket Paşa to take the initiative. Halil did this upon his return from Paris, where French Socialist leader and Deputy Jean Jaurés had apprised him of the sway of anti-turkish opinions in Europe with respect to the Turko-Armenian conflict. The Grand Vizier on April 2/15, 1913 had decided to take up the issue and accordingly launched, albeit futilely, a program which was to enlist the help of Great Britain in handling the matter of effecting a new reform scheme. Lest Russia be disturbed by such British involvement, Great Britain declined. *Halil Menteşénin Anıları* (Istanbul, 1986), 37.

11. See Chapter 10, n. 3.

12. Tunaya, [n. 7] 296.

13. *Ibid.*, 294–95.

14. L. von Sanders, *Five Years in Turkey* (Annapolis, 1927), 8.

15. Halil Paşa, *Ittihad ve Terakkiden Cumhuriyete: Bitmeyen Savaş* (From Ittihad ve Terakki to the Republic: The Unending Fight) (Istanbul, 1972), 125; Tunaya, [n. 7] 123, 275, 294. See also Ihsan Birinci, "Cemiyet ve Çeteler" (Ittihad party and the Brigands), *Hayat* 2 (October 1, 1971): 33. On p. 29 the author admits that one of the principal missions of the Special Organization was to carry out the deportation scheme.

16. J. Viscount Bryce, *The Treatment of Armenians in the Ottoman Empire, 1915–16* (compiled by Arnold Toynbee, British Governmental Document Miscellaneous no. 31) (London, 1916), 636.

Part VI

THE INITIATION AND CONSUMMATION OF THE GENOCIDE UNDER COVER OF THE FIRST WORLD WAR

A Note on the Limitations of International Law Relative to the Problem of Impunity

Although the Armenian massacres preceding World War I were significant in many respects, they underscored two especially important facts. First, the massacres were not subjected to the test of criminal proceedings, either nationally or internationally; the resulting impunity accorded the perpetrators became a form of negative reward. Second, no deterrence materialized in anticipation of the genocide of 1915. Current international law on genocide revolves around these twin principles of prevention and punishment. The examination of the special case of the Armenian Genocide, in which both of these principles failed to operate, brings into question the adequacy of international law and the efficacy of international efforts to deter genocide.

The classification of genocide as a crime under international law in the U.N. Convention Against Genocide poses a number of difficulties in current international jurisprudence, where the principle of state sovereignty remains powerful. While a variety of new principles, doctrines, conventions, and covenants have emerged in the post-Nuremberg period and provided some help in this area, these difficulties remain substantial. Specifically, some of the obstacles to countering genocide under international law include:

a) The fact that international law has been largely confined to the level of declaratory principles. As Cardozo explained: "International law ... has at times ... a twilight existence during which it is hardly distinguishable from morality or justice, until at length the imprimatur of a court attests its jural quality." New Jersey v. Delaware, 291 U.S. 361, 383 (1934);

b) The uncertainties attending the "self-executing" provisions in certain treaties, which have somewhat diminished the usefulness of these treaties as legally binding instruments in municipal courts;

c) The fact that treaties, lacking the force of legislation, often cannot effectively specify a crime, assign jurisdiction, or provide the machinery for the administration of punitive justice;

d) The absence in international law of criminal statutes and jurisdiction;

e) The lack of international criminal courts competent to deal with offenders.

As indicated above, however, the major impediment to successful prevention or punishment of genocide under international law are the principles of state sovereignty and *raison d'état*. These principles allow a state substantial latitude in the treatment of its own subjects and substantial immunity from extra- or supra-national jurisdiction over such actions. Lauterpacht succinctly spelled out the abuses that can emerge from this system, abuses which are by no means obsolete in our times. These abuses involve the "cruder forms of treacherous violence, brazen perfidy, and outright deceit."[1] Nor is the U.N. exempt from the propensity to countenance such abuses. See Kuper's observation on this issue (Introduction n. 15).

It is only recently that the crime of genocide has even been considered a crime under international law. As Willis states:

> Not until 1948 would genocide ... be clearly defined as an international crime, and in 1919 adherence to time-honored notions of sovereignty placed limitations upon the scope of traditional laws and customs of war. The Hague conventions ... [did not deal] with a state's treatment of its own citizens .... . From this perspective, Turkish action against Armenians was an internal matter, not subject to the jurisdiction of another government.[2]

As indicated in this study, this deference to state sovereignty was ever-present in the international reaction to the Armenian genocide. See the exchange between U.S. Secretary of State Lansing and President Wilson during World War I. (See Introduction, n. 14).

Notes to Part VI

1. Lauterpacht, "The Grotian Tradition in International Law," in *International Law: A Contemporary Perspective*, (R. Falk., F. Kratochwil & S. Mendlowitz, eds. Boulder, CO, 1985), 21; *see also* Moore, "Law and National Security," in *ibid.*, 47–58 (discussion of legal ramifications of national security problems with particular emphasis on U.S. government policies).
2. J. Willis, *Prologue to Nuremberg: The Politics and Diplomacy of Punishing War Criminals of the First World War*, (Westport, CT, 1982), 157.

Chapter 12

The Legal-Political Context
of the Initiation

Evidence suggests that Turkey's entry into World War I was substantially influenced by a desire to create a suitable opportunity to resolve once and for all certain lingering domestic conflicts. The recent literature analyzing the problems of genocide is replete with discussions recognizing this historical fact. Several of these discussions singled out the 1894–96 Abdul Hamit-era massacres as a historical antecedent of contemporary issues of genocide, while others focus on the World War I massacres.[1]

The Alliance with Imperial Germany and the Opportunity Factor

When World War I broke out in July 1914, Turkey was neither prepared militarily nor disposed to commit itself instantly and unconditionally to the camp of the Central Powers led by Imperial Germany. But sympathies for Germany among the most powerful leaders of Ittihad, especially War Minister Enver and some of his close associates in the ministry, as well as Dr. Nazım, the shadowy arch power-wielder in the supreme directorate of the party, were omnipresent. Following the declaration of "holy war" against the "infidel" Allies (November 14, 1914), for example, the large crowd proceeded to the German Embassy from the balcony of which Dr. Nazım, consistent with his predilections for Kaiser's Germany, gave a speech depicting Germany as the genuine friend of the three hundred million Muslims for whom the Kaiser had sworn his allegiance. Dr. Nazım had already dsplayed his veneration for Germany, and especially for the Kaiser, at the 1910 annual congress of the Ittihad party (October

31/November 1). His cohort, Dr. Şakir, was in the same frame of mind. Even in the throes of defeat, Şakir in February 1916, when Erzurum, the strategic fortress city, was about to be captured by the Russians, haughtily declared to Stapleton, Acting American consul at Erzurum: "It is imperative that from Istanbul to India and China there be only one unitary Muslim population with Syria serving as a nexus between the Muhammedan worlds of Asia and Africa. This vast project will be accomplished through the scientific genius and organizational talent of the Germans and the valiant arm of the Turks."[2] Several factors additionally favored the adoption of a pro-German Turkish stance. Foremost among these was the German Emperor Wilhelm II's legacy of diplomatic support of the regime of Sultan Abdul Hamit at a time when most of the other Powers of the Concert of Europe were aghast at the wholesale Armenian massacres carried out under the aegis of that regime which they had condemned. Moreover, it was an Ottoman tradition to entrust the reorganization and rebuilding of the Ottoman Army mainly to German officers, among whom Moltke and Goltz stand out. Perhaps most important, the Ittihadists' first major move, after they overthrew the government of their opponents in January 1913, was to seek German military assistance in reorganizing once more the Ottoman Army, then directly under the control of Enver. Enver's sympathies for the Germans bordered on exaltation of Germany as a formidable military machine, which he had an opportunity to observe and assess when serving in Berlin twice as Turkish Military Attaché prior to World War I. The arrival in the Ottoman capital in December 1913 of a German Military Mission to Turkey, following the signing of a contract, more or less foreshadowed the Turkish intent to forge a partnership with Germany. That partnership materialized in fact when, on August 2, 1914, following a series of stringent negotiations, whereby the Turks secured German commitments for massive monetary and other types of economic help to Turkey, the secret Turko-German political and military alliance was signed.[3] It was followed by a similar alliance with Austria.

The dividends of these twin alliances for the unfolding of Turkish designs and aspirations were multifarious. First and foremost, Germany now offered a protective shield to Ittihad's wartime plans. For the Young Turk Ittihadist leaders that alliance was to serve as a "shield" (*Schutz*) for their own overt and covert designs. In a report marked "very confidential" (*streng vertraulich*), the Austrian Ambassador on April 8, 1916, informed Burian, his Foreign Minister in Vienna, that the Turks were "exploiting" the Alliance as a "prop" (*Stütze*) to "proceed in the severest manner" against the Armenians.[4] In a July 27, 1915, "confidential" report, Aleppo's German consul Rössler complained to his Chancellor in Berlin, Hollweg, that the Turks in fact were bent on "resolving the Armenian Question during the war as the government is utilizing the alliance with the Central Powers for this purpose." Accusing the Ittihadist power-wielders of the crime of "the ruination (*Untergang*) of hecatombs of innocent people" he declared them "unworthy" (*unwürdig*) of an alliance with Germany.[5] Internally, the centerpiece of these plans was the homogenizing of the ethnic make-up of what was left of the Ottoman empire. As events later were to demonstrate, by explicit and strict orders from the German High Command in Berlin, the multitudes of German officers affiliated with the German Military Mission to Turkey were forbidden to intervene in the process of the extermination of the Armenian population of the empire. This policy of non-intervention was approved at the highest level of the German government and sanctioned by the Kaiser. As disclosed in an October 2, 1919, personal letter by General Bronsart von Schellendorf, the German emperor enjoined a group of high ranking German officers, who were received in audience by him on the eve of their departure to Turkey as members of the German Military Mission to Turkey, "not to interfere in Turkey's internal affairs." General Bronsart added that this prohibition extended to "the Armenian Question.[6] Furthermore, Maximillian Harden, the noted publisher and editor of the German weekly *Die Zukunft*, levelled a scathing criticism against the Imperial German government for "tolerating and condoning this Turkish affront, this most infamous instance of vileness in history [through which] nearly 1.5 million Armenians were slaughtered." In this connection he made the following disclosure in an editorial: "I personally heard a minion of the Kaiser ... [at a banquet] tell in a low voice the Director of the Bureau of Wartime Press 'I just came from the Supreme Headquarters where I had an audience with His Majesty. In accord with the High Command, it has been decided that nothing will be said in the press about the Armenian issue.'"[7] The same prohibition applied to the thousands of other German officers assisting in the Turkish war effort, whether as commanders in combat, or as administrative support personnel. The following account by Ludwig Schraundenbach, the commander of 14th Ottoman Infantry Division, epitomizes the case. It depicts the fate of Armenians who supposedly were being driven to Mesopotamia for purposes of temporary wartime "relocation." The narration belongs to Lieutenant Pfeifer, the commander of a 300-man strong motorized column, who was a witness to the incidents described. His journal entry on January 28, 1917, reads: "Turkish officers and gendarmes each evening were picking out dozens of Armenian men from the ranks of the deportees and were using them as targets for practice games (*auf sie ein Scheibenschiessen veranstaltete*)."[8]However, the German commander had received specific instructions not to discuss the case of the Armenians. "It was one of the very few instructions ... the Armenian Question was to be treated as *noli me tangere*" (touch me not).[9]

This directive of the German emperor was adopted as a general rule by the Supreme Board of Censorship of the Wartime Press (*Obere Zensur-Stelle des Kriegspresseamtes*), an outfit comprising the representatives of the Foreign Ministry, the General Staff, the High Command, and the Prussian Ministry of Defense. In a press conference on October 7, 1915, the members of the German press were exhorted as follows: "Our friendly relations with Turkey ought not only not to be endangered through an involvement in such administrative matters, but in the present, difficult moment even it ought not to be examined. Therefore, for the time being it is your duty to remain silent."[10] In another conference on December 23, 1915, the same press people were told: "It is better to remain silent over the Armenian Question. The conduct of the Turkish power-wielders in this Question is not particularly praiseworthy."[11] This order was rationalized by twin arguments. First, unconditional support of the Turkish ally for the sake of a common victory in a war in which the issue was survival, was to be regarded as a matter that takes precedence over everything else. Second, Germany can ill-afford to ignore "Turkish sensitivities" with regard to the Armenian issue. In fact, in a lengthy report to Berlin, German Ambassador Hans Freiherr von Wangenheim, on April 15, 1915 declared that, by intervening in "a hopeless case *(aussichtslose Sache)*, we may jeopardize interests which are more important and crucial for us."[12]

Apart from these attitudes of indulging the Turks and thereby granting them a laissez faire license, German intelligence operatives helped the Ittihadists to set up a surveillance bureau within the General Police Directorate in the Ottoman capital. Operating in close association with The Political Section *(Kısmı Siyasi)*, which represented one of the three branches of the Directorate [the other two were called Administrative *(Idare)* and Legal *(Adli)*], that bureau extended its surveillance to all major centers of Armenian political activity within and without Turkey, including the Armenian Patriarchate in Istanbul, political parties in Egypt, and anti-Ittihadist opponents in Paris.[13] As noted above, the purpose was to prepare lists and dossiers on Armenian community leaders to be treated as potential foes of Turkey.[14] Furthermore, encouraged by the Germans, War Minister Enver reactivated and expanded the residual Special Organization *(Teşkilatı Mahsusa)* as an instrument of wartime agitation, sabotage, and murder, within and without Turkey.[15] According to the candid account of a Turkish author familiar with the operational plans of that organization, one of its missions was the execution of the Armenian "deportations."[16]

Thus, taking advantage of the general crisis generated by the outbreak of the war in July 1914, the mobilization in the wake of the signing of the Turko-German alliance, and the state of siege and the corollary martial law, the Turkish authorities proceeded to prepare the ground for the final reckoning with the Armenians while furiously preparing themselves for preemptive war. The opportunity was not only at hand, but it was considerably maximized.

External War as A Crucible for Targeting the "Internal Foe"

Vice-Field Marshal Pomiankowski, the Austrian Military Plenipotentiary attached to the Ottoman General Headquarters during the War, alluded in his memoirs to the unabating antagonism between the Muslims and the non-Muslim nationalities. He said that since 1909, up to the end of the war "I had ample opportunity to get to know the land and the people of Turkey. During the war, however, I was from start to finish eyewitness of practically all the decisions and activities of the Turkish government." Referring to "the spontaneous utterances of many intelligent Turks," Pomiankowski conveyed their view that these conquered people ought to have been forcibly converted into Muslims, or "ought to have been exterminated *(ausrotten)*" long ago. His conclusion is noteworthy:

> In this sense there is no doubt that the Young Turk government already before the war had decided to utilize the next opportunity for rectifying at least in part this mistake ... . It is also very probable that this consideration, i.e., the intent, had a very important influence upon the decisions of the Ottoman government relative to joining the Central Powers, and upon the determination of the exact time of their intervening in the war.[17]

Ambassador Morgenthau, whose contacts with high-ranking Young Turk officials were frequent and intimate, was even more explicit in this regard:

> The conditions of the war gave to the Turkish Government its longed-for opportunity to lay hold of the Armenians ... . They criticized their ancestors for neglecting to destroy or convert the Christian races to Mohammedanism at the time when they first subjugated them. Now ... they thought the time opportune to make good the oversight of their ancestors in the 15th century. They concluded that once they had carried out their plan, the Great Powers would find themselves before an accomplished fact and that their crime would be condoned, as was done in the case of the massacres of 1895–96, when the Great Powers did not even reprimand the Sultan.[18]

Morgenthau's opinion was unequivocally confirmed by the Young Turk party leader Talât, one of his chief sources in Turkish government circles. Talât told Dr. Mordtman, the man in charge of the Armenian desk and the dragoman at the German Embassy at Istanbul, that Turkey was "intent on taking advantage of the war in order to thoroughly liquidate its internal foes, i.e., the indigenous Christians, without being thereby disturbed by foreign intervention."[19] In a joint memorandum to Berlin requesting the removal of German Ambassador Metternich, on account of the envoy's unceasing efforts to intercede on behalf of the Armenians, Talât (along with war lord Enver) re-emphasized this point: "the work must be done *now;* after the war it will be too late."[20]

The observations of two prominent German experts also merit special attention. In explaining Turkey's motivation for entering World War I on the side of Germany, K. Ziemke, a renowned German political scientist, described Turkey's desire to extricate itself from the bondage of the Armenian Reform Agreement of January 26/February 8, 1914, an agreement initiated in the wake of the 1912 Balkan war, as a contributing factor. He in fact recognized the massacre and destruction of "one million Armenians" during that war as "the radical solution" of the Armenian question delivering Turkey from the burden of all future vexations; by so doing the Turkish Government eliminated the conditions for future reform projects and the allied pressures.[21] More significantly, a German officer serving as Vice Consul of Erzurum (where a large Armenian population was destroyed) informed Berlin that "the Armenian question which for decades occupied the attention of Europe's diplomats is to be solved in the course of the present war ... . [M]easures undertaken by the Turkish government ... are tantamount to the total destruction of the Armenians."[22]

This view is further corroborated by sources within the Ittihadist regime itself. Cemal Paşa, who served both as a member of the Young Turk triumvirate running the Ittihadist regime between 1908–18 and also as the Commander of the Fourth Army and Marine Minister during the war, states in his memoirs that, "our sole objective (*bizim yegâne gayemiz*) was to free ourselves from all the measures [imposed upon us] in this war and which constituted a blow to our internal independence."[23] These shackles involved the international stipulations on the autonomy of Lebanon, and the Armenian reform agreement signed on February 8, 1914 between Turkey and Russia, with the concurrence of the other Powers. As Cemal stated, "We wanted to tear up that Agreement."[24] Enver, also a member of the ruling Ittihad triumvirate, likewise denounced the reforms stipulated by the international agreement of February 8, 1914. During an exchange on August 6, 1915 with Hans Humann (German naval attaché and Enver's childhood friend), the Minister admitted that the main rationale of the anti-Armenian measures was "the total elimination of any basis" for future interventions by the Powers on behalf of the Armenians.[25] As a departmental head in the Turkish Justice Ministry declared, "There is no room for Armenians and Turks in our state, and it would be irresponsible and thoughtless for us if we didn't take advantage of this opportunity [afforded by the war] to do away with [the Armenians] thoroughly."[26]

All these assertions, allegations and attributions are confirmed, however cautiously, within the framework of a set of memoirs posthumously edited and published in Istanbul on behalf of Talât. In them the Ittihadist boss indicates that his support of Enver's plan to intervene in the war on the side of the Central Powers, led by Germany, was strongly prompted by a sense of urgency, put forth by Enver, about the perils issuing from the perceived disloyalty of non-Muslims, whom they branded as the internal enemy. They had to be dealt with. The main target was, of course, the Armenians. Talât goes on to indicate that in order to facilitate the elimination of that peril, they decided to suspend the Parliament, after which he railroaded through the Cabinet the decree of deportation.[27] As he, Talât, explicity stated to German Ambassador Wangenheim, the Ittihadists "were getting rid of the Armenian" because it was necessary to end "the presence in our midst of an internal enemy."[28]

Notes to Chapter 12

1. See A. Jacoby, "Genocide," *Schweizerische Zeitschrift für Strassrecht* 4 (*Revue Penale Suisse* 4) (1949): 472; Cervantes Rio, "Etude sur l'Article 175 du Code Penal Mexicain 'Genocide,'" *Etudes Internationales de Psycho-Sociologie Criminelle* 16–17 (1969): 52. See A. Pflanzer, *Le Crime de Genocide*, 15, 18, 20 (St. Gallen, Switzerland, 1956); The United Nations War Crimes Commission, *History of the United Nations War Crimes Commission and the Development of the Laws of War*, 35, 45 (1948) [hereinafter *War Crimes Commission*]; S. Toriguian, *The Armenian Question and International Law* (2nd ed. 1988); Bassiouni, "International Law and the Holocaust," *Case W. International Law Journal*, 9 (1979): 210; A.K. Kuhn, "The Genocide Convention and State Rights," *American Journal of International Law* 43(1948):501; R. Lemkin, "Genocide: A New International Crime: Punishment and Prevention," *Revue Internationale de Droit Pénal*, 10 (1946): 367; E. Schwelb, "Crimes Against Humanity," *British Year Book of International Law* 1946: 181–82, 198; K. Stillschweig, "Das Abkommen zur Bekämpfung von Genocide," *Die Friedenswarte Für Zwischenstaatliche Organisation*, 3 (1949): 97, 99.

2. Nazım's speech was reported in *Deutsche Tageszeitung*, November 16, 1914. His words of veneration for Germany and the Kaiser are mentioned in the Ittihad Congress of 1910 and in the September 14, 1910 report of Dr. Schwörbel, German consul at Saloniki. See A.A. Türkei 158/11, A15682. Dr. Şakir's statement is in J. de Morgan, *Contre les barbares de l'Orient* (Paris, 1918), 188.

3. For a detailed discussion of the circumstances under which this pact was signed see Ulrich Trumpener, *Germany and the Ottoman Empire, 1914–1918.* (Princeton, NJ, 1968, chapter 2, 21–61; Y. H. Bayur, *Türk Inkilâbı Tarihi* (The History of the Turkish Revolution) vol. 2, Part 4 (Ankara, 1952), 629–647. For the general political developments leading to the signing of the treaty of alliance see Frank G. Weber, *Eagles on the Crescent* (Ithaca, NY, 1970), chapters 1 and 2, 5–16, 17–58.

4. *Austrian Foreign Ministry Archives* (*DAA* henceforth), Political Department (PA), XII (Türkei), File (*Karton*) 218, or XII Türkei/210, No. 28/P.A.

5. *German Foreign Ministry Archives* (Bonn). (*A. A.* henceforth). Türkei 183/38, A23991.

6. A.A. Göppert Papers, VI/1, p. 3 of the General's 7-page letter to Dr. Karl Axenfeld, a leader in the German missionary movement.

7. Maximillian Harden. "Zwischen Ost und West. Armenien in Moabit" *Die Zukunft*, 29, 37 (11 June, 1921): 300–301.

8. Ludwig Schraudenbach, *Muharebe* (War) (Berlin, 1924), 315. This form of atrocity was confirmed by a Turkish grocer who after the war had migrated and settled in Portland, Maine, U.S.A. As recounted to his Irish-American friend, this is what he personally experienced during the World War I Armenian genocide. "As a young soldier in the Turkish army he was part of a unit escorting a large group of Armenians into the countryside where they were to be left to die of starvation. At a pause in the march, he told me, an officer in his company walked over to him and told him and his companions to go into the group and bayonet some of them for practice, since they were going to die anyway. 'God help me', he said almost in tears, 'I did.'" William J. McLaughlin, *Boston Globe*, 18 September, 1987. Schraudenbach's book of recollections is full of narrations

of similar acts of atrocities which evoked in him images of "Dante's Inferno," he said
(p. 345). Referring to Salihzeki, the governor of the district of Der Zor in the desert,
who "greeted us very politely and was wearing elegant European clothes," the author
states that "shocking atrocities" (*haarsträubende Greuel*) were perpetrated in that
region, including "the tying of the Armenian children between wooden boards and setting them on fire" (pp. 351–52).

9. *Ibid.*, 147.

10. Kurt Mühsam, *Wie Wir Belogen Wurden. Die Amtliche Irreführung des deutschen Volkes*
(How we Were Deceived. The Official Acts of Misleading the German People)
(Münich, 1918), 76. The practice of this censorship was evidently extended to foreign
journalists as well. In his memoirs the War Correspondent of the Associated press in
Constantinople describes how the German Embassy refused to help him relay his
wartime report on the Armenian massacres to his bureau chief in Berlin. George A
Shriner, *From Berlin to Bagdad* (New York, 1918), 333.

11. *Ibid.*, Mühsam, 13, 79.

12. A. A. Türkei 183/36, A13922.

13. This highly sensitive information was revealed in the post-war memoirs of an Armenian police lieutenant who early in February 1915 was recruited by the Turkish Security
and Intelligence Bureau (*Emniyeti Umumiye*) to help round up the members of the
Armenian intelligentsia of Turkey by way of compiling the requisite lists; he later
assisted the Turkish police in tracking down those who had managed to evade it and
who were in hiding. Haroutiun Mugurditchian, "Kaghdniknerou Gudzigu" (The Thread
of the Secrets) *Hairenik* (an Armenian daily published by the author during the
Armistice for a very short period in Istanbul). Instalments Nos. 1 and 2, October
28/November 10, and October 30/November 12, 1918, issues.

14. Special attention was paid to the members of the Ottoman Chamber of Deputies, some
of whom reportedly were observed of having visited the Russian Embassy in Istanbul.
Fethi Okyar, *Üç Devirde Bir Adam* (A Man of Three Eras) C. Kutay ed., (Istanbul,
1980), 106, n. 1; Cemal Kutay, *Talât Paşanın Gurbet Hatıraları* (The Memoirs of Talât
Paşa in Exile) vol. 2(Istanbul, 1983), 523, 906–07.

15. Doğan Avcıoğlu, *Milli Kurtuluş Tarihi* (History of the National Liberation) vol. 3 (Istanbul, 1974), 1135; Ilber Ortaylı, *Osmanlı İmparatorluğunda Alman Nüfuzu* (The German
Influence in the history of the Ottoman Empire) (Istanbul, 1983), 122; Ziya Şakir,
1914–1918 *Cihan Harbini Nasıl İdare Ettik* (How Did We Direct the 1914–1918 World
War) (Istanbul, 1944), 46–51.

16. Ihsan Birinci, "Cemiyet ve Çeteler" (The Party and the Irregulars [Brigands mostly])
Hayat 2 (October 1, 1971): 33. For similar Turkish views acknowledging the involvement of the Special Organization in the liquidation of Ottoman Armenians see Vahakn
N. Dadrian, "The Role of the Special Organization in the Armenian Genocide during
the First World War" in *Minorities in Wartime*, P. Panayi, ed. (Oxford, 1993).

17. J. Pomiankowski, *Der Zusammenbruch des Ottomanischen Reiches* (Vienna, 1969), 162.

18. H. Morgenthau, "The Greatest Horror in History," *Red Cross Magazine* (March, 1918):
9. Louis Heck, the U.S. High Commissioner in Istanbul and a Special Assistant of the
Department of State, also pointed out the opportunity factor provided by World War I:
"[T]he Young Turk Government soon availed itself of the opportunity afforded by war
conditions to try to exterminate the Armenian population of Asia Minor and thus rid
itself once and for all of the 'Armenian question.'" FO 371/3658/75852, Folio 441, p.
2, May 19, 1919.

19. The Talât statement is in German Ambassador Wangenheim's June 17, 1915 report to
his Chancellor in Berlin. A.A. Türkei 183/37, A19744; J. Lepsius, *Deutschland und
Armenien 1914–1918* (Potsdam-Berlin, 1919), 84. The same Talât in a Cabinet meeting in the Fall of 1915, when the anti-Armenian extermination campaign had all but run
its course, is reported to have declared that he was aiming at the creation of a solidly
Turkish nation, cleansed from alien elements, so that the Powers will have no more
cause to intervene in the internal affairs of Turkey. A. A. Türkei 159, No. 2, vol. 14,
Neurath's November 5, 1915 report to Berlin.

These disclosures are confirmed by Ernst Jäckh, the German expert on Turkey who
undertook several inspection trips to Turkey during the war, relaying the gist of his con-

versations with high ranking Turkish officials and his observations to Kaiser Wilhelm II at his Headquarters, to the German Chamber of Deputies, and to the Foreign Office. In his 22-page report covering his September-October 1915 trip he stated, "Indeed Talât openly hailed the destruction of the Armenian people as a political relief." A.A. Türkei 158/14, 18, Oct. 17, 1915. Another German author, the last German Ambassador to Turkey in World War I, commented in his memoirs: "When I kept on pestering him [Talât] on the Armenian Question, he once said with a smile, 'What on earth do you want? The question is settled. There are no more Armenians.'" The ambassador later explained this assertion of having solved the Armenian Question in terms of the ancestral territories of the victims, namely, "Armenia where the Turks have been systematically trying to exterminate the Christian population." Despite his expressions of esteem for Talât, the ambassador conceded Talât's role in that extermination: "His complicity in the Armenian crime he atoned for by his death." *Memoirs of Count Bernstorff*, Eric Sutton trans. (New York, 1936), 176, 180, 374. All these admissions and testimonies are confirmed by a Turkish newspaper which was able to gain access to a pile of secret documents hidden in a suitcase which was found and impounded by the Turkish judicial police during a raid at the home of attorney-at-law Ramiz, the brother-in-law of Dr. B. Şakir. In its December 14, 1918 issue, *Sabah*, the newspaper in question, concluded that, "Talât has ordered the extermination of the Armenians."

20. U. Trumpener, *Germany and the Ottoman Empire* [n. 3], 127. (Emphasis in original).

21. K. Ziemke, *Die Neue Türkei 1914–1929* (Stuttgart, 1930), 271–72. The French text of the February 8, 1914 Agreement is in A. Mandelstam, *Le sort de l'Empire Ottoman* (Lausanne, 1917), 236–38.

22. A.A. Türkei 183/39, A28584 (Aug. 10, 1915 report by Dr. Max Erwin von Scheubner Richter). *See also* J. Lepsius, *Deutschland* [n. 21], 123–24.

23. C. Paşa, *Hatıralar*, (Istanbul, 1977), 438.

Cemal in the September-December 1913 period, during which the Armenians were again pressing for reforms to be executed under European control, repeatedly threatened the Armenian leaders with massacres through "the Muslim populations of the six provinces," which were targeted for reforms. The threat was made to Vartkes, one of the Armenian Deputies serving in the Ottoman Parliament. Being an ardent Ittihadist, Vartkes, who was also a nationalist Dashnak leader, was advised by Cemal to inform his party of this threat, warning it against further solicitation of European intervention. A. Karo, *Abruadz Orer* (Lived Days) (Boston, 1948), 191–92. This threat was confirmed by K. Zohrab, another Armenian Deputy and a professor of international law at Istanbul's law school. In his pre-World War I secret diary, Zohrab, in anticipation of the genocide, called attention to Cemal's threat. "Zohrabee Orakroutiunu Yegernee Nakhoriageen" (K. Zohrab's Diary on the Eve of the Genocide), *Nayiri* (Armenian literary weekly in Beirut) 22 (May 1975): 2–6. Both Vartkes and Zohrab were arrested and summarily killed during the war by agents of the Special Organization.

In December 1913, Cemal had several Armenian students arrested for leading the festivities celebrating the 1500th anniversary of the invention of the Armenian alphabet. When exhorting them to stop their "traitorous activities," Cemal again threatened to "exterminate the Armenians, sparing neither infants nor the old." L. Mozian, *Aksoraganee mu Votisaganu: Sev Orerou Hishadagner* (An Exile's Odyssey: Memories of Dark Days) (Boston, 1958), 9–10. Cemal's threat is further confirmed by another Armenian deputy of the Ottoman Parliament who, along with 5 other Dashnak leaders, had met Cemal in a private session after dinner in Prinkipo (Büyükada) island. Cemal at that meeting repeated his threat. V. Papazian, *Eem Housherus* (My Memoirs) vol. 2 (Beirut, 1952), pp. 191–92. For a Turkish account of this series of meetings between Ittihadist and Dashnak leaders see Bayur, *Türk* [n. 3], vol. 2, Part 3 (Ankara, 1983), 71–2, excerpted from the November 2, 1946 issue of the Turkish daily *Cumhuriyet* which was then serializing the memoirs of Economics Minister Cavid.

24. C. Paşa, *Hatıralar* [n. 23], 438.

25. A.A. Botschaft Konstantinopel, 170, folio 52; J. Lepsius, *Deutschland* [n. 19], 122.

26. J. Lepsius, *Der Todesgang des Armenischen Volkes* (Potsdam, 1930), 230.

27. Kutay, *Talât Paşanın* [n. 14], 522–23, 906–09.

28. A.A. Türkei 183/38, A23991.

Chapter 13

International Law as a
Crucible of Legal Liabilities

The Annulment of the Treaties

The Ottoman government's intransigence, which had gathered momentum through the diplomatic crises and associated Armenian pogroms, found a violent outlet in the pursuit of World War I, into which Turkey willingly plunged by unilaterally provoking and initiating hostilities. The Ottoman government saw the war as a way to end once and for all the grounds for foreign intervention. The preemptory wartime annulment of the Treaties of Paris and Berlin and of the 1914 Agreement attested to this intent inasmuch as these acts deprived the Armenians of their last vestiges of hope. Through a December 3/16, 1914, Imperial Rescript, the Agreement of February 8, 1914, was cancelled.[1] The cancellation coincided with the termination of the contract of the two inspectors, a Dutchman, L.C. Westenenk, Assistant Resident in the Dutch East Indies, and a Norwegian, Nicolai Hoff, Major, later Lieutenant Colonel, in the Norwegian Army and the Secretary General of the Norwegian Ministry of War; these inspectors were to implement the reforms. However, as Toynbee pointed out, the two Inspectors' mission was intentionally handicapped by the Turkish authorities so as to derail and abolish it at an opportune moment:

> A clause was inserted in the Inspectors' contract of engagement, empowering the Government to denounce it at any moment upon payment of an indemnity of one year's salary—a flat violation of the ten years' term provided for under the scheme; and the list of "superior officials" was inflated until the patronage of the Inspectors, which, next to their irrevocability, would have been their most effective power, was reduced to an illusion. The unfortunate nominees were

were spared the farce of exercising their maimed authority. They had barely reached their provinces when the European War broke out, and the Government promptly denounced the contracts and suspended the Scheme of Reforms, as the first step towards its own intervention in the conflict. Thus, at the close of 1914, the Armenians found themselves in the same position as in 1883. The measures designed for their security had fallen through, and left nothing behind but the resentment of the Government that still held them at its mercy.[2]

In Austrian Ambassador Pallavicini's May 16, 1914 report, he informed Vienna that "many of the competencies agreed upon by the Powers were not included in the contract," and in his May 25, 1914 report he complained that the two Inspectors were being treated as subordinate civil servants under the authority of the Turkish government, not as European Inspectors-General.[3] Westenenk in his diary quoted Talât as describing Hoff and him as "just our officials," with Hoff repeatedly expressing doubt about the seriousness of the Turkish rulers.[4] Interior Minister and Party Chief Talât's two appointments were revealing in this respect, portending ominous developments for the Armenians. Diyarbekir Deputy Feyzi and Bitlis province Governor Mustafa Abdulhalik, his brother-in-law, were assigned to the staff of Hoff as Deputies. Both men were subsequently to play pivotal roles in the destruction of the largest concentration of Armenians in southeastern and eastern Turkey, involving the provinces of Diyarbekir and Bitlis. Abdulhalik was later assigned to the post of Governor of Aleppo province, directing the ancillary liquidation of the remnants of the Armenian population who had survived the ordeal of an exacting forced trek from the interior of Turkey to the deserts of Mesopotamia in 1915–16.[5]

Interior Minister Talât's highhanded breaches of the February 8 Reform Agreement, involving a contract with the two European Inspectors-General, were challenged by Boghos Nubar in a protest-letter to German Deputy Foreign Minister Zimmermann on June 22, 1914. In it, Nubar, who in 1912 had been appointed by the Catholicos of All Armenians in Russian Armenia to revive and pursue in Europe the outstanding problem of Armenian Reforms, pointed out that the stipulations of the Reform Act were grossly violated by the provisions of the contract. As an international Agreement, the Act had precedence over an internal contract and the Turkish government had no legal basis to circumvent that Act. Nubar was mainly objecting to the willful reduction of the international status of the European inspectors to that of mere Ottoman functionaries whereby they would lose their power of control over the administration of the Reform Act as well as their ten-year tenure set forth in that Act. He warned Zimmermann that should the Turks be allowed to get away with these breaches, the reforms would once more prove moribund.[6]

The protest was an exercise in futility. Long before World War I broke out, Talât let the Armenian leaders know that they were wasting their time and that under no circumstances would Turkey allow European or, for that matter, any foreign control of the provincial administration. He told an Armenian deputy of the Ottoman Parliament "Don't you realize that there are a thousand ways to derail the reforms in the course of their implementation?"[7] The Turkish biographer of Talât confirmed this obstructive stance of the Ittihadist party boss who avowedly was biding his time to dismantle the whole plan.[8] Talât, then Interior Minister, justified this move of the cancellation of the contract by declaring to Dr. Mordtman, "*C'est le seul moment propice.*"[9]

In a report to Berlin on February 2, 1915 German Ambassador Wangenheim stated that pursuant to article 5 of the contract, signed with the two Inspectors-General, the Turkish government had the right to cancel that contract.[10]

According to a Turkish historian, the contract was signed on May 25, 1914 and provided for a monthly salary of 400 Turkish gold pounds, plus a supplementary allocation for lodging.[11]

The use of the word "propitious" is significant as it reveals a frame of mind geared to the incidence of a suitable opportunity to proceed with the execution of a plan. In his account of the existence of such a plan, another Armenian deputy of the Ottoman Parliament relates Talât's vehement reaction to the Reform Act and all that is implied by it. He quotes Talât as declaring, "Don't Armenians realize that the implementation of the reforms depends on us; we shall not respond to the proposals the Inspectors may put forward ... the Armenians are trying to create a new Bulgaria. They don't seem to have learned their lessons; all undertakings opposed by us are bound to fail. Let the Armenians wait, opportunities will certainly come our way too. Turkey belongs only to the Turks."[12] This watchword "Turkey for the Turks" was the standard rationale on which other Ittihadist leaders based their campaign against the Armenians. Dr. Nâzım, a cohort of Talât, is reported to have declared, "The Ottoman state must be exclusively Turkish. The presence of foreign elements is a pretext for European intervention. They [the foreign elements] should be forcibly Turkicized."[13] This stance reflected a general determination during the war to abrogate the international treaties that had resulted from the application of the principle of "humanitarian intervention." On September 5, 1916, Ottoman Foreign Minister Halil informed German Ambassador Wolff Metternich that "the Ottoman Cabinet had decided to declare null and void the Paris Treaty of 1856, the London Declaration of 1871, and the Berlin Treaty of 1878."[14] As Halil explained, "all three of these international treaties had imposed 'political shackles' on the Ottoman state which the Porte intended to be rid of."[15] Halil on the same day departed to Berlin to seek German support for the annulments. In informing his government of this move in his September 5, 1916 report, German Ambassador Metternich directed attention to the Turkish concern for article 61 of the Berlin Treaty involving Turkey's "engagements for Armenia," and to Halil's justification of the act on grounds of "the effect of war" (*Kriegszustand*).[16]

These acts of annulment may technically be attributed to the effect of war; international law has no explicit or uniform rules for the preservation or annulment of treaties during war.[17] The annulments acquire critical significance, however, when placed in the context of Ottoman Turkey's continuous flouting of treaty provisions in the decades preceding the war. The episodic prewar massacres of Armenians occurred when these treaties were in force but not enforced. The European Powers elected to substitute expressions of outrage for any initiation of sanctions. While it must also be pointed out that the relevant treaties lacked self-executing provisions in case of violation, the fact remains that the Powers' inaction was not due to any sensitivity to legal niceties but rather to mutual suspicions and rivalries.[18] The full text of the repudiation of the treaties is available in German.[19] Halil predicates his abrogation of the Paris and Berlin Treaties on the following main arguments:

(1) The Paris Treaty provisions proscribing interference in the internal affairs of Turkey were violated through some of the provisions of the Berlin Treaty. (2) While the Ottoman Empire scrupulously adhered to the two treaties, Italy, England, France and Russia repeatedly violated them. (3) France coerced Turkey to grant limited autonomy to Lebanon illegally; moreover, the provisions of the autonomy were not part of any international treaty or agreement but rather internal administrative adjustments. Hence, they could be revoked and cancelled. (4) Russia blatantly violated the Paris Treaty by acts of agitation in the Balkan provinces, an aggressive war against Turkey, a series of interventions in the internal affairs of Turkey, and by illegally subverting the status of the Black Sea port city of Batum. (5) The present conditions have altered the situation in that Turkey was no longer under the Powers' tutelage and as a totally independent state could act with all the rights and privileges conferred upon such a state. (6) This new situation justified the conclusion that the two treaties forfeited their right to exist.

It is important to note that Kühlmann, the German Ambassador at Istanbul, pointed to the relationship between the Armenian reform movement and the imposition of these "shackles" on Turkey, especially the February 8, 1914 Reform Agreement, as a fact that provided the rationale for the ensuing genocide. Six months before he became Foreign Minister, Kühlmann, in a February 16, 1917 report reviewing the history of the Turko-Armenian conflict, traced "the destruction of the Armenians, which has been carried out on a large scale, resulting from a policy of extermination," to "Armenian reform endeavors, especially those launched during the 1912 Balkan war."[20] In his memoirs Talât confirms the arousal of many Turks, including himself and his cohorts, in face of the Armenian attempt at reviving the reform issue at that time.[21] Nor were the Armenians themselves unaware of the dangers looming in the horizon; the years 1913 and 1914 up to the fall, when Turkey unilaterally intervened in the war joining the camp of the Central Powers, were periods of anxiety bordering on apprehension. Turkish threats of retaliation as a response to the revival of the reform issue were especially aggravating in this respect.[22] Of particular significance are the threat letters sent to the Armenian press and to the Armenian Patriarch. In a communication of November 12, 1913, the Patriarch was addressed as follows, "... You Armenians ... never forgot where you live ... you accursed ones (*melunlar*) have brought many perils on the head of our esteemed government ... paved the way for foreign assault (*tecavüzat*) ... . You must know that the Young Turks have awakened now ... Turkish youth ... shall not delay the execution of their assigned duties"; it was signed, Islam Young Turks. Four days later, a more threatening letter was sent in which, among others, the following menacing lines were included. "The Turkish sword to date has cut down millions of *gâvurs* [infidels], nor has it lost its intention to cut down millions more hereafter. Know this that the Turks have committed themselves, and have vowed to subdue and to clean up the Armenian gâvurs who have become tubercular microbes for us."[23] In one of the series of articles, published in the Armistice period in a newspaper edited by himself, "Harun Efendi Komiser," an Armenian agent of the Turkish secret police hinted that these letters, inspired by Dr. Nazım, were the work of Hüseyin Azmi, at the time the Director General of Istanbul Police, who played an important role in the preparation and initiation in Istanbul of the World War I genocide; after the war, on November 1/2, 1918, Azmi, along with six other Ittihadist leaders, escaped to Germany.[24] An Armenian historian indicates that already in December 1913 a number of British leaders had warned the British government that Turkey was bent on destroying wholesale the Ottoman Armenian population in the event the Powers imposed upon Turkey the Reform Act. According to this account, Aneurin Williams, a member of Parliament, on September 18, 1914 informed British Foreign Minister Grey of the prevalence in Turkey of a "great fear of a massacre."[25]

The Allies' Warning and the Introduction of the Principle of "Crimes Against Humanity"

As the genocide was beginning, the Allies issued a joint declaration on May 24, 1915 condemning "the connivance and often assistance of Ottoman authorities" in the massacres. "In view of these new crimes of Turkey against humanity and civilization," the declaration continued, "the Allied governments announce publicly ... that they will hold personally responsible ... all members of the Ottoman government and those of their agents who are implicated in such massacres."[26]

This declaration had several important features. 1) It was a public and joint commitment to prosecute after the war those responsible for the crimes perpetrated; 2) it acknowledged the complicity of Ottoman authorities in terms of "connivance and often assistance"; 3) it acknowledged the legacy of Turkey, involving an established record of past massacres, by appending the adjective "new" to the words "crimes of Turkey"; 4) it created a new framework of international law by ushering in the codification of the term "crimes against humanity"; 5) that concept was later to serve as a legal yardstick to prosecute under an emerging international law the top strata of the Nazi leadership at Nuremberg. Consequently, it was fully embraced by the United Nations, forming the core of the preamble of its convention on the Prevention and Punishment Convention on Genocide (December 9, 1948).

Notes to Chapter 13

1. G. Jäschke, "Das Osmanische Reich vom Berliner Kongress bis zu seinem Ende (1878–1920/22)," *Handbuch der Europäischen Geschichte*, 6 (1968): 543, 545–56, n. 36. See also Y. Bayur, *Türk Inkılâbı Tarihi* vol. 3, Part 3 (Ankara, 1956), 12; British Ambassador Mallet's September 23, 1914 report to Grey is in FO 371/226/56207.

2. J. (Viscount) Bryce, *The Treatment of Armenians in the Ottoman Empire 1915–16*. Compiled by A. Toynbee, Miscellaneous 31, Government Publication (London, 1916), 635–36.

3. *Austrian Foreign Affairs Archives*. Political Department. (hereafter DAA). 12 Türkei, Karton 463.

4. See Van der Dussen, "The Westenenk File," *Armenian Review* 39 (1986): 46, 57, 69, 72.

5. A. A. Türkei 183/38, A24658, Enclosure VI of Aug. 20, 1915 report; *Zhamanag* (Istanbul) 6/19 July 1914, also describes the other, i.e., Abdulhalik's assignment, whose complicity in the Armenian genocide is sketched in V. Dadrian, "The Naim-Andonian Documents on the World War I Destruction of the Ottoman Armenians-The Anatomy of a Genocide," *International Journal of Middle East Studies* 18, 3 (1986): 342, 336–38.

6. A. A. Botschaft Konstantinopel, vol. 168, A12314.

7. V. Papazian. *Eem Hoosherus* (My Memoirs) vol. 2 (Beirut, 1952) 235–36. An Armenian political executioner assigned by the Dashnak party to duties involving the "avenging" of the crimes perpetrated against the Armenians by assassinating the arch perpetrators, in his memoirs claims to have encountered in the prison a Turkish agent sent there to spy on him and establish his true identity. Hasan Burhaneddin, the agent, reportedly was induced to confess that he was assigned to the task of assassinating in Romania one of the two Inspectors. K. Merdjanof, *Eem Gudagu* (My Testament) (Beirut, 1972), 28–9.

8. T. Çavdar, *Talât Paşa* (Ankara, 1984), 308–11.

9. A. A. Türkei 183/46, A5043.

10. *Ibid.*, 183/36, A5043.

11. Ismail Danişmend, *Izahlı Osmanlı Tarihi Kronolojisi* (The Annotated Chronology of Ottoman History) 2nd ed. (Istanbul, 1961), 409.

12. "*Kegham Der Garabedianee Vugayutounu*" (the Testimony of Kegham Der Garabedian) in G. Sassouni, *Badmoutiun Daronee Achkharee* (History of Daron) (Beirut, 1957), 838–39.

13. René Pinon, "La liquidation de l'Empire Ottoman," *Revue des Deux Mondes* 53 (September 1919): 131.

14. U. Trumpener, *Germany and the Ottoman Empire*, (Princeton, N. J., 1968), 134–39; Frank Weber, *Eagles on the Crescent*, (Ithaca, N. Y., 1970), 201, n. 105.

15. *Ibid.*, Trumpener.

16. A. A. Türkei, 183/44, A24061.

17. L. Oppenheim, *International Law*, vol. 2, paragraph 99, 7th ed., ed. by Lauterpacht (London, 1952).

18. See chapter 7, section on Abortive Treaty Engagements.

19. Kraelitz-Greifenhorst, "Die Ungültigkeitserklärung des Pariser und Berliner Vertrages durch die Osmanische Regierung," *Österreichische Monatsschrift für den Orient*, 43 (1917): 56–60. For the English text of Halil's statements, see *Current History*, N. Y. Times monthly publication 5 (February 1917): 822–24.

20. A. A. Türkei 183/46, A5919.

21. *Talât Paşanın Hatıraları* (The Memoirs of Talât Paşa), E. Bolayir, ed., (Istanbul, 1946), 51, and 50–55.

22. *Mecheroutiette* (Paris, monthly, organ of Itilaf) 6, 50 (January 1914): 44–45.

23. Haigaz K. Kazarian, "How Turkey Prepared the Ground for Massacre" *Armenian Review* 18, 4 (Winter 1965): 31–2.

24. H. Mugurditchian "Kaghdnikneroun Gudzigu" (The Thread of the Secrets) *Hairenik*. Instalments nos. 1 and 2, October 28/November 10 and October 30/November 12, 1918, issues.

25. A. Nassibian, *Britain and the Armenian Question 1915–1923* (London, 1984), 30–31.

26. *Guerre 1914–1918, Turquie*, 887. *Arménie*, 1, (May 26, 1915); FO 371/2488/51010 (May 28, 1915); A. A. Türkei 183/37, A17667; *Foreign Relations of the United States*, 1915 Supp., 981 (1928); U.S. National Archives, Record Group 59, 867. 4016/67 (May 28). See also the report of Polish jurist Litawski, the Legal Officer of the U.N. War Crimes Commission, who, in addition to writing Chapter 11 in The United Nations War Crimes Commission, *History of the United Nations War Crimes Commission and the Development of the Laws of War* (London, 1948), prepared a separate report, U.N. Doc. E/CN. 4/W. 20/ Corr. 1, p. 1, no. 3 (1948). (The May 28, 1915, date is a misprint for May 24, 1915, in these works, including that of E. Schwelb, "Crimes Against Humanity," *British Yearbook of International Law* (1946): 181).

Chapter 14

The Implementation
of the Genocide

Alleging treasonable acts, separatism, and other assorted acts by the Armenians as a national minority, the Ottoman authorities ordered, for national security reasons, the wholesale deportation of the Armenian population of the empire's eastern and southeastern provinces. This act resulted from a concerted drive by the military authorities, in collusion with the Central Committee of the Ittihad party, to divest Anatolia of its Armenian population under cover of the war. The drive was linked to a protracted deliberative process in which were involved the highest organs of the party, the military, and Interior ministry, and national security authorities. In a major, top secret conference a concrete blueprint was hammered out to serve as a general guideline for the benefit of officials and their party overseers in the interior who were charged with the execution of the genocide scheme. The conference was attended by five top decision makers and power-wielders of Turkey, namely, Talât, the two physician-politicians Şakir and Nazım, national security chief Canbolat, and the head of Department II (Intelligence) at the Ottoman General Headquarters, Colonel Seyfi.[1] The scheme was subsequently extended to virtually all of the empire's Armenian population, including such far away cities as Bursa, Eskişehir, Konya, and the Ottoman capital, Istanbul.[2]

The disguising of this order, ostensibly a wartime emergency measure of relocation, served to mask the planned execution of the Armenian population. The vast majority of the deportees perished through a variety of direct and indirect atrocities perpetrated during the deportations. As Winston Churchill wrote,

> In 1915 the Turkish government began and ruthlessly carried out the infamous general massacre and deportation of Armenians in Asia Minor ... the clearance

of the race from Asia Minor was about as complete as such an act, on a scale so great, could well be ... . There is no reasonable doubt that this crime was planned and executed for political reasons. The opportunity presented itself for clearing Turkish soil of a Christian race opposed to all Turkish ambitions, cherishing national ambitions that could be satisfied only at the expense of Turkey, and planted geographically between Turkish and Caucasian Moslems.[3]

A secret propaganda campaign operated by Department II of the Turkish War Office followed the deportation order. The campaign sought to deflect blame from the Turkish government by labeling the Armenians a national security threat. As one Turkish naval captain attached to the office recounted:

> In order to justify this enormous crime (*bu muazzam cinayet*) [of the Armenian genocide] the requisite propaganda material was thoroughly prepared in Istanbul. [It included such statements as:] "the Armenians are in league with the enemy. They will launch an uprising in Istanbul, kill off the Ittihadist leaders and will succeed in opening up the straits [to enable the Allied fleets to capture Istanbul]." These vile and malicious incitements [were such, however, that they] could persuade only people who were not even able to feel the pangs of their own hunger.[4]

The main vehicle of this anti-Armenian agitation was the Ottoman propaganda weekly *Harb Mecmuası* (War Magazine). Edited by Colonel Seyfi, the head of Department II at the War Office, this weekly's influence went well beyond its 15,000 subscribers. A Turkish newspaper during the Armistice declared that it was Seyfi who, as director of the Political Department at Ottoman General Headquarters, mapped the strategy of the massacres against the Armenians, mobilizing the *çetes* (brigands) of the Special Organization, in close cooperation with Dr. B. Şakir, and under the auspices of the Ittihad party's Central Committee.[5] Even more significant, the German Military Plenipotentiary at the German Embassy at Constantinople, Colonel, later Major General, Otto von Lossow, confirmed this fact. In a communication to the German General Headquarters, dated November 16, 1916, Lossow indicated that Seyfi and his Department II at Ottoman General Headquarters were in charge of the "Armenian deportations" (*Armenierverschickungen*). "He handles this matter and knows exactly about it" (*der diese Sachen bearbeitet und genau orientiert ist*).[6] Moreover, Colonel Fuat Balkan, one of the top leaders of the Special Organization operating in the Balkans, in his memoirs, published in *Yakın Tarihimiz* (vol. 2, 1962, p. 297), stated that Seyfi directed the operations of the Special Organization from his office at the General Headquarters.

Mobilization and Deportation

Invoking the principle of "armed neutrality," Turkey, with the assistance of German staff officers, launched a general mobilization on August 2-3,

1914. Among those affected by this scheme were male Armenians, who were inducted in three stages. First called were those between 20 and 45 years of age, followed by those between 15 and 20, and finally those in the 45 to 60 age group, who were used as pack animals for the transport of military equipment.[7] About a month later, on September 6, 1914, the Interior Ministry instructed the provincial authorities, through a cipher circular, to keep Armenian political and community leaders under surveillance. When Turkey finally entered the war by a preemptive attack on Russian seaports and shipping in the Black Sea some two months later,[8] the military's emergency measures assumed inordinate dimensions of severity. The requisitions in particular stripped the provincial Armenian population of most of their accumulated goods; the confiscations included almost anything subsumed under the general category of supplies and provisions for the Army.[9] Widespread governmental provocations, during which some Armenians clashed with gendarmes and soldiers who were harassing them, accentuated these hardships. As one Turkish author recently observed, "Under the pretext of searching for arms, of collecting war levies, of tracking down deserters, there had already been established a practice of systematically carried-out plunders, raids and murders [against the Armenians] which had become daily occurrences."[10] There were also sporadic acts of sabotage by isolated individuals and groups of Armenians.[11] This unrest culminated in the Interior Ministry order of April 24, 1915 authorizing the arrest of all Armenian political and community leaders suspected of anti-Ittihad or nationalistic sentiments. Thousands of Armenians were seized and incarcerated; in Istanbul alone in a matter of weeks 2,345 such leaders were arrested[12] only to be executed subsequently in large part. A large number of them were neither nationalists nor in any way involved in politics. None of them was charged with wartime sabotage, espionage, or any other crime and tried accordingly.

The last and decisive stage of the process of reducing the Armenian population to helplessness was deportation. In a Memorandum dated May 26, 1915, (new style, i.e., n.s.) the Interior Minister requested from the Grand Vizier the enactment through the Cabinet of a special law authorizing deportations. The Memorandum was endorsed on May 29 by the Grand Vizier even though the Cabinet did not act on it until May 30. The press, meanwhile, had already announced the promulgation of the new emergency law, called the Temporary Law of Deportation,[13] on May 27. Without referring to the Armenians, the law authorized the Commanders of Armies, Army Corps, Divisions, and Commandants of local garrisons to order the deportation of population clusters on suspicion of espionage, treason, and on military necessity. The key word was "sensing" (*hissetmek*); the authorities, empowered to order deportations, had merely to have a feel or a sense of the offense or danger.[14] This vague but sweeping authorization resulted in the deportation of the bulk of Turkey's Armenian population. As one Turkish historian admitted, the Interior Minister "was intent on creating an accomplished fact," and "railroad[ed] the Cabinet approval of the law" by beginning to administer the deportations prior to submitting his draft bill.[15] The Temporary Law of Deportation, it should be noted, was eventually repealed "on account of its unconstitutionality" in a stormy November 4, 1918 session of the postwar Ottoman Parliament, during which the Armenian massacres, the scope of the victims, and the responsibility of the government were debated; the motion for repeal of that law was made by the Interior Minister Fethi Okyar.[16] Thus, without irony, the Turkish Parliament cancelled a law which it had not debated or approved before, and when its object, the victim population, was all but eliminated.

Expropriation and Confiscation of Goods and Assets

A supplementary law enacted on June 10, 1915 contained instructions on how to register the properties of the deportees, how to safeguard them, and how to dispose of others through public auctions, with the revenues to be held in trust for remittance to the owners upon their return after the war.[17] Another Temporary Law promulgated on September 26, 1915 disposed of the deportees' goods and properties. It provided for the handling of the debts, credits, and assets of the deportees. In relaying this new law to the German Foreign Office, Arthur von Gwinner, the Director of Deutsche Bank, sarcastically stated that the eleven articles might well have been compressed into the following two: "1. All goods of the Armenians are confiscated. 2. The government will cash in the credits of the deportees and will repay (or will not repay) their debts."[18]

Unlike the Temporary Law of Deportation which, though approved by the Cabinet, was never promulgated by the Ottoman Parliament as required by article 36 of the Ottoman Constitution, the Ottoman Senate publicly debated the Temporary Law of Expropriation and Confiscation. Over a two month period, from October 4 through December 13, 1915, a lone Senator, Ahmed Riza, raised his voice in opposition to the proposed measure.[19] The course of the debate sheds further light on the political forces and biases that shaped the Ottoman government's decisions.

In the September 21/October 4, 1915 session of the Senate, Senator Riza pleaded with his government to allow the deportees, "hundreds and thousands of whom, women, children and old people, are helplessly and miserably wandering around in the streets and mountains of Anatolia, to return to their original places of residence or to settle wherever they wish before the onset of the winter."[20] He then submitted a draft bill that proposed to postpone the Temporary Law's application until after the end of the war.[21]

Senator Riza claimed that the Temporary Law was contrary to article 16 of the Ottoman Constitution because it was announced two days before the convening of the Parliament. He further argued that "[i]t is also inimical to the principles of law and justice. This law must, therefore, pass first through the Parliament and go into effect only after the end of the war. Hence, on the basis of Article 53 of the Constitution, I request the change as proposed in the bill before us."[22] The ensuing debate revealed that the Parliament knew nothing about the Temporary Law in question, and that nobody knew when, if ever, it would come to the Parliament for consideration. Therefore, no proposal for change would be entertained. Following Senator Riza's expression of concern that the Temporary Law might either come too late or not at all to the Parliament, the Senate voted to transmit the Senator's bill to the Legislative Acts Committee of the Senate.

In the October 19/November 1, 1915 session of the Senate, Senator Riza again urged his fellow legislators to consider the suffering of the wretched deportees in and around the Anatolian mountains before the onset of the winter season. He requested that the Senate expedite relief which, according to the President of the Senate, the government had formally promised to provide.[23] In discussing these debates, prominent Turkish historian Bayur noted the pressures brought to bear upon Senator Riza to withdraw his bill; one Deputy shouted at Riza "this is not the time to provoke rumors"[24]—alluding to the delicate political matter of the massacres that were still in progress. Bayur states that Senator Riza was especially harrassed during the November 24/December 7, 1915 session, when the Senate decided to consider the bill only after the bill was reported to it. As Bayur observed, "[t]wo and a half months had elapsed since the bill was introduced and the Chamber of Deputies hadn't even begun to consider it. Clearly, the Parliament was intent on sanctioning the application of the Temporary Law while putting Riza's bill 'to sleep.'"[25]

During the November 30/December 13, 1915 session, Senator Riza once more raised his voice, this time protesting the subversion of the Constitution, which forbade the implementation of any law before the Parliament passes it in session. Since the law had been introduced in the Chamber of Deputies after the Chamber had convened, Riza argued, the matter became the concern of the Legislative branch. Focusing on the key elements of the Temporary Law, the Senator raised the following objection:

> It is unlawful to designate the Armenian assets and properties as 'abandoned goods' *[emvalı metruke]* for the Armenians, the proprietors, did not abandon their properties voluntarily; they were forcibly, compulsively [*zorla, cebir ile*] removed from their domiciles and exiled. Now the government through its officials is selling their goods … . Nobody can sell my property if I am unwilling to sell it. Article 21 of the Constitution forbids it. If we are a constitutional regime functioning in accordance with constitutional law we can't do this. This is atrocious. Grab my arm, eject me from my village, then sell my goods

and properties, such a thing can never be permissible. Neither the conscience of the Ottomans nor the law can allow it.[26]

In his November 4, 1915 communication to the State Department, Morgenthau confirmed the occurrence of these debates. He further disclosed that Talât himself exerted the greatest pressure upon Senator Riza by threatening to initiate more severe measures against the Armenians should Riza continue his agitation on their behalf: "From other sources it is stated that the Cabinet promised to modify their attitude towards the Armenians if Ahmed Riza and his friends would agree not to interpellate the government. This Ahmed Riza and his friends did."[27] The Temporary Law on Abandoned Goods was thus left intact. A Turkish Armistice government facing the victorious Allies subsequently annulled the law on January 8, 1920,[28] but the insurgent Kemalists reversed the anullment on September 14, 1922.[29]

During the November-December 1918 hearings of the Fifth Committee of the Ottoman Chamber, investigating, among other things, the wartime massacres, several Turkish Deputies took former Justice Minister Ibrahim to task over the illegal aspects of the expropriation. One of them pointed out the widespread "robberies and plunders" that were committed in the course of the confiscations.[30] Ibrahim conceded that "abuses" occurred which his government investigated.[31] Other observors were less charitable in their analysis. The Swiss historian Zurlinden, in a detailed study of the Armenian genocide, quoted "a knowledgeable German" source who stated: "What really happened was an expropriation carried out on the greatest scale against 1.5 million citizens."[32] American Consul Jackson pointed to the major role the confiscation played in the genocidal scheme of the Turkish government, identifying the genocide as "a gigantic plundering scheme as well as a final blow to extinguish the [Armenian] race."[33] Turkish historian Doğan Avcıoğlu confirms this point stating that after the European interventions of 1856–78, "[t]here emerged a need to radically solve this problem. The nationalization of the economy was the complementary part of this policy … . Among those who quickly enriched themselves in the process of the expropriation of the Armenians were [Ittihad] party influentials, ex-officers serving as party operatives, and Turkish immigrants."[34]

Neither the Temporary Law on Deportations nor the Temporary Law of Expropriation and Confiscation referred specifically to the Armenians or, in fact, to any nationality. During the secret Parliamentary debates of the fledgling Turkish Republic after World War I, however, Turkish Deputies were told that the general terms were used in order to conceal the true purposes of the law from the Armenians. This fact emerged during the debate on April 3, 1924, when Deputy Musa Kâzım objected to article 2 of a draft fiscal bill which used the cover formula, "a political body of people" (*siyasi zümre*) to target non-Muslim minorities. He argued that: "[t]he guilt of a person should be determined in a court of law. In my opinion, the insertion in a bill of economic character of a clause smacking of politics is very much out of place. It is a shame. I implore you to let us remove it."[35] In responding to this objection, former Finance Minister Hasan Fehmi, representing the Parliamentary Commission in charge of preparing the bill in question, explained the rationale of secretly targetting non-Muslims, given the risks of specifically identifying them in the bill. He said that the Commission had secretly made a deal with the Finance Minister to the effect that the Muslims were to be excluded from the application of the law. In this connection, he revealed the fact that the same procedure had been adopted during the war when the September 13/26, 1915 Temporary Law on Expropriaton and Confiscation was instituted:

> Not a single Muslim's goods were liquidated ... you can establish these facts by examining the old records of the secret deliberations. The Parliament at that time secretly secured reassurances from the Finance Minister that the law would not apply to Muslims who had fled as a result of war. Only after registering this assurance did we proclaim to the world that law. Presently, we are repeating that procedure.[36]

Deputy Kazım withdrew his motion and the bill was approved.[37]

The Genocidal Killings

Contrary to the avowals of Ottoman authorities who promulgated these emergency laws, the Armenians did not return from the deportations.[38] The deportations proved to be a cover for the ensuing destruction. As American Ambassador Morgenthau observed:

> The real purpose of the deportation was robbery and destruction; it really represented a new method of massacre. When the Turkish authorities gave the orders for these deportations, they were merely giving the death warrant to a whole race; they understood this well, and, in their conversations with me, they made no particular attempt to conceal the fact.[39]

By official Turkish accounts alone, those directly killed numbered about 800,000,[40] not counting the tens of thousands of wartime conscripts liquidated by the military. To quote Morgenthau again:

> In many instances Armenian soldiers were disposed of in even more summary fashion, for it now became almost the general practice to shoot them in cold blood. In almost all cases the procedure was the same. Here and there squads of 50 or 100 men would be taken, bound together in groups of four, and then marched out to a secluded spot a short distance from the village. Suddenly the sound of rifle shots would fill the air, and the Turkish soldiers who had acted as the escort would sullenly return to camp. Those sent to bury the bodies would find them almost invariably stark naked, for, as usual, the Turks had stolen all their clothes. In cases that came to my attention, the murderers had

added a refinement to the victims' sufferings by compelling them to dig their graves before being shot.[41]

In a message to his Ambassador in Istanbul (October 2, 1916), German Undersecretary of Foreign Affairs Zimmermann, who six weeks later replaced Jagow as Foreign Minister, denounced the exterminations accompanying the deportations, including the forcible "mass conversions" to Islam of Armenian children whose parents had been killed, as cause for "indignation in the entire civilized world."[42] He added that he had discussed his feelings on this point with Turkish Foreign Minister Halil. In that communication Zimmermann used the expression "with an appearance of legality" when describing the official deportation measures.[43]

And yet here too there is evidence of German assistance when one considers the connection between the illegal decree of general mobilization on the one hand, and the illegal decree of deportation on the other (see note 15). As attested to by historian Bayur, the general mobilization was designed, detailed, and administratively organized through the help of the German officers attached to German Military Mission. The department in the Ministry of War, which was in charge of the general mobilization initiative, was headed by Colonel Kress von Kressenstein.[44] Though that mobilization had many other objectives, it served a major purpose for the swift execution of the plan of genocide. By removing all able-bodied Armenian males from their cities, villages, hamlets, and by isolating them in conditions in which they virtually became trapped, the Armenian community was reduced to a condition of near-total helplessness, thus an easy prey for destruction. It was a masterful stroke as it attained with one blow the three objectives of the operation of trapping the victim population: a) dislocation through forcible removal; b) isolation; c) concentration for easy targeting. This is one reason why war represents an optimal opportunity for a dominant group bent on liquidating a vulnerable minority by labeling it as "the internal foe."

Notes to Chapter 14

1. Vahakn N. Dadrian, "The Secret Young-Turk Ittihadist Conference and the Decision for the World War I Genocide of the Armenians" *Holocaust and Genocide Studies* 7, 2 (Fall 1993). An Armenian member of Smyrna's (Izmir) wartime *Deutscher Verein*, with access to knowledgeable Germans, specifies February 26, 1915 as the date when 75 top ranking Ittihadists reportedly convened on the initiative of the War Minister Enver to discuss "a very urgent matter." The genocide plan was finalized at this secret gathering, according to this source. The participants reportedly agreed by exclaiming "it's about time" (*vaktı gelmiştir*) "Hai Aghedeen Usguspnabadjaru" (The Rudiments of the Armenian Catastrophe) *Tashink* (Smyrna Armenian daily) January 30, 1919. This date jibes with a more or less identical date supplied by two well informed Turkish sources

indicating the time frame of Dr. B. Şakir's return to Istanbul from Erzurum. The purpose of this trip, according to Filibeli Hilmi, an Ittihadist Inspector of Erzurum and Şakir's Assistant in the organization of the genocide in the eastern provinces of Turkey, was to persuade Ittihad's Supreme Directorate to allow him to proceed with his plans by granting Special Organization East, a force created by him and placed under his command, complete autonomy, i.e., a free hand. At this point Şakir's cardinal plan was to pounce on the Armenians as "the internal enemy ... which was threatening the rear of the Turkish army." A. Mil, "Umumi Harpte Teşkılâtı Mahsusa," installment no. 100, *Vakit* February 12, 1934. His departure to Istanbul is described in installment no. 98 (which is a misprint for 96), February 8, 1934. General Ali Ihsan Sabis, in *Harp Hatıralarım* (My War Memoirs), vol. 2 (Ankara, 1951), p. 192, specifies February 28/March 13, 1915 as the date of Şakir's conference trip to Istanbul.

2. German Embassy Chargé von Neurath informed Berlin on November 12, 1915: "According to a reliable source, the Turkish Government has, contrary to all assurances, decided to deport the Armenians of Constantinople also." A.A. Türkei, 183/40, A33705. On December 7, 1915, German Ambassador Metternich informed Berlin that four thousand Armenians had recently been removed from Constantinople, that the total number of those deported from the Ottoman capital up to that time had reached thirty thousand, and that "gradually a clean sweep will be made of the remaining 80,000 Armenian inhabitants" of the Ottoman capital. A.A. Türkei, 183/40, A36184. For additional corroboration of this pattern of deportation of Istanbul's Armenians, see S. Zurlinden, *Der Weltkrieg*, vol. 2 (Zürich, 1918), p. 705. *See also* A. Toynbee, *Armenian Atrocities: The Murder of a Nation* (London, 1915), 77-78; Ambassador Morgenthau's October 4, 1915 cipher No. 1121. U. S. National Archives. R.G. 59, 867.4016/159; A. Refik, *Iki Komite Iki Kıtal* (Istanbul, 1919), 23–24. This Turkish intelligence officer recounts his own observations about "atrocious" deaths of the victims of these cities "so far removed from the war zones." Far more significant, however, is his declaration, "I even heard that the entire Armenian population of Istanbul was slated for removal." *ibid.*, p. 40. In an Austrian report, the cautious operations of rounding up in the Ottoman capital of multitudes of Armenians of lower classes and the possibility of the apprehension and removal of Armenians of higher social strata at an opportune moment is underscored. *Foreign Ministry Archives of Austria*. XL Interna. Konfidentenberichte 1914-1918, No. 272. Forderung zur Türkisierung des Reiches. Situationsbericht No. 312. Konstantinopel, August 27, 1915. See also the following works containing the eyewitness accounts of German correspondents and an American diplomat stationed in Istanbul. In a "very confidential" report, the correspondent of *Kölnische Zeitung*, a major German newspaper, narrates the procedures of the gradual liquidation of the Armenian population of the capital, concentrating first on the provincials, the singles, then, the married ones, with their families. Ridiculing the government's claim that only those suspected of disloyalty are being arrested, the correspondent argues that "the most harmless people are being deported in a very systematic way, such as the two caretakers of my household; they just disappeared after being taken in custody ... I have authentic information that the arrests are being carried out absolutely at random. The cautious procedure is due to the presence of ambassadors; once the measures in the interior are brought to a completion, then it will be the turn of the capital. This is the general impression among the pro-Turkish Germans." A. A. Türkei 183/38, A30432. The correspondent was Ernst von Nahmer whose two reports, September 5 and 6, comprise together 22 pages; the quotations are from pp. 3-4. He has a *Nachlass* (Papers) at *Deutsches Zentralarchiv*, Potsdam. Another correspondent provides graphic details of the mass arrests in Constantinople based on daily quotas of "two hundred or a thousand—to be delivered up daily from a certain quarter of the town—as I have been told was the case by reliable Turks who were in full touch with the police organization and knew the system of these deportations." H. Stürmer, *Two Years in Constantinople*, E. Allen trans. (New York, 1917), 51, 53-55, 62-63; the German original is in *Zwei Kriegsjahre in Konstantinople* (Lausanne, 1917), 44, 46-49, 54-55. A French demographer likewise maintains that the Armenian population of Constantinople was subjected to "round-ups in the streets and to executions." Daniel Panzac, "L'enjeu du nombre. La population de la Turquie de 1914 à 1927," *Revue du Monde Musulman de la Mediter-*

ranée 50, 4 (1988): 61. Finally, reference may be made to an American diplomat stationed in Turkey during most of the genocide. In the August 23, 1915 entry of his diary he notes that "in the capital ... the arrests of Armenians are of daily occurrence." In the September 8 entry, he speaks of new wholesale arrests, "and there is fresh consternation." Lewis Einstein, *Inside Constantinople* (New York, 1918), 253, 285. In an effort to dispute genocidal intent in the wartime anti-Armenian measures, some scholars, bent on defending Turkey's reputation and interests, are adding Smyrna (Izmir) to the case of Constantinople to assert that it too was spared, inasmuch as no deportation took place there, and hence no comprehensive plan of destruction could have existed. As German, Austrian, and American documents demonstrate, however, the exemption from deportation given to most of the Armenian population of Smyrna was not granted because of Ittihadist good will but in spite of Ittihadist efforts of deportation. These efforts were foiled by the intervention of German General Liman von Sanders who was the regional commander at the time. He threatened to use military force if new convoys of Armenians were assembled and deported from the city, adding that he was not eager to protect the Armenians but was anxious to protect military interests and objectives that might be imperiled by such "massive deportations." The deportations stopped forthwith. A.A. Türkei 183/45, A31127, No. 703; Austrian Foreign Ministry Archives PA 12. Karton 463, No. 89/P.; U.S. National Archives, RG. 59.867.00/802.5. General Sanders was supported in his move by then German Foreign Affairs Minister Zimmermann. Türkei 183/45, A30700, No. 1301.

3. W. Churchill, *The World Crisis: The Aftermath* (London, 1929), 405.

Three massive volumes in English, German, and French document these atrocities, relying mostly upon neutral observers (Swiss, American, Swedish), and German and Austrian civilian and military officials stationed in Turkey as war-time allies. (1) J. (Viscount) Bryce, *The Treatment of Armenians in the Ottoman Empire 1915-16*, His Majesty's Stationery Office, Miscellaneous No. 31, A. Toynbee, compiler (London, 1916) (Viscount Bryce, also author of the classic *The American Commonwealth* (1888), was Regius Professor of Civil Law at Oxford from 1870–1893, entered Parliament in 1880, and during 1907–1913 was Ambassador to the United States, signing the Anglo-American Arbitration Treaty in 1911. After the war he was appointed Chairman of a Royal Commission on German atrocities in Belgium and subsequently became a member of the Hague Permanent Court of Arbitration); (2) J. Lepsius, *Deutschland und Armenien 1914-1918* (Berlin, 1919); (3) A. Beylerian, *Les Grandes Puissances, L'Empire Ottoman, et les Arméniens dans les Archives Françaises 1914-18* (Paris, 1983). Because the first volume was compiled during the war, some critics questioned the impartiality and balance of its contents. To prove the veracity of the work, Bryce submitted the material before publication to a number of scholars for evaluation. Among them was Gilbert Murray, Regius Professor at Oxford, who declared: "I realize that in times of persecution passions run high ... But the evidence of these letters and reports will bear any scrutiny and overpower any skepticism. Their genuineness is established beyond question ... " p. xxxi. H.A.L. Fisher, Vice-Chancellor of Sheffield University, declared: "The evidence here collected ... will carry conviction wherever and whenever it is studied by honest enquirers ... It is corroborated by reports received from Americans, Danes, Swiss, Germans, Italians and other foreigners ... It is clear that a catastrophe, conceived upon a scale quite unparalleled in modern history, has been contrived for the Armenian inhabitants of the Ottoman Empire." p. xxix. Moorfield Storey, the former President of the American Bar Association, observed:

> I have no doubt that, while there may be inaccuracies of detail, these statements establish without any question the essential facts. It must be borne in mind that in such a case the evidence of eye-witnesses is not easily obtained; the victims, with few exceptions, are dead; the perpetrators will not confess ... Such statements as you print are the best evidence which, in the circumstances, it is possible to obtain. They come from persons holding positions which give weight to their words, and from other persons with no motive to falsify, and it is impossible that such a body of concurring evidence should have been manufactured ... In my opinion the evidence which you print ... establishes beyond any reasonable doubt, the deliberate purpose of the Turkish authorities practically to exterminate the Armenians, and

their responsibility for the hideous atrocities which have been perpetrated upon that unhappy people.

pp. xxxi, xxxii. In commenting on Toynbee's competence and scrupulousness in compiling the material, Bryce declared "[n]othing has been admitted the substantial truth of which seems open to reasonable doubt. Facts only have been dealt with; questions of future policy have been carefully avoided." p. xvi. In his note to Vice-Chancellor Fisher, Toynbee himself described the volume as "an awful piece of history. Fortunately, one gets absorbed in the work of editing and arranging the documents and half deadened to things themselves." FO 96/206/ IV, Aug. 4, 1916. In the circular attached to the volume and sent to 250 American publications, Toynbee noted, "The fiendish character of the atrocities committed and the deliberate, systematic plan on which they were organized from Constantinople appear to me to be the most striking features that emerge." *Ibid*. In a report from Samsun, dated May 26, 1917, Austria's well-informed Consul General, Ernst von Kwiatkowski, advised his government in Vienna that "insofar as I was able to familiarize myself with the contents of this book, and on the basis of my own perceptions and the information I have at my disposal, the book to a great extent does reflect but the truth." *Austrian Foreign Ministry Archives* PA 12. Karton (or box) 463. Z.21/P.

4. A. Refik (Altınay), *Iki Komite Iki Kital* (Two Committees and Two Massacres) (Istanbul, 1919), 40. Dismissing these pieces of agitation as crass propaganda that "defies every logic," Refik returns to his central theme, that under the guise of deportation and wartime relocation, Ittihad pursued the goal of "destroying (*imha*) the Armenians." *Ibid*., 23. Refik later became a Professor of History at the University of Istanbul. In his memoirs Interior Minister Talât repeats this charge of an imminent Armenian uprising in Istanbul and opening up the Straits for the fleet of the Allies to make the anti-Armenian measures look preemptive in nature and as borne out of military necessity. *Talât Paşanın Hatıraları* (The Memoirs of Talât Paşa) E. Bolayır, ed. (Istanbul, 1946), 73.

5. The newspaper is the daily *Sabah*, from which an Armenian daily probably a day or two later, repeated that declaration in summary form. *Ariamard* (namesake of *Djagadamard*), Dec. 13, 1918. This shows the enormous power of Colonel Seyfi, a graduate of the Istanbul Turkish War Staff Academy and a longtime Ittihadist supporter of war lord Enver; he later became General Düzgören in the Turkish Republic. According to U.S. Acting Secretary of State William Phillips, Seyfi "was vested with great power." FO 371/4173, folio 345 (March 20, 1919) (report to U.S. Ambassador to England John Davis assessing Seyfi's liability as a top war criminal). As observed in note 1, British intelligence during the Armistice obtained a document from the Turkish Interior Ministry's National Security Office files in which Seyfi is described as one of the five top Ittihadist leaders plotting the genocide against the Armenians. FO 371/4172/ 31307. folio 386. On the provocative contents of the military periodical *Polis Mecmuası*, edited by Seyfi, see H. Sirounee, "Yegern Mu Yev Eer Badmoutyunu" (A Genocide and its History) *Etchmiadzin* (the official periodical of the Catholicosate in Armenia) (February-March-April joint issue, 1965): 20, and G. Kapigian, *Yegernabadoum* (The Chronicle of the Genocide ... in Sıvas), (Boston, 1924) 89. The Turkish government also worked to deflect blame for the eventual killing of the Armenians through its use of the Special Organization. The members of the Special Organization, mostly ex-convicts, would be identified as the actual villains and portrayed as "beyond the authority and control of the government." An American author noted this method and described the unruly "group of brigands" who made up the Special Organization as "a secret, rather disreputable group." P. Stoddard, *The Ottoman Government and the Arabs, 1911 to 1918: A Preliminary Study of the Teşkilâtı Mahsusa* (Ann Arbor, 1964), 49.

6. A. A. Botschaft Konstantinopel, vol. 174. The editor of the wartime publication, *Die Nationalverteidigung* (a German-language periodical promoting German interests in Turkey), and of its politically oriented offshoot, the daily French-language newspaper *La Defense*, denounces Seyfi in his postwar memoirs as a ruthless potentate holding sway at the Ottoman General Headquarters. According to this editor, as the Chief of Department II there, Seyfi organized the liquidation of Ottoman Armenians through "systematic massacres." Colonel Seyfi reportedly was in charge of the notorious "fedayis," most of whom comprised the killer bands of the Special Organization, the principal instrument of the Armenian Genocide. In these accounts Seyfi is also por-

trayed as an arch plunderer who amassed a huge fortune through the appropriation of the vast riches of the victims of his lethal measures as well as through a web of wartime black market deals in Germany and Sweden. Mehmed Zeki Bey, *Raubmörder als Gäste der deutschen Republik* (Berlin, 1920), 35, 37. Zeki is described by a German newspaper correspondent as a tool of the German Embassy at Constantinople, on whose behalf he reportedly operated as intelligence agent (*Gewährsmann*), collecting secret information from many influential Turks with whom he was dealing at many levels, including business transactions. Stürmer, *Two Years* [n. 2], 142; in the original German, *Zwei Jahre* [n. 2], 124.

7. American Ambassador Morgenthau describes the use of these Armenian conscripts as pack animals and their eventual destruction as follows:

> Army supplies of all kinds were loaded on their backs, and, stumbling under the burdens and driven by the whips and bayonets of the Turks ... almost waist high through snow ... If any stragglers succeeded in reaching their destinations, they were not infrequently massacred. In many instances, Armenian soldiers were disposed of in even summary fashion, for it now became almost the general practice to shoot them in cold blood.

H. Morgenthau, *Ambassador Morgenthau's Story* (New York, 1918), 302. For the conscription order see Morgenthau's August 10, 1915 dispatch to Washington in U. S. National Archives. RG 59. 867.4016/74, and G. Vardar, *Ittihad ve Terakki İçinde Dönenler* (The Inside Story of Ittihad), S. H. Tansu, ed., (Istanbul, 1975), 271.

8. U. Trumpener, *Germany and the Ottoman Empire 1914-1918* (Princeton, 1968), 51.

9. In discussing these requisitions, Dr. Henry Stürmer, the Istanbul correspondent of the influential German daily newspaper *Kölnische Zeitung,* noted,

> When I speak of requisitioning, I do not mean the necessary military carrying off of grain, cattle, vehicles, buffaloes, and horses, general equipment, and so on ... I do not mean that, even though the way it was accomplished bled the country far more than was necessary, falling as it did in the country into the hands of ignorant, brutal, and fanatical underlings, and in the town being carried out with every kind of refinement by the central authorities. Too often it was a means to violent "nationalisation" and deprivation of property and rights exercised especially against the Armenians, Greeks, and subjects of other Entente countries.

H. Stürmer, *Two Years* [n. 2], 115.

10. Taner Akçam, *Türk Ulusal Kimliği ve Ermeni Sorumu* (Turkish National Identity and the Armenian Question) (Istanbul, 1992), 109. *See also* J. (Viscount) Bryce, *Treatment* [n. 3], 33–36 (American nurse Grace Knapp's eyewitness account); *see also* C. Ussher, *An American Physician in Turkey* (Boston, 1917), 264–65; R. De Nogales, *Four Years Beneath the Crescent*, M. Lee, trans., (New York, 1926), 60–70, 80–89, 95 (detailed description by Venezuelan officer who led Turkish artillery in reducing Armenian defenses in Van).

11. As Morgenthau related, "some Armenians proposed to defend their own lives and their women's honor against the outrages ... Nothing was sacred to the Turkish gendarmes under the plea of searching for hidden arms, they ransacked churches, treated the altars and sacred utensils with the utmost indignity ... They would beat the priests into insensibility." H. Morgenthau, *Ambassador* [n. 7], 304–05. Commenting on his intimate exchanges with "authoritative Turkish personalities," Erzurum's German Vice Consul, Captain von Scheubner-Richter, in a December 4, 1916 summary report to his Chancellor in Berlin, reveals Turkish plans to provoke Armenians into "acts of self-defense" which then were used as a basis for "inflated descriptions" of Armenian insurgency and, therefore, as "pretexts" for the subsequent mass murder. A.A. Türkei 183/45, A33457. On April 26, 1915, the German Consulate at Adana relayed to the German Embassy the German text of a lengthy report in which the Armenian Supreme Patriarch of the See of Cilicia bitterly complains to the Armenian Patriarch in Istanbul of "the outrageous atrocities and mistreatments the sole purpose of which is to provoke the peaceful people of the region to extreme acts in order to provide the government an excuse for annihilation. A.A. *Botschaft Konstantinopel*, 168 (No. 2540); *see also* J. Lepsius, *Deutschland* [n. 3], 53–54. The purpose of these provocations evidently was the cre-

ation of a basis to send to the Ottoman High Command and the party leadership in Istanbul highly inflated reports of Armenian acts of rebelliousness. In his affidavit, prepared at the request of the post-war Turkish Military Tribunal, the military commandant of Yozgat district in Ankara province, and at the same time the head of the local Draft Board, exposed the resort to "the preparation of official and unofficial reports to military authorities, mainly Armee Corps and divisional commanders, vilifying the Armenians and thereby paving the ground for drastic measures against them." Major Mehmed Salim, *(Yozgat Şube Reisi ve Mevki Kumandanı)* Affidavit copy is deposited at Jerusalem Armenian Patriarchate Archive, indexed under the Armenian alphabet character H (pronounced Ho, the 16th letter, and not its variant Hee, the 21st), File 21, M572, bearing January 5, 1919 date.

12. E. Uras, *Tarihte Ermeniler ve Ermeni Meselesi* (The Armenians and the Armenian Question in History) 2d ed., (Istanbul, 1976), 612.

13. For the English text of the law, see R. Hovannisian, *Armenia on the Road to Independence 1918* (Berkeley, CA, 1967), 51.

14. *Takvimi Vekâyi*, No. 2189 (May 19/June 1, 1915).

15. Y. Bayur, *Türk* [n. 44], 3, Part 3 (1957), 38. In T. Z. Tunaya, *Türkiyede Siyasal Partiler* (The Political Parties in Turkey) vol. 1, 2nd enlarged ed., (Istanbul, 1984), 579, the author characterizes this "accomplished fact" as typical of Ittihad prone to bypassing the regular channels of the government. According to the testimony of Finance Minister Cavid, the General Mobilization on August 2/3, 1914 was likewise ordered prior to the approval of the Cabinet. Vakit (Istanbul), *Harb Kabinelerinin Isticvabı (The War Cabinets' Hearings)* (Istanbul, 1933), 81 [hereinafter *War Cabinets Hearings*].

16. *Meclisi Mebusan Zabıt Ceridesi* (Transcripts of the Proceedings of the Chamber of Deputies) Third Election Period. Fifth Session. Eleventh Sitting. November 4, 1918, pp. 114-16. This fact contradicts Kamuran Gürün's assertion that on September 15, 1915, when the Ottoman Parliament reconvened, it took up this Temporary Law and "accepted" it. Kamuran Gürün, *The Armenian File. The Myth of Innocence Exposed* (New York, 1985), 209; p. 104 in the Turkish version.

17. FO 371/4241/170751. The 34 Articles are reproduced in *Documents*, vol. 1, (Ankara, 1982), 76-80. (A compilation of ciphers and letters, assembled by the Press and Information Office of Turkey's Prime Minister to justify or explain away the anti-Armenian measures). See also *Takvimi Vekâyi* of October 1/14, 1916.

18. A.A. Türkei 183/39, A29127 Oct. 7, 1915 report. The French text of the 11 articles is provided in A.A. Türkei 183/39, A29127, and J. Lepsius, *Deutschland* [n. 3], 214–16. In reacting to the same law, the Austrian Military Plenipotentiary dismissed "the whole thing [as] a comedy." J. Pomiankowski, *Der Zusammenbruch des Ottomanischen Reiches* (Vienna, 1969), 169.

19. J. Lepsius, *Deutschland* [n. 3], 216–18. Senator Ahmed Riza was one of the original founders of Ittihad. Subsequently, however, he became a dissident fighting vigorously against Ittihad excesses. On October 19, 1918, in his first post-war speech in the Senate, Riza invoked the memory of "the Armenians who were murdered in a savage manner." A.A. Türkei 201/9, A46488. Quoting the Senator directly, Tunaya reproduces the original Turkish words, *"vahşice öldürülen"*. *Türkiyede* [n. 15], vol. 3, 156. The actual words the Senator used were *"vahşiyane öldürülen Ermeniler."* *Meclisi Âyan Zabıt Ceridesi* (Transcripts of the Proceedings of the Senate) Third Election Period. Fifth Session. Second Sitting. October 19, 1918, p. 8.

20. J. Lepsius, *Deutschland* [n. 3], 216.

21. For this purpose, the bill amended article 2 of the Temporary Law to read as follows: "This law goes into operation after the end of the World War and one month after the signing of the peace treaty." *Meclisi Âyan* [n. 19], First Session. Twenty Eighth Sitting. September 28, 1919, p. 441.

22. *Ibid.*, 441. See also Lepsius, *Deutschland* [n. 3], 217. For specific references to the Transcripts of the Records of the Senate covering the sessions during which Senator Ahmed Riza interpellated on behalf of the Armenians, see Tunaya, *Türkiyede* [n. 15], 577 n. 48, and S. Akşin, *Istanbul Hükümetleri ve Milli Mücadele* (The Istanbul Governments and the National Struggle), vol. 1 (Istanbul, 1983), 42-43 n.59.

23. A.A. Türkei 183/39, A33514, October 19/November 1, 1915 report.

24. Y. Bayur. *Türk* [n. 15], 46.

25. *Ibid.* 46–49, 522 *Meclisi Âyan* [n. 19], Second Session. Tenth Sitting. November 30, 1915, pp. 133-34.

26. Turkish historian Ahmed Refik, an eyewitness of the many procedures of expropriation, relates a scene in the city of Ankara where the Armenians were reportedly forced to give back the money they had gotten right after selling their property to local Turks. Expressing dismay and shame, Refik wrote, "No government in history had at any time committed such a vicious crime (*gaddarane bir cinayet*). There is going to be a day of reckoning for this crime against humanity (*beşeriyet namına bir cinayet.*)" *Iki Komite* [n. 4], 41-42.

27. *U. S. National Archives.* R.G. 59, 867.00/797 1/2; U.S. Foreign Relations. L. p. 763. Further confirmation of the purported accommodation between Senator Riza and the Ittihad government can be found in A.A Türkei 183/39, A33514.

The importance of economic motives in the genocide is highlighted by the following incident as Ambassador Morgenthau wrote in the diary he kept during the war:

> One day Talaat made what was perhaps the most astonishing request I had ever heard. The New York Life Insurance Company and the Equitable Life of New York had for years done considerable business among the Armenians. The extent to which this people insured their lives was merely another indication of their thrifty habits.
>
> "I wish," Talaat now said, "that you would get the American life insurance companies to send us a complete list of their Armenian policy holders. They are practically all dead now and have left no heirs to collect the money. It of course all escheats to the State. The Government is the beneficiary now. Will you do so?"
>
> This was almost too much, and I lost my temper. "You will get no such list from me," I said and I got up and left him.

H. Morgenthau, *Ambassador* [n. 7], 339.

28. G. Jaeschke, *Türk Inkilâbı Tarihi Kronolojisi 1918–1923* (The Chronology of the Turkish Revolution), N. R. Aksu, trans. (Istanbul, 1939), 61 *(citing* Takvimi Vekâyi, No. 3747).

29. *Ibid.* 136 (citing *Kavanin Mecmuası,* vol. 1, 482 (1922) (the Code of Public Laws of the newly established Ankara government)). There are several works treating the issue of confiscations during the war. After extensive legal debate, four prominent experts in international law (three of them were from the University of Paris and one from the University of St. Petersburg) decided that the Armenian survivors were entitled to reclaim their properties and assets, and to massive indemnities. These arguments are compiled in a book by Comité Central des Refugiés Arméniens, *Confiscation des Biens des Refugiés Armeniens par le Gouvernement Turc* (Paris, 1929). Some more recent works are K. Baghdjian, *La Confiscation par le Gouvernement Turc des Biens Arméniens ... Dits Abandonnés* (Montréal, 1987); S. Toriguian, *The Armenian Question and International Law* 2d ed., (La Verne, CA, 1988), 85–96; L. Vartan, *Haigagan Dasnuhinku yev Hayeru Lukial Kouykeru* (The Armenian 1915 and the Abandoned Goods of the Armenians) (Beirut, 1970).

30. *War Cabinets' Hearings,* [n. 15], 527. These abuses were brought out in the open in some memoirs and public debates in the aftermath of the war. In the Grand National Assembly on December 6, 1920, Trabzon's Deputy Ali Şükrü lamented the fact that "The so called Abandoned Goods ended up becoming the property of the grabbers. What was the result of your shouts and protests?" *Yakın Tarihimiz,* 4, (1962): 77. A similar observation was made at the November 18, 1922 session of the Assembly by Yozgad Deputy Feyyaz Ali. *Türkiye Büyük Millet Meclisi Gizli Celse Zabıtları,* (The Transcripts of the Secret Sessions of the Grand National Assembly of Turkey) vol. 3 (Ankara, 1985), 1065. Moreover, in his memoirs Economics Minister Cavid admitted that on November 9, 1918 he ordered using up 1 million Turkish Pounds from the proceeds of the Abandoned Goods scheme. *Tanin,* August 30, 1945. During a public debate in which a number of prominent Turks were accusing each other of theft and plunder of the possessions and wealth of the deported Armenians, the former governor-general of Erzurum province, Hasan Tahsin (Uzer) in an open letter in a Turkish newspaper made the following statement as a means of refuting accusations levelled against him on the basis of some suspicions. "Prior to the deportations the Armenians of Erzurum had their

gold possessions and jewelry committed to the care of Bank Ottoman against which they were given receipts. Following the deportations the Financy Ministry invoked the Law of Abandoned Goods to place a claim on these deposits. The Bank refused. However, after protracted negotiations and the remittance by the ministry of material guarantees, it was agreed that all the bank deposits of Erzurum Armenians would be transferred to the Finance Ministry. Consequently, Cemal Bey, the military governor of Erzurum, and Celal Bey, the director of Ottoman Bank's Erzurum branch, have jointly sealed the packets and Cemal Bey took them to Istanbul and delivered them to the Finance Ministry for which he was given a receipt. I still have that receipt and am prepared to publish a copy of it." *Cumhuriyet*, December 19, 1924.

31. *War Cabinet's Hearings* [n. 15], 519.

32. S. Zurlinden, *Der Weltkrieg*, vol. 2 (Züurich, 1918), 596.

33. *U. S. National Archives.* R.G. 59.807.4014/148 (enclosure in Ambassador Morgenthau's August 30, 1915 report).

34. D. Avcıoğlu, *Milli Kurtuluş Tarihi*, (History of the National Liberation) vol. 3 (Istanbul, 1974), 1137, 1141. Sina Akşin likewise maintains that the Armenian deportations were implemented in pursuit of economic goals which eliminated minority dominance and competition in business and industry, allowing Muslims to control these areas. *See* Sina Akşin, *100 Soruda Jön Türkler ve Ittihat ve Terakki* (Ittihad ve Terakki in the Context of 100 Questions) (Istanbul, 1980), 283.

35. *Türkiye Büyük Millet Meclisi Gizli Celse Zabıtları*, [n. 30], vol. 4, p. 429 (Transcripts of the Secret Sessions of the Grand National Assembly of Turkey, March 2, 1923-October 25, 1934) (28th secret session, second sitting).

36. *Ibid.* The explanations of former Finance Minister Hasan Fehmi (Ataç) are as significant as the fact that his elevation to a ministerial post by Mustafa Kemal Atatürk on April 24, 1922 raised eyebrows among other associates of the latter on account of the fact that he was "uneducated." Avcıoğlu, *Milli* [n. 34], vol. 2, p. 640n.

37. *Türkiye* [n. 35], 430. The Finance Minister at the time was Mustafa Abdulhalik, who was present at the sitting and promised to execute the law as formulated. His pivotal role in the Armenian Genocide as governor of two large provinces, Bitlis and Aleppo, and as deputy to Talât in the Interior Ministry is discussed in Dadrian, "The Naim-Andonian Documents on the World War One Destruction of the Ottoman Armenians—The Anatomy of a Genocide," *International Journal of Middle East Studies* 18, 3 (1986): 331–32, 336–38. It is noteworthy that during the debate several Deputies singled out the Jews with the derogatory Turkish epithet "Mişon," denouncing them as the real "bloodsuckers" of Turkey and insisting that the law should apply to them with special emphasis. *Türkiye* [n. 35], 430–31.

38. S. Shaw and E. Shaw, *History of the Ottoman Empire and Modern Turkey*, vol. 2, (Cambridge, 1977), 315. In the light of the outcome of the deportations, it is significant that the authors chose to completely ignore the deceptiveness of these avowals.

39. H. Morgenthau, *Ambassador* [n. 7], 309.

40. This figure was released by a post-war Turkish Interior Minister relying on statistics compiled by his Ministry. *See* Dadrian, "Naim-Andonian" [n. 37], 342, and *idem.*, "The Documentation of the World War I Armenian Massacres in the Proceedings of the Turkish Military Tribunal" 23, 4 (November 1991): 552. In a recent volume by a Turkish historian this figure is confirmed as a more or less accurate computation by Turkish authorities. Y. Bayur, *Türk* [n. 44], 3, Part 4, p. 787 (1983). This 800,000 figure was likewise confirmed by Mustafa Kemal himself in an exchange with American Major General Harbord, the chief of the American Military Mission to Armenia, in September 1919. *Yakın Tarihimiz*, 3, (1962): 179. Excluded from this figure are all other categories of victims such as those executed while serving in the Turkish army, the multitudes of young females forced into concubinage, Muslim marriages, or adoption, victims of coercive religious conversions, and countless others who eventually perished as a result of the extraordinary hardships of deportation.

41. H. Morgenthau, *Ambassador* [n. 7], 302-03.

42. Two prominent Turkish authors likewise denounced the practice of forcing Islam on Armenian orphans. *See* H. Edib, *The Turkish Ordeal* (New York, 1928), 16; D. Avcıoğlu, *Milli* [n. 34], 1141.

43. A.A. *Botschaft Konstantinopel*, 174/27, and A.A. Türkei 183/44 A26071. In one of his candid statements, Dr. B. Şakir, one of the principal architects of the genocide, indicated that he expected that many people would be indignant at his role, denouncing it as contrary to, to use his own words, "the laws of the nation and of humanity." A.E. Yalman, *Yakın Tarihte Gördüklerim ve Işittiklerim*, vol. 1 (The Things I Saw and Heard in Recent History), 332.
44. Yusuf H. Bayur, *Türk Inkilâbı Tarihi* (The History of the Turkish Revolution) vol. 3, Part 1 (Ankara, 1953), 476.

Chapter 15

The Disguises of the Law of Deportation and Ancillary Acts

Ultimate Responsibility for the Deportation

Ultimate responsibility for these measures must lie with members of the Ittihad party. Ittihad was able to accomplish the anti-Armenian measures through its powerful stranglehold on the Turkish government. Indeed, to fully understand the de facto power structure of the Ottoman government in wartime emergency conditions, one must recognize that the executive branch's actions were substantially freed from the restraints of the already emasculated legislature.[1] At the same time, the military and the quasi-military gained a preponderance of authority, legitimized by the very same executive. Superseding these institutions was the autocracy of Ittihad, a monolithic political party that dominated the state apparatus.

As noted above, the Temporary Law of Deportation[2] was railroaded through the Cabinet Council in May, 1915, when the deportations were already well underway. By resorting to this unauthorized tactic "Interior Minister Talât singlehandedly assumed a very grave responsibility … he probably wanted to forestall some opposition in the Cabinet."[3] The fourth article of that law, rarely publicized in pertinent literature, contains two stipulations. The first charged the War Minister with executing the deportations (*meriyeti ahkâm*). This stipulation was consonant with the Monarch's prerogatives spelled out in article 7 of the Constitution. Nevertheless, the Interior Ministry and its subsidiary offices, including the provincial centers of administration, security, police, and gendarmery forces, actually organized and administered the deportations.[4] The second stipulation refers to the formal promulgation of the law by the Parliament "in its next session," as provided by article 36 of the Ottoman Constitu-

---

Notes for this chapter begin on page 243.

tion. There is no evidence that this formal promulgation occurred when the temporarily suspended Parliament reconvened on September 28, 1915.

Interior Minister Talât in his memoirs supplies a hint that the suspension of Parliament was directly connected to the intended anti-Armenian measures.[5] The architects of the "deportation" felt that as long as the Parliament was in session, they could take no effective counter-measures against the Armenians in response to the anti-Turkish acts that were being attributed to them. Moreover, suspending Parliament allowed the deputies to return to their electoral districts and inform their constituencies about the Armenian danger. The Supreme Directorate of Ittihad made the decision to suspend Parliament on March 1, 1915 to facilitate the deportations.[6] This marks an instance in which Ittihad, a monolithic political party, substituted its will for government policy, thereby preempting the legislative branch which was thus prevented from debating and thereafter formally promulgating the temporary law. Instead, Ittihad expediently circumvented the Parliament until the task of destroying the victim population was all but completed and Turkey ended up losing the war. Only then, and not on September 15, 1915, as claimed by Kamuran Gürün and other Turkish and non-Turkish authors (see note no. 16 of chapter 14), a weak and meek Ottoman Parliament representing a vanquished and partly occupied country, expeditiously proceeded to debate the law, only to cancel it promptly by a negative vote of rejection. The comical aspects of this parliamentary parody were exceeded only by the grim tragedy surrounding the fate of the population to which that sham law was inexorably applied during the war.

The Special Organization (Teşkilâtı Mahsusa)

During this time, Ittihadist leaders secretly formed a unit called the Special Organization, one of whose principal purposes was resolving the Armenian question. Equipped with special codes, funds, cadres, weapons, and ammunition, they functioned as a semi-autonomous "state within the state."[7] Their mission was to deploy in remote areas of Turkey's interior and to ambush and destroy convoys of Armenian deportees.[8] The cadres consisted almost entirely of convicted criminals, released from the Empire's prisons by a special dispensation issued by the Ministries of both Interior and Justice.[9] In his testimony before the Fifth Committee of the Ottoman Chamber of Deputies on November 10, 1918, ex-Justice Minister Ibrahim acknowledged such a release of convicts from the prisons.[10] The application for Imperial Legal Authorization (*Irade*) to form the Special Organization was deliberately framed in a "vague formula to deflect attention from its secret goals"; this formula invoked "national ideals and objectives to be ensured through solidarity and cohesiveness to secure which will be the purpose of the Organization."[11] When, in 1916, the draft bill to enlist convicted murderers in the Special Organization was being discussed, that organization already had all but completed its mission against the Armenians. In denouncing the rationale of the bill, Senator A. Riza stated that "murderers and criminals do not belong in the army," inasmuch as the bill was framed in such a way as to convey the impression that the recruitment was for the benefit of the army. However, Colonel Behiç (Erkin) of the Supply Department of the War Ministry (*Ikmal Şubesi*) proudly declared in the Parliament that the majority of the convicts was being recruited not for the benefit of the army but for the *Teşkilatı Mahsusa*, the organization in which "they had proven their usefulness." Hence, he argued, it was impossible for these criminals to prove pernicious to the overall morality of the army soldiers. Angered by this admission, Riza retorted: "We know about the nature of that organization. We shall call it to account in the future" (*O teşkilatın ne olduğunu biliyoruz. Ilerde hesabını soracağız*). This notwithstanding, the bill was declared as "lawful" by the undersecretary of the Justice Ministry who requested and secured its passage as "an emergency" bill (*müstaceliyet*).[12]

During the second sitting of the trial series of the top Ittihadists (May 4, 1919) Colonel Cevad's defense counsel introduced a document signed by the same Colonel Behiç. Dated November 25, 1914, and addressed to the directorate of the Special Organization, it let it be known that henceforth the *valis* in the eastern provinces will be able to participate in the work of the Special Organization since a law is being passed which authorizes the engagement of convicts. It appears that some eastern governors, anxious about the risks of their complicity, were hedging and were demanding some legal protection. The document ends with a request to return it after taking cognizance of its contents.[13] In his testimony at the second sitting of the same tribunal (May 4, 1919), Colonel Atıf admitted that eastern *valis* were involved in the work of the Special Organization.[14]

The stated responsibilities of the Special Organization included intelligence, counter espionage, and the prevention of sabotage. The writings of two Turkish authors, who had access to secrets of the Special Organization indicate, however, that its principal duty was the execution of the Armenian genocide. Kutay alluded to the Ittihad Central Committee's covert objectives in setting up the Special Organization as involving "the vital interests of Turkey which could not be openly acknowledged as being part of Ittihad's program".[15] The other, a principal Special Organization chief, who "had assumed duties" in connection with the Armenian deportations, admitted to having accomplished things which the government and law enforcement agencies "absolutely couldn't," namely, "the execution of measures against non-Turkish nationality population clusters."[16] Turkish historian Avcıoğlu was even more direct. He wrote:

In order to radically solve the Armenian question, Ittihad through the Special Organization resorted to systematic and large scale deportations. Hundreds of thousands of Armenians were in a very short time and *en masse* taken to spots outside Anatolia. This policy, supported by the Germans, was sponsored in the Councils of Ittihad by Dr. Behaeddin Şakir ... .

As to the sweeping character of this decision and the manner of implementation, Avcıoğlu declared.

> ... the liquidation of the Christian elements was decided upon outside the auspices of the official government and at the headquarters of the Ittihad, following deliberations that lasted months. Young officers whom the Ittihad trusted were recalled to Istanbul and were briefed [on the missions with which they were] entrusted.[17]

These covert missions of the Special Organization were first exposed through the efforts of the Turkish press. On November 4, 1918, five days after the signing of the Armistice, the Turkish daily *Hadisat*, the organ of the Association for the Defense of National Rights of Eastern Provinces, in an open letter to Grand Vizier Izzet, first mentioned publicly the existence and wartime criminal activities of this organization.[18] In December, the press reported the statements, made during a debate in the Chamber by the Turkish Deputy from Trabzon, mentioning the Special Organization as the principal tool of the massacres and admitting that "up until now we had remained silent about all this."[19] In an open letter to the Justice Minister, the opposition daily *Sabah* provided the most explicit public exposure of the Special Organization's existence and the complicity of the Justice Minister in its activities:

> Did you not drop by every morning at Talât's home to receive your atrocious orders from that brigand chief [*çetebaşı*]? Did you not, as a result of a decision reached at Ittihad's party headquarters, release from the central prison of Istanbul the most ferocious murderers so that they could kill with axes the innocent Armenians in the vicinity of towns and villages of which they were the inhabitants? Did you not order similar releases from prisons in the provinces? Was it not the general purpose to select the most bloodthirsty murderers and enroll them in the brigand cadres [of the Special Organization] for which end you appointed the procuror-general of the Appellate Court, whereas [the] War Minister was represented by a high ranking officer? Furthermore, was not a physician appointed also to determine whether the selected convicts would be fit to apply a degree of savagery of killing you required? Did not the formation of the brigand criminals take place in the office of the same procuror-general of the Appellate Court which was located just below your own office? Did not this organizational work continue for weeks during which one could observe the prison convicts being brought to the corridors located outside of the offices of the procuror-general, the chamber of the Criminal Court, and the Courtroom itself?[20]

In his November 9, 1918 testimony before the Ottoman Parliament's Fifth Committee investigating "the misdeeds" of the Cabinet Ministers, Grand Vizier Sait Halim twice stated that the Cabinet had not authorized the formation of the Special Organization. The Organization, which he called "a very bad thing," was thus constituted outside the purview of the government.[21] The Justice Minister made the same statement.[22] Both officials admitted that the purpose of the deportations was subverted, as the Grand Vizier clearly testified, to "killing." In this connection, in one paragraph he used the term "massacre" three times, dropping entirely the term "deportation."[23]

A captain of the Ottoman War Office's Intelligence Department, subsequently a professor of history at Istanbul University and a prolific author, wrote of the massacres:

> The criminal gangs who were released from the prisons, after a week's training at the War Ministry's training grounds, were sent off to the Caucasian front as the brigands of the Special Organization, perpetrating the worst crimes against the Armenians ... . The Ittihadists intended to destroy the Armenians, and thereby to do away with the Question of the Eastern Provinces.[24]

For a detailed discussion of the origin, organization, function and command and control setup of the Special Organization, see a recent contribution in a book dealing with the fate of minorities in wartime.[25] The estimates on the number of Special Organization men vary.[26]

Efforts to Disguise Responsibility and Intent: A Challenge for Punishment
The argument of national security and the weapon of holy war

On May 24, 1915, the Allies declared the Turkish government and its officials responsible for the massacres then in progress. Despite the continuance of the government-sponsored destruction, the Ottomans responded to the declaration by carefully disguising the intent behind the anti-Armenian massacres. The Turkish response stated that the Ottoman government "considers its principal duty to resort to any measure it deems appropriate for safeguarding the security [*muhafazai emniyet*] of its borders, and feels, therefore, that it has no obligation whatsoever to give an account to any foreign government."[27] This statement implicitly relied upon the rule of international law that "the state is entitled to treat its own citizens at discretion."[28] At the same time, the Turkish declaration served as an artful deflection, hedging against the criminal consequences of intent. Ultimately, the question of intent became the cardinal challenge to the ensuing prosecution. As one legal scholar pointed out, "governments less stupid than that of National Socialist Germany will never admit the intent to destroy a group as such, but will tell the world that they are acting against the traitors ... ."[29]

Laws enacted under such conditions and rationale are but sham laws transforming the principle of legality into willful license. The intent of the crime of genocide can be located precisely in that particular zone which separates the stated purposes of the law from the consequences of its application. When massive deportations culminate in mass destruction, the law covering the former betrays a criminal intent to achieve the latter.

The religious strain in the Ottoman-Turkish martial legacy only reinforced that intent. The proclamation of holy war (*cihad*) on November 11, 1914, carefully planned beforehand, proved an expedient catalyst in that respect, despite the fact that it was formally aimed at the Entente powers, i.e., France, England and Russia, while excluding Turkey's equally Christian allies Germany and Austria. In his testimony at the trial in Berlin of Soghomon Teilerian, the "avenger", who had assassinated Talât, Marshal Liman von Sanders, the head of the German Military Mission to Turkey, declared that the men escorting the Armenian deportee convoys were influenced by the spirit of *cihad* when attacking their Armenian charges as Christians.[30] In his memoirs Sanders describes a scene of destructiveness against Armenian property in Constantinople, immediately in the wake of the declaration of holy war, adding that "as usual the processions were organized by the police."[31] The excitatory features of *cihad*, directed especially against the Armenians, are narrated by a number of other eyewitnesses.[32]

Deportation and the governmental pledge of "relocation"

The disguise which proved most perilous for the victim population was the air of solicitousness with which the Turkish authorities officially pledged to "relocate" that population whose deportation they had decreed under a plea of wartime military necessity. The outcome of these deportations and the actual fate of the targeted population are matters of historical record which is being examined and highlighted in the present study. The discussion below, reviewing the significance of this governmental pledge of "relocation" for the issue of genocidal planing, is part of this effort. Such planning certainly includes the need of trapping the targeted group through resort to deception, bordering on perfidy. Presently, the citizen subjects of the Ottoman-Turkish state were betrayed by their own government which chose to deliberately subvert the principles of trust and good faith.

The strategem employed here had a broader compass of goal-directedness, however. Apart from the end of deflecting from its covert intent of genocide, it aimed at establishing the grounds for post-genocide claims of exculpation. Generally speaking, the argument of deportation as a wartime emergency measure has a tinge of persuasiveness, if not legitimacy, which tends to confound outsiders as to the incidence of perpetrator-intent, at the same time obfuscating historical analysis and judgement. This fact is reflected in the writings of some contemporary Ottomanists, identified with "the Turkish point of view." Stanford Shaw and Ezel Shaw, for example, offer the following description on this issue. The order to deport the Armenians was attended by

> arrangements made to settle them in towns and camps in the Mosul area of northern Irak ... to provide them with sufficient food and other supplies to meet their needs during the march and after they were settled ... the Armenians were to be protected and cared for until they returned to their homes after the war ... the government would provide for their return once the crisis was over.[33]

By reproducing through these statements standard Turkish assertions, the authors are not only insisting on the validity of the pledge of relocation but, beyond it, are also maintaining that the government indeed intended to have the deported masses returned to their homes after the war. Even Turkish historians, including K. Gürün, do not go so far, indicating instead that the dislocation of the deportees was final and terminal.[34] But the persistence in routinely echoing—after so many decades of discovery of facts—the claim of the Turkish government about "relocation" is a condition that needs to be dealt with briefly. At stake is the very integrity of scholarship touching on one of the most critical aspects in the enactment of the genocide at issue here.

Even if one were to discount the vast corpus of data obtained from Armenian survivors, the aggregate testimony supplied on this issue by German, American, and Turkish officials, who were on duty in Turkey during the war, in stark terms expose the falsehood of the claim of relocation. Here are some examples. In responding to a governmental declaration, made in the course of the ongoing deportations, that the deportees were going to be provided, free of charge, new housing facilities at their new destinations, Dr. Otto Göppert, the legal councillor at the German Embassy in the Ottoman capital, in so many words characterized this promise of relocation as a farce when reporting about it to Berlin.[35] Lewis Einstein, the Special Agent of the State Department on duty at the American Embassy in the Ottoman capital during the enactment of the genocide, decried that promise of relocation, stating:

> New homes would be provided for them, [the deportees], at Zor and in the desert land, through which follows the Euphrates. Such was the official euphemism ... the grim humor of paternal solicitude which usually covers the most barbarous massacres in Turkey ... . [What was involved here was] an armed policy of deportation, and its implied sequel, extermination ... . The diabolical plot aimed at making the Armenians run the whole gauntlet of Asia Minor, where the country had been aroused to murder.[36]

Another American official, Leslie Davis, American consul at Harput in southeast of Turkey, personally had observed how huge clusters of Armenian populations, deported from the other provinces of Turkey, on their way to the deserts of Mesopotamia were rerouted in Harput "only to be butchered in this province." In his lengthy report, prepared at the request of his superior, Wilbur J. Carr, the director of the Consular Bureau of the U.S. State Department, Davis concluded, "The term 'Slaughter-house Vilayet' (Province) which I applied to this vilayet ... has been fully justified by what I have learned and actually seen ... ."[37] Vice Marshal Pomiankowski, the Austrian Plenipotentiary attached to the Ottoman General Headquarters throughout the war, in his memoirs stated that "the barbaric order to deport and resettle in the northern desert regions of Arabia, i.e., Mesopotamia, where the Euphrates flows, the entire Armenian population of Asia Minor in reality entailed the extermination [*Ausrottung*] of Asia Minor's Armenian population."[38] Theodore A. Elmer, a professor at the American Anatolia College in Marzuan (Merzifon), recounted how the commander of the gendarmerie of that city "who had the business of their [Armenians] deportation in charge, called at the mission compound, and talked freely about the deportation of the Armenians in the presence of all the American men in our station. He said that not one out of a thousand would ever reach Mosul ... ."[39] In a similar vein, Austrian author Wolfdieter Bihl, in his massive treatise examining the Armenian genocide, stated that "the manner, in which the deporations were carried out, was a mockery of the arrangements" the government claimed to have made for relocation and shelter. Continuing on, Bihl declared that "often there was no 'effort' to deport the Armenians as the victims in an outburst of unprecedented bloodlust were tortured and slaughtered—one has to use this word—on the spot."[40]

Given the gargantuan task of destroying such a huge population with rather primitive means, there were significant numbers of victims who had survived both the acts of intermittent massacres en route, and the decimation and attrition resulting from the exacting treks of deportations throughout the length and breadth of Anatolia. For these survivors the authorities had created a string of waystations in the deserts from which they were regularly dispatched to their ultimate death by a variety of methods.[41] A German employee of the American consulate at Aleppo, Mr. Bernau, was commissioned to inspect these waystations and report back on the conditions he observed. In a lengthy report he prepared he said that he couldn't even bring himself to call these waystations "camps" (*Lager*). He adjudged the conditions there "so fiendish that the most cruel of the Mongols could not have imagined them." Bernau then wrote:

> The entrance of these concentration camps could well bear the legend imprinted on the gates of Dante's hell 'Ye who enter here, abandon all hope.'"[42]

Nor are all Turkish authors in accord with the posture of Turkish authorities, past and present, and that of their advocates in the West, pretending that the government was serious about relocation. Turkish general Ali Fuad Erden, who at the time was Chief of Staff of Cemal Paşa's IVth Army, whose areas of jurisdiction included most of the deserts of Mesopotamia, in his memoirs concedes that "there was neither preparation, nor organization to shelter the hundreds of thousands of the deportees ... ."[43] Ahmet Refik (Altınay), a wartime intelligence officer at Department II, Ottoman General Headquarters, likewise stated that those deportees who escaped massacre "were driven to blazing deserts, to hunger, misery and death."[44]

Taner Akçam, the most maverick of all these dissenting Turkish authors, and perhaps the most promising rising star in a new firmament of Turkish historiography, succinctly summed up the picture in this conclusion of his:

> The fact that neither at the start of the deportations, nor en route, and nor at the locations, which were declared to be their initial halting places, were there any single arrangement, required for the organization of a people's migration, is sufficient proof of the existence of this plan of annihilation.[45]

Commenting on the operation of the waystations which he calls "the death camps" (*ölüm kampları*), Akçam notes that though labeled as "concentration camps," they were an alternate method of killing off the victims in the deserts through artificially induced privations and epidemic diseases; "for anyone to emerge alive from them was tantamount to a miracle."[46]

Notes to Chapter 15

1. Turkish historian Bayur cites this attitude of War Minister Enver as typical in this respect. Enver's contempt for the procedures of the orderly enactment of laws was expressed in his motto: "If there is no [corresponding] law, then make up law and [thus] you have law" (*yok kanun, yap kanun, var kanun*). Y. Bayur, *Türk Inkilâbı Tarihi* (The History of the Turkish Revolution)vol. 3 Part 2 (Ankara, 1955) 400. See also F. Atay, *Zeytindağı* (Istanbul, 1981), 78. Dr. Harry Stürmer, the Istanbul correspondent of the German daily newspaper *Kölnische Zeitung*, relates an incident at the same Parliament when war lord Enver, Talât's acolyte, "went so far as to hurl the epithet 'shameless dog' [*edebsiz köpek*] at Ahmed Riza in the Senate without being called to order by the President." H. Stürmer, *Two Years in Constantinople*, E. Allen trans. (New York, 1917), 256; *see also ibid., Zwei Kriegsjahre in Konstantinopel. Skizzen Deutsch-Jung-Türkischer Moral und Politik* (Lausanne, 1917), 232.

2. For the English text of the law, see R. Hovannisian, *Armenia on the Road to Independence 1918* (Los Angeles, 1967), 51.

3. Y. Bayur, *Türk*, [n. 1], vol. 3, Part 3 (1957), 38. Turkish political scientist Tunaya likewise points out the Ittihadist method of by-passing the Cabinet when enacting a governmental decision on its behalf through the initiative of a single minister. T. Tunaya, *Türkiyede Siyasal Partiler* (The Political Parties in Turkey), vol. 1, Part 1, 2nd enlarged ed. (Istanbul, 1984), 579.

4. *Ibid.*, (Bayur), 40; *see also* C. Paşa, *Hatıraları* (Istanbul, 1977), 440. Historian Bayur indicates that at the start of World War I, Süleyman Askeri, the original chief of the Special Organization, had his headquarters in one of the branches of the Interior Ministry, created for the handling of the missions of that organization. Bayur, *Türk* [n. 1] vol. 3, Part 1 (1953), 398.

5. C. Kutay, *Talât Paşanın Gurbet Hatıraları* (The Memoirs of Talât Paşa in Exile), vol. 2 (Istanbul, 1983), 907. Specifically, the proposal for suspension was made by Ittihad General-Secretary Mithat Şükrü (Bleda).

6. This termination one and a half months earlier than stipulated by the law (February 11, 1915 Amendment of Article 35 of the Constitution), necessitated the reconvening of the Parliament on September 28, 1915, one and a half months sooner than the normal date. Jäschke, *"Die Entwicklung des osmanischen Verfassungstaates von den Anfängen bis zur Gegenwart", Die Welt des Islams*, 5 (1917): 37. The Parliament was actually recessed the first time on August 2, 1914, the day when the secret Turko-German military and political alliance was signed. *Takvimi Vekâyi* No. 1946, September 12, 1914.

7. C. Kutay, *Birinci Dünya Harbinde Teşkilâtı Mahsusa* (The Special Organization During World War I) (Istanbul, 1962), 38. Most of the data contained in this book was supplied by one of the Special Organization's founders and chiefs, E. Kuşcubaşı. For a detailed discussion of the origin, development, function and direction of the organization see Tunaya, *Türkiyede* [n. 3], vol. 3, 275–292. For a description of the Ottoman legacy of using irregulars regularly in all kinds of wars *see* James Reid, "The Concept of War and Genocidal Impulses in the Ottoman Empire, 1821–1918" *Holocaust and Genocide Studies* 4 (1989): 177–182.

8. In his July 27, 1915 report to his Chancellor in Berlin, Germany's Aleppo Consul Rössler described the Special Organization massacre details as "convicts, released from the prisons, and put in military uniform. They were deployed on locations through which the doomed deportee convoys were scheduled to pass." A.A. Türkei 183/38, A23991; *see also* J. Lepsius, *Deutschland und Armenien 1914–1918* (Berlin-Potsdam, 1919), 111; A. Yalman, *Yakın Tarihte Gördüklerim ve Işittiklerim*, (The Things I Saw and Heard in Recent History) vol. 1 (Istanbul, 1970), 331. This method of deployment and ambush of the deportee convoys is described in a recently published comprehensive study of the Ottoman Empire, a collaborative work by French area experts. *Histoire de l'Empire Ottoman*, R. Mantran, ed. (Paris, 1989), 623. Turkish Military Intelligence Officer Ahmed Refik in his post-war account of the role of this organization declares that "the worst crimes against the Armenians were perpetrated by the brigand cadres of this organization (*Ermeni mezaliminde en büyük cinayetleri bu çeteler ika ettiler*). A. Refik (Altınay) *Iki Komite Iki Kıtal* (Two Committees and Two Massacres) (Istanbul, 1919), 23. Reed describes "the operational aspect" of a Turkish tradition of "total war" … through "the usual localized attacks" as "a key to understanding of the Armenian Genocide." "Total War, the Annihilation Ethic, and the Armenian Genocide, 1870–1918," in R. Hovannisian ed., *The Armenian Genocide: History, Politics, Ethics*, (New York, 1992), 39–40. For an account on the technique of ambush by an American diplomat stationed in one of the provinces, whose Armenian population was subjected to wholesale destruction, *see* L. A. Davis, *The Slaughterhouse Province* S. Blair, ed. (New Rochelle, N. Y., 1989), 58.

9. F. Atay, *Zeytindağı* [n. 1], 35–36. The preponderance of convicts in the ranks of the organization is mentioned in A. Toynbee, *The Western Question in Greece and Turkey* (Boston, 1922), 265–66, 279–80. S. Sonyel concedes the employment of convicts, attributing it to the lack of gendarmes who were sent to the front for war duties. "Armenian Deportations: A Reappraisal in the Light of New Documents," *Belleten* (January 1972): 60.

10. *Harb Kabinelerinin Isticvabı* (War Cabinets' Hearings) (Istanbul, 1933), 537. (*Vakit* newspaper special documentary publication series, No. 2).

11. C. Kutay, *Birinci*, [n. 7], 39. In touching on this point of deflection, political scientist Melson argues with reference to the massacres of the Hamidian era, that thereby "massacre could achieve the desired results without clearly implicating the central government." R. Melson, "A Theoretical Inquiry into the Armenian Massacres of 1894–1896," *Comparative Study in Society & History* 24 (1982): 507. Stoddard, another American author specializing in the missions of the Special Organization, suggests that the authorities used the organization to shift the onus for their perpetrations to "groups of brigands" which could not be controlled from Istanbul. P. Stoddard, *The Ottoman* [n. 26], 49, 50. In a scathing criticism of Ittihad political and military leaders for their use of the Special Organization, of the officers in charge of the cadres of the organization, and above all, of the convicts comprising these cadres, a high ranking Turkish staff officer challenged the legality of the use of convicts. He was the Chief of Staff of the Army Corps of the Reserve Cavalry whose ranks were also filled with convicts released from

the prisons. "Military Penal Law deprives criminals of the honor to bear arms ... yet in order to be delivered from the shackles of prison life, these criminals made all sorts of pledges only to discard them upon release ... The regiment of Yakub Cemil, for example, consisted of bloodthirsty criminals (*kanlı katil*)." A. Samih, *Büyük Harpte Kafkas Cephesi Hatıraları* (The Causasus Front in the Great War) (Ankara, 1934), 3, 67–68, 104.

12. *Meclisi Âyan Zabıt Ceridesi* (Transcripts of the Proceedings of the Senate) Third Perod. Session 3. Fifteenth Sitting. December 12, 1916, pp. 186–88.

13. *Takvimi Vekâyi* No. 3543, p. 28.

14. *Tarihi Muhakeme* (Historical Trial) (Istanbul, 1919), 60.

15. C. Kutay, *Talât* [n. 5], vol. 3, p. 1299. The writings of two officers within the Special Organization also confirm the direct involvement of the Ittihad Central Committee. In his memoirs, one of them, a lieutenant colonel of the Special Organization, conceded that the Central Committee authorized the anti-Armenian measures which led to the massacres, describing these measures as reprisals against Armenian "insurgents." H. Ertürk, *Iki Devrin Perde Arkası* (Behind the Scenes during Two Eras) S. Tansu, ed. (Istanbul, 1957), 294–98, 306. The lieutenant colonel's right hand man likewise maintained that the Ittihad's Central Committee, a sort of directorate under Talât, formulated special plans for the Special Organization's missions. G. Vardar, *Ittihad ve Terakki İçinde Dönenler* (The Inside Story of Ittihad ve Terakki), S. Tansu, ed. (Istanbul, 1960), 244–46, 274. For a similar view see M. R. Esatlı, *Ittihad ve Terakki Tarihinde Esrar Perdesi* (The Curtain of Secrecy in the History of Ittihad), 258 (Istanbul, 1975).

16. C. Kutay, *Birinci* [n. 7], 38, 78.

17. D. Avcıoğlu, *Milli Kurtuluş Tarihi* (History of the National Liberation), vol. 3 (Istanbul, 1974), 1114, 1135. Reference should be made to the following findings made by British political and military intelligence. When reporting to London about the Court Martial death sentence against Şakir, British High Commissioner Admiral John de Robeck wrote, "He was a member of the small secret Committe known as Teshkilati Mahsusa [the Special Organization] formed by the Central Committee of the Committee of Union and Progress [the Ittihad] to organize the extermination of the Armenian race." FO 371/5089/E949, Feb. 18, 1920 report. An intelligence report prepared by the Istanbul branch of the M.I.L.C. likewise stated: "Teshkilati Mahsusa [was] created by the CUP in 1914 for the extermination of the Armenians and was controlled by the infamous Behaeddin Shakir." FO 371/5171/E12228, p. 7 (August 29, 1920). Turkish sociologist and publicist Yalman, who held intimate conversations with many of the Ittihadists (severely implicated in the organization as well as implementation of the Armenian Genocide), while being detained with them in Malta by the British, stated that "two influential" Ittihadists helped to create the Special Organization. While Dr. Şakir is the all too familiar one, the allusion to the other one is most probably Dr. Nazım. Yalman candidly states that the anti-Armenian measures reflected a "policy of general extermination" to remove "the danger" to Turkey of "a dense Armenian population in the Eastern Provinces." A. E. Yalman, *Turkey in the World War* (New Haven, 1930), 220.

18. *Hadisat* (Istanbul), November 4, 1918.

19. *Zhamanag* (Istanbul), December 12, 1918; *Ariamard* (Istanbul), December 12, 1918. The deputy was Hafız Mehmet, who later became the Justice Minister in the fledgling Turkish Republic and was executed in July, 1926 on charges of conspiring against the life of Mustafa Kemal, the founder of the Republic. E. Zürcher, *The Unionist Factor* (Leiden, 1984), 154.

20. *Sabah* (Istanbul), November 21, 1918. *Renaissance*, January 19, 1919.

21. *War Cabinets' Hearings* [n. 10], 308, 309. Economics Minister Cavid declared likewise before the Fifth Committee that there was no governmental authorization for the formation of the Special Organization. *Ibid.*, 170.

22. *Ibid.*, 534, 535.

23. *Ibid.*, 290, 293–94.

24. A. Refik, *Iki Komite* [n. 8], 23.

25. Vahakn N. Dadrian, "The Role of the Special Organization in the Armenian Genocide during the First World War" in *Minorities in Wartime. National and Racial Groupings*

in Europe, North America and Australia during Two World Wars (P. Panayi, ed. (Oxford, 1993), 50–82.

26. Western sources estimate the number of these convicts between thirty thousand, E. Doumergue, *L'Arménie, les Massacres et la Question D'Orient*, (Paris, 1916), 24–25, and thirty-four thousand, S. Zurlinden, *Der Weltkrieg*, vol. 2 (Zürich, 1918), 657. According to P. Stoddard the total number of men enrolled in the organization was "about 30,000." *The Ottoman Government and the Arabs, 1911 to 1918. A Preliminary Study of the Teşkilât-ı Mahsusa* (Ann Arbor, MI, 1963), 58.

27. E. Uras, *Tarihte Ermeniler ve Ermeni Meselesi* (The Armenians and the Armenian Question in History)(Istanbul, 1950), 621; in the 1976 edition the editors instead of the terms "safeguarding the security of its borders," use the expression "public safety" *(genel güvenlik)* (Ankara), 612.

28. L. Oppenheim & H. Lauterpacht, *International Law* vol. 1, 7th ed. (London, 1948), 583.

29. G. A. Finch, "The Genocide Convention," *American Journal of International Law* 43 (1949): 743.

30. *Der Prozess Talaat Pascha*. Stenographischer Prozessbericht (Berlin, 1921), 62.

31. Liman von Sanders, *Five Years in Turkey* (Annapolis, 1927), 35.

32. Rafael de Nogales, *Four Years Beneath the Crescent*, Muna Lee, trans. (New York, 1926), 14; Ulrich Trumpener, *Germany and the Ottoman Empire* (Princeton, 1968), 118; a confidential, internal German Foreign Office memo stated that "cihad excited the passions of the Turkish people against the Armenians." A. A. Türkei 183/49, August 1917; Simon Khoren, "Hishoghutiunner" (Memories) in Teotig ed., *Amenoun Daret-zouytzu* (Everyone's Almanac) vols. 10–14, 1916–1920, p. 133.

33. S. Shaw and E. Shaw, *History of the Ottoman Empire and Modern Turkey*, vol. 2 (Cambridge, 1977), 315.

34. Kamuran Gürün, *The Armenian File. The Myth of Innocence Exposed* (New York, 1985), 209. Idem. *Ermeni Dosyası* (Ankara, 1983), 217; Avcıoğlu, *Milli Kurtuluş* [n. 17], 1140.

35. A. A. Türkei 183/45, A28792. October 20, 1916 report.

36. Lewis Einstein, "The Armenian Massacres," *Contemporary Review* 616 (April 1917): 490.

37. Leslie A. Davis, *The Slaughterhouse Province. An American Diplomat's Report on the Armenian Genocide, 1915–1917*. Susan K. Blair, ed. (New Rochelle, N.Y., 1989), 181. see also pp. 83, 160.

38. Joseph Pomiankowski, *Der Zusammenbruch des Ottomanischen Reiches* (Vienna, 1969 [reissue of the original 1928 edition]), 160.

39. Viscount Bryce, *The Treatment of Armenians in the Ottoman Empire 1915–16*, A. Toynbee, compiler (London, 1916, government publication Miscellaneous No. 31), Doc. No. 87, p. 341.

40. Wolfdieter Bihl, *Die Kaukasus-Politik der Mittelmächte* Part I (Vienna, 1975), 172.

41. For a brief description of these methods see Vahakn N. Dadrian, "The Naim-Andonian Documents on the World War I Destruction of Ottoman Armenians: The Anatomy of a Genocide," *International Journal of Middle East Studies*, 18, 3 (August 1986): 351, notes 60 and 61.

42. A. A. Türkei 183/46, A8613, German consul Rössler's February 14, 1917 report; the full text of the extensive report is in Johannes Lepsius, *Deutschland and Armenien. Sammlung Diplomatischer Aktenstücke* (Potsdam-Berlin, 1919), 486–493. The English translation of the report is in Dickran Boyajian, *Armenia-The Case for a Forgotten Genocide* (Westwood, N.J., 1972), 117–124. In addition, there is a remarkable State Department document exposing the fiendish character of the "relocation" scheme. It originates from the Chargé of the American Embassy at the Ottoman capital, Constantinople, and is relayed via Copenhagen as "confidentially" secured information. Here are some excerpts from it:

> In "wide districts including Deir Zor and other places on Euphrates and in the Desert … agents found them [the Armenian deportees] eating grass, herbs, and locusts and in desperate cases dead animals and human bodies … death rate from starvation and sickness very high and increased by brutal treatment of the authorities whose bearing toward the exiles as they are being driven back and forth [in the] desert is not unlike

that of slave drivers. With few exceptions no shelter of any kind is provided and the people coming from cold climate are left under scorching desert sun without food and water ... Misery and hopelessness of the situation is such that many are reported to resort to suicide ... Boat loads sent from Zor down the river arrived at Ana, one thirty miles away, with three fifths of passengers missing. *There appears in short steady policy to exterminate these people but to deny charge of massacre. Their destruction from so-called natural causes seems decided upon"* (Italics added). Cipher telegram of Hoffman Philip, the American Chargé at Constantinople. July 12, 1916. *U.S. National Archives,* R.G. 59.867.48/356.

43. Orgeneral Ali Fuad Erden, *Birinci Dünya Harbinde Suriye Hatıraları* (Syrian Memoirs of World War I), vol. 1 (Istanbul, 1954), 122.

44. Refik (Altınay), *Iki Komite* [n. 8], 30.

45. Taner Akçam, *Türk Ulusal Kimliği ve Ermeni Sorumu* (Istanbul, 1992), 106.

46. *Ibid.,* 111.

Chapter 16

The Issue of German Complicity

The Revival of the Armenian Question and the New Turko-German Partnership

The Turkish impulse to consider the Armenians as an "internal foe" was only in part a reflection of the state of exigencies of the war animating that impulse. More critical in this respect was the political fallout of the revival of the Armenian Question in the period interposed between the first Balkan War and World War I. Furthermore, there was a new line-up among the Powers marking the re-emergence of Russia as the advocate of the Armenian cause which issued from that revival; it was supported in this new role, albeit passively, by England and France. The new alignment was this time free from the cryptic acts of sabotage Russia, and to a lesser degree France, were wont to indulge in during the turbulent era of Abdul Hamit, thereby frustrating England's effort to force the Sultan to carry out the reforms in the provinces.

That legacy of shielding Turkey from the presumed inroads of alien reforms, portending an encroachment on Turkish sovereignty, was borne by Emperor William II's Germany which for some time had been cultivating a new and invigorated partnership with the Young Turk regime. In this new shift of alignments, the Turko-German common objective was to place constraints on Russian designs of reform which were suspected to be Russian imperial designs in disguise. The man entrusted with this task was Hans Freiherr von Wangenheim, the German Ambassador to Turkey. In the unending chain of ironies, characteristic of the vicissitudes and frailties of diplomacy, Russia was now being administered the same dose of frustration it had administered to England in the 1894–96 period, especially when Salisbury was in office several times during that period.

Notes for this chapter begin on page 294.

Ambassador Wangenheim, in a manifest gesture of optimal support of Turkey, went so far as to declare at one stage of the negotiations for Armenian reforms (September 1913) that Germany would agree to the terms of the proposed Reform Agreement act only to the extent to which Turkey itself voluntarily would agree. In the period December 1912–June 1913 Russian diplomacy was actively engaged in efforts to prepare the ground for a new conference on Armenian Reforms. While encouraging the Armenians to pursue their cause inside and outside Turkey through the media and through appeals to governments and public figures, the Russian ambassador to the Ottoman Empire explicitly warned them to refrain from provocative acts through which their condition could but deteriorate, adding: "It is important that in the eyes of Europe the Armenians appear as victims of Turkish willfulness rather than as political revolutionaries who are out to exploit current Turkish military setbacks with a view to realizing their national aspirations."[1]

Following the dispatch on June 6, 1913 by Neratof, the Deputy Foreign Minister of Russia, of a circular Note to the governments of Europe, a Reform Commission, consisting of the representatives of the six Powers, was set up in Constantinople to come up with a new reform project. In order to accommodate the positions, taken by Turkey and Germany, the original terms of the project, which was conceived and elaborated by André Mandelstam, the legal expert of the Russian Embassy, were considerably diluted during a series of grueling negotiations. Having ironed out most of their major differences, the Powers, along with Turkey, finally embraced, through the signatures of the Russian representative and the Turkish Grand Vizier, who were acting on behalf of the two camps separating the Powers, the January 26/February 8, 1914 Reform Agreement.

The fate of this accord has been described in part 3 of chapter 12. Its relevance for the present discussion derives from the significance the Russians, the Turks and the Germans attached to this document. In relaying the news of the completion of the accord to his Foreign Minister, Gulkevitch, Russian Chargé at the Ottoman capital, was relishing in what he considered to be the preeminent role Russia played in forging an internationally binding legal document. He redefined Russia's new Armenia policy as one animated by "an appreciation of the great importance for Russia of the Armenian Question, from the point of view of humanitarianism, as well as of Russian interests." He then for the first time injected in the picture the idea of the urgency of pushing through the reforms, to be executed under Russian or European control, with due regard to such principles as "the integrity of Turkey" (*sans porter atteinte à l'integrité de la Turquie*) and "the Sultan's sovereignty."

From a Turkish, and indirectly, a German perspective, the most ominous element of this new policy declaration was the assertion that the Reform Agreement was an act "preparatory for the occupation of Armenia [eastern Turkey], in the event the reform should fail to materialize in consequence of the inability, or the ill-will, of the Turkish government or, in the event the country should lapse into anarchy, imperilling the security of Russia's neighboring provinces."[2] The acuteness of the need for Armenian reforms was exceeded only by the severity of the dangers this Russian stance signaled as far as the future of Turkey's eastern provinces was concerned, not to speak of the future of Turkey as a whole. By a curious twist of circumstances the Armenian Question had thus become the Russian Question inasmuch as the two questions became entwined, especially in the minds of the Young Turk leaders. The threat, emanating from Russia, the historical nemesis of Turkey, was now, more than ever, intimately associated with an Armenian threat flowing from the urgency of the provisions of the accord which was more or less masterminded by the Russians.

The German partnership with Turkey, which culminated in the wartime enactment of the August 2, 1914 secret Turko-German military alliance, was the direct result of an evolving, historical process which was considerably accelerated as a response to the re-emergence of this Russian threat. German national interests tended to converge with Turkish national interests. As determined by William II and his advisers, the Russian threat was such as to be reckoned with, and to confront it while the war appeared to be imminent.

The Inroads of the German Military Mission to Turkey

From a strictly military point of view, the event which catalyzed this confrontation in a rudimentary form was the creation of the German Military Mission to Turkey whose arrival in Turkey (December 1913) coincided with the onset of the very last stages of the negotiations on the new Armenian Reform accord. Essentially led by veteran Prussian officers, the group was to reform and reorganize the Turkish army. This mission was nothing new in the history of Turko-German relations. The German involvement in the task of reforming the Ottoman-Turkish army in modern times dates back to 1882 when then Major von der Goltz was commissioned by Sultan Abdul Hamit to reorganize the Turkish army and the training of its officers corps. From a Turkish point of view the military alliance treaty, which first was proposed by War Minister Enver (July 22, 1914) was almost entirely aimed at Russia. The Turks were seeking German protection, but the Germans, though unimpressed with the Turkish military potential at the time, insisted on a commitment by Turkey to intervene militarily should a Russo-German war break out. The centerpiece of the treaty was an understanding that the officers of the German Military Mission were to assume responsibility for the operative command of the Turkish army. The passage reads: *influence effective sur la conduite générale de l'armée.*[3]

The acerbity with which the Russians reacted to this arrangement in a sense foreshadowed the Russo-German confrontation which was shaping up at the time. The incremental influx of German military cadres in Turkey eventually led to the cultivation of many connections to the German industrial-military complex, especially Krupp, which became the principal supplier of the munitions and armaments of the Turkish army. German military missions to Turkey thus emerge as special harbingers of German power and influence enveloping a struggling and weary nation-state. The authority of the German Military Mission was further enhanced by the injection in the respective contract a clause by virtue of which German officers could be entitled to a rank one grade higher in the Turkish army than their grade in the German army. The higher echelons of the German Mission included a Prussian Field Marshal (von der Goltz), two generals, who likewise became marshals, i.e., *müşir* (Liman von Sanders and von Falkenhayn) and three admirals (Usedom, Souchon, and Mertens), and about ten generals, i.e., those of lower ranks advancing to the Turkish *ferik* rank of various grades. The original complement of 70 officers of the mission had expanded to such a degree that at the height of its wartime operations the mission had at its disposal 7–800 German officers and some 12,000 troops.[4]

The most tangible and consequential influence these German military leaders, especially the admirals, had, was that they preempted Turkey's ability to chart its own course relative to the choice of intervening in the war. Indeed, they managed to embroil Turkey in a war with Russia—perhaps too soon and, therefore, prematurely. By launching naval assaults against Russian ships and military installations in and around the Black Sea, without legal authorization by the Turks, they forced the hands of the latter in terms of a precipitate intervention in the war.[5] Another condition of the contract involved the understanding that when a Turkish officer served as field commander of a unit, his chief of staff was to be a German, and vice versa.

These descriptions and numbers do not tell, however, the entire story of the German influence at issue here. Superseding them in significance was one factor through which the sway of German influence was not only ensured, but it was amplified substantially. It was War Minister Enver's personal relationship to the German Emperor, combined with his exaggerated assessment of the potential of the German war machine, and his overall admiration of what he perceived to be distinct German attributes, such as organizational skills and military prowess and discipline. While a colonel, Enver in the 1909–1913 period twice served as a military attaché at Berlin. During these terms of service William II at times went out of his way to cultivate a special relationship to him, virtually pampering him, in anticipation of the latter's ascendancy in the ranks of the Young Turk power-wielders.[6]

After having attained that position Enver in many, but not all, respects became a kind of proxy of the German strategists in Berlin and in the Imperial German General Headquarters. Postwar accounts by several Turkish generals, who were part of the military apparatus, bitterly inveigh against Enver, portraying him as a subservient puppet of the Germans, who prematurely dragged Turkey into the war in pursuit of dubious objectives and personal glory.[7] One of these generals even asserts that in private conversations Enver disclosed to him that he was planning to "settle in Anatolia many (*bir hayli*) Germans,"[8] presumably in areas vacated through "the Armenian deportations." Another general complained that Enver in all of his trips to the front studiously avoided taking along Turkish officers, and except for his adjutants and some secretaries, was always accompanied by high ranking German officers.[9] Still another general, Ismet, deplored the fact that "The German Military Mission was in a position to follow day by day all that was transpiring in the country," that the Germans were "entrusted with all the secrets of the state, be they political or military secrets."[10] The extraordinary importance of this privileged German position for the present inquiry into the matter of German complicity calls for emphasis. It brings into special relief the import of the role of the General Headquarters in view of the duties assigned to a particular department within those headquarters, namely, Department II, Intelligence (*Istihbarat*). This was one of the few departments which simultaneously was Department II in both the Ministry of War and the General Headquarters, thus belonging to two overlapping military jurisdictions with but one identity, function, and staff. It was run by Enver's friend and cohort, Colonel Seyfi, and Seyfi was one of the key organizers of the genocide.

Moreover, according to the account of a Turkish historian, "A German officer was appointed to head Department II, which was the center where all the political and military secrets of the state converged. This was tantamount to surrendering the state to the Germans."[11] The officer in question was Lieutenant Colonel Sievert. One of the functions of Department II was the organization, deployment, and direction of the brigand units of the Special Organization,[12] carrying out the operations in the killing fields. The participation of Colonel Seyfi, the Turkish chief of Department II, in the secret Young Turk Ittihadist conference at which the decision for the mass murder was spelled out in terms of a blueprint is one of the indicators of the nature of that department's involvement in the planning and execution of that mass murder.[13]

The Bearings of the German Ideological Perspectives

To the extent that it may be possible to ascertain a degree of German complicity under review here, to that extent an examination of certain underlying attitudes affording such complicity may be warranted. There are a number of categories of attitudes to be considered. One of them refers to those which were vestiges of the Abdul Hamit era and to the massacres of that era. Two personalities stand out in terms of embodying in this regard the legacy of that era inasmuch as that legacy in effect carried over into the era of the wartime genocide. The views of Friedrich Naumann have already been exposed (in section 6, chapter 6). But the attitude of the other, Emperor William II (discussed in the same section), deserves a special review, especially on two separate but interconnected levels. First to be considered is his general perspective on Islam and Turkey, which gradually evolved and eventually crystallized itself in the course of his two trips to the Sultan's domain, especially the second one (1898). William II's monarchical affinities for the Turkish monarch sufficiently overwhelmed him to re-examine and recast his views on Islam and on theocracy within a new perspective. Identifying himself with the Turkish sultan in some respects, William II, through this new perspective, came to view the latter as a ruler whose power emanated from and was preordained by God, whose Regent on earth he was, and in whom converged sacred and secular authority in the highest form. Within this perspective he also came to appreciate Islam as a unifying force, beckoning to the true believers with the appeal of a set of ideals, the magnetism of which he compared to the spell of the ascetic virtues of an idealized Prussia. In fact he regarded Turkey as the Prussia of the Orient; he compared the Islamic attributes of self-denial to his notions of Prussian puritanism. His November 8, 1898 Damascus speech, proclaiming his solidarity with three hundred million Mohammedans worldwide, was emblematic of this seemingly ideological embrace of Turkey, as a theocratic wonderland, committed to the task of consecrating the ideals and aspirations of Islam.

These indulgences in exaltations of religious ideals and puritanism were, however, as liable to transmutation into an indulgence in ferocity as the release of the passions, suppressed by the exertions of such puritanism, whether Prussian or Islamic, would allow. The history of the wartime deportations is but an aspect of this phenomenon of transmutation. By inquiring into the German role in the carrying out of these deportations it may be worth considering some evidence of the German emperor's attitude on the idea of such deportations. Before the occurrence of the German military setback at Marne (September 5–12, 1914) he was seriously considering at the Imperial German General Headquarters the possibility of "clearing" (*evakuieren*) from certain occupied regions of France and Belgium the indigenous populations involved and of "settling [there] in their stead" (*ansiedeln*) "deserving" Germans. Equally significant, his Chancellor described the suggestion as "intriguing" and, therefore, worth exploring as one of the dividends of military victory. This penchant for uprooting people en masse was even more pronounced with respect to

Alsace. In the April 2, 1915 entry of his diary Admiral Tirpitz writes; "The Kaiser said the other day, that he would have every French man cleared out of Alsace."[14] In other words, the emperor and his coterie of rulers were already toying with the idea of what in today's parlance is called "ethnic cleansing" through forced deportations.

The ideological rudiments of the Turkish scheme to divest Turkey of its indigenous Armenian population in this respect bear a German imprint. In the immediate aftermath of the 1894–96 Armenian massacres General von der Goltz, whom German ambassador Marschall at the time described as the guru of patriotic Turkish officers,[15] in a lengthy article advocated a new doctrine of Turkish national renewal; he indicated the perils for Turkey in the event the latter failed to chart the new course Goltz was expounding. The gist of this doctrine was that Turkey's future lay   in the Asiatic part of its empire and that, therefore, it should give up the European part, turn inward, and consolidate herself in Anatolia. The goal is, he said, to transform a weak Byzantine realm into a Turkish-Arabic one by way of cementing the Islamic ties among the peoples of the regions in question. His advice was: concentrate on the quintessential provinces of Asiatic Turkey to achieve the goal of inner strength. Goltz repeated this view when he stated that "the core of Turkey is to be found not in Europe but in Asia Minor. Turkey has greater chances of military success in Transcaucasia, where Russia is militarily weak, and her ethnic and religious ties with the local Muslim populations would come in handy."[16] A similar view was expounded by German Colonel von Diest, and especially Paul Rohrbach, a champion of the idea of German expansionism in the Near East. Rohrbach is in fact suspected to have been the theoretician who implanted in Turkish minds the idea of the expediency of the evacuation of the Armenians from their ancestral territories in eastern Turkey and their relocation in Mesopotamia for the purpose of populating and cultivating the areas through which the Baghdad Railway system was to be established. French author René Pinon asserted, for example, that in a lecture given in Winter 1913 Rohrbach proposed this deal as a solution to the lingering Armenian Question by virtue of which the interests both of Germany and Turkey could be served simultaneously.[17] American Ambassador Morgenthau, citing the French newspaper *Temps*, made the same attribution to Rohrbach.[18] The Armenian Patriach of Istanbul made a similar assertion. In a meeting on May 28–June 10, 1915 with Dr. Mordtmann, the head of the Armenian desk at the German embassy at Constantinople, the Patriach told the latter that the deportations which the Turkish government was embarking upon at that time were the realization of the Rohrbach plan which Rohrbach in a lecture to the German Geographic Society had presented sometime ago.[19] Echoing these speculations, and adding a new detail, namely, that Rohrbach allegedly made his proposal during a presentation to the German emperor, Germany's Vice

Consul at Erzurum, Scheubner Richter, in a report to Berlin disputed the allied claim that the deportations were the result of this advice.[20] Perhaps the most plausible speculation attaches to a similar proposal attributed to General von der Goltz. He is reported to have outlined such a proposal in a public lecture in Berlin in February 1914. The lecture was delivered under the sponsorship of the German-Turkish League *(Deutsch-Türkische Vereiningung)* and was attended by members of the Turkish embassy, prominent German public figures and the members of the League. The League itself was created on the instance of the German Foreign Office, with Goltz serving as a member of the Board of Directors. The main points of the reported proposal were:

1) Russia for almost a century now has been intervening in the internal affairs of Turkey under the pretext of wanting to protect the subject nationalities.

2) As a result, all non-Turkish nationalities of the empire have emancipated themselves from Turkish dominion and Turkey's territories shrunk substantially.

3) Exploiting the Balkan War crisis Russia has recently taken up the Armenian problem, and is covertly aiming at the further truncation of Turkish territories by bringing up a new reform project.

4) In order to spare Turkey a new disaster, it is necessary to remove from the Russo-Turkish border areas, once and for all, the half a million Armenians who inhabit the provinces of Van, Bitlis and Erzurum that are contiguous to these areas. They should be transported to the south and resettled in the areas of Aleppo and Mesopotamia.

5) In return, the Arabs of these areas should be resettled along the Russo-Turkish borders.

Even though presently there is no other source to corroborate this account of a lecture by Goltz, his main thesis, expounded in his 1897 article, is a sort of corroboration itself as it more or less squares with the thrust of the reported lecture. In addition, the background of the source is such as to lend a measure of credence to the veracity of that source. That source is an Armenian priest who at the time was a student of theology at the University of Berlin. A German professor, who had attended the lecture, "confidentially" had apprised him of the contents of the lecture and he in turn had promptly relayed the information to his superiors at the Armenian Patriarchate at Constantinople.[21]

The Complicity of the Military. The Order for the "Deportations"
General Bronsart von Schellendorf's role

Despite the lengths to which German authorities in Constantinople and Berlin went to avoid appearing being in any way involved in the launching of the wartime anti-Armenian measures, two sets of evidentiary material attest to such an involvement. The first is contained in the edited memoirs of the Young Turk Ittihadist party chief and boss, Interior Minister, and subsequently Grand Vizier (February 1917–October 1918), Talât. According to this account, in December 1914 General Major Fritz Bronsart von Schellendorf, the Chief of Staff at Ottoman General Headquarters (*Umumi Karargâh*), requested from Enver, War Minister, and de facto Commander-in-Chief of Ottoman Armed Forces, that he "convene an emergency, secret conference to be attended by competent Ministers." Attending that conference were, among others, German generals Goltz and Liman von Sanders, and Turkish power-wielders Talât and Enver. Reportedly, the German military at that conference supplied evidence of Armenian acts of sabotage and atrocities, committed in the rear of the army; they, therefore, requested the initiation of counter-measures (*tedbir*) to stamp out this danger that avowedly seemed to them to threaten the sinew of the Turkish war effort.[22] Again, no other document is available to substantiate this particular account in which General Bronsart is depicted as the actual initiator of the scheme of Armenian deportations. However, in an interview Talât granted Aubrey Herbert, a member of the British Parliament, and an intelligence operative, he made the same assertion, namely, that the Germans had pressed for the initiation of anti-Armenian measures.[23] Without specifying the Germans as the people involved, Said Halim, the Grand Vizier at the time told the Armenian Patriarch likewise that the deportations were the result of "months of pressure by military authorities"; the Patriarch on April 13–26, 1915, i.e., that is two days after the mass arrests in the Ottoman capital of the leaders of the Armenian community, was in the Grand Vizier's office to present a petition on behalf of the Armenian people. (on page 98 of the Patriarch's source cited in Note 19). The second is an official document, unearthed by the officials of the British High Commissioner's office towards the end of the Turkish Armistice. In it, General Bronsart is seen ordering, in his capacity as Chief of Staff at Ottoman High Command, the deportation of the Armenians, urging that "severe" (*şedide*) measures be applied against those Armenians, who were then part of labor battalions, to prevent their being troublesome in connection with deportation procedures, and to keep them under strict surveillance.[24] The significance of this document cannot be overemphasized given the unusual circumspection the Germans exercised in structuring their relationship to the Turkish scheme involving the whole array of anti-Armenian measures, as noted above. This issue of circumspection will further be discussed later. What needs to be emphasized at this point is that the document clearly demonstrates the very direct involvement, whether intentional or inadvertent, of one of the highest ranking German officers, subject to the jurisdiction of the

German Military Mission to Turkey, in the authorization of the Armenian deportations. It also demonstrates something which is critical for understanding the real intent of these deportations: the mutual understanding between the German Chief of Staff and his Turkish cohorts at the headquarters on the need to impose a measure of "severity" in the application of the deportation measures.[25] Ordinarily, the word "severe" could denote the idea of strictness. But in Turkish phraseology, especially adopted and used during the Abdul Hamit era massacres against the Armenians, it also connoted for the officials the idea of license for lethal violence. Moreover, General Bronsart instructed Count von Schulenburg, who had replaced Scheubner Richter as Germany's Consul at Erzurum, not to follow in the footsteps of his predecessor and hence not to intercede on behalf of the Armenians.[26] As will be seen later in the chapter, General Bronsart, fully aware of the actual outcome of the deportations he authorized, not only did not express any regret, not to speak of any remorse, but to the end of his life, with unrepentant truculence, acted as a committed apologist for the Turks.

The genocidal consequences of the order and the issue of legal liability

An order, one way or another intended to authorize the violent elimination of a targeted group, if framed carefully, may be, after the fact, defended on semantic, if on no other, grounds. Implied injunctions or instructions, in substitution of explicit exhortations, have this function. Indeed, by the nature of things, orders of the latter type are the exception rather than the norm. Even the Nazis relied on the use of the covert term *Unschädlichmachung*, i.e., rendering the subject "harmless," to mask the actual liquidation scheme involved. In such situations the test of intent lies in the actual end result of the order, in the simple fact that exterminatory intent is best revealed in outcomes that have exterminatory character. Thus, the nature of an intent cannot be separated from the nature of its consequences. General Bronsart's order had, apart from its reference to "the Armenian people" (*Ermeni ahalinin*), whose deportation has been "determined upon" (*mukarrerdir*), the additional specific purpose, namely, targeting "the Armenians in the labor battalions" who, for security reasons, were to be subjected to "severe" treatment. An inquiry into the fate of these Armenians should provide, for instance, a basis for assessing the purpose of the order. From the welter of available material relating to that fate, the adducing of a few examples may assist in this task; they are furnished by sources which were identified with the German camp and, equally important, were actual eyewitnesses.

In one of his reports to his Chancellor in Berlin, Dr. Walter Rössler, Germany's veteran consul at Aleppo, relayed the account of a German captain of cavalry on the murder "through cutting off the throats" (*durchschnittene Hälse*), of countless young Armenians who were part of a labor battalion and whose corpses were strewn on both sides of the road he was riding through on his way from Diyarbekir to Urfa.[27] In another report, Rössler on September 3, 1915 relates the story of "the murder of hundreds of Armenians engaged in road construction" in his district.[28] The account of a Venezuelan officer who, under German sponsorship had volunteered to fight alongside the Turks, personally observed, while serving as a commanding officer in the eastern and southeastern sectors of the war front in Turkey, case after case of systematic destructions of these Armenian contingents of labor battalions. Focusing on a particular case whereby he observed those "thirteen or fifteen hundred unarmed Armenian soldiers, breaking stone and mending road," he declared that shortly thereafter they had become the victims of "a massacre," of a "so hideous a crime against humanity."[29] German state archives are replete with documents with similar testimonies on the near uniformity of this pattern of elimination of the Armenian able-bodied men, namely, conscription, disarming, isolation, and liquidation. That this arrangement of assigning the Armenians to construction work was not in any way related to insurrections in the rear of the Turkish army, as often claimed by Turkish sources, is indicated by Lieutenant Commander Hans Humann, Marine Attaché to Turkey, and a close friend of War Minister Enver. In a report on October 16, 1914, i.e., several weeks before even Turkey entered the war, he disclosed that the Armenians, along with the Greeks, were already being segregated in labor battalion formations, i.e., long before the Armenians had either any reason or occasion to think of any insurrection, let alone to mount an insurrection.[30]

Before closing this discussion, a comment or two on the cipher telegram sent by General Bronsart is called for; after all, the consequences described above are foreshadowed in the text of that cipher. First, neither Turkish authorities, nor Turkish, or pro-Turkish authors, hitherto disputed the authenticity of it. On the contrary, many of them directly or indirectly accepted or validated them by invoking them to prove a certain point or to advance a certain argument. Moreover, the Turkish Historical Society, a quasi-arm of the Turkish government, in one of its publications, *Belleten*, reproduced the set of documents, of which the Bronsart cipher is part, and Turkish author Sonyel, reworked them in a new pamphlet containing translations of that set in French and English (see note 25).

Beyond these considerations, there is the fundamental legal issue. By identifying himself as the author of the cipher telegraph in question, the German general assumed a level of responsibility which transcends the political and military ramifications of the problem, posing the problem of the legal liability of office. He was not only the chief of staff at the General Headquarters and at the General Staff, but also temporarily, i.e., during the 1914–15 Sarıkamış offensive, chief of staff of the Ottoman Third

Army mounting that offensive. The operations had manifold repercussions for the Armenian population of the six provinces which the Third Army's zone of command encompassed. In addition, he was contractually a representative of Imperial Germany. He was first and foremost a member of the German Military Mission to Turkey to which he was accountable, and through it, to Emperor William II and his military and civilian high command. Indeed, that mission was authorized and sanctioned by the very same emperor who appointed its chief, Marshal Liman von Sanders, investing him with enough of a high level of competency to afford him the privilege to bypass the German Embassy and other intermediary channels and to report directly to the emperor. As Sanders relates in his memoirs, first he was "authorized by H. M. the Emperor to sign" the contract. Then, in November 1913, "I was called before H. M. the Emperor" who briefed him on the mission. Before his departure for Constantinople General Sanders and the first contingent of German officers, including Bronsart von Schellendorf, was once more called before the emperor to be formally charged with the mission.[31]

General Bronsart's exculpatory rationale blaming the victim after the fact

The attribution of guilt to the Armenians is the basis on which Bronsart predicates his justification of the manner in which they were treated during the war. However, the victims are not only accused of acts of provocation but are also blamed on account of certain negative images which clearly fall into the category of prejudice and typecasting. According to this rationale, the Armenians deserved the fate befalling them. This posture merits special attention as it sheds light on the social psychological mechanisms through the dynamics of which the act of the complicity in question appears to be generated and subsequently rationalized. It is evident that the general's hostility to the victim population did not only not abate in the post-war years, but was sustained throughout. As if frustrated at the incompleteness of the destruction of that population, Bronsart continued to lash out against the Armenians as a corporate entity. One of the methods he used for this end was to compare them with the Jews, vilifying them both through the assertion,

> Namely, the Armenian is just like the Jew, a parasite outside the confines of his homeland, sucking off the marrow of the people of the host country. Year after year they abandon their native land—just like the Polish Jews who migrate to Germany—to engage in usurious activities. Hence the hatred which, in a medieval form, has unleashed itself against them as an unpleasant people, entailing their murder.[32]

Elsewhere, he called the Armenians as "agitators" who rightly were much more hated throughout Turkey than the worst Jews. Extending his rancor to American Ambassador Morgenthau, who had been trying to intercede on behalf of the Armenians, Bronsart disdainfully called him "the Jew Morgenthau." By a pun on words, he also described the United States as "the corrupted United States" (*ver-un-reinigten*), i.e., by inserting the negative *un* and the letter *r* between *Ver* and *einigten*.[33] One reason for this invective was the fact that Morgenthau in his memoirs had called General Bronsart "the evil spirit," interfering in the affairs of the Turks and influencing some of their decisions.

But under the conditions prevailing in wartime Turkey, no foreign general could venture to interfere without a power base affording such intervention. In his capacity as Chief of Staff at Ottoman General Headquarters, Bronsart had that base. His close, personal ties with Enver, War Minister and *de facto* Commander-in-Chief of Ottoman Armed Forces, served to solidify that base. As noted above, the power emanating from that base included the power of authorizing Armenian deportations which he exercised without any hesitation. A wartime German document reveals in this connection that General Bronsart sought to extend the deportation measures also to the Greek population. On August 2, 1916, the Ottoman General Headquarters issued a request to General Liman von Sanders, the Commander of the 5th Ottoman Army, which guarded the entire west coast of Asia Minor to Adalia on the Mediterranean inclusive. It concerned the deportation "of Greeks from the coastal zones;" the request was signed by General Bronsart. For a variety of reasons, including political and military considerations, the request was not complied with—for the time being.[34]

The roles and attitudes of other high-ranking
German officers

VON DER GOLTZ. FIELD MARSHAL

Foremost among these were Marshal von der Goltz and Lieutenants Colonel Feldmann and Boettrich. Goltz's involvement was first brought up in a German language Armenian periodical; it essentially confirmed what Talât reportedly had disclosed in his memoirs (note 22). According to this periodical, Goltz's involvement was a certainty. "In fact, the plan had been presented to the field marshal, and had been approved by him."[35] Goltz had acquired a reputation as being more a Turk than the Turks themselves. According to the Austrian Military Plenipotentiary to Turkey, he was dubbed by others a "Turkified" (*vertürkt*) German.[36] When War Minister Enver in the first week of February 1915 appointed him as "Advisor" to himself, Goltz not only received an office in the Ministry of War, but upon Enver's special order he was made an integral part of the group at the Ottoman General Headquarters. Enver further ordered the German Chief of Staff, General Bronsart, to keep Goltz "apprised" (*unterrichten*) on all matters that concerned [the direction of] the war."[37] It should be noted that the final decision to "deport" the Armenian population of the empire is believed to have been made towards the end of February or early March, 1915. However uncertain the exact nature and extent of his involvement in such decision making may be, Goltz in his memoirs gives expression to the chagrin he felt "from the bottom of [my] heart" at the sight of "the boundless misery" (*grenzenloses Elend*) of the Armenian deportees he came across at the southern tip of the Taurus mountains, characterizing the whole thing as a "terrible national tragedy."[38] Dr. Otto Göppert, German Foreign Office councillor, and former Privy Legation Councillor at the German Embassy at Constantinople, saw fit to distinguish between the act of advising and that of consenting (*Zustimmung*). He then stated, "It appears to be true that Enver Paşa showed the order ... to Goltz, asking him for his opinion ... [Goltz] did, then, think of the evacuation [of the Armenians] as a possibility. Of course we must bear in mind that the Turks would hide behind the utterance of the field marshal."[39]

FELDMANN. LIEUTENANT COLONEL

The role of Lieutenant Colonel von Feldmann, who was the head of Department I, Operations, at the Ottoman General Headquarters, is less ambiguous as he himself in 1921 openly declared that he personally was involved in the act of "advising" Turkish authorities on the necessity of "clearing certain regions ... of Armenians." Equally significant is his concomitant admission that other "German officers" were likewise involved.[40] This admission is the more significant as Feldmann, like Bronsart, had accompanied Enver to eastern Turkey and served as staff officer in the 1914–15 campaign against Russia. According to a German military historian Bronsart and Feldmann were "the confidants of Enver, and in daily consultations with him had been exchanging views with him in minute detail."[41]

BOETTRICH. LIEUTENANT COLONEL

The case of Lieutenant Colonel Boettrich, Chief of Railroad Services at Ottoman General Headquarters, is both striking and considerably more revealing than in the cases discussed above. Like Bronsart, he is another high-ranking German officer who ordered the deportation of the Armenians, and placed his signature on that order. Involved was the fate of those thousands of Armenians who were working on the Baghdad Railway construction project. Boettrich, discharging his duties, ordered the deportation in two stages of these Armenians and just like Bronsart, used the words "severe application of the measures" relative to the deportation procedures. The degree of severity of these measures is narrated by an eyewitness of the successive carnages to which the Armenian workmen of the Baghdad Railway in the thousands were subjected for the purpose of extermination. "Like the hundreds of thousands of their brothers before them, they shared the same kind of fate near Viranşehir. They were all dispatched with the knife" (*Mit dem Messer wurden sie alle erledigt*).[42]

There are several points to be made about this document. First of all it demonstrates the willingness of a German officer to accommodate the demands of the Turkish ally, irrespective of the costliness of such accommodation to the Turko-German joint war effort. Many of the Armenians in question were skilled laborers, technicians, engineers, and railroad traffic administrators. The speedy completion of the Baghdad Railway project was of the highest strategic importance for that war effort, a compelling necessity for winning the war in the Turkish theater of operations. The German authorities, military and civilian, were fully aware of this. Yet, for reasons of their own, they joined the Turks in the decision to deport these craftsmen. Tens of thousands perished as a result, and the project was delayed for several costly months as the authorities found it most difficult to replace those who were disposed of.

Second, German military and civilian authorities of the highest rank, apparently unaware of General Bronsart's much more serious blunder, became alarmed and upset when they learned about Boettrich's direct involvement in the issuance of deportation orders. These authorities were alerted by Franz Günther, the Deputy General Director of the Anatolian Railway, who complained that Boettrich was foolish enough to put his signature on this document thereby sanctioning the order, giving it a German attribute, and creating a liability for the German state. As he put it,

> Our enemies will some day pay a good price to obtain possession of this document … they will be able to prove that the Germans have not only done nothing to prevent the Armenian persecutions but they even issued certain orders to this effect, as the [Turkish] Military Commander has ecstatically pointed out.[43]

German Foreign Minister von Jagow immediately transmitted the document to Falkenhayn, the chief in the German High Command, for action to be taken against Boettrich. The former refused, however, to dismiss the latter, as recommended by Treutler, German diplomat in the Foreign Office.[44] In commenting on these indiscretions, Count von Lüttichau, the chaplain of the German Embassy, whom German Foreign Minister Kühlmann described as "a symbol of German genius,"[45] declared:

> Indeed German officers consented to the measures of evacuation for military strategic reasons. And, it is possible that … the Turks distorted this consent so as to make it look like a German wish or order. Should it develop that the Turks thrust the German officers to the forefront and the latter allowed themselves to be so pushed without being aware of the political consequences, as I am afraid, might unfortunately be the case, then any attempt of concealment [*Verheimlichung*] will not do because of the existence of written orders, bearing signatures.[46]

Professor Richter, one of the Editors of *Allgemeine Missions-Zeitung* had asserted that German officers had in fact "dispensed advice" (*den Rat gaben*) to the Turks to deport the Armenians.[47]

GUIDO VON USEDOM. ADMIRAL

One of the three German admirals engaged by the Turks, Usedom was to help defend the Straits and the coastal fortifications of the area. He first became Inspector General of coastal artillery and mining. Later, he took charge of the High Command for the Defense of the Straits at the Dardanelles and the Bosphorus, for which purpose there was created for him the Special Navy Task Force Admiral von Usedom. (*Marine-Sonderkommando* Admiral von Usedom.) Usedom embodied many of the Prussian military traditions. Before being assigned to duties in Turkey he served as the German emperor's aide-de-camp, was commander of the latter's yacht Hohenzollern, and was made part of the emperor's official retinue.

During a series of exchanges with the German admiral, American Ambassador Morgenthau brought up the subject of the deportations, just before the outbreak of the war, of some 100,000 Greeks from the Asiatic littoral in the Aegean. Usedom admitted that "the Germans had suggested this deportation to the Turks." As to "the Armenian massacres," Morgenthau relates the following, "Usedom ... discussed the whole thing calmly, merely as a military problem, and one would never have guessed from his remarks that the lives of a million human beings had been involved. He simply said that the Armenians were in the way, that they were an obstacle to German success, and that it had, therefore, been necessary to remove them, just like so much useless lumber."[48]

WILHELM SOUCHON. REAR ADMIRAL

He was commander-in-Chief of the Turkish Fleet, and the Chief of the Mediterranean Arm of the German Navy (*Mittelmeer Division*), which was spearheaded by the battle cruiser Goeben (which later was renamed *Yavuz* and was appropriated by the Turkish Navy), and the light cruiser Breslau (likewise renamed *Midilli*). Souchon was the man who directed the naval assault against Russia in October 1914, deliberately triggering the ensuing Russo-Turkish war.

Commenting on the Armenians and their fate in the war, Souchon is quoted as saying, "Turkey is acting against the Armenian with thoroughness and utmost discretion. I hope that this drama will soon come to an end." Four days later, in August 1915, he reportedly added this note in his diary: "It will be salvation for Turkey when it has done away with the last Armenian; it will be rid then of subversive bloodsuckers."[49]

SEECKT. LIEUTENANT GENERAL

Lieutenant General Hans Friedrich Leopold von Seeckt came to Turkey in 1917 following a meteoric rise in the ranks of the German field army, serving as chief of staff in the armies commanded by Mackensen on the eastern front and subsequently in Serbia where Seeckt played a major role in the German victory. Having succeeded Major General Fritz Bronsart von Schellendorf as Chief of Staff at Ottoman General Headquarters,

Seeckt quickly acclimatized himself at his post, establishing a more or less smooth working relationship with War Minister Enver, his superior. In commenting on the liquidation of the Armenians of the Ottoman Empire, Seeckt is quoted as saying: "The requirements of the war made it necessary that Christian, sentimental, and political considerations simply vanish" (... *Rücksicht der Kriegsnotwendigkeit halber verschwinden*).[50] His sense of loyalty to the Turks was strong enough to motivate him to offer War Minister Enver and his cohort—at the time Grand Vizier—Talât German help which was needed to enable them to flee the country at the end of the war.

COUNT EBERHARD WOLFFSKEEL VON REICHENBERG. MAJOR
He arrived in Turkey in January, 1915 and was appointed Chief of Staff to the governor of Syria in February, 1915. Four months later he became Chief of Staff of the 8th Army Corps with the rank of major of the Ottoman army, but remaining a member of the German Military Mission to Turkey.

His involvement in anti-Armenian activity in the April-October 1915 period is significant in two respects. First, it was active participation in military operations in which he played a leading role in obliterating the opposing Armenians. Second, he performed this task by the orders of a Turkish general to whom he was assigned as an Adjutant.

The reference is to the suppression of the defensive uprisings of the Armenians at Mussa Dagh, August-September, at which operation Wolfskeel was an observer, and Urfa, September-October 1915. Faced with imminent deportation and destruction, the Armenians of these two areas decided to sell their lives dear by rising up against the regular units of the Ottoman army. General Fahri, Chief of Staff of the 4th Army Commander Cemal Paşa, and later, Commander of the Expeditionary Force in the Hedjaz, and defender of Medina, was given the task of supressing and reducing the Armenians who were thus resisting deportation. When three battalions of the regular standing army and countless irregulars, equipped with two field guns and a howitzer, proved unable to defeat the Armenian defenders of Urfa, Fahri, at the time the commander of the 12th Army Corps, ordered Major Wolffskeel, to bombard and reduce the city's Armenian Quarter. In executing that order, the German artillery officer blasted that Quarter into the stone age. "Repeatedly" denouncing them as "traitors" *(Verräter),* the major portrayed the Armenians as a source of "trouble" *(Scherereien)* for the Turks, whose methods of dealing with the Armenians he described as "internal Turkish matter" (*innertürkische Angelegenheit*). He concluded that the best solution to the problem would be the wholesale deportation of the Armenians. It is most significant that in German Ambassador Métternich's November 29, 1915 report to Berlin the two references to Wolffskeel with regard to the Urfa episode are crossed out, signaling deletion. Likewise, German Chargé Neurath's extensive paragraphs, containing Major Wolffskeel's account of the military operations against the Urfa Armenians, are excised in Lepsius's volume in which Neurath's November 20, 1915 communication to German Chancellor Bethman Hollweg is reproduced.[51]

The Political Indicators of Complicity

Despite the sway of Prussian militarism in the unfolding German national aspirations, in the months preceding World War I there was sufficient scope for manoeuvring politically, rather than militarily, and for calibrating foreign policy in such a way as to attune political to military desiderata, and vice versa. The status of William II provided the connecting link between the two spheres of expedients. He was not only the Supreme Ruler of Imperial Germany but, by entitlement at least, also the Supreme War Lord (*Oberster Kriegsherr*), a status proudly acquired and instituted in modern times by Frederick the Great. William II often visited the German Headquarters at Coblenz, Luxembourg, Spa and Pless and Kreuznach. The Chief of the German General Staff daily reported to him. William II was nominally the Commander-in-Chief, as he was also the Head of the State, by virtue of which he did not hesitate to interfere in the conduct of military affairs—for reasons of state.

The role performance of the high ranking German officers, stationed in Turkey during the war, inevitably had political implications, given the terms and thrust of the August 2, 1914 secret Turko-German alliance treaty. Their very presence in Turkey during the war was in itself a foremost political act with subsidiary military implications. Within this perspective, military service in Turkey entailed adaptations to the ancillary political designs of the Turkish ally, including such operations as "ethnic cleansing." In this sense, the attitudes and doctrines of the architects of German foreign policy call for a comment. The chief architect was, of course, the emperor himself who set the stage for casting the foundations of that policy as discussed above (chapter 6, section 6). The formation of the German Military Mission to Turkey and the staffing of its top echelons through the appointment of several Prussian officers was an extension of this will to chart the course of German wartime alliance policy.

Included in this policy design was the imposition of censorship on the German media with a view to suppressing or withholding information on the unfolding mass murder of the Armenians (as discussed in chapter 12, section 1). Sometimes reticence in this respect is more functional for concealment purposes than joining the campaign of disinformation and denial. The German policy on the Armenian issue essentially was and remained one of studious avoidance of discussion and debate. For this very reason utterances, made in this connection on rare occasions, do acquire special significance. The following statement, attributed to the German emperor by British Intelligence officials, was reportedly made on the occasion of the emperor's third visit to Turkey (October 15–18, 1917). In a compressed manner it tells of the emperor's attitude towards the destruction of Ottoman Armenians, epitomizing the German policy on that problem. Relying on a "sure source," the Political Intelligence Department at the British Foreign Office, in a memorandum, dated May 25, 1918, declared that William II on October 17, 1917, the second day of his visit at the Ottoman capital, told his Turkish hosts that "Armenia ... should be dealt with by the Ottoman government at its discretion."[52]

This German permissiveness prefigures in the diplomatic correspondence of German Foreign Minister Jagow. In a March 14, 1914 report, sent to a group of German businessmen, he stated that if the Turkish government should continue disregarding German wishes and commercial interests, the German government will become "gravely alienated" (*ernstes Befremden*). As a result, "It will be impossible for us to maintain our friendly policy toward Turkey." He then warned that "unless Turkey undertakes a speedy and fundamental change in her attitude, she won't be able to continue counting on us [in the handling of] such matters as the Armenian and other questions."[53] The Turks yielded, the Germans prevailed and the alliance was forged in less than five months thereafter.

One of the consequences of the alliance was the inevitable politicization of some German military officers with propensities to identify with ardor with the Turks and Turkish interests—beyond the thresholds of obligations and duties arising from the alliance. Foremost among these were Goltz and Bronsart, who jealously tried to protect the prestige and reputation of Turkey against attempts by fellow Germans and others to belittle or discredit Turkey. In a April 22, 1915 report, marked "top secret" (*streng geheim*), Prince Gottfried Hohenlohe, Austria's ambassador to Germany, apprised his foreign minister in Vienna of a major incident, with serious ramifications for the future of the Turko-German alliance. Before relating it, Hohenlohe pleaded as follows: "I beg you not to avail yourself of this information in such a way that the German Embassy in Constantinople may learn that I supplied this information." It develops that during Goltz's visit at the headquarters of the German High Command, some German officers "in the presence of the emperor held the alliance with Turkey of very little value (*sehr gering bewertet*) and actually considered it a burden (*Last*) for Germany." Goltz was "very upset" about these utterances but, upon his return to Constantinople he "incomprehensibly" complained about them to Enver.

This deed produced "a tremendous resentment in the circle of competent Turkish authorities [*eine ungeheuere Verstimmung*]." Hohenlohe added that Turkish Economics Minister Cavid, when in Berlin recently, declared that the people at the German Foreign Office are "very accommodating" but that the circle of military officers are "not appreciative at all" of the Turkish contributions to the war effort and consider the alliance as "completely superfluous." "In the German Foreign Office people are very angry over the blunder, especially over the inopportune talkativeness of the field marshal."[54]

General Bronsart had a similar pathos for Turkey, and was equally jealous of its reputation. He went out of his way to challenge the German language daily in Constantinople, *Osmanischer Lloyd*, which was more or less financed by the German Embassy and represented German interests in Turkey. In a letter of protest, addressed to the German Embassy, Bronsart took issue with an editorial in that newspaper in which the theme is developed that "in Europe there is a tendency to ignore in Turkey the real needs." The German newspaper evidently picked up that theme from the Turkish daily *Sabah* and expanding on it, wrote that "despite the fact that thousands of Germans have returned home after three years of service in Turkey, people in Germany have no understanding for the Turkish national soul." Bronsart felt that the German newspaper should "under no circumstances (*keinesfalls*) be permitted" to write such things. Not satisfied with this rebuke, Bronsart raised the issue of another Turkish newspaper article (in *Tercümanı Hakikat*) which evidently was reproduced in the same *Osmanischer Lloyd*. Bronsart urged the Embassy to be vigilant about such indiscretions which he characterized as "political impoliteness" towards the Turkish ally.[55]

Though incidental in character, these displays of extreme sensitivity for the imagery of Turkey are actually quite significant for they are symptomatic of powerful underlying attitudes. Goltz and Bronsart emerge here as military men who have become partisan politicians. More important, they appear to have personalized the conditions and objectives of the partnership with Turkey to a point of optimum identification with Turkey and things Turkish in general. There is evidence here of a confluence of militarism and politics in which the stakes for the alliance are confounded with personal stakes, mainly through the cultivation of highly personal friendship ties with Turkish leaders.

In such circumstances, it seems inevitable that some military leaders end up becoming ardent politicians, and political leaders, including diplomats, adopt militaristic postures. The discussion in the next section of this chapter will focus on two such Germans who may be viewed as the outstanding exponents of the idea of *laissez-faire* regarding the Turkish scheme of liquidation of the Armenian population.

An Ambassador and a Marine Attaché: The Issue of Paramountcy in Complicity

The formal initiation of an alliance in itself does not ensure its continuity or survival. The pragmatic consummation of the terms of that alliance is a more consequential task, especially in times of war, but more especially when there are religious cleavages and cultural disparities separating the allies from each other. In such situations the alliance needs to be nurtured and cultivated to prevent or obviate the onset of crises threatening or undermining the alliance. In brief, committed watchdogs are needed. One such watchdog was the German ambassador to Turkey.

Ambassador Hans Freiherr von Wangenheim

American Ambassador Morgenthau described him as "this perfect embodiment of the Prussian system," even though Wangenheim was a Thuringian and not a Prussian by birth and background. But he had served in the cavalry as a young man and "like all of his social order, Wangenheim worshipped the Prussian military system; his splendid bearing showed that he had himself served in the army, and, in true German fashion, he regarded practically every situation in life from a military standpoint." To him the Prussian legacy, "the great land-owning Junker" system, "represented the perfection of mankind," and deserved "to be venerated and worshipped."[56]

Due to political expediency, largely occasioned by military necessity, Wangenheim overcame his initial low opinion of the Turkish military potential and in July 1914 recommended to Berlin that Turkey seriously be considered a candidate for an alliance with Germany. His modus operandi pursuant to the terms of that alliance is a vast subject and reaches beyond the scope of this study. But his method of bullying the Grand Vizier, presumably with the tacit support of Enver, to secure Turkish governmental consent to the German scheme to push Turkey into war with Russia through a foray into Russian territorial waters in the Black Sea, stands out as a monument to his ability to be overbearing and even ruthless in pursuit of higher German national interests. As Wangenheim reported to Berlin, "I told him that the purpose of the foray into the Black Sea was to pursue German interests which on occasion we will be forced to superordinate to the Turkish ones. Though they are at the disposal of Turkey, the ships involved have German identity and, therefore, cannot take direct orders from the Turkish Minister of Marine.... My declarations, which I repeated to other Cabinet ministers, appear to have made an impact." In point of fact, Wangenheim was executing the direct orders of the Emperor William II. The order was relayed through Admiral Hugo von Pohl, Chief of the German Naval Staff, later Commander of the German High Sea Fleet.[57] A Turkish author acknowledges Wangenheim's propensity to "even bully Cabinet ministers," adding, "As the typical personification of German militarism, Wangenheim proceeded to intervene in the conduct of the affairs of the Ottoman government. He was the despot of Istanbul."[58]

These details demonstrate the ambassador's aptitude for bellicosity, and his readiness to manifest it, when needed. They also demonstrate, however, his uncanny ability to confront the leaders of the government and with resolve and forcefulness impose upon that government the will of his own government. As noted above, he most probably was supported in some of these bold moves by such other leaders as Enver, and to some extent even Talât and Dr. Nazım, the omnipotent Ittihadist leader operating behind the scenes. But this very fact of support from within the Young Turk Ittihadist power structure evinces the built-in advantages Germany enjoyed in the alliance, affording her a certain measure of preponderance and even some control in the determination of war-related Turkish priorities. Turkey was substantially more dependent upon Germany than the other way. This sense of dependence, and an allied appreciation, is crisply encapsulated in these words Talât during the war uttered to Colonel Otto von Lossow, the German Military Attaché to Turkey. "Germany is our father, but Austria is just a neighbor" (*L'Allemagne est notre père, L'Autriche, c'est un voisin*).[59] The resulting Turkish vulnerability to German exertions and demands is attested by Talât who in his famous interview with British member of parliament Aubrey Herbert is reported to have declared that "he found himself completely handcuffed by the Germans and said to the Council of Ministers, 'I often wondered why the English wanted to fight the Germans, but now I know.'"[60]

This notwithstanding, Wangenheim studiously avoided interceding on behalf of the Armenians; he had raised that avoidance to a level of firm policy. More than that, whether out of inner conviction or by virtue of constraints imposed upon him by his superiors in Berlin, or on account of a combination of both factors, he unhesitatingly sided with the Turks, even when he was receiving harrowing reports from his consuls in the provinces about the unfolding genocide, and even when he dutifully was forwarding these reports to Berlin. In this sense, his communications to Berlin on this subject are but the formal and official expression of his stance, and indirectly the stance of his government. As described above (chapter 6, section 6, n. 101), Wangenheim in April 1915, the month that ushered in the episode of the Armenian genocide, bluntly told Berlin that the situation of the Armenians was more or less hopeless and that higher German interests required that the German government does not intervene.

That characterization of hopelessness was somewhat consistent with his diagnosis of the nature of the general plight of the Armenians in Turkey. In an exchange with the Austrian Military Plenipotentiary to

Turkey, Vice Marshal Pomiankowski, which coincided with the then ongoing negotiations on Armenian reforms in 1913, Wangenheim told the
latter that the only salvation for the Armenians of Turkey was "conversion to Islam."[61] In the reports on informal conversations with Ambassador Morgenthau, however, a more truculent, if not sinister, picture
emerges. As in the case of German General Bronsart, Wangenheim too
appears to be opposed to the Armenians, with sentiments ranging from
mere antipathy to sheer hatred. Having simply accepted as true Turkish
charges and decrials against the Armenians, and having adopted their
concomitant epithets, Wangenheim told Morgenthau that "the Armenians
were simply traitorous vermin."

By a remark he made to Morgenthau, Wangenheim clearly indicated
that if he wanted to, he could help intervene on behalf of any nationality posing problems for Turkey. The Jews, for example, are a case in
point. Even though on account of geography and demography they
posed much less of a threat, their aspirations for Palestine, harnessed to
the Zionist movement, did pose a territorial problem as far as the
steadily shrinking Ottoman Empire was concerned. Moreover, Talât har-
bored an acute dislike against Russian Jews, whose role in the cultivation of designs on Palestine was substantial; in his interview with
Aubrey Herbert, mentioned above, he described "the majority of the
Russian Jews" as "degenerate."[62] Nevertheless, Wangenheim self-confi-
dently reassured Morgenthau that he could intervene. "'I will help the
Zionists' he said, thinking that this remark would be personally pleasing
to me, 'But I shall do nothing for the Armenians.'"[63] Wangenheim then
shifted the burden of interceding for the Armenians to the United States.
"The U.S. is apparently the only country that takes much interest in the
Armenians." Referring to "your people [who] have constituted their
guardians," Wangenheim suggested that helping the Armenians was an
American responsibility. In a twist of logic, Wangenheim blamed the
U.S. government for selling munitions to England and France and the
use of shells by the Allies against the Turks at the Dardanelles, adding
that "As long as your government maintains that attitude we can do
nothing for the Armenians." It is noticeable that throughout these
exchanges, Wangenheim did not say, or even intimate, that he would like
to help but that he couldn't in face of insurmountable obstacles erected
by the Turks. Instead, he bluntly reiterated the point that he does not
wish to. For his part, Marshal Liman von Sanders credited Wangenheim
with the ability to know "how to gain his ends in Turkey."[64] Morgenthau
was astounded at this display of absurdity by the German ambassador
who dared to link American help to the Allies to "Turkey's attacks upon
hundred of thousands of Armenian women and children." He had tried
to sensitize Wangenheim to the fact that the issue was not "military
necessity, state policy, or else" but simply "a human problem." He

appealed to him to consider the fact that at issue was the extirpation mostly of "old men, old women and helpless children. Why can't you, as a human being, see that these people are permitted to live?" Wangenheim was intransigent as he retorted, "I shall not intervene," reciting in English the oft repeated maxim of the militarists: "Our aim is to win this war." The stress and strain attending these events apparently damaged the German ambassador's health, afflicting him with some infirmity. According to Morgenthau, who was host to Wangenheim in his office at the American Embassy, upon signaling to Wangenheim that there was no point in carrying on the conversation, "I turned from him in disgust, Wangenheim rose to leave. As he did so he gave a gasp, and his legs suddenly shot from under him. I jumped and caught the man just as he was falling. For a minute he seemed utterly dazed; he looked at me in a bewildered way, then suddenly he collected himself and regained his poise. I took the Ambassador by the arm, piloted him down stairs, and put him into his auto... Two days afterward, while sitting at his dinner table, he had a stroke of apoplexy; he was carried upstairs to his bed, but he never regained consciousness." Wangenheim died on October 25, 1915, and, after a huge funeral in the Ottoman capital, he was buried on the grounds of the German summer embassy in Therapia, on the shores of Bosphorous. As Morgenthau concluded, "He was the one man and his government was the one government, that could have stopped these crimes ... the massacre of a nation...."[65]

Some may dispute this judgement which also implies a verdict. One can only wonder, however, about the irony of a coincidence involved here. Two diplomats, a Russian and a German, a Foreign Minister and an Ambassador, vested with enormous powers, deliberately allowed the perpetration in a span of two decades of two instances of mass murders against the Armenians, thereby sharing in a major onus of complicity. They also shared the same experience of illness that culminated in their death as that illness, stroke, proved fatal. (See chapter 6, notes 31, 32 for the fate of Wangenheim's Russian counterpart, Lobanof).

Lieutenant Commander and Marine Attaché Hans Humann

Of all the German military personnel appointed to posts in wartime Turkey, Humann was the most important in one respect: he was connected to War Minister Enver with bonds of friendship that dated back to the days of Enver's two tours of duty in Berlin where he served as Turkish Military Attaché (1908–1909 and 1909–1912). Antedating this relationship was the heritage of Karl Humann, whose archeological interests had many times brought him to Turkey, where his son Hans was born (Smyrna-Izmir), and where he did much excavation work, with a focus on the memorable edifices of ancient Greek civilization. He eventually became Director of the Oriental Museum of Berlin. His son, Hans Humann, spent a great deal of his childhood in Turkey, developing an affinity for the Turks, which eventually evolved and crystallized itself around a friendship with Enver, first in Berlin and later in Constantinople. Before being assigned to duties in Turkey, Humann had a key position in the intelligence service of the German Navy which was headed by the powerful Grand Admiral von Tirpitz, whose loyal and admiring protégé Hans Humann was, and to whose Pangermanist doctrines he subscribed.

Following the Ittihadist seizure of power in 1913, he was appointed commander of Loreley, the embassy guard-ship in Constantinople. Subsequently, Humann was appointed Marine Attaché at the embassy. As his friend Ernst Jäckh stated, Humann "became the unofficial German envoy ... he had direct access to the Kaiser's entourage over the head of any ambassador. It was an outstanding position of extraordinary influence, to say the least." In this connection Humann is credited with an act that paved the ground for Turkey's intervention in the war. He proposed and pushed through a scheme whereby the German squadron under Rear Admiral Souchon's command escaped the pursuit of British naval forces, entering through the Straits and subsequently joining the Turkish Navy into which it eventually became incorporated only to trigger within weeks the Russo-Turkish war.

His unhampered access to Enver, with whom he communicated in intimate, first-name and German *Du*, i.e., thou, form, enabled him to mediate between such conflicting parties as the head of the German Military Mission, the German ambassador, Enver and General Bronsart. Yet, he was consorting with those who one way or another supported Enver and his cohorts in the initiation and execution of the wartime anti-Armenian measures, such as Bronsart, Goltz, and Wangenheim. To him, the main challenge consisted in the endeavor to provide optimum accomodation of Turkish needs and demands; everything else was of subsidiary import, or not important at all as far as the requirements of the alliance was concerned. In a note to Ambassador Kühlmann, he urged him not to alienate the leaders of Turkey for the sake of "our political interests. We can't afford to alienate them and jeopardize our Near Eastern policies which here in the Orient is always predicated upon personal relations."[66]

In exchanges with American Ambassador Morgenthau, he too "discussed the Armenian problem with the utmost frankness and brutality." He declared that based on his intimate knowledge of the Turks and Turkey, he concluded that "Armenians and Turks cannot live together in this country. One of these races has to go. And I don't blame the Turks for what they are doing to the Armenians. I think that they are entirely justified. The weaker nation must succumb." Morgenthau observed that callous as German ambassador Wangenheim proved to be, he was not so implacable and truculent as Humann, who was "a man of great influence." A German diplomat once told the American ambassador that "Humann was more of a Turk than Enver and Talât."[67] In his refutation of these allegations Humann in a 12-page report[68] tried to dispute nearly everything said by Morgenthau, thereby raising doubts about the seriousness of his disclaimer. In the process, he parroted the most incredulous charges made by the Turks during the war against the Armenians, such as the claim that "out of 130,000 Turks in Van province, 100,000 were massacred by the Armenians." Moreover, in denying that he was ever involved in consultations about the anti-Armenian measures, he was careful to use the word "official" (*amtlich*), thereby leaving open the possibility that he might have been involved unofficially. As has been pointed out above, however (chapter 6, note 98), Wangenheim himself admitted that he used Humann for consulting and relaying important information to Enver—unofficially. In other words, he avoided official channels when critical issues were involved. It is evident that in this report Humann tried to avail himself of his experience as a veteran Navy intelligence man (*Admiralstab, Marineamt*) to obfuscate issues while trying to dispute charges levelled against him, and even to dispense disinformation, when deemed necessary.

After examining Morgenthau's allegations against Humann in the official records of the German archives covering the 1914–15 period, a Swiss author concluded that these records "confirm Morgenthau's perception" of Humann. He cites, for example, Humann's response to the news that the Armenians are being "more or less exterminated"; Humann is quoted as saying, "This is harsh but useful."[69] Two days later, i.e., June 17, 1915, Humann added to that statement this note, "… the Turkish government utilizes the time of war and Europe's pre-occupation to settle the entire Armenian question by force." According to this author, Humann, like General Bronsart, sustained the tempo of his enmity against the Armenians for many years after the war through the medium of the postwar nationalist German newspaper *Deutsche Allgemeine Zeitung*. He concluded that Humann "welcomed and supported the extermination of the Armenian people in the Ottoman Empire."[70] Ambassador Metternich worked with Humann, observing his contacts, his relationship to Enver, and to other potentates. His judgement on Humann is also a decrial of him for he characterized Humann as an "arch scoundrel."[71]

Turkish Assertions on German Complicity

The German government on a number of occasions requested from the Turkish leadership that they publicly deny growing number of reports

and hints that the Germans advised the Turks to proceed with the liquidation of the Armenian population. The Turks obliged without hesitation.
To underscore such denials they insisted that the wartime treatment of the
Armenians by the government was a strictly internal matter and that,
therefore, there was no legal basis or justification for any foreign government, including the German, to intervene in any manner in the decision-making processes of the Turkish government. The picture changed,
however, in the aftermath of the war as numerous Turks came forward to
implicate Germany in a number of respects. Foremost among these was
party boss, Interior Minister, and since February 1917 Grand Vizier Talât.
(See notes 22, 23, and 60 above).

Journalistic Accounts

Some of the assertions were in the form of journalistic pokes, containing
unsubstantiated simple declarations. During the Armistice, for example,
the noted Turkish writer Cenab Şahabeddin, who in 1915 had visited
Germany as a member of a delegation of Turkish newspaper men and
editors, stated that German military officers were responsible for the initiation of anti-Armenian measures.[72] Another Turkish editor recently
likewise asserted that it was the German General Staff which requested
that the Armenians be removed in order to make the rear of the Turkish
army safe and secure.[73] Still another Turkish editor in the most explicit
terms implicated the Germans, especially "the German orientalists who
even before the outbreak of the war had brought up the matter of the
deportation of the Armenians within the framework of the analysis of the
issues at hand. A member of the German Military Mission to Turkey had
declared that 'the plan to exile the Armenians was a German idea.'"[74]
Finally, reference may be made to a monographic study on the German
influence in Turkey in which the author maintains that in face of the outbreak of disorders, Germans influenced Turkish decision making, operating behind the scenes and pulling the strings (*akıl hocalığı*). It is
noteworthy that this author uses the same word "severely" (*şiddetle*) to
relate the idea that when the German General Staff urged the Turks to
repress the Armenians, they advised severity.[75]

The reported disclosure of a former Turkish Foreign Minister

In the archives of the British Foreign Office lies the record of a protracted correspondence between British and American sources on "the
complicity of Berlin in the Armenian massacres." The correspondence
revolves around Asım, who in 1911 was Minister of Foreign Affairs of
Turkey and subsequently was entrusted by the Young Turk leadership
with the task of winning over the Iranians for an alliance with Turkey,
for which purpose he was appointed ambassador at Teheran. In one of

the pieces of this correspondence there is a cipher telegram, stating emphatically that "Assim Bey can afford and has afforded definite information as to instigation and complicity of German Government on Armenian massacres." British sources describe him as having been disappointed with the overall conduct of the Ittihadists, their "scoundrelism," to quote one of these sources, that he is prepared to expose them. Conversant in German, and with access to both the ambassadors of Turkey and Germany in Washington D.C., he reportedly obtained the information on German complicity from the German ambassador.[76] The cipher telegram cited above on "the complicity of Berlin" was sent by Dixon, the editor of the *Christian Science Monitor* in Boston, to G.H. Locock, the British Consul General at Boston, but on leave in London at the time.[77] According to A. Harvey Bathurst, the Chief of *Christian Science Monitor's* London bureau, the whole episode of willingness to reveal a state secret exploded as a result of a conflict at the Turkish section of the 1915 Panama Pacific Exhibition at San Francisco, whose Armenian director, Vahan Cardashian, was ejected from his post as a result of the intervention of the German ambassador in Washington, D.C. It is not clear, however, how Asım came to be involved in this episode. According to Bathurst, a British source and a lawyer, Asım in the past had some quarrels with Ittihad, was knowledgeable about some of their secrets and learned more in 1915 through his contacts with the German ambassador.

The latter evidently received the documents in question from the Turkish ambassador. Asım is described as being cognizant of "the inside of the secret plan" against the Armenians, and as having communicated "to a few people" his knowledge thereof. Bathurst also indicated that the U.S. government is "none too anxious to add to the feeling on the subject of the Germans here by the disclosures."[78] However, there is no resolution of the issue as far as the correspondence in question is concerned. Beyond the general assertion that a former Turkish Foreign Minister claimed to have documents in his possession regarding German complicity in the destruction of Ottoman Armenians, nothing specific is in fact disclosed or even described. One has to depend upon the perceptions and faith of the British and American sources involved, as well as upon their integrity.

The intimations of two Turkish deputies—before and after the fact

The possibility that some sort of a deal was struck with some German authorities in Germany prior to the war and months before a Turko-German military alliance materialized was hinted at by a member of the Turkish Parliament. He was Deputy Feyzi, representing the province of Diyarbekir. In two successive exchanges with Diyarbekir's British Vice Consul, who happened to be an Armenian, Feyzi threateningly forecast the demise of the Armenian population of Turkey in the event the Armenian leaders should continue to orient themselves to the British and their allies. In the meeting on August 27, 1914, Feyzi reiterated Turkey's reasons for identifying with Germany and in that vein he disclosed that he was part of a delegation of Turkish deputies who had visited Berlin in the spring of that year. When the Armenian vice consul expressed surprise at his uninhibitedness with which he was uttering such ominous things, the Turkish deputy retorted: "On the basis of what I saw, heard and learned there [in Berlin], I have absolutely reached this conclusion." This forecast gains added significance by the fact that Deputy Feyzi subsequently proved to be one of the most ferocious organizers of the Armenian genocide. According to a British Intelligence report, "Deputy Feyzi was received by the Kaiser and decorated with the Iron Cross."[79]

Another Turkish deputy serving in the new Parliament of the fledgling Kemalist regime is on record on having made a similar intimation about German permissiveness as a factor in the successful execution of the Turkish plan against the Armenians. In the course of a secret session (June 10, 1922) at which the deputies were debating the problem of deporting the Greek population of Pontus in the Trabzon area, Ali Şükrü, the deputy from Trabzon, expressed regrets that the Turkish government failed to tackle this Greek problem during the war when the conditions were so much more favorable. He deplored the reliance on half-hearted and intermittent measures, and with a sense of nostalgia invoked the period of the war when "Germany was behind us, complying with everyone of our wishes. But now, we are on our own. Yet, no matter what, we at once have to resolve this problem."

The allusion was, of course, to the drastic methods through which the deportation of the Armenians was enacted to achieve the goal of destruction. Commenting on this end result, Finance Minister Hasan Fehmi, during one of the further stages of the same debate compared the pending Greek issue with the successful Armenian deportations. He expressed satisfaction that the success was due "to the army being all over the country and the Armenians having no inkling as to what awaited them."[80]

The assertion of a Turkish cabinet minister

Cavid, the Minister of Economy, was in constant touch with the representatives of Germany, negotiating and renegotiating economic and fiscal matters to sustain Turkey amid incremental wartime hardships. He even went to Berlin and had high-level consultations with German officials for the same purpose. In an interview with Folley, the Special Correspondent in the Ottoman capital of the British newspaper *Morning Post*, Cavid in the Armistice period maintained that the Germans are the ones who first brought up the matter of liquidating the Armenian population of Turkey.[81]

A Turkish historian's input

In his multi-volume studies on the subject of Turkish struggles for liberation in modern times, Doğan Avcıoğlu appears to be one of the few chroniclers who had, or was allowed to have, access to some of the innermost secrets of the Young Turk Ittihadists. In one of his discussions on the Armenian deportations, he stated that these deportations were of a wide scope, were carried out systematically and whose aim was "the radical solution of the Armenian question." According to the evidence at his disposal, the plan was championed in the councils of Ittihad by Dr. Şakir, and was "endorsed" (*onaylandığı*) by the Germans.[82]

These Turkish allegations and assertions are unofficial in character and as such lack the quality of authenticity. But, given the nature of the complicity at issue here, one may be hard put to secure any other type of evidence to ascertain definitively any degree of complicitous involvement. As will be discussed in the next section of this chapter, the German Chief of Staff at the Ottoman General Headquarters removed substantial quantities of files and carried them with him to Berlin upon departure from Turkey at the end of the war. As with the rest of the material relative to the issue of culpability in general, one has to learn to make the best out of what can only be circumstantial evidence.

Incidents of Concealment and Disclosure

The conditions of war, and preparations for war, are such as to magnify the need for ordinary secrecy attending the patterns of international diplomacy and related activities of military cooperation. The Turkish plan against the Armenian population was not only part of a war-related secrecy but it was one of the centerpieces of such secrecy. The German involvement in the genesis and execution of that plan, irrespective of its nature and extent, made German efforts to help the Turks conceal the evidence of the crime, which that plan entailed, an almost compelling necessity. By the same token, such concealment was bound to be even more critical for protecting ancillary German interests insofar as the issue of German involvement was concerned.

The deletions in the main foreign office documentary tome

One of the major targets to which German efforts of concealment were directed was the German public, and even German officialdom. Even though German diplomats, i.e., a succession of German ambassadors to Turkey, and a host of German consuls, stationed in the interior of Turkey, were inundating the German Foreign Office and the office of the German chancellor in Berlin, with details of the mass murder in progress, the authorities, including the High Command at the General Headquarters had issued orders to suppress the evidence by withholding it from the German public. A protestant missionary historian, Dr. Johannes Lepsius, set out to contest his government by secretly assembling and compiling documentation for the purpose of alerting the public, in the hope that public indignation and a resulting public pressure may induce the government to intervene and stop the carnage. Lepsius was not a novice in the matter of the history of Armenian massacres. In the wake of the Abdul Hamit-era massacres he had undertaken a two-month inspection trip to the sites of the atrocities and published his findings in a book (see chapter 8, n. 146). He undertook a similar trip to Turkey in July 1915; the German authorities relented considerably before issuing a permit to travel. In the course of his visit in Constantinople Lepsius managed to secretly gather incriminating evidence against the Turkish authorities by contact with the American Embassy, the Armenian Patriarchate, German, Swiss, and American missionaries, and some Turkish officials; included in this activity was a meeting with War Minister Enver who defiantly told him that he assumes full responsibility for what is happening to the Armenians in the provinces.

With inordinate courage Lepsius prepared *A Special Report* which in the form of a 303-page booklet was printed and secretly mailed to the members of the Reichstag (German Parliament), the receipt of which was barred by the government, and to 10,000–20,000 other Germans, including church leaders, public figures, etc.[83] Many more copies were scheduled for distribution when Ibrahim Hakkı Paşa, Turkish ambassador at Berlin, lodged a vigorous protest in which he invoked the interests of "our common cause" for "the triumph" of which this "most infamous" piece of propaganda should be suppressed. Within days Foreign Minister Jagow obligingly informed the ambassador that the books in question have been "confiscated."[84] Furthermore, Lepsius was subjected to pressures from all sides, especially the German Foreign Office, to cease and desist; at times these pressures took on the form of intimidation and veiled threats. In Holland, where he was in self-imposed exile, he was subjected to a humiliating treatment by Friedrich Rosen, the German ambassador there, who was demanding that Lepsius refrain from making public statements for the duration of the war.[85] While refusing to remain silent, Lepsius promised not to do or say anything that may undermine German foreign policy and also "offend the sensibilities of the Turkish ally"; he meant to confine himself to charity and relief work to succor the wounds of the survivors.

In the process Lepsius was led, however, onto a path which constrained him to perform the task of sanitizing to a certain degree official German records whereby Germany could be purged of any guilt or complicity regarding the fate of the Armenians. In this sense, he was impelled to play the role of an apologist for Germany, while emphasizing the fact that Turkey alone was responsible for the crimes attached to that fate. The result was the publication in 1919 of a massive compilation of German Foreign Office documents, containing 444 pieces of diplomatic and military correspondence and five pertinent Annexes.[86]

The conditions surrounding the publication of this work betray the symptoms of a profound German concern to exculpate Germany under all circumstances and focus instead on the primacy and magnitude of Turkish culpability and responsibility. The German Foreign Office, through its representative, Dr. Wilhelm Solf, made a deal with Lepsius whereby it would relinquish its plan to publish a White Book on the Armenian deportations and massacres, and allow instead Lepsius to have access to its files to produce a substitute volume for which he personally would be responsible. Lepsius accepted, with the stipulation that nothing would be withheld from him and that he would have complete access. The German official who haggled with Lepsius over the need to omit certain documents and delete portions from other documents was Privy Legation Councillor Dr. Otto Göppert.[87] In a mood to accommodate him, Lepsius in his response from Holland to Göppert's June 28, 1919 letter reassured Göppert that "from the very outset I intended to relieve [i.e., exonerate] (*entlasten*) Germany ... I believe the book will adequately serve the purpose of dispelling the calumnies against German officials and military officers."[88] When Göppert expressed appreciation for this intent of Lepsius he informed the latter that he has decided to withhold new material from the files of German consuls which would have been supplementary to the material already supplied. Assembled by former Aleppo Consul Rössler, these new files were deemed to be of no value for the end of serving German interests (*ohne Nutzen für uns*) while capable of "further inculpating the Turks" by injecting into the picture material that "replenishes the chapter of Turkish atrocities" (*zur Vervollständigung des Kapitels der türkischen Greuel*).[89]

Lepsius volume is indeed deficient in this respect. Some crucial portions are lifted from certain documents to conceal instances of German attitudes and actions betraying various levels of German consent or involvement, whether direct or indirect; at other places sentences or words are substituted in altered forms. Authors such as Trumpener,[90] Dinkel[91] and Bihl have noticed these omissions and deletions, with the latter providing a detailed illustration of the method used.[92] A close scrutiny of the condition of the originals of these documents, deposited at the Foreign Office at Bonn, reveals that the deletions were effected by the insertion at chosen spots of faintly penned brackets. While some blame Lepsius for these modifications, the cryptic intervention by someone from the Foreign Office, directly dealing with the publisher, cannot be ruled out.[93]

The issue of financial liability

Perhaps the most outstanding reason prompting the German authorities to withhold and suppress evidence (wartime concealment through censorship was discussed in Chapter 12, notes 9, 10, 11) was revealed by Göppert. He expressed his deep concern about the ramifications of the charge of complicity leveled against Germany "in the whole world, and especially America...." He then spelled out the fundamental source of that concern: "This is a heavy charge from which we must free ourselves not least for financial reasons, since otherwise we will be liable for the damages."[94]

The removal by the Germans of Ottoman General Staff files

The bulk of the material adduced in this chapter points to the complicity in various ways and degrees of some high-ranking German officers, especially those on duty at Ottoman General Headquarters. This being the case, the records assembled in the archives of that headquarters would be of critical significance. Yet Major General Seeckt, the last German Chief of Staff at that office, whisked away substantial parts of these records when departing from Turkey at the end of the war. Turkish Cabinet ministers, especially Education Minister Dr. Riza Tevfik, and postwar Grand Vizier Izzet Paşa, publicly denounced this move when they became cognizant of it. On November 6, 1918 Grand Vizier Izzet lodged a formal protest to Berlin, accusing Seeckt of a transgression i.e., of carrying with him "*tous les dossiers du Quartier Général Ottoman,*" despite Seeckt's formal promise not to take away these pieces "which are the property of the government." Seeckt on November 24, 1918 promised to return only those files which basically concern the Turkish military.[95] There is no indication as to the category of the items these files did contain or to the language or languages in which the documents in question were framed. Nor could it be ascertained as to whether these files were in fact returned, and if so, to what extent, when, and to what branch of the Turkish government. This element of uncertainty makes it impossible to probe deeper into the problem and its implications, except to say that it is part of a broad sweep of efforts of concealment.

A German document with a revelatory hint

The extraordinary value of this document lies in its rarity. In all the relevant files perused by this author in the archives at Bonn, or Potsdam, there is no other official document that approximates the inclination for frankness with which a German intelligence operative in it intimates that there is some truth about the prevalent rumors and allegations on German complicity. The document originates from the office of Otto Günther Wesendonck, a specialist on nationalities in the Political Section of the German Foreign Office, and the principal exponent of insurrectionary movements in the border areas of Russia. In a report, dated May 4, 1916, he quotes O. von Schmidt as declaring that "insightful Turks are contending that the annihilation (*Vertilgung*) of the Armenians was ordered by the Germans" (*auf deutshen Befehl*).[96]

There are several aspects to this caustic remark deserving special attention. First of all the declaration is somewhat accurate when one takes into account the deportation order of General Bronsart (described above)—in terms of its consequences. Second, the position of Schmidt renders the declaration more or less reliable insofar as the contacts he had with Turkish and German intelligence operatives, involved in special, secret missions, are concerned. He was the agent of Count Friedrich Werner von Schulenburg, who, apart from temporary consular services, was involved in the work of organizing and deploying guerillas; the latter's mission was to undermine Russia's war effort through sabotage and insurrectionary acts on its Transcaucasian borders. The umbrella organization coordinating these activities was the Turkish Special Organization, the principal instrument for the implementation of the Armenian genocide. Equally important, Schmidt was associated with two men, a German and a Turk, i.e., Dr. Nazım and Humann, likewise implicated at various levels in the liquidation of the Armenian population. On the occasion of a trip to Berlin, which Schmidt took with Nazım, for example, Humann wrote a letter to Jäckh, a Turkophile German operative enjoying the benefits of the sponsorship of the German Foreign Office, recommending Dr. Nazım. Humann pleaded with Jäckh to "watch over him with a tender loving eye. I don't need to say anything about the foremost importance of this man in the entire political life of Turkey."[97]

The most revealing feature of the document is the adjective Schmidt uses to characterize those Turks who at the time were blaming Germany for "the annihilation," of the Armenians. The adjective he used was the German word "*einsichtig*" which means "insightful," or "perceptive." There is not only a total absence of the standard German disclaimer in face of such Turkish assertions, but evidence of an urge to praise those making these assertions. These people are not dismissed out of hand but are acknowledged as people with keen minds. As if to punctuate this fact, von Wesendonck, who was one of the leaders directing the anti-Russian insurrectionary plots, is seen in this document as agreeing with Schmidt, if by default; despite his responsible position, he has not chosen to contradict or dispute anywhere in that document Schmidt, who clearly is seen here adopting the Turkish rationale thereby implicitly concurring with the charge of German complicity. Finally, the same point may be made about Eugen Mittwoch, Professor of Egyptian Studies at the University of Berlin, who had taken charge of the bureau dealing with matters of intelligence and propaganda in the east. His statement, appended to Wesendonck's report in the same document, simply glosses over Schmidt's declaration.

It is conceivable that this was a confidential piece of communication, intended strictly for in-house use, but was somehow inserted in regular record files. It is likewise conceivable that both Wesendonck and Mittwoch were more preoccupied with the other aspects of the document, treating the Schmidt statement as a side issue not worthy of any particular comment. Therefore, their failure to disclaim or refute Schmidt's view is not necessarily proof of concurrence with it. Nevertheless, the fact remains that Schmidt, an intelligence official with ties to certain Turks and Germans, who was knowledgeable about the extermination of the Armenians, tacitly acknowledged German complicity, thereby adding another link in the chain of fragments of evidence which is being explored in this chapter.

Disclosure through the medium of two veteran Austrian consuls

Dr. Ernst von Kwiatkowski was the Dual Monarchy's Consul General at Trabzon and was very active in the gathering of reliable information on the conditions of the Armenian deportations and massacres in the entire province. Of all the Austrian consuls stationed in wartime Turkey he was the most conscientious about this task; his reports to Vienna were both numerous and focused in this respect. In a number of these reports he advised his Foreign Minister, Stephan Baron Burian, that the German consuls at Trabzon and Erzurum, Dr. Heinrich Bergfeld and Dr. Max Erwin von Scheubner Richter, respectively, were being pressured by their government to "tone down" their reports about Turkish massacres.[98] In several other reports Kwiatkowski informed Vienna that the assertion about German complicity is gaining ground in all Turkish circles, including official quarters.[99]

The one particular report which is the principal subject of the present discussion was sent from Trabzon on October 22, 1915; it is marked "confidential," and was addressed to Burian, with a copy to Pallavicini, the Austrian ambassador in the Ottoman capital. In order to appreciate the significance of the provenance of the source, i.e., the port city of Trabzon, the following fact should be taken into account. Trabzon was a central location for the marshaling of the resources, logistics and the deployment of the guerilla bands of the Special Organization. Several of its leaders on the field, such as Dr. Behaeddin Şakir, Yakub Cemil, Yusuf Riza, and Yenibahçeli Nail, met and mapped their plans in that city, which thus became a hub for Special Organization-related traffic. Equally significant, German intelligence operatives and agents, one way or another involved in the activities of that organization, converged in Trabzon as the place of rendezvous, including Colonel Stange of the German army who was in command a Turkish regiment comprising a contingent of Special Organization guerillas; at one time during the war, both Yusuf Riza and Dr. Şakir were under his command.[100] This is the text of the report of Trabzon's Austrian consul:

I learned from a German source, which usually is reliable, that the first suggestion for the *Unschädlichmachung* of the Armenians—certainly not in the manner in which it was actually carried out—came from the German camp.[101]

As noted above, in German parlance the word *Unschädlichmachung* denotes the idea of rendering the subject incapable of causing any injury; but it also connotes the idea of summary liquidation of that subject, as likewise evidenced in the spoken and written words as well as the deeds of the Nazis during World War II. This piece of document is significant on two grounds. It is based on what appears to be a credible German source; its content is in accord with the statement of the German functionary Schmidt discussed above. The Austrian consul's effort to protect the identity of that source from his superiors, at least in terms of official records, is also noteworthy.

The other Austrian consul involved is Dr. Arthur Chevalier de Nadamlenzki, on duty at Adrianople (Edirne), in the European part of Turkey. Unlike the case of his colleague at Trabzon, his source is not German but Turkish, namely, "a very influential personality, who has close ties with the Ittihadist clique, and knows all their secrets." Nadamlenzki received the disclosure through one of his confidential informants (*Gewährsman*), probably a Turkish official, whom he could not persuade to reveal the identity of the source; the informant would merely stress the high profile of that source in such terms as quoted above. The disclosure consists in the simple and crude assertion that "Germany wanted the enactment of the anti-Armenian measures." The consul sent this report both to his ambassador and to his foreign minister.[102] The need to exercise some caution, if not suspicion, is warranted in the case of this document, given the origin and nature of the source described.

The necessity for such a caveat is indicated by the contents of the report German Embassy chaplain Count von Lüttichau compiled on the entire wartime episode of Armenian deportations and massacres. After describing the many cases where Turks from all walks of life are seen persisting in their eagerness to blame Germany as the arch instigator against the Armenians, Lüttichau focuses on a particular instance. Relying on Turkish sources, who claim to have been present at a meeting Malatya's deputy Haşim is reported to have convened upon his return from the Ottoman capital in the wake of the spring 1916 recess of the Parliament, the chaplain provides the following account. The Turkish deputy reportedly told the notables of Malatya he had gathered together that he personally was present when German ambassador Wangenheim one day [it has to be before his sudden death in October 1915] appeared at the seat of the Ottoman government, the Sublime Porte, in order to "convey his government's congratulations for the comprehensive manner and the crowning glorious success with which the Armenian people were

exterminated." Lüttichau in his report, disputing the veracity of the statement attributed to Wangenheim, responds with the retort, "Such shame-
lessness exceeds all bounds."[103]

The Anti-Russian Ideology in the Turko-German Partnership and its Anti-Armenian Repercussions

The quest for credible sources is further redeemed by adding to the array
of sources used thus far a source which differs from the latter. It involves
a source which did forecast the fate of the Armenians six months before
the outbreak of World War I. Relying on information, presumably supplied by the agents of the Russian Secret Service, the Russian periodical
Golos Moskoi in its January 1914 issue directed attention to a "Turko-
German scheme to deport the Armenians of the Ottoman provinces to
Mesopotamia." According to the editors of the newspaper, this plan was
in line with Turkish and German designs to establish homogenous Muslim masses of populations in the east of Turkey, contiguous to those of
the Caucasus, thereby enabling these Muslim kinsmen to confront
together the Slavic peoples exactly as advocated by Marshal Goltz (see
his proposal earlier in this chapter). Through a reference to this Russian
source he made in an editorial on October 17/30, 1918, a former lieutenant of the Turkish security police, an Armenian, who during the war
had assisted the Turks in the liquidation of the Armenian notables in the
Ottoman capital, confirmed the allegation of a Turko-German scheme to
resettle the Armenians in Mesopotamia. It appears that an Armenian
newspaper, *Gohag*, had been punished by the Turkish Court-Martial
which, invoking the state of martial law existing at that time, had banned
that paper for republishing the Russian forecast; the Armenian newspaper
then reappeared under the new name of *Taylaylig*.[104] What is even more
significant, *Ikdam*, a Turkish newspaper, which after the war published an
open letter to President Wilson admitting the culpabilities of Turkey, in
its January 17, 1914 issue took *Golos Moskoi* to task for publishing such
"absurdities."[105] It should be noted that *The Okhrana*, the Russian
Department of Police, otherwise called the Imperial Russian Secret
Police, not only had agents in the Ottoman capital, but had available a
number of Turkish sources affiliated one way or another with the
Ottoman security system. As if to indirectly corroborate the forecast of
Golos Moskoi, the *Okhrana* on January 23, 1914, relayed a secret report
through its contacts in the Russian Interior and Foreign Affairs ministries,
declaring, "Today, at a secret meeting of panislamists and Ittihadists at
Nuri Osmaniye [the party headquarters of Ittihad], several delegates
spoke up, lambasting the Russians and the Christians … . At the end of
the conclave Talât stated that Turkey is opposed to any type of foreign

control in Anatolia [the reference is to the imminent February 8, 1914 Accord on Armenian Reforms in the provinces].[106]

This matter raises the issue of ideology seen as a factor facilitating at another level the growth of a Turko-German partnership under review here; it involves an ideology that is punctuated by anti-Russian elements. A brief commentary may, therefore, be in order. In surveying the whole picture, the Turkish sociologist Ismail Beşikci discerned a Turko-German conspiracy in "the deportation of hundreds of thousands of Armenians which in actuality was a genocide in its truest meaning [*tam anlamıyla bir soykırım*] ... it was the result of an undertaking in which German imperialism, in a collision course with Russian imperialism ... enabled the Ittihadists to solve the Armenian question by spurring Turkism and panturanism."[107] Moreover, the founder of the ideology of panturanism, the Tatar political leader and journalist from Russia, Yusuf Akçura, espoused the same doctrine. Akçura had joined the Ittihadists after the latter's successful 1908 revolution. He also had founded *Türk Yurdu*, the organ of the panturanists who rallied under the banner of the Turkish Hearth (*Türk Ocağı*). While studying in Paris he had absorbed the racial superiority views of the pangermanists. He too believed that the Germans could help the Turkic peoples of Russia achieve emancipation and freedom from Tsarist rule and oppression. In the first issue of *Türk Yurdu* it was declared that "the rulers of the universe have always been the representatives of only two great nations—Turks and Germans." Akçura in the same issue stated that Russian Turks had great expectations from a new coalition of Turks and Germans.[108] One such expectation involved the removal of Armenians and Armenia from the paths of Ottoman Turks who were gravitating towards their kinsmen in the Caucasus and beyond, i.e., to the dreamland of Turan. In a speech on January 29, 1920, delivered at a mass meeting in Istanbul, Akçura stated that the Turkish soldiers sacrificed themselves to secure independence for Azerbaijan. He then declared, "It is necessary to destroy Armenia which the Allies want to erect as a barrier between the two brotherly segments of Turkdom, Anatolia and the Caucasus."[109] In fact Zenkovsky, as noted earlier, explicitly concluded that "the massacre in 1914–16 of one and a half million Armenians was largely conditioned by the desire of the Young Turks to eliminate the Armenian obstacle" in this respect (see note 5, chapter 20).

The chief exponent of an alliance of the forces of pangermanism and panturkism was Tekin Alp who argued that the Slavs were the historical common enemy of both the Turks and the Germans and that, therefore, an alliance between the two nations was "a geographical and historical necessity. The condition of the Germans and Turks vis a vis the Slavic peoples has not changed in a millennium of history. They still remain the common enemy of the Slavic power and must, therefore, protect themselves against the Moscowite bear ... panturkism cannot attain a full measure of fruition before the Moscowite monster is overpowered. Russia for her part is impeded in her development by two obstacles: the Germans and the Turks ... . So long as there is a Slavic danger, panturkism and pangermanism must remain partners and follow the same path." Completely embracing this ideological blueprint the Young Turk Ittihadists under German tutelage and through the prodding of the German High Command unilaterally intervened in World War I when they precipitated the outbreak of hostilities against Russia.

In a secret circular that was brought to light by Alp himself and, thus far, is to be found nowhere else, the Ittihadists notified their provincial branch offices that it was inevitable for Turkey to get involved in the war for reasons they framed as follows:

> Let us not forget that one of the most important reasons for which we are intervening in the war is related to our national objective which is twofold. On the one hand, we are anxious to destroy the Moscovite enemy in order to create natural borders which allow us to unite with our kinfolk and to incorporate them in our domain. On the other hand, we are driven with a religious zeal to free the Islamic world from the bondage imposed upon them by the infidels and to secure the independence of the Muslim faithful.[110]

This work appeared in German in Weimar with a view to familiarizing the Germans with the tenets of panturkish nationalism and thereby to cement a new mold of Turko-German partnership, the rudiments of which have been described in section 1 of this chapter. The Germans not only adopted the idea of an alliance with Turkey for the purpose of confronting the perceived threat from Russia, but assisted in the process of liquidating the Ottoman Armenians who were considered to be a subsidiary part of the overall Russian threat. The responses to the outcome of that liquidation by some other representatives of German society, adduced below, may shed further light on this problem.

German Political Economists and the Armenian Genocide

One type of such response involved the manifestation of a sense of affinity with the Turks in terms of a model personality presumed to be embodying certain common character traits. German Ambassador Wangenheim had admiringly told Grand Vizier Said Halim, for example, that "Turkey was the Prussia of the Islamic world." When reporting on this ambassadorial tribute, a German economics professor who was also a Reichstag deputy, and who had just completed a visit in Turkey, proceeded to assess the significance of "the Armenian massacres" which by then had largely run their course. He declared that as the Turkish leaders had through exterminatory massacres eliminated the Armenians, they had enabled "this old master race [*Herrenvolk*]" to achieve a certain level of "a national, or rather a religious cohesiveness" (*eine nationale, oder vielmehr, religiöse Geschlossenheit*).[111] Another economist, and a leader of the German Association for Defense (*Wehrverein*), for five weeks (and at about the same time as the professor mentioned above) had conducted an inspection tour of Turkey. In his 26-page report he reproved European attitudes which, he complained, routinely condemned Turkey for the massacre of the Armenians on the basis of Western standards. As a counter-argument, he directed attention to the fact that "the political party ruling in Turkey willfully can dispose over the possessions and lives of their subjects." In other words, he meant that there was nothing unusual about these massacres. After echoing the Turkish charges of Armenian treason and enmity against Turkey, the author stated that "by February 1916, 1.5 million Armenians were destroyed." Wholeheartedly approving it as "the first step toward the recovery of the [levers of] economic predominance in Turkey," the German author added that "there was 'joy' (*Freude*) in the government circles that the long-desired opportunity (*langgewünschte Gelegenheit*) finally presented itself...." It is noticeable that, while approving of the mass murder he was describing, the author used for that purpose such words as "horrors" (*Greuel*), "butchery" (*Niedermetzelung*), and "extermination" (*Ausrottung*), thereby dispensing with the repetition of the Turkish euphemism "deportation" used by the Turkish authorities to disguise the intended act of genocide.[112]

The Views of German Experts of Criminal and International Law on German Complicity as a By-Product of Militarism

Perhaps the most common element in the cultivation of the Turko-German partnership was the legacy of militarism dominating many aspects of both German and Turkish cultures, which otherwise were quite disparate in many other respects. This convergence, however narrow in scope, was sufficient to afford many high-ranking German officers the latitude to go along with their Turkish counterparts or to spur them on the matter of the elimination of the Armenians as "a military necessity." In sections 4 and 5 of this chapter this issue has been dealt with at some length. It may be relevant at this point to revisit and reinterpret briefly the legal liability aspect of this factor of militarism that was specifically examined as an ancillary problem above.

That relevance issues from the significance of a precedent-setting trial that took place in a district criminal court in Berlin in 1921. It involved the prosecution of a young Armenian who, in broad daylight, had assassinated Talât, the architect of the Armenian genocide, on a major boulevard in Berlin, and was acquitted after a mere one-hour deliberation by a German jury on grounds of temporary insanity, as provided for in article

51 of the German penal code. As stated elsewhere (Chapter 22, note 6), the German Foreign Office had declined the request of the postwar Ottoman government to have Talât extradited to Turkey for trial as a war criminal; he subsequently was tried in Istanbul in absentia and was sentenced to death. Several aspects of the Armenian genocide came to light during the trial. Foremost among these were the declarations of the defense counsel on the matter of the Turko-German alliance and the issue of German complicity. Dr. Johannes Werthauer, a Legal Councillor and a member of the defense team, rejected the prosecutor's plea to be mindful of the fact that Talât represented a valued ally and was a guest of Germany.[113] He argued instead that Talât and his cronies who had taken refuge in Germany and were "fugitives of justice," were the allies of a government that was "Prussian in make-up, and militaristic." Inveighing against "militarists" as proponents of violence who disdain the notions of right and justice, are eager to wage war, and are prepared to destroy anything and everything under a plea of "military necessity," Werthauer in his closing arguments declared: "We too have men prone to violence, men whom we have sent to Turkey so that they could drill the Turkish military into the art of violence … and it so happens that these men of violence (*Gewaltmenschen*) were the ones who destroyed the Armenian people … the order to deport an entire people is the vilest thought that can ever enter the mind of a militarist … the German people too are being accused of having allowed the issuance of such orders of deportation. Only by way of a total and unreserved repudiation of such principles and a renunciation of such mean-spirited, criminal orders can we regain the respect to which, I believe, we are entitled."[114]

Another member of the defense team was Dr. Niemeyer, Government Privy Councillor and a Professor of Law at the University of Kiel; he was a world-renowned authority on international law. In his closing argument he conceded two points which underscore the relevance of this entire chapter while at the same time accentuating its significance. The Attorney General, Gollnick, had not only tried to defend the reputation of Talât, the murder victim, but had extolled the virtues of the Turko-German alliance which, he said, Talât embodied. Consequently, he said, Talât was catapulted to "the elevated heights of history."[115] Declaring that he feels constrained to respond to this assessment by the Attorney General, Niemeyer stated: "During the war in Turkey military authorities here at home, and over there [in Turkey], maintained silence over and covered up [*verschwiegen und verdeckt*] the Armenian horrors, to an extent which bordered on approval" (*an die Grenze des Zulässigen heranreichenden Weise*).[116] Thus, he concurred with Dr. Werthauer, his partner on the defense team, about this aspect of German complicity. Equally important, he submitted for consideration the argument that, in adjudicating a crime under the German penal code, "the generally accepted rules of international law are to be treated as binding integral parts of the law of the German Reich, as provided by Article 4 of the constitution of the empire."[117]

In commenting on these proceedings, the *New York Times* wrote, "The damning German angle to the Turkish war atrocities in Armenia was patent to all present...."[118]

The Significance of Emperor William II's Secret Activities

The matter of secrecy and concealment has its most abiding test in the evaluation of the role of Emperor William II. In section 5 of this chapter his dual status as civilian head of the nation as well as commander-in-chief of the armed forces was briefly sketched. There are indications, however, that he was involved also in activities which border on conspiracy and involve the supervision of plots, authorization of "special missions," and acts of espionage and sabotage outside Germany. One German agent in his memoirs describes, for example, how he was received by William II, performed "secret" missions "for the Kaiser," including one at Constantinople. He provides graphic details of an encounter with William II at the German Foreign Office at Wilhelmstrasse where the emperor personally charged him with a secret mission in Morocco, and reportedly added these words: "Outside Count Wedel [Count von Botho Wedel at the time was emperor's Privy Councillor and head of the Secret Service, that was run by the emperor], no one is to know anything of your mission. No one is to know that you are carrying a verbal message from me to the Captain of the warship Panther. Understand?" After inducing the agent to memorize the contents of the slip of paper, William II reportedly asked, "Have you memorized it?" "Yes, Sir." "Then taking the note from me, he at once struck a match and held it under the paper until it was reduced to ashes." With respect to his previous 1905 mission at Constantinople, the same agent states, "I was bidden to keep away from all official German intercourse in Constantinople." This agent also disclosed that William II kept a privy purse to finance these operations. After four months of operations, he returned to Berlin with a report on Abdul Hamit, palace spies, Russian and French gold for bribery, the Young Turk dissidents and Enver.[119]

The disclosures of another German agent are more pertinent. He performed secret service work in Constantinople on three different occasions, namely, in the latter half of 1908, the first half of 1909, and the closing months of the second Balkan war, i.e., during the Spring of 1913. He had established contact with Enver and was told by his superior in Berlin that the latter was considered a key person for fulfilling German ambitions in Turkey, and as a nemesis to Russian ambitions there. He further maintains that German Ambassador Wangenheim was "a personal friend" of his. It is against this backdrop that the agent's following revelations need to be assessed. In the Spring of 1914 Enver undertook "a secret" trip to Germany. "I took him to the station.... He told me he had had a long talk with the Emperor, and he seemed particularly cheerful in consequence. More than once I have wondered what bearing that talk had upon subsequent events on the Bosphorus." The agent also states that at the end of June, or early July 1914, "William II caused a ciphered message to be forwarded to Enver Pasha, who in obedience thereto hastened to Berlin," spending two days in conference with General Moltke, the Chief of the German General Staff. All this may be better understood in the light of the fact that "Enver Bey had always cherished a grudge against Russia.... He sent secret messengers to Berlin with an offer of service to the Kaiser, declaring to him that the forces of Turkey were at his disposal...." Finally, the author notes that in the fall of 1913, when Ittihad was firmly entrenched in power, large secret funds were remitted to Enver and his Ittihad party.[120]

Some of these assertions are independently verified by other agents or historians. Captain Franz von Rintelen from the German Naval Staff (*Admiralstab*), for example, states that he received a "*Kaiserpass*," an exceptional passport given to people with special missions, entitling the bearer to all manner of assistance from German embassies and legations around the world. Though Bernstorff, German ambassador at Washington D.C., was kept in the dark about the nature of his mission, which was sabotage, Zimmermann, William II's confidant in the Foreign Office, knew about it.[121] Another German author wrote that the German High Command through the Central Office of Censorship "confidentially" directed the German newspapers not to say anything about Enver's presence in Berlin in April 1917.[122] Enver's submissiveness to the desiderata of the German High Command is confirmed by General Bronsart in a "top secret" (*streng geheim*) December 15, 1917 memorandum in which Enver is praised for his accomodating stance towards the German General Staff and his Germanophile attitude, "borne by an inner conviction."[123] Historian Gottlieb for his part maintains that Enver, along with Talât, was completely under the influence of German ambassador Wangenheim,[124] with a Turkish author, a former army officer, maintaining that Enver was beholden to the German secret service.[125]

All these manifestations of acute influence converge in a single knot; they reflect the exertions of a central source of authority, namely, the institutionalized power of the German Emperor directing Germany's foreign policy and its war effort. Significant, for example, is his retort to Prince Bernhard von Bülow who had just resigned as Chancellor of Germany in June 1909 and William II, accepting Bülow's recommendation, had appointed Bethmann Hollweg as Reich's Chancellor, after giving up on General Colmar von der Goltz, the Turkophile Prussian General, who was his first choice. Bülow was praising Hollweg's merits and aptitudes

in terms of domestic matters but pointed out what he believed to be Hollweg's ignorance on foreign policy matters. The Emperor dismissed this
admonition, smugly declaring: "Foreign policy. You can leave it to
me."[126] His penchant for autocratic and secret deals in the conduct of the
war is epitomized by the manner in which he engineered the creation of
the German Military Mission to Turkey in 1913 and undertook to appoint
the Prussian general Liman von Sanders as the Chief of that Mission
without the knowledge of the Chancellor or the Foreign Affairs Ministry.[127] Whether military officers or diplomatic representatives, German
functionaries collaborating with the Turkish leaders in Turkey were in the
final analysis the underlings of their emperor; they were the executioners
of his policy designs. This fact is clearly evinced in the dispatch of the
following "top secret" (*ganz geheim*) order.

To the Naval War Staff

Through the medium of the Foreign Office the following telegram has
been sent to Admiral Usedom:

> His majesty the Emperor expects that you, in close conjunction with Admiral
> Souchon, do submit [*unterordnen*] to the ambassador's political views which
> His Majesty approves. His Majesty considers this as a first condition for a suc-
> cessful performance in Turkey.
>
> In discharge of the Supreme Order
v. Müller[128]
>
> (Admiral Georg Alexander v. Müller, head of the German Naval Cabinet)

A Final Commentary on the Issue of German Complicity

By any definition, a crime, resulting from an act of conspiracy of one
kind or another, does not easily lend itself to probing and, consequently,
to the establishment of probative evidence; uncertainties and ambiguities
often surround the crime. In fact these are part of the make-up of the act
of conspiracy itself; often they are deliberately created and structured so
as to avoid or encumber detection and apprehension, or to deflect them.
Furthermore, one is dealing here with sets of records which are quintessential state secrets; they have the potential to prove highly compromising, if not inculpatory, as far as the reputations of the governments of
both Turkey and Germany are concerned. The wartime destruction of the
Ottoman Armenian population clearly involved a secret scheme. Despite
the incidence of certain ambiguities, the realities of a Turko-German
political and military alliance are significant enough to overcome the
problem these ambiguities tend to create. To be considered in this respect
are: the condition of the secrecy of the genesis of that alliance, the close
cooperation at the Ottoman General Headquarters between Turkish offi-

cers, especially War Minister Enver on the one hand, and high-ranking German officers on the other, and the evidence that the deportation of the victim population was the result of the pressures and initiatives of these military leaders. These are paramount considerations. They favor the acceptance of the view that German authorities cannot entirely be seen as divorced from a degree of involvement in the decision making processes relating to the deportations and massacres. This view becomes even more plausible when one brings to bear upon the inquiry a historical perspective focusing on the distinct and aberrant conduct of German authorities in the face of, and, particularly in the aftermath of, the 1894–96 Abdul Hamit-era Armenian massacres (see Chapter 6, last section, and Chapter 12, first section); it is difficult to overlook the significance of the attendant evolution of a new German policy on Turkey, reflecting the emergence of strong new German affinities for Turkey.

The ambiguities alluded to above are further dissipated at two other levels of consideration; they refer to concrete German attempts at concealing any role German military might have played in the deportation of the Armenians. The case of Lieutenant Colonel Boettrich's indiscretion, and the ensuing panicky reaction of the German Foreign Office, has been examined above. The vehemence of that reaction did not so much attach to the cooperation of Boettrich with his Turkish colleagues at the headquarters on the authorization of the deportation of a particular segment of the Armenian population, but rather to his foolishness to reveal his active role by placing his signature on the respective order. The post-war efforts by German authorities to remove or withhold pertinent files and documents, or alter or modify portions of documents, have also been examined above. The significance of these attempts and efforts is twofold. First, they contradict the spirit and the letter of the series of protests the German government dutifully lodged with the Turkish government, thereby exposing the pro-forma character (and the allied intent to create a basis for postwar alibis) of these diplomatic remonstrances and protests. Second, they betray certain anxieties that imply a sense of fear of discovery of complicity, if not genuine guilt. In the absence of such anxieties, the procedure warranting credibility is to let the records speak for themselves—without any interference.

The condition of the relevant records in terms of complete accessibility was and is a factor which continues to pose a problem at another level. That level refers to the formidable obstructions resulting from the Turkish denial syndrome. The persistence with which the Turks continue to deny the historical fact of the Armenian genocide has served to obfuscate the central issues of the Armenian genocide, including the issue of German complicity. No party can afford to confirm the possession of any pertinent records on a crime whose very occurrence it sees fit to negate. Hence, the issue of German complicity is reduced to irrelevance, as far as the Turks are concerned, even though they may concede that there is complicity only at the level of the problem of deportations, as distinct from a deliberate act of genocide. This conditional concession is as untenable, however, as the undergirding argument that the anti-Armenian measures merely involved deportations for the sole purpose of wartime temporary locations. As reiterated throughout this study, however, the real purpose of an undertaking is best gauged by the actual outcome of that undertaking, and not by the label appended to mask the purpose of that undertaking.

For reasons described above the issue of German complicity has ultimately to be resolved in relation to the position of William II as the supreme instance of German authority. He was vested with requisite powers to prescribe or proscribe, to allow or to disallow, to exercise control or to relax control over certain of the patterns of the behavior of his representatives—patterns that could have consequences for the fate of a minority facing annihilation by a close ally of Germany. In other words, he was not only responsible for his own conduct, but also for the conduct of his subalterns. As far as these subalterns are concerned, the available evidence on the matter of directly ordering the deportation of the Armenians is such as to overshadow the issue of complicity and directly inculpate two high ranking German military officers, namely, General Bronsart and Lieutenant-Colonel Boettrich, as actual, or first degree perpetrators. [See above in this chapter.] Those German officers who one way or another participated in consultations or deliberations, leading up to the decision to deport the Armenians, are liable to the charge of co-conspirators, especially Marshal von der Goltz and Lieutenant Colonel Feldman.

These are but the known cases where the evidence is direct, authentic and verifiable, as far as the deportations are concerned. The web of indirect evidence, however, is no less significant. As underscored throughout this study, the nature of the crime warrants a degree of reliance on indirect evidence or, in legal-technical language, circumstantial evidence. Criminal law and justice has always allowed the marshaling of such evidence in the presence of unusual conditions such as the gravity of a crime and the quality of the ensemble of the pieces of circumstantial evidence. The wealth of fragments of testimony by American Ambassador Morgenthau on Admirals Usedom, Souchon, Navy Lieutenant Commander Humann, and on Ambassador Wangenheim, committed to writing through daily entries in his diary, may in some quarters be subject to dispute. But the array of corroborative evidence from a host of diverse and independent sources, including Trabzon's Austrian Consul Kwiatkowski, and German intelligence operative O. Schmidt, is too compelling to doubt the veracity of Morgenthau's accounts or to discount the relevance and significance of the corpus of circumstantial evidence, or to question its reliability. One is faced here with a configuration of bids of evidence, including an incriminating statement attributed by British Intelligence to the Emperor, in which the quantity of diverse sources and data tends to acquire qualitative value, thereby rendering the sources even more credible.

What stands out in that evidence is a central feature of German complicity, namely, the willingness of a number of German officials, civilian and military, to aid and abet the Turks in their drive to liquidate the Armenians. They thus qualify to be regarded as co-perpetrators and "accessories to the crime," the bearers of the onus of what the Germans call "*Mitschuld*," i.e., complicity. Subsumed in this general category of inculpation are not only those German officers who actually signed deportation orders and as such are in fact co-perpetrators but are also the two major variants depicting the twin modalities of German involvement. One is described as "suggestion" (*Anregung*); the involvement here is active as the actor is seen taking the initiative to sensitize or incite the Turks against the Armenians. The other is in the form of consent (*Zusage*); the actor is in a passive role as he merely is responding, albeit positively, to the scheme presented to him by the Turks. This notwithstanding, the difference is such as to subside into insignificance, if not irrelevance, when one considers the oneness of the consequence afforded by the underlying indistinguishability of both types of roles, namely, the role of abettors in the Turkish enactment of the genocide against the Armenians.

Still in bondage to the shackles of obdurate atavism, and still profiting from the fruits of the negative reward, i.e., the impunity accruing to it, Turkey may continue for a while to deny any and all culpability. The expectations from Germany in this respect are rightly of a different order for it has demonstrated a capacity for redemption, a large measure of which it attained with respect to the cataclysm of the Holocaust. Such a capacity cannot be separated, however, from an underlying commitment to the quest for unmitigated truth, extending to and punctuating the tragic fate of another but less potent and influential victim nation. Perhaps the historians and perhaps even the statesmen of Germany will find it pertinent and seemly to reconsider the central issue raised here. In the final analysis what is at stake here is the triumph of the forces of civilization over a legacy of barbarism which almost succeeded in bringing about the extirpation of an ancient nation.[129]

Notes to Chapter 16

1. *Russian Imperial Archives* (St. Petersburg). Ministerstvo Inostranikh Del. Spornik diplomaticheskikh dokumentof. Reformee v Armenyee, 26 noiabria 1912 goda—10 maia 1914 goda. (The Orange Book). Collection of Diplomatic Documents. The Reform

in Armenia. November 26, 1912 to May 10, 1914. (Hereafter cited as *DAR*). (1915). Docs. No. 8, 22, 32.

2. André Mandelstam, *Le sort de L'Empire Ottoman* (Lausanne, 1917), 236, 243.

3. Carl Mühlmann, "Deutschland und die Türkei 1913–1914." *Politische Wissenschaft* 7 (1929): 70–80.

4. *Ibid.*, 39–43; A. A. Türkei 142/40, A21135, Wangenheim to the Foreign Office, September 8, 1914; *ibid.*, A25509, his October 6, 1914 report. In 1917 a fourth admiral, Hubert von Rebeur-Paschwitz, was engaged.

5. Joseph Pomiankowski, *Der Zusammenbruch des Ottomanischen Reiches* (Graz, 1969), 54–55; A. A. Türkei, No. 139/39, (Überlassung) report No. 123, January 29, 1916.

6. Şevket Süreyya Aydemir, *Makedonyadan Ortaasya'ya Enver Paşa* (Enver Paşa. From Macedonia to Central Asia), vol. 2 (Istanbul, 1971). On pp. 531–35, the author describes a scene of such deliberate pampering. It seems that the Emperor wanted to inflate Enver's ego through a public display of preferential treatment at a banquet he had staged for that purpose. He had seated Enver at the head of the table, which was reserved for the principal guest of the evening, and offered the following rationale to the other attachés present: "You have higher ranks than Enver, but he will soon be catapulted into the position of head of a great empire. That is why I accorded him the honor of principal guest." Following the banquet, William II picked him out, locked arms, and nudging him into an adjoining room, declared, "Enver, I will furnish you all the assistance you may ask after you take charge." Burhan Oğuz, *Yüzyıllar Boyunca Alman Gerçeği Ve Türkler* (The German Reality Throughout Centuries) (Istanbul, 1983) 265.

7. Ali Ihsan Sabis, *Harb Hatıralarım* (My War Memoirs) (Istanbul, 1943) vol. 1, 130–32; *idem.* vol. 2, (Ankara, 1951), 68, 101; Kâzım Karabekir, *Istiklâl Harbimizde Enver Paşa ve Ittihad Terakki Erkânı* (Enver Paşa and the Leadership of Ittihad ve Terakki During the Independence War) (Istanbul, 1967), 139.

8. Kâzım Karabekir, *Istiklâl Harbimizin Esasları* (The Essentials of Our Independence War) (Istanbul, 1933–1951), 23–24.

9. Ahmet Izzet Paşa, *Feryadım* (My Lamentation) vol. 1 (Istanbul, 1992), 94.

10. Şevket Süreyya Aydemir, *Ikinci Adam* (Second Man), vol. 1, 3rd ed. (Istanbul, 1973), 86.

11. Alptekin Müderrisoğlu, *Sarıkamış Dramı* (The Drama of Sarıkamış) vol. 1 (Istanbul, 1988), 193.

12. *Sabah*, December 12, 1919; Fuat Balkan, "Beş Albaylar" (Five Colonels) *Yakın Tarihimiz* 2 (1926): 297; Mehmed Zeki, *Raubmörder als Gäste der deutschen Republik* (Berlin, 1920), 35.

13. Vahakn N. Dadrian, "The Secret Young-Turk Ittihadist Conference and the Decision for the World War I Genocide of the Armenians" *Holocaust and Genocide Studies* 7, 2 (Fall 1993): 173–201.

14. The reference to deportations for France and Belgium is in Fritz Fischer, *Griff nach der Weltmacht* (Düsseldorf, 1967), 99; the reference to Alsace is in Grand Admiral von Tirpitz, *My Memoirs* vol. 2 (New York, 1919) 329.

15. *German Foreign Ministry Archives.* (*Die Diplomatischen Akten des Auswärtigen Amtes*) Die Grosse Politik der Europäischen Kabinette 1871–1914 (Hereafter cited as *DAG*) vol. 12 (2), Doc. No. 3339, "Confidential" report No. 57, p. 562. March 5, 1898.

16. The first view is in C. Freiherrn von der Goltz, "Stärke und Schwäche des türkischen Reiches" (The Strength and Weakness of the Turkish Empire) *Deutsche Rundschau* XXIV, 1 (October 1897): 104, 106, 109, 110, 118. The second view on Russia and Transcaucasia is in Goltz, *Denkwürdigkeiten* [n. 37], 111–12.

17. René Pinon, *La Suppression des Arméniens. Méthode allemande-travail turc* (Paris, 1916), 12–3.

18. Henry Morgenthau, *Ambassador Morgenthau's Story* (Garden City, N. Y., 1918), 366–67.

19. Zaven Archbishop, *Badriarkagan Housherus. Vaverakirner yev Vugayutiunner* (My Patriarchal Memoirs. Documents and Testimonies), (Cairo, 1947), 104. See also A. S. Baronigian, *Blicke ins Märtyrerland* (Lössnitzgrund i. Sachsen, 1921), 3, 4, 6.

20. A. A. Türkei 183/39, A28384, enclosure No. 2, August 5, 1915.

21. Rev. Krikoris Balakian, *Hai Koghkotan. Trouakner Hai Mardirosakroutiunen. Berlinen Tebee Zor 1914–1920* (The Armenian Golgotha. Episodes from the Armenian Martyril-

ogy. From Berlin to Zor 1914–1920) vol. 1 (Vienna, 1922), 32–3. The author was a Berlin-educated Armenian priest, a survivor of the genocide, who subsequently became the Primate of the Armenian Diocese of Manchester and later Marseille, France. Upon the outbreak of the war he returned to Constantinople and was among those Armenian leaders who on April 24, 1915 were arrested and deported to be destroyed. But through the assistance of a German major he escaped and survived.

22. Cemal Kutay, *Talât Paşanın Gurbet Hatıraları* (The Memoirs of Talât Paşa in Exile) vol. 3 (Istanbul, 1983), 1197.

23. Aubrey Herbert, "Talât Pasha" *Blackwood's Magazine* CCXIII (April, 1923): 426, 436. See also *idem. Ben Kendim. A Record of Eastern Travel.* 2d. ed. (London, 1924), 309.

24. FO371/9158/E5523, folios 106–7, British High Commissioner Neville Henderson's May 22, 1923 dispatch.

25. In reproducing Bronsart's order for deportation Turkish author Salahi Sonyel, apart from deleting some words, incorrectly translated the word *şedide* into the word "necessary", thus divesting the composition of the order of its hidden intimation as described in the text. *Displacement of the Armenians. Documents* (pamphlet) (Ankara, 1978), 1. In the orders issued during the Abdul Hamit-era massacres the same word *şedide* was used to convey the sense of massacre being inflicted upon the victims as a method of exterminatory terror. J. Lepsius, *Armenien und Europa* (Berlin, 1897), 125.

26 . *Austrian Foreign Ministry Archives.* Vienna. PA 12. Karton 380, Zl.21, folio 209. May 26, 1917 report of Austrian Consul General Kwiatkowski.

27. A. A. Türkei 183/44, A24663, enclosure No. 3. The English translation of portions of this report is in *Germany, Turkey and Armenia* (A selection of documentary evidence relating to the Armenian atrocities from German and other sources) (London, 1917), 80–85.

28. *Ibid.,* 183/38, A28019, K. No. 90/B. No. 1950, enclosure No. 1.

29. Rafael de Nogales, *Four Years Beneath the Crescent* Muna Lee, transl. (New York, 1926), 141, 150.

30. A. A. Türkei 142/41, A27535. Report No. 241. October 16, 1914.

31. Liman von Sanders, *Five Years in Turkey* (Annapolis, 1927), 2, 3.

32. A. A. Bonn. Göppert Papers (*Nachlass*), vol. VI, file 5 (files 1–8), p. 4, February 10, 1919.

33. *German Federal Military Archive* (Freiburg at Breisgau) BA. MA. MSg, 1/2039, from his diary. Cited in Christoph Dinkel, "German Officers and the Armenian Genocide" *Armenian Review* 44, 1/173 (Spring, 1991): 103.

34. For Morgenthau's remark on Bronsart, see Morgenthau, *Ambassador* [n. 18], 148. Bronsart's request regarding Greek deportations is in A.A. Türkei 168/15; General Sanders' and German Ambassador Metternich's, August 3 and 4, 1916, negative responses are in *ibid.*

35. Dinkel, "German Officers" [n. 33], 79.

36. Pomiankowski, *Der Zusammenbruch* [n. 5], 216–17.

37. Colmar Freiherr von der Goltz, *Denkwürdigkeiten* (Memoirs) Friedrich v. d. Goltz, W. Foerster eds. (Berlin, 1929), 393, n. 1; Sanders [n. 31], 49, 133.

38. *Ibid.,* 428.

39. Dinkel, "German Officers" [n. 33], 80–01.

40. *Allgemeine Missions-Zeitschrift* (monthly, published by Professor Julius Richter and J. Warneck) (June 30, 1921), quoted in Dinkel, "German Officers" [n. 33], 26.

41. Carl Mühlmann, *Das Deutsch-Türkische Waffenbündnis im Weltkriege* (Leipzig, 1940), 292.

42. Boettrich's order is in A. A. *Grosses Hauptquartier*, vol. 194, Türkei 41/I, A32610, registry No. 6882, enclosure No. 3, October 3, 1915, folios 137,138. The narrative on the slaughter of the Armenian workers of the Baghdad Railway is provided by the Swiss pharmacist of the area, Jacob Künzler, *Im Lande des Blutes und der Tränen. Erlebnisse in Mesopotamien während des Weltkrieges* (Potsdam-Berlin, 1921), 76.

43. The document was discovered by the officials of the British High Commissioner in Istanbul during the Armistice and was promptly sent to London with a translated version. FO371/5265/E7556, July 22, 1920. The Günther's letter itself is dated October 28, 1915.

44. A. A. *Grosses Hauptquartier*, [n. 42], Registry No. 209, folio 136, November 13, 1916, von Jagow's dispatch; *ibid.,* folio 140, Treutler's communication; Falkenhayn's refusal is in *ibid.,* folios 139–40, November 19, 1915.

45. Richard von Kühlmann, *Erinnerungen* (Memoirs) (Heidelberg, 1948), 467.
46. A. A. Türkei 183/55, A4156, February 6, 1919 in Dr. Karl Axenfeld's report to General B. v. Schellendorf. See also Lüttichau's own report. *Ibid.*, 183/54. A44066, p. 8, of 20 pp. report, Summer 1918.
47. *Allgemeine Missions-Zeitschrift* (February 1919): 36.
48. Morgenthau, *Ambassador* [n. 18], 49, 365, 395.
49. Dinkel, "German Officers" [n. 33], 116.
50. Hans Meier-Welcker, *Seeckt* (Frankfurt am Main, 1967), 154.
51. While serving in Turkey in the March-October, 1915 period, Major Wolffskeel wrote a number of letters to his family, especially to his wife and father. His suggestion on the deportation of the Armenians is excerpted from his September 15, and the other on "internal Turkish matter" is excerpted from his October 16, 1915 letter. *German Federal Military Archive* [n. 33], Papers (*Nachlass*) Wolffskeel N138/2, N138/6. His remark on Armenians as being "traitors" was repeatedly made in the presence of a German eyewitness of the Urfa bloodbath. Bruno Eckart, *Meine Erlebnisse in Urfa* (Berlin-Potsdam, 1922), 27. Another eyewitness was the Swiss medic-pharmacist who observed the arrival in Urfa of Wolffskeel along with General Fahri, whose "German Adjutant" he was. Ida Alamuddin, *Papa Kuenzler and the Armenians* (London, 1970), 67. See also the work of another Swiss author who underscores the fact that Wolffskeel was in charge of "the Turkish battery that roared for days on end." Karl Meyer, *Armenien und die Schwiez* (Bern, 1974), 95. Still another Swiss, a professor, who had investigated the matter, described Wolffskeel's devastating role through German canons (*da kartätschte deutsche Artillerie alles zusammen*). A. A. Türkei 183/54, A38243, registry no. 2228, September 7, 1919 report of the lecture which was given by Prof. Ragaz. Finally reference may be made to a British subject who was interned in Urfa during the war as an enemy alien. He witnessed the carnage and in his report to the British Foreign Office he made repeated references to "the bombardments" directed against the Armenians and the role of "a German officer" in this onslaught. F0608/78/2610, February 10, 1919 report, folios 152–154.
52. FO371/4363. Confidential. Foreign Office Political Intelligence Department. May 25, 1918. Memorandum on the Present State of Mind in Turkey. The P. I. D. is particularly indebted to Sir H. Rumbolds' weekly reports and to another "sure source" for preparing this memo.
53. A. A. Türkei 158/13, A5135, cipher No. 72.
54. *Austrian Foreign Ministry Archives.* Vienna. (Hereafter cited as *DAA*) P. A. 1. Karton Rot. 947 (f). Secret report No. 5139, cipher No. 189.
55. *A. A. Botschaft Konstantinopel.* 434, No. 15994. October 5, 1917.
56. Morgenthau, *Ambassador* [n. 18], 5, 6, 383. Two studies have at length discussed many of these areas. See Ulrich Trumpener, *Germany and the Ottoman Empire 1914–1918* (Princeton, 1968) and F. Weber *Eagles on the Crescent* (Ithaca, 1970).
57. *Grosses Hauptquartier.* vol. 185, Türkei 18, Registry No. 505, September 21, 1914, Wangenheim to Undersecretary Zimmermann; the emperor's order is in *Ibid.*, 18/1, Registry No. 93. September 12, 1914. These details are more or less confirmed by Grand Vizier Said Halim who was being detained at Malta by the British for later trial on charges of complicity on crimes associated with the Armenian deportations and massacres. In his letter of protest from Malta Said Halim referred to "the treacherous staging by the Germans of the Black Sea incident which irretrievably compromised the neutrality of Turkey." FO371/4174/127758, folios 408–09. The 8-page letter of protest was written on August 12, 1919 in Malta and was addressed to the British Prime Minister Lloyd George.
58. Ilber Ortaylı, *Osmanlı Imparatorluğunda Alman Nüfuzu* (The German Influence on the Ottoman Empire (Istanbul, 1983), 137, and 137 n. 13.
59. A. A. Türkei 158/15, A14133, folio 126. April 25, 1916.
60. Herbert, "Talât Pasha" [n. 23], 430; *idem., Ben Kendim* [n. 23], 314.
61. Pomiankowski, *Der Zusammenbruch* [n. 5], 163.
62. Herbert, "Talât Pasha" [n. 23], 435; *idem., Ben Kendim* [n. 23] 321.
63. Morgenthau, *Ambassador* [n. 18], 370.
64. Liman von Sanders, *Five Years in Turkey* (Annapolis, 1927), 14.
65. Morgenthau, *Ambassador* [n. 18], 370–73, 378–79, 382–83.

66. A. A. Botschaft Konstantinopel. vol. 137, Doc. No. 240. February 22, 1917. Deutsches
    Militär in der Türkei. Jäckh's remark on Humann is in Ernst Jackh, *The Rising Crescent*,
    (New York, 1944), 119.
67. Morgenthau, *Ambassador* [n. 18], 375–76.
68. For this report of denial see A. A. Türkei 183/55, A11259.
69. Dinkel, "German Officers" [n. 33], 113.
70. *Ibid.*, 110, 115.
71. Ulrich Trumpener, *Germany and the Ottoman Empire 1914–1918* (Princeton, 1968), 127.
72. *Hadisat*, November 7, 1918.
73. Çetin Altan, *Sabah*, January 20, 1992.
74. Dilek Zabıtcıoğlu, *Cumhuriyet*, April 20, 1993.
75. Ilber Ortaylı, *Osmanlı İmparatorluğunda Alman Nüfuzu* (The German Influence in the
    Ottoman Empire) (Istanbul, 1983), 122.
76. FO371/2488/161837 Nov. 1, 1915; *ibid.*, /171151, November 15, 1915.
77. *Ibid.*, /148432, October 12, 1915.
78. *Ibid.*, /161837, November 1, 1915; *ibid.*, 171151, November 15, 1915.
79. Feyzi's remark about his trip to Berlin is in Tovmas Mugurditchian, *Deekranagerdi
    Nahankin Tcharteru Yev Kiurderou Kazanioutounneru* (The Massacres in Diyarbekir
    Province and the Savageries of the Kurds) (Cairo, 1919), 22–26. The author's attribu-
    tions to Deputy Feyzi are independently confirmed by an Armenian, a Civil Inspector
    of the First Class, who was spared the fate of his co-nationals by virtue of his close ties
    to Ittihad. See his affidavit prepared at the request of the office of the British Commis-
    sion in Istanbul. F0371/6500, folios 77–81/344–48. Feyzi's decoration by the Kaiser is
    in F0371/4172/24597, no. 63490, folio 304.
80. *T. B. M. M. Gizli Celse Zabıtları* (The Transcripts of the Secret Sessions of the Grand
    National Assembly of Turkey) vol. 3, (Ankara, 1985), 377, 394.
81. The content of the interview was published in instalments in a Turkish newspaper.
    Tanin, September 8, 1945.
82. Doğan Avcıoğlu, *Milli Kurtuluş Tarihi* (History of the National Liberation) vol. 3 (Istan-
    bul, 1974), 1135.
83. A missionary monthly put the number 10,000. see Dinkel in n. 40, p. 40; but in Richard
    Schäfer, *Persönliche Erinnerungen an Johannes Lepsius* (Potsdam, 1935), 12, the
    20,000 number is given.
84. A. A. Türkei 183/44, A24404, September 9, 1916, *ibid.*, September 15, 1916. The piece
    involved is *Bericht über die Lage des Armenischen Volkes in der Türkei* (Potsdam,
    Berlin, 1916).
85. A. A. Türkei 183/45, A31131, November 16, 1916; A34247, November 28, 1916,
    November 30, 1916, December 2, 1916; A32822, December 2, 1916; 183/47, A178182,
    May 18, 1917. The order to confiscate Lepsius booklets is in *ibid.*, 183/44, A24404 Sep-
    tember 15, 1916.
86. Johannes Lepsius, *Deutschland und Armenien 1914–198. Sammlung Diplomatischer
    Aktenstücke* (Berlin-Potsdam, 1919). Some eleven years later, and four years after his
    death, an enlarged version of his wartime *Bericht* was published post-humously under
    the new title, *Der Todesgang des Armenischen Volkes* (Berlin-Potsdam, 1930).
87. *Göppert Papers* [n. 32], February 13, 1919, vol. VI, file 1, p. 2.
88. A. A. Türkei 183/56, A20906. The Haag. July 13, 1919.
89. *Ibid.*, July 26, 1919.
90. Trumpener, *Germany* [n.71], 206 n. 15; an example of the case is a quotation from
    Undersecretary Zimmermann on p. 219, the second part of which is deleted in the Lep-
    sius volume, p. 136, without Trumpener indicating the deletion.
91. Dinkel, "German Officers" [n. 33], 86.
92. Wolfdieter Bihl, *Die Kaukasus-Politik der Mittelmächte* Part I (Vienna, 1975), 176, n. 402.
93. In the production of the volume were involved, beside Lepsius, Dr. Solf, Dr. Göppert
    and Dr. W. Rössler from the German Ministry of Foreign Affairs. While doing research
    in Berlin in 1978, this author raised the question of omissions and deletions with Ms.
    Gitta Lepsius, one of Lepsius' daughters who at the time had served as his secretary,
    typing the entire manuscript for him. She categorically denied receiving any instruc-

tions from anyone regarding omissions or deletions about which, she asserted, she was hearing for the first time. In other words, she maintained she didn't even know about their incidence.

94. Dinkel, "German Officers" [n. 33], 82.
95. A. A. Türkei 158/21, A48179, folios 158–59, 175; Tevfik, Çavdar, *Talât Paşa* (Ankara, 1984), 435–37.
96. A. A. Türkei 183/42, A11715.
97. *Ibid.*, 158/16, A31746, folio 095–96. Humann's November 15, 1916 report.
98. Bihl, *Die Kaukasus-Politik* [n. 92], 334, n. 405.
99. *DAA* [n. 54], PA XXXVIII/368 No. Zl. 54/P. September 4, 1915; *ibid.*, XII/380, No. 84/P., December 17, 1915.
100. Sanders, *Five Years* [n. 31], 106; Bihl, *Die Kaukasus-Politik* [n. 92], 351, n. 24; Sabis, *Harp Hatıralarım* [n. 7] vol. 2, 191; A. A. Botschaft Konstantinopel, vol. 23, I5845, Military Mission. October 27, 1917.
101. *DAA* [n. 54], XII/463, No. 70/P. Trabzon, October 22, 1915.
102. *Ibid.*, PA. XII/209, Z.100/P, and No. 96/P. C. November 10, 1915, Cipher Telegram Nos. 20 and 23.
103. A. A. Türkei, 183/54, A44066, pp. 8, 9 of the reports October 18, 1918.
104. *Hairenik*, October 17/30, 1918.
105. *Houshartzan Abril Dasnumegi* (In Memoriam of April 24) (Istanbul, 1919), 96.
106. *The Hoover Institution on War, Revolution and Peace*. Stanford. Interior Ministry. Foreign Affairs Department of the Secret Service of the Police. Section 4. Doc. No. 16609. January 23, 1914.
107. Ismail Beşikci, *Kürdistan Üzerinde Emperyalist Bölüşüm Mücadelesi: 1915–1925* (The Fight over Kurdistan's Imperialist Partition 1915–1925) vol. 1 (Ankara, 1992), 88–101.
108. S. A. Zenkovsky, *Pan-Turanism and Islam in Russia* (Cambridge, MA, 1967), 110–11.
109. Quoted in René Pinon, "L'Offensive de l'Asie" *Revue des deux Mondes* (April 15, 1920): 810–11.
110. Tekin Alp, *Türkismus und Pantürkismus* (Weimar, 1915), 46–7, 50, 53. The author, whose original name was Moise Cohen, was from Saloniki and following the defeat of the Turks at the first Balkan war settled in Istanbul in 1912. He was a strong advocate of the need for "the Turks [to pursue their] economic independence in their own land," and for "the economic lifting" (*Hebung*) of Turkey through Turkish nationalism, to be applied by ministers adhering to the ideology of Turkism, pp. 38, 39, 43, 45.
111. *German Foreign Ministry Archives*. A. A. Türkei 134/35, A8212, pp. 9 and 10 of the "confidential" report. The author was Privy Councillor of the Treasury Department Prof. Dr. von Schulze Gaevernitz who had visited Turkey in March 1916 and conducted "detailed interviews" with "leading Turkish statesmen," among others.
112. A. A. Türkei, 134/35, A18613, pp. 1, 2, 3, 4. The report, titled "Volkswirtschaftliche Studien in der Türkei" (Political Economic Studies in Turkey), was anonymously written on July 2, 1916 and submitted to the Foreign Office on July 14, 1916. Another German author, likewise examining the economic aspects of the liquidation of the Ottoman Armenians, decried the complicity of "the political and military instruments of German imperialism" in the crime of genocide against the Armenians. As he put it, "In order to pave the ground for the turanist invasion of the Caucasus, the Ittihadist leaders proceeded to "ruthlessly and completely exterminate the Ottoman Armenians … By the explicit order of the Turkish government, in the June 1915–March 1916 period more than one million men, women and children were murdered with unprecedented ferocity (*beispiellose Grausamkeit*), and under the pretext that they were being taken to Mesopotamia for the purpose of resettlement." Lothar Rathmann, *Stossrichtung des deutschen Imperialismus im ersten Weltkrieg* (Berlin, 1963), 138.
113. *Der Prozess Talaat Pascha*. Stenographic account of the trial. (Berlin, 1921), 84.
114. *Ibid.*, 109, 112, 113, 123.
115. *Ibid.*, 84.
116. *Ibid.*, 125.
117. *Ibid.*, 118.
118. *The New York Times*, June 3, 1921.
119. Dr. Armgaard Karl Graves, *The Secrets of the German War Office* (with the collaboration of E. L. Fox) 4th ed. (New York, 1914), 56, 73, 118–19, 121.

120. **** (n.a.), *The Near East From Within* (New York, n. d., probably winter 1914–15), 51, 59, 83–84, 235.
121. Captain von Rintelen, *The Dark Invader. Wartime Reminiscences of a German Naval Intelligence Officer* (New York, 1933), 74, 81, 83, 84.
122. Dr. Kurt Mühsam, *Wie Wir Belogen Wurden* (Münich, 1918), 149.
123. Ernst Werner, "Ökonomishce und Militärische Aspekte der Türkei-Politik Österreich-Ungarns 1915 bis 1918" *Jahrbuch für Geschichte* 10 (1974): 396.
124. Wolfram W. Gottlieb, *Studies in Secret Diplomacy during the First World War* (London, 1957), 44.
125. Hasan Amca, *Doğmayan Hürriyet. Bir Devrin İç Yüzü 1908–1918* (Freedom Unborn, The Inside Story of an Era 1908–1918) (Istanbul, 1958), 123, 155, 180.
126. Fürst Bernhard von Bülow, *Denkwürdigkeiten.* vol. 2 (Berlin, 1930), 512.
127. Erich Eyck, *Das persönliche Regiment Wilhelms II: Politische Geschichte des deutschen Kaiserreiches von 1890 bis 1914* (Zürich, 1948), 682–83.
128. *German War Ministry Archives.* Bundesarchiv Militärarchiv. Kaiserliche Marine-Kabinets. Archiv der Marine. RM 2/V. 1115, 4995/14. August 22, 1914.
129. It is a historical fact that under certain sets of circumstances almost any nation is capable of committing acts of barbarism, including mass murder. In this sense scholarly efforts may benefit from undertakings that are descriptive or analytical, or both, without being unduly sanctimonious. The following two comments on Turkish proneness to barbarism are significant in two respects. First they emanate from two key diplomats whose knowledge of the horrors of the Armenian genocide did not prevent them from persisting in their Turkophile attitudes. Here the affirmation of genocidal behavior is separated from any consideration of condemnation and punishment. Second, they are identified with two nation-states whose governments are manifestly on record, however, for publicly registering their sense of contrition for past instances of mass murder of one kind or another, and for concomitantly instituting prodigious packages of indemnities. Naturally, the issue of indemnity is of subsidiary significance in the context of the present discussion. Barbarism perpetrated on a sweeping scale cannot be meaningfully remedied by any measure of material compensation but it may be atoned by the test of genuine remorse. But atonement presupposes acknowledgment of guilt. The Turkish refusal in this respect is not only categorical and persistent but it is punctuated by a defiant truculence. This raises the question whether the perpetration of the Armenian genocide was a lapse into barbarism or something other than a mere lapse. Here are the two comments alluded to above. In a long and intimate letter to a "dear friend" at the German Foreign Office Ambassador Wangenheim on December 30, 1914, i.e., a few months before the launching of the genocide, referred to the eruption of "Turkish fury the extent of which cannot always be predicted given the barbarous condition of the population." A. A. Türkei, 139/34, A46. In the Armistice period when Kemalist insurgents were resuming the massacres against the remnants of the Armenian population in the interior of the country, their principal champion in the Ottoman capital, Admiral Bristol, the U.S. High Commissioner, felt constrained to advise Washington "It is known that the Turks will rob, pillage, deport and murder Christians whenever the opportunity is favorable from their point of view... It is my opinion that, knowing the character of the Moslem Turks,... if you arouse the brutal instincts of the Turks, together with his fanatical tendencies, he will attack the Christian races if he is not restrained by absolute force." *U.S. National Archives.* Record Group (RG) 59. 867.00/1361. Bristol's October 23, 1920 report to Washington, pp. 1 and 2. For details of these massacres by the Kemalists see the two reports of C. von Engert, an official attached to Admiral Bristol's U.S. High Commissioner's Office in the Ottoman capital. He made reference to the massacre of "several thousand Armenians" whom he described as victims of the same "insolent spirit" that had run amuck during World War I and had imperiled the Ottoman Armenians. For the February 28, 1920 cable see *ibid.* 867.00/1127; for the March 15, 1920 cable, likewise dispatched from Beirut, see *ibid.* 867.00/1165.

Part VII

THE QUEST FOR JUSTICE
IN THE AFTERMATH
OF TURKISH MILITARY DEFEAT

Chapter 17

Allied Attempts
at Retributive Justice

As World War I ended, the Allies focused attention on the task of punishment for the war crimes committed against the Armenians. At first, the Allies attempted to apply principles of international law to the perpetrators of the massacres. The initial impulse to seek justice, however, faded in the months after the war and eventually gave way to political expediency. The Turkish government's attempts to bring its own nationals to justice also faltered. The rise of nationalism, and the Turkish populace's increasingly defiant attitude toward the Allies, weakened the government's resolve in its quest for justice. This weakened resolve and the Allies' own waning interest hampered the efforts of prosecution.

When Turkey signed the Armistice on October 30, 1918, it lay at the mercy of the European Allies. Having declared war against Turkey only in April 1917, the United States did not at that time maintain a belligerent status toward Turkey, and could, therefore, not participate in the issuance of the May 24 declaration by the Entente Powers. Churchill described Turkey as being "under the spell of defeat, and of deserved defeat."[1] Similarly, British Foreign Minister Curzon denounced Turkey as "a culprit awaiting sentence."[2] Andrew Ryan, a dragoman and a political-legal officer at the British High Commission in the Ottoman capital, describes the wariness of the Turks in the earlier part of the Armistice, "so wary that many would have welcomed a (peace) settlement on any terms."[3] Turkey's "culpability," in Allied eyes, involved mainly war crimes and crimes against her own citizens. The Allies, pursuant to their warning on May 24, 1915, initiated criminal proceedings against Turkish officials suspected of complicity in the Armenian massacres.

The Judicial Arm of the Paris Peace Conference

In January, 1919, the Preliminary Peace Congress in Paris established the Commission on Responsibilities and Sanctions. Chaired by U.S. Secretary of State Lansing, its First Subcommission (also known as the Commission of Fifteen) examined, among other offenses, "barbarous and illegitimate methods of warfare." This included the category of "offenses against the laws and customs of war, and the principles of humanity," which the French representative of the Third Subcommission, Larnaude, insisted was "absolutely" necessary to ensure human rights.[4]

The Commission of Fifteen proceeded in its investigation according to the terms of the Fourth Hague Convention. This Convention, part of the 1907 Second Peace Conference, was intended to give "a fresh development to the humanitarian principles [towards] evolving a lofty conception of the common welfare of humanity." In the Preamble of the Convention, the Contracting Parties attempted to guarantee that "the inhabitants and belligerents remain under the protection and governance of the principles of the law of the nations, derived from the usages established among civilized peoples, from the laws of humanity, and from the dictates of public conscience."[5] As Bassiouni pointed out, however, the juridical roots of the concept of "crimes against humanity" are to be found in the First Hague Convention of 1899 on the Laws and Customs of War where "humanity" is invoked as a general norm and where "the laws of humanity" and "the requirements of public conscience" are identified as a matrix of "the principles of international law."[6] It was in this context that Nicolas Politis, a member of the Commission of Fifteen and Foreign Minister of Greece, proposed the adoption of a new category of war crimes meant to cover the massacres against the Armenians, declaring: "Technically these acts did not come within the provisions of the penal code, [but they constituted grave offenses against] the law of humanity."[7] Despite the objections of American representatives Lansing and Scott, who challenged the ex-post facto nature of such a law, the majority of the Commission "hesitatingly" concurred with Politis.[8] The Commission based its decision upon a Hague Convention principle which allowed for reliance upon "the laws of humanity" and "dictates of public conscience"[9] whenever clearly defined standards and regulations to deal with grave offenses were lacking.

A March 5, 1919 report by the Commission specified the following violations against civilian populations: systematic terror; murders and massacres; dishonoring of women; confiscation of private property; pillage; seizing of goods belonging to communities, educational establishments, and charities; arbitrary destruction of public and private goods; deportation and forced labor; execution of civilians under false allegations of war crimes; and violations against civilians as well as military personnel.[10] The Commission's final report, dated March 29, 1919, spoke of "the clear dictates of humanity" which were abused "by the Central Empires together with their allies," especially Turkey, "by barbarous or illegitimate methods in violation of ... the elementary laws of humanity."[11] The report concluded that "all persons belonging to enemy countries ... who have been guilty of offenses against the laws and customs of war or the laws of humanity, are liable to criminal prosecution."[12] Prompted by the Belgian jurist Rolin Jaequemeyns, the Commission included, but did not sharply highlight, the crimes which Turkey was accused of having perpetrated against its Armenian citizens.[13]

As a result of the Commission's efforts, several articles stipulating the trial and punishment of those responsible for the genocide were inserted into the Peace Treaty of Sèvres, signed on August 10, 1920.[14] Under article 226, "the Turkish government recognize[d]" this right of trial and punishment by the Allied Powers, "notwithstanding any proceedings or prosecution before a tribunal in Turkey." Turkey under the same article was obligated to surrender "all persons accused of having committed an act in violation of the laws and customs of war, who are specified either by name or by rank, office or employment which they held under Turkish authorities."[15] Under article 230 of the Peace Treaty, Turkey was further obligated

> to hand over to the Allied Powers the persons whose surrender may be required by the latter as being responsible for the massacres committed during the continuance of the state of war on territory which formed part of the Turkish Empire on August 1, 1914. The Allied powers reserve to themselves the right to designate the tribunal which shall try the persons so accused, and the Turkish Government undertakes to recognize such tribunal. The provisions of Article 228 apply to the cases dealt with in this Article.[16]

The Treaty of Sèvres, therefore, provided the legal basis for international adjudication of the crimes perpetrated by the Ottoman Empire against the Armenians during World War I. These provisions never came into force, however. As discussed in the following section, political tensions within the Allied Powers and nationalistic passions in Turkey eventually led to the scrapping of this treaty.

The Legal Gropings of the British

While the international community was attempting to pursue the punishment of the Turkish war criminals under international law, the British were likewise attempting to bring these accused mass murderers to justice. Their efforts, however, proved no more successful than those required by the Treaty of Sèvres.

The High Commission and the Law Officers of the Crown

The immediate task facing the Allies following the Armistice was the treatment of the enemies' accused war criminals. The crimes charged fell into two major categories. The first concerned "the mistreatment" of war prisoners, mostly British; the second referred to "deportations and massacres," principally against the Armenians.[17] The sudden escape from Istanbul of the seven top Young Turk leaders aboard a German destroyer on the night of November 1-2, 1918, catalyzed action against the remaining high ranking officials and party leaders. As Richard Webb, Rear Admiral and Deputy High Commissioner at Istanbul, wired then British Foreign Secretary Arthur James Balfour: "There is hardly an organ of the Press which is not vehemently attacking these men ... for their share in the massacres."[18] Describing the flight of these seven Turks in his memoirs, the Secretary-General of Ittihad, who stayed behind, indicated that the complicity of the fugitives in Armenian "deportations" was the chief reason for their flight.[19]

On January 18, 1919, British High Commissioner Admiral Calthorpe told the Turkish Foreign Minister, "His Majesty's Government are resolved to have proper punishment inflicted on those responsible for Armenian massacres."[20] Ten days later, Calthorpe wired London, "It was pointed out to [the Turkish] Government that when [the] massacres became known in England, British Statesmen had promised [the] civilized world that persons connected would be held personally responsible and that it was [the] firm intention of H.M. Government to fulfil [that] promise."[21] On March 20, 1919, the Director of British Military Intelligence relayed to the U.S. State Department a February 27, 1919 report form British Military Attaché Brigadier-General W. H. Deedes to General Allenby in which Deedes declared, "H. M. Government not only desired the punishment of massacrers, but intended to secure it ... they would never forget what had been done during the war, much less condone it."[22] Deputy High Commissioner Webb, in an April 3, 1919 cipher telegram to the Peace Conference in Paris, declared:

> To punish all persons guilty of Armenian atrocities would necessitate wholesale execution of Turks and I therefore suggest punishment should rather take the form of, nationally, dismemberment of [the] late Turkish Empire and, individually, in trial of high officials such as those on my lists whose fate will serve as an example.[23]

Punishment, however, required appropriate jurisdiction, legal evidence, penal codes, and the machinery to administer the applicable laws. The British were quite sensitive to the need to separate executive from judicial acts and to bar, as much as possible, political considerations from intruding into legal proceedings. Many British jurists insisted that the British Military Courts in occupied zones carry out the trial and punishment of Turkish offenders in accordance with the "Common Law of War." The "Common Law of War," it was argued, subsumed the violations of the customs and laws of war.[24] An authoritative opinion, issued by the Law Officers of the Crown in response to a detailed inquiry from the Foreign Office, clarified the legal ramifications of the alternatives. The Law Officers maintained, for example, that British Military Courts in occupied territories could proceed with such trials "if this course has the sanction of the British Government. The matter is not within the sphere of municipal law, but is governed by the customs of war and rules of international law, [hence] there is no *legal* objection."[25] In addition, such courts could try persons for any offenses committed outside the zones of occupation, provided that there is "the consent of the Turkish Government to the exercise of the jurisdiction."[26]

Speaking strictly of crimes such as the Armenian massacres, the Law Officers considered it preferable that such crimes "be reserved for disposal under the provisions of the Peace Treaty, and that there is no legal objection to the detention of these offenders. Such detention is an act of State, the propriety of which cannot be questioned by any court of law."[27] Because the British felt that the Turkish government was incapable of dealing with their own offenders, the Crown Law Officers concluded that it would be "practicable and desirable" to "insert ... a provision quashing the [Turkish criminal proceedings]," and stipulating that "the offenders should be disposed of in the same manner as is decided upon for offenders in Allied custody."[28]

Transfer of the prima facie suspects from Turkish to British custody

Beginning in January, 1919, Turkish authorities, directed and often pressured by Allied authorities in Istanbul, arrested and detained scores of Turks. Those arrested comprised four groups: 1) the members of Ittihad's Central Committee; 2) the two wartime Cabinet Ministers; 3) a host of provincial governors; and 4) high-ranking military officers identified as organizers of wholesale massacres in their zones of authority. The suspects were first taken to the Military Governor's headquarters and were subsequently transferred to the military prison maintained by the Turkish Defense Ministry. Their custody and the disposal of their case by the Turkish judiciary, however, posed serious problems.[29] Furthermore, events were complicated by political developments including: 1) Greek occupation of Smyrna (Izmir) in May, 1919; 2) the massive and demonstrative funeral, on April 12, 1919, of a district commissioner (*mutasarrıf*) following his trial, conviction, and execution by the Turkish Military Tribunal for having been a principal perpetrator of Armenian massacres in his district; and 3) the series of mass demonstrations at various locations in Istanbul in the May 20-23, 1919 period, challenging the Allied occupation forces and asserting Turkish national rights. As one Turkish author wrote, the danger of "storming the Bekirağa military prison in the style of the Bastille raid" to free the high ranking prisoners was imminent.[30] To mollify the public, on May 21 the Ottoman Grand Vizier ordered the release of 41 prisoners.[31] Following that, the Interior Minister instructed the Director of Police not to proceed with new arrests for the time being.[32] These events prompted the British to initiate measures for the transfer of the detainees to British custody in Mudros and Malta.[33]

Turkish officials resisted handing over the offenders for trial before an international or inter-allied tribunal. They claimed that such a surrender of Turkish subjects contradicted the sovereign rights of the Ottoman Empire as recognized by England in the Armistice Agreement. As the Turkish Foreign Minister argued, compliance with the demand for surrender by the Turkish Government

> would be in direct contradiction with its sovereign rights in view of the fact that by international law each State has [the] right to try its subjects for crimes or misdemeanors committed in its own territory by its own tribunals. Moreover, His Britannic Majesty having by conclusion of an armistice with the Ottoman Empire recognized [the] latter as a *de facto* and *de jure* sovereign State, it is incontestably evident that the Imperial Government possesses all the prerogatives for freely exercising [the] principles inherent in its sovereignty.[34]

Despite this argument, the Commission of Responsibilities and Sanctions of the Paris Peace Conference held that trials by national courts should not bar legal proceedings by an international or an allied national tribunal. On April 2, 1919, Foreign Minister Balfour stated that, should the Turks persist in their recalcitrant attitude, "pressure should at least be brought to bear upon them to refrain from instituting any form of proceedings against [the accused war criminals] until the Peace Conference has decided as to their ultimate disposal."[35]

On May 28, 1919, 67 detainees were seized by surprise by the British and removed from the military prison. Twelve of them, mostly ex-Ministers, were taken to the island of Mudros, the rest to Malta. The 12 ministers were eventually transferred to Malta, where the number of prisoners rose to 118 by August, 1920.[36]

The effects of national and international politics

In the months following the removal of Turkish suspects to Malta, the political climate in Istanbul, and particularly in the interior of Turkey, began to change to the Allies' detriment. As insurgent Kemalism[37] gained a foothold throughout Turkey, the Sultan's government steadily weakened. Moreover, the Allies began to bicker among themselves. Delays in the final peace settlement with Turkey complicated this volatile situation. France and Italy began to court the Kemalists in secret; the Italians lent the new regime substantial military assistance, and both the French and the Italians sabotaged British efforts to restore and strengthen the authority of the Sultan and his government.[38] Willis summed up the situation as follows:

> During the two years between the armistice and Mudros and the signing of the treaty of Sèvres, the Turkish Nationalist movement grew into a major force, and the Allied coalition virtually dissolved. By 1920 most of the victors no longer included among their aims the punishment of Turkish war criminals ... the Italians evaded a British request for the arrest of former Young Turk leaders then reported as meeting within their territory. The French and Italians hoped to secure concessions in Asia Minor and did not want to antagonize powerful factions in Turkey unnecessarily, particularly the rising Nationalists.[39]

Historian Toynbee, who participated as a British delegate at the Paris Peace Conference, castigated the hidden agendas of the Allies as vices revolving around "covetousness." This vice "resulted, likely, in nothing more substantial than the precarious honor among thieves who find their business threatened by a vigorous and talented competitor. Some of the thieves, at any rate, never got out of the habit of picking their temporary partner's pockets."[40] In the face of these developments, Britain's resolve to secure justice in accordance with the May 24, 1915 Allied declaration was progressively attenuated.

Toward the end of September, 1919, the demise of pro-Sultan Damad Ferid's Cabinet became imminent. On November 17, 1919, the new High Commissioner Admiral de Robeck, told Curzon that

> the present Turkish Government ... [is] so dependent on the toleration of the organisers of the [Kemalist] National Movement that I feel it would be futile to ask for the arrest of any Turk accused of offences against Christians, even though he may be living openly in Constantinople ... I do not consider it politically advisable to deport [to Malta] any more prisoners.[41]

Notwithstanding, the British Admiral stated almost prophetically that unless a legal process was initiated "it may be safely predicted that the question of retribution for the deportations and massacres will be an element of venomous trouble in the life of each of the countries concerned."[42]

The problem of probative and legal evidence

Political considerations were not the only impediments to the commencement of retributive justice. In mid-1920, Lamb, the political-legal officer of the British High Commission at Istanbul, enumerated in a detailed Memorandum the evidentiary difficulties encumbering the effective prosecution of the authors of the Armenian genocide. These conditions were: 1) the impossibility of obtaining any Turkish documents regarding pertinent orders and instructions issued by the Central Government or provincial authorities; 2) the reluctance of the Allied Governments to participate in prosecuting the suspects accused of the massacre; 3) "the apparent apathy of our Authorities in the Middle East as evidenced by their replies to the High Commissioner's queries in the matter"; 4) the massacre of the great majority of the adult male Armenian population in the provinces and of practically all the intellectuals; 5) the lack of public security and want of confidence about the intention of the Allies to exact punishment from the perpetrators, for those who could come forward and supply evidence; and 6) the indications of eventual release of prisoners from Malta.[43] Alarmed by the implications of these impediments, Lamb warned his superiors:

> Unless there is whole-hearted co-operation and will to act among the Allies, the trials will fall to the ground and the direct and indirect massacres of about one million Christians will get off unscathed. Rather than this should happen, it were better that the Allies had never made their declarations in the matter and had never followed up their declarations by the arrests and deportations that have been made.[44]

In a report to London on March 16, 1921, High Commissioner Rumbold confirmed several of the points that Lamb made in this memo.[45]

Lamb did state in his Memorandum that the British High Commission had gathered through its Greek-Armenian section a large mass of information concerning the 118 prisoners on Malta and some 1,000 others, all alleged to have been directly or indirectly guilty of participation in massacres. Despite his concerns, Lamb concluded, "[i]t is safe to say that very few 'dossiers,' as they now stand, would not be marked 'no case' by a practical lawyer."[46]

Perhaps the most difficult evidentiary problem was the inability of the British to gather incriminating evidence held by the Turkish government. As W.S. Edmonds, Undersecretary in the Eastern Department of the Foreign Office, observed on August 3, 1921, "there is probably some evidence in the archives of the [Turkish] court martial at Constantinople [but] the really important documents could no doubt be smuggled away before we begin to examine them."[47] On August 10, 1921, the British Secretary of State expressed his agreement with this view to the High Commissioner in Istanbul, adding that it would be "useless" to seek help from the French in exacting justice against the war criminals, considering "the general attitude observed by the French Government as regards Turkey."[48] Similarly, British judge Lindsey Smith asserted his belief that "a considerable amount of incriminating evidence was collected by the Turkish Government but it is idle to expect to get it. The only alternative is, therefore, to retain them as hostages only and release them against British prisoners." He recommended, therefore, the abandonment of the plans to prosecute the Malta prisoners. As he judged, "an abortive trial would do more harm than good."[49]

The Ultimate Suspension of Prosecution

In the end, the May 24, 1915 Allied declaration proved the *brutum fulmen* (empty, hollow threat) of the entire episode; the urgency of retributive justice gave way to expediency of political accommodation. Abandoned by their allies, and pressured domestically to seek the release of some British prisoners held hostage by the Kemalists, who in the meantime had gained national, political, and military ascendancy, the British sought a deal with Kemalist representatives for the total release of the Malta detainees. Mustafa Kemal refused, however, to honor the former government's Exchange Agreement of March 16, 1921,[50] since this agreement had excluded several Ittihadists implicated in Armenian massacres, as well as eight others accused of mistreating British prisoners during the War. Instead, new Foreign Minister Yusuf Kemal (Tengirşek) pressed for an "all for all" exchange.[51] Meanwhile, 16 Ittihadists, excluded from the exchange and slated for trial before an International Tribunal, had collectively fled from Malta on September 6, 1921, following an initial, partial exchange.[52] This group included two army commanders, four governors, one district commissioner, one deputy and Şükrü Kaya, the wartime Director of Deportations. Two other prisoners who would have been candidates for trial, labelled "the most notorious members of the group," (one of whom was Tahir Cevdet, the former Governor of Van), had escaped earlier.[53] In a final opinion relayed to the Cabinet, the Law Officers of the Crown argued that for the reasons described above, the Turks could not be tried and found guilty, and that the only remedy was the implementation of the Sèvres Treaty.[54]

The "all for all" exchange agreement ensued on October 23, 1921, and the remaining 53 Turks were released on November 1, 1921. British shame and guilt set in immediately afterwards. Calling some of the Turks whom they had set free "notorious exterminators" of Armenians,[55] the British officials involved in the negotiations and decision-making appended their reactions to the relevant documents. Foreign Minister Curzon scolded himself for having made "a great mistake" in pushing for the release of the Turks from British custody; he attributed his act "to a pressure which I always felt to be mistaken." Another British official commented as follows:

> The less we say about these people the better ... I had to explain why we released the Turkish deportees from Malta, skating over thin ice as quickly as I could. There would have been a row I think ... . [T]he staunch belief among Members [of the Parliament is] that one British prisoner is worth a shipload of Turks, and so the exchange was excused.[56]

A major source of pressure was the maneuvering of Winston Churchill, then Secretary of State of War, who persuaded the Cabinet to adopt a lenient attitude toward "less guilty Turks."[57] It is equally significant that one of the Turkish internees gleefully stated after his release that the British were duped by "a sly trick" of the Ankara government whose "British prisoners" to be exchanged included "six Maltese laborers and their Greek wives and children."[58]

A Commentary on the Abortiveness of Allied Justice

From a strictly legal point of view, the British failure to bring the Malta detainees to trial before a national or international tribunal was due to evidentiary problems resulting from a lack of prosecutorial powers and jurisdictional competence. These constraints were, however, self-imposed on two accounts. First, the Allies did not assert their belligerent status strongly from the very start through a complete occupation and control of Turkey, as was done in Germany and Japan at the end of World War II. Second, they studiously refrained from any involvement in the Turkish Courts Martial prosecutions.

The British statements on the relative worth of Turks and Britons quoted above epitomize the subversion of justice by national and international politics. The May 24, 1915 Allied declaration was, to a considerable degree, a politically motivated act akin to the nineteenth-century tradition of proclaiming the doctrine of humanitarian intervention on behalf of oppressed nationalities and minorities. That declaration repeatedly cited throughout the war,[59] served as the forerunner of the principle of "crimes against humanity and civilization" adopted first by the 1919 Commission (of Fifteen), which depicted for future prosecution the "offenses" against "laws of humanity" resulting from the treatment by the Turkish authorities of Armenian subjects during World War I;[60] subsequently, it was made part of the Nuremberg Charter (article 6c) and the U.N. Convention on Genocide (preamble). Nevertheless, the declaration proved ephemeral in the case of the Armenian genocide. In this sense, the declaration suffered the fate of many rules of international law that declare general principles but lack compulsory force. As victors who had exacted from the vanquished a virtually unconditional surrender, however, the Allies missed a rare opportunity to create with their May 24 declaration a new touchstone of international jurisprudence calling for forceful intervention in cases involving organized mass murder.[61] The Sèvres Treaty, signed by the representatives of the Ottoman government, had included the rudiments of such an international jurisprudence. As noted above, however, the treaty was jettisoned as the victors chose political and economic gain over effectuation of their promises and principles.

The ascendancy of Kemalism may be traced directly to the consequences of certain clauses in the Armistice of 1918,[62] which allowed Turkey to escape total Allied occupation, to maintain and refurbish a number of Army Corps and associated divisions and their staffs, and to effectively sabotage the stipulated processes of demobilization and disarmament. Above all, the Allies left the Ottoman state system intact, granting it *de facto* and *de jure* sovereign rights. In so doing, the Allies relinquished the power needed to carry out the pledges contained in the 1915 Allied Note.

The failure of the Allied prosecutorial efforts illustrates the inherent weakness of international law as a deterrent to crimes committed by the various agencies of sovereign governments. The political and practical limitations that exist in a system that respects independent state sovereignty will almost always prove more tenacious than the call for humanitarian intervention.

Notes to Chapter 17

1. W. Churchill, *The World Crisis: The Aftermath* (London, 1929), 367.
2. *Documents on British Foreign Policy 1919–1939*, vol. 4. First Series, W. Woodward & R. Butler, eds. (London, 1952) (Statement of Minister Curzon, July 4, 1919), 661.
3. Sir A. Ryan, *The Last of the Dragomans*, (London, 1951), 130.
4. FO 608/246, Procès-Verbal no. 6, p. 57 (folio 417)(Mar. 8, 1919). For a description of the gradual emergence in the Allied countries' political and legal circles of an agreement to punish the Central Powers' civilian and military officials suspected of war- or atrocity-crimes, see J. Read, *Atrocity Propaganda 1914–19*, 240-84 (New Haven, CT, 1941); for details of the Commission deliberations see *ibid.* pp. 254-65. The work of the Commission was divided into three areas with three corresponding subcommittees: (1) Criminal Offenses respecting (a) violation of peace through aggression and (b) war crimes; (2) Responsibilities of the War involving the offenders covered under (1)(a) above and their criminal liabilities and their possible prosecution; (3) Violations of the laws of war affecting the offenders covered under (1)(b) above and their criminal liabilities and possible prosecution. Lansing headed this last Sub-committee, otherwise called the Commission of Fifteen.
5. The United States War Crimes Commission, *History of the United States War Crimes Commission and the Development of the Laws of War* (London, 1948), 24, 25. See also *Final Act of the Second Peace Conference, The Hague* (1907) (Cmd. 4175) (1914), *reprinted in* 36 Stat. 2277, Treaty Series No. 539, with Annex.
6. M. C. Bassiouni, *Crimes Against Humanity in International Criminal Law* (Boston, 1992), 166–67. For excerpts from the texts of both Conventions see 634–37 (1899 Convention) and 634–41 (1907 Convention).
7. J. Willis, *Prologue to Nuremberg: The Policy and Diplomacy of Punishing War Criminals of the First World War* (Westport, CT, 1982), 157.
8. *Ibid.*
9. When a Committee of Jurists in 1920 was commissioned by the Council of the League of Nations to prepare the Statute of Permanent Court of International Justice, the issues of humanity and civilization surfaced again. Baron Descamps of Belgium, the Chairman, injected into the concept of international law not only such rules as were "recognized by the civilized nations but also by the demands of public conscience [and] the dictates of the legal conscience of civilized nations." After much debate, including the objections of Elihu Root, the American representative, the Committee adopted his revised version, the third point of which referred to "the general principles of law recognized by civilized nations." P.C.I.J., Advisory Committee of Jurists, Procès-Verbaux of the Committee, June 16-July 24, 1920, pp. 310, 318, 331, 344.
10. See Articles 1, 23, 46, 53, and 56 of the Fourth Hague Convention, FO 608/246, Procès-Verbal, Annexe. 2e Rapport, p. 60.
11. Carnegie Endowment for International Peace, *Violations of the Laws and Customs of War: Report of the Majority and Dissenting Reports of the American and Japanese Members of the Commission on Responsibilities at the Conference of Paris, 1919*, Pamphlet No. 32, p. 19.

12. *Ibid.* The dissenting American members were Robert Lansing and James Scott, who felt that the words "and the laws of humanity" were "improperly added." *Ibid.* p. 64. In their Memorandum of Reservations, they maintained that the laws and principles of humanity were not "a standard certain" to be found in legal treatises of authority and in international law practices. They argued that these laws and principles do vary within different periods of a legal system, between different legal systems, and with different circumstances. In other words, they declared that there is no fixed and universal standard of humanity, and that a judicial organ only relies on existing law when administering it, "leaving to another forum infractions of the moral law and actions contrary to the laws and principles of humanity." *Ibid.*, 73.

13. *See* FO 608/246, Third Session, Feb. 20, 1919, p. 20 (folio 163).

14. The Treaty of Peace Between the Allied Powers and Turkey. *American Journal of International Law.* Supplement. 15 (1921): 179; 1920 Gr. Brit. T.S. No. 11.

15. Willis, *Prologue* [n. 7], 180-81.

16. *Ibid.*, p. 181.

17. FO 371/4174/129560, p. 2 (acting Assistant Secretary of State for Foreign Affairs Tilley's July 10, 1919 communication to the Law Officers of the Crown).

18. FO 371/3411/210534 (folio 334). Historian Bayur characterized the fugitives as "thieves" (*hırsızlar*), excepting only Talât. Y. H. Bayur, *Türk Inkilâbı Tarihi* vol. 3 Part 4 (Ankara, 1983), 780, n. 91.

19. M. Bleda, *Imparatorluğun Çöküşü* (The Collapse of the Empire) (Istanbul, 1979), 124.

20. FO 371/4174/118377 (folio 253).

21. *Ibid.*

22. FO 371/4173/44216 (folio 50).

23. FO 371/4173/53351 (folios 192-93). There was similar agitation in the United States where in the fall of 1918 Charles H. Livermore of the World Peace Foundation drew up a list of eleven "outlaws of civilization" meriting "condign punishment." The list included the three leading Young Turk leaders comprising the Ittihad triumvirate, *i.e.*, Talât. Enver and Cemal. Willis, *Prologue* [n. 7], 43. A similar, but larger list, was prepared in 1917 in France by Tancrède Martel, an international law expert, who argued that the men he indicted deserved to be tried as common criminals by ordinary civil and criminal courts of the Allied countries because of the type and scope of the atrocities they were accused of having perpetrated. In its final report, completed on March 29, 1919, the Commission on Responsibilities through Annex I, Table 2, identified thirteen Turkish categories of outrages liable to criminal prosecution. Read, *Atrocity* [n. 4], 245, 266.

24. FO 608/244/8493 (folio 423), May 9, 1919 (Minutes by Lieutenant-Colonel J.H. Morgan).

25. FO 371/4174/129560, pp. 2-3 (folio 430-31) (all emphasis in the original). The Foreign Office inquiry was sent on July 10, 1919, by Acting Assistant Under-Secretary J.A.C. Tilley. The August 7, 1919, response of the Law Officers was signed by Gordon Hewart and Ernest M. Pollock.

26. *Ibid.* (folio 431).

27. *Ibid.*

28. *Ibid.*

29. *See* note 31 of this chapter.

30. B. Şimşir, *Malta Sürgünleri* (The Malta Exiles), (Istanbul, 1976), 113. Another Turkish author avers that 150,000 demonstrators upon the slightest signal would with love and zest have stormed the prison in the style of Bastille but that the police had blocked the streets leading to it. T. M. Göztepe, *Osmanoğullarının Son Padişahı Sultan Vahdeddin Mütareke Gayyasında* (The last monarch from the Ottoman Dynasty, Sultan Vahdeddin in the Impasse of the Armistice) (Istanbul, 1969), 163.

31. *Ibid.* Of these, twenty-six were ordered released by the Court Martial itself with the assertion, "There is no case against them." *Spectateur d'Orient* (Istanbul), May 21, 1919. Admiral Calthorpe informed London regarding the forty-one Turks released from military prison by Ottoman authorities that "there was every reason to believe, [they] were guilty of the most heinous crimes ... mainly in connection with massacres." FO 371/4174/88761 (folio 9) (May 30, 1919). Referring to the Malta exiles, Foreign Office Near East specialist Edmonds declared, "There is probably not one of these prisoners who does not deserve a long term of imprisonment if not capital punishment." FO 371/6509/E8745 (folios 23-24).

32. U.S. Admiralty Weekly Intelligence Report No. 15, *U.S. National Archives,* R.G. 256, 867.002/10 (May 27, 1919). The British had decided in a February 25, 1919 conference that "it was undesirable to leave it to the Turkish authorities to try to punish such offenders as could not be competently tried by Military Courts." FO 608/244/3700 (folio 311-2). The participants of the conference included representatives of the Admiralty, War Office, and Foreign Office.

33. FO 371/4174 No. 1302/1 G. (folio 125) (May 22, 1919), and FO 371/4174/88761 (May 30, 1919). For British apprehension regarding further releases of Turkish detainees from the military prison ("some or all of them"), see FO 371/4173/76582 (folio 381) (May 19, 1919 report by Rear Admiral Webb).

34. FO 608/244/3749 (folio 315) (Rear Admiral Webb's February 19, 1919 telegram to London, quoting from the Turkish Minister's February 16 note whose original, full text in French is in FO 608/247/4222 (folio 177)).

35. FO 371/4173/47590 (folio 89).

36. Fourteen of the latter group were accused of mistreatment of British prisoners during the war.

37. The main tenets of Kemalism are summarized in two documents framed as the movement was crystallizing the emergent post-war Turkish nationalism: the Declaration of the Kemalist Congress at Sıvas (Sep. 9, 1919) and the subsequent National Pact (Jan. 28, 1920). *See* E. G. Mears, "Select Documents," in *Modern Turkey: A Politico-Economic Interpretation, 1908–1923 Inclusive,*, E. G. Mears, ed. (New York, 1924), 627–31.

38. *See* D. Lloyd George, *Memoirs of the Peace Conference,* vol. 2, (London, 1939), 871, 878.

39. Willis, *Prologue* [n. 7], 158.

40. A. Toynbee, *The Western Question in Greece and Turkey* (Boston, 1922), 46.

41. FO 371/4174/156721 (folios 523-24).

42. FO 371/4174/136069 (folio 470).

43. FO 371/6500/, W. 2178, appendix A (folio 385-118, 386-119), Aug. 11, 1920.

44. *Ibid.* In discussing the evidentiary difficulties, Lamb stated further: "Though none of this information is in itself of strict legal value, still no prosecution could get to work without it." *Ibid.*

45. FO 371/6500/E3557 (folios 63-64).

46. *Ibid.* (folio 385-118).

47. FO 371/6509/E8745 (folios 23-24).

48. *Ibid.* (folio 29).

49. FO 371/6509/E10023 (folios 100-01) (Aug. 24, 1921 opinion).

50. FO 371/6500/E3375 (folio 284/15).

51. FO 371/6509 (folio 47) (Aug. 4, 1921 summary of the negotiations); Şimşir, *Malta* [n. 30], 447.

52. FO 371/6509/E10319 (folios 122-23).

53. FO 371/5091/E16080 (folio 85). In announcing this escape the British Foreign Office noted that the first two "have broken parole"; on the occasion of the subsequent escape of the sixteen, the Office wondered out loud "how little Turkish sense of honor can be relied on." FO 3071/6509/E10662 (folio 159).

54. Willis, *Prologue* [n. 7], 162.

55. FO 371/7882/E4425 (comment by D. Osborne, May 23, 1922).

56. FO 371/7882/E4425 (folio 182). This attitude is also evident in the remark General Campbell inserted in his letter to Lloyd George, whom he was pressuring for the release of his son, Captain Campbell, from Turkish custody. Captain Campbell had written his father, who repeated it to Lloyd George, "I am more valuable than any of these miserable Turks." FO 371/6509/E8562 (folio 16). Captain Campbell, in the Spring of 1920, was serving as an Intelligence Officer in Anatolia. He was detained by the Kemalists in March as the Letter of Recall failed to reach him.

57. Willis, *Prologue,* [n. 7], 160.

58. A. Yalman, *Turkey in My Time* (Norman, OK, 1956), 106.

59. Less than three months before the onset of the Turkish Armistice, French Premier Clemenceau publicly declared that France and Great Britain intend to secure justice for the Armenians *"selon les règles supérieures de l'Humanité et de la justice."* K. Ziemke, *Die Neue Türkei 1914–1929* (Berlin, 1930), 273. (Letter from Clemenceau to Armenian

National Delegation, Paris, July 14, 1918). *See also* The American Committee Opposed to the Lausanne Treaty, *The Lausanne Treaty, Turkey and Armenia* (New York, 1926), 195. Echoing the May 24 Allied declaration, this large pledge proved as inconsequential as its predecessor. The forsaking of Armenia and Armenian claims was a classic instance of adaptive politics in which the military challenge of the erstwhile vanquished Turkish nation paradoxically emerged as the determining factor in the capitulation of the victors. As noted elsewhere, Lloyd George decried that capitulation by excoriating the Lausanne Peace Treaty, in which neither Turkish war crimes nor Armenia were mentioned, as "abject, cowardly and infamous." D. Lloyd George, *Memoirs* [n. 38], 872.

60. E. Schwelb, "Crimes Against Humanity." *The British Yearbook of International Law* 23 (1946): 181–82; Bassiouni, *Crimes Against* [n. 6] 170 n. 78, 173.

61. *See* J. L. Brierly, "The Rule of Law in the International Society," *Nordisk Tidskrift for International Ret, Acta Scandinavica Juris Gentium* 7 (1936).

62. *See* Mears, "Select," [n. 37], 624-26; *British General Staff Files, W.O.* 100, *Execution of the Armistice with Turkey* app. I (30 Oct.-30 Nov. 1918). Some of these key clauses were Nos. 5, 16, and 20. A British diplomat offered another line of explanation. " … the Foreign Office renewed its orders to cut down all expenditure incurred for the protection of the minorities, and the War Office were prepared to abandon the Anatolian Railway, measures which we found it difficult to reconcile with the brave words of Mr. Lloyd George … 'Anatolia, Armenia and the Christian communities would be protected.'" Sir R. Graves, *Storm Centers of the Near East*, (Personal Memoirs 1879–1929) (Constantinople, 1933), 328.

Chapter 18

The Recourse to the Machinery of Turkish Justice

The efforts to prosecute those responsible for the Armenian genocide under Turkish domestic law also faltered as a result of domestic and international political considerations. The Turkish trials were successful in documenting the crimes that had been committed against the Armenian people. They failed dismally, however, in punishing the perpetrators. Domestically, the rise of a strong nationalist movement, led by Mustafa Kemal, conflicted with legal efforts to prosecute Turkish military and government officials. The nationalist aspirations of unity and national pride were inconsistent with the internal impulse to fix blame and apportion responsibility for the Armenian genocide on Turkish leaders. In the international sphere, political considerations outweighed the Allies' desire to force the Turks to acknowledge and effectively prosecute the war criminals. In their zest to win favor with the Kemalist government, France and Italy undermined the efforts of Britain, and to a lesser extent the United States, to bring about retributive justice for the Armenians through the use of the Turkish Courts. Britain, lacking the support of its allies and facing Turkish opposition, eventually sacrificed the pursuit of justice to political expediency.

A parallel can be drawn between the Istanbul and Leipzig trials, where the German war criminals were prosecuted. At Leipzig, domestic and international forces combined to thwart efforts to prosecute alleged war criminals. As with Turkey, nationalist feelings in Germany militated against prosecuting one's own nationals, especially under foreign pressure. The Allies, during both the Turkish and Leipzig trials, allowed political considerations to prevail over the efforts to prosecute the enemy's officials. The Leipzig parallel shows that the failure of the Turkish

---

domestic efforts should not be seen as an exception. Rather, their joint lesson is that it is difficult to achieve effective punishment for genocide and other crimes against humanity through domestic processes.

Although ultimately ineffectual, the prosecution of the Turkish leaders implicated in the Armenian Genocide before Turkish Courts Martial, which resulted in a series of indictments, verdicts, and sentences, was of extraordinary, though unrecognized, significance. For the first time in history, deliberate mass murder, designated "a crime under international law,"[1] was adjudicated in accordance with domestic penal codes, thus substituting national laws for the rules of international law. These trials, therefore, provide a perspective on the developing efforts to criminalize genocide under domestic laws. In 1949, the Special American Bar Association Committee on Peace and Law through the United Nations, defined the U.N. Convention on Genocide as "a code of domestic crimes, which are already denominated in all countries as common law crimes."[2] Lemkin likewise asserted that "genocide is a composite crime and consists of acts which are themselves punishable by most existing legislation."[3]

In 1988, Congress added the crimes of genocide and attempted genocide to the U.S. criminal code. Such legislative efforts, however, can only be effective to the degree that they are enforced. As noted above, international and domestic political structures work against such enforcement. In post-World War I Turkey, however, there were countervailing pressures which could have provided enough momentum for the initiation and ultimate success of enforcement efforts. By agreeing to try Turkish war criminals, the Ottoman authorities expected to be treated less sternly at the Peace Conference, a fact confirmed by both contemporary Turkish historians[4] and British officials involved.[5] These Ottoman authorities reasoned that the Turkish nation could not be held responsible for the crimes of a political party and its governmental agents.[6] Commenting on the first sentence of capital punishment imposed by the Turkish Military Tribunal, British High Commissioner Admiral Calthorpe maintained that the Turks, including the Grand Vizier and his supporters, "consider executions a mere concession to the Entente rather than as punishment justly meted out to criminals."[7]

In addition, the surreptitious flight in November, 1918 of the principal architects of the Armenian genocide created a furor among many sectors of the Turkish public still suffering the hardships of war and defeat. The anti-Ittihadist factions that had been persecuted and oppressed before and during the war demanded speedy trials. Others, including many journalists, simply lamented the atrocities perpetrated against the Armenians. For example, the journal *Minber*, published jointly by Mustafa Kemal (Atatürk) and by F. Okyar, Interior Minister in the first postwar Cabinet and subsequently Prime Minister of the Turkish Republic from 1924–25, denounced "the attempt to exterminate the Armenians [which] was fraught with grave consequences "(*Ermeni milletini ... kırmak sevdâsı ... imha etmek ... renki vehâmet.*)"[8] Thus, the domestic trials against the perpetrators of the Armenian genocide were not without political, public, and media support within Turkey. The failure of these trials, therefore, is doubly instructive.

Pretrial Inquiries and Investigations
The Parliament's Fifth Committee

Article 31 of the Ottoman Constitution detailed procedures through which one or more Deputies could lodge allegations of misconduct against a Minister. These allegations ultimately would lead to a trial before the High Court, whose composition, jurisdiction, and function were spelled out in articles 92–95. If a Committee of the Chamber of Deputies decided to investigate the allegations, the Constitution required a two-thirds vote of the full Chamber and the sanction of the Sovereign for an actual trial.

On the very day the seven top leaders of Ittihad fled from Istanbul (November 1–2, 1918), causing there "a great tumult,"[9] a Muslim Deputy introduced a motion for the trial before the High Court of the Ministers of the two wartime Cabinets. He attached to that motion ten charges against these Ministers referring to their misdeeds related to the Turkish participation in World War I, including aggression, military incompetence, political abuses, and economic crimes. Two of these charges related to the Armenian massacres. Number 5 challenged the enactment of the Temporary Laws[10] as "completely contrary to the spirit and letter of our Constitution." In denouncing "the disasters" that followed this enactment, and the associated "orders and instructions," the Deputy invoked "the rules of law and humanity." Charge No. 10 indicted the Ministers for the creation of "brigands [*çetes*] whose assaults on life, property and honor rendered the Ministers guilty as co-perpetrators of the tragic crimes that resulted."[11]

To investigate these charges, the Fifth Committee of the Chamber of Deputies was created, its 20 members having been selected by the drawing of lots. Its slow pace and digressions, however, gave rise to public complaints. Further, by the time of the full Chamber's vote to institute High Court trials, only 156 Deputies remained of the 256 who had been elected before the war; the corresponding ratio for the Senate was 30 out of 48.

In response to these concerns, the Sultan dissolved the Chamber on December 21, 1918, and transferred jurisdiction to the Courts Martial. The Sultan's action precluded High Court jurisdiction, since there was no Chamber to vote on the findings of the Fifth Committee and to recommend trials under the jurisdiction of that Court. This move also served the political interests of the Sultan by cutting off the Ittihadists' Parliamentary power and giving the Sultan's government a free hand to control the country by edict.

Notwithstanding the preemption of its procedural sequence, the Fifth Committee's work had already yielded some results. From November 9 to December 12, 1918, the Committee conducted 14 hearings in which it interrogated 15 ministers, including two Şeyhulislams.[12] These interrogations resulted in a number of important admissions. For example, former Justice Minister Ibrahim admitted to the release from the prisons of "an appreciably large number of convicted common law criminals upon the instance of the Army claiming to be needing them."[13] Ibrahim further accepted responsibility for the atrocities resulting from the Temporary Law of Deportation, collectively for the Cabinet, and individually as a Minister, although he argued that the excesses were perpetrated "without the knowledge of the government."[14] When a Deputy retorted, "What do you mean 'the government was not cognizant of them,' the problem did not occur in one day, but dragged on for eighteen months," Ibrahim shifted the blame to the military, which in turn persistently denied "the vile deeds."[15] Another Deputy raised the question of the military "willfully carrying out deportations and executions in areas outside the theaters of military operations." To this the ex-Minister of Justice responded, "we are unaware of such things."[16]

In addition to the revelations and confessions exacted from the ministers during these hearings, the Committee also secured a number of documents, some of which were top-secret orders and instructions regarding the massacres. These documents were eventually turned over to the prosecutors attached to the Courts Martial.[17]

The Administration's Inquiry Commission

The Administration's Inquiry Commission, which came into being on November 23, 1918 and operated concurrently with the Parliamentary investigation, was charged with the investigation of the misdeeds (*seyyiat*) of governmental officials irrespective of rank. As mandated by paragraphs 47, 75, and 87 of the Ottoman Code of Criminal Procedures,[18] the Commission, headed by Hasan Mazhar, was vested with broad powers. These powers, including subpoena, search and seizure, and arrest and detention, were executed by the judicial police and the agency of the Military Governor. Over two months, the Commission secured coded and decoded telegraphic orders from dozens of provincial locations identified as centers of deportations and massacres in Asiatic and European Turkey. The Commission obtained a batch of 42 ciphers from the Ankara province alone. In addition, the Commission compiled a mass of pre-trial evidence through interrogatories administered orally and in writing to suspects by examining magistrates (*sorgu hâkimi*). Among these suspects were 26 Chamber Deputies whose possible escape was averted by a Cabinet order denying them permits to travel to their electoral districts.[19] Through a set of ten questions directed to the Defense Ministry, the Commission also sought information on the organization, function, command-and-control of the Special Organization.

When finished with its task, the Commission forwarded to the Courts Martial the dossiers of the suspects; by mid-January, 1919, it had compiled separate dossiers for 130 suspects.[20] In the meantime Reşid Akif Paşa, President of the State Council, had determined that Ittihad, and its party chief Talât, should be prosecuted as prima facie suspects. This transfer of pre-trial evidence was accompanied by a recommendation, as stipulated by the Criminal Procedure Code, that evidence was incriminating enough to warrant the commencement of criminal proceedings against the suspects.[21]

The Formation of the Court Martial

The next steps of martial justice originated in early December, 1918 from the office of the Procuror-General of the Court of Appeals in the Ottoman capital, and were subsequently formalized in a conference between the head of the Criminal Affairs division of the Justice Ministry and the Chief Legal Counsel of the Interior Ministry.[22] The Court Martial was initially formed by Imperial authorization on December 16, 1918.[23] A subsequent authorization, dated December 25,1918, declared that jurisdiction for areas not under martial law would devolve upon existing criminal courts as stipulated by article 88 of the Constitution.[24] A third decision, dated January 8, 1919, rendered the Extraordinary (or Special) Court Martial operational.[25] In March, however, the Sultan installed a new government which he believed would bring about a more efficient and expedited trial of the accused; by Imperial authorization, the statutes of a new Court Martial were set forth on March 8, 1919.[26] Pursuant to the provision of article 371 of the Ottoman Code of Criminal Procedures, the Court Martial ordered the seven top leaders of the Young Turk regime "presently being fugitives," to appear before the Court within ten days. Otherwise, they would be treated as rebels against the law, tried in absentia, lose all their civil rights, and their properties would be confiscated without right to appeal.[27] "Part of the task of this Tribunal" (*cümlei vazife*) was the investigation of the charges of "massacres and unlawful, personal profiteering" (*taktil ve ihtikâr*).[28] On May 26, 1919, the new Procuror-General framed a new indictment which added more comprehensive allegations, centering around the main charge of "overthrow of the government" (*taklibi hükümet*)."[29] This revision was in line with the terms of paragraph

311 of the Code of Criminal Procedures providing for the amendment of charges in the event that new crimes should come to light during a trial.[30] Finally, on April 23, 1920, the charges were expanded to include "rebellion" and "violation of public order."[31] The target of this move were the insurgent Kemalists in the interior of Turkey.

The Initiation of the Proceedings

The evidence obtained in preparation for the trials was indexed and cross-indexed along the lines of 1) *ratione personae,* or accomplices (*cerayim failleri*); 2) *ratione loci,* or location of the crimes; and 3) *ratione materiae,* involving the classification and itemization of the evidence. The Court Martial adopted broad standards concerning the laws of evidence. Relying on longstanding Ottoman judicial tradition, it applied the principle of "intimate conviction" (*hukuku takdiriye,* or *kanaatı vicdaniye*), by which a judge can, to the best of his conscience, assess the probative value of the evidence available to him. Further, nearly every document obtained by the Inquiry Commission was authenticated by the legal experts of the Interior Ministry with the standard notation of "it conforms to the original" (*aslına muvafik* or *mutabık*). In the seventh, eighth, and ninth sittings of the Yozgat trial series (February 18, 20 and 22, 1919), for example, several of the military cipher-telegrams were introduced as prosecution exhibits and, as with all prosecution exhibits, read aloud in court. The presiding judge also decided to allow public trials, stating that while "[i]t is not customary, nor is there any legal obligation for a Court Martial, to allow the proceedings to be public … . In order to demonstrate the intent of the Court to conduct the trials impartially and in a spirit of lofty justice [*kemali adil ve bitaraf*], I am going to use judicial discretion and conduct public trials. The Court is simply trying to help the defendants and facilitate their defense" (*teshil ve istiane*).[32]

The defense, coordinated during the "Cabinet Council" sessions that were held in the prison, amounted to a form of stonewalling: individually and collectively, the defendants steadfastly denied the charges.[33] In commenting on the display of a near uniform defense stance in their court appearance, Tunaya uses the words "in unison" (*bir ağız halinde*), or "unanimously" (*oybirligi*).[34] In trying to overcome this defense, the Military Tribunal used three methods: 1) surprising the defendants through the sudden production of cipher telegrams bearing their signatures; 2) confronting them with their statements and confessions from the oral and written pretrial interrogatories they had signed;[35] and 3) isolating a defendant at the dock and rigorously questioning him. The admissions extracted were then used in the examination of the other defendants, leading some of the defendants to amend their testimony.

The Key Indictment

Although separate indictments were framed for the series of subsidiary trials on massacres which took place in different locales, the Key Indictment focused on the Cabinet Ministers and the top leaders of the ruling Ittihad party. The League For the Defense of Ottoman Interests pointed to this indictment as "a historical document" through which "the country" will be tried and judged.[36] The cardinal feature of the Key Indictment, not present in any other indictment, was the set of documents lodged within it. In support of the charges spelled out, the Indictment cited 41 specific documents in the possession of the Court. Most of these documents consisted of decoded telegrams sent to and from the Interior Minister, the IIIrd and IVth Army Commanders, the Deputy Commanders of the Vth Army Corps and the XVth Division from Ankara province, (both of whom subsequently testified regarding their ciphers), the Directors of the Special Organization, two Military Governors of Istanbul, and a host of governors and district commissioners. An editorial in a Turkish daily described the impending court martial proceedings against high-ranking officials and party leaders as "the most important trial in the six-hundred year history of the Ottoman empire."[37]

The charges

The charges in the indictment centered on the Ittihad party, sometimes called *Cemiyet* (meaning a close knit community of party members). In declaring the party's objectives and methods criminal, the Procuror-General specifically cited its Central Committee, General Assembly, and two provincial control groups headed by Responsible Secretaries and Inspectors. The Defense Ministry, the War Office, particularly the Special Organization, and the Interior Ministry were likewise included in these charges since they were all led and directed by the two principal chiefs of the party, War Minister Enver and Interior Minister (later Grand Vizier) Talât.[38] "The evidence gathered yields the picture of a party whose moral personality is mired in an unending chain of bloodthirstiness, plunder and abuses."[39] By way of a brief digression it may be relevant to inject here the assessment of American Ambassador Morgenthau who, in a lengthy analysis (November 4, 1915) of the omnipotence, of the Central Committee of the Young Turk Ittihad party, mentions these men as the arch leaders of "an invisible and irresponsible government." That omnipotence, with particular reference to organizing the "Armenian atrocities," is accounted for in terms of "an absolute control of the army, navy and civil government of the country. They have removed many governors of interior *vilayets* [provinces] who would not obey their orders. They also completely control the Chamber of Deputies, whose members are absolutely selected by them ... they have frightened almost everyone into submission ... . There is no opposition party in existence. The Press is carefully censored and must obey the wishes of the Union and Progress Party ... . They have annihilated or displaced at least two thirds of the Armenian population ... ."[40] The principle charges are discussed below.

Conspiracy

This charge was two-pronged: the defendants were first accused of having deliberately engineered Turkey's entry into the war "by recourse to a number of vile tricks and deceitful means"; they were also accused of using "this vantage ground to carry out their secret intentions."[41] In accord with a central plan, the indictment stated, the party proceeded to implement its "covert and conspiratorial" goals.[42] The conspiracy was thus extended to the point of subverting the legitimate authority of the government whose "high ranking officials submitted" (*inkiyad*) to the dictates of the party.[43] The principal objective of Ittihad was "the massacre and destruction of the Armenians"[44] for which purpose they further conspired to "release gangs of convicts from the prisons,"[45] ostensibly for combat duty. In reality, "the prisons were emptied ... of these criminals and outlaws"; they were then assigned "massacre" duties in the Special Organization.[46] The indictment alleged that the conspiracy included self-enrichment not only for the members of the units but also for the principal leaders of the party who "likewise tried to pile up fortunes" for themselves through "the pillage and plunder" of the goods and possessions of their victims.[47] As noted above, the indictment, therefore, emphasized that "the investigation of massacres and illegal, personal profiteering is the principal task of this Tribunal."[48] The provincial organization and supervision of the plan of "extermination" was entrusted to the Responsible Secretaries, carefully selected by the party leadership.[49]

Premeditation and intent

The Indictment further alleged that "[t]he massacre and destruction of the Armenians were the result of decisions by the Central Committee of Ittihad."[50] The decision process involved "extensive and profound deliberations," in consequence of which the scheme against the Armenians "has been determined upon."[51] It is worth to consider in this connection the August 3, 1915 entry of American Ambassador Morgenthau's diary which reads, "Talât ... told me that the Union and Progress Committee [Ittihad party] had carefully considered the matter in all its details and that the policy which was being pursued was that which they had officially adopted. He said that I must not get the idea that the deportations had been decided upon hastily; in reality, they were the result of prolonged and careful deliberation."[52] In order to conceal that decision, the

Indictment maintained, Ittihad leaders relied on the party's tactic of "disguise." The execution of the central plan was "ensured and directed through oral and secret orders and instructions."[53] These orders, sent via coded ciphers, were at times accompanied by the instruction to "destroy" (*iptal*) them after reading.[54]

On the issue of intent, the Indictment countered two possibilities that were later advanced by the defense. One was military necessity, which the defense argued necessitated massive relocation through deportations; the other was the justified punishment of a disloyal community. The Indictment asserted that "the deportations were neither a measure of military necessity, nor a punitive, disciplinary act."[55] Rather, they entailed "massacres ... as acts subsidiary to a centrally directed plan."[56] That plan had nothing to do with "a particular incident" provoked by the Armenians; nor were the massacres "limited to a particular locality."[57] The Indictment's allusion to a comprehensive and centrally directed plan of destruction was based on Ittihad's overt purpose of "solving once and for all [*hall ve fasl*] unresolved problems and conflicts" of which Ittihad considered the lingering Armenian question the most troublesome.[58] The Indictment cited as proof for this the Ittihad Central Committee's intent of "solving the Eastern question."[59] The plan of wholesale destruction was eventually confirmed in two separate verdicts: 1) one was based, in part, on a cipher telegram in which the Chief of the Special Organization asked the Responsible Secretary of Harput province whether the Armenians of his province "are being annihilated, or are they being merely deported and exiled."[60] The governor of Harput province, Sabit, had supplied this and another cipher when being interrogated by an examining magistrate. It appears that he had saved them for use for defense in the event of an arrest following Turkey's military defeat.[61] 2) Documentary evidence was adduced to substantiate the charge that Ittihad party Chief and Interior Minister Talât had given oral instructions to interpret the order for "deportation" as an order for "destruction" (*imha*).[62]

The military commander in whose command zone the massacres were carried out substantiated these charges of premeditation and intent. When informed that a contingent of two thousand Armenian soldiers assigned to labor battalion duties were trapped and slaughtered on their way to a new assignment on the Baghdad Railroad, General Vehib of the IIIrd Army's command zone launched an investigation that led to a court-martial and some executions. It was in the course of this investigation that General Vehib learned of the large-scale massacres that had taken place in the six provinces of the IIIrd Army's command zone in the months preceding his assuming command in February 1916. In his detailed affidavit prepared at the request of the Administration's Inquiry Commission and repeatedly cited in the Key Indictment and two Verdicts, Vehib summed up his findings as follows:

The massacre and destruction of the Armenians and the plunder and pillage of their goods were the results of decisions reached by Ittihad's Central Committee ... . The atrocities were carried out under a program that was determined upon and involved a definite case of premeditation [*mukarrer bir program ve mutlak bir kasd tahtında yapılan işbu mezalim*]. It was [also] ascertained that these atrocities and crimes were encouraged [*teşvik*] by the district attorneys whose dereliction of judicial duties in face of their occurrence and especially their remaining indifferent [*lâkayd*] renders them accessories to these crimes [*feren zi methal*].[63]

Murder and personal responsibility

The top leaders of Ittihad were also accused of having committed statutory crimes in their capacity as members of the party's Central Committee. Two members of the triumvirate, Enver (the War Minister and de facto Supreme Commander of Ottoman Armed Forces), and Cemal (the Marine Minister and Commander of the IVth Army), were military leaders. Talât, the third member, was Interior Minister and the ultimate coordinator of the Special Organization's ties with the party's Central Committee and the War Office. Both the Military Governors of Istanbul, attached to the War Office, and the head of Public Security, were prominently mentioned in the Indictment as organizers of the Special Organization cadres in the Ottoman capital. The most prominently mentioned Ittihad Central Committee members were the two physician-politicians, Nazım and Şakir. The Indictment cited both of them eight times as the foremost organizers of the Special Organization,[64] which itself was cited a dozen times as the principal tool used in association with the crimes of "murder, arson, gutting, rape, and all sorts of torture."[65]

The Responsible Secretaries were identified as the key group directing these crimes. The following description by a Turkish author remarkably familiar with many of the secrets of Ittihad and the Special organization, may help to underline the importance of this role, somewhat akin to that played by the *Gauleiters* of Nazi Third Reich:

> The title [Responsible Secretary] was created to avoid the appearance of overshadowing the state authority while investing the holder with powers required for the direction of the course of events. In fact, in all matters of consequence, *the last decision* belongs to them. These men ... in line with this practice made *final decisions*. They were selected by the Central Committee, the shadow Cabinet, on the basis of experience, age, brains and familiarity.[66]

A similar view is expressed by another Turkish historian who was in opposition to Ittihad. He described the Responsible Secretaries as omnipotent provincial commissars "exercising control over the army." As to the members of the party's Central Committee, "they became powerful enough to be compared to ministers."[67] For this reason, the Military Tribunal remanded their case to a separate series of trials after repeatedly underscoring in the Key Indictment their pivotal role. In the separate and subsidiary Indictment, framed for this series, the Court depicted the participation of these provincial commissars in "the decision of the Central Committee … [in that t]hey created a secret arm of the government and subverted that government [*tagayyür*], operating within the party as a special cadre of high ranking officials" (*erkânı mahsusa*).[68] In describing their role in the destruction of the victims under the cloak of "deportation," the Procuror-General in his closing argument described these deportations as "a pretext for the massacres," adding "[t]his established fact is as clear as the equation $2 + 2 = 4$."[69] The Indictment concluded that as the crimes were specified as "personal" (*şahsi ceraim*) or "ordinary" (*ceraimi adiye*), the defendants would not be entitled to immunity under the doctrine of act of state.

The prosecution's exclusive reliance on domestic penal codes

In seeking to punish the perpetrators involved, the prosecution relied solely on the Ottoman Penal Code.[70] The Code, paralleling the French Penal Code's classification of offenses and corresponding criminal sanctions, had three major divisions. The first 47 articles defined the principles of culpability, delineating individual responsibilities, and liabilities for violations. The second division, articles 48–167, defined general offenses directed against institutions, such as the government. The third division, articles 168–253, mainly prescribed the specific penalties. Of these, articles 168–191 dealt with acts of coercion and violence against persons.

The Court Martial classified the defendants as either principal co-perpetrators or accessories. For the first category, the Court invoked article 45, paragraph 1 of the Penal Code:

> If several persons together commit a crime or if a crime is composed of several acts and each of a gang of persons perpetrates one or some of such acts with the object of the accomplishment of the offense, such persons are styled accomplices and all of them are punished as sole perpetrators.[71]

Further, the Procuror-General proposed to apply article 170 to the offenders of the first category. This article reads:

> If a person's being a killer with premeditation is proved according to law, sentence for his being put to death is passed legally.[72]

Most importantly, the Procuror-General added the last paragraph of article 55 to cover the charge of "forcible alteration of the government" that was subsequently incorporated into the amended bill of charges. That paragraph reads:

> The person whose forcible attempt to alter, change or destroy the Constitution, or the shape or form of the Government, or the system of succession of the Ottoman Empire is [to be] put to death.[73]

The Court designated the defendants in the second category, "accessories in the first degree" (*feren zi methal*), subjecting them to paragraph 2 of article 45, which read:

> Those who are accessories in the commission of a crime become subject to punishment in the following manner where there is no explicitness in the law … the punishment of temporary forced labor for not less than ten years if the principal act calls for the punishment of death or perpetual forced labor … .[74]

The Jurisdictional Challenge by the Defense: The Constitutional Argument

Before accepting the post offered him on March 3, 1919, Damad Ferit, the new Grand Vizier, stipulated that he wanted, the defense's apparent stalling notwithstanding, a "[s]peedy judgment of the crisis so as to be able to deal with the authors of a crime that drew the revulsion of the entire humankind."[75] A month later the Grand Vizier went so far as to entertain the possibility of prosecuting, as a collective entity, all the "active" members of Ittihad under the charge of having belonged to "a criminal organization."[76] The procedures adopted to satisfy Ferit provided grounds for charges of constitutional violations. Defended by 16 lawyers, the Ministers repeatedly challenged the competence of the Tribunal and criticized the procedures under which they were apprehended and were being prosecuted.

Led by Turkish Bar Association President and Istanbul University Law Professor C. Arif (later Deputy, Parliament President and Minister of the Ankara government), the defense lawyers invoked several articles of the Constitution to support their challenge. The defense argued that article 31 of the Ottoman Constitution[77] set forth the procedures for bringing to trial a Minister charged with misconduct, specifying the High Court as the requisite venue for trial. The defense further claimed that the crimes charged in the indictment were not "ordinary crimes,"[78] but rather revolved around the implementation of the Law of Deportation which had been enacted by the government and sanctioned by an Imperial *Irade* (authorization). Since the massacres incident to the deportations were part of an act of state, guilt or innocence depended on the scope of ministerial duties and authority; as a result, they were not subject to article 33 but rather to article 92 which defined the function and composition of the High Court.[79] Indeed, the defense argued that even if one assumed that article 33 would apply, the article stipulated that in the event misconduct was not related to official acts, and a High Court is ruled out, existing criminal courts, not a court martial, must have jurisdiction.[80] Finally, the defense argued that the Court did not have the authority to determine which article of the constitution should be applied in the case because article 117 specifies the Senate as the ultimate interpreter of the exact meaning of an article of the Constitution.[81]

The Court first rejected the "act of state" argument. Even if it granted that the massacres were incidental to the deportation, the Court noted that massacre was still murder, a separate and distinct state act. Only if new evidence established that the massacres were not intended but were merely inevitable results attending the fulfilment of official duties, would the Court consider the argument. The Court found, however, that the available evidence demonstrated that the massacres were part of policies and decisions arrived at by the defendants, not as Ministers conducting official work, but as members of a secret, conspiratorial association (*cemiyet*).[82] The Court also noted that the act of state defense was inconsistent with the indictment, which defined "the principal task" of the Court to be the investigation of "massacres and illegal, personal profiteering" (*taktil ve ihtikâr*).[83] Further, the bill of particulars singled out "the moral personality" of the Ittihad party of which they were the leaders, and asserted that in the course of exercising that leadership the defendants committed "personal crimes" (*şahsi ceraim*).[84]

The Court then rejected the remaining constitutional and jurisdictional challenges. Since martial law had been imposed by the Ittihad regime itself, and was still in force, neither article 32 nor 33 could be invoked for the purpose of effecting a change of venue or for transferring the defendants to the jurisdiction of regular criminal courts, as motioned by the defense. Further, article 113, concerning the imposition of martial law, provided for the temporary suspension of civil rights. The Court again pointed to the language of the indictment: "wherever martial law is in force, civil and judicial laws are entirely muted" (*kavanini mülkiye ve adliye tamamile sakin*), and courts martial become the only penal recourse (*mercii ceraim*).[85] (Ittihad itself had further revised the original martial law in 1909 in order to have greater authority in suspending regular laws.[86]) The Court also rejected the defendants' claim that the Fifth Committee of the Chamber opted for the High Court. The Court noted that the Deputies had merely conducted an investigation without a final decision; since the Sultan had dissolved the Parliament, the impossibility of a Parliamentary vote invalidated the claim in question. Finally, consistent with the Court's holding, a special Imperial *Irade* with the force of a decree-law vested the Court with the requisite authority and competence to try the accused. On May 4, 1919, at its second sitting, the Court again rejected the Constitutional argument and that of challenging the competence of the Court. In doing so it swore to proceed "without deviating at all from the glorious precepts of the Koran and with fear of God" (*Ahkâmı celilei Kuraniyeden zerre kadar inhiraf etmeksizin … Allah korkusu ile dolu … .*).[87]

In rejecting the defense arguments, the Court overlooked or ignored a major consideration. It is true that article 31 of the Ottoman Constitution sets the condition of a trial before the High Court for Ministers accused of misconduct—as opposed to a Court Martial. But it contains a contingency element—"if"—at the very beginning. It reads: "If one or more Deputies wish to level a complaint against a Minister whose responsibility is at issue on matters touching the domain of the Chamber … ." (*şikayet beyan ettiği halde*). Thus, the Constitution neither compels nor precludes any particular line of procedure. Its provisions are binding only for Parliamentary procedures; other procedures, such as recourse to regular criminal courts, are not addressed. A Deputy may or can, but is not directed to take the High Court route. Consequently, the statute is not preemptory in its thrust; other options are available to Deputies or to judicial officials wanting to exercise criminal jurisdiction. Moreover, there is no record of any constitution with any provision affording an official, high or low, the privilege of being placed beyond the reach of public law for common offenses or crimes. This may be the chief, if not the only reason why article 31 is prefaced with the prepositon "if." The prosecution failed to make this point, even though in the Key Indictment it had declared emphatically that the crimes associated with the Armenian deportations did "constitute the real purpose of these court proceedings," (*Takvimi Vekâyi*, No. 3540, May 5, 1919), p. 8, and as such were justiciable in courts other than the High Court.

The Key Verdict

Following a prolonged trial of the Cabinet Ministers, marked by a series of amendments of the Key Indictment in May and June, 1919, the Court entered its Key Verdict on July 5, 1919.[88] The Court found the Ministers guilty of both orchestrating the entry of Turkey into World War I and of committing the genocide of the Armenians. The Key Verdict traced Ittihad's wartime crimes to its 1908–1914 prewar career. The Court cited the betrayal of the ideals of the Ittihad revolution which had overthrown the regime of Abdul Hamit in 1908, and the subsequent imposition of "arbitrary rule and tyranny to such a point that people began to yearn"[89] for the overthrown regime. It focused especially on Ittihad's violent reseizure of power in January, 1913, in the course of which War Minister Nazım and one of his Adjudants were killed.[90] By creating "a fourth instance of authority, above and beyond the three [branches of government] that comprise the legal framework of the Ottoman government, [Ittihad] resorted to coercive intimidation [*kuvvei tehdidiye*] in altering [*tağyir*] the machinery of the government … which amounts to altering the form of the government."[91] The Court also found that the Ittihadists "maintained almost without interruption the state of siege which necessarily was declared at the start of the revolution."[92]

This domination of the state apparatus, the Court reasoned, was in line with "the special aspirations and objectives" of the party.[93] The engineering of Turkey's entry into World War I through "aggression" was cited as a principal objective.[94] The Tribunal cited the testimony of Trabzon province's delegate, who had been a key Special Organization leader, when it alluded to the incidence of "crime against peace."[95] As this delegate testified, Ittihad had organized, before the onset of the Russo-Turkish war in November 1914, guerilla forays into the Russian Caucasus in anticipation of the war it was set to provoke: "It was Ittihad's predilection and intent that led to the declaration of war."[96] At the end of the second sitting of the Military Tribunal, May 4, 1919, defendant Atıf, a member of the Central Committee and one of the four directors of the Special Organization in the Ottoman capital, likewise admitted on the witness stand to forays of sabotage inside Russian territories.[97]

The second objective, "the organization and execution of crime of massacre [*taktil cinayeti*] by the leaders of Ittihad" against the Armenians, had been exposed during the preceding trials.[98] "This fact," the Court noted, "has been proven and verified [*tahakkuk*] by the Court Martial."[99] The Verdict focused attention on two subsidiary facts: 1) "The Armenians in particular suffered disaffection as the constitutional provisions guaranteeing security and justice proved ill-founded; as a result, they were prompted to assume a posture of waiting for an opportunity to fall back on their national aspirations."[100] 2) "The Ittihadists deliberately exacerbated racial and national differences and cleavages,"[101] implicitly stigmatizing anyone who was against Ittihad as anti-Moslem. In this connection, the Verdict cited the Şeyhulislam's testimony that "to resign from Ittihad meant to resign from Islam."[102]

In the conviction and sentencing of the principal co-perpetrators, the Verdict relied on articles 45 (paragraph 1), 55, and 170 of the Penal Code, as had been demanded by the Prosecution in the Key Indictment. Talât, Enver, Cemal, and Dr. Nazım, the top leaders of Ittihad and Cabinet Ministers, were condemned to death in absentia. The lesser Ittihadists, also Cabinet Ministers, were convicted under article 45, paragraph 2. The Court imposed a sentence of fifteen years of imprisonment with hard labor on the second category of offenders. The ex-Ministers of Post and Commerce were acquitted.

Ancillary Verdicts and the End of the Proceedings

The legal arguments and procedures applied to the trials of the Cabinet Ministers, especially the Key Indictment and the Key Verdict, set the tone for other trials that were occurring during this time. The common element in all the verdicts was the finding that the deportations were a cloak for the central plan of the destruction of the deportees.[103] As the Yozgat Verdict declared, "there can be no doubt and no hesitation" about this fact. Furthermore, the real purpose behind the deportations had been proven by documents personally written and signed by the defendants (*hattı destiyle mukarrer vesika*).[104] That same Verdict, besides relying on specific Ottoman penal codes (articles 45 and 170 of the Penal Code and article 171 of the Military Code, concerning the offense of plunder of goods and provisions), invoked "the sublime precepts of Islam" as well as "humanity and civilization" to condemn "the crimes of massacre, pillage and plunder."[105]

The Yozgat judgment, like the subsequent Key verdict, deplored the Ittihadist defendants' agitation "not only among local Muslims, but among Muslims in general," in favor of murdering the Armenians, calling such agitation "a mortal sin."[106] The Yozgat Verdict likewise repudiated the defense's argument that the murders of innocent people were reprisals against Armenians elsewhere who had committed sabotage and other acts of rebellion.

> These circumstances do not justify the commission of the crimes with which the defendants are charged. Besides, only a trifling portion of the Armenian people is implicated in these acts; the majority of them demonstrated their loyalty ... . Such transfer of blame in any event is against the dictates of law and conscience.[107]

The Trabzon Verdict also invoked "the high principles of Islam and the provisions of the Ottoman Civil Code" to emphasize "the rights of all Ottoman elements to the protection of their honor, lives and properties, without discrimination, by the officials of the state, that protection being a matter of duty of the first order for the latter."[108] The Armenian deportees, the Court found, were instead handed over to gangs of "repeat criminals" who methodically robbed, raped and murdered their charges, usually by drowning them in the Black Sea (*bahra ilka etmekle boğdurup mahv ettikleri*).[109]

The Responsible Secretaries Verdict found the defendants guilty of "the massacre and destruction of the Armenians and the plunder and looting of their goods and belongings ... they had a free hand in their criminal activities [involving mainly] the organization and engagement [*tertip ve ihzar*] of the gangs of brigands assigned to massacre duty."[110]

The actual sentences of those found guilty, however, provided a striking contrast to the concept of retributive justice which had motivated the prosecution. In the Harput trial, Dr. Şakir, the Political Director of the Special Organization, was convicted and sentenced to death in absentia. In all the ancillary verdicts only two relatively minor provincial officials and one gendarmery commander were executed for their complicity in the Armenian massacres.[111] In reference to light sentencing, Rear Admiral and British Acting High Commissioner at Istanbul, Richard Webb, stated "It is interesting to see ... the manner in which the sentences have been apportioned among the absent and the present so as to effect a minimum of real bloodshed."[112]

These trials were but a fragment of the many other trials for which only the preparations were completed as Kemalism emerged to displace the Sultan's government. On January 13, 1921, the Courts Martial were abolished altogether, with jurisdiction reverting to regular military courts.[113] Nearly all of the key figures of Ittihad managed to escape Turkey before being brought to trial.[114] Scores of other, lesser Ittihadists were likewise condemned to death in absentia or sentenced to prison terms. Many of these eventually escaped or were set free. The July 24, 1923 Treaty of Lausanne,[115] which preempted and replaced that of Sèvres, was framed in such a way so as to avoid treating the subject of war crimes and massacres. With Declaration VIII of Amnesty and the Protocol attached to this treaty,[116] and as Kemalism gained the upper hand and eventually ended the Ottoman Empire, the pursuit of justice for the Armenians within international law was abandoned.

Political Impediments to the Domestic Trials

The promise of domestic retribution could not be redeemed for the same reasons that the international efforts had failed. The insistence on prerogatives of national sovereignty on the part of Turkey overwhelmed the weak commitment of the European Powers to exact punishment. The force of the national sovereignty argument is especially strong in the present cases where the criminal act was committed by Turkish subjects upon Turkish subjects and within the territorial boundaries of Turkey. Furthermore, a nation will generally be unwilling to assume the collective guilt that domestic punishment of its former leaders implies. In this setting, the political infighting, both within Turkey and between the Allied Powers, often played a larger role in the criminal trials than the appreciation of the need to adhere to and uphold the standards of justice.

The preliminary stages of the trials

From the very first stages of the criminal prosecution in Turkey, the proceedings were subject to the pressures of internal Turkish politics. The enemies of the discredited Ittihad party, comprising journalists, intellectuals, civil servants, and retired military officers, were in the forefront of the campaign aimed at punishing the leaders of that party. Himself a foe of Ittihad, the Sultan encouraged that effort. Further, for most of the critical period of the trial (March 4, 1919–October 17, 1920), Damad Ferit, himself an avowed foe of Ittihad, occupied the office of Grand Vizier. In fact, the desire for retribution was at first so strong that in the first few months after the Armistice, prosecution threatened to give way to persecution. The headquarters of the Ittihad party as well as several branches were raided, the inventories impounded, and the properties of the fugitive leaders confiscated.[117] Further, at one point "ten political dignitaries" appealed to the Sultan to punish the Ittihadists by recourse to speedy justice.[118]

These efforts, however, were more than offset by the residual authority and influence of Ittihad, whose partisans and sympathizers still dominated the Civil Service, the War Office, and especially the police.[119] After temporarily receding into the background, Ittihad began to form a network of resistance cells in many wards of the Ottoman capital. Many key officials in the Interior and Justice Ministries, co-opted by Ittihad, began to obstruct the pace and direction of the trials. These officials withheld crucial documents, impeded communication with provincial authorities, delayed compliance with court orders for production and certification of secret and top secret cipher telegrams, and altogether encumbered the proceedings. In addition, they helped a host of key suspects escape.[120]

While the suspects awaited trial in the military prison, the British military authorities in charge of implementing Armistice terms issued a report that noted:

> All prisoners of whom there are 112 are allowed to walk about the prison and mix freely during the day. Except for a casual glance at their passes, individuals are not subjected to any inspection on entering the prison, and large packets are often to be seen being carried in by individuals, stated to be food, but might be anything. Women are allowed in all times during the day, and are never inspected.[121]

The privileges enjoyed by these suspects extended to the conditions of their detention. They were not subject to the close confinement and stern control ordinarily imposed upon suspects awaiting criminal proceedings. In his memoirs, one inmate relates how the Cabinet ministers were able to gather together in a large room for what the inmate sardonically labeled the prison's "Cabinet Council" sessions to discuss defense strategy. The ministers even invited Osman, the Legal Counsellor of the Interior Ministry, for consultation.[122]

The trials

Despite their seemingly good intentions, the Turkish tribunals lacked the strength for the full prosecution of those charged with carrying out the Armenian genocide. This weakness reflected the relative impotence of the postwar government. No government called upon to represent the interests of a vanquished nation can be strong; rather, it can function at best as a shock-absorber. By assigning blame and fixing punishment, the

Turkish Courts Martial were expected to alleviate the devastating domestic consequences of military defeat through "catharsis," and, at the same time, mollify the victors. They were, therefore, placed in a position which, by its very nature, tended to weaken the judicial will to adjudicate the criminal charges.[123]

Generally, no nation can adjudge impartially and condemn itself, directly or indirectly, on charges of complicity in atrocities unless it is strictly constrained to adhere to the law and the facts of the case.[124] This tendency often emerged in the course of the trials in the Turkish Courts Martial. For example, following the relatively mild Yozgat Verdict of the Turkish Military Tribunal, in which one minor official received a death sentence, the Secretary-General of the defunct Ittihad party indignantly labelled the Verdict a "self-condemnation by the Government and the Court, and a condemnation of the Turkish nation."[125] A Prime Minister of the Ankara government described the Verdict as "a concession and certification of guilt by our own government."[126]

The abortiveness of the Istanbul trials also reflected the Turks' increasingly defiant attitude toward the Allies. The sources of this defiance were only in part attributable to nationalism. To a much greater degree, they can be traced to the irresoluteness of the victorious Allies. The Allies' failure to completely occupy Turkey left the state system intact, thus implicitly recognizing Turkish sovereign rights. Further, the interminable delays in the signing of a peace treaty as well as the treaty terms providing for the surrender and trial of war criminals before Allied tribunals caused unnecessary delays, allowing suspects to disappear, witnesses to disperse, incriminating evidence to be removed or rendered inaccessible, and the immediate post-war public shock and revulsion regarding the atrocities to dissipate. The Allied Powers also neglected to insert criminal sanctions into the Armistice Convention, incorporating them instead into the terms of the Versailles and Sèvres Treaties. At times, the Powers seemed almost wilfully abandoning their power over postwar Turkey. For example, the British returned "over 100,000 prisoners of war ... to Anatolia without any condition whatever despite the fact that a state of war still exists."[127]

Addressing the same issue, British High Commissioner Thomas Hohler wrote to London, "I never contemplated that the Allies would reduce their military forces so thoroughly before they had made peace and imposed their conditions. We have acted on the reverse principle of the Japanese, whose old proverb is that the end of the fight is the right time to tie on your helmet."[128] Another British diplomat registered his dismay that "scores of thousands of Turkish prisoners of war in Egypt were being released and returned to Turkey, and it seemed strange that we made no attempt to prevent them from being at once enrolled in Mustafa Kemal's Nationalist Army to fight the Greeks in Anatolia, thus providing him with a large contingent of more or less trained soldiers.[129] The chief Turkish negotiator at the Mudros armistice talks, Captain Rauf, Turkish naval hero, is reported to have expressed the view that the Armistice terms he got were "very favorable for Turkey."[130] British High Commissioner Admiral de Robeck felt that the surest way Turkey could be pacified and made amenable to peace was "only by means of an army of occupation."[131]

The disagreements, feuds, and rivalries among the Allies further emboldened the Turks to flout the terms of Armistice. Within six months after the Armistice, the British, French, and Italians began to work at cross-purposes, often undermining each other's efforts. The French and the Italians began to support, at first secretly and then openly, the rival Kemalist government in Ankara, thereby hastening the demise of the Istanbul government and its Sultan. These diplomatic efforts crippled the retributive justice process. The British Attorney-General advising the Foreign Office in London, and indirectly the British High Commission at Istanbul, of the effects of these efforts, stated: "There is the improbability that the French and the Italian Governments would agree to participate in constituting the court provided for in article 230 of the Treaty of Sèvres."[132] The British were thus left in the lurch.

The signing of the Lausanne Peace Treaty was the Allies' final act of acquiescence to Turkey's new national policy. The principle of retributive justice, solemnly heralded during World War I, and reiterated after the end of hostilities, was lost in the aftermath of the war.

Notes to Chapter 18

1. R. Lemkin, "Genocide as a Crime Under International Law," *American Journal of International Law* 41 (1947): 150.
2. G. A. Finch, "The Genocide Convention," *American Journal of International Law* 43 (1949): 735.
3. Lemkin, "Genocide," [n. 1], 150.
4. S. Akşin, *Istanbul Hükümetleri ve Milli Mücadele* (The Istanbul Governments and the National Struggle) vol. 1 (Istanbul, 1983), 140–41; I. Danişmend, *Izahlı Osmanlı Tarihi Kronolojisi* (The Annotated Chronology of Ottoman History) vol. 4, 2d ed. (Istanbul, 1961), 457.
5. FO 371/4173/44216, folio 51 (Mar. 20, 1919, report by W. H. Deedes). In folio 50, Deedes explicitly states the official British position of non-interference in Turkey's internal affairs. In an interview with a local newspaper, Lewis Heck, U.S. Commissioner, took issue with this attitude, arguing that the Turks should try the Ittihadist culprits for justice's sake, not in expectation of milder peace terms. He then advised not to use Armenian revenge acts as an excuse to explain away the wholesale extermination of the Armenians that preceded these acts, adding that the two episodes should not be equated or confused with each other as the Armenian reprisals were a distinct and separate category. *Le Journal d'Orient*, April 12, 1919.

6. In response to this repeated claim that only the Ittihadist authorities were responsible, the U.S. Commissioner in Constantinople. Lewis Heck, in two separate ciphers to Washington disputed that claim. On January 20, 1919 he stated that the mass murder of the Armenians was "heartily approved at the time by the vast majority of the Turkish population of the country." *U. S. National Archives* (hereafter cited as R. G. only) R.G. 256. 867.00/59, p. 3 of the report. Eleven days earlier he had conveyed his view that not only top Ittihadist leaders but "the great majority of the Turkish officials in the interior are also the same officials who either actively participated in or at least condoned the massacre of the Armenians ... " p. 1 of the January 9, 1919 report. R.G.256.867.4016/12.

7. FO 608/246, folios 654, 656, cipher No. 799 A (April 19, 1919).

8 . "Ermeni Terbiyei Milliyesi" (The Armenian National Culture). *Minber*, November 9, 1918. See also A.A. Türkei 167/14, p. vi (Istanbul German Embassy review of Turkish press, based on reproduction in *Le Soir* (French language Istanbul daily) (Nov. 12, 1918).

9. See A. Yalman, *Yakın Tarihte Gördüklerim ve Işittiklerim*, vol. 1 (Istanbul, 1970), 314–15. Two days before this collective escape, two former heads of the General Directorate of Istanbul Police, Osman Bedri and Hüseyin Azmi, likewise fled but were captured and charged for travelling without valid passports. They were released shortly thereafter on account of this minor charge and fled once more. Danişmend, *Izahlı* [n. 4], 451.

10. Vakit, *Harb Kabinelerinin Isticvabı* (War Cabinet's Hearings), (Istanbul, 1933), 6, 7.

11. *Ibid.* (referring to the Special Organization). The Deputy was Fuad, who represented the Divaniye district. His motion was drafted on October 28, submitted on November 2, and entertained on November 4, 1918. He died December 14, 1918.

    Fuad was part of that group of Arab Deputies in the Ottoman Parliament which, unlike any other group, boldly pursued the task of holding high ranking officials accountable for the crimes against the Armenians; this was most evident during the Fifth Committee hearings. Fuad's motion was initially resisted by Halil (Menteşe) who was an ardent Ittihadist and at that time was Acting President of the Chamber of Deputies (During the war he held several ministerial posts but was mostly Minister of Foreign Affairs). He tried to table the motion and yielded only upon the insistent demands of Deputy Fuad. Necmeddin Sahir Silan "Ikinci Meşrutiyette Divanı Ali Hareketleri" (The High Court Venue Initiatives during the Second Constitution Era) 2d instalment. *Tarih Konuşuyor* 5, 29 (June 1966): 2472–73. The Senate, the upper chamber of the Ottoman Parliament, by coincidence or design, on November 4, 1918, likewise debated the matter of investigating and possibly prosecuting the wartime crimes. General Çürüksulu Mahmud, former Minister of Public Works, on that day submitted a respective motion, *Ibid.* instalment 3., 6, 31 (August 1966): 2568. During the course of a subsequent debate, i.e., on November 7, 1918, Mahmud proposed that the investigation of the abuses be related to "the conduct of internal affairs policy (*dahiliye siyaseti*) and governance." He was supported in this regard by Senator Reşit Akif, who referred to "certain calamities inflicted upon the children of this land." *Ibid.* instalment 8., 6, 36 (October 1966): 3011–12.

12. *Harb Kabinelerinin* [n. 10], 3–4.

13. *Ibid.*, 537.

14. *Ibid.*, 534–35.

15. *Ibid.*, 520.

16. *Ibid.*, 523.

17. M. Gökbilgin, *Milli Mücadele Başlarken* (As the National Struggle Began) vol. 1 (Ankara, 1959), 57.

18. G. Young, *Corps de Droit Ottoman, Code de Procédure Pénale* (Treatise of Ottoman Law, Code of Criminal Procedure) vol. 7 (Oxford, 1906) 235, 239.

19. FO 371/4141/49194, p. 4 (part II of extensive, six-part report of British Saloniki Force Intelligence Section, March 8, 1919).

20. R. G. 256, 867.00/59, p. 3 (U.S. Commissioner at Istanbul Lewis Hecks' January 20, 1919 report to the State Dept.).

21. Young, *Corps* [n. 18], 247.

22. Gökbilgin, *Milli* [n. 17], 15.

23. *Takvimi Vekâyi*, No. 3424. For the overall composition of the Court Martial see Akşin, *Istanbul* [n. 4], 141–42, and *Takvimi Vekâyi* Nos. 3424 and 3433.

24. *Takvimi Vekâyi*, No. 3430.
25. *Takvimi Vekâyi*, No. 3445.
26. There were two formations of the Court Martial in March 1919. (1) March 8; it was presided over by Fevzi Paşa. R.G. 256, 867.00/27, R.G. 59, 867.4011/408; *Takvimi Vekâyi*, No. 3493. (2) March 19, presided over by Nazım Paşa, *Journal D'Orient* (Istanbul), April 23, 1919; *Takvimi Vekâyi*, No. 3503.
27. *Journal D'Orient* (Istanbul), (April 15, 1919): 1.
28. *Takvimi Vekâyi*, No. 3540, May 5, 1919, p. 8.
29. *Takvimi Vekâyi*, No. 3571, June 13, 1919, p. 128.
30. Young, *Corps* [n. 18], 273.
31. *Takvimi Vekâyi*, No. 3837.
32. *Takvimi Vekâyi*, No. 3540, May 5, 1919, p. 4.
33. This denial prompted Aka Gündüz (Enis Avni), the celebrated nationalist writer, to mock them in an article imitating their defense style, "Oh alas, oh alas, oh alas, oh alas. We didn't see, we didn't know, we didn't hear" (*"Vah vah, vah vah. görmüyorduk, bilmiyorduk, işitmiyorduk"*). *Alemdar* (Istanbul), May 10, 1919. For a description of "Cabinet Council" sessions, *see* Yalman, *Yakın* [n. 9], 339–41.
34. T. Tunaya, *Türkiyede Siyasal Partiler*, vol. 3, 2nd enlarged ed. (Istanbul, 1984), 210, 281.
35. Ottoman criminal procedure codes stipulated secrecy in the trial preparations; defense counsel were therefore barred from access to the pre-trial investigatory files and from accompanying their clients to the interrogations conducted as preparatory to the trials. The discretionary powers of the presiding judge of a criminal court are set forth in the Code of Criminal Procedure articles 232–34 and address the matters of reliance on one's conscience in the quest for probative evidence, including the authority to hear witnesses whose testimony is "informational" and whose oath-taking can be dispensed with. Young, *Corps* [n. 18], 216–62. Article 269 of the same code provides for new judicial measures in case of detection of discrepancies or inconsistencies between pre-trial depositions and court testimony. *Ibid.*, 266.
36. *Le Courrier de Turquie* (Istanbul), April 30, 1919.
37. *Hadisat* (Istanbul), April 26, 1919.
38. The entire discussion of the Indictment is based on the text as published as supplement in *Takvimi Vekâyi*, No. 3540; the citations are from pp. 4–8 of that issue.
39. *Takvimi Vekâyi*, No. 3540, p. 4.
40. R.G. (L.) 59, 867.00/797 1/2; L. p. 762–66. On December 1, 1915, Morgenthau changed his language in a report to Secretary of State Lansing to use the words "the destruction of the Armenians" as a near completed fact. R.G. (L.) 59, 867.00/799 1/2; L. p. 771.
41. *Takvimi Vekâyi*, No. 3540, p. 4.
42. *Ibid.*
43. *Ibid.*, p. 7.
44. *Ibid.*, p. 6.
45. *Ibid.*, p. 5.
46. *Ibid.*
47. *Ibid.*, p. 4.
48. *Ibid.*, p. 8.
49. *Ibid.*, p. 6.
50. *Ibid.*, p. 8.
51. *Ibid.*
52. H. Morgenthau, *Ambassador Morgenthau's Story* (New York, 1918), 333.
53. *Takvimi Vekâyi*, No. 3540, p. 5.
54. *Ibid.*, p. 6.
55. *Ibid.*
56. *Ibid.*, p. 7.
57. *Ibid.*, p. 6.
58. *Ibid.*, p. 4.
59. *Ibid.*, p. 8.
60. *Takvimi Vekâyi*, No. 3771, February 9, 1919, p. 2.
61. *Ariamard*, December 12, 1918.

62. *Takvimi Vekâyi*, No. 3772, February 10, 1919, p. 5.

63. Vehib's affidavit (dated December 5, 1918) was read in its entirety at the second sitting of the Trabzon trial series (March 29, 1919). Portions of it were incorporated in (1) the Key Indictment, *Takvimi Vekâyi*, No. 3540, May 5, 1919, p. 7, within which the 12 page, handwritten document was lodged, (2) the Harput verdict, *Takvimi Vekâyi*, No. 3771, February 9 1919, p. 1 and (3) *Le Courrier de Turquie*, April 1 and 2, 1919. The copy of the full text in its original Ottoman Turkish is in the Jerusalem Armenian Patriarchate Archive, indexed under the Armenian alphabet character H (pronounced Ho, the 16th letter, and not its variant Hee, the 21st), pp. 171–182 of the "H" file. The citation used here is from page 5 of the affidavit, whose rough Armenian translation is in *Hairenik*, April 13, 1968. The details of the Court Martial set up by General Vehib are in *Ariamard*, December 10, 1918, including the text in Ottoman Turkish of the General's proclamation through which he informed, as a warning, his Third Army units of the verdict of the court and the execution of the gendarmery commander involved.

64. For a detailed discussion of the leading role of these two party leaders, see Vahakn N. Dadrian, "The Role of Turkish Physicians in the World War I Genocide of the Armenians," *Holocaust and Genocide Stud*ies, 1 (1986): 169–92.

65. *Takvimi Vekâyi*, No. 3540, pp. 4–8.

66. C. Kutay, *Celal Bayarın Yazmadığı ve Yazmayacağı Üç Devirden Hakikatler* (Facts on Three Eras About Which Celal Bayar Did Not and Will Not Write), 12 (1982) (emphasis in original). Bayar himself was a Responsible Secretary in Izmir (Smyrna), Aydın Province, and was 1950–1960 President of the Turkish Republic.

67. A. B. Kuran, *Osmanlı İmparatorluğunda ve Türkiye Cumhuriyetinde Inkilâp Hareketleri* (Revolutionary Movements in the Ottoman Empire and the Turkish Republic) (Istanbul, 1959), 479.

68. *Takvimi Vekâyi*, No. 3586, June 28, 1919, p. 164.

69. *Renaissance* (Istanbul), January 6, 1920.

70. *The Imperial Ottoman Penal Code*, J. Bucknill & H. Utidjian, trans. (Oxford, 1913). Article 13 of the original martial law provides for the application of civil penal codes whenever courts martial do not dispose over corresponding military codes. *See* A. Biliotti and A. Sedad, *Législation Ottoman depuis la rétablissement de la Constitution*, vol. 1 (Paris, 1912), 197.

71. *The Imperial Ottoman Penal Code*, [n. 70], 32.

72. *Ibid.*, p. 125.

73. *Ibid.*, p. 47.

74. *Ibid.*, p. 32.

75. A. Türkgeldi, *Görüp İşittiklerim* (The Things I Witnessed and Heard) (Ankara, 1951), 197. In an exchange with the Chief Rabbi of Ottoman Jews, Grand Vizier Izzet Paşa likewise avowed "on my word of honor that I will prosecute the accomplices, even if they are Cabinet Ministers." The Rabbi was on his way to the United States where he said "public opinion is against us on account of the deportations and massacres" and where he was supposed to create good will for Turkey. *Yakın Tarihimiz*, 2(1962):389.

76. Akşin, *Istanbul* [n. 4], 201.

77. Ottoman Constitution (Midhat), *American Journal of International of Law* 2 (supplement 1908): 367.

78. *Takvimi Vekâyi*, No. 3540, pp. 10, 11.

79. *Ibid.*, p. 13.

80. *Ibid.*, p. 12.

81. *Ibid.*, p. 11.

82. *Ibid.*, p. 14.

83. *Ibid.*, pp. 8, 9.

84. *Ibid.*, pp. 8, 14.

85. *Ibid.*, p. 8.

86. The Martial Law of August 19/September 1, 1910, article 1, reprinted in A. Biliotti and A. Sedad, *Législation* [n. 70], 483. Article 2 of the original martial law of October, 1877 specifically declares as "temporarily suspended" those provisions of the Constitution and other laws and administrative regulations that contravene martial law. *Ibid.*, 195.

87. See *Takvimi Vekâyi*, No. 3540, May 5, 1919, p. 8; *Takvimi Vekâyi*, No. 3543, May 8, 1919, p. 17.
88. *Takvimi Vekâyi*, No. 3604, pp. 217–20.
89. *Ibid.*, p. 218.
90. *Ibid.*, p. 217.
91. *Ibid.*, p. 219.
92. *Ibid.*, p. 218.
93. *Ibid.*, p. 219.
94. *Ibid.*, p. 218.
95. *Ibid.*
96. *Ibid.*
97. *Tarihi Muhakeme*, K. Sudi, ed. (Istanbul, 1919), 63.
98. *Takvimi Vekâyi* No. 3604, p. 218. This reference is to the Yozgat and Trabzon trials that preceded the trial of Ministers, *see* text accompanying note 103.
99. *Ibid.*
100. *Ibid.*
101. *Ibid.*
102. *Ibid.*, p. 219.
103. Trabzon Verdict, *Takvimi Vekâyi*, No. 3616, August 6, 1919, pp. 1–3; Yozgat, *Takvimi Vekâyi*, No. 3617, August 7, 1919, pp. 1–2; Harput, *Takvimi Vekâyi*, No. 3771, February 9, 1919, pp. 1–2; Responsible Secretaries, *Takvimi Vekâyi*, No. 3772, February 10, 1919, pp. 1–6, Erzincan, *Takvimi Vekâyi*, No. 3917, July 27, 1920, pp. 5–6. Portions of the Court Martial proceedings are embodied in *Tarihi Muhakeme* [n. 97].
104. *Takvimi Vekâyi*, No. 3617, August 7, 1919, p. 2.
105. *Ibid.*
106. *Ibid.*, p. 1.
107. *Ibid.*
108. *Takvimi Vekâyi*, No. 3616, August 6, 1919, p. 2.
109. *Ibid.*
110. *Takvimi Vekâyi*, No. 3772, February 10, 1919, p. 3.
111. Those executed were: (1) Mehmed Kemal, county executive (*kaymakam*) of Boğazlıyan, and during the massacres, Deputy District Commissioner (*mutassarrıf*) of Yozgat. *Takvimi Vekâyi*, No. 3520.

(2) Abdullah Avni, nicknamed Hayran Baba, who was in charge of the Erzincan gendarmery. He was the brother of Abdul Gani, a prominent Ittihadist and the Responsible Secretary of Edirne. *Takvimi Vekâyi*, No. 3917, July 27, 1920, pp. 5–6.

(3) Behramzade Nusret, Bayburt county executive, later District Commissioner of Ergani and subsequently of Urfa. *Takvimi Vekâyi*, No. 3924. After the debacle of the Damad Ferit regime and the ascendancy of Kemalism, the military Appeals Court overturned Nusret's July 20, 1920 verdict on January 7, 1921. *See* G. Jaeschke, *Türk Inkilâbı Tarihi Kronolojisi 1918–1923*, 95 (1939). Both Kemal and Nusret were then declared "national Martyrs" (*milli şehid*). Jaeschke, "Beiträge zur Geschichte des Kampfes der Türkei um ihre Unabhängigkeit," *N.S. Die Welt des Islams*, 5:16 6 (1958). On December 25, 1920, the Ankara regime allocated a pension for Nusret's family. *See* G. Jaeschke, *Türk*, 95. For some details on the two men subsumed under (2) and (3) above see F. R. Atay, *Çankaya,* (Istanbul, 1980), 225–26, and 228–29. Through public subscription, initiated by the newspaper *Tasviri Efkâr*, the Turkish people raised 20,000 Turkish gold pounds for Kemal's family.
112. FO 371/4174/118392, folio 267 (July 7, 1919 communication).
113. The abolition was part of a series of related political acts: (1) On April 29, 1920, a bill was introduced in the new Kemalist National Assembly in Ankara to declare the official decisions and decrees of the Sultan's Istanbul government null and void. (2) On June 7, 1920, the Ankara government enacted Law No. 7, which declared the Istanbul government, its Treaties and Agreements, invalid as of March 16, 1920, when the Allies formally occupied the city and assumed full control of it. (3) On January 3, 1921, the Kemalist Ankara Government decided to have its Independence Court supplant the Court Martial in the judgement of the crimes alleged to have occurred in the Armistice period in Yozgat (Ankara province). (4) On April 25, 1922, the last Cabinet

of the last Grand Vizier was impelled by the Kemalists to declare military Tribunals incompetent to try "nationalists," meaning adherents of Kemalism. (5) On November 6, 1922, Ankara laws were introduced in Istanbul and proclaimed to be the new laws of the land. (6) Finally, on March 31, 1923, general amnesty was announced for all those convicted by Courts Martial as well as civilian courts. Jaeschke, *Türk* [n. 111]. All six acts are described on pp. 76, 80, 95, 128, 142, and 148 respectively.

114. Most of these war criminals, however, were tracked down and executed by Armenian "avengers." These executions occurred in Germany and Russia, where all of the condemned men cited in the text had fled. Talât was assassinated in Berlin on March 15, 1921. The Grand National Assembly in Ankara reportedly praised Talât, approved of his initiative of "deportations," and allocated a pension for his family. A. Ryan, *The Last of the Dragomans* (London, 1951), 219. Dr. Şakir was assassinated in Berlin on April 17, 1922. Cemal was gunned down in Tbilissi (Tiflis) on July 21, 1922. Enver is said to have been tracked down by Agabekof, an Armenian operative of the Communist Secret Service, in the Emirate of Bukhara, and killed on August 4, 1922 during the ensuing fight. This role by Armenian Agabekof is confirmed by a Turkish author. Ihsan Ilgar, "Ermeni Meselesi" *Hayat Tarih Mecmuası* 11, 2, no. 11, (November 1, 1975): 78. Though the literature on Enver's end is imprecise, the following sources are instructive: Esad Bey, *Die Verschwörung Gegen die Welt* (Berlin, 1932); "Wie der Klassenkampf im Emirat Buchara entschieden wurde," *Frankfurter Allgemeine Zeitung* (Frankfurt), (February 6, 1980): 9; *Sovetagan Hayasdan* (Yerevan, monthly publication), (August 1984): 8.

Ten days after the execution of Şakir, Dr. Nazım, who had also taken refuge in Berlin and for a while was hiding in Batum, together with Enver, fled back to Turkey to escape a similar fate after accepting the Kemalist condition that he as well as other Ittihadists would be welcome to the fatherland if they would integrate themselves into the new regime. But Nazım, constantly denouncing Kemal and agitating against him, was charged with conspiracy in connection with the Ittihadist attempt on the life of Mustafa Kemal and was hanged in Ankara on August 26, 1926, by the order of the Independence Court. FO 371/11528/E5141. Only one of the commandos of these carefully planned and accomplished series of executions was apprehended, but the German Criminal Court acquitted the self-confessed culprit who had tracked down and assassinated ex-Grand Vizier Talât in Berlin. Commenting on this event, Robert Kempner, U.S. Deputy Chief of Counsel, Nuremberg War Crimes Trials, stated that the incidence "focused global attention on a particularly important development in international law." From the foreword of a soon-to-be published book on this trial (on file with author). For details on the assassination and trial see V. Dadrian, "The Naim-Andonian Documents on the World War One Destruction of the Ottoman Armenians—The Anatomy of a Genocide," *International Journal of Middle East Studies* 18 (1986): 359, n.113.

115. Treaty of Lausanne, 28 L.N.T.S. 12, 117 Brit. and For. St. Papers 543, reprinted in *American Journal of International Law*, 18 (Supplement 1924): 1.

116. *Ibid.*; Declaration of Amnesty is in article 1. In commenting on the failure of the feeble Allied efforts to secure a measure of justice for the Armenians at Lausanne, an author wrote: "it became a matter of the highest importance from the humanitarian standpoint that liberal provisions be made regarding the treatment of the Armenians ... as determined by the Treaty of Peace." E. Turlington, "The Settlement of Lausanne," *American Journal of International Law*, 18 (1924): 699–700. The three articles of the Lausanne Treaty Amnesty are reproduced in F. Kandemir, *Istiklâl Savaşında Bozguncular ve Casuslar* (Defeatists and Spies in the Fight for Independence) (Istanbul, 1964), 172–73.

117. M. Gökbilgin, *Milli Mücadele Başlarken*, vol. 1 (Ankara, 1959), 8–10; *Takvimi Vekâyi*, No. 3462. The respective official documents on these acts of confiscation are reprinted in Tunaya, *Türkiyede* [n. 34], vol 2, 55–59.

118. Akşin, *Istanbul* [n. 4], 151. The message was relayed on January 23, 1919.

119. A *London Times* correspondent stated that the organizational network of the Ittihad in Turkey was "almost intact." *Times* (London), January 1, 1919. American High Commissioner Heck confirms this observation in his report to the U.S. Ambassador in

Paris, complaining that "the great majority of officials [are] still members of the C.U.P. [Ittihad] organization." FO 608/342/8514 (Curzon memorandum, enclosure no. 2, April 18, 1919). Turkish author Göztepe likewise stated that the War Office, i.e. the War Ministry, was filled with Ittihadists. T.M. Göztepe, *Osmanoğullarının Son Padişahı Sultan Vahdeddin Mütareke Gayyasında* (Istanbul, 1969), 89. A French historian with personal experience in Turkey during the Armistice maintains that Turkish police were beholden to Ittihad and that the excessive legalism of the High Commissioners of the Allies in the Ottoman capital made them dependent upon the Turkish police. E. Pech, *Les alliés et la Turquie* (Paris, 1925), 25, 27.

120. The escapees included three top Party leaders heavily implicated in Armenian massacres: Trabzon's Responsible Secretary Yenibahçeli Nail, Erzurum's Delegate Filibeli Ahmed Hilmi, and one of that region's Chief of the Special Organization, Ebuhintli Câfer; they obtained documents (*vesika*) from the government to flee by ship. Masterminded by the residual leadership of the Special Organization, these ventures also involved escapes from War Ministry's Bekirağa prison by other prominent perpetrators. Among these were Sixth Army Commander Halil, Ittihad Central Committee member Küçük Talât, and former Diyarbekir province governor Dr. Mehmed Reşid. H. Ertürk, *Iki Devrin Perde Arkası* (Behind the Scenes During Two Eras) S. Tansu, ed. (Istanbul, 1957), 213, 326–27. General Halil's August 8, 1919 escape is recorded in *Takvimi Vekâyi*, No. 3731; his hiding prior to his arrest and the organization of his escape is described in Halil Paşa, *Ittihad ve Terakki'den Cumhuriyet'e: Bitmeyen Savaş* (From Ittihad to the Republic: The Unending Fight) M.T. Sorgun, ed. (Istanbul, 1972), 265, 280–82. Sultan's order to prosecute Halil is in *Takvimi Vekâyi*, No. 3480.

121. FO 371/4174 (folio 149), June 28, 1919.

122. Yalman, *Yakın* [n. 9], 339–41.

123. Adaptive justice can exert itself in the opposite direction as well. A very strong government with dictatorial powers can cause judicial sternness to transform prosecution into persecution. Wartime governments inherently possess such unlimited or near-unlimited powers. As weak as the post-war Turkish Courts Martial were, their wartime counterparts, fully propped up by the dictatorial Ittihadist regime, mustered sufficient strength to stage show trials in order to execute countless numbers of Armenians on charges of treason without regard to the elementary rules of due process and the law of evidence (most victims, of course, were simply executed). In his memoirs American Ambassador Morgenthau refers to "public hangings without trial." *Ambassador* [n. 52], 311.

124. On May 20, 1919, the British Foreign Office counselor referred in his minutes to "the incompetence of the Turkish tribunals," and to "the Gilbertian methods of the Turkish judiciary." FO 371/4173/76582, folio 380. On May 21, 1919 the British Foreign Office in a cable marked "urgent" apprised Foreign Minister Balfour in Paris that the Turkish Court Martial proceedings required "embarrassing supplementaries as to ability of Turkish authorities to ensure satisfactory results … " FO 371/4173/77213, folio 388. On May 27, 1919 a British Foreign Office expert noted on the margin of a FO document that "common to all Turkish judicial proceedings" is the habit of "beating around the bush." FO371/4173/80105, folio 419. On July 10, 1919, Tilley, the Acting Undersecretary, stated in a report to the Law Officers of the Crown that "the great majority [of the suspects] are either under remand or have been released on bail, or have been acquitted or escaped." FO 371/4174/129560, folio 430/2. On August 1, 1919, the British High Commission at Istanbul, in a historical review of the status of Turkey, informed London that "trial by the Turkish Court Martial was proving to be a farce and injurious to our own prestige and to that of the Turkish government." FO 371/4174/118377, folio 256. On September 21, 1919, British High Commissioner Vice Admiral de Robeck told Foreign Minister Curzon that the Court Martial proceedings are "in many respects unsatisfactory and chaotic; … such a dead failure that its findings cannot be held of any account at all, if it is intended to make responsibility for deportations and massacres of inter-Allied concern … it is generally thought now that little can be expected from Court Martial … " FO 371/4174/136069, folios 466, 469–70. On November 17, 1919, Vice Admiral de Robeck reiterated to Curzon that "the Turkish Court Martial … was never efficient and whose President and members are continually being changed, has become more of a farce than ever." FO

371/4174/158721, folio 524. This outcome was anticipated by the U.S. High Commissioner in the Ottoman capital, Lewis Heck, at the very start of the Courts Martial when on February 7, 1919, he sent a telegram stating, "proceedings conducted characteristically dilatory fashion and attitude of court ... showing little disposition to be severe or rapid in judgement." *U.S. National Archives.* R.G. 256, 867.00/81.

125. M. Bleda, *Imparatorluğun Çöküşü*, (The Collapse of the Empire) (Istanbul, 1979), 62.

126. *See* F. Okyar, *Üç Devirde Bir Adam* (A Man of Three Eras), 280 C. Kutay, ed., (Istanbul, 1980). This point is one that has no German parallel; as the Leipzig trials did not result in any death sentences, there was no cause for a similar reaction in Germany.

127. FO 371/6509, folio 130 (British General Harrington's cipher No. 982 to the War Office, September 14, 1921).

128. P. Helmreich, *From Paris to Sèvres* (Columbus, OH, 1974), 236.

129. R. Graves, *Storm Centers of the Near East* (Constantinople, 1933), 328.

130. B. Şimşir, *Malta Sürgünleri* (Istanbul, 1976), 18–19.

131. A. Attrep, "'A state of Wretcheness and Impotence' A British View of Istanbul and Turkey, 1919" *International Journal of Middle East Studies* 9 (1978): 6.

132. FO 371/6509. folio 29, No. 851.

Part VIII

THE PUSH BEYOND DOMESTIC GENOCIDE. THE TARGETING OF THE RUSSIAN ARMENIANS

Chapter 19

The Ittihadist Thrust against Russian Armenia

The 1917–18 collapse of the Russian army attending the Bolshevik Revolution had dramatically changed the military, political, and economic conditions surrounding the eastern provinces of Turkey and the Transcaucasus. In the period preceding the onset of the revolution the Turkish IIIrd Army (or what was left of it) had, in the course of a series of lost battles, withdrawn all the way to the area encompassing Sıvas province, thereby yielding to the Russians substantial territories in the east of Turkey. That army had thus become the Achilles heel of an empire facing imminent defeat after three years of debilitating warfare. The eruption of the Russian revolution was one of those surprises of history which served to rescue Turkey from the liabilities of an impending major disaster. More important, it also enabled that army to reorganize and to sufficiently reinvigorate itself to launch a new offensive—in violation of a temporary truce—in order to regain the lost territories and push even further east. The emergence of a vacuum in the military landscape in the wake of the collapse and dissipation of the Russian Caucasus Army on the one hand, and the revival of Ittihadist designs of panturanism on the other, were factors which combined to motivate the Turks to invade the Transcaucasus.

When executing the operations of this offensive (spring and summer 1918), the IIIrd Army which had been recast in the Caucasus Army Groups (*Kafkas Ordular Grubu*), was once more expanded and restructured to become Army Groups East (*Şark Ordular Grubu*). The Commander-in-Chief was Halil (Kut), War Minister Enver's uncle who had replaced General Vehib, the preceding IIIrd Army Commander. The new Army Groups East consisted of four sub-units.1) The IIIrd Army, commanded by General Esad, General Vehib's older brother.2) The Caucasus Islam Armies, led by 27-year-old Honorary Divisional General (*Fahri Ferik*) Nuri (Kıllıgil), War Minister Enver's brother, 3) The IXth Army, commanded by General Şevki, and 4) The VIth Army, commanded by General Ali Ihsan (Sabis); that Army was previously commanded by Halil (Kut), now in charge of the entire Army Groups East. One of the immediate targets of the new Turkish offensive were those territories in the Transcaucasus which were inhabited by Russian Armenians, territories, otherwise called Russian Armenia. The collapse of the Tsarist regime and the ensuing disintegration of the overall economy in the region, compounded by the cumulative effects of wartime hardships, had considerably enfeebled Russian Armenia economically. Moreover, the turmoil and social unrest, resulting from the advent of bolshevism and its inroads in the Caucasus, were such as to intensify the crisis. But there was another crisis the gravity of which was exceeded only by the enormity of the perils it portended for the survival of the Armenian people.

The source of this other crisis was directly connected to the wartime genocide in Turkey whose estimated 300,000 survivors, having escaped the mass murder, and having taken refuge in the contiguous area of Russian Armenia, had aggravated the overall plight of Armenia. Destitute to the utmost, they were perishing day by day in the throes of hunger and disease which were assuming epidemic proportions throughout landlocked Russian Armenia. In brief, the Armenian population of the area was in the grip of a crisis that was nothing short of being existential in nature.

This is the backdrop against which the genocidal thrust of the invasion by the Turkish armies, and their subsequent capture and occupation in the Transcaucasus of territories, largely occupied by the Armenians, must be examined and assessed. Two salient features of this military undertaking merit special attention. 1) The description below of the role in this undertaking of 1918 by the Turkish military as a lethal instrument underscores the preeminence of the Ottoman legacy of destroying the Armenian population of the empire by recourse to the functional efficiency of the military.[1] 2) The quality of the sources attesting to this role is of paramount significance as these sources are identified not with the enemies of the Turks, not with neutral observers or bystanders, but with the camp of Turkey's two political and military allies, i.e., Imperial Germany and Imperial Austria (Hungary). These sources could neither wish nor afford to falsely discredit their Turkish counterparts; if anything, it was incumbent upon them to protect rather than impugn the reputation of that partner. They felt constrained, if not compelled, however, to inform their governments otherwise. Furthermore, their "confidential" and "secret" reports were for in-house, internal purposes; they were not expected at that time to be aired in public. This aspect of the attribute of these sources alone bespeaks of the high level of authenticity and veracity of the reports in question, which additionally bear the stamp of officialness.

What follows is a constellation of relevant excerpts garnered from the reports of high-ranking German and Austrian military authorities, who at the time were stationed in *locus in quo*, as well as of a high ranking German diplomat, namely, the Foreign Minister. They all converge in their ultimate judgement that the Turkish generals commanding the Turkish occupation forces in Russian Armenia were bent on extending the genocide of Ottoman Armenians to the Russian Armenians; their verdicts are as explicit as they are consistent. In evaluating the reasons of the German military and civilian authorities of the highest order for not only exposing but unreservedly condemning the genocidal acts of their Turkish ally, the onset of a slight change in the texture of the alliance towards the end of the war needs to be borne in mind. Because of an acute disparity in their mutually incompatible designs for the Transcaucasus and the resulting rivalries especially with respect to the enormous oil reserves at Baku, the German and Turkish wartime leaders began to clash with one another. This critical fact caused the German concern for the reputation of Turkey to subside considerably, and with it their compulsion to be reticent about or to cover up the Turkish plan of annihilation of the Armenians. The experience of acute disappointment and conflict once more proved a catalyst for transforming the latent inclination to conceal to a patent urge to reveal.

German Military Testimony

Otto von Lossow, Major General, Military attaché; and, March 1916-September 1918, "German Military Plenipotentiary in Turkey"; German Representative at Batum Conference May, 1918. In Turkish military services, 1911–1914:

> The Turks have embarked upon "the total extermination of the Armenians in Transcaucasia also" (*Völlige Ausrottung der Armenier auch in Transkaukasien*).[2] "The aim of Turkish policy is, as I have always reiterated, the taking of possession of Armenian districts and the extermination of the Armenians." (*Ausrottung*).[3] "Talât's government party wants to destroy all Armenians (*alle Armenier ausrotten will*), not only in Turkey, but also outside Turkey."[4] After "completely encircling" (*völlige Abschliessung*) the remnants of the Armenian nation in Transcaucasus "The Turkish intention (*Absicht*) … to starve off the entire Armenian nation, is evident" (*liegt klar zu Tage*).[5] "On the basis of all the reports and news coming to me here in Tbilissi [Tiflis, Georgia] there hardly can be any doubt that the Turks systematically are aiming at the … extermination of the few hundred thousand Armenians whom they left alive until now." (*die Türken systematisch darauf ausgehen … auszurotten.*)[6]

Friedrich Freiherr Kress von Kressenstein. Major General, July 1914. Chief of Operations, Turkish General Headquarters; later Chief of Staff of Turkish IV, the Army in Syria and Palestine; September 1917, Commander in Chief of 8th Army, Palestine; June 1918, Chief of the German Imperial Delegation in the Caucasus:

> The Turkish policy of causing starvation is an all too obvious proof, if proof was still needed as to who is responsible for the massacre, for the Turkish resolve to destroy the Armenians [*ein zu augenfälliger Beweis für den Vernichtungswillen der Türkei gegenüber dem armenischen Element ... als dass noch Zweifel darüber bestehen konnten auf wen die Massakres zurückzuführen sind*].[7] The Turkish intention is ... quite obvious. Turkish General Esad with flimsy excuses refused relief. It is the urgent mandate of humanity to have the Central Powers exert the strongest pressure upon the Turks.[8] The Turkish policy vis a vis the Armenians is clearly outlined [*zeichnet sich klar ab*]. The Turks have by no means relinquished their intention to exterminate the Armenians [*ihre Absicht ... auszurotten*]. They merely changed their tactic. Wherever possible, the Armenians are being aroused, provoked in the hope of thereby securing a pretext for new assaults on them [*Man reizt die Armenier, wo nur irgend möglich, man provoziert sie in der Hoffnung dadurch einen Vorwand zu neuen Angriffen ... zu erhalten*].[9]

As to the scenes of deportation he witnessed while travelling with Cemal Paşa, the Commander of the IVth Army of which he was the Chief of Staff, Ambassador Metternich describes the general's state of mind from a letter he received from him that "the memories of the dreadful scenes of the Armenian horrors" will probably remain with him as long as he lives (*die schauderhaften Bilder des Armenierelends ihn wohl sein Leben lang nicht verlassen würde*).[10] In the following very comprehensive report General Kress underscores the Turkish resort to "unconscionable" methods of disinformation about the Armenians by Turkish civilian and military authorities reporting to their superiors in the Ottoman capital. He scorns the use of such clichés as "military necessity," "threat to our communication and supply lines," and "other similar pretexts," which, as he avers in that report, are being advanced in order "to justify the murder of thousands of human beings." In an appended declaration, co-signed by the Austrian diplomat in the Caucasus, Georg Freiherr von Franckenstein, Turkish generals Esad, Şevki and War Minister Enver's brother Nuri, are taken to task for spreading "distorted information" (*entstellte Meldungen*) about Russian Armenia. "The perfidy [*Hinterhaltigkeit*] of General Esad was revealed when his explanations about Armenian refugees without any danger of being slaughtered being able to return, proved false" (*unwahr*).[11]

Ernst Paraquin, Lieut. Colonel, Chief of Staff of General Halil (Kut), Commander-in-Chief of Army Groups East:

> His report on the September 15–17, 1918 Baku Massacre exposed in most inculpatory language the annihilation of the Armenians in Turkey and subsequently the massacre of Baku Armenians. For the occurrence of the latter, Paraquin specifically blamed the Turkish military commanders, particularly General Nuri, Enver's 27-year-old brother who, as the Commander-in-Chief

of the Army of Islam, together with General Halil, his uncle, had marched into Baku and occupied it. According to Paraquin, Turkish General Mürsel, Commander of the 5th Division, and in charge of Baku City Fortifications, informed him of Tatar plans to massacre the Armenians of Baku as soon as it was captured by the Turkish Army. Only after three days of unrelenting butchery did the Turkish Commander and War Minister Enver's bother, Nuri, who had been forewarned about it by Paraquin, decree Martial Law. The Turkish Command indeed allowed the Tatars this opportunity of revenge. This view was openly and repeatedly suggested [*die vielfach offen ausgesprochene Ansicht*]. "The carnage [*Gemetzel*] was foretold weeks earlier and had no relationship whatsoever with the tactical phases" of the military operations [*ohne jeden Zusammerhang mit taktischen Vorgängen*]. That carnage was confirmed by a Turkish major who upon returning from a tour of inspection on September 17, 1918, told the German Chief of Staff: "You are right. It has been terrible in the city. One cannot deny it" [*... ist es schrecklich zugegangen. Man kann es nich leugnen*]. Paraquin was eventually relieved of his post by Halil for protesting against the Baku massacre.

Lieut. Col. Ernst Paraquin after the war published a two-part article in a German newspaper in Berlin. Here is an excerpt from installment 1:

> With hypocritical indignation [*geheuchelter Entrüstung*] the Turkish government ment denies all barbarous conduct against the Armenians. The evacuation of Anatolia by the Russians furnished the desired opportunity to clear out also the Russian Armenians ... . The annihilation campaign against the Armenians proceeded ... with inexorable ruthlessness.[12]

It is most significant that Dr. Behaeddin Şakir, the head of Special Organization East, and one of the chief architects of the World War I Armenian Genocide, was acting as General Director of Police in the ranks of Halil's army which in September 1918 captured Baku, triggering the September 15–17 massacre of the city's Armenian population.[13]

Erich Ludendorf, General, Chief of Staff, German High Command 1916–1918:

> Turkey plunged into a war of murder and looting (*Mord und Beutekrieg*) in the Caucasus.[14]

Paul von Hindenburg, Generalfeldmarschall. Chief of the German High Command, (1916–1918):

> The atrocious events ... which transpired in the entire domain of the Ottoman Empire and towards the end of the war occurred also in the Armenian part of the Transcaucasus ... [they] were defined by the Turks as merely an internal affair ... .[15]

Other Accounts

Kühlmann. Foreign Minister:

> Following a high level conference in Berlin, Kühlmann issued the following report to General Headquarters and to the German Ambassador to Turkey.

"The information supplied to us by our absolutely reliable agent ... asserts that in violation of their promises the Turks systematically are pursuing their plan of annihilation of the Armenians in the Caucasus ... ." [*die Vernichtung planmässig betreiben.*][16]

Austrian Testimony

Austrian Ambassador to Germany, Hohenlohe, to Austrian Foreign Minister Burian:

According to reports, "Turkey wants to annex the Caucasus entirely and exterminate the Armenians [*ausrotten*] with all means available; massacres and bloodbaths are the order of the day."[17]

Vice Marshal Pomiankowski, the Austrian Military Attaché and Plenipotentiary in Turkey, to the Chief of the Austrian General Staff:

In such a case we would be forced not only to protect the Armenians in the Caucasus against massacre but also against hunger ... .[18]

The Political Abetment of the Military

The evidence of the instrumental role of the Turkish generals in the comprehensive destruction of the Armenians within and without Turkey raises questions about the issues of authority and authorization in this regard. It appears that the generals were at least cognizant of a general policy of annihilation against the Armenians, and they felt confident enough about this to persist in their effort, and when necessary, to assert themselves in face of obstacles or opposition. Paraquin's altercations with Halil about the barbaric atrocities being perpetrated in Baku city and Halil's defiant responses are one more indication of the near-omnipotence of these generals, enjoying the protective shield of the party. If Halil's account is to be believed, he hinted to Paraquin that if he did not stop bickering, he himself might end on the gallows, following a court martial.[19] As far as it is known, this is the only instance during the war where a high-ranking German officer, serving as chief of staff to a Turkish general, departed from established guidelines and challenged his military superior in face of an ongoing massacre against the Armenians. The threat to punish the German officer through court martial casts in relief the career of General Halil who claims to have issued the threat. By his own admissions, that career is punctuated by strong loyalties to Ittihad as a political party and by a major role in the implementation in the preceding war years of the Armenian massacres.[20] In response to a charge relayed to him by a British captain visiting him in the Bekirağa prison where he, along with other top Ittihadists, was being kept in custody for later court martial, Halil in 1919 proudly and caustically asserted, in writing, that the number of his victims included, "300,000 Armenians ... . It can be more or less, I didn't count ... ."[21] In the summer of 1918 in Yerevan, capital of Armenia, he boasted to an Armenian audience that "I have endeavored to wipe out the Armenian nation to the last individual" (*Son ferdine kadar yok etmeye çalıştığım Ermeni milleti*).[22]

It is worth noting that the wartime exterminatory activities of General Ali Ihsan (Sabis), one of the commanders of the units of the Army Groups East, more or less coincide with those of General Halil. The two were in charge of the 51st and 52nd divisions, respectively. All the Armenians attached to these units, including physicians and pharmacists, were executed cold-bloodedly. Ihsan later assumed the command, first of the 13th, and subsequently of the 4th Army Corps (47th and 48th divisions). In September 1918, when in charge of the VIth Army (2nd and 14th divisions), Ihsan through deliberate measures of exhaustion and starvation caused the expiration of tens of thousands of Armenians. German Embassy chaplain Lieutenant von Lüttichau, details his experiences and observations during an extended inspection trip in the interior of Turkey. In it he focuses on the atrocities committed by General Ali Ihsan (Sabis). "General A. Ihsan countless times and purposefully let the Germans know that he would not allow a single Armenian stay alive in his command zone." He bragged to German officers that "he had killed Armenians with his own hands" (*rühmte sich mit eigener Hand Armenier getötet zu haben*).[23] For his part the French Consul at Tabriz reported on March 8, 1919: "Ali Ihsan Paşa, formerly the Commander of the Army Corps stationed at Van, entered Tabriz at the end of June 1918 in the capacity of Commander-in-Chief of the Ottoman Forces in Azerbaijan ... . In an address to an Armenian delegation he said approximately the following: 'Let it be known that during my entry into Khoi I had the Armenians of the area massacred, without distinction of age and sex ... .' A few days later, during a reception of the Armenian Prelate Mgr. Nerces, the Paşa told him: 'I had a half a million of your coreligionists massacred. I can offer you a cup of tea.'"[24]

What emerges from this compilation is tangible evidence of not only of a legacy of genocidal role performance in the conduct of a number of Turkish generals, but also of evidence of the type of consequences associated with the condition of impunity which are described in the last part of Ch. 21. Here are two generals, with one of them having risen to the rank of Commander-in-Chief of Army Groups in the Turkish High Command, who are portrayed as having openly boasted of that role performance. This is a fact which may go a long way in explaining the repetition of genocidal massacres in Russian Armenia under the aegis of men with an outstanding record of previous acts of perpetration.

The concept of legacy not only denotes historical antecedents but it also connotes the idea of a continuum in a certain behavioral pattern by certain people. Presently, the maintenance of that pattern is intimately connected with the incidence of impunity accruing to the perpetrator. Barring a change in the equation, such as a decline in the power leverage of the perpetrator, or a drastic change in the victim's condition of vulnerability, the impulse to repeat the crime remains acute, acquiring a more or less self-sustaining potentiality.[25] As in all other comparable situations, the activation of a legacy, i.e., a critical transition from impulse to enactment, becomes a function of situational determinants involving specific contingencies.

Notes to Chapter 19

1. Vahakn N. Dadrian, "The Role of the Turkish Military in the Destruction of Ottoman Armenians: A Study in Historical Continuities" *Journal of Political and Military Sociology* 20 (Winter, 1992): 257–288.
2. German Foreign Ministry Archives. *A. A. Türkei* 183/51, A20698, May 15, 1918. His first report.
3. *A. A. Türkei* 183/51, A21877, May 23, 1918.
4. *Deutsches Zentralarchiv* (Potsdam) Bestand Reichskanzlei No. 2458/9, Blatt 202, June 3, 1918 report, p. 2.
5. *A. A. Türkei* 183/53/ A32123, July 10, 1918.
6. *A. A. Türkei* 183/53, A31345, July 11, 1918.
7. *A. A. Türkei* 158/20, A31679, July 13, 1918.
8. *Deutsches* [n. 4] Blatt 287, July 31, 1918.
9. *A. A. Türkei* 183/54, A34707, August 5, 1918.
10. *A. A. Türkei* 183/40, A36483.
11. *A. A. Türkei* 183/54, A39244, September 3, 1918.
12. The details on the Baku massacre, furnished by Paraquin, are in *A.A. Türkei* 183/54, September 26, 1918. Report to General Seeckt, Chief of Staff, Ottoman General Headquarters. The second statement on extending the genocide to Russian Armenia is in "Politik im Orient." *Berliner Tageblatt*. In two installments, January 24 and 28, 1920. Excerpt used is from January 24. A summary of the contents in synopsis form is to be found in *A.A. Türkei* 158/24, A1373.
13. Murat Çulcu, *Ermeni Entrikalarının Perde Arkası "Torlakyan Davası"* (Istanbul, 1990), 240. In confirming Şakir's role as Baku's Chief of Police in the days following "the liberation" of that city on September 15, 1918, another Türkish chronicler offers some additional comments. After stating that he lived in the Caucasus for about two and a half years and got to know the Azeri people, this author declares that of all the Turks the Azeris came in contact with, they liked most Dr. B. Şakir and his cohort Nuri Paşa, the supreme ruler in Baku at that time. Muhittin Birgen, "Bizimkiler ve Azerbaycan" (Our People and Azerbaijan) *Yakın Tarihimiz* 2 (1962):158. Given Şakir's decisive role in the conception, organization and implementation of the World War I Armenian genocide in Ottoman Turkey, his entering into Baku with the armies of the two principle commanders, Halil and Nuri, War Minister Enver's uncle and brother, respectively, indicates, if not demonstrates, Ittihad's resolve to extend the genocide beyond the borders of Turkey. Otherwise, one is prompted to ask what a Turkish physician is doing in Azerbaijan, and what qualifications such a physician has to function as police chief? The answer is, of course, to be found in the outcome of his temporary and brief performance as police chief: the ferocious massacre of the Armenian population of that city and the attendant massive plunder of the goods and possessions of the victims. (See note 20 for some details.)
14. Erich Ludendorf, *Urkunden der Obersten Heeresleitung über ihre Tätigkeit. 1916–18 (Documents of the High Command on its Activities 1916–18)*. (Berlin, 1922), 500.

15. Paul von Hindenburg. *Aus Meinem Leben.* (Leipzig, 1934), 168.
16. *A. A. Türkei* 183/51, A28533, No. 1178, June 3, 1918.
17. *Austrian Foreign Ministry Archives* (Vienna), 10 Russland/155, No. 61/P.A., May 29, 1918.
18. *Ibid.*, Kriegsarchiv, KM. Präs. 47/–I/26–1917, August 20, 1918.
19. Halil Paşa, *Ittihad ve Terakki'den Cumhuriyete: Bitmeyen Savaş* (From Ittihad to the Republic: The Unending Struggle) M. Taylan-Sorgun, ed. (Istanbul, 1972), 229.
20. Halil started his World War I career as military governor of the Ottoman capital (*merkez kumandan*). In December 1914 he was asked by War Minister Enver, whose uncle he was, to form the Fifth Expeditionary Force for the purpose of invading the Caucasus by way of Iran; the idea was to encircle and help destroy the Russian Caucasus Army, in pursuit of the Ittihadist Turanian dreams. Having disastrously failed in this endeavor, mainly because of the defeat at Dilman, which was being defended by an Armenian volunteer contingent led by the legendary hero Antranik, Halil in the summer of 1915 withdrew to the provinces of Van and Bitlis. The ensuing massacres against the heavy concentrations of Armenians in these provinces were particulary ferocious as the victims were slaughtered en masse near their towns and villages, instead of being deported. Taking over the command of the right wing of the IIIrd Army, comprising the 51st and 52nd divisions (the former Expeditionary Corps Nos. 1 and 5) and the Gendarmerie division at Van, Halil, with the active assistance of the governors of the two provinces, took the initiative in this lethal enterprise in the summer of 1915. He then commanded the 18th Army Corps in which the 51st and 52nd divisions were reconstituted. In January 1916 Halil became Commander of the VIth Army in Iraq. Finally, in the summer of 1918 he was promoted to Commander-in-Chief of the Army Groups East that marched into the Caucasus and remained there until the Armistice. Throughout this period (1916–18) Halil, with the scheming of his Chief of Staff, Lieutenant Colonel Vasfi Basri, systematically destroyed the Armenian populations of the areas falling under his control; he was especially methodical about the killing of Armenian officers and soldiers serving in his units, including those of the Russian Caucasus Army who were captured as prisoners of war.
21. Halil, *Ittihad* ... [n. 19], 274.
22. *Ibid.*, 241. Halil's genocidal activities are independently confirmed by the following sources. *German Foreign Ministry Archives. A. A Botschaft Konstantinopel*, vol. 171. No. 60. German Musul Vice-Consul Holstein's November 4, 1915 report: "A colonel in the staff of Halil [probably his chief of staff Basri. V.N.D.] told me just now that the Armenians in Musul too must be slaughtered ... Halil's troops have already perpetrated massacres in the north." German Vice-Consul Scheubner Richter's 4 December 1915 report to Berlin: "Halil's expedition to northern Iran entailed the massacre of his Armenian and Syrian battalions ... ." *A. A. Türkei* 183/45, A33457.
23. *A. A. Türkei* 183/54, A44066. pp. 12–13 of the summer 1918, 20–page, report.
24. *French Foreign Ministry Archives*, Series E. Levant 1918–1940. Arménie 4. 1919 (folios 41–42). The same quotation is in Etienne Radap, "La question arménienne reste ouverte," *Etudes* (August-September 1970): 208. According to *Renaissance* (Istanbul French-language Armistice daily), January 14, 1919, General Ihsan had 10,000 Christian labor battalion soldiers killed in the VIth Army command zone.
25. The likelihood of a repetition of the crime of genocide is recognized by an American psychologist as follows: "A society not facing up to atrocities it committed and not dealing with its own inhumanity is likely to continue or repeat such actions." Ervin Staub, *The Roots of Evil, The Origins of Genocide and Other Group Violence* (Cambridge, MA, 1989), 187.

Chapter 20

The Kemalist Thrust against Russian Armenia

The Armenian massacres had been a paramount fact of World War I, in cognizance of which the victorious Allies had publicly committed themselves to punish after the war that crime and those responsible for it. The genocidal dimensions of these massacres, compounded by the enormity of the scope of the collateral material losses, were such as to prompt the Armenians to entertain hopes for amends at the expense of vanquished Turkey. Their high expectations in this regard included the incorporation in the territories of the fledgling Armenian Republic of vast tracts of Turkish territories. These territories comprised those provinces in eastern Turkey the high-density Armenian populations of which were obliterated during the war with the goal of ending once and for all suspected or assumed Armenian aspirations to forge out of these provinces a new Armenia, and thereby reconsecrate these provinces as the hollowed birthplace of the ancient Armenian nation. Led by American President Wilson, many statesmen among the Allies, notably Lord Curzon, from Great Britain and Alexandre Millerand and Philippe Berthelot, respectively Premier and Foreign Minister of France, were favoring such a redrawing of boundaries, especially with respect to the arch-prize, the province of Erzurum. The August 10, 1920 Sèvres Treaty in fact made allowance for such an Armenia, bestriding eastern Turkey and the Caucasus; at the same time it authorized Wilson to draw the final boundaries, which he did in late November 1920, creating a vast Armenia that among other provinces and districts encompassed Erzurum, Erzincan, and the Black Sea port city of Trabzon.

This development was the very condition which the Ittihadists during the war had resorted to wholesale massacres in these regions to avert, as attested to by an Ittihadist publicist.[1] The urge to prevent the realization of this plan of an aggrandized new Armenia was one of the prime movers in the genesis, growth, and ultimate sway of the Kemalist insurgency movement. Even though that movement was largely buttressed by a sizable group of Ittihadists, civilian and military, and above all, Special Organization operatives, who were *prima facie* suspects in the matter of the wartime genocide and, therefore, Kemalism for them was both a shield and a refuge, this was only part of the picture. More significant, the top leadership of the Kemalist movement was animated with the same impulses of nationalism that drove the Ittihadist to commit genocide: the prevention by all means of the loss of the eastern provinces, considered to be part of the heartland of Turkey.

Ankara's Secret Order to "Physically Annihilate Armenia"

The Kemalist insurgency was not only initiated, organized and directed by generals, all graduates of the Turkish War Academy (the *Harbiye* Staff College), but it was also anchored on the residual army corps of the Turkish army which were about to be refurbished and recast as an army of liberation. It all began to take shape in Erzurum in eastern Turkey where General Karabekir in May 1919 established his new headquarters as Commander of the 15th Army Corps (the former IXth Army). The primary target of the offensive preparations, thus set in motion, was naturally the newly established independent Armenian Republic, which was expected to benefit from the terms of the Sèvres Peace Treaty. This treaty was more or less imposed upon the Sultan's government representing vanquished Turkey. Six weeks thereafter began the invasion of Armenia which General Karabekir was prevented from launching on three previous occasions in 1920 by the veto of his superior, Mustafa Kemal. The latter was concerned that an attack on Armenia may mean "a new Armenian massacre" (*yeniden bir Ermeni kıtalı demek olan bu hareket*), and that consequently "the entire Christian world and especially America will turn against us."[2] Having been persuaded in the meantime of the improbability of such an adverse response, he finally allowed Karabekir to proceed. Ill-equipped, ill-trained, and ill-prepared, the fledgling army of the fledgling Armenian Republic couldn't stem the tide of the invasion. When the shaky government sued for an armistice, in response Karabekir, on November 6, transmitted to the Armenians his own set of armistice terms. But Ankara's instructions obliged him to withdraw these terms, which the Armenians had accepted a day before; these instructions contained new terms that were deliberately harsh so as to preclude their acceptance. Following the anticipated rejection of these new terms by the Armenians on November 10, Karabekir resumed his military campaign in a drive to Yerevan, the capital of Armenia,[3] forcing the Armenians to sue for armistice a second time. They were now trapped in the clutches of a new conspiracy of genocide, as the recent discovery of an official document, emanating from the Foreign Affairs Minister of the Kemalist government, unmistakably revealed. In virtual replication of the genocidal designs of the previous Ittihadist regime, the document embodied a new blueprint for genocide, directed against the Russian Armenians of the Transcaucasus.

Here are the essential components of this new conspiracy. First, the ground was prepared to justify the crime through the following assertions:

> By virtue of the provisions of the Sèvres Treaty Armenia will be enabled to cut off Turkey from the East. Together with Greece she will impede Turkey's general growth. Further, being situated in the midst of a great Islamic periphery, she will never voluntarily relinquish her assigned role of a despotic gendarme, and will never try to integrate her destiny with the general conditions of Turkey and Islam.

After the enumeration of these rationales the following decision was transmitted. "Consequently, it is indispensable that Armenia be annihilated politically and physically "(*siyaseten ve maddeten ortadan kaldırmak*)." The General was further advised on the requisite methods to be employed:

> Since the attainment of this objective is subject to [the limitations of] our power and the general political situation, it is necessary to be adaptive in the implementation of the decision mentioned above [*tevfiki icraat*]. Our withdrawal from Armenia as part of a peace settlement is out of the question. Rather you will resort to a modus operandi intended to deceive the Armenians [*Ermenileri iğfal*] and fool the Europeans by an appearance of peacelovingness. In reality, however, [*fakat hakikatde*] the purpose of all this is to achieve by stages the objective [stated above] … . [I]t is required that vague and gentle-sounding words [*mübhem ve mülâyim*] be employed both in the framing and in the application of the peace settlement, while constantly maintaining an appearance of peacelovingness towards the Armenians.

The cipher ends with the exhortation that "[t]hese instructions reflect the real intent [*makasidi hakikiyesi*] of the Cabinet. They are to be treated as secret, and are meant only for your eyes."[4]

Compressed in this single, official document is a succinct portrayal of the most salient features of the established genocidal legacy that has been examined throughout the body of this work. The recurrence of the World War I Ittihadist pattern of genocide is evident, and may be outlined as follows.

1) Lethal decision making at the highest executive level of government, involving collective deliberations, crystallization of genocidal intent, authorization of exterminatory measures, and standard rationalizations to lend an appearance of legitimacy to the decision.

2) The opportunities afforded by a war, especially through reliance on the military machinery as the most convenient instrument of destruction

and as an efficient command-and-control system; an optimum mobilization of resources under a plea of national emergency; and the compelling rationale of "military necessity" as a license for radical measures.

3) Efforts to conceal the incriminating material evidence of the secret intent of annihilation. The chief reason for this recourse was the need to eliminate any basis for post-war accusations of culpability. The document advocated use of the classic stratagem, namely trapping of the victim population, and lulling them into a manufactured sense of security.

4) The use of subterfuges highlights another cardinal feature of the genocidal legacy under review here. Under "the pretext" (*vesile*) of protecting the rights of Azerbaijanis, who are related to the Turks by ethnic and religious ties, the General was advised to: militarily occupy the entire territory of Armenia; temporarily arrange the frontiers of Armenia in such a way that "under the pretext of protecting the rights of Muslim minorities there is ground for constant intervention [on our part]" (*hukuku muhafaza vesilesiyle daimi müdahaleye zemin*); and disarm the Armenians, at the same time "arming the Turks of the area little by little, toward the goal of linking up east and west in the area, and moulding Azerbaijan into an independent Turkish government through the creation of a national force structure."[5]

5) The Treaty of Sèvres which the Ottoman government signed on August 10, 1920 but failed to ratify, was mentioned in the cipher as a sore point for Turkey and her future. As with the 1878 Berlin Treaty, Sèvres began as an effort to improve the lot of the Armenians, but ended up compounding their misfortunes. However long overdue and deserved its terms might have seemed to the Armenians, its promise of restoring to the Armenians a large chunk of historic Armenia fueled extravagant Armenian hopes and irredentist aspirations. Placing too much faith in the resolve of the victorious Allies to make the treaty operational, the Armenian Republic ultimately became a victim again of the vagaries of international politics, barely two years after the end of the World War I genocide.

The genesis of the document coincides with the defeat of Damad Ferit's Cabinet representing the Sultan's government in Istanbul which had initiated the prosecution against the authors of the Armenian genocide. From that period on, the Court Martial proceedings slackened considerably, gradually disappearing. It was a period in which retributive justice within domestic law was being undermined by resurgent nationalism reacting to the devastating consequences of military defeat. The passive attitude of the victorious Allies in the face of this developing judicial fiasco was matched by their reluctance to come militarily to the rescue of imperiled Armenia. As Kazemzadeh caustically observed, "While Armenia was dying under Turkish blows the Western Powers who had made so many promises of help and assistance merely talked about her fate in the First General Assembly of the League of Nations [but] the fate of Armenia was sealed by defeat and Sovietization … ."[6] As Helmreich observed also, "None of the European states had ever intended to become heavily involved in Armenia, despite all their pious pronouncements. Now, finally faced with the necessity of making a decision, they coldly and ruthlessly pushed aside the Armenians and their newborn state."[7] In fact, the decision to destroy Armenia was made in Ankara following protracted deliberations which led to the firm conclusion that neither England nor any other Allied Power was likely to intervene on behalf of Armenia.[8]

The design of that Turkish government to deliver a final blow to the rest of the Armenian people was foiled, however, by the last-minute intervention of the 11th Red Army that was stationed nearby. By precipitously sovietizing Armenia in the wake of the Turkish military victory, the Army averted the Armenian nation's all-but-certain extinction. Notwithstanding, Soviet Armenian sources have furnished evidence of a vast scale of devastation in the area of Alexandropol (until recently Leninakan, and now renamed Gyumri, the site of the December 7, 1988 Armenian earthquake) which remained under Turkish occupation for five months until a Soviet ultimatum put an end to that occupation.

The dimensions of this miniature genocide are documented in many sources. In a telegram sent in June, 1921 to K.V. Chicherin, Soviet Foreign Affairs Minister, Alexander Miassnigian, the President of the Council of People's Commissars of Soviet Armenia, presented the following list of casualties in the wake of the withdrawal of the Turkish occupation forces from Alexandropol and environs:

> [T]he total number killed by the Turks reached 60,000, of which 30,000 were men, 15,000 women, 5,000 children, and 10,000 young girls. Of the 38,000 wounded, 20,000 were men, 10,000 women, 5,000 young girls, and 3,000 children. Some 18,000 men were carried away as prisoners. Only 2,000 have survived; the rest have died either from starvation, exposure to the elements, or by the sword.[9]

In his memoirs, Lieutenant Colonel Rawlinson, a British officer, provided a glimpse of the fate of these eighteen thousand men, most of whom were deported to Erzurum in eastern Turkey as military prisoners. The Colonel was being held captive in that city as a hostage for the purpose of trading him for Turks being detained in Malta by the British as war criminals:

> On leaving our old quarters we first saw "Armenian prisoners." Those we saw were being used as labourers (slaves would be the proper word), and accustomed as I had become to see starvation, misery, and privations of every description, yet the appearance of these men gave me, even at that time, a shock such as I had never before experienced, and a memory which will remain with me whilst life lasts. It was then midwinter, the snow everywhere lying deep, the force and temperature of the arctic wind being beyond description; yet those miserable spectres were clothed, if that word can be applied to their condition, in the rottenest and filthiest of verminous rags, through which their fleshless bones protruded in many places, so that it seemed impossible that humanity could be reduced to such extremities and live.

The Colonel concluded that the ultimate purpose was "to exterminate" the Armenians, which purpose "is, and has long been a deliberate policy of the Turkish Government."[10]

In one of the documents of the ministry of foreign affairs of the former USSR it is stated that the Armenian populations of Kars and Alexandropol have been subjected to a two-pronged campaign of extirpation, namely, through "massacre" on the one hand and starvation through "total economic ruin," on the other. The Armenians "of some tens of towns in various regions of Armenia have been put to the sword."[11] In another document, supplied by the Academy of Sciences of the former Republic of Soviet Armenia, one reads the following: "They force parents to hand over to these executioners their eight-year-old daughters and 20-to 25-year-old sons. They rape the girls and murder the young men—all this in the presence of parents. This is the way they conducted themselves in all the towns. Young girls and women up to the age of 40 are snatched away … . These towns are depopulated. The situation has no precedent; it is beyond description."[12] A clue to the magnitude and ferocity of the destruction is provided in a document from the central archives of the former Armenian SSR which reveals that "*çetes* and "irregulars," which to a large extent consisted of convicts released from the prisons, were involved in the task of destruction. "In the Olti district" alone there were "close to 1000" such "irregulars," and in the Bartus and Olti districts alone there were engaged "4,500 regular soldiers and 3,000 to 3,500 irregulars."[13] The relentlessness of the pace of human and material destruction was such that A.A. Bekzadian, the Foreign Minister of the infant republic of Soviet Armenia, felt compelled to dispense with the farcical avowals of sentiments of "brotherhood" both sides, the Kemalists and the Bolsheviks were indulging in, and issue three strongly worded protest notes to Ankara. In them he accused the Turks of pursuing "the old policy of implacable hostility toward Armenia" as a result of which, he declared, Turkish army is devastating the land, where "violence and murder" as well as "organzied plunder and real carnage" have taken "a general character."[14] According to the 1961 edition of the *Soviet Encyclopedia of History*, these Armenian losses are summed up as follows:

> on the basis of incomplete data the number of victims in just the areas occupied by the Turks, as a result of the Turco-Armenian war, was close to 198,000 lives, [and] the value of the properties destroyed and appropriated by the Turks is estimated at eighteen million gold rubles.[15]

The Reengagement of the Old Ittihadist Chieftains

The plan to destroy Russian Armenia emerged from the interplay of a number of factors animating the Kemalist insurgency movement in the wake of the defeat of Turkey in October 1918. The acts of vengeance by the Armenian volunteer bands, however limited in scope, in some respects were severe enough to strike terror in the hearts of multitudes of Turks still living in the theaters of war in the eastern provinces. These "avengers" were remnants of the contingents of Armenian troops which were made part of the Russian Caucasus army at the start of the war; especially involved were hundreds of Turkish Armenians who upon their re-entry into Turkey, found their villages and homes ruined, and whose families had simply vanished. Another factor was the emergence of the Armenian Republic as a claimant at the Paris Peace Conference, which in so many ways had signaled a willingness to accommodate Armenian territorial claims put forth against vanquished Turkey. But from the point of view of energizing the Kemalist insurgency movement and providing it the organizational nucleus, a far more important factor needs to be taken into account. The reference is, of course, to the residual leaders of the Special Organization that had played a pivotal role in the wartime campaign of extermination against the Armenian people. As will be seen below, the massacres, pillages, and the rapes en masse perpetrated in connection with the Fall 1920 invasion of Armenia by General Karabekir's Eastern Army, i.e., the 15th Army Corps, was largely the work of Special Organization units, led by many of the wartime chieftains of that organization who somehow managed to insinuate themselves in the Kemalist insurgency movement under a new banner of exigent patriotism.

Their solemn assurances notwithstanding, their motives for joining the Kemalist movement were not free from impulses of self-preservation, to be achieved through the refuge and shield which that movement was destined to provide them. The fact is that several of these leaders were "fugitives of justice." The Sultan's government at Constantinople through the agency of the Special Court Martial had issued arrest warrants against them; they were to be prosecuted on charges of complicity in the crimes associated with "Armenian deportations and massacres" (*tehcir ve taktil*). There are ample indications that the invasion of Armenia was envisaged not only as a military campaign but also as a political undertaking, with the intent to deliver the *coup de grâce* to the existence of the remnants of the Armenian nation. Equally important, there are also indications that the invasion was essentially masterminded by these operatives of the Special Organization, especially by Eyublu "Deli" Halit (Karsıalan), one of the foremost destroyers of the Armenian population of eastern Turkey. He was a former Special Organization chieftain, had practically no schooling whatsoever,[16] and he was made Commander of the 9th Division, one of the four divisions of the Eastern Army that invaded Armenia. According to one knowledgeable source about that invasion, Halit was one of those organizers of the invasion whose talents were more responsible for the success of that invasion than those of Karabekir, the Commander-in-Chief.[17]

The willingness of Mustafa Kemal and some members of his coterie to embrace these former Special Organization operatives is a phenomenon that is best explained in terms of a symbiosis. Both sides needed each other, and hence, used each other in the name of patriotism, with Kemal being more circumspect lest his open avowal of wanting to dissociate himself and his movement from former Ittihadists might be belied. Moreover, there was the problem of the ballast of old loyalties. In consideration of this fact, Kemal was willing to avail himself of old Ittihadists up to a point, and under the strict condition that they make a choice between him and such erstwhile Ittihadist leaders as Enver and Talât—in terms of a binding and exclusive loyalty. For this reason alone many collaborators in the incipient stages of the Kemalist movement were treated with a degree of suspicion as potential Trojan horses. Deli Halit and Colonel Seyfi (Düzgören), the chief of Department II (Intelligence) at the Ottoman General Headquarters, were shuffled around on account of their former ties to Enver.[18]

Despite these Kemalist anxieties, however, the symbiotic relationship, which was sustained, served its purpose for the duration of the insurgency and beyond it. At the level of verbal and moral support, the symbiosis even extended to the pillars of the Special Organization who at the same time were the principal leaders of Ittihad, namely, Talât, Enver, and Dr. Behaeddin Şakir. These men by personal letters encouraged Mustafa Kemal and Kâzım Karabekir in their campaign to rescue Turkey from the perils of the military defeat it suffered at the end of the World War I.

The Proddings of the Top Ittihadist Leaders

More than anyone else, it was General Karabekir who relentlessly pushed for a military showdown with Armenia for which he had been preparing since his arrival in Erzurum on March 13, 1919. Shortly thereafter, i.e., on April 3, the existing 9th Army of General Yakub Şevki was abolished and reconstituted as the 15th Army Corps in which were incorporated the 3d, 9th and 11th Caucasian and 12th divisions. The provinces of Trabzon, Erzurum and Van comprised the military zone that was subject to the authority of the 15th Army Corps, which was headquartered in Erzurum. After four insistent requests within the space of six months in 1920 for permission to attack and invade Armenia Karabekir finally received from Ankara the permission and on September 28 the invasion was launched without a formal declaration of war. Within two months Armenia was crushed and was forced to sign the Alexandropol (Gümrü) peace treaty. This initiative was tacitly supported by the Ministry of War of the Sultan's regular government in the Ottoman capital, some of whose top staff

officers were secretly consorting with the generals of the Kemalist movement. It was Ankara's first external military venture and as such it served
as a crucible of the Kemalist defiance against the victorious Allies who
had embraced the cause of Armenia. This notwithstanding, three top Ittihadists, and foremost Special Organization leaders at the same time, who
had fled from Turkey at the end of the war, sent three separate letters urging General Karabekir and the Kemalists to proceed against Armenia,
without hesitation and without further delay.

The first two letters were sent from Berlin by Talât and Enver sometime in the spring of 1920. After stating that Armenia was vulnerable as
no one was likely to come to its aid, Talât urged, "My dearest Karabekir,
if your military preparations are complete, begin your attack."[19] Shortly
thereafter the Turkish general received a second letter written by Enver
who at that time was staying as a guest in Talât's home. After explaining
how through the medium of their Patriarch he, Enver, had warned the
Armenians during the war to behave themselves, he likewise urged, "My
dearest [*azizim*] Karabekir, I have given this explanation so that your
conscience is in no way burdened with any torment in the course of the
military operation you are to embark upon in order to preserve the
integrity of the country. Longing for the news of your victory ... . "[20] The
third letter, bearing the date of June 4, 1920, and sent from Moscow, is
written by Dr. Behaeddin Şakir. One of the persons, to whom it is
addressed, is his former friend Colonel Rüştü, the Commander of Trabzon's 3rd division. In the military campaign against Armenia, Rüştü was
promoted to the position of Deputy Commander of the 15th Army Corps
with duties at the Sarıkamış sector of the front and following the capture
of the fortress of Kars he became the commander of that fortress. The
other person to whom the letter was addressed was Filibeli Hilmi, a notorious Ittihadist fedayi and wartime deputy director of Special Organization East, serving directly under Şakir. At the time Hilmi was a deputy in
the Kemalist National Assembly, representing Ardahan; he was agitating for the return to Turkey of former War Minister Enver and Enver's
cohorts to reclaim Ittihad's control in war-torn Turkey.[21] Like the other
two Ittihadist leaders, Şakir was urging the Kemalists to proceed "with
resoluteness and severity" (*azim ve şiddetle*), otherwise, "nothing can be
achieved." Equally significant, he was pressing the point that there was
absolutely no chance that the Allies would intervene inasmuch as they
were feuding among themselves, with France and Italy opposing England's eastern policy, and America completely withdrawing. "Our leadership in Berlin is entirely in touch with the forces in the interior of the
country."[22] In still another communication, his second letter to Karabekir,
Enver on September 7, 1920 from Baku chided Karabekir for not having
launched the attack against Armenia sooner. "You shouldn't have allowed
Armenia to gather strength."[23]

The Cooperation of the Sultan's Government

Mustafa Kemal had barely arrived in Samsun as Inspector General of the IXth Ottoman army, thus still a member of the armed forces identified with the Sultan's government, when he urged his government to bolster the 15th Army Corps against the eventuality of an assault by Armenian military forces. In his May 24, 1919 telegram to the head of the Turkish General Staff, Arabkirli Cevad Paşa (Çobanlı), he expressed concern that the eastern provinces may be in jeopardy and that the Armenians may be aided in their territorial claims by the British in the same way as the Greeks who at that time had landed in Smyrna (Izmir). Cevad and his two deputies, Kâzım and Basri, the same day jointly appealed to the prime minister for permission to undertake appropriate measures.[24] On May 29 and 30, 1919, Mustafa Kemal notified Karabekir in the same manner, adding in the latter communication the assurance that the Cabinet in Istanbul decided to "supply secret funds" (*tahsisatı mestureden para*) to conduct intelligence operations in the area.[25] Mustafa Kemal on June 5 again warned his superiors in Istanbul of Greek-Armenian designs on Turkey. Responding to his first warning, Mustafa Sabri, the Şeyhulislam and at the same time the deputy prime minister, on June 9 authorized the adoption of new security measures, including the strengthening of the 15th Army Corps in Erzurum. Thereupon, the War Ministry on June 11 sent a seven-point order to the Commander of the 15th Army Corps. Point five provides for "the adoption of all initial measures, without arousing the suspicion of the outside world." Point six advises that "the preventive and security measures as well as the requisite preparations be launched in such a way that they deflect attention from the real purpose [*başka sebeplere istinat*]; they should be undertaken with utmost secrecy [*gayet gizli*]."[26] The outlines of a covert order to prepare for a preemptive strike against Armenia are discernible in this communication from the military authorities in Istanbul.

Karabekir. The Foe of Armenia and the Patron of Azerbaijan

The role of this Turkish general in galvanizing the Turkish population in the eastern provinces, especially the remnants of the former IXth Army, for an energetic military action against Armenia was crucial. He made ample use of his intimate knowledge of the conditions of the area and of the people involved. More important, he was the victorious commander of the First Caucasian Army Corps, which was part of General Vehib's Army, and which had marched into Armenia in the summer of 1918. He was confident that he could once more overwhelm Armenia with the armed forces at his disposal. Furthermore, Karabekir at that time was subject to the authority of the Ministry of War in Istanbul and was, therefore, an agent of the Sultan's government.

In his massive volume on the Turkish War of Independence, Karabekir reiterates again and again the theme that Armenia is both a threat and an obstacle for Turkey's paramount need to establish contiguous frontiers with Azerbaijan and other Turkic countries in the Caucasus. (*Kafkaslarda ebediyen yerleşmek lâzımdır*). He berates Halil Kut, the Commander of Army Groups East at the time, for hindering his plan to capture Zankezour at the end of World War I and to establish the link with Azerbaijan. That goal could have been accomplished so very easily, he claims. "I had my headquarters in Nakhitchevan ... and the act of disallowing my plans for Zankezour was a political and military crime." Karabekir further believed that Nakhitchevan should be in Turkish hands, as an inseparable part of the bridge to the east.[27] By the same token Karabekir described Nakhitchevan as "an entirely pure Turkish land" (*kâmilen öz Türk*), and as a corridor to Azerbaijan.[28] Evidently, Halil himself was trying to capture Zankezour in 1920 for which purpose he was seeking from Karabekir an auxiliary force of 2,000 men, but the latter felt that under the conditions then prevailing that job should be left to the Azeris, even though "I am not convinced at all that they [the Azeris] are capable of achieving any positive results."[29] For his part Halil Kut in April 1920 informed Karabekir from his military command post in Karabagh that his "soldiers are intent on liquidating [*temizledikten*] the Armenians of Karabagh ... . The people and soldiers here are eagerly awaiting the crossing of the borders by the Ottoman armies so as to achieve this goal in a short period of time."[30] This attitude was entirely in line with the thinking of Karabekir who on April 28, 1920 told the commander of the 3rd division of his Army Corps that "the aim of all Turks is to unite with the Turkic brothers. History is affording us today the last opportunity. In order for the Islamic world not to be forever fragmented it is necessary that the campaign against Karabagh be not allowed to abate. As a matter of fact drive the point home in Azeri circles that that campaign should be pursued with greater terror and severity (*daha azim ve şiddetle*). Impress upon them the point also that the Armenians should be kept busy until such time when we are ready to launch our own campaign."[31]

The most dominant theme punctuating Karabekir's volume relative to his designs against Armenia is his pledge to destroy Armenia in fulfilment of what he considered to be a national imperative. Describing the continued existence of Armenia as "a curse for us" (*belâ*),[32] Karabekir in the May 1919 to August 1920 period at least 12 times vowed to destroy Armenia using such terms as "crush" (*ezmek*), "finish off" (*bitireceğiz*) "trample down" (*çignememize*), "ruination" (*mahv*) "expire under the heel of the Turk" (*can vereceksiniz*), "annihilate" (*imha*).[33]

The Reactivation of the Leadership of the Wartime Special Organization

In preparing the attack on Armenia, Karabekir undertook to incorporate in the organization of his 15th Army Corps, which eventually was renamed the Eastern Army, several leaders of the wartime Special Organization, some of whom had done staff work, developing tactical plans and administering the logistical parts of the mission of that organization. Chief among these was Colonel Seyfi, who was the head of Department II in the War Office, and as such played a pivotal role in the organization of the genocide. Seyfi had been arrested in 1919 for his complicity in the Armenian deportations and massacres but through his connections to the Ministry of War was set free subsequently. Following the formal occupation of Istanbul by the British in March 1920, he fled and joined the Kemalists in Anatolia. On May 6, 1920 Karabekir informed the Presidium of the Grand National Assembly in Ankara that he had appointed Seyfi to the post of Chief of Department II, Intelligence, at his headquarters in Erzurum; Seyfi was to direct undercover activities, including propaganda, in connection with the projected invasion of Armenia.[34]

The Return of the Special Organization Field Officers

General Karabekir's plan to invade Armenia was a welcome opportunity for a host of people seeking relief at two interrelated levels. One of these was, as noted above, escape from the clutches of criminal prosecution through court martial, set up by successive Ottoman governments in the aftermath of the war, to punish the authors of the Armenian Genocide. The other was the readiness to effect that escape through a new engagement against Armenians within the framework of a military operation which had a new patriotic tag but offered the same old opportunities of Armenian massacres and attendant plunders implicit in anticipated military victories and conquest. Practically all of them were part of the wartime Special Organization leadership, in charge of the actual killing operations in the eastern provinces of Turkey.

Foremost among these were three high ranking Special Organization leaders namely Halil Paşa, Yenibahçeli Nail, and Filibeli Hilmi who promptly accommodated Karabekir and joined his command organization.[35] All three were military men, with the last two having resigned from the military to carry out Ittihad's secret and clandestine schemes. All three had distinguished themselves during the war as efficient administrators of the genocidal massacres against the Armenians. Nail was in charge of Trabzon, and Hilmi of the Erzurum province massacres, while Halil annihilated the Armenians of Bitlis province, as well as those serving as soldiers and officers in the army contingents under his command. No data is available about their specific roles in the invasion and subsequent occupation of Armenian territories, except to observe that, after a while, two of them, Halil and Nail, transferred their hostile activities to Azeri bases in the Transcaucasus. However, on three other Special Organization operatives there is sufficient data to briefly sketch their roles. They are Eyublu "Deli" Halit (Karsıalan), Ebuhintli Câfer and Topal Osman; Karabekir himself described these men as "swashbucklers who during the Ittihad era enriched themselves by engaging in brigandage" (*çetecilik*) and are now claiming to be part of the national liberation struggle.[36]

"Deli" Halit (Karsıalan)

Halit was a close friend of Dr. Nazım, one of the co-founders of that arm of the Special Organization whose mission it was to liquidate the provincial Armenian population. During World War I he served as a Special Organization officer; in the spring of 1915 he, as a major, was in charge of the Artvin contingent,[37] and in the spring of 1916 he was in command of the 1st and 2nd Regiments of the Special Organization which comprised the Çoruh Contingent (*Müfreze*).[38] Several Turkish authors point out that there was a warrant for his arrest which was issued by the Sultan's government on account of his complicity in "Armenian massacres."[39] Historian Avcıoğlu likewise indicates that Mustafa Kemal tried to snatch Halit from Karabekir's grip and use him for his own needs but that Halit for a while remained in hiding in Bayburt because of his involvement, "as a Special Organization leader," in the atrocities against the Armenians;[40] according to Kansu, he was also in hiding in Trabzon.[41]

Halit's involvement in brigand-type activities in connection with Karabekir's invasion of Armenia is even more exposed in relevant accounts. In order to understand this type of involvement it is necessary to understand the force structure of Karabekir's army of invasion. It had three components: the regular army units (3rd, 9th, 11th, and 12th divisions); the auxiliary forces, involving two regiments and three companies about 5,000 men; and the irregulars comprising several brigades, a few independent regiments and contingents from the Kurdish Sadkan, Hatkan, and Keçeran tribes, altogether, 4–5,000 armed men, some on foot, some on horses.[42] The irregulars are, as a rule, subsumed under the category "milis," i.e., home guard or militia, which during World War I was coterminous with brigands who were enrolled in the Special Organization. As his biographer indicates, Yakub Cemil, for example, entered the ranks of the Special Organization as a "milis" commander,[43] having at his disposal 2,000 regimental men at the time he was engaged in the extermination of the Armenians in the eastern provinces of Turkey during World War I. And Halit was a close cohort of Yakub Cemil[44] during these operations.

General Karabekir assigned Halit to special duties involving the conduct of military actions against Armenia and Armenians. He was not only the Commander of the 9th division but, more important, "Halit gathered together brigands [*çetes*] and reorganized them into 'milis detachments' [*milis müfreze*]; they were attached to the regular army units. When ordering the execution of an Armenian prisoner, he would use the euphemism 'send him to school.'"[45] In organizing the annihilation of the Armenians during the military operations Halit among other brigand chiefs, who were notorious for their efficiency in mass murder, engaged "Mehmed Sungur who had massacred many Armenians and who joined Halit in the capture of Kars."[46]

Two points emerge here as undisputed facts as attested by Turkish historians. 1) Halit, the commander of the 9th division during the invasion of Armenia (at the outset when the 15th Army Corps was being reorganized he was commander of the 3rd division) was entrusted with the task of "organizing brigands."[47] 2) The purpose of this arrangement was to employ them "against the Armenians."[48]

Ebuhintli Câfer

He was active in the organization and implementation of the massacre against the Armenians of Erzurum province, by virtue of which "he amassed considerable wealth." He was "a culpable one on the Armenian matter" (*Ermeni suçlusu*),[49] with strong ties to Halit and Mustafa Kemal.[50]

Topal Osman

Like Halit and Câfer, discussed above, Osman too was on the list of those former Special Organization brigands whose apprehension was being sought by the Turkish Court Martial in Istanbul. The charge pending against him, as against all the others, was crimes arising out of his involvement in the operations of "deportation and massacre" (*tehcir ve taktil*); he was, therefore, a fugitive of justice.[51] As noted above, Osman was a Special Organization man during World War I; had the rank of Milis colonel in command of a Special Organization contingent comprising 150 convicts, recruited from Trabzon prison, and some 100 "volunteers" recruited from Giresun.[52]

Following his execution by the Kemalists (in March 1923 he was decapitated and hanged in front of the Turkish parliament after he was trapped and killed in a house from which vantage ground he fought off Kemal's security forces; these forces were trying to arrest him for the murder of Ali Şükrü, Trabzon's deputy in the Turkish parliament) a Turkish newspaper called him "an ordinary criminal."[53] Avcıoğlu declared that he would have been prosecuted for the "atrocities and evil deeds" he committed against the Armenians.[54]

However, the Kemalists, especially Mustafa Kemal, were appreciative of his potential as a fearless fighter, even though they knew of his proneness to plunder and rob. In one of his reports to the Sultan's government, at a time when he was still Inspector of the IXth Army, Kemal stated that "the brigand group of Topal Osman, who had escaped in order to avoid arrest for his involvement in [Armenian] deportations, is important … ."[55] He later ended up becoming the commander of Mustafa Kemal's personal security detail. Unable to read or write, and crippled by his right leg, hence his name *topal* (lame), Osman too played a role in the conquest and decimation of the Armenian populations of Kars and beyond. According to the biographer of Osman, the latter's Gieresun contingent of *çetes* "for four months served under the authority and command of Karabekir in his fight against the Armenians." Osman and his *çetes* were slated to join the western forces in the Kemalist war of independence but were "diverted to Kars as needed."[56] Another Turkish author refers to a "Samsun battalion of 1,000 volunteers" being sent to Kars for the same purpose.[57]

Küçük Kâzım

Another Special Organization *fedayi* ("self-sacrificing") officer, Kâzım, not to be confused with two other Kâzıms, Özalp and Dirik, was a gendarmery major; at the same time he was Ittihad's Responsible Secretary at Muş in Bitlis province. He was "thoroughly" involved in the Armenian deportation and massacres, was one of those "Ittihadist villains" (*Ittihatcı suçlular*) and, therefore, "his throat was in peril" (*kellesi tehlikede*).[58] Like Halit and Câfer, he too returned to his old redoubt, Erzurum, and ingratiated himself with the Kemalists. Küçük Kâzım played a major role in the destruction of the Armenian population of Muş and Bitlis as a result of which his detachment was dubbed as "the butcher battalion" (*kasab taburu*).[59]

Nuri Paşa's Azeri Regiment

After a number of clashes with the units of the Bolshevik Red Army in Azerbaijan, Nuri in June 1920 fled to Erzurum through Iran. He took with him his 2,000-man strong Azeri Regiment and joined Karabekir's forces for the invasion of Armenia.[60] On July 31, 1920 a contingent of Azerbaijan's Tatarski regiment arrived at Karabekir's headquarters, as did another infantry detachment join his Army Corps at Horasan. As Karabekir announced, "I will be utilizing these in my invasion of Armenia."[61]

Notes to Chapter 20

1. Speaking of "the deportations," that publicist wrote:

   "But for certain influential Turkish politicians they [the deportations] meant the extermination of the Armenian minority in Turkey with the idea of bringing about racial homogeneity in Asia Minor. Other politicians accepted this point of view, while others again took the opposite side, with varying degrees of consistence. Those who put forward the policy of general extermination were said to take this stand: 'A dense Armenian population, in the Eastern Provinces, has proved to be a danger to the very existence of Turkey. We are acting as instruments to remove this danger. We know that, successful or not successful, we shall be universally despised and condemned.'"

   Ahmed Emin (Yalman), *Turkey in the World War* (New Haven, CT, 1930), 220. Another Ittihadist, who later became a life-long confidant of the founder of the Republic of Turkey, Mustafa Kemal (Atatürk), likewise wrote,

   "Şakir was bent on eliminating the Armenian nation in order to prevent the formation of a future Armenia ... Had the Armenians remained concentrated in the East, there is no doubt that in 1918 at the time of the Armistice they undoubtedly immediately would have created an Armenia ... Genocide is one of the gravest crimes against humanity. ... I don't believe in the right of retaliation" (alluding to Turkish genocidal killings as reprisals against the Armenians).

   Falih Rıfkı (Atay) *Dünya*, December 17, 1967. Atay's weekly column *Pazar Konuşması* (Sunday talk). Writing on the formation and missions of the Special Organization, the top-secret wartime Ittihadist outfit in charge of the killing fields in the interior of Turkey, an American author for his part singled out one of those missions, which was, to "thwart any Russian-Armenian plans for an independent Armenia carved out of Ottoman Turkey." Philip H. Stoddard, *The Ottoman Government and the Arabs, 1911 to 1918: A Preliminary Study of the Teşkilâtı Mahsusa.* (Ann Arbor, MI, 1963), 56.

2. Kâzım Karabekir, *Istiklâl Harbimiz* (Our War of Independence) (Istanbul, 1969), 663, May 6, 1920 cipher.

3. K. Lazian, *Haiasdan Yev Hai Tadu Usd Tashnakirneru* (Armenia and the Armenian Question According to Treaties) (Cairo, 1942), 191–202. *See also* FO406/44/E15522. Colonel Stokes to Curzon.

4. Buried in a 1200-page tome, the document consists of a cipher telegram, dated November 8, 1920, sent by Ahmet Muhtar, then Ankara's Foreign Affairs Minister, to General Kâzım Karabekir. Karabekir was the Commander in Chief of the Eastern Front Army, and the compiler of a volume documenting the military campaign of the insurgent Kemalist movement. The first phase of that military campaign involved the invasion in September, 1920 of Armenia which, since May, 1918, had acquired the status of a free and independent Republic. The inexperienced Armenian army, was unable to muster any substantial resistance. The set of instructions that comprise the blueprint for a new cycle of genocide were inserted in the cipher telegram which was sent Karabekir at the start of negotiations for an armistice. For Ankara's secret order to annihilate Armenia, see K. Karabekir, *Istiklal* [n. 2], 844–45 (2d ed. 1969). In the 1960 1st ed. the same cipher is on p. 961.

   Precisely why this document was included in the book is unclear. It is conceivable that Karabekir was simply trying to be meticulous by making his documentary compilation as complete as possible without paying too much attention to the myriad details. It is most noteworthy that as far as it is known the document in question appears nowhere else, and that until now no one seems to have tried to assess its inordinate significance.

5. Karabekir, *Istiklâl Harbimiz* [n. 2], 845. The kinship ties between the Turks and the Azeris, their "cousins" in Soviet Transcaucasus, are reflected in the transfer of the Turko-Armenian conflict to the domain of Armeno-Azeri relations. The current flare-up of hostility between these two peoples within the former Soviet Union, highlighted by the February, 1988 massacres of the Armenians in the Azerbaijani city of Sumgait, has jolted the Armenians into rediscovering the perils of their geopolitical vulnerabilities. The ferocity and heinous methods employed in the course of the massacre, and the inability of the Soviet security forces to prevent the carnage, were agonizing enough to

resuscitate in the Armenian psyche the memories of the World War I genocide, and most particularly, the sense of total abandonment and helplessness. Called "pogroms" by Soviet Deputy Procuror-General Alexander Katusov, *Bakinski Rabotichi* (Baku daily), March 12, 1988, the outbreak was exacerbated by the Azeris who "carried posters of Khomeini of Iran to indicate that they considered the dispute a matter of Islamic pride and solidarity." *N.Y. Times*, January 13, 1989. Other demonstrators in Baku carried Turkish flags. *Moscow News*, November 30, 1988. The painfulness of the episode was described by Times correspondent Keller as follows:

> Like the Israelis, the Armenians are united by a vivid sense of victimization, stemming from the 1915 Turkish massacre of 1.5 million Armenians. Armenians are brought up on this story of genocide, and have a feeling of being surrounded ... by the Islamic Azerbaijan, Iran and Turkey. This was reinforced in February by an anti-Armenian pogrom in the Azerbaijani city of Sumgait ... .

N.Y. Times (Sept. 11, 1988): S E, p. 3. The linkage of enmity against Armenia to the Turkish perception of Armenia as a geographical obstruction to Turkey's direct access to other Turkish peoples in the Caucasus, and Turkey's resort to genocide as a device for removing that obstruction, were underlined by a noted expert on Russia and Panturkism. "The massacre in 1914–1916 of one and a half million Armenians was largely conditioned by the desire of the Young Turks to eliminate the Armenian obstacle which separated Ottoman Turks from the Turks of Azerbaijan, and to prepare the way for the territorial unification of the 'Oguz,' or southeastern group." S. Zenkovsky, *Pan-Turkism and Islam in Russia*, (Cambridge, MA, 1967), 111.

6. F. Kazemzadeh, *The Struggle for Transcaucasia (1917–1921)* (New York, 1951), 292.

7. Paul C. Helmreich, *From Paris to Sèvres. The Partition of the Ottoman Empire at the Peace Conference of 1919–1920.* (Columbus, OH, 1974), 295–96.

8. K. Karabekir, *Istiklal Harbimizin Esasları* (The Essential components of our War of Independence) (Istanbul, 1951), 32, 35.

9. E. Sarkisian and R. Sahakian, *Vital Issues in Modern Armenian History*, (Watertown, MA, 1965), 55–56 (E. Chrakian, transl.). The reference to the Soviet ultimatum, which ended the five-month Turkish occupation of the city, is on page 70.

10. A. Rawlinson, *Adventures in the Near East 1918–1922*, (London, 1923), 307, 335. See also FO371/7877 p. 7 (folio 148) (February 1922). Another source describes the carnage in Kars following its capture when "for two full weeks the peaceful civil population of that city and the surrounding town was subjected to massacres. Sarkisian & Sahakian, *Vital* [n. 9], 54, 55–56.

11. Sarkisian and Sahakian, *Vital Issues* [n. 9], 54–5.

12. *Hoktemperian Sotzialisdagan Medz Revolutzian Yev Sovetagan Ishkhanoutian Haghtanagu Haiasdanum* (The Great Socialist October Revolution and the Victory of the Soviet Regime in Armenia) (Yerevan, 1960), 447–48.

13. *Haigagan SSR Bedagan Gentronagan Badmagan Archiv* (Armenian SSR Historical Archives), series 200, list 1, file 867, no. 19.

14. A. L. Zapantis, *Greek-Soviet Relations, 1917–1941* (Boulder, CO, 1982), 72, 73. The protest notes were issued on November 29, December 10, 1920, and January 19, 1921.

15. *Sovetskaya Istoricheskaya Enciklopediya*, vol. 1 (Moscow, 1961), 748.

16. Celal Bayar, *Ben de Yazdım* (I Too Have Written) vol. 6, (Istanbul, 1968), 1893 n. 2. As Bayar put it, "*tahsili yok denecek kadar azdı.*" But, this may be a different Halit.

17. The source is Recep Zühtü. He is quoted in Nurşen Mazıcı, *Belgelerle Atatürk Döneminde Muhalefet (1919–1926)* (Istanbul, 1984), 48–9.

18. Kâzım Karabekir, *Istiklâl Harbimizde Enver Paşa ve Ittihat Terakki Erkânı* (The Positions of Enver Paşa and the Leadership of Ittihad ve Terakki in our Independence War) (Istanbul, 1967), 136, 137. In these three communications of May 22, May 24, and May 25, 1921, Mustafa Kemal and Deputy Chief of Staff, Fevzi Paşa, respectively, are raising objections to Colonel Seyfi's assuming command of a division to be constituted at Trabzon—on account of the latter's "devotion to Enver Paşa."

19. Cemal Kutay, *Karabekir Ermenistan'ı Nasıl Yok Etti?* (How Karabekir Wiped Out Armenia?) (Istanbul, 1956), 27.

20. *Ibid.*, 29–30.

21. Karabekir, *Istiklal Harbimizde Enver* [n. 18], 139, Karabekir's long personal communication at the telegraph machine on May 25, 1921.
22. Karabekir, *Istiklâl Harbimiz* [n. 2], 751–52.
23. Karabekir, *Istiklâl Harbimizde Enver* [n. 18], 40.
24. Mehmed Hocaoğlu, *Arşiv Vesikalırıyla Tarihte Ermeni Mezâlimi ve Ermeniler* (The Armenians and Armenian Atrocities in History in the Light of Archive Documents) (Istanbul, 1979), 830.
25. Karabekir, *Istiklâl Harbimiz* [n. 2], 35, 37.
26. Hocaoğlu, *Arşiv* [n. 24], 831–32.
27. Karabekir, *Istiklâl Harbimiz* [n. 2], 31, 882; idem, *Istiklâl ... Esasları* [n. 8], 27.
28. Karabekir, *Istiklâl Harbimiz* [n. 2], 394, 609.
29. *Ibid.*, 315.
30. *Ibid.*, 608.
31. *Ibid.*, 631.
32. *Ibid.*, 671.
33. *Ibid.*, 67, 287, 373, 713, 749, 783, 805 in the context of the general's discussions. In specific correspondence, the following instances may be cited. To the Ankara government on April 13, 1920, in which communication Karabekir declared that "we will have to trample down Armenia in order to revitalize Azerbaijan," pp. 584–85; his order of the day on April 18, 1920, p. 603; to the Ankara government on May 15, 1920, p. 684; to the Armenian regimental commander on May 30, 1920, p. 715 where he uses the term "wipe out for eternity" (*ebediyen mahv*); to his armed forces on August 4, 1920, p. 722.
34. *Ibid.*, 653, 661–62, 667. It should be noted that before Seyfi was made chief of Department II at the Ottoman General Headquarters in 1914, that post was occupied by Karabekir himself. Upon the latter's transfer to the combat zone, Seyfi succeeded him. Seyfi later became a member of the Turkish delegation which conducted negotiations with the Bolshevik leadership in Moscow to secure through them large-scale military assistance for the Kemalist insurgents. Following the completion of these negotiations Seyfi was appointed Commander of the 9th division of the 15th Army Corps, pp. 893, 896.
35. Ihsan Ilgar, "Bir Asır Boyunca Ermeni Meselesi. Karabekir Paşanın Bulduğu Çare" (The Armenian Problem Throughout a Century. Karabekir Paşa's Remedy) *Hayat ve Tarih Mecmuası* 11, 2 (October 1, 1975): 70. All three men would subsequently be discarded by the Kemalists, however, on account of their machinations on behalf of Enver who seemed anxious to reclaim the center stage as the arch Ittihadist leader.
36. Karabekir, *Istiklâl Harbimiz* [n. 2], 411–12.
37. Ali Ihsan Sabis, *Harp Hatıralarım* (My War Memoirs) vol. 2 (Ankara, 1951), 192.
38. General Fahri Belen, *Birinci Cihan Harbinde Türk Harbi* (The Turkish War During the First World War) vol. 3 (Ankara, 1965), 34.
39. Mazhar Müfit Kansu, *Erzurum'dan Ölümüne Kadar Atatürk'le Beraber* (From Erzurum On Up to his Death With Atatürk) vol. 1, 2d ed. (Ankara, 1986). Halit is accused of responsibility for the massacres at Ardahan and Ahıska, pp. 301–02. Kansu cites a letter from Karabekir to Mustafa Kemal, dated September 20, 1919, to explain the circumstances; Ihsan Birinci, "Ermenistan Seferi" (The Invasion of Armenia) *Hayat ve Tarih Mecmuası* 2, 7 (August 1, 1967): 31.
40. Doğan Avcıoğlu, *Milli Kurtuluş Tarihi 1838 den 1995e* (The History of National Liberation from 1838 to 1995) vol. 3 (Istanbul, 1974), 1183–84.
41. Kansu, *Erzurum'dan* [n. 39], 301.
42. Karabekir, *Istiklâl Harbimiz* [n. 2], 754, 789.
43. Mustafa Ragıp Esatlı, *Ittihat ve Terakki Tarihinde Esrar Perdesi* (The Curtain of Secrecy in the History of Ittihat ve Terakki) (Istanbul, 1975), 460, n. 1.
44. Feridun Kandemir in *Resimli Tarih* 2, 21 (September, 1951): 947–49.
45. Birinci, "Ermenistan Seferi" [n. 39] 1, (February 1, 1967): 90.
46. *Ibid.*, [n. 39]: 68.
47. *Ibid.*, 67.
48. Avcıoğlu, *Milli* [n. 40], 1184.
49. *Ibid.*, 1185–86; Karabekir, *Istiklâl Harbimiz* [n. 2], 411 where Mustafa Kemal likewise acknowledges his liability to prosecution by the Military Tribunal in Istanbul.
50. *Ibid.*, 83; Avcıoğlu, *Milli* [n. 40], 1185–86.

51. Sina Akşin, *Istanbul Hükümetleri ve Milli Mücadele* (The Governments of Istanbul and the National Struggle) vol. 2 (Istanbul, 1992), 182; Cemal Şener, *Topal Osman Olayı* (The Topal Osman Affair) (Ankara, 1968), 48–9, 61, 65; Ömer Sami Coşar, *Osman Ağa* (Istanbul, 1971), 9–12 where the author indicates that the district attorney of Giresun warned him of the designs of the Istanbul government, coaxing him to flee.
52. *Ibid.*, (Şener), 55, 61, 65, 105.
53. *Ileri*, April 4, 1923.
54. Avcıoğlu, *Milli* [n. 40], 1187–1192.
55. Şener, *Topal Osman* [n. 51], 49.
56. *Ibid.*, 76, 147.
57. Mahmut Gologlu, *Üçüncü Meşrutiyet 1920* (The Third Constitution, 1920) Ankara, 1970), 284.
58. Avcıoğlu, *Milli* [n. 40], 1181, 1183.
59. Vahan Papazian, *Eem Husheru* (My Memoirs) vol. 2 (Beirut, 1952), 291.
60. Gologlu, *Üçüncü* [n. 57], 282.
61. Karabekir, *Istiklâl Harbimiz* [n. 2], 775.

Part IX

A REVIEW OF THE ARMENIAN GENOCIDE IN A COMPARATIVE PERSPECTIVE

Chapter 21

The Saliency
of Some of the Determinants
of the Armenian Genocide

This study essentially focused on the historical, political, and legal aspects of the Armenian genocide to emphasize the convergence and interplay in the incidence of that genocide of a complex web of factors. As a result, the study acquired a degree of comprehensiveness which does not allow a brief and meaningful recapitulation; the very organization of the study does not lend itself to it. Nevertheless, it is worth trying to distill from it a few observations and thoughts to serve as possible connecting links to other studies focusing on other genocides. Such links are essential for venturing into the domain of comparative studies with a view to elaborating certain generalizations that transcend the limitations intrinsic to single-case studies and illuminate the universal features of genocide. Rather than delving into the overall comparative aspects of the Armenian Genocide, however, this segment of the study will basically be confined to the depiction of those problems which revolve around the issues of prevention and punishment of genocide.

Throughout this study the Armenian genocide has been examined in the context of the Turko-Armenian conflict. Religious cleavages, despite official and other Turkish assertions to the contrary, were crucial in the origin and growth of that conflict. Claims of proverbial Ottoman liberality regarding the coexistence in the empire of a host of religious systems and creeds among the various ethnic groups of the empire are belied by the thin veil of tolerance with which the non-Muslim subjects and their religious institutions were treated. One may even speak of the disdain, if not the contempt, that multitudes of Turks felt towards them, the *raia gâvurs*, the "infidel" non-Muslim subjects. No society is free from stresses and strains arising from myriad conditions of interpersonal and intergroup conflicts. In the history of nationality conflicts of the Ottoman Empire, the slightest incident of such a conflict was more often than not a suitable opportunity for Muslim Turks to freely ventilate their hostility based on such feelings of contempt towards non-Muslims. That contempt was intense enough to erupt into belligerent hatred and enmity with the advent of the era of Armenian reforms which revolved around the fundamental principle of liberalism, namely, equality. Neither the theocratic canons of Islam, as interpreted and applied by the Ottoman Turks, nor the vested interests of the vast provincial strata of the religious leaders of the empire would or could allow such equality, however. The stakes were high and the Turko-Armenian conflict intensified progressively, defying solutions.

Like other major religious systems of beliefs, Islam embodied a wide range of precepts and dogmas which were neither entirely consistent, nor always compatible with each other. These incongruities allowed scope for any leader, religious or secular, to select, distort or magnify certain aspects of Islam's canonic laws, especially its deprecations of and militancy against non-Muslims. Needless to say that the protracted Turko-Armenian conflict was such as to allow broad scope for the use of religion as a leverage in this sense. Even though to a significant degree religious differences helped engender that conflict, only the deliberate and sinister manipulation of Islam rendered the Turko-Armenian conflict explosive and lethal. During the era of Abdul Hamit, the notion of Turk or Turkish was in fact inoperative; the conflict was portrayed in terms of Islam, or Muslims, as being challenged by "infidel" Armenians. The attendant massacres were accordingly defined as acts of self-defense by the Muslims, which category remarkably included an amalgam of such non-Turkic peoples as Kurds, Circassians and Lazes. Abdul Hamit misused and exploited Islam especially in his modus operandi as a Sultan-Khalif, blending theocracy and autocracy, and exacerbating existing religious cleavages. As one Turkish historian conceded, in order to justify his method of rule he resorted to "a reinterpretation and perversion of Ottoman Islamic political theory."[1]

That this pattern of handling the Armenians became a legacy is evident in the developments pertaining to the successor regime of the Young Turk Ittihadists. They too came to appreciate the expediency of "a manipulative instrumental attitude toward ... institutional Islam," to quote Mardin again. (See Ch. 1, n. 9). They too expressed the conviction, through the vehicle of a secret speech Talât delivered in August 1910, that "equality of Mussulman and gâvur ("infidel" non-Muslims) ... is an unrealizable ideal," and, therefore, the empire needs to be "Ottoman-ized." (See Ch. 10, n. 7). Apart from these considerations, there was the factor of Turkish nationalism, the bearers of which insisted on the supremacy of the Turkish element in the affairs of the multi-ethnic Ottoman Empire. By declaring themselves as "the ruling nation" (*milleti hâkime*), they supplanted the notion of equality with that of a nation of overlords, who were preordained to dominate the rest of the peoples comprising the empire.

On account of its complexion, the Turks had to treat the Turko-Armenian conflict at two levels which in many ways were interconnected, namely, internal and external. The external treatment involved reckoning with the Powers, many of which had adopted the principle of humanitarian intervention. That treatment was such as to test the depths of Oriental cunning and the allied Ottoman resolve to circumvent the Powers and ultimately to prevail.

The nineteenth-century "humanitarian interventions" of the Concert of Europe to protect the Armenians failed in large part because the Powers involved did not give due consideration to the socio-political forces which compelled the Armenians into assuming an inferior position. By failing to address this central factor, the Europeans allowed the Ottoman state to pursue the more expedient but far less effective route of responding to the symptoms of the crises the socio-political system was producing. The Turkish authorities, while feigning concurrence with the need for reforms, ensured that these reforms never took actual effect. The manipulative tinge of the diplomatic acumen of Ottoman foreign ministers, ambassadors and sultans, developed in the latter stages of the turbulent career of the empire, proved quite useful in this regard. A Belgian legist described "the distinguishing characteristics of modern Ottoman diplomacy—great facility in assimilating the administrative and constitutional jargon of civilized countries; consummate cunning in taking advantage of this cunning to conceal, under deceptive appearances, the barbarous reality of deeds and intentions; cool audacity, making promises which there is neither the power nor the desire to make good and finally, a paternal and oily tone, intended to create the impression that the Turkish Government is the victim of unjust prejudices and odious calumnies."[2] Another author discerned three phases of Turkish diplomatic tactics on the matter of reform. 1) Defiance of the Powers insisting on faithful performance of stipulated compacts, when this can be resorted to with impunity. 2) An assurance of compliance with the demand, given with all the solemnity of a devout Muslim. No semblance even of performance is ever attempted. 3) The most desperate stage, from the Muslim point of view, along with the solemn pledge there is some deceptive appearance of performance.[3] By pursuing a strategy of stalling and temporizing, while at the same time playing the Powers against each other, the Turks managed to defuse internationally explosive situations without taking any action which could be contrary to their traditional beliefs and related interests. At issue for the Turks was not the formal introduction of reforms, a series of which were in fact enacted and promulgated, but their effective implementation. The Armenians were not "entitled" to, and hence were not going to be accorded, equality in the Ottoman system. When deception and deferral were ineffective, the Turks resorted to violent measures of repression, culminating first in the 1894–1896 Hamidian massacres. The failure of the Powers to prevent the massacre of Ottoman Armenians, despite their adoption of the principle of humanitarian intervention, compounded the problem of the Armenians in a critical way. To their condition of internal vulnerability was added the condition of external vulnerability; they remained dangerously unprotected by outside forces. Far more critical was, however, another non-event associated with this failure. The Powers not only failed to prevent the massacres but they also avoided punishing the massacrers. Thus, lack of external deterrence on the one hand, and the certainty of impunity, on the other, combined to render "Armenian massacres" affordable for the Turks. These massacres are important not only because they foreshadowed the subsequent genocide, but also because the perpetrators were not prosecuted. Given this precedent, the Turks had strong reason to believe that there would likewise be no punishment for subsequent killings.

The intransigence of the Ottoman government, which gathered momentum through the diplomatic crises and associated Armenian pogroms, found a violent outlet in the pursuit of World War I, into which Turkey willingly plunged by unilaterally provoking and initiating hostilities. The climax of the European ritual of alternately remonstrating and threatening Turkey, with a tenor that patently lacked credibility, came in May, 1915 with the initiation of the Armenian genocide. The genocide was consummated irrespective of Europe's threats, and the perpetrators once more escaped punishment.[4]

This historical perspective employed in this study demonstrates the fact that the episodic Armenian massacres served both as a crucible and a prelude to the World War I holocaust. Had the Powers interceded in concert after any one of these episodes, as they did in Lebanon in the aftermath of the 1860 massacre, the issues of prevention and punishment in all likelihood would not have arisen. They were impeded, however, by the vagaries of politics, among themselves and in relation to the Turkish state. While they pretended to pursue "humanitarian intervention," they frequently engaged in *Realpolitik*; the Turks understood the resulting cleavage between purport and intent and took it into account when considering radical preemptive measures. This aspect of the conduct of the Powers introduced a third element into the picture, one which was counterpoised to prevention and punishment but which distorted them both: the inadvertent aggravation of a domestic conflict by perfunctory interventions whose latent functions produced disaster instead of relief. An additional reason for the disastrousness of the humanitarian intervention approach, warranted as it was by certain rules of international law, was the fragility of the substructure of the treaties involved on which that law was predicated. A series of treaties and agreements signed between the European Powers and Turkey in the 1856 and 1914 period nominally obligated the Ottoman authorities to extend equality to their non-Muslim subjects.

The problem, however, was that these treaties were not legislative enactments but merely contracts between states; thus they did not specify a crime, assign jurisdiction, or provide the machinery for the administration of punitive justice. These limitations, still intrinsic to the field of international law, spelled disaster for the Armenians. Rather than resulting in a resolution of the Armenian Question, these treaties served only to internationalize the issue, thereby gravely exacerbating the Turko-Armenian conflict.[5]

A domestic conflict for the Ottomans was thus transformed into an international adversity. Fridjof Nansen, who as High Commissioner of the League of Nations tried very hard to succor the wounds of Armenia and rehabilitate the survivors of the holocaust along with the other refugees of the war, for which he was awarded the Nobel Peace Prize in 1922, ended his volume on the Armenian tragedy with this lamentation: "Woe to the Armenians, that they were ever drawn into European politics! It would have been better for them if the name of Armenia had never been uttered by any European diplomatist."[6]

The Armenian experience is also instructive in that the failure to prevent a particular instance of genocide does not ensure its subsequent punishment. Although Nuremberg provides a striking counter-example of international consensus, the Armenian experience of noble talk without substantive action is far more common. The international efforts at retribution following World War I, both in the case of Turkey and its ally Germany, reveal the weakness of available legal and political means capable of ensuring international punishment—as an effective deterrent to future acts of genocide. The international efforts of the European Powers to bring the perpetrators of the Armenian genocide to justice fell victim to the overarching principle of national sovereignty and the machinations of international politics. By allowing the Ottoman government to remain in place following its defeat in the war, the European Powers gave up the authority that they needed to effectuate retribution for the massacre. The presence of a sovereign government in Turkey impeded the initiation of international trials through standard legal barriers, such as issues of jurisdiction, and practical impediments, such as difficulties in securing the evidence needed for international prosecution. It likewise led to the splintering of European resolve by fostering political maneuvering between the powers to curry favor with the emerging forces of Turkish nationalism bent on inaugurating a new Turkish government.

The efforts at domestic retribution for the Armenian genocide were similarly ineffective. Although Courts Martial were instituted in Turkey, and a great deal of damning evidence concerning the genocide was revealed, its perpetrators emerged relatively unscathed. The fact that these trials were held at all likely was due only to the efforts of a weak postwar government to secure more promising terms for peace. Thus, the Courts were never given the power they needed to prosecute effectively the perpetrators. Instead, the trials served only to stir a new ground swell of nationalist fervor among the Muslims which helped ensure the sway of the Kemalist regime. The Turks, like the Germans following World War I, were unwilling to accept the collective guilt that these domestic trials represented. Thus, after the Kemalist regime took power, the large number of the Courts Martial that had not reached the verdict stage were dismantled, and the last opportunity at retribution disappeared. The European Powers, having lost the necessary cohesion and authority, were unable to prevent this result and abjectly acquiesced to it.

The uniformity of the response to Armenian clamors of reforms by two avowedly diverse Ottoman regimes is instructive for understanding the nature of that response which involved the initiation of the exterminatory massacres in the Abdul Hamit- and the Young Turk Ittihadist-eras. At issue here is the significance of the incidence of a basic pattern. When two diverse regimes over a period of several decades converge in their resort to the same method of victimization, i.e., massacres, the convergence acquires critical significance, requiring an examination of the common propensity for massacre as a method of conflict resolution. This is even more true when one considers the allied fact that such a *propensity* over a period of time is likely to evolve into a *proclivity* for massacre. The Armenian experience demonstrates that when it comes to resolving a lingering nationality conflict, most differences, separating one regime from another, will attenuate themselves for the purpose of forging a common response. Involved in such a response are pervasive cultural values that, as a rule, eclipse other and less potent values and traditions. The traditional Turkish proneness for lethal violence in conflict situations went hand in hand with Turkish martial traditions, eventually crystallizing itself into a core element of Turkish culture. The Turkish maxim "by the right of my sword" (*kılıcımın hakkı ile*) aptly epitomizes this historical fact. Here, the reliance on the sword is elevated to the altar of righteousness, thereby equating violent might with justice. This attitude explains the alpha and omega of a culture of massacre. The Armenians were expected to remain humble, docile and submissive; for the Turks that was a cultural imperative. When they began to assert themselves, they were meted out punishment through incremental massacres. Yet as the Powers became more and more entangled in Turkish internal affairs in the quest for, among others, remedies to the unending nationality conflict afflicting the Ottoman Empire, the culture of massacre gradually submerged. Eventually it became a clandestine operation in the sense that the authorities disclaimed responsibility, or even outright denied, the very massacres they surreptitiously had sanctioned and helped organize. Thus, with the advent of modern times the legacy of a culture of manifest massacre assumed a latent character, functioning more often than not covertly. One may, therefore, characterize modern Turkish episodes of massacre as subcultural undertakings whereby official decisions and state policies are seen as being channeled into diversionary avenues and vehicles for the sole purpose of concealment and deflection.

When a crime is steadily crowned with success, it becomes its own reward. Unabating Armenian vulnerability, more or less predictable inaction by the Powers, and the resulting impunity accruing to the Turks, were the main factors which combined to ensure such success. It is most significant that the two principal architects of the two genocides of the twentieth century, i.e., of the Armenians and of the Jews, are on record exalting the experience of success as a warrant for mass murder which they justified in terms of higher national interests. Deferring the citation of Hitler's respective exaltation for later use in the chapter on Nuremberg, (see Chapter 23 in paragraph preceeding note 15, p. 404), at this point reference may be made to a statement by Talât which he is reported to have made when summarizing his sentiments about the issue of "the extermination" of the Armenians. He reportedly was discussing the issue with Halide Edib, the Turkish feminist writer. Here is Talât's rationale: "I have the conviction that as long as a nation does the best for its own interests, *and succeeds*, the world admires it and thinks it moral."[7] (italics added).

Success in genocidal undertakings cannot be taken for granted, however. The preparations must include, as noted above, gimmicks and devices through which the victims are more or less caught unawares and trapped. Moreover, in order to obviate the problems of responsibility and accountability, the perpetrator camp must secure and unobtrusively deploy proxies with the mission to carry out the operations of destruction. To deflect attention from the real purposes of a scheme, euphemisms, code language, and maximum reliance on oral instructions are utilized as standard procedures. In other words the method of deception permeates the whole enterprise. The history of the Armenian genocide in all its stages of development is punctuated with a whole range of techniques of deception, diversion and deflection which the perpetrators applied to secure and optimize success. Foremost among these were, for example, the twin terms of deception that were used in World War I, namely, "deportation" (*tehcir*) and "relocation" (*tebdili mekân*); they were intended to conceal from the multitudes of the victims the real intent of the massive dislocations. Even Mustafa Kemal (Atatürk) could not bring himself to refrain from indulging in similar techniques of deception and deflection. In the cipher of May 6, 1920 (cited in Ch. 20, n. 2) he suggested that the attack on Armenia be carried out "as secretly as possible (*mümkün olduğu kadar sureti hafiyede*) by the *milis* [militia] forces formed with our help in the districts" surrounding Armenia, and "by the Muslim Bolsheviks ... ." In other words finish off Armenia through proxies while counting on the help of Ankara.

Perhaps the most striking aspect of deceptiveness in the entire episode under review here was the practice of two-track communications. For public purposes only the central authorities in Istanbul would frame their orders in such benign sounding terms as "deportation," "relocation," "protect the convoys," "supply bread and olive to the deportees," "punish the transgressors," etc. But subsequently these orders were superseded by secret orders decreeing the destruction of the convoys through massacre. Assurances given to the German and Austrian ambassadors regarding Turkish willingness to exempt from deportation Catholic and Protestant Armenians suffered the same fate.[8] This line of behavior prompted some German and Austrian consuls as well as ambassadors to decry Talât and his cronies as people routinely indulging in "brazen lies" and "double-dealing" (*krasse Lügen, Doppelspiel treiben*), with German Ambassador Metternich bluntly denouncing Talât as a "double-dealer" (*ein Doppelgänger*). [9] Even Grand Vizier Said Halim, who in February 1917 was relieved of his post and was supplanted by party boss and Interior Minister Talât, during a parliamentary inquiry held in the aftermath of the war complained that the legitimate orders for "deportations" were being perverted into orders to "kill" the deportees.[10]

The most incriminating evidence about this modus operandi was provided by Reşit Akif Paşa, one of the foremost Ottoman-Turkish statesmen who held such positions as provincial governor-general and cabinet minister (Interior), and twice was appointed to the Council of State, the second time serving as its President. In the course of one of the debates in the Senate (November 21, 1918) on the crime of wartime massacres against the Armenians, he disclosed that during a routine examination of official papers at his office, i.e., President of the Council of State, he was surprised to uncover a damning document. As he explained "It was this official order for deportation, issued by the notorious Interior Ministry and relayed to the provinces. However, following [the issuance of] this official order, the Central Committee [of Ittihad party] undertook to send an ominous circular order to all points [in the provinces], urging the expediting of the execution of the accursed mission of the brigands [*çetes*]. Thereupon, the brigands proceeded to act and the atrocious massacres were the result."[11]

In order to carry out such deceptive stratagems the two foremost Ittihadist leaders, Talât and War Minister Enver, had installed in their homes telegraphic apparatuses through which they issued their clandestine and informal orders and instructions. In the case of Talât, this became public when American Ambassador Morgenthau one day during the war surprised Talât at his home to transact some urgent business, and later noted in his memoirs, "I shall never forget the picture ... this huge Turk ... working industriously his own telegraph key, his young wife gazing at him through a little window."[12] Hayriye, the wife, confirmed Talât's use of such an apparatus at home when she subsequently wrote her own memoirs.[13]

Enver's duplicitous use of the telegraphic apparatus, installed in his home, is revealed in the memoirs of a Turkish author who obtained the information from the Aide-de-Camp of Halil Paşa, the commander of the Turkish troops which in September 1918 had attacked and had helped in the capture of Baku. According to the terms of the March 3, 1918 Brest-Litovsk Treaty, Baku was to be left to the Russians and the Germans, the ally of the Turks, did not want the Turks to seize Baku. Nevertheless, Enver sent the following telegraphic order, "Without delay organize local forces and try to seize Baku. However, you personally and ostensibly keep an appearance of neutrality. Local Azeri forces should handle the fighting." After Halil on September 15, 1918 informed the Turkish High Command of the capture of Baku, "Enver, the supreme commander, sent this order at midnight: 'Baku was to be given to the Russians ... Why did you find it necessary to invade there? Your place is in Kars. What business do you have in Baku. Return at once to Kars.' However, after a lapse of three hours, Enver Paşa sent the following telegram: 'With the greatest joy have I received the news of the capture of Baku city, lying at the shores of the Caspian Sea, and belonging to the Turanian Empire. This great service of yours will not be forgotten in Turkish and Islamic history. I kiss the eyes of our war veterans and offer the verses of the opening chapter of the Kuran to invoke the memory of our fallen heroes.'" As the Turkish author indicates, the first and third telegraphic orders were sent from the privacy and secrecy of Enver's home, the second, a veritable charade, was sent from the General Headquarters,[14] in all likelihood for the purpose of throwing dust in the eyes of German Lieutenant General Seeckt, the Chief of Staff at the headquarters. It should be noted that one of the reasons the Germans tried (and failed) to control the Turks by way of sending in a cavalry force was to avert the anticipated massacre of Baku Armenians; the Turks sabotaged that effort by blowing up one or two bridges, and proceeded with the massacre as planned. (See Chapter 19, n. 12).

This legacy of duplicity manifested itself in an even more blatant form in the design of the fledgling Ankara government which was bent on completing the destruction of the Armenian people by extending the Ittihadist genocide to Russian Armenia. On November 8, 1920, Ankara had sent two cipher telegrams, one of which went to General Karabekir who had invaded Armenia, defeating its newly formed but ill-prepared and ill-equipped army. The sinister character of the contradictoriness of the contents of these twin ciphers is exceeded only by the gravity of the peril this deceptive ploy portended for the Armenians. In notes 2-5 of Chapter 20 one of these ciphers has already been dissected in detail; it was also noted in this chapter above. The dominant theme there is: to achieve the destruction of Armenia it will be necessary to mislead and deceive (*iğfal*) them, the Armenians, as well as the Europeans, by appearing friendly, at the same time, however, proceeding gradually and covertly for the fulfillment of the real mission. The other telegram, sent to the Armenian government, is full of conjurations of "profound and genuine friendship" (*amik ve samimi*), of "humanity" (*insaniyet*) and promises of economic assistance to help Armenia recover and achieve "complete independence and security" (*temamii istiklâl ve emniyet*).[15]

It may be observed that these instances of official duplicity and deceptiveness, revealing as they do a patent aptitude for lethal cunning, are illustrative of the incidence of subcultural factors whereby the resort to exterminatory massacres is handled surreptitiously and deviously, thereby attempting to exempt society at large and its culture from any onus of blame, accountability and responsibility.

A Note on the Dynamics of Impunity

In examining the processes and conditions of the Armenian genocide, the shortcomings of the rules of international law incident to defective treaty clauses and abortive treaty engagements were examined as major contributing factors. The failure to prevent the genocide, and the antecedents of that genocide, was related to the absence of a predictable pattern of deterrence by the European Powers, and to a resulting increase in the vulnerability of the targeted Armenian population. The post-genocide judicial proceedings, though incomplete, sufficiently documented the fact of that genocide; but they failed to produce retributive justice to any significant degree. This double failure to prevent or to punish is perhaps the most important feature of the Armenian case, needing to be restated and re-emphasized. To the extent that prevention of a crime is contingent upon the predictability of the punishment of that crime, retributive justice acquires critical significance in the control of future outbreaks of genocide.

The impunity with which Ottoman Turkey was treated in the wake of the 1894–96 empire-wide Hamit-era series of massacres served to embolden the Young Turks to commit the subsequent 1909 Adana holocaust, testing once more the thresholds of impunity accorded Turkey by the rest of the world. The negligible outcome in terms of retributive justice, applied to the perpetrators of that holocaust, was but indicative of the permissiveness of the outside world in face of such mass murders. The ensuing World War I genocide was the logical culmination of this chain of episodic massacres. The post-genocide twin attempts to extend the compass of Armenocide to the Transcaucasus, i.e., beyond the borders of Turkey, must be understood in this context.

When a crime such as genocide goes more or less unchallenged while being committed and unpunished afterwards, the crime becomes consequential in a dual sense. Not only is the victim's quest for justice denied but even more important, the perpetrator is encouraged to redefine the offense in such a way that the criminality of the act is either diluted or denied altogether. Such a proclivity to redefine is almost always accompanied by a host of rationalizations, producing what might be called a denial syndrome. The perpetrator is wont to deny the crime, deny the victim and deny anyone else the right to question such denials, and recognize much less the right to condemn the act of the criminality involved. The portents of such denials have not been adequately appreciated by legists or statesmen. The denials may be pregnant with incentives for potential perpetrators to consider the initial crime a precedent warranting emulation. The graver threat issuing from such denials concerns, however, the surviving victim population and its progeny that may be targeted for new and even more potent strikes. Lacking remorse, and emboldened by an erosion of existing inhibitions, afforded by an absence of prosecution and punishment, the perpetrator resorting to denials may have little hesitation in repeating the crime under circumstances he may deem propitious.

The persistence of clamors for justice by the Armenians, who, on account of the equally persistent disinterest in their cause by the rest of the world, have been rendered impotent for so long, cannot restore a sense of remorse in the Turkish psyche. Obversely, such clamors are capable of functioning as a major source of aggravation for the same Turks. Aroused in this way, the latter may be tempted to entertain ideas of new and perhaps even more radical strikes against the Armenians, with a view to permanently extirpating that source of grievance and challenge.

Notes to Chapter 21

1. Kemal H. Karpat, "The Transformation of the Ottoman State, 1789–1908" *International Journal of Middle East Studies* 3 (1972): 271.
2. M. Rolin-Jaequemeyns, *Armenia, the Armenians, and the Treaties* (London, 1891), 87. The international law expertise of the author of this statement lends it special significance. He was the editor of *Revue de droit international et de législation comparée*, and twice the President of the Institute of International Law. In 1899 he took part in the First Peace Conference of the Hague and was appointed Reporter for the Fourth Convention on the Laws and Customs of War. At the end of World War I, he went to the Peace Conference at Paris as the Secretary-General of the Belgian delegation, was later appointed Belgian High Commissioner in the Occupied Territory of The Rhineland, and subsequently became Belgian Minister of Internal Affairs. In 1930 he reached the pinnacle of his career when he was elected to be a judge of the Permanent Court of International Justice. *British Year Book International Law* 18 (1937): 156–57 (obituary).
3. An old Indian, *Historical Sketch of Armenia and the Armenians (With Special Reference to the Present Crisis)*(London, 1896), 132–33.

4. The viability of recourse to humanitarian intervention in contemporary settings of domestic conflict and mass murder is discussed by a number of experts of international law. Falk, for example, enumerates the obstacles to effective intervention in the face of genocidal killings, underscoring his assertion that unless the world order becomes amenable to structural changes providing new standards of international law, the obstacles are likely to persist. R. Falk, "Responding to Severe Violations," in *Enhancing Global Human Rights* (1979). After surveying the history of humanitarian intervention and the present state of the law respecting the resort to coercive force on humanitarian grounds, two legal scholars conclude that such intervention, especially when unilateral, is not sanctioned historically or by current standards, except with the sanction of the United Nations. They, therefore, dispute the merits of arguments defining as precedent-setting India's use of military force against Pakistan and in favor of Bangladesh. T.M. Franck and N.S. Rodley, "After Bangladesh: The Law of Humanitarian Intervention by Military Force," *American Journal of International Law* 67 (1973): 302.

The example these two authors set in incorporating the Armenian case of genocide into their arguments was followed by two others who, in their most recent contributions to the field of international law, depict the "full-scale extermination of ... approximately one million Armenians ... in Turkey." Bazyler, "Reexamining the Doctrine of Humanitarian Intervention in Light of the Atrocities in Kampuchea and Ethiopia," *Stanford Journal of International Law* 23 (1987): 593, and emphasize the fact that "the [U.N.] Convention [on the Prevention and Punishment of Genocide] would cover the Armenian Genocide." LeBlanc, "The United Nations Genocide Convention and Political Groups: Should the United States Propose an Amendment?" *Yale Journal of International Law* 13 (1988): 270, 290, 293. See also D. Matas, "Prosecuting Crimes Against Humanity: The Lessons of World War I" *Fordham International Law Journal*, (1990): 86–104; L. B. Sohn and T. Buergenthal "Human Intercession on Behalf of Armenians" in *International Protection of Human Rights* (1973), 185–191; L. S. Wiseberg, "Humanitarian Intervention: Lessons from the Nigerian Civil War" *Revue des Droits de l'Homme. Human Rights Journal*, 70, 1, (1974): 61–98.

5. Historian Danişmend maintains that the first rift between Ittihadist leaders, especially Dr. Nazım, and the Armenians occurred in a 1902 congress where the Armenians insisted on the implementation of Article 61, and Ahmed Riza and Dr. Nazım adamantly rejected it as unwarranted intervention by the Powers in the internal affairs of Turkey. I. Danişmend, *Izahlı Osmanlı Tarihi Kronolojisi* (Annotated Chronology of Ottoman History) vol. 4, 2nd ed. (Istanbul, 1961), 358–59.

Commenting on this issue in 1920, Brown deplored "the intrusive and fruitless friendship of Great Britain for the Armenians" as being responsible for the 1895–96 and World War I massacres. P.H. Brown, "The Mandate Over Armenia," *American Journal of International Law* 14 (1920): 396, 397–98. Secretary of State (later Chief Justice) Charles Evans Hughes, in a 1924 address to the Council of Foreign Relations, likewise attributed "a large part of the distress" at issue here to the "encouraging action [of the British] which failed of adequate support ... . [The victims were] left to their own devices." C.E. Hughes, "Recent Questions and Negotiations," *American Journal of International Law*, 18 (1924): 229, 239.

6. F. Nansen, *Armenia and the Near East* (New York, 1976), 324. During his engagement as League of Nations' High Commissioner for Relief for Russia, Nansen tried to seek justice and redemption for Armenia, whose fate he defined as "the betrayal of a nation." His exchange with Lord Robert Cecil, then Assistant Foreign Minister of Great Britain, epitomizes his disdain and bitterness with regard to foreign policies of governments. The irony of his remark stems from the fact that Lord Cecil, the son of the famous nineteenth century British Statesman Lord Salisbury, who is regarded as the architect of Article 61 of the 1878 Berlin Treaty, was one of the very few British diplomats who tried to implement the "Charter for Armenian Justice." The four clauses of that charter are described in R. Hovannisian, *Armenia on the Road to Independence 1918* (Berkeley, CA, 1967), 248–49. Nansen is reported to have chastised Lord Cecil with the words, "Your damned rotten government. Well, all governments are rotten." Cited by his daughter Liv Nansen, who under the married name Heoyer wrote and published the book *Nansen Og Verden* (Nansen and the World) (1955), (cited in Yayloian, *Medz Der-*

outiunneri Goğme Moratzuadz Jhogovourt (A People Forsaken by the Great Powers), *Sovetakan Haiasdan*, 4 (1987): 31). Commenting on this problem of being forsaken after receiving vague assurances of support, American philosopher of pragmatism John Dewey observed, "Happy the minority which has had no Christian nation to protect it." *The New Republic* 40 (November 12, 1928): 268.

7. Halide Edib, *Memoirs of* (New York, 1926), 387.

8. See Vahakn N. Dadrian, *The Armenian Genocide in Official Turkish Sources*. Collected Essays. Special Issue of *Journal of Political and Military Sociology*, Roger Smith, guest ed., Vol. 22, 1 (Summer, 1994): 137, 143–45 n. 12.

9. Vahakn N. Dadrian, "The Naim-Andonian Documents on the World War I Destruction of Ottoman Armenians: The Anatomy of a Genocide" *International Journal of Middle East Studies* 18, 3 (August 1986): 327, 339, 349 notes 37 and 38, 355–57 n. 104; Metternich's denunciation of Talât is in *German Foreign Ministry Archives*. Türkei 159 no. 3/4, A24679, September 7, 1916.

10. *Harb Kabinelerinin Isticvabı* (Wartime Cabinets' Hearings) Special *Vakit* Publication Series No. 2 (Istanbul, 1933), 290–91, 295, 325–26.

11. Dadrian, *The Armenian Genocide* [n. 8], 85. Culled from *Meclisi Ayan Zabıt Ceridesi* (Transcripts of the Proceedings of the Senate). Third Election Period. Fifth Session. Eleventh sitting. vol. 1, p 125, left column.

12. Henry Morgenthau, *Ambassador Morgenthau's Story* (New York, 1918), 140, 143–44.

13. *Hürriyet* (Istanbul Turkish daily) December 21, 1982.

14. Burhan Oğuz, *Yüzyıllar Boyunca Alman Gerçeği ve Türkler* (The German Reality in the Course of Centuries and the Turks) (Istanbul, 1983), 325–26. The author is the stepson of Yenibahçeli Şükrü, a prominent leader of the notorious Special Organization, and the brother of Nail, another leader of that organization. He learned many of the latter's secrets by his exposure to this family circle.

15. Kâzım Karabekir, *Istiklâl Harbimiz* (Our War of Independence) 2d ed. (Istanbul, 1969), 844.

Chapter 22

Parallel Problems in the Post-War Prosecution of World War I German War Criminals

The crimes with which nearly 1,000 Germans were charged at the end of World War I in several respects differed from those with which the Ottoman Turks were charged. In the German case the victims, for instance, were almost entirely people who were neither Germans by nationality, nor subjects or citizens of the German state. There was no evidence of a centrally conceived and organized scheme to commit the alleged criminal acts. The atrocities in question were essentially war-related and had no significant relationship to prewar ideology or designs. In brief, there was no evidence of a comprehensive initiative targeting a victim population in its entirety. But, in many other respects, there emerged some similarities when the Allies tried to prosecute the offenders. Indeed, in some respects the history of the 1921–1922 Leipzig trials was remarkably similar to that of the 1919–1921 Istanbul trials. In both cases, the domestic governments were reluctant to accede to foreign pressure and institute criminal proceedings against their own nationals for wartime crimes against humanity. Both nations, however, finally agreed to prosecute the cases. The Germans did so as a way of placating public opinion in the Allied countries, while the Turks did so in expectation of being rewarded by lenient peace terms.

By refusing to surrender German nationals to the Allies for trial, the German government virtually repudiated article 228 of the Versailles Treaty, which stipulated such a surrender. Field Marshal von der Goltz's [sic] scornful declaration, "The world must realize that … no catchpoll shall hand Germans over to the Allies,"[1] was symptomatic of the powerful resistance among Germans to which the Allies eventually succumbed. The Turkish response to the demand for the surrender of criminal suspects paralleled the German response. Not only did the Foreign Minister of the Istanbul government object to surrendering Turkish nationals to the Allies, but Mustafa Kemal, the head of the antagonistic Ankara government, rejected the very idea of "recognizing a kind of right of jurisdiction on the part of a foreign government over the acts of a Turkish subject in the interior of Turkey herself."[2]

Instead, both "vanquished states" offered internal proceedings against the war criminals. On June 11, 1921, the Ankara government informed the British that when the Malta internees are released in exchange for British civilian and military persons, "those accused of crimes would be put on impartial trial at Ankara in the same way as German prisoners were being tried in Germany."[3] A similar assurance was given by Ankara's Foreign Minister Bekir Sami on March 10, 1921.[4] These, as well as subsequent assurances, proved to be mere negotiating ploys. Beyond nationalist politics, a legal issue worked in Turkey's and Germany's favor: the ex *post facto* character of the provisions of both the Versailles and Sèvres treaties in that they were not predicated on existing national or international laws. Article 15 of the Ottoman Penal Code, for example, explicitly prohibited that type of procedure ("punishment is not to be effected in accordance with a subsequent law"). Neither the Versailles nor the Sèvres treaties specified the jurisdiction and laws by which conviction and sentence rendition could be effected.

Attempts at extradition raised comparable difficulties. The Dutch government refused to surrender Emperor William II who had taken refuge in Holland after fleeing Germany at the end of the war. The Dutch rejected not only the concepts of "international policy" and "international morality" upon which the Allies proposed to try and punish the emperor, but they also invoked the domestic laws and national traditions of Holland as further justification. The Dutch defined the offense with which the emperor was charged as "political" and hence exempt from extradition.[5]

Similarly, Germany refused to surrender Talât Paşa, who as Grand Vizier was the de facto head of the Ottoman state when he fled to Germany at the end of the war. German Foreign Minister Solf invoked paragraph 2 of article 5 of the 1917 Turko-German Extradition Treaty which permitted extradition under three conditions: an arrest order, a verdict against the person whose extradition is being sought, or the submission of related judicial documents. As the Court Martial had not yet taken place, there was no judicial documentation of a verdict. At any rate, added Solf, "Talât stuck with us faithfully, and our country remains open to him."[6]

As the trials progressed, internal pressures in both countries, caused by resurgent nationalism, strongly affected the proceedings. From similar beginnings, the Leipzig trials resulted in failures similar to their counterparts in Istanbul. "The German public showed indignation that German judges could be found to sentence the war criminals and the press brought all possible pressure to bear on the Court."[7] Many of the defendants were cheered upon entering or leaving the courtroom, while representatives of the Allies attending the trials were hooted. Those acquitted often departed the courtroom with bouquets of flowers offered to them by an admiring public. Prison guards who assisted in the escape of some defendants before or after conviction were publicly congratulated.[8] The most famous case involved the Llandovery Castle Hospital Ship, which had been torpedoed and sunk, with two naval lieutenants firing upon the survivors in the lifeboats. The two lieutenants proudly accepted the *London Times* decrial of them as "barbarians," while the German press hailed them as "U-Boat Heroes" following their being sentenced to four years' imprisonment.[9]

The outcome of the Leipzig proceedings was dismal by any standard of retributive justice. Out of a total of 901 cases,[10] 888 suspects were either acquitted or summarily dismissed. Only 12 trials were held; half resulted in acquittals and half in convictions with light sentences. Allied disappointment at the popular exaltation of the defendants and subversion of justice in Turkey, also applied to Germany. In the latter case the Allies appointed a Commission of Allied jurists to examine the effect of the popular response on the proceedings. The Commission unanimously recommended to the Supreme Council that the Leipzig trials be suspended and the remaining defendants be tried before Allied Courts. As in Turkey, the Commission's recommendations failed to yield the desired results.[11]

Perhaps the most signal feature of commonality interconnecting the two cases has reference to the overarching principle of impunity through which it may be explained how genocides are rendered viable and affordable undertakings in the minds of actual or potential perpetrators: an unpunished mass murder has the potential of serving as a precedent and at the same time a warrant for a future enactment of genocide.

After his conviction at Nuremberg, Albert Speer, reflecting on the crime of the World War I deportations Germany had carried out against populations in occupied territories, deplored the failure of the Allies to prosecute the violators. Such prosecution "would have encouraged a sense of responsibility on the part of leading political figures if after the First World War the Allies had actually held the trials they had threatened … ."[12]

Notes to Chapter 22

1. United Nations War Crimes Commission, *History of the United Nations War Crimes Commission and the Development of the Laws of War*, (London, 1948), 48. It is possible that this reference to Goltz is an error. As far as it is known, there was only one Field Mar-

shal von der Goltz and he died from typhus in Baghdad in April 1916. The Goltz meant is in all likelihood General Rudiger von der Goltz who in 1919 was leading military operations against the Bolsheviks in Lituania and Latvia; his forces included German Free Corps units, Baltic militia, and army troops organized by the Baltic governments.

2. *Speech delivered by Mustafa Kemal Atatürk 1927* (Istanbul, 1963), 497.
3. FO 371/6504/E9112, folio 47. Three months later, i.e., on September 14, 1921, Rafet Paşa, the Interior Minister of the Ankara government repeated the same pledge when he informed General Harrington, then the highest military authority at Istanbul, that those Malta exiles implicated in war crimes "will be tried on arrival." FO 371/6504/E10411, folio 130.
4. FO 371/6499/E3110, p. 190; *see also* FO 371/5049/E6376, folio 187; A. Yalman, *Turkey in My Time* (Norman, OK, 1956), 106.
5. See Quincy Wright, "The Legal Liability of the Kaiser," *American Political Science Review* 13 (1919): 120; *N.Y. Times*, January 22, 1920.
6. A. A. Türkei 183/54 A45718; *Takvimi Vekâyi* No. 3407. For the protracted exchange on this subject between the German Foreign Office and the Ottoman Foreign Ministry, see FO 371/4173/82190, 371/4174/98910, 371/5173/E6949, 618/113/1941, folios 404–15; *see also* Y. Bayur, *Türk Inkilâbl Tarihi*, 3, Part 4 (Ankara, 1983), 782.
7. War Crimes Commission, [n. 1], 51–52.
8. See J. Willis, *Prologue to Nuremberg: The Politics and Diplomacy of Punishing War Criminals of the First World War* (Westport, CT, 1982), 126–47.
9. *Times* (London). July 9, 1921; "German War Trials: Report of the Proceedings before the Supreme Court in Leipzig," *American Journal of International Law* 16 (1922): 628–40, 674–724; *see also* C. Mullins, *The Leipzig Trials* (London, 1921); Ann. Dig. 2: 436 (Reichsgericht 1921).
10. The lists of these suspects were, in part, compiled and transmitted to the Germans by Britain (97), Belgium (334), Poland (57), France (332), Italy (29) and Rumania (41). The remaining suspects were fugitives.
11. *German War Crimes: Report of the Proceedings*, Brit. Parl. Papers, Cmnd. 1450 (1921).
12. Willis, *Prologue* [n. 8], 173.

Chapter 23

The Armenian Genocide in Relation to the Holocaust and the Nuremberg Trials

The discussion in the preceding chapter revolved around coteries of Germans and Turks who in the aftermath of World War I were tried in Istanbul and Leipzig in connection with wartime crimes. The focus there was on the category of perpetrators and the objective of the trials was punishment. But the issue of the other and twin category, i.e., prevention, is by no means a separate issue. Indeed, implicit in the condition of punishment is the reality that the crime of mass murder was not or could not be prevented. Thus, there are some interconnections between the phenomenon of prevention and that of punishment and that, therefore, a fuller understanding of genocide requires a change of focus, namely, shifting the attention from the perpetrator to the victim whose victimization could not be prevented. Such a shift is specially warranted for the examination of the Armenian and Jewish cases of genocide in a comparative framework which for the limited purposes of this study can only be in an outline form. The genocidal victimization of these two peoples has many facets and characteristics the comparative analysis of which would be a challenging and at the same time an edifying task. Here the effort will be limited to the issue of the incidence of the interconnection of the two instances of genocide in relation to the twin concepts of prevention and punishment. In this sense it is to be observed that the two cases converge as well as diverge. They converge in relation to prevention because the Jewish and Armenian peoples were the victims of genocides which could not be averted. They diverge, however, on account of the fact that in the Armenian case the perpetrators escaped punishment, in spite of the respective solemn and public pledge of the Entente Powers (by France, England, and Russia on May 24, 1915), whereas in the Jewish case, as promised, such punishment was meted out internationally and judicially.

Two related questions pose themselves in this connection: 1) Was the impunity, accorded to the perpetrators of the Armenian genocide, portentous enough to influence the dispositions and mentality of the Nazis, in particular Adolf Hitler, and facilitate thereby the latter's eventual adoption of a genocidal scheme akin to that applied against the Armenians? 2) To what extent the institution of the Nuremberg trials by the victorious Allies in the wake of World War II was, among other reasons, the result of a perception that there was an interrelationship between the Armenian genocide and the Jewish Holocaust in the sense outlined under 1 and that it was, therefore, imperative that genocide, a "crime against humanity," be no longer tolerated and be punished forthwith? There are many indications that Hitler and his cohorts were fully aware of the Armenian cataclysm and that they drew from it lessons suitable for wanting to emulate the Turkish model of enacting a "final solution." Before delving into the treatment of these questions, however, a note on the conditions under which Jews and Armenians have historically become recurrent targets of persecution may be in order. One should not underestimate the ramifications of this accumulation of a historical record when examining the circumstances of these peoples' genocidal demise in the twentieth century.

The Problem of the Vulnerability of the Jews and Armenians as Potential Targets of Victimization

The significance of the vulnerability factor derives from the cardinal fact that genocide in any form and under any circumstance is first and foremost an exercise of power with lethal consequences. It therefore presupposes a substantial disparity in the power relations between a potential perpetrator and a potential victim. One of the most common elements in the vulnerability syndrome of the Armenians and the Jews has been the inferior status to which for centuries they have been relegated as disdained minorities by nation-states and dominant groups operating within such states. The liabilities issuing from this condition had a statutory character and the vulnerability in question, therefore, involved a structural problem. Yet the overall consequences of this structural setup were considerable. For one thing, assigned or imposed inferiority implies a host of prejudices and entails a range of discriminatory practices which are bound to debilitate the collective psyche of the affected population. It is a social psychological fact that when a group of people over a period of time are treated differently the chances are that after a while many of them will begin to think of themselves as being different and, indeed, even begin to act differently. An offshoot of this process of differentiation was the rise and growth of an ethnocentrism which was distinctly adaptive. In order to accommodate and at times to placate the abusive strata of the dominant groups they were stuck with, Jews and Armenians learned to be submissive externally while developing an inner toughness which, though mostly subdued, spelled ethnic assertiveness. The result was an inveterate resistance to assimilation and the perpetuation of an ethnic identity which, depending on changing circumstances, including the onset of acute national crises, continued to disconcert, irritate or even provoke their potential victimizer groups.

These social liabilities were not the only problem; they were often compounded by legal disabilities attending them. In the case of the Armenians this included the denial of the right to bear arms in a land where their adversaries were armed to the teeth, especially in the interior and the distant provinces. For extended periods Armenians and Jews were politically disenfranchised people and, barring some incidental exceptions, they were excluded from any manner of engagement in the power structure of their respective societies. This impotence often sharply contrasted with the economic ascendancy of certain segments of these two minorities. In such situations economic preponderance and power paradoxically function to amplify the vulnerability of the minority, especially when large segments of the respective dominant group are in the grip of sustained economic hardships. In this sense, it may be argued that the combination of economic ascendancy and political impotence is intrinsically explosive. But one has to recognize that, as causative factors, what are involved here are structural constraints. The discriminations imposed upon the Jews and Armenians effectively barred them from entry into certain occupations such as civil service, the military, and government. This arrangement of preemption was restrictive enough to impel the Armenians and Jews to forego these fields of endeavor where income was regulated by fixed salaries and to channel their ambitions into trade, commerce, and industry, in other words, into strictly profitable economic activities with no limits to the pursuit of riches. In stigmatizing the respective talents that evolved and the successes that were attained as a result of these constraints the detractors and antagonists involved have simply been oblivious to the fact that this development largely came about in default. More important to consider, the larger masses of the Armenian and Jewish minorities were neither affluent nor inordinately prosperous, especially in the case of the Armenians of whom 70–80% were apolitical, simple peasants engaged in agricultural work in their ancestral territories. In his ground-breaking essay which ushered in the era of panturkish ideology, displacing the ideal of Ottomanism and eclipsing panislamism, Yusuf Akçura explained the main reason for this exclusionary stance. "Equality with non-Muslims not only would legally put an end to the 600-year-old domination of Ottoman Turks but would afford the non-Muslims access to jobs in the military and the civil service which were the monopoly of the Turks."[1]

In the equation on genocide, in which power is a critical component, there is a twin component which in a sense functions to control the exercise of power. The reference is to what sociologists call the opportunity structure. As in the case of any premeditated crime, unless there is a suitable opportunity at hand, no perpetrator will venture to proceed to a level of action, irrespective of substantial advantages of power. The sway of more or less normal conditions such as peace, stability, and order, is unproductive in this respect. However, the outbreak of a war, often purposively precipitated by a potential perpetrator, is, by the very nature of war itself, pregnant with myriad emergencies which together constitute an ideal opportunity structure. It is no accident that the destruction of the Armenians and the Jews was consummated in the vortex of two global wars. In both cases the perpetrator groups had precipitated the respective wars.[2] Indeed, the nature of warfare is such that, as a rule, it allows legislative authority to subside, if not to vanish entirely, with the executive branch of the government as the main beneficiary of the "emergency powers" accruing to it. In a war the bastion of power is usually the Executive. As the authority of the Legislative either subsides or vanishes altogether, the power of the Executive increases substantially. Emergency powers are expressive of the supreme opportunities a war yields in this regard. In both systems, the Nazi and the Ittihadist, the principal agents of these powers have been the so-called "security forces" comprising a vast network of outfits; they were invested with levels of authority that in most cases bordered on license for criminal abuse. Perhaps the greatest source of power in times of war in an oppressive society is the military establishment identified with the authorities in charge. To the extent that the outcome of the war hinges on their performance, to that extent they will acquire inordinate power and accordingly will be catapulted into relative predominance. Genocide not only requires opportunistic decision making but its execution depends on functional efficiency. In addition to planning and administering the logistics involved there has to be a command-and-control setup to ensure a reasonably smooth operation. The goal is optimal destruction at minimal cost. This is a task for which the specialized skills of the military are needed. In both cases of genocide the military played a crucial role. Involved were not just regular officers but officers who were intensely committed to the respective ideologies and goals of the Nazis and Ittihadists. Within this framework of loyalty and dedication they did critical staff work, maintained secrecy and discipline, and participated in field operations as commanders of killer bands. Such terms as "Nazi officers" and "Ittihadist officers" are descriptive of the potentially lethal process of indoctrinating military officers with party credos and teachings and in general politicizing the military, or segments of it. War emerges here as an ideal opportunity for harnessing political power into military power as an instrument of genocide.[3]

The dynamics of such a process of power amplification were such that the vulnerabilities of the Jews and Armenians as minorities increased in proportion to this growth of power; the stronger the victimizers became, the weaker became the victims. This is a mechanism which ultimately leads to what might be called victim trapping. In the Armenian case the Turks used four devices for this purpose. 1) They suspended the Parliament; it was prorogued just before the initiation of the genocide and was reconvened when that genocide had all but run its course. 2) They introduced a system of Temporary Laws, the framing of which became the prerogative of the Executive, i.e., the Ittihadist power-wielders. 3) Armed with these powers, they launched a program of massive arrests in all parts of the Ottoman Empire; nearly all community leaders, intellectuals, educators, ranking clergymen and political activists were simultaneously rounded up in nightly surprise raids, were deported and liquidated. 4) To further emasculate the victim population and reduce it to an easy prey for subsequent annihilation, all able-bodied Armenian males were conscripted in three stages as part of the general mobilization; very few of them survived the ensuing operations of summary executions or extirpation through other lethal measures.

In the Jewish case similar procedures were adopted. The emasculation of the Jewish community in Germany was more progressive in its course as its initiation dated back to the prewar years. In its first stage, i.e., the promulgation of the March 23, 1933 Enabling Act, it had a general thrust, and was not specifically directed against the Jews. As in the case of the Ittihadist initiative described above, the Nazis managed to institute an Act through which they would be empowered to make laws without the approval of the German parliament, the *Reichstag*. The five articles of the Act all but destroyed the German constitution. As in the case of the Young Turk Ittihadists, the Nazis subsequently embarked upon their scheme of *Gleichschaltung* whereby they substituted Nazi power for parliamentary power. With the outbreak of World War II, however, the Enabling Act acquired special significance for the Jews as it was renewed in 1939 and 1942 in conformity with its Article 5 which required renewal every four years. These renewals imparted a semblance of legitimacy to the array of anti-Jewish measures adopted by the various agencies of the Nazi dominated government.

The Nuremberg Laws, which came into force on September 15, 1935, and which were a by-product of the Enabling Act, comprised a series of laws specifically targeting the Jews. Since the formal emancipation of the Jews in Germany in the 1869–1871 period, by virtue of which the latter were to enjoy about the same civil rights as the Germans, the Jews for the first time were divested of their normal citizenship rights and were declared second-class subjects of the state. In the 1935–1943 period the promulgation of some 250 decrees ensued; they provided for the exclusion of the Jews from official positions and professions and progressively from economic activities, forcing them to wear the Star of David. In a final decree they were reduced to the non-status of "outlaw." It is noteworthy that both victim nations were with relative ease lulled into a sense of false security by the code word "deportation" that was to disguise the destruction awaiting them.

The vulnerability of the Jews and Armenians was not merely determined by the internal conditions of the German and Turkish nation states and the attendant coercive measure of the Nazi and Ittihadist regimes. For similar reasons but under dissimilar circumstances both minorities over extended periods of time had developed and fostered pools of support groups abroad, including political groups, diasporas, and occasionally governments acting for reasons of expediency, or on grounds of purported humanitarianism. These were factors the perpetrators had to reckon with. Precisely for these reasons, however, both instances of genocide were ushered in by the perpetrators gradually rather than precipitately, cautiously rather than carelessly. In the case of the Nazis it all started with a scheme of expulsion attended by expropriation. Then came the plan and the related negotiations for a massive relocation undertaking (the Madagascar plan). As Hilberg noted, "Hitler did not order the annihilation of the Jews immediately upon the outbreak of the war. Even Hitler shrank from such a drastic step. Even Hitler hesitated before the 'final solution.'"[4] The lack of tangible cooperation by the West in connection with these Nazi initiatives combined with the onset of new war-related exigencies to generate a situation which encouraged the Nazis to consider more radical options. As a new phase of deportation was evolving, one of the foremost Nazi leaders, Joseph Goebbels, on December 13, 1942 noted in his diary that there is an apparent concern by the media in Europe on "the persecution" of the Jews, "At bottom, however, I believe both the English and the Americans are happy that we are exterminating the Jewish riff-raff."[5] As American sociologist W.I. Thomas postulated, "If men define situations as real, they are real in their consequences." One can hardly underestimate the effect this Nazi perception had upon the subsequent crystallization of a Nazi resolve to proceed against the Jews in a more drastic way, discounting the onset of gravely adverse consequences. The resort to the "Final Solution" was a feat which was undertaken with near-complete abandon. The gigantic dimensions of the war against the Soviet Union and the confrontation with a new demographic problem, the treatment of the millions of Soviet Jews, certainly were considerations in this matter. But the paramount fact remains that the failure of the external world to mount a persuasive and effective attempt at deterrence considerably emboldened the Nazis. For a long time the Nazis had been testing the waters, expecting some counteractions or a display of credible threats.

The initiation of the Armenian genocide also involved developmental stages in the course of which the Ittihadists likewise tested the waters and released trial balloons. One such signal stage was the mass arrest on April 24, 1915 of the Armenian notables in the Ottoman capital and their immediate dispatch to the interior of the country. Given the legacy of Ottoman Turkey in the handling of such matters, the mass arrest was a harbinger of worse things to come. The ominousness of the measure did not move Turkey's allies and the neutral States in Europe and in the Americas. The promulgation on May 26, 1915 of the Temporary Law of Deportation was the next stage, the grim portentousness of which likewise made very little dent. The Turks then began the cycle of their sporadic massacres, destroying a number of deportee convoys. For nearly six weeks the Ittihadists thus continued to probe the conscience, solidarity, and resolve of the rest of the world. The Central Powers, Turkey's allies, pretended not to know; the Entente Powers, Turkey's wartime adversaries, were handicapped in terms of their preoccupation with the goal of winning the war; and the neutrals preferred to remain aloof and uninvolved. It is, therefore, no coincidence that the genocide against the Armenians swung in full gear only after the perpetrators persuaded themselves that they could afford to proceed. Beginning with the first week of June 1915 and for months on end the annihilation of the bulk of the Armenian population of the Ottoman Empire proceeded systematically, relentlessly, and implacably by a variety of means.

In both cases the forbidding specter of external deterrence failed to materialize not only because other powers and nation-states were disinclined to intervene but also because neither the Armenians nor the Jews had a parent state to counteract effectively and in a timely manner. As members of minorities, which were identified with two orphan nations, they had reached the optimum level of their vulnerability at the time of their peril and doom.

The cumulative aspects of the vulnerability issue highlight the historical dimensions of the problem. The logical counterpart of the notion of a notorious perpetrator is that of a notorious victim. For a host of reasons, some of them described above, the Armenians and the Jews acquired a notoriety as suitable, if not ideal, targets for potential perpetrator groups. This is the more significant when one takes into account the many differences separating the two peoples in terms of origin, religion, culture, and demography. By the same token one may point out the vast differences separating the victimizers, the Germans and the Turks, in terms of levels of culture and civilization.

It is evident that in genocide victim differences, whether among members of a single victim group or among several victim groups, are of little significance. The differences simply collapse into an abyss of irrelevance as they are levelled by the mechanisms and claws of a mammoth engine of destruction.[6] In this connection it may be observed in conclusion that the most salient feature of the two genocides in terms of the circumstances under which neither genocide could be prevented is the identity of the agents who designed, installed, and effectively ran that engine of destruction. Contrary to generally accepted assertions, these agents were not primarily affiliated with the respective state apparatuses but with two monolithic political parties, those of the Nazis and the Ittihadists. The leaders of these parties simply overwhelmed these apparatuses by gaining control of the state organizations, permeating the ministries, controlling the latters' functions and altogether imposing upon the respective governments the party programs at issue. One should not confound the boundaries which, as a rule, circumscribe the functions of a state and the operations of a government with the license a monolithic and dictatorial political party can allow itself in its effort to implement its ideals and goals. Nor can one equate the rules of accountability governing the affairs of a state with party regulations, party reward system, party secrecy, and party discipline as the main, if not sole, standards for running public affairs and directing the destiny of a nation. The sections to follow may further vindicate this argument. A Turkish author who was Minister of Defense in the pre-World War I years, who served as Army Commander during that war, and was the first Grand Vizier in the Armistice period, aptly diagnosed this problem in his memoirs. According to him "the principal reason of the Ittihadist government's failure was its insistence on the implementation of decisions which Ittihad had reached as a secret [conspiratorial] committee but which it tried to implement after gaining control of the government. It ran that government through the secret levers of power with which its party centers were invested."[7]

Considerations on the Armenian Genocide Seen as a Precedent and a Precursor of the Holocaust

This is an issue with acute significance, an acuteness which is matched by the largeness of the difficulty of providing a clear and definitive answer to it. The main difficulty is that, given the nature of the problem, one is fully dependent upon the perpetrators of the Holocaust, especially Hitler, for such a definitive answer; they, or Hitler, would have had to volunteer the requisite information, credibly and unambiguously, which, of course, they didn't. It is a historical fact that Hitler in particular was, as a rule, extremely secretive about the details of his conspiratorial ideas and plans. As will be seen below, this obsession for secrecy came into play in an incident in which he had made an allusion to the successfulness of the scheme of the World War I genocide against the Armenians. His inadvertent witness subsequently ended up dying in dubious circumstances.

The record of Hitler's allusions to the fate of the Armenians

Hitler's ideology was no secret as it was broadcast in general terms, including the expression of his inveterate urge to destroy the Jews. But when it came to blueprints, mechanics, instructions and orders, there is either silence or the abiding veil of stealthiness. One is faced with this duality of a personality characteristic, "an inimitable mixture of brutal honesty and the art of concealment" (*eine unnachahmliche Mischung von brutaler Ehrlichkeit und Kunst des Verbergens*).[8] Joachim Fest, who called attention to Hitler's "characteristic mania for secrecy" (*Verheimlichungs-manie*), maintains that Hitler was cognizant of the record of the past involving "acts of physical annihilation" denoted by the terms "elimination or extermination," and he was thus cognizant "much earlier than his closest followers … . Even at the beginnings of the thirties Hitler had, among his intimates, called for the development of a 'technique of depopulation' and explicitly added that by that he meant the elimination of entire races."[9]

A number of utterances Hitler made in the 1920s and 30s indicate that he was knowledgeable about both Armenians and Turks in general, about the historical record of the persecution of the Armenians, and their demise in Turkey through "annihilation." In one of the earliest surviving written documents containing statements or speeches by Hitler and covering the period up to 1924, the future Nazi leader made an allusion to the Armenians as victims of their lack of courage for combativeness. The "solution of the Jewish question," he added, requires, therefore, "a bloody clash." Otherwise, Hitler noted, "the German people will end up becoming just like the Armenians" (… *das deutsche Volk wird ein Volk wie die Armenier …*).[10] Hitler made an analogous remark some two decades later. At the Klessheim Conference (April 17, 1943), he plunged into a speech full of invectives against the Jews as depraved parasites, as "tubercular bacilli that threatened a healthy body." He was arguing in the sense that nations which could not defend themselves against what he viewed as the pernicious influence of the Jews were doomed to suffer the fate of "once so proud a people as the Persians, who now had to continue their miserable existence as Armenians."[11] In an interview in July 1933 Hitler told the editor of a Turkish newspaper that he admired the movement in modern Turkey which fostered the virtues of primitivity among native peasants in Anatolia. For him, Hitler, the example of that movement was "a shining star."[12] The situation for the Jews of Germany in 1935 was ominous enough to prompt two British officials, who were negotiating with German officials in the Economics Ministry about the financial aspects of emigration of German Jews to Palestine, to express their despair about the future of the Jews in Nazi

Germany. One of them, Eric Mills, the Commissioner for Migration and Statistics in Palestine, wrote in a private letter after the negotiation, "... the fate of German Jews is a tragedy for which cold, intelligent planning by those in authority takes rank ... with the elimination of the Armenians from the Turkish Empire."[13]

Hitler's much debated key statement on the annihilation of the Armenians. Genghis Khan as a role model.

The statement in question has been extensively used by many authors for the purpose of establishing a link of one kind or another between the Armenian genocide and the subsequent genocidal initiatives of Hitler, who is presumed to have been influenced by that genocide, but, more particularly, by the outcome of that genocide (as far as the perpetrators were concerned), namely, impunity. The debate was prompted by the uncertainties surrounding the provenance and venue of the document in question, and the identity of the source obtaining and transmitting the material embedded in the document. These issues had arisen in connection with the task of the prosecutors at the Nuremberg trials to ascertain the criminal intent and conduct of the Nazis prior to and in the course of the war. As will be explained below, however, documentary evidence emerging since the Nuremberg trials episode has dispelled the doubts in this regard, duly establishing the authenticity of the statement which reads as follows: "Who after all is today speaking of the destruction of the Armenians" (*Wer redet heute noch von der Vernichtung der Armenier*). The document was for the first time transmitted to British diplomats in Berlin in August 1939 by Louis Lochner. For more than two decades Lochner was chief of the Berlin Bureau of The Associated Press and for many years he was president of the Foreign Press Association there. Sir Neville Henderson, British Ambassador at Berlin, transmitted the document to London on August 25, 1939.[14]

The document purports to be the summary of one or two speeches Hitler delivered to the Chief Commanders and Commanding Generals at Obersalzberg, August 22, 1939, in preparation for the impending invasion of Poland. In essence, Hitler in that speech is admonishing the high ranking military officers to be brutal and merciless for a quick victory (*Seien Sie hart, seien Sie schonungslos, handeln Sie schneller und brutaler als die andern*).

The imminent invasion is portrayed as the initiation of the first step for the implementation of a wide-ranging visionary scheme to "secure the living space we need" (*gewinnen wir den Lebensraum den wir brauchen*). The overall purpose is to "redistribute the world" (*eine Neuverteilung der Welt*). The explicit reference to the Armenians is made in a paragraph furnishing the context of one of Hitler's notions that the creation of a new world order calls for a resort to mass murder for which he cited the example of Genghis Khan who "sent millions of women and children into death knowingly and cheerfully (*fröhlichen Herzens*). Yet, history sees in him only the great founder of States." This line of thought is introduced to conclude that the extermination of the Armenians served a similar purpose. The Turks destroyed them mercilessly allowing Mustafa Kemal to establish a new Turkish state system and the world not only consigned the annihilation of the Armenians to oblivion but has accepted the new order of the things because "The world believes only in success" (*Die Welt glaubt nur an den Erfolg.*) (Note an identical remark on success Talât, the architect of the Armenian genocide, has made in connection with the extermination of the Armenians. Ch 21, note 7.)

This sort of affinity which Hitler seemingly felt for Genghis Khan was of the kind which also allowed him to extend it to Mustafa Kemal Atatürk whom he extolled in the same speech as a true statesman, as the founder of modern Turkey, while dismissing as idiots (*Kretins*) those who succeeded him as stewards of that modern Turkey.[15] His treatment of M. Kemal as a sort of model for him at the time of the November 1923 Putsch in Münich is mentioned by Fest; Hitler reportedly drew inspiration from the Turkish leader to overcome his hesitations and to act boldly and forcefully.[16] Despite important differences between Genghis Khan and Atatürk there are certain elements of correspondence in the circumstances of the two which call for some comments. For one thing, Atatürk himself exalted the historical figure of Genghis in a November 1, 1922, speech in the Grand National Assembly, describing him as a source of pride for the Turkish nation.[17] Moreover, the three foremost pioneers of modern Turkish nationalism, Akçura, Hüseyinzade, and Ziya Gökalp, in prose and verse, glorified the Mongol war lord Genghis Khan as the primordial symbol of the capacity of "Turkic-Turanian" warriors to proceed against people with boundless ferocity during sweeping martial operations. In a poem titled *Turan*, Ziya Gökalp described him as a genius who has "crowned my race with conquests." In another poem, likewise titled *Turan*, Hüseyinzade Ali, using the pen-name A. Turani, marvelled at how Genghis "shook the horizons end to end." Akçura likewise "exalted" (*yüceltmiş*) the figure of Genghis, calling him "a Turk." In 1914, at the outbreak of World War I, another nationalist poet, and a cohort of Atatürk, Mehmet Emin, in his ringing call, O Turk, Wake Up (*Ey Türk Uyan*), which found an echo in the Nazi emblem, Germany, Awake (*Deutschland, Erwache*), appealed to "all the Turks" to be inspired by the heroic feats of the Mongolian conqueror and emulate him by ascending "the heights of the Altais," (that conqueror's natural habitat), "and raise your voice ferociously … . No flower grows ever without blood … . Let all the Turks of this planet come and unite 'round your banner.'"[18]

Clearly, Genghis and his feats of conquest were such as to impress not only Turks but other national leaders also aspiring to be conquerors.

Awed by the size of the successful outcome, such leaders were bound to be influenced by the sanguinary and ferocious methods which Genghis used to secure that outcome. This is the rationale linking Hitler to the historical legacy of Genghis and through it to the idea of genocide as a viable vehicle for the execution of grandiose schemes. According to Wanda von Baeyer, a German psychologist, Hitler himself had introduced the SS practice of *Blutkitt*, Genghis Khan's tradition of cementing solidarity among his hordes through the perpetration of merciless mass murder. Reportedly, Hitler "had discovered in a book about Genghis Khan ... as early as his Landsberg Prison days" (February 2-December 20, 1924).[19] Another German author discerned a pattern of continuity of the Genghis legacy in the emergence of the Ottoman dynasty, thereby indicating the incidence of a Mongol-Ottoman Turk connection. As he relates, "The Ottoman dynasty began at a time when the hordes of Genghis Khan—the Pan-Asiatic Mongol—was sweeping westward and carrying the swastika in Asia Minor. It ended when the modern Genghis Khan—the Pan-European Hitler—was laying plans for the drive of his swastika-bearing armies toward the ends of the earth."[20]

The thread of devastation running through all these episodes of history is exemplified in the stance of some of the foremost organizers of the Armenian genocide. One of them, Halil Kut, the uncle of Enver, the wartime de facto Commander-in-Chief of Ottoman Armed Forces, was Commander-in-Chief of Army Group East and had invaded Russian Armenia in the spring of 1918. Before a large crowd of Armenians in the capital city of Yerevan in the summer of that year, General Halil boastfully declared "I have tried to wipe out the Armenian nation to the last individual."[21] When being detained in a military prison in the Ottoman capital during the Armistice (along with other Ittihadist leaders, implicated in the organization of the Armenian genocide) for what would be his later court martial, this Turkish general, as noted above, defiantly and in writing told a British captain that the number of his victims of mass killings may have reached "300,000 Armenians ... . It can be more or less. I didn't count."[22] As confessional as these truculently framed admissions are, they are even more telling when placed in a context in which General Halil's veneration, bordering on idolatry, of Genghis Khan is revealed. The source for such a revelation is Colonel Ernst Paraquin, the German Chief of Staff of General Halil. Colonel Paraquin in exposing the horrors of the Armenian genocide—"the solution of the Armenian Question through annihilation"— alludes to Halil's grandiose plans of "a Panturkish Empire," stretching from Anatolia and the Caucasus to "the extreme outposts of Turkdom in the East ... as far as the Siberian Jakuts." He states that the Armenians were destroyed with "inexorable ruthlessness," which was consistent with a predilection for "barbarous behavior"; all the carnage was carried out in the name of "this great, nationally

exclusive Turkish Empire." It is against this backdrop that one may interpret the significance of Halil naming his youngest son after the ferocious
war lord Genghis. As the German staff officer relates in his essay, Halil's
zest for panturanist drives and assaults was reflected in this motto of his:
"Let us push to Turkestan; there I will found the new empire for my little Genghis" (*Dort will ich das neue Kaisertum für meinen kleinen
Dschingis gründen*).[23] Halil evidently repeated to his Turkish friends his
conjurations for Genghis Khan. According to a Turkish historian, Halil
"was dead serious when he vowed to 'have my son Genghis sit on the
throne of Turkistan.' He was deceiving neither himself nor anyone else ... .
He was speaking his own true language."[24] (Turkistan in Persian means
"land of the Turks," a land that encompasses most of the areas subsumed
under the term Central Asia. All of it fell to the Mongol armies of
Genghis Khan in the thirteenth century. Tamerlane, another conqueror
with a taste for merciless carnage, is said to be descended from him.)

    The annihilative spirit of Genghis Khan had permeated the frame of
mind of many of the Ittihadist leaders, likewise driven by panturkism and
likewise committed to the task of liquidating the Armenians, the principal and troublesome obstacle on the road to "Turkistan." The speech
delivered by Ittihadist chieftain Yenibahçeli Nail one week before the
start of the annihilation of the Armenian population of the province of
Trabzon epitomizes this frame of mind. On June 5/18, 1915, Nail
addressed a mass meeting in the public park of the city of Trabzon. After
explaining the reasons for Turkey's intervention in the war, praising the
Germans as Turkey's friends and ally, and tongue-lashing the British, but
especially the Russians, he finished the speech with the intonation: "Oh
people [*Ey ahali*]. We are the progeny of the likes of Genghis Khan,
Tamerlane and Osman; we are their worthy scions. In our veins flows
their blood. We shall demonstrate to the world the might of our arms; the
palpitations of our horses' hoofs will echo in the lands of our foes. The
hour has come to show to the Europeans of Christian faith, to the infidel
Russians, and to their friends [amongst us] the power of our sword."[25]
The allusion to the Armenians as the internal enemy in the last sentence
was all too transparent to escape attention. In fact, Nail at this time was
touring the various districts of the province, of which he was Ittihad's
Responsible Secretary, i.e., the omnipotent party commissar with veto
power over the Governor-General, inciting the Muslim population
against the Armenians in secretly held assemblies and conclaves.

    Nail's omnipotence was exceeded only by the ferocity with which he
exercised that omnipotence. This fact is illustrated in one of the reports
Oscar S. Heizer, the American consul at Trabzon, filed with the State
Department. Through the intercession of many people, including the
Greek Primate of Trabzon, foreign diplomats and Turks, the governor-
general had agreed to exempt from deportation the Armenian children, at

least for the time being. According to the American consul, "Nearly 3,000 children were installed in empty houses of which there were many … . This plan did not suit Nail Bey … . Many of the children were loaded into boats and taken out to sea and thrown overboard. I myself saw where 16 bodies were washed ashore and buried by a Greek woman near the Italian Monastery."[26] The testimony of a Greek merchant, a native of Trabzon, is even more striking. He had heard of the murder through multiple mutilations of the remaining three Armenian employees of the local branch of Bank Ottoman, all of them recent college graduates. When afterwards Nail dropped in to make some purchase, the merchant, with whom Nail was acquainted, inquired about the fate of these victims. Nail is reported to have answered as follows: "Were it within my powers [*elimden gelirse*], I would recreate the Armenians so that I may exterminate them anew."[27]

As in most cases of capital crime in which the perpetration requires a corresponding frame of mind, so too in the case of genocide, the perpetration requires the presence of a genocidal frame of mind. The preceding discussion indicates, if not demonstrates, a certain interconnection, at the level of genocidal frames of minds, between the incidence of the Armenian genocide and that of the Jewish Holocaust in which the murderous legacy of the Mongol war lord Genghis Khan emerges as a nexus, as a functional link. There are, of course, a whole range of factors through the operational configuration of which both genocides evolved and materialized, including the ideologically conditioned belief that the ushering in of a radically new order may necessitate destruction and cataclysm on a grand scale. But there can be no doubt that the example of Genghis had a foremost impact upon the organization and implementation of not only the Armenian genocide but also the Nazi-engineered cataclysm of World War II in which the Jewish Holocaust occupies the center stage. In his overall assessment of that cataclysm, Lord Wright, the Chairman of United Nations War Crimes Commission, in March 1948, i.e., in the wake of the Nuremberg Trials, acknowledged this fact. He attributed the horrors of World War II to a lapse into barbarism, reminiscent "of the days of Attila, Genghis Khan or Tamarlane."[28]

It was noted above that Hitler's August 22, 1939 statement, upon which this entire discussion is predicated, has been subject to dispute. The debate arose in connection with the attempt by the prosecution at the Nuremberg trials to introduce as an exhibit the document, from which the statement was excerpted. For the reasons described above, the document was not accepted as authentic, thereby questioning, but not denying, the veracity of Hitler's statement contained in it. Two detailed studies tackled this problem of veracity. One of them, by Winfried Baumgart, concluded that there were five versions of the document in question. The first was the one procured by Lochner; the second consisted of a set of two versions originating from the repositories of the German High Command; the third from Admiral Böhm; the fourth from General Halder, Chief of Army General Staff; and the fifth from the Army's War Diary which was compiled by H. Greiner, the man in charge of it. After a meticulous scrutiny, Baumgart concluded that Lochner's document or version was essentially identical with the set of the two versions originating from the repositories of the German High Command as well as with Greiner's fifth version and that in all likelihood all these versions were commonly based on the handwritten notes which Admiral Canaris, the Chief of Counterintelligence, secretly took down during the conference on August 22.

Baumgart proved to be less than accurate, however, when he ventured to suggest that the reference to the Armenians in Hitler's speech in all likelihood was an act of editorial "coloring up" (*Ausmalen*) by those who prepared reports on the speech.[29] Indeed, at the time Baumgart's article appeared (1968), Edouard Galic was publishing his book, *Ohne Maske,* in which the texts of two newly uncovered confidential interviews with Hitler in 1931 were published. It develops that fully eight years earlier than the speech he delivered at Obersalzberg Hitler had made exactly the same statement as he brought forth the historical fact of "the extermination the Armenians." During the second interview in June 1931 he was discussing his future plans of massive deportations and the inevitable ruination of the victim populations involved. He was being interviewed by Richard Breiting, the powerful editor of the great German daily *Leipziger Neueste Nachrichten*, the organ of the conservative-nationalist Germans. Departing from his rigid policy, Hitler allowed Breiting to take short-hand notes swearing him, however, to secrecy. Here is his remark:

> Everywhere people are awaiting a new world order. We intend to introduce a great resettlement policy ... . Think of the biblical deportations and the massacres of the Middle Ages ... and remember the extermination of the Armenians [*erinnern Sie sich doch an die Ausrottung Armeniens.*][30]

The veracity of this statement issues from the conditions of authenticity surrounding it. After a lapse of several years the Leipzig Gestapo was mobilized to retrieve the notes of Breiting which the Nazi leadership by retrospection felt to be revealing of Hitler's projective designs and, therefore, liable to all sorts of interpretations and reactions by the West. Breiting in 1937 died under suspicious conditions after meeting two Gestapo agents to whom he unsuccessfully pretended that he had destroyed the notes. These were supplied after the war, however, by his sister. Calic produces a full list of people, including the former chief of the Reichstag stenographic bureau, who through sworn statements and affidavits certify the authenticity of the notes; especially detailed is the memorandum of the Reichstag stenographic bureau chief.[31]

The confirmation of the accuracy of the portion on the Armenians in Hitler's speech extends to that on Genghis Khan as well. The context is the same, the words are uttered in the same vein, and Hitler on other occasions acknowledged the legacy of the latter as a source of inspiration for him. The entire debate in terms of the origin, conditions, and authenticity of the document, containing Hitler's speech, and the range of arguments about its merits are examined in the other study undertaken by K. Bardakjian, who concluded that the document is authentic.[32] Even though the motives of Hitler in wanting to destroy the Jews were not in every respect identical with those of the Ittihadists wanting to destroy the Armenians, the two victim nations share one common element in Hitler's scheme of things: their extreme undesirability. He emphasized the urgency of "the task of protecting the German blood from contamination, not only of the Jewish but also of the Armenian blood."[33]

The sources of knowledge in Nazi Germany regarding the fate of the Armenians

The relative ease with which the Armenian genocide was consummated and the perpetrators escaped retributive justice was such as to impress the higher strata of Nazi leadership contemplating a similar initiative with respect to the Jews. As Abram Sachar wrote, " ... the genocide was cited approvingly twenty-five years later by the Fuehrer ... who found the Armenian 'solution' an instructive precedent."[34] It was instructive primarily because, as noted above, it was indirectly rewarded with impunity. As David Matas, a Canadian expert on international law, observed, "Nothing emboldens a criminal so much as the knowledge he can get away with a crime. That was the message the failure to prosecute for the Armenian massacre gave to the Nazis. We ignore the lesson of the Holocaust at our peril."[35] Richard Lichtheim, one of the German Jews who, as a young leader of the Zionist movement, feverishly negotiated with Ittihadist leaders in wartime Turkey, described the "the cold-bloodedly planned extermination of over one million Armenians" (*kaltblütig durchdacht*) as an act of perpetration "akin to Hitler's crusade of destruction against the Jews in the 1940–1942 period."[36]

Even though the story of the Armenian genocide was suppressed in wartime Germany by the authorities, the German missionary and historian Lepsius had already in 1916 spread the word in limited circles on the nature and scale of the Turkish anti-Armenian measures. With the end of the war the picture changed dramatically as a plethora of German missionaries, especially protestant, flooded the market with a stream of accounts on "the Armenian martyrdom." The trial in 1921 in Berlin of the assassin of Talât, and particularly his acquittal by a jury, were events galvanizing large segments of the German public which thus became acquainted with the details of the horrors of the genocide. As one expert on the Holocaust noted, "during the 1920's authors had ... popularized the history of the genocide: and Franz Werfel, the German-Jewish novelist did the same in the 1930's through his *Forty Days of Musa Dagh*."[37] Werfel not only wrote about "this incomprehensible destiny of the Armenian nation" (his introductory note to this novel) but through a lecture tour in German cities in the Fall of 1933 he broadcast and belabored the details of the Armenian genocide within a literary framework of description and interpretation. In reacting to this role of Werfel, the Nazi periodical *Das Schwarze Korps* denounced him as a propagandist of "alleged Turkish horrors perpetrated against the Armenians," and berated "America's Armenian Jews for promoting in the U.S.A. the sale of Werfel's book.[38]

When one moves from the German public as an audience learning about the Armenian genocide to the arena of German officialdom as the locus of authoritative sources on the Armenian genocide, the possibilities for the higher-echelon Nazi leaders, including Hitler, to come into possession of intimate details of the Armenian genocide proliferate. Some of these German officials functioned as agents of transition from war to Armistice; others from the Weimar Republic to the Nazi era. Still others acquired a double identity; they served consecutively, both Emperor William II and Adolf Hitler. Most of them were stationed for different periods of service in wartime Turkey and thus knew a great deal about the operations of liquidating the Armenians. The channels and manner of communicating their knowledge of the Armenian genocide to Nazi decision makers is an issue of circumstantialness; a central element of contingency in this regard is the degree of their identification with the Nazi regime and ideology, and the nature of their access to these decision makers. The potential of communication is there for all of them; the likelihood of it applies to many of them, and the probability to some of them. (Within these parameters of ambiguity the officials involved are listed and briefly described in the Appendix attached to this study.)

The special case of Dr. Max Erwin von Scheubner Richter

Of all the German World War I veterans who had served in allied Turkey in a military and/or diplomatic capacity and who at the same time were in a position to influence in some way Hitler's frame of mind at the rudimentary stages of the Nazi movement about the possibilities of eliminating the "alien" elements of Germany, Scheubner Richter is most prominent. As Vice Consul in Erzurum, and later as Co-Commander of a joint Turko-German Expeditionary guerilla force he was afforded exceptional opportunities to gain insight in the overt as well as covert aspects of the Ittihadist scheme of the Armenian genocide. During the march of the Expeditionary units to the zone of operations he even witnessed scenes of massacre in the Bitlis province which he described in his last report to Chancellor Hollweg.[39] In the April 30-November 5, 1915 period he had sent to his superiors 15 major reports on the details of the ongoing deportations and massacres, and in his last lengthy report, noted above, he declared that "except for a few hundred thousand survivors, the Armenians of Turkey for all practical purposes have been exterminated" (*ausgerottet*). In the same report Scheubner provides details about the Ittihadist design of violently homogenizing Turkey, the web of contrived excuses, pretexts, deflections, and concealments with respect to that design, techniques of lulling and trapping the victim population, the use of criminal gangs, and the active involvement in all this of the Ittihadist party machinery. In brief, Scheubner learned all that needs to be learned about motivation, organization, mechanics, and cover-up in the enactment of a genocide.

Whether he transmitted all that knowledge to Hitler thereby contributing to the emergence of a frame of mind from the recesses of which came forth Hitler's repeatedly made declaration that, based on the Armenian example, one may commit mass murder with impunity, is a question which is still being debated. Focusing on that August 22, 1939 declaration made in Obersalzberg, a German publication recently answered the question rather affirmatively. It stated that "Hitler must have known exactly" *(Hitler muss genau Bescheid gewusst haben)* about the Armenian case of genocide "because one of his closest collaborators at the early stages of the National Socialist movement was Dr. Max Erwin von Scheubner Richter, i.e., Germany's former consul at Erzurum whose awful reports on the massacre of the Armenians are preserved."[40] The periodical went even one step further asserting that the skills used in the Armenian episode served as an example for Hitler's similar initiative against the Jews. In this connection the periodical depicts such analogous features as "wartime deportations; extirpation through exhaustive labor; death marches; incitement of other peoples for the purpose of enlisting their help in the destruction of the victim population; decimation through attrition by way of artificially induced hardships involving exposure to harsh climactic conditions, starvation and epidemics; the creation of concentration camps; and shameless acts of enrichment through the appropriation of the possessions of the deportees."

The issue of Scheubner's direct and effective influence upon Hitler's frame of mind requires a brief review of the origin, nature, and outcome of the relationship that developed between Hitler and Scheubner. It was Alfred Rosenberg, a fellow Baltic German, and the guru of Nazi ideology, who in 1920 in München introduced Scheubner to Hitler. Scheubner and his wife on November 22 of the same year joined the Nazi party following their attendance of a Nazi gathering at which Hitler spoke. The initial impetus for both Hitler and Scheubner to involve themselves in the launching of a nationalist movement in Bavaria was the revolutionary agitation throughout Germany on the part of the German socialists, especially the communists. In one of his editorials in his paper *Aufbau-Korrespondenz*, which he had established in München in 1920, Scheubner warned against the dangers of communism behind which, he maintained, lurked "the international-Jewish plot of world domination." Both nations, German and Russian, he continued, should, therefore, beware of the threat of "a Jewish-Bolshevik dictatorship."[41] In yet another editorial published in early 1923, Scheubner adopted a more militant posture. Blaming alien elements for what he called the gradual corrosion of Germany, he urged the resort to "a ruthless and relentless" campaign against these elements so that "Germany is inexorably cleansed" (*rücksichtslose Reinigung Deutschlands*). He wrote, "We have to wage a merciless fight against all that is alien to the corporate entity of the German people—for the sake of the German nation and the Great German Reich."[42] It is noteworthy that Scheubner in one of his World War I reports to his ambassador characterized the city-dwelling Armenians as "these Jews of the Orient, these wily businessmen" (*gerissene Handelsleute*).[43] It is equally noteworthy that in the printed version of this report in the German Foreign Office compilation of documents on the Armenian genocide, edited by Lepsius, this remark, along with some others, is deleted.

When in February 1920 the Nazis in Bavaria struck up an alliance with a string of militantly nationalistic societies and other outfits with a fascistic bent, and the S.A. became the military arm of this new Fighting League (*Kampfbund*), Hitler appointed Scheubner as the general manager of it. From then on the relationship between the two intensified with Scheubner securing for the League "enormous sums of money" through his network of extensive contacts with German industrialists. At the November 8–9, 1923 abortive Putsch in München, at which such foremost Nazis as Rosenberg, Julius Streicher, Hermann Göring, Ludendorff, were trying to overthrow the Bavarian government, Scheubner was marching with his arm linked with Hitler's. He was one of the first to be hit by the local police, struck in the heart by a bullet that killed him immediately. "As he fell, he pulled Hitler down with him so hard that the Führer dislocated his shoulder and screamed with pain."[44]

As Joachim Fest observed, "His influence on Hitler was considerable; he was the only one of those killed at the Feldherrnhalle on November 9, 1923, whom Hitler held to be irreplaceable."[45] A similar view is expressed by Trumpener who noted that "Scheubner Richter, like so many other German officials in wartime Turkey, later became a prominent figure in German politics. In the early years of the Nazi movement he was one of Hitler's closest advisers ... ."[46]

The Nuremberg Crucible

If the Jews and Armenians shared a common fate because their victimization could not be prevented, that commonality vanished with the institution of the Nuremberg trials as a result of which a large dose of retributive justice was administered to the phalanx of the Nazi perpetrators involved. The scale of that justice was considerable because of its by-products and after-effects; a host of other, ancillary sets of trials were launched in Germany and elsewhere in Europe.

The series of mistakes and failures on the part of the European victors in World War I rendered the Armenian genocide impervious to both prevention and punishment. The failure of the justice process in this case (compounded by the dismal results of the German Leipzig trials) prompted the Allies to employ different methods at Nuremberg following World War II. This change was considerably facilitated by maintaining a modicum of consensus and unison among the victors. The German State and its subsidiary organizations were challenged on the main issue of the criminal abuse of sovereignty, whereby its own citizens had become victims of "murder, extermination, enslavement, deportation." United States Supreme Court Justice Robert Jackson played a key role in this respect. Questioning the relevance of the World War I arguments of the American members of the Commission on Responsibilities, who adhered to the doctrine of the inviolability and immunity of the sovereign state, he declared, "[S]entiment in the United States and the better World opinion have greatly changed since Mr. James Brown Scott and Secretary Lansing announced their views … ."[47] In his opening statement, he counterposed to that doctrine the following arguments:

> Of course, it was under the law of all civilized peoples a crime for one man with his bare knuckles to assault another. How did it come that multiplying this crime by a million, and adding firearms to bare knuckles, made a legally innocent act? The doctrine was that one could not be regarded as criminal for committing the usual violent acts in the conduct of legitimate warfare … . An International Law which operates only on states can be enforced only by war because the most practicable method of coercing a state is warfare … . The only answer to recalcitrance was impotence or war … . Of course, the idea that a state, any more than a corporation, commits crimes is a fiction. While it is quite proper to employ the fiction of responsibility of a state or corporation for the purpose of imposing a collective liability, it is quite intolerable to let such a legalism become the basis of personal immunity. The Charter recognizes that one who has committed criminal acts may not take refuge in superior orders nor in the doctrine that his crimes were acts of states … . The Charter also recognizes a vicarious liability, which responsibility is recognized by most modern systems of law, for acts committed by others in carrying out a common plan or conspiracy to which a defendant has become a party … . [M]en are convicted for acts that they did not personally commit but for which they were held responsible because of membership in illegal combinations or plans or conspiracies.[48]

The Nuremberg Tribunal was not only a military court of occupation, but an international court as well. As such it pioneered in some crucial ways in overcoming areas of tension between national and international law to impose penal sanctions for crimes against humanity committed by a state. The procedural adaptations embedded in the Nuremberg Charter illustrate the point.

The Agreement, an outgrowth of the work of the London Conference, was concluded at London, August 8, 1945. The Charter, under which the 1945–1946 Nuremberg trials were held, was annexed to the agreement. The Nuremberg principles, which emerged from a series of decisions associated with these trials, are significant in terms of both precedence and codification. In the Judgment, for example, it is stated that,

> The jurisdiction of the Tribunal is defined in the Agreement and Charter, and the crimes coming within the jurisdiction of the Tribunal, for which there shall be individual responsibility, are set out in Article 6. The law of the Charter is decisive, and binding upon the Tribunal. The making of the Charter was the exercise of the sovereign legislative power by the countries to which the German Reich unconditionally surrendered; and the undoubted right of these countries to legislate for the occupied territories had been recognized by the civilized world.[49]

This decision is entirely in accord with the 1919 recommendation of the Commission on Responsibilities, cited in Carnegie Endowment for International Peace, *Violations of the Laws and Customs of War: Report of the Majority and Dissenting Reports of the American and Japanese Members of the Commission on Responsibilities at the Conference of Paris.* The following procedural adaptations spelled out in the Charter are likewise noteworthy:

Art. 3   Neither the Tribunal, its members nor their alternates can be challenged by the prosecution, or by the defendants or their counsel.

Art. 18 The Tribunal shall
(a) Confine the trial strictly to an expeditious hearing of the issues raised by the charges.
(b) Take strict measures to prevent any action which will cause unreasonable delay, and rule out irrelevant issues and statements of any kind whatsoever.
(c) Deal summarily with any contumacy imposing appropriate punishment, including exclusion of any defendant or his counsel from some or all further proceedings, but without prejudice to the determination of the charges.

Art. 19 The Tribunal shall not be bound by technical rules of evidence. It shall adopt and apply to the greatest possible extent expeditious and non-technical procedure, and shall admit any evidence which it deems to have probative value.[50]

The resulting legal precedents circumscribed the primacy and exclusivity of domestic laws concerning personal responsibility, international accountability, and criminal liability for wartime conduct. These princi-

ples extended criminal liability to the highest officials of a state, including
the sovereign, imposing severe restrictions on such defenses as superior
orders, act of state, and military necessity. The legal nuances of these
restrictions, treated as a matter of customary international law, were extensively debated in the wake of World War I by British, French, and German
jurists grappling with the proposed terms of the Versailles Treaty.[51]

The Nuremberg Charter stipulation that crimes against humanity, in
order to be prosecuted, have to be war-related, i.e., "in execution or in
connection with the war," was treated in general terms by the 1919 Turkish Military Tribunal. In its Key Indictment, it scorned the covert goals of
the conspirators in their catapulting Turkey into war by a preemptive
strike against Russia. *Takvimi Vekayi*, No. 3540, May 5, 1919. In its Key
Verdict, it reiterated this point by citing the evidence supplied by one of
the members of Ittihad party's Central Committee. *Takvimi Vekayi*, No.
3604. The final report of the Commission on Responsibilities likewise
underscored the fact that the war was "premeditated by the central powers together with their allies," especially Turkey, "and was the result of
acts deliberately connected in order to make it unavoidable." It then
linked these premeditated designs with the wartime perpetration of "barbarous methods in violation of the established laws and customs of war
and the elementary laws of humanity."[52] Above all the Tribunal paved the
way for the affirmation of crimes against humanity as a supreme offense
under international law, treating it as subsidiary to common and uncommon types of war crimes, and as a source of the law of nations.

The historical roots of this development, with particular reference to
the nineteenth-century Armenian Question, deserve to be emphasized
once more. When British Foreign Secretary Grey decided, after some
hesitation, to join his French and Russian colleagues in endorsing the
May 24, 1915 public warning against Turkey regarding a new wave of
Armenian massacres, he "saw the threat of punishments as a continuation
of nineteenth century policies against Turkish atrocities."[53] Even more
significant, Sir Hartley Shawcross, the British Chief Prosecutor at
Nuremberg, singled out the Armenian case as the basis of the emergence
of the Nuremberg law on crimes against humanity. Quoting Grotius to the
effect that intervention is justified when atrocities are perpetrated by dic-
tators against their own subjects, he declared:

> The same view was acted upon by the European Powers which in time past
> intervened in order to protect the Christian subjects of Turkey against cruel
> persecution. The fact is that the right of humanitarian intervention by war is
> not a novelty in International Law ... .

This argument was preceded by his analysis of the limits of state sovereignty in relation to international law:

> Normally International Law concedes that it is for the State to decide how it
> shall treat its own nationals; it is a matter of domestic jurisdiction ... . Yet Inter-

national Law has in the past made some claim that there is a limit to the omnipotence of the State and that the individual human being, the ultimate unit of all law is not disentitled to the protection of mankind when the State tramples upon his rights in a manner which outrages the conscience of mankind.[54]

The success of Nuremberg, however, should not obscure the ever present dangers that led to the failure of international law during the Armenian genocide. Given the nature of genocide, the practical problems attending the enforcement of legal sanctions are issues which continue to render questionable the viability of efforts at deterrence. Nor is there any great likelihood that any future initiatives of retribution will benefit from the degree of consensus among the participating states as existed at Nuremberg. The Nazi crimes were too extensive, the victim categories too numerous, and the resulting devastation too cataclysmic to permit the intrusion at Nuremberg of consequential disagreements among the Allies. Most important, the nations partaking in the judicial prosecution of Nazi crimes were, next to the Jews, the principal victims of Nazi atrocities. It is appropriate to wonder whether Nuremberg might have been contemplated at all, let alone instituted, if only the Jews and to some extent the Gypsies (at that time two vulnerable minorities with no parent-state to press for punitive justice) had been the sole victims of the Nazis. As Holmes articulated, there is no substitute for lived experience as an animus for law-making.

Notes to Chapter 23

1. Yusuf Akçura, *Üç Tarzı Siyaset* (Three Pathways of Policy) (Ankara, 1987), 28. The 32 pp. essay first appeared as a series of articles in the May-June, 1904 nos. 24–34 issues of *Türk*, a Cairo newspaper whose editors were identified as Young Turks (*Genç Türkler*).
2. Even though Turkey intervened in World War I belatedly, that intervention served to precipitate the war with Russia, a war which was deliberately provoked. Abandoning her pretended neutrality Turkey, with German goading and the help of substantial German naval forces, on October 29, 1914, launched a preemptive strike against Russian ports, coastal installations and ships in the Black Sea, destroying several of the targets. As expected, Russia a few days later declared war against Turkey, with France and England, her allies, following suit.
3. For a discussion of this problem with respect to Turkey see Vahakn N. Dadrian, "The Role of the Turkish Military in the Destruction of Ottoman Armenians: A Study in Historical Continuities" "*Journal of Political and Military Sociology* 20, 2 (Winter 1992): 257–288; idem., "The Role of the Special Organization in the Armenian Genocide" in *Minorities in Wartime* P. Panayi ed. (Oxford, 1993), 50–82.
4. R. Hilberg, *The Destruction of the European Jews* (Chicago, 1969), 127, 250–60.
5. *The Goebbels Diaries*, L. Lochner, ed., trans. (New York, 1948), 241.
6. For a recent study on the comparative aspects of the Armenian genocide and the Jewish Holocaust, see Robert F. Melson, *Revolution and Genocide. On the Origins of the Armenian Genocide and the Holocaust* (Chicago, 1992). For a Review Article on this work see Vahakn N. Dadrian, *Holocaust and Genocide Studies* 8, 3 (Winter, 1994): 410–17. For a general, historical discussion of the topic see Vahakn N. Dadrian, "The

Convergent Aspects of the Armenian and Jewish Cases of Genocide. A Reinterpretation of the Concept of Holocaust" *Holocaust and Genocide Studies*, 3, 2 (1988), 151–169.

7. Ahmet Izzet Paşa, *Feryadım* (My Lament) vol. 1, (Istanbul, 1992), 310–11.

8. Golo Mann, Foreward to Edouard Calic's *Unmasked*, R. Barry trans. (London, 1971), 10. The original is in Edouard Calic, *Ohne Maske. Hitler-Breiting Geheimgespräche 1931* (Frankfurt am Main, 1968), 8.

9. Joachim C. Fest, *Hitler*. Richard and Clara Winston translators (New York, 1975), 679, 681.

10. Eberhard Jäckel and Axel Kuhn eds., *Hitler. Sämtliche Aufzeichnungen 1905–1924* (Stuttgart, 1980), 775. The respective document is identified as one emanating from German Federal Archives (*Bundesarchiv*) R48 I, Reichs Chancellor's Office (*Reichskanzlei*), dossier no. 2681, pp. 85 ff.

11. Hilberg, *The Destruction* (n. 4], 524. The data are culled from a summary prepared by Dr. Paul Otto Schmidt, German Foreign Office interpreter, on the meeting at Klessheim. Hitler and Foreign Minister Ribbentrop were trying to induce Admiral Horty, the Hungarian Regent, to proceed against the Jews of Hungary mercilessly, namely, to have them killed off.

12. *Frankfurter Zeitung*, July 22, 1993; the Turkish newspaper was *Milliyet*. Quoted in *The Speeches of Adolf Hitler. April 1922–August 1939*. vol. 1. Norman H. Baynes. trans. and ed. (Oxford, 1942), 868.

13. Martin Gilbert, *The Holocaust. The Jewish Tragedy* 3d. edition (London, 1987), 48–9. The other official was Frank Foley, Passport Control Officer in Berlin. The letter is dated November 12, 1935 and is in FO 371/19919.

14. *Documents on British Foreign Policy. 1919–1939*. E.L. Woodward, R. Butler and A. Orde eds. Third Series. vol. VII, 1939 (London, 1954). Doc. No. 314, enclosure. pp. 258–260.

15. *Ibid.*, p. 259. This view of the extermination of the Armenians as a factor affording the establishment of the new Turkish Republic, a view which is implied by Hitler, is shared by a number of prominent Turkish authors. In an essay in which he described the exterminatory measures against the Armenians as "genocide," using exactly this composite Latino-Greek term, one such author, (a former Ittihadist and subsequently an ardent Kemalist and a confidant of Mustafa Kemal Ataturk), noted that "there was no doubt" (*şüphe yoktu*) about this relationship between the liquidation of the Armenians and the establishment of the new Kemalist Turkey. Falih Rıfkı Atay, "Pazar Konuşması" (Düşünce Yorum), *Dünya*, December 17, 1967. A contemporary Turkish author went even so far as to declare that "the foundations of the edifice of the Turkish Republic rest on the story of the extermination of a people ... " In the same vein he maintained that the Turkish War of Independence, which led to the establishment of that Republic, "was largely organized by the Ittihadists ... who played an extremely important role (*son derece önemli bir rolü ...*) ... the outfit providing its most crucial support was the Special Organization which previously had enacted the Armenian genocide." Taner Akçam, *Türk Ulusal Kimliği ve Ermeni Sorumu* (The Turkish National Identity and the Armenian Question) (Istanbul, 1992), 156, 161. Even Atay, cited above, admitted that without the success of the plan of the Ittihadists to eliminate the Armenians, Atatürk's movement to create a new nation-state could not have succeeded; even though the Armenians brought upon themselves "this tragedy by cooperating with the Tsarist armies, what a painful thing it was though (*ne acıklı şey*)." Falih Rıfkı Atay, *Çankaya* (Istanbul, 1980), 450. Even more significant in this respect is the admission of Ittihadist Foreign Minister and President of the Chamber of Deputies, Halil Menteşe. In his memoirs he conceded that "the Armenians were liquidated." *Hayat Tarih Mecmuası* 9, 2 (September 1973): 20. In another instalment of the series of his memoirs Halil further declared that without this operation of "liquidation" (*temizlemek*) "it would have been impossible to bring into being (*tekevvün*) our nation-state (*milli devlet*)." *Cumhuriyet*. November 9, 1946. Instalment No. 24.

16. Fest, *Hitler* [n. 9], 156–57. A French author states that Atatürk's bullying tactics against the French in 1936 and 1937 in connection with his design to annex Alexandrette, which was part of French-mandated Syria (which annexation he achieved by simply sending in Turkish troops of occupation), influenced Hitler's own handling of the annexation (*Anschluss*) of Austria. Paul du Véou, *Le désastre d'Alexandrette 1934–1938* (Paris, 1938), 2, 136–39.

17. *Nutuk. Kemal Atatürk* (Speech K. Atatürk) vol. 3, 7th ed. (Istanbul, n.d.), 1250.

18. The first reference to "conquests" from Ziya Gökalp's poem on *Turan* is on p. 34; the second on shaking "horizons" from a poem by Hüseyinzade is on p. 25; Mehmet Emin's poem and his words are on p. 133. Zarevand, *United and Independent Turania. Aims and Designs of the Turks*. V.N. Dadrian trans. (Leiden, 1971). Akçura's exaltation of Genghis Khan is in Ercümend Kuran, "Yusuf Akçuranın Tarihçiliği" (The Historicism of Yusuf Akçura) in the Proceedings of the Symposium on the 50th anniversary of Akçura's death (Ölümünün Ellinci Yılında Yusuf Akçura Sempozyumu Tebliğleri) (Ankara, 1987), 48.

19. Leo Alexander, "War Crimes and Their Motivation. The Social Psychological Structure of the SS and the Criminalization of Society," *Journal of Criminal Law, Criminology and Police Science, XXXIX* (September-October 1948): 300.

20. Ernst Jackh, *The Rising Crescent* (New York, 1944), 64–5.

21. Halil Paşa (Kut), *Bitmeyen Savaş* (The Unending Fight) (Istanbul, 1972), 241.

22. *Ibid.*, 274.

23. Ernst Paraquin, "Politik im Orient," *Berliner Tageblatt* January 24, 28, 1920 instalments. A synopsis of the series is filed in the German Foreign Ministry Archives. A. A. Türkei 158/24, A1373. It is worth noting in this connection that Nesimi, the Muslim *kaymakam* of Lice county in Diyarbekir province, made a similar reference to Genghiz Khan when refusing to obey the order of that province's governor-general, Dr. Reşid, a veterinarian, to have the Armenians of his area massacred. He is quoted as saying, "I would like to be excused from carrying out such Genghiz-style orders." *(Cengizhane verilen böyle emirlere mazurum)*. He was subsequently ambushed and killed by the henchmen of the governor. Krieger, *Houssaper* (special issue) on the 50th anniversary of the Armenian genocide. (Cairo, 1965) :27. *See also* A.A. Türkei 183/43, A17939.K No. 61/No. 1703, Aleppo's German Consul Rössler's June 17, 1916 report.

24. Şevket Süreyya Aydemir, *Makedonyadan Orta Asya'ya Enver Paşa* (Enver Paşa. From Macedonia to Central Asia) vol. 3 (Istanbul, 1972), 541.

25. Ghazar Magountz, *Trabezonee Hayotz Deghahanoutinu* (The Deportation of the Armenians of Trabizon) H. Gosoyian ed. (Teheran, 1963), 60–61.

26. *U.S. National Archives.* R.G. 59. 867. 4016/411. April 11, 1919 report.

27. *Badmoutiun Haigagan Bondosee* (History of the Armenian Pontus) H. Hovagimian ed. (Beirut, 1967), 240.

28. *History of the United Nations War Crimes Commission and the Development of the Laws of War* (London, 1948), iv.

29. Winfried Baumgart, "Zur Ansprache Hitler's vor den Führern der Wehrmacht Am 22. August 1939. Eine quellenkritische Untersuchung" *Vierteljahreshefte für Zeitgeschichte* 12, 2 (1968), 121–24, 126, 128, 138, 139.

30. Calic, *Unmasked* [n. 8], 81; in the German original *ibid.*, 101.

31. *Ibid.*, 16 (in *Unmasked*). Here is an excerpt from Ludwig Krieger's memorandum:

> The transcript checks with the original … Having been a shorthand writer at Hitler's briefing conferences in his headquarters during the Second World War, I recognize Hitler's style and reactions throughout the record. Breiting's papers as a whole confirm the sequence of events. Both from the factual and political points of view the checking of these papers has been of extreme interest to me. Breiting's shorthand record is assuredly of great historical value since, as far as I know, no shorthand notes of private discussions with Hitler in the pre–1933 period exist.

32. Kevork B. Bardakjian, *Hitler and the Armenian Genocide* (Cambridge, MA, 1985).

33. Henry Picker, *Hitler's Tischgespräche im Führerhauptquartier* 3rd. ed. (Stuttgart, 1977), 422. quoted in Bardakjian. *ibid.*, 30. Consistent with this portrayal of the Armenians, Hitler's subordinates are on record deprecating the Armenians as a race. Rosenberg, the Nazi ideologue, equated the Jews and the Armenians as "the people of the wastes." Alfred Rosenberg, *Der Mythus des Zwanzigsten Jahrhunderts* (Münich, 1930), 213, and the German High Command in one of its declarations stated that the "Armenians were even worse than the Jews." Robert Cecil, *The Myth of the Master Race: Alfred Rosenberg and Nazi Ideology* (London, 1972), 200. Both quotations are cited by Bardakjian, *Hitler* [n. 32], 30.

34. Howard M. Sachar, *The Emergence of the Middle East, 1914–1924* (New York, 1969), 115.

35. David Matas, "Prosecuting Crimes Against Humanity: The Lessons of World War I," *Fordham International Law Journal* (1990): 104.
36. Richard Lichtheim, *Rückkehr. Lebenserinnerungen aus der Frühzeit des deutschen Zionismus* (Stuttgart, 1970), 287, 341.
37. Sybil Milton, "Armin T. Wegner: Polemicist for Armenian and Jewish Human Rights," *Armenian Review* 42, 4 (Winter 1989): 17.
38. *Das Schwarze Korps* (November 1936).
39. A. A. Türkei 183/45, A33457. See also Botschaft Konstantinopel K 174, folio 53; the report was filed from Münich on December 4, 1916.
40. *Die Zeit* (German weekly in Hamburg), No. 50, "Dossier," December 7, 1984.
41. Paul Leverkuehn, *Posten auf Ewiger Wache. Aus dem abenteuerlichen Leben des Max von Scheubner-Richter* (Essen, 1938), 186.
42. *Ibid.*, 190–91.
43. A. A. Türkei 183/39, A28584, enclosure no. 2, in "secret report" No. 23, pp. 11–12 of the 15 pp. report of August 5, 1915 filed from Erzurum.
44. John Dornberg, *Münich 1923. The Story of Hitler's First Grab for Power* (New York, 1982), 295.
45. Fest, Hitler [n. 9], 137.
46. U. Trumpener, *Germany and the Ottoman Empire 1914–1918* (Princeton, 1968) [n. 44], 207 n. 19.
47. U.S. Department of State, *Report of Robert H. Jackson, United States Representative to the International Conference on Military Trials*, London, 1945 (1949), 18–20.
48. R. Jackson, *The Nürnberg Case as Presented by Robert H. Jackson, Chief of Counsel for the United States* (New York, 1971), 8–83, 88–89.
49. M.C. Bassiouni, "International Law and the Holocaust" *California Western International Law Journal* 9, 2 (Spring 1979): 283.
50. Department of State Publication No. 2420. Reprinted in *American Journal of International Law* 39 (Supplement 1945): 257.
51. For a detailed analysis of the exchanges see J. Garner, *International Law and the World War*, vol. 2, 483–501 (paras. 588–94) (1920); *see also* Wright, "War Crimes Under International Law," *Law Quarterly Review* (January 1946): 40–52, *reprinted in* United Nations War Crimes Commission, *History of the United Nations War Crimes Commission* [n. 28], 550–51.
52. *Ibid.*, (Garner), 550–51.
53. James F. Willis, *Prologue to Nuremberg. The Politics and Diplomacy of Punishing War Criminals of the First World War* (Westport, CT, 1982), 26.
54. H. M. Stationery Office, *Speeches of the Chief Prosecutors at the Close of the Case Against the Individual Defendants*, 63 Cmd. 6964 (H.M. Attorney-General, 1946).

CONCLUSION

A brief recapitulation of the central theme of this study is in order.

In assessing the future tasks of national and international law as they relate to genocide as a crime, the fundamental and universal mission of law must be underlined. That mission is to restrain human behavior under a system of sanctions or legal consequences. The negative assumption about the human potential for criminal acts implied by this view was cogently articulated by Aristotle some 23 centuries ago: "When separated from law and justice man is the worst of all animals."[1] In the absence of such legal sanctions, however, the concept of criminal behavior is bound to be diluted in the minds of offenders. The progressive escalation of the level of genocidal killing of the Armenians in Ottoman Turkey through episodic and recurrent massacres in the eras of Abdul Hamit and the Young Turk Ittihadists in particular is a paramount fact in this respect. In accounting for that fact Toynbee, who during the war (in 1916) compiled one of the most massive volumes documenting and detailing the Armenian genocide, recognized in this regard the intimate connections between Turkish official denials and more radical subsequent resorts to mass murder.

When challenging the wartime Turkish protestations of innocence, for example, Toynbee virtually dismissed the associated Turkish charges of treason and rebellion leveled against the Armenians as fabrications which will not "bear examination," are "easily rebutted," and are "found to rest on the most frivolous grounds," only to conclude that "it is evident that the war was merely an opportunity and not a cause."[2] Restating his firm conviction that what was involved here was in fact a premeditated act of genocide this is what he wrote a half a century later in an autobiographical account:

> The massacre of Armenian subjects in the Ottoman Empire in 1896 … was amateur and ineffective compared with the largely successful attempt to exter-

minate [them] during the First World War in 1915 ... . [This] genocide was carried out under the cloak of legality by cold-blooded governmental action. These were not mass-murders committed spontaneously by mobs of private people ... .[3]

One reason the massacres of the era of Sultan Abdul Hamit (1894–96) were "amateur" was because the planning was less thorough and the experience for organizing them on a genocidal scale was lacking. More important, there was some lingering apprehension that unrestricted and indiscriminate mass murder at that time might provoke the Powers to proceed against Turkey militarily under certain treaty rights as interpreted by them under those circumstances. (Art. 1 of the Cyprus Convention of Defensive Alliance, June 4, 1878, Great Britain and Turkey; Art. 61 of the Berlin Treaty, July 13, 1878, the six Powers and Turkey.) They had already established a legacy of "humanitarian intervention" in Europe and the Near East. This element of uncertainty imparted to the entire episode of massacres a more or less experimental character, as far as the perpetrators were concerned. In the end, however, the outcome proved quite reassuring for the latter. The victim population could be regarded as fair game when projecting more effective future operations of that kind.

The era of World War I proved even more reassuring in this regard. The consuming preoccupation of the Allies with effective warfare and the end of victory obviated the chances of their intervention. Moreover, the alliance with Imperial Germany had secured the engagement of a powerful protective shield, allowing the Ittihadists optimal scope for unhampered operations against the Armenians defined as "the internal enemy." In one of his cogent appraisals of the situation, American Ambassador Morgenthau touched on this problem in a "private and confidential" letter to Secretary of State Robert Lansing on November 18, 1915. For reasons unknown, the State Department chose to excise these portions in the volume in which this and other official reports are published.[4]

> Unfortunately the previous Armenian massacres were allowed to pass without the great Christian Powers punishing the perpetrators thereof; and these people believe that an offense that has been condoned before, will probably be again forgiven.

Reflecting further on this interrelationship between the series of massacres, Morgenthau confirmed what other credible sources have repeatedly asserted, namely, that this time, i.e., World War I, the perpetrators were thorough in their planning and organization; there was long-standing premeditation and careful deliberation. After declaring, "I am firmly convinced that this is the greatest crime of the ages," Morgenthau went on to state:

> ... now, while four of the great Powers were fighting them [i.e., the Turks] and had unsuccessfully attempted to enter their country [to Constantinople through the Straits], and the two other great Powers [Germany and Austria]

were their Allies, it was a great opportunity for them to put into effect their long cherished plan of exterminating the Armenian race ... .[5]

Perhaps the most daunting lesson of the history of the Armenian genocide is the grim evidence of consistency with which the victimization of the Armenians has proven unpreventable but also has proven impervious to punishment. One is faced here with the persistence of the dismal reality of impunity perversely functioning as a negative reward benefiting the camp of the perpetrators, past and present, and rendering the latter as remorseless as ever. It is within this context that the Turkish denial syndrome needs to be understood and dealt with. The impulse to deny the crime is entwined with and sustained by the reality of impunity.

Presently what makes the impunity consequential is not that it is the by-product of passive indifference or inaction by the rest of the world but because that impunity has been invested with a semblance of legal aegis. The reference is, of course, to the Lausanne Treaty (July 24, 1923). The victorious Allies for a variety of reasons yielded to the pressures of the implacable Kemalists, who in less than three years had managed to convert a crippling military defeat at the end of World War I into a signal victory. As a result, the Allies abjectly discarded the Sèvres Treaty, which they had signed two years earlier and through which they had set out to prosecute and punish the authors of the Armenian genocide and at the same time redeem their promises for a future Armenia. After expunging any and all references to Armenian massacres, and to Armenia from the draft treaty, they put their signatures on the Lausanne Peace Treaty, thereby insidiously helping to codify the condition of impunity by obversely pleading *nolo contendere*, i.e., they would not contest the Turkish insistence to consign to oblivion the episode of the Armenian genocide. The respective international law, flowing from this international treaty, however a sham law in essence, has thus lent an aura of respectability to the mantle of impunity because there is the imprimatur of a peace conference attached to it. In this respect it is worth noting the following observation of a French jurist reacting to the fact that through the terms of the Lausanne Treaty Turkey escaped the threat of punishment for the mass murder of the Armenians. "This Treaty, it is the assurance for impunity for (the crime of) massacre; especially, it is the exaltation of the crime. An entire race, the Armenians, was systematically exterminated ... ."[6] In this sense the Lausanne Treaty is also a monument to the triumph of political expediency over fundamental principles of justice, the pretended ramparts of Western civilization.

To conclude, the core problems of genocide transcend considerations of the fate of individual victim groups, or the peculiarities of a particular perpetrator-victim relationship. The mitigation, if not the elimination, of these problems devolves upon the further development of international law, the prime matrix of all human rights, including the rights of potential or actual genocide victims. Addressing the problem of impunity, the United Nations passed a resolution redefining and indefinitely postponing the criminal liabilities of the offenders on November 26, 1968—the Convention on the Nonapplicability of Statutory Limitations to War Crimes Against Humanity.[7] Article 1(b) includes the crime of genocide, even if it does "not constitute a violation of the domestic law of the country in which [it was] committed." The Convention implicitly inspires hopes for ultimate justice, belying the general maxim that justice delayed is justice denied. Counterposed to these hopes, however, is the specter of political forces whose traditions may continue to thwart the initiation of effective relief, indefinitely postponing the redemption of these hopes.

Notes to Conclusion

1. Aristotle, *Politics*, Book. 1., chapter 2, p. 6, B. Jowett and T. Twining, trans. (New York, 1959).
2. Viscount Bryce, *The Treatment of Armenians in the Ottoman Empire 1915–16* A. Toynbee, compiler (London, 1916), 627, 629, 631, 633.
3. A. Toynbee, Experiences (Oxford, 1969), 241, 341.
4. *Papers Relating to the Foreign Relations of the United States. The Lansing Papers 1914–1920.* vol. 1 (Washington, 1939), 762–66.
5. *U.S. National Archives.* R.G. (Records of the State Department) 867.00/798 $\frac{1}{2}$, p. 7 of 9ff report.
6. C. H. Lebeau, *Essai sur la justice en Turquie* (á propos du Traité de Lausanne) (Paris, 1924), 109–110. According to the disclosure of a Turkish historian the precluding from the Lausanne Peace Treaty any and all references to Armenian massacres, and even simply to Armenia, was not a chance circumstance but the result of a private, secret, agreement reached during a luncheon between Ismet Inönü, the head of the Turkish delegation, and Lord Curzon, the head of the British delegation. When Curzon the next day nevertheless made a furtive reference to the Armenian question, Ismet was amazed and upset. Trying to mollify him after the end of the session, Curzon is reported to have quipped, "Can't you bear to hear even such a trivial funeral oration?" Şevket S. Aydemir, *Makedonyadan Orta Asyàya Enver Paşa* (Enver Paşa from Macedonia to Central Asia) vol. 3 (Intanbul, 1972), 109, n. 2.
7. General Assembly Resolution 2391 (XXIII), 23 United Nations General Assembly Official Records (GAOR), Supp. (No. 18) 40, U.N. Doc. A/7218 (1968).

APPENDIX

The Pool of Potential Sources in Nazi Germany Regarding the Facts of the Armenian Genocide

Three such officials were prominent in the Nazi Foreign Service. Franz von Papen helped the Nazis seize power when he was Chancellor in postwar Germany (June 1932). He was Chief of General Staff of the IVth Turkish army in World War I.[1] Konstantin Freiherr von Neurath, an aristocrat, occupied the post of Foreign Minister in Papen's cabinet and continued on in that post when Hitler became Chancellor, thus imparting respectability to Hitler's regime. Following the occupation of Czechoslovakia by the German army, he became Protector of Bohemia and Moravia where he had to give cover to the terror of Reinhard Heydrich who eventually replaced him. In World War I Neurath served as Councillor at the German Embassy in Constantinople 1915–16, and was instructed by Chancellor Hollweg to monitor the operations against the Armenians.[2] Count F.W. von der Schulenburg, an army captain, had a long career in German Foreign Service before becoming ambassador to Russia (1934–1941), serving as Minister to Iran and Minister to Rumania. In World War I he was Interim Consul at Erzurum, Turkey, August 1915–February 1916, and at the same time was involved in the organization of guerilla operations in eastern Turkey and the Caucasus.

There were two other German officials who during the war directed from Berlin German policy in Turkey and Turko-German insurgency actions against Russia but who, after the war, became diplomats, both of them serving as ambassadors to Turkey. Privy State councillor Frederic Hans von Rosenberg was the head of the Eastern Department at the German Foreign Office, and Rudolf Nadolny, an army captain, was in charge

Notes for this section begin on page 427.

of the Political Section in the Reserve General Staff (*Stellvertretender Generalstab*) conducting intelligence and sabotage undertakings against Russia from Turkish bases.[3]

Preceding these men in a transition from service in World War I to post-World War I diplomatic service in Germany was Wilhelm Solf, Real Privy Councillor, and Minister of Colonial Affairs (*Reichskolonialamt*). In October 1918 he became Foreign Minister of Germany. During World War II Solf served as Ambassador to Japan. On two occasions he became involved in developments surrounding the World War I Armenian massacres. In the spring of 1916 Chancellor Hollweg sent him to Constantinople to investigate the Turkish complaints against Ambassador Metternich who repeatedly had been remonstrating against the atrocities which were then being committed against the Armenians. The Turkish authorities were demanding the recall of the Ambassador. Solf recommended against it, and his friend Metternich stayed-for a while at least. During his tenure as Foreign Minister Solf adamantly refused to extradite Talât who in the Fall of 1918 had fled to Germany and whose surrender was being demanded by post-war Turkish authorities. His rationale was that Talât was a loyal friend of Imperial Germany and in the absence of valid legal documents he could not be extradited.[4]

There were a host of high-ranking military officers who, having served in wartime Turkey, likewise stand out as connecting links between the German army of World War I and the subsequently emerging Wehrmacht as well as the SS military formations. Foremost among these was Lieutenant General Hans von Seeckt, whose record as a brilliant staff officer was matched by his reputation as an ideal Prussian military leader imbued with the ethics of duty and service to the state. In the last year of the war he served as Chief of Staff at Ottoman General Headquarters. But upon his return to Germany at the end of the war he set out to prevent the dissolution of the German army and proceeded to rebuild it instead. In the 1919–1926 period he laid the ground-work for the emergence of the Wehrmacht through a carefully crafted restructuring of the Reichswehr, the 100,000 German army allowed by the Versailles Treaty. Even though Seeckt initially had some misgivings about Hitler, after his second meeting with him in 1931, he expressed his approval of the Nazis as "saviors" of a Germany which was beset by crises. He believed in "the task of German policy" which must be "to prepare for the next war."[5] Utilizing his ties with former War Minister Enver, who at that time was, like Talât, a fugitive in Berlin also, Seeckt secured Enver's mediation for reaching a secret agreement with Russia to procure weapons for the projected buildup of the German army.[6] When he died in 1936, Hitler honored him by ordering a state funeral which he attended.

General Seeckt was to a great degree politically identified with the Ittihadist top leaders; he offered them at the end of the war German naval

units to effect their escape from Turkey.[7] That help was extended to Enver
in 1920 again when through the intervention of Seeckt the intelligence
department of the residual German High Command arranged for his
escape by plane from a prison at Kaunas, Lithuania, and subsequently for
his trip to Russia.[8] Moreover, Seeckt was well informed of the wartime
fate of the Armenians of Turkey but consistent with his ideals of Prussian
militarism, he in so many words justified the calamity by invoking the
principle of "military necessity." (See Chapter 16, n. 50.)

Two other German generals who were Seeckt's colleagues in wartime
Turkey were key players in the emergence of Bavaria as a center of anti-
Berlin insurrectionary movements. As the city of Munich, the capital of
Bavaria, became a center of gravitation for rightist nationalists (including
a number of high-ranking Prussian officers) in the aftermath of the March
1920 abortive Kapp *Putsch*, Hitler's relationship with Bavaria's civilian
and military authorities became a test case for the future of the Nazi
movement. These developments adversely affected the authority of General Seeckt who was in charge of the *Reichswehr*. One of them was Major
General Otto von Lossow who during the war was Military Attaché to
Turkey. During the insurrectionary turmoils in Bavaria he was the commander of the 7th district and was in charge of the district's 7th infantry
division. The other was Major General Kress von Kressenstein who at
one time during the war was Chief of Operations at Ottoman General
Headquarters and later served as Chief of Staff of the IV Turkish Army
and finally as Commander-in-Chief of the VIIIth Turkish Army. During
Hitler's troubles in Münich in 1923 Kressenstein was the artillery commander of the military district in Münich. Both generals had conducted
extensive correspondence with Berlin on the Armenian genocide.[9]

Some of the highest ranking military officers serving Hitler and Nazi
Germany, but with a background of military services in the Armed Forces
of wartime Turkey, deserve special attention. Foremost among them was
Karl Dönitz, Grand Admiral and Supreme Commander of the German
Navy. In his Last Will and Testament Hitler elevated Dönitz to the rank
of President of the Reich and Supreme Commander of the German
Armed Forces. At the start of World War I Dönitz was an ensign on duty
on board of the light cruiser Breslau (later assigned the Turkish name
Midilli). In a 1917 pamphlet on *Die Fahrten der Breslau,* Dönitz describes
the combined Turko-German preemptive naval assault against Russian
ships and coastal installations in the Black Sea (October 28–29, 1914)
that served to precipitate the intended Russo-Turkish war a few days
later. At the end of the war Dönitz was promoted to the rank of captain.
Moreover, General Alfred Jodl, Hitler's chief of Wehrmacht operations,
Chief of Staff of the High Command, was assigned to a tour of duty
(1934–1937) in Turkey as part of a military exchange program. Likewise
to be mentioned is Pfeffer von Wildenbruch, who was a first lieutenant in

wartime Turkey but in World War II he had become SS Obergruppen-führer (General) and the military governor of Budapest.[10] World War II general, Alexander von Falkenhausen, also served in Turkey in the 1916–18 period and in the 1940–44 period was military governor in Belgium. Finally, reference may be made to Rudolf Höss, the Commandant of the Auschwitz extermination camp 1940–43 and Deputy Inspector of concentration camps at SS Headquarters 1944–45. After running away from a home, dominated by his authoritarian father, in 1916 he joined the German forces serving in Turkey when he was only 16, and after the war he joined the Freikorps. These were private armies in post-war Germany, consisting of ex-soldiers, and led by former regular officers, with Münich becoming a refuge for them.[11]

Of these officials and officers in Nazi Germany, who were tried at Nuremberg, General Jodl was sentenced to death, Neurath to fifteen and Dönitz to ten years in prison. Von Papen was acquitted but in January 1947 he was retried by a German de-Nazification court and sentenced to eight years' hard labor; he was released in 1949. Höss was convicted and hanged by the Poles at Auschwitz camp in 1947.

Notes to Appendix

1. In the January 30, 1933–June 1934 period Papen served as Hitler's Vice Chancellor and as President of Prussia. In 1934 he became Special Ambassador to Austria where he paved the ground for the 1938 *Anschluss*, the annexation of Austria to the Nazi Reich. When the funds of the Nazi party ran out, Papen arranged the delivery of financial help from the big industrialists of the Rhine and Ruhr regions. Prior to his engagement in the Turkish army in World War I, he was military attaché at Washington D.C., but upon the discovery of some espionage activities in which he was implicated, he was expelled from the U.S.A. in 1915. See Franz von Papen, *Der Wahrheit eine Gasse* (Münich, 1952).
2. A. A. Türkei 183/39, A33278; 183/40, A33705.
3. Rudolf Nadolny, *Mein Beitrag* (Wiesbaden, 1955).
4. For Solf's correspondence with Metternich, see *Gegen die Unvernunft. Der Briefwechsel zwrischen Paul Graf Wolff Metternich und Wilhelm Solf 1915–1918*, E. von Vietsch ed. (Bremen, 1964), 7, 42. On the matter of extradition, see Ch. 22, n. 6, p. 391.
5. Walter Goerlitz, *History of the German General Staff 1657–1945*, B. Battershaw, trans. (New York, 1953), 174, 260.
6. *Ibid.*, 231; Ulrich Trumpener, *Germany and the Ottoman Empire 1914–1918* (Princeton, 1968), 362–63.
7. *Ibid.*, 359, n. 17; Frank G. Weber, *Eagles on the Crescent* (Ithaca, 1970), 253.
8. Şevket S. Aydemir, *Makedonyadan Orta Asya'ya Enver Paşa* (Enver Paşa. From Macedonia to Central Asia) vol. 3 (Istanbul, 1972), 545.
9. For excerpts from their reports to Berlin on the extermination of the Armenians see Vahakn N. Dadrian, "Documentation of the Armenian genocide in German and Austrian Sources" in *The Widening Circle of Genocide. Genocide: A Critical Bibliographic Review*. vol. 3, Israel W. Charny ed. (New Brunswick, N.J., 1994), 123–24.
10. Some of the data about these officers were culled from Werner Haupt, "Deutsche unter dem Halbmond," *Deutsches Soldatenjahrbuch* (1967), 216, 217.
11. Gerald Reitlinger, *The SS. Alibi of a Nation. 1922–1945* (New York, 1957), 283, 468.

BIBLIOGRAPHY

PRIMARY SOURCES. STATE AND NATIONAL ARCHIVES. OFFICIAL DOCUMENTS

I. AUSTRIA
Österreichisches Staatsarchiv. *Die Akten des k. u. k. Ministeriums des Äussern, 1848–1918* (Foreign Ministry Archives of Austria, in Vienna) Abteilung XII: Türkei, Kartons (files) 462,463; XL. Interna, File 272; Konsulate 38, file 303; Karton Rot 947.

II. EUROPE
European Parliament Resolution. Doc. No. A2–33/87. 31(1987). Agenda Item 10. Resolution on a Political Solution to the Armenian Question.

III. GERMANY
German State Archive (Staatsarchiv) vols. 31, 32, 33 H.V. Kremer-Auenrode and Hirsch, eds. Leipzig, 1877.

The Diplomatic Archives of the Foreign Ministry of Germany (Die Diplomatischen Akten des Auswärtigen Amtes), vols. 9, 10, 11, 12 (1), 12 (2).

Orientalia Generalia. No. 5. vol. 30. (1896).

Federal Republic of Germany, *Akten des Auswärtigen Amtes 1867–1920* (West Germany's Foreign Office Archives, Bonn) Abteilung IA (Political Dept.)

Türkei, file numbers 158 and 183, with sets of volumes (Band), and corresponding entry numbers, preceded by letter A, attached to them.

Botschaft Konstantinopel (K) Consular documents.

Grosses Hauptquartier, (German General Headquarters) vols. 185, 187, 194.

German Military Archives (Bundesarchiv-Militärarchiv), i.e., BA/MA.

Deutschland und Armenien, 1914–1918: Sammlung diplomatischer Aktenstücke. J. Lepsius ed., 1919. (German Foreign Office archive documents dealing almost entirely with the World War I Armenian deportations and massacres).

The German Documents on the Outbreak of the War 1914. (Die deutschen Dokumente zum Kriegsausbruch 1914), compiled by K. Kautsky, Max Graf von Montgelas, and Walter Schückling, eds., 2nd expanded ed, vol. 1. Berlin, 1922.

The Talât Paşa Trial (Der Prozess Talaat Pascha) Stenographic Records. Berlin, 1921.

IV. FRANCE
Archives du Ministère des Affaires Étrangères. Quai d'Orsay, Paris (Foreign Ministry Archives)

Documents Diplomatiques. Affaires Arméniennes. Projets de Réformes Dans l'Empire Ottoman 1893–1897 (Livre Jaune) Paris, 1897.

Documents Diplomatiques. Affaires Arméniennes (Supplément) 1895–1896. Paris 1897.

Documents Diplomatiques Français 1871–1900. vols. XI, XII, Paris, 1947, 1951.

Nouvelle Série: *Correspondance politique et commerçiale 1897: Turquie. Politique intérieure. Dossier General,* vols. 7 and 8. Jeunes Turcs.

Guerre 1914–1918: vols. I, II, III. *Turquie.* 887–889 Arménie. August 1914–December 1915, January 1916–March 1917, April 1917–May 1918.

Les Grandes Puissances, L'Empire Ottoman et les Arméniens dans les archives françaises (1914–1918). (A. Beylerian, ed. 1983). (French Foreign, War, and General Headquarters Office documents dealing with the Armenian genocide).

V. GREAT BRITAIN

British Documents on Ottoman Armenians, vol. I. 1856–1880 (Ankara, 1982); vol. 2. 1880–1890. 1983. B. Şimşir, ed.

Blue Book Series on Turkey. 1877–1881, 1895–1897. (Reports by Her Majesty's Diplomatic and Consular Agents in Turkey Respecting the persecution, oppression and massacres of the Armenians in the Ottoman Empire)

Foreign Office (FO) *Archives.* Public Record Office, London and Kew.

Class 371 Files. Political: *General Correspondence, 1915–1920.* (persecution, deportation, massacres of Armenians in Turkey)

Class 608 Files. *Paris Peace Conference Records, 1919–1920*

WO 106. *War Office Directorate of Military Operations and Intelligence.*

Great Britain, Parliament. *The Treatment of the Armenians in the Ottoman Empire: Documents Presented to Viscount Grey of Fallodon, Secretary of State for Foreign Affairs.* (Compiled by A. Toynbee, Miscellaneous No. 31, 1916). (A massive collection of accounts on the Armenian genocide up to summer 1916 by European and American observers in wartime Turkey.)

Armenia. Parliamentary Debates, House of Lords. (November 13, 1918); House of Commons (October 23, 24, 30, 31, November 6, 7, 12, 14, 18, 1918) A. Raffi, ed. London, 1918.

British Documents on the Origins of the War 1889–1914. Part I, vol. 9. Gooch and Temperley, eds. London, 1926.

Documents on British Foreign Policy 1919–1939, vol. 4. First Series, W. Woodward and R. Butler, eds. London, 1952.

VI. TURKEY (OTTOMAN EMPIRE AND THE TURKISH REPUBLIC)

Ottoman Archives. Yıldız Collection. The Armenian Question, vol. 1. Tailori Incidents. Istanbul Research Center, 1989.

Corps de Droit Ottoman, Code de Procédure Pénale (Treatise of Ottoman Law, Code of Criminal Procedure) G. Young, vol. 7. Oxford, 1906.

Ottoman Constitution (Midhat). reprinted in American Journal of International Law. 2 (Supp. 1908): The French text of the Constitution is in Schopoff, *Réformes.*

Türkiye Büyük Millet Meclisi Gizli Celse Zabıtları (The Transcripts of the Secret Sessions of the Grand National Assembly of Turkey) (Türkiye Iş Banka Cultural Series, Publ. No. 267), 4 vols.; vol. 4. (March 2, 1923–Oct. 25, 1934) Ankara, 1985.

Takvimi Vekâyi issues (Ottoman government's official gazette whose supplements *[ilâve]* served as judicial journal, recording the proceedings of the Turkish Military Tribunal that tried the authors of the Armenian genocide Istanbul, 1919–20).

Meclisi Mebusan Zabıt Ceridesi (Transcripts of the Proceedings of the Chamber of Deputies) Third Election Period. Fifth Session. 1918.

Meclisi Âyan Zabıt Ceridesi (Transcripts of the Proceedings of the Senate) Third Election Period. Fifth Session. 1918.

Harb Kabinelerinin Isticvabı (War Cabinet Ministers' Hearings) by Ottoman Chamber of Deputies Fifth Committee. November–December, 1918 (1333). (This is an abbreviated version of the transcripts of the hearings which the Istanbul Turkish daily *Vakit* in 1933 published in the form of a Special Supplement. The complete version of the transcripts was published by the Fifth Committee itself under the title *Meclisi Mebusan Zabıtları* [Records of the Proceedings of the Chamber of Deputies] Third Parliament, 5th session, No. 521) Istanbul, 1918.

Nutuk. Kemal Atatürk (Speech, K. Atatürk), vol. 3, 7th ed. Istanbul, n.d.

Tarihi Muhakeme (Historical Trial [of the authors of the Armenian genocide]) (Kit. Sudi ed.) Istanbul, 1919 (This volume contains the transcripts of the first two sessions of the Cabinet Ministers' trials described under V1, Takvimi Vekâyi).

K. Karabekir, *Istiklâl Harbimiz* (Our War of Independence). Istanbul, 1st ed. 1960; 2d ed. 1969. (A massive compilation of official documents covering mainly the political and military correspondence between the fledgling Ankara government and the Commander in Chief of Ankara's Eastern Front Army 1919–20).

A Speech Delivered by Mustafa Kemal Atatürk 1927 (Istanbul, 1963) (Contains the pertinent documents in support of Mustafa Kemal's account of the direction of the Turkish War of Independence and its aftermath, 1919–1924. The speech lasted six days, Oct. 15–20, 1927, and was delivered before the Deputies and Representatives of the Republican Party that was founded by him. The volume is published under the auspices of the Turkish Ministry of Education).

The Imperial Ottoman Penal Code. J. Bucknill and H. Utidjian trans. Oxford, 1913.

Documents. (purporting to demonstrate Armenian guilt and the relative innocence of the Ittihad government), vol. I. Compiled by The Office of Press and Information, Directorate General, Prime Ministry. Ankara, 1982.

Sonyel, Dr. Salahi, *Displacement of the Armenians: Dcouments* (pamphlet in English, French and Turkish) Ankara, 1978.

VII. UNITED NATIONS

Escor Comm. on Human Rights, Sub-Comm. on Prevention of Discrimination and Protection of Minorities.

U.N. ESCOR Comm. on Human Rights, Sub-Comm. on Prevention of Discrimination and Protection of Minorities (38th sess.) (Item 57) 7, U.N: Doc. E/CN.4/Sub.2/1985/SR.36 (1985) (summary record of 36th meeting, Aug. 29, 1985).

Agenda Item 4, Prevention and Punishment of the Crime of Genocide (1985) (the Whitaker report reviewing the historical antecedents of genocide).

Summary Record of the 36th Meeting of Sub-Comm. (1985) (the Sub-Commission's favorable response to the Whitaker report defining the World War I massacre against the Armenians as genocide). *Revised and updated report on the question of the prevention and punishment of the crime of genocide,* 38 U.N. ESCOR Comm. on Human Rights, Subcomm. on Prevention of Discrimination and Protection of Minorities, (Agenda Item 4), 8–9, U.N. Doc. E/CN.4/Sub.2/1985/6 (1985).

The United Nations War Crimes Commission, History of the United Nations War Crimes Commission and the Development of the Laws of War. London, 1948.

VIII. UNITED STATES

United States, Dept. of State, National Archives, Record Groups, i.e., R.G. 59 and R.G. 256, Relating to the:

Internal Affairs of Turkey 1910–1929 R.G. 59. 867.4016, Race Problems (persecution, deportation, massacres and expulsion from Turkey of the Armenians).

The American Commission to Negotiate Peace at the Paris Peace Conference R.G. 256. 867.00. Turkey (political affairs).

United States, Dept. of State. *Papers Relating to the Foreign Relations of the United States. 1915 Supplement. The World War.* Washington, 1928.

United States, Dept. of State. *Papers Relating to the Foreign Relations of the United States. The Lansing Papers. 1914–1920.* (L.) (In two volumes) vol. 1. Washington, D.C., 1939.

132 Cong. Rec. (1986) (Statements by a host of U.S. Senators noting the Armenian genocide in their arguments in support of the U.S. ratification of the U.N. Convention on Genocide).

The Hoover Institution on War, Revolution and Peace. Stanford. Imperial Russian Interior Ministry. Foreign Affairs Department of the Secret Service of the Police. Section 4.

SECONDARY SOURCES. PUBLISHED BOOKS IN:

Turkish

Akçam, T. *Siyasi Kültürümüzde Zulüm ve İşkence*. (Atrocity and Torture in Our Political Culture). Istanbul, 1992.

_____. *Türk Ulusal Kimliği ve Ermeni Sorunu*. (Turkish National Identity and the Armenian Question). Istanbul, 1992.

Akçura, Y. *Üç Tarzı Siyaset* (Three Pathways of Policy). Ankara, 1987.

Akşin, S. *100 Soruda Jön Turkler ve Ittihat ve Terakki* (The Young Turks and Ittihad ve Terakki in the Context of 100 Questions). Istanbul, 1980.

_____. *Istanbul Hükümetleri ve Milli Mücadele* (The Istanbul Governments and the National Struggle), vol. 1. Istanbul, 1983; vol. 2 .Istanbul, 1992.

Amca, H. *Doğmayan Hürriyet. Bir Devrin İç Yüzü 1908–1918* (Freedom Unborn, The Inside Story of an Era 1908–1918). Istanbul, 1958.

Atay, F.R. *Çankaya*. Istanbul, 1980.

_____. *Zeytindağı* (Mount Olive). Istanbul, 1981.

Avcıoğlu, D. *Milli Kurtuluş Tarihi*. (History of the National Liberation), vol. 3. Istanbul, 1974.

Aydemir, Ş.S. *Makedonyadan Ortaasya'ya Enver Paşa* (Enver Paşa. From Macedonia to Central Asia), vol. 2. Istanbul, 1971; vol. 3. Istanbul, 1972.

Bayar, C. *Ben de Yazdım* (I Too Have Written), vol. 6. Istanbul, 1968.

Bayur, H.K. *Sadrazam Kâmil Paşa. Siyasi Hayatı* (Grand Vizier Kâmil Paşa. His Political Life). Ankara, 1954.

Bayur, Y.H. *Türk Inkilâbı Tarihi* (The History of the Turkish Revolution), vol. 2. Part 4. Ankara, 1952; vol. 3. Part 1. 1953; vol. 3. Part 3. 1957; vol. 3. Part 4. 1983.

Belen, General F. *Birinci Cihan Harbinde Türk Harbi* (The Turkish War During the First World War), vol. 3. Ankara, 1965.

Beşikci, I. *Kürdistan Üzerinde Emperyalist Bölüşüm Mücadelesi: 1915–1925* (The Fight over Kurdistan's Imperialist Partition 1915–1925), vol. 1. Ankara, 1992.

Bleda, M. *Imparatorluğun Çöküşü* (The Collapse of the Empire), Istanbul, 1979.

Cemal, P. *Hatıralar*. Istanbul, 1977.

Cevdet Paşa, A. *Tezâkir* (Memoirs), vol. 1. C. Baysun, ed. Ankara, 1953.

Çulcu, Murat. *Ermeni Entrikalarının Perde Arkası "Torlakyan Davası* (The Inside Story of Armenian Intrigues. "The Torlakyan Trial") Instanbul, 1990.

Çavdar, T. *Talât Paşa*. Ankara, 1984.

Coşar, S. *Osman Ağa*. Istanbul, 1971.

Danişmend, I. *Izahlı Osmanlı Tarihi Kronolojisi* (The Annotated Chronology of Ottoman History), vol. 4, 2d ed. Istanbul, 1961.

Duru, K. *Ziya Gökalp*. Istanbul, 1949.

Erden, Orgeneral A.F. *Birinci Dünya Harbinde Suriye Hatıraları* (Syrian Memoirs of World War I), vol. 1 Istanbul, 1954.

Ertürk, H. *Iki Devrin Perde Arkası* (Behind the Scenes During Two Eras). S.H. Tansu, ed. Istanbul, 1957.

Esatlı, M.R. *Ittihad ve Terakki Tarihinde Esrar Perdesi* (The Curtain of Secrecy in the History of Ittihad). Istanbul, 1975.

Galib, A.R.M. *Geçen Asırda Devlet Adamlarımız* (Our Statesmen of the Past Century). Istanbul, 1979.

Gökbilgin, M.T. *Milli Mücadele Başlarken* (As the National Struggle Began), vol. 1. Ankara, 1959.

Gologlu, M., *Üçüncü Meşrutiyet 1920*. (The Third Constitution 1920). Ankara, 1970.

Göztepe, T.M. *Osmanoğullarının Son Padişahı Sultan Vahdeddin Mütareke Gayyasında* (The Last monarch from the Ottoman Dynasty Sultan Vahdeddin in the Impasse of the Armistice). Istanbul, 1969.

Gürün, K. *Ermeni Dosyası* (The Armenian File). Ankara, 1983.

Halil Menteşénin Anıları. Istanbul, 1986.

Halil Paşa. *Ittihad ve Terakki'den Cumhuriyet'e: Bitmeyen Savaş* (From Ittihad to the Republic: The Unending Fight). M.T. Sorgun, ed. Istanbul, 1972.

Hocaoğlu, M. *Arşiv Vesikalarıyla Tarihte Ermeni Mezâlimi ve Ermeniler* (Armenians and Armenian Atrocities in History Through Archive Documents). Istanbul, 1976.

Izzet, P.A. *Feryadım* (My Lamentation), vol. 1. Istanbul, 1992.

Jaeschke, G. *Türk Inkilabı Tarihi Kronolojisi 1918–1923* (Chronology of the Turkish Revolution). Niyazi R. Aksu, trans. Istanbul, 1939.

Kadri, H.K. *Balkanlardan Hicaz'a Imparatorluğun Tasfiyesi. 10 Tennuz Inkilâbı ve Netayici* (The Liquidation of the Empire from the Balkans to Hejaz. The July 10 Revolution and its Results). K. Büyükcoşkun ed. Istanbul, 1992.

Kâmil, P. *Hatıratı Sadrı Esbak Kâmil Paşa* (The Memoirs of former Grand Vizier Kâmil Paşa) Ottoman Script. Istanbul, [1913].

Kandemir, F. *Istiklâl Savaşında Bozguncular ve Casuslar* (Defeatists and Spies in the Fight for Independence). Istanbul, 1964.

Kansu, M.M. *Erzurum'dan Ölümüne Kadar Atatürk'le Beraber* (From Erzurum On Up to his Death With Atatürk), vol. 1, 2d ed. Ankara, 1986.

Karabekir, K. *Istiklâl Harbimiz* (Our War of Independence), lst ed. Istanbul, 1960, 2d ed. Istanbul, 1969.

―――. *Istiklâl Harbimizin Esasları* (The Essential Components of Our War of Independence). Istanbul, 1951.

―――. *Istiklâl Harbimizde Enver Paşa ve Ittihat Terakki Erkânı* (Enver Paşa and the Leadership of Ittihad ve Terakki During the Independence War). Istanbul, 1967.

Kaynar, R. *Türkiyede Hukuk Devleti Kurma Yolundaki Hareketler* (Movements in Turkey for the Creation of a Legal State). Istanbul, 1983.

Kocaş, S. *Tarih Boyunca Ermeniler ve Türk-Ermeni Ilişikleri* (The Armenians Throughout History and Turko-Armenian Relations). Ankara, 1967.

Kuran, A.B. *Osmanlı Imparatorluğunda ve Türkiye Cumhuriyetinde Inkilâp Hareketleri* (Revolutionary Movements in the Ottoman Empire and the Turkish Republic). Istanbul, 1959.

Kutay, C. *Birinci Dünya Harbinde Teşkilatı Mahsusa* (The Special Organization During World War I). Istanbul, 1962.

―――. *Celal Bayarın Yazmadığı ve Yazmayacağı üç Devirden Hakikatler* (Facts on Three Eras About Which Celal Bayar Did Not and Will Not Write). Istanbul, 1982.

―――. *Talât Paşanın Gurbet Hatıraları* (The Memoirs of Talât Paşa in Exile), 3 vols., vols. 2 and 3. Istanbul, 1983.

Küçük, Y. *Türkiye Üzerine Tezler 1908–1978*, vol. 1. 3d ed. Istanbul, 1980.

Müderrisoğlu, A. *Sarıkamış Dramı* (The Drama of Sarıkamış), vol. 1. Istanbul, 1988.

Oğuz, B. *Yüzyıllar Boyunca Alman Gerçeği ve Türkler* (The German Reality in the Course of Centuries and the Turks). Istanbul, 1983.

Öke, Dr. Mim Kemâl, *Ermeni Meselesi 1914-1923* (The Armenian Question 1914-1923), Instanbut, 1986.

Ökte, F. *Varlık Vergisi Faciası* (The Tragedy of the Wealth Tax). Istanbul, n.d.

Okyar, F. *Üç Devirde Bir Adam* (A Man of Three Eras). C. Kutay, ed. Istanbul, 1980.

Orel, Ş. and S. Yuca. *Ermenilerce Talât Paşa'ya Atfedilen Telegrafların Gerçek Yüzü* (The Real Nature of the Telegrams Attributed to Talât Paşa by the Armenians). Ankara, 1983.

Ortaylı, I. *Osmanlı Imparatorluğunda Alman Nüfuzu* (The German Influence in the history of the Ottoman Empire). Istanbul, 1983.

Osman N. *Abdulhamid Sani ve Devri Saltanatı. Hayatı Hususiye ve Siyasiyesi.* (Abdulhamit the Second and His Period of Rule. His Private and Political Life). Ottoman script. vol. 2. Istanbul, 1328/1912.

Refik, A. (Altınay), *Iki Komite Iki Kıtal* (Two Committees and Two Massacres) Ottoman Script. Istanbul, 1919.

Sabis, A.I. *Harb Hatıralarım* (My War Memoirs), vol. 1. Istanbul, 1943;*idem*, vol. 2. Ankara, 1951.

Şakir, Z. *1914–1918 Cihan Harbini Nasıl Idare Ettik* (How Did We Direct the 1914–1918 World War). Istanbul, 1944.

Samih, A. *Büyük Harpte Kafkas Cephesi* (The Caucasus Front in the Great War). Ankara, 1934.

Şener, C. *Topal Osman Olayı* (The Topal Osman Affair). Ankara, 1968.

Şimşir, B. *Malta Sürgünleri* (The Malta Exiles). Istanbul, 1976.

Sultan II Abdülhamid Han, *Devlet ve Memleket Görüşlerim* (My Views on State and Country). A.A. Çetin and R. Yıldız, eds. Istanbul, 1976.

Tahsin, P. *Abdülhamit Yıldız Hatıraları* (Abdul Hamit's *Yıldız* [Palace] Memoirs). Istanbul, 1931.

Talât Paşanın Hatıraları. (The Memoirs of Talât Paşa). E. Bolayir ed. Istanbul, 1946.

Tarihi Muhakeme. (Historical Trial [of the authors of the Armenian Genocide]). Ottoman Script. K. Sudi, ed. Istanbul, 1919. The first two sessions of Cabinet Ministers' trials.

Tunaya, T.Z. *Türkiyede Siyasal Partiler* (The Political Parties in Turkey), 3 vols., 2d enl. ed. Ankara, 1984.

Türkgeldi, A.F. *Görüp Işittiklerim* (The Things I Witnessed and Heard). 2d ed. Ankara, 1951.

Uras, E. *Tarihte Ermeniler ve Ermeni Meselesi* (The Armenians and the Armenian Question in History), lst ed. Istanbul, 1950; 2d ed. 1976.

Vakit. Harb Kabinelerinin Isticvabı (The War Cabinets Hearings). Istanbul, 1933. (Special Supplement on Memoirs and Documents, no. 2.)

Vardar, G. *Ittihad ve Terakki Içinde Dönenler* (The Inside Story of Ittihad ve Terakki). S.H. Tansu, ed. Istanbul, 1960.

Yalman, A.E. *Yakın Tarihte Gördüklerim ve Işittiklerim* (The Things I Saw and Heard in Recent History), 4 vols. Istanbul, 1970.

English

Ahmad, F. *The Young Turks*. Oxford, 1969.

Alamuddin, Ida. *Papa Kuenzler and the Armenians,* London, 1970.

Argyll, Duke of (George John Douglas Campbell, formerly Secretary of State for India and Lord Privy Seal), *Our Responsibilities for Turkey*. London, 1896.

Aristotle. *Politics*. Jowett and Twining, trans. New York, 1959.

Armenian National Delegation. *The Lausanne Treaty, Turkey and Armenia*. New York, 1926.

Bailey, F.E. *British Policy and the Turkish Reform Movement: A Study in Anglo-Turkish Relations 1826–1853*. New York, 1970.

Bardakjian, K. *Hitler and the Armenian Genocide*. Cambridge, Mass., 1985.

Bassiouni, M.C. *Crimes Against Humanity in International Law*. Boston, 1992.

Bat Ye'or [Y. Masriya]. *The Dhimmi: Jews and Christians Under Islam*. D. Maisel, P. Fenton, D. Littman, trans. London, 1985.

Berkes, N. *The Development of Secularism in Turkey*. Montreal, 1964.

Bernstorff, J. *Memoirs of Count Bernstorff*. E. Sutton, trans. New York, 1936.

Boyajian, D. *Armenia. The Case for a Forgotten Genocide*. Westwood, New Jersey, 1972.

British Documents on the Origins of the War 1889–1914, vol. IX: 1. Gooch and Temperley, eds. London, 1926.

Bryce, J. *Transcaucasia and Ararat*. London, 1896.

——. *The Treatment of Armenians in the Ottoman Empire 1915–16*. Compiled by A. Toynbee. London, 1916.

Calic, E. *Unmasked*. R. Barry, trans. London, 1971.

Campbell, G. (Duke of Argyll). *Our Responsibilities for Turkey*. London, 1896.

Carnegie Endowment for International Peace. *Violation of the Laws and Customs of War: Report of the Majority and Dissenting Reports of the American and Japanese Members of the Commission on Responsibilities at the Conference of Paris*. Pamphlet No. 32. Oxford, 1919.

Cecil, Lady G. (Salisbury's daughter) *Life of Robert, Marquis of Salisbury,* 4 vols. London, 1921–1931.

Chaliand, G. and Y. Ternon. *The Armenians from Genocide to Resistance*. London, 1981.

Charny, Israel W., ed., *Geoncide: A Critical Bibliographic Review,* vol. 1, London 1988; vol. 2, London and New York, 1991.

Churchill, W. *The World Crisis. The Aftermath*. London, 1929.

Davis, L. *The Slaughterhouse Province*. S. Blair, ed. New Rochelle, New York, 1989.

Davis, W.S. *The Roots of the War*. New York, 1918.

Dawson, W.H. *The Cambridge History of British Foreign Policy*, vol. III. Cambridge, 1923.

De Nogales, R. *Four Years Beneath the Crescent*. M. Lee, trans. New York, 1926.

Documents on British Foreign Policy 1919–1939. First Series. W.L. Woodward and R. Butler, eds. London, 1952.

Dornberg, J. *Munich 1923. The Story of Hitler's First Grab for Power.* New York, 1982.

Edib, H. *The Turkish Ordeal.* New York, 1928.

———. *Memoirs of New York*, New York, 1926.

Einstein, L. *Inside Constantinople.* New York, 1918.

Encyclopedia of World History. W. Langer. rev. ed. Boston, 1948.

Fawaz, Leila. *An Occasion for War. Ethnic Conflict in Lebanon and Damascus.* Berkeley, 1994.

Feis, H. *Europe, the World's Banker 1870–1914.* New Haven, 1930.

Fenwick, C. *International Law.* Rev. enl. ed. New York, 1934.

Fest, J.C. *Hitler.* Richard and Clara Winston, trans. New York, 1975.

Festinger, L. *A Theory of Cognitive Dissonance.* Stanford, California, 1957.

Garner, J. *International Law and the World War*, vol. 2. London, 1920.

Genocide. A Critical Bibliographic Review. W. Charny, ed. vol. 1, London, 1988.

George, L. *Memoirs of the Peace Conference*, vol. 2. London, 1939.

Germany, Turkey and Armenia (A selection of documentary evidence relating to the Armenian atrocities from German and other sources) London, 1917.

Gibb, H.A.R. and H. Bowen. *Islamic Society and the West*, vol. 1: 2. Oxford, 1962.

Gilbert, M. *The Holocaust. The Jewish Tragedy*, 3d. ed. London, 1987.

The Goebbels Diaries. L. Lochner, ed., trans. New York, 1948.

Goerlitz, W. *History of the German General Staff 1657–1945*, B. Battershaw, trans. New York, 1953.

Gökalp, Z. *Turkish Nationalism and Western Civilization.* N. Berkes, trans., ed. London, 1959.

Gooch, G.P. *History of Modern Europe 1878–1919.* New York, 1923.

Gottlieb, W.W. *Studies in Secret Diplomacy during the First World War.* London, 1957.

Grant, A.J. and H. Temperley, *Europe in the Nineteenth and the Twentieth Centuries (1789–1914).* London, 1962.

Graves, Dr. A.K. *The Secrets of the German War Office* (with the collaboration of E. L. Fox) 4th ed. New York, 1914.

Graves, Sir R. *Storm Centers of the Near East* (Personal Memoirs 1879–1929). Constantinople, 1933.

Grey, Viscount of Fallodon, *Twenty-Five Years. 1892–1916*, vol. 1. New York, 1925.

Gürün, K. *The Armenian File. The Myth of Innocence Exposed.* New York, 1985.

Hackworth, G.H. *International Law*, 8 vols. vol. 1. Washington, D.C., 1940–1944.

Hartunian, A.H. *Neither to Laugh Nor to Weep. A Memoir of the Armenian Genocide.* Vartan Hartunian, trans. Boston, 1968; 2d. ed. Cambridge, MA, 1986.

Helmreich, P.C. *From Paris to Sèvres.* Columbus, Ohio, 1974.

Hepworth, G.H. *Through Armenia on Horseback*, New York, 1898.

Herbert, A. *Ben Kendim. A Record of Eastern Travel*, 2nd. ed. London, 1924.

Hertslet, E. *The Map of Europe by Treaty*, vol. 4. (1875–1891) London, 1891.

Hilberg, R. *The Destruction of the European Jews.* Chicago, 1969.

Hovannisian, R. *Armenia on the Road to Independence 1918.* Berkeley, Calif., 1967.

———. ed. *The Armenian Genocide: History, Politics, Ethics.* New York, 1992.

———. *The Armenian Holocaust. (A Bibliography Relating to the Deportation, Massacres, and Dispersion of the Armenian People, 1915–1923).* Cambridge, Mass., 1980.

Hurewitz, J.C. *Diplomacy in the Near and Middle East, A Documentary Record; 1535–1914*, vol. 1. Princeton, New Jersey, 1956.

The Imperial Ottoman Penal Code. J. Bucknill and H. Utidjian trans. Oxford, 1913.

Ismail, K.B., *The Memoirs of Ismail Kemal Bey.* S. Story, ed. London, 1920.

International Law: A Contemporary Perspective. R. Falk, F. Kratochwil, and S. Mendlowitz, eds. Boulder, Colorado, 1985.

Jäckh, E. *The Rising Crescent.* New York, 1944.

Jackson, R. *The Nürnberg Case as Presented by Robert H. Jackson, Chief of Counsel for the United States. Together with Other Documents*. New York, 1971.

Karpat, K. *Ottoman Population 1830–1914*. Madison, WI, 1985.

Kazemzadeh, F. *The Struggle for Transcaucasia (1917–1922)*. New York, 1951.

Kinross, Lord. *The Ottoman Centuries*. New York, 1977.

Kuper, L. *Genocide: Its Political Use in the Twentieth Century*. New Haven, Conn., 1981.

_____. *The Prevention of Genocide*. New Haven, Connecticut, 1985.

Langer, W. *The Diplomacy of Imperialism 1890–1902*, vol. 1. New York, 1935.

Lauterpacht, H. *The Grotian Tradition in International Law: A Contemporary Perspective*. R. Falk, F. Kratochwil, and S. Mendlowitz, eds. 1985.

League of Nations, Permanent Court of International Justice, Advisory Committee of Jurists. *Procés-Verbaux of the Proceedings of the Committee, June 16–July 24*. Geneva, 1920.

MacColl, M. *The Sultan and the Powers*. London, 1896.

Marriott, J. *The Eastern Question* (An Historical Study in European Diplomacy), 4th ed. Reprinted. Glasgow, 1958.

Maurois, A. *Disraeli*. H. Miles, trans. Chautauqua, N.Y., 1930.

Mears, E.G. *Modern Turkey: A Politico-Economic Interpretation 1908–1923 Inclusive*. New York, 1924.

Melson, R. *Revolution and Genocide. On the Origins of the Armenian Genocide and the Holocaust*. Chicago, 1992.

Midhat, A.H. *The Life of Midhat Pasha*. London, 1903.

Morgenthau, H. *Ambassador Morgenthau's Story*. New York, 1918.

Morley, J. *The Life of Gladstone*, vol. 1. New York, 1909.

Mullins, C. *The Leipzig Trials*. New York, 1921.

Nalbandian, L. *The Armenian Revolutionary Movement*. Berkeley, 1963.

Nansen, F. *Armenia and the Near East*. London, 1928. Reprinted, New York, 1976.

Nassibian, A. *Britain and the Armenian Question 1915–1923*. London, 1984.

n.a. *The Near East From Within*. New York, n. d. (probably winter 1914–15).

An Old Indian, *Historical Sketch of Armenia and the Armenians* (With Special Reference to the Present Crisis). London, 1896.

Oppenheim, L. *International Law*, vol. 2. H. Lauterpacht, ed. 7th ed. London, 1952.

Oppenheim-Lauterpacht, *International Law*. 7th ed. London, 1948.

Paneth, P. *Turkey. Decadence and Rebirth*. London, 1943.

Parliamentary Debates. *Armenia*. A. Raffi, ed. London, 1918.

Pears, Sir E. *Forty Years in Constantinople. The Recollections of Sir Edwin Pears 1873–1915*. New York, 1916.

The Permanent Peoples Tribunal. *A Crime of Silence*. London, 1985.

Ramsaur, E.E. *The Young Turks. Prelude to the Revolution of 1908* Beirut, 1965.

Ramsay, W.M. *Impressions of Turkey During Twelve Years' Wanderings*. New York, 1897.

Rawlinson, A. *Adventures in the Near East 1918–1922*. London, 1923.

Read, J.M. *Atrocity Propaganda 1914–1919*. New Haven, Conn., 1941.

Reitlinger, G. *The SS. Alibi of a Nation. 1922–1945*. New York, 1957.

von Rintelen, Captain. *The Dark Invader. Wartime Reminiscences of a German Naval Intelligence Officer*. New York, 1933.

Rolin-Jaequemeyns, M.G. *Armenia, The Armenians, and the Treaties*. London, 1891.

Ryan, Sir A. *The Last of the Dragomans*. London, 1951.

Sachar, H.M. *The Emergence of the Middle East, 1914–1924* New York, 1969.

Sahakian, R. and E. Sarkisian. *Vital Issues in Modern Armenian History*. E. Cherakian, trans. Watertown, MA, 1965.

Salt, Jeremy. *Imperialism, Evangelism and the Ottoman Armenians 1878–1896*. London, 1993.

von Sanders, L. *Five Years in Turkey*. Annapolis, Maryland, 1927.

Sarkissian, A.O. *History of the Armenian Question to 1885*, reprint, Urbana, IL, 1938, *University of Illinois Bulletin*, vol. xxxv. 1938.

Sarkisian, E.E. and R.G. Sahakian. *Vital Issues in Modern Armenian History*. E. Chrakian, trans. Watertown, MA, 1965.

Scott, J. *Cases on International Law*, 2nd ed. St. Paul, Minn., 1922.

Seymour, C. *The Diplomatic Background of the War 1870–1914*. New Haven, Connecticut, 1927.

Shaw, S. and E.K. Shaw *History of the Ottoman Empire and Modern Turkey*, vol. 2. Cambridge, England, 1977.

Shriner, G.A. *From Berlin to Bagdad*. New York, 1918.

Sohn, L.B. and T. Buergenthal. *International Protection of Human Rights*. New York, 1973.

Sonyel, Dr. Salahi, *Displacement of the Armenians*. Documents (pamphlet in English, French and Turkish) Ankara, 1978.

Sontag, R. *European Diplomatic History 1871–1932*. New York, 1933.

Speech Delivered by Mustafa Kemal Ataturk 1927. Istanbul, 1963.

Staub, E. *The Roots of Evil. The Origins of Genocide and Other Group Violence*. Cambridge, 1989.

Stoddard, P. *The Ottoman Government and the Arabs, 1911 to 1918: A Preliminary Study of the Teşkilatı-Mahsusa* (Special Organization). Univ. Microfilms. Ann Arbor, Mich., 1963.

Stürmer, H. *Two Years in Constantinople*. E. Allen, trans. New York, 1917.

Tirpitz, A. *My Memoirs*, vol. 2. New York, 1919.

Toriguian, S. *The Armenian Question and International Law*, 2nd ed. La Verne, Calif., 1988.

Toynbee, A. *Armenian Atrocities. The Murder of a Nation*. London, 1915.

————. *The Western Question in Greece and Turkey* Boston, 1922.

————. *Experiences*. Oxford, 1969.

Trumpener, U. *Germany and the Ottoman Empire 1914–1918*. Princeton, 1968.

The United Nations War Crimes Commission. *History of the United Nations War Crimes Commission and the Development of the Laws of War*. London, 1948.

Ussher, C. *An American Physician in Turkey*. Boston, 1917.

Walker, C. *Armenia. The Survival of a Nation*. New York, 1980; 2nd, rev. ed. 1990.

Watt, M. *Islam and the Integration of Society*. Evanston, Illinois, 1961.

Weber, F.G. *Eagles on the Crescent*. Ithaca, NY, 1970.

Williams, T. *Turkey. A World Problem of Today*. Garden City, N.Y., 1921.

Willis, J.F. *Prologue to Nuremberg. The Politics and Diplomacy of Punishing War Criminals of the First World War*. Westport, Conn., 1982.

Yale, W. *The Near East. A Modern History*. New and rev. Ann Arbor, Michigan, 1968.

Yalman, A.E. *The Development in Modern Turkey as Measured by the Press*. New York, 1914.

————. *Turkey in my Time*. Norman, Okla., 1956.

————. *Turkey in the World War*. New Haven, Connecticut, 1930.

Zapantis, A.L. *Greek-Soviet Relations, 1917–1941*. Boulder, CO, 1982.

Zarevand, *United and Independent Turania. Aims and Designs of the Turks*. V.N. Dadrian trans. Leiden, 1971.

Zenkovsky, S. *Pan-Turkism and Islam in Russia*. Cambridge, Mass., 1967.

Zürcher, E. *The Unionist Factor*. Leiden, 1984.

German

Alp, T. *Türkismus und Pantürkismus*. Weimar, 1915.

Baronigian, A.S. *Blicke ins Märtyrerland*. Lössnitzgrund i. Sachsen, 1921.

Bihl, W. *Die Kaukasus-Politik der Mittelmächte*. Part I. Vienna, 1975.

Bismarck. *Denkwürdigkeiten* (Memoirs). P. Liman, ed. (Culled from his letters, speeches, and personal recollections) Berlin, 1899.

————. *Anhang zu den Gedanken und Erinnerungen*. Stuttgart, 1901.

von Bülow, F.B. *Denkwürdigkeiten*, vol. 2. Berlin, 1930.

Das Staatsarchiv. *Sammlung der Officiellen Actenstücke*, vols. 30 and 32 (1874). Kremer-Aunrode and Hirsch, eds. Leipzig, 1877.

Die Grosse Politik der Europäischen Kabinette 1871–1914, vol. 9, Der Nahe Osten; vol. 10, Das Türkische Problem 1895. J. Lepsius, A.M. Bartholdy, F. Thimme, eds., 3rd ed. Berlin, 1927.

Esad Bey, *Die Verschwörung Gegen die Welt*. Berlin, 1932.

Eyck, E. *Das persönliche Regiment Wilhelms II: Politische Geschichte des deutschen Kaiserreiches von 1890 bis 1914. Zürich,* 1948.

Fischer, F. *Griff nach der Weltmacht.* Düsseldorf, 1967.

Giesl, W. *Zwei Jahrzehnte im Nahen Orient* (Two Decades in the Near East. The Notes of General Of Cavalry). Major-General R. V. Steinitz ed. Berlin, 1927.

von der Goltz, C.F. *Denkwürdigkeiten* (Memoirs). Friedrich v. d. Goltz, W. Foerster eds. Berlin, 1929.

Guttmann, B. *Schattenriss einer Generation* (The Silhouette of a Generation). Stuttgart, 1950.

Herzl, T. *Tagebücher 1895–1904,* 3 vols.; vol. 1. Berlin, 1922, vols. 2 and 3, 1923.

von Hindenburg, P. 1934. *Aus Meinem Leben.* Leipzig, 1934.

Hohenlohe-Schillingshurst, C. *Denkwürdigkeiten der Reichskanzlerzeit* (Memoirs from the Time of Service as Chancellor). Stuttgart, 1931.

Institut für Armenische Fragen. *The Armenian Genocide. Documentation,* vol. I. Munich, 1987; vol. II. 1988.

Jäckel, E. and Axel Kuhn, eds. *Hitler. Sämtliche Aufzeichnungen 1905–1924.* Stuttgart, 1980.

Jäckh, E. *Der Aufsteigende Halbmond,* 6th ed. Berlin, 1916.

———. *Der Goldene Pflug* (The Golden Ploughshare). Stuttgart, 1954.

von Kampen, W. *Studien zur Deutschen Türkeipolitik in der Zeit Wilhelms II* (Studies on Germany's Policy on Turkey in William II's Time). (doctoral thesis at the University of Kiel), 1968.

von Kühlmann, R. *Erinnerungen* (Memoirs). Heidelberg, 1948.

Künzler, Jacob. *Im Lande des Blutes und der Tränen. Erlebnisse in Mesopotamien während des Krieges.* Potsdam-Berlin, 1921.

Lepsius, J. *Armenien und Europa.* Berlin-Westend, 1897.

———. *Deutschland und Armenien 1914–1918.* Berlin-Potsdam, 1919.

———. *Der Todesgang des Armenischen Volkes.* Berlin-Potsdam, 1930.

Leverkuehn, P. *Posten auf Ewiger Wache. Aus dem abenteuerreichen Leben des Max von Scheubner-Richter.* Essen, 1938.

Lichtheim, R. *Rückkehr. Lebenserinnerungen aus der Frühzeit des deutschen Zionismus.* Stuttgart, 1970.

Ludendorf, E. *Urkunden der Obersten Heeresleitung über ihre Tätigkeit. 1916–18* (Documents of the High Command on its Activities 1916–18). Berlin, 1922.

Ludwig, E. *Wilhelm der Zweite.* Berlin, 1926.

Marquart, J. *Die Entstehung und Wiederherstellung der armenischen Nation.* Berlin-Schöneberg, 1919.

Meier-Welcker, H. *Seeckt.* Frankfurt am Main, 1967.

Meyer, Karl. *Armenien und die Schweiz.* Bern, 1974.

Muhtar Pascha, Mahmud. *Meine Führung im Balkankrieg 1912.* 5th ed. Imhoff Pascha trans. Berlin, 1913.

Mühlmann, C. *Das Deutsch-Türkische Waffenbündnis im Weltkriege.* Leipzig, 1940.

Mühsam, Kurt. *Wie Wir Belogen Wurden.* Munich, 1918.

von Müller, G. A. *Der Kaiser ... Aufzeichnungen des Chefs des Marinekabinetts Admiral G. A. V. Müller über die Ära Wilhelms II.* (Navy Cabinet Chef Admiral Müllers Notes on William II's Era of Rule) W. Görlitz ed. Göttingen, 1965.

Nadolny, R. *Mein Beitrag.* Wiesbaden, 1955.

Naumann, F. *Asia.* Berlin-Schoneberg, 1911.

von Papen, Franz. *Der Wahrheit eine Gasse.* Munich, 1952.

Picker, H. *Hitler's Tischgespräche im Führerhauptquartier,* 3rd. ed. Stuttgart, 1977.

Pomiankowski, J. *Der Zusammenbruch des Ottomanischen Reiches.* Original Edition 1928, Vienna. Reprint, Graz, 1969.

Rathmann, L. *Stossrichtung des deutschen Imperialismus im ersten Weltkrieg.* Berlin, 1963.

von Sanders, L. *Fünf Jahre in der Türkei.* Berlin, 1920.

Saupp, N. *Das Deutsche Reich und die Armenische Frage* (The German Empire and the Armenian Question). Cologne or Köln, (doctoral thesis at the University of Köln), 1990.

Schäfer, R. *Persönliche Erinnerungen an Johannes Lepsius.* Berlin-Potsdam, 1935.

Schraudenbach, L. *Muharebe.* (War) Berlin, 1924.

Solf, W. *Gegen die Unvernunft. Der Briefwechsel zwrischen Paul Graf Wolff Metternich und Wilhelm Solf 1915–1918.* E. von Vietsch, ed. Bremen, 1964.

Stürmer, H. *Zwei Kriegsjahre in Konstantinopel. Skizzen Deutsch-Jungtürkischer Moral in Politik.* Lausanne, Switzerland, 1917.

von Tirpitz, A. *Erinnerungen* (Memoirs). Leipzig, 1919.

Wallach, J. L. *Anatomie einer Militärhilfe. Die preussisch-deutschen Militärmissionen in der Türkei 1835-1919.* Düsseldorf, 1976.

von Waldersee, A.G. *Denkwürdigkeiten* (Memoirs), vol. 1. H.O. Meisner, ed. Stuttgart, 1923.

Zeki, M. *Raubmörder als Gäste der deutschen Republik.* Berlin, 1920.

Ziemke, K. *Die Neue Türkei 1914–1929.* Stuttgart, 1930.

Zurlinden, S. *Der Weltkrieg,* vol. 2. Zürich, Switzerland, 1918.

French

Baghdjian, K. *La Confiscation par le Gourvernement Turc des Biens Arméniens ... Dits "Abandonnés."* Montreal, 1987.

Bérard, V. *La politique du Sultan* (Paris, 1897)

_____. *La Mort de Istamboul.* Paris, 1913.

Beylerian, A. *Les Grandes Puissances, L'Empire Ottoman, et les Arméniens dans les Archives Françaises 1914–1918.* Paris, 1983.

Biliotti, A. and A. Sedad. *Legislation Ottoman Depuis la Rétablissement de la Constitution,* vol. 1. Paris, 1912.

Cambon, P. *Correspondance 1870–1924,* vol. I. (1870–1898) Paris, 1940.

Choublier, M. *La Question D'Orient depuis le Traité de Berlin,* 2nd ed. Paris, 1889.

Comité Central des Refugiés Arméniens. (M.M. Gidel, A. de LaPradelle, L. Le Fur). *Confiscation des biens des refugiés Armeniéns par le gouvernement Turc.* Paris, 1929.

Destrilhes, M. *Confidences sur la Turquie.* Paris, 1855.

Documents Diplomatiques Français 1871–1900. Paris, 1951.

Doumergue, E. *L'Arménie, les Massacres et la Question D'Orient.* Paris, 1916.

Engelhardt, E. *La Turquie et le Tanzimat ou histoire des réformes dans L'Empire Ottoman,* vols. I. 1882 and II. Paris, 1884.

French Foreign Ministry Archives. Nouvelle Série. Turquie, Politique Interieure, Jeunes Turcs, Paris. vols. 7 and 8.

de la Jonquière, Le Vte. *Histoire de l'Empire Ottoman depuis les origines jusqu'a nos jours,* vol. II. new, enl. ed. Paris, 1914.

Karal, E.Z., *La Question Arménienne (1878–1923).* K. Dorsan, trans. Ankara, 1984.

C. H. Lebeau, *Essai sur la justice en Turquie* (á propos du Traité de Lausanne) Paris, 1924.

Livre Jaune. Affaires Arméniens, Projets de Réformes dans L'Empire Ottoman 1893–1897. Paris, 1897.

Mandelstam, A. *La Société des Nations et les Puissances devant le Problème Arménien.* Paris, 1926.

_____. *Le Sort de L'Empire Ottomane.* Lausanne, 1917.

Mantram, R., ed. *Histoire de l'Empire Ottoman.* Paris, 1989.

Morgan, J. *Contre les barbares de l'Orient.* Paris, 1918.

Nicol, E. *Angora et la France.* Paris, 1922.

Nolde, B. *L'Alliance franco-russe.* Paris, 1936.

Noradounghian, G. *Recueil D'Actes Internationaux de L'Empire Ottoman,* vol. 2, 1789–1856. Paris, 1900; vol. 3, 1856–1878. 1902.

Özkaya, I.C. *Le Peuple Arménien et les Tentatives de Rendre en Servitude le Peuple Turc* (The Armenian People and the Attempts to Subjugate the Turkish People.) Istanbul, 1971.

Pech, E. *Les Alliés et la Turquie.* Paris, 1925.

Pinon, R. *La Suppression des Arméniens. Méthode allemande-travail turc.* Paris, 1916.

Pflanzer, A. *Le Crime de Génocide.* St. Gallen, Switzerland, 1956.

Renouvin, P., E. Preclin, G. Hardy, *L'Epoque contemporaine.* La paix armée et la Grande Guerre (1871–1919), 2nd ed. Paris, 1947.

Schopoff, A. *Les réformes et la protection des Chrétiens en Turquie 1673–1904.* Paris, 1904.
Ternon, Y. *Enquête sur la négation d'un génocide.* Marseille, France, 1989.
_____. *Les Arméniens, histoire d'un génocide.* Paris, 1977
Vandal, A. *Les Arméniens et la Réforme de la Turquie.* Paris, 1897.
Young, G. *Corps de Droit Ottoman. Code de Procédure Pénale,* vol. 7. Oxford, 1906.

Armenian

Aghassi. (Garabed Tour-Sarkissian). *Zeitoun yev eer Shurtchanakneru* (Zeitoun and its Environs). Paris, 1968.
Andonian, A. *Untartzag Badmoutiun Balkanian Baderazmeen.* (Comprehensive History of the Balkan War), vol.3. Istanbul, 1912.
ARF. *Houshabadoum Hai Heghapokhagan Dashnaktzoutian* (Commemorative Tome of the Armenian Revolutionary Federation. 1890–1950). Boston, 1950.
Badmoutiun Haigagan Bondosee (History of the Armenian Pontus). H. Hovagimian ed. Beirut, 1967.
Balakian, Rev. K. *Hai Koghkotan. Trouakner Hai Mardirosakroutiunen. Berlinen Tebee Zor 1914–1920* (The Armenian Golgotha. Episodes from the Armenian Martyrilogy. From Berlin to Zor 1914–1920), vol. 1. Vienna, 1922.
Haigagan SSR Bedagan Gentronagan Badmagan Archiv (Armenian SSR Historical Archives).
Hoktemperian Sotzialisdagan Medz Revolutzian Yev Sovetagan Ishkhanoutian Haghtanagu Haiasdanum (The Great Socialist October Revolution and the Victory of the Soviet Regime in Armenia). Yerevan, 1960.
Houshartzan Abril Dasnumegi (In Memoriam of April 24, 1915). Istanbul, 1919.
Kapigian, G. *Yegernabadoum* (The Chronicle of the Genocide ... in Sivas). Boston, 1924.
Karo, A. *Abruadz Orer* (Lived Days). Boston, 1948.
Lazian, K. *Haiasdan yev Hai Tadu usd Tashnakirneru* (Armenia and the Armenian Question According to Treaties). Cairo, 1942.
Leo (Arakel Babakhanian). *Turkahai Heghopokhutian Kaghaparapanoutiunu* (The Ideology of the Revolution of Turkish Armenian), vol. 1. Paris, 1934.
Magountz, G. *Trabezonee Hayotz Deghahanoutinu* (The Deportation of the Armenians of Trabizon). H. Gosoyian, ed. Teheran, 1963.
Merdjanof, K., *Eem Gudagu* (My Testament). Beirut, 1972.
Mozian, L. *Aksoraganee mu Votisaganu: Sev Orerou Hishadagner* (An Exile's Odyssey: Memories of Dark Days). Boston, 1958.
Mugurditchian, T. *Deekranagerdi Nahankin Tcharteru Yev Kiurderou Kazanioutounneru* (The Massacres in Diyarbekir Province and the Savageries of the Kurds). Cairo, 1919.
Papazian, V. *Eem Housherus* (My Memoirs), vol. 2. Beirut, 1952.
Teotig, ed. *Amenoun Daretzouytzu* (Everyone's Almanac), vols. 10–14, 1916–1920. Istanbul, 1921.
Varantian, M. *Hai Heghapokhagan Dashnakzoutian Badmoutiun* (History of the Armenian Revolutionary Federation), vol. 1. Paris, 1932.
Vartan, L. *Haigagan Dasnihunku Yev Hayeru Lukial Kouykeru* (The Armenian Fifteen [Referring to the 1915 Genocide] and the Abandoned Goods of the Armenians). Beirut, Lebanon, 1970.
Yegarian, A. *Housher* (Memoirs). H. Adjemian, ed. Cairo, 1947.
Yeramian, H. *Houshartzan Van-Vaspourakanee* (Memorial for Van-Vaspourakan), vol. 1. Alexandria, Egypt, 1929.
Zaven Arkyebiskobos. *Badriarkagan Houserus. Vaverakirner yev Vugayoutiunner* (Patriarch Zaven's Memoirs. Documents and Testimonies), vol. 1. Cairo, 1947.

ARTICLES

Turkish

Balkan, F. "Beş Albaylar" (Five Colonels). *Yakın Tarihimiz* 2 (1962).
Birinci, I. "Cemiyet ve Çeteler" (Ittihad party and the Brigands), *Hayat* 2 (October 1, 1971).
Birgen, M. "Bizimkiler ve Azerbaycan" *Yakın Tarihimiz* 2 (1962): 158.

Ilgar, I. "Bir Asır Boyunca Ermeni Meselesi. Karabekir Paşanın Bulduğu Çare" (The Armenian Problem Throughout a Century. Karabekir Paşa's Remedy), *Hayat ve Tarih Mecmuası* 11, 2 (October 1, 1975).

_____. "Ermeni Meselesi," *Hayat ve Tarih Mecmuası* 11, 2 (November 1, 1975).

Kuran, E. "Yusuf Akçuranın Tarihçiliği" (The Historicism of Yusuf Akçura), in the Proceedings of the Symposium on the 50th anniversary of Akçura's death *(Ölümünün Ellinci Yılında Yusuf Akçura Sempozyumu Tebliğleri)* Ankara, 1987.

Sertoğlu, M. "Türkiyede Ermeni Meselesi" (The Armenian Question in Turkey), *Belgelerle Türk Tarih Dergisi* 2 (November, 1967).

Silan, Neameddin Sahir "Ikinci Meşrutiyette Divanı Ali Hareketleri" (High Court Actions during the Second Constitution Era) *Tarih Konuşuyor.* 2nd installment 5, 29 (June 1966).

English

Ahmad, F. "Unionist Relations with the Greek, Armenian and Jewish Communities of the Ottoman Empire, 1908–1914." In *Christians and Jews in the Ottoman Empire*, vol. 1. B. Braude and B. Lewis, eds. New York, 1982.

Alexander, L. "War Crimes and Their Motivation. The Social Psychological Structure of the SS and the Criminalization of Society," *Journal of Criminal Law, Criminology and Police Science*, XXXIX (September-October 1948).

Attrap, A. "'A State of Wretchedness and Impotence': A British View of Istanbul and Turkey, 1919." *International Journal of Middle East Studies* 9 (1978).

Bassiouni, M.C. "International Law and the Holocaust." *California Western International Law Journal* 9 (1979).

Bazyler, "Reexamining the Doctrine of Humanitarian Intervention in Light of the Atrocities in Kampuchea and Ethiopia." *Stanford Journal of International Law* (1987).

Bosworth, C.E. "The Concept of Dhimma in Early Islam." In *Christians and Jews in the Ottoman Empire*, vol. 1. B. Braude and B. Lewis, eds. New York, 1982.

Brierly, J.L. "The Rule of Law in the International Society." *Nordisk Tidskrift for International Ret, Acta Scandinavica Juris Gentium* 7 (1936).

Brown, P.H. "The Mandate Over Armenia." *American Journal of International Law* 14 (1920).

n.a. "The Constantinople Massacre," *Contemporary Review* 70 (October 1896).

Dadrian, V.N. "The Anticipation and Prevention of Genocide in International Conflicts." *International Journal of Group Tensions* 18, 3 (1988).

_____. "The Convergent Aspects of the Armenian and Jewish Cases of Genocide. A Reinterpretation of the Concept of Holocaust." *Holocaust and Genocide Studies* 3, 2 (1988).

_____. "The Naim-Andonian Documents on the World War I Destruction of Ottoman Armenians—The Anatomy of a Genocide." *International Journal of Middle East Studies* 18, 3 (1986).

_____. "The Role of Turkish Physicians in the World War I Genocide of the Armenians." *Holocaust and Genocide Studies* 1, 2 (1986).

_____. "The Role of the Turkish Military in the Destruction of Ottoman Armenians: A Study in Historical Continuities," *Journal of Political and Military Sociology* 20 (Winter, 1992).

_____. "The Role of the Special Organization in the Armenian Genocide during the First World War" in *Minorities in Wartime*, P. Panayi, ed. Oxford, 1993.

_____. "The Secret Young-Turk Ittihadist Conference and the Decision for the World War I Genocide of the Armenians," *Holocaust and Genocide Studies* 7, 2 (Fall, 1993).

_____. "Documentation of the Armenian Genocide in German and Austrian Sources" in *The Widening Circle of Genocide* I. Charny, ed. New Brunswick, N.J., 1994.

_____. *The Armenian Genocide in Official Turkish Sources*. Collected Essays. Special Issue of *Journal of Political and Military Sociology*, Roger Smith, guest ed., vol. 22, 1 (Summer, 1994).

Davison, R. "The Armenian Crisis, 1912–1914." *American Historical Review* 53, 3 (1948).

_____. "Turkish Attitudes Concerning Christian-Muslim Equality in the Nineteenth Century." *American Historical Review* 59 (1954).

Des Pres, T. "Introduction, Remembering Armenia." In *The Armenian Genocide in Perspective*. R. Hovanissian, ed. New Brunswick, New Jersey, 1987.

_____. "The Governing Narratives: The Turkish Armenian Case." *The Yale Review* 75 (1987).

Dewey, J. "The Turkish Tragedy." *The New Republic* 49 (November 12, 1928).

DeZayas, "International Law and Mass Population Transfers." *Harvard International Law Journal* 16 (1975).

Dillon, E.J. "The Condition of Armenia," *Contemporary Review* LXVIII (1895).

Dinkel, C. "German Officers and the Armenian Genocide," *Armenian Review* 44, 1/173 (Spring, 1991).

Douglas, R. "Britain and the Armenian Question 1894–7," *The Historical Journal* 19, 1 (1976).

van der Dussen, W.J. "The Westenenk File. The Question of Armenian Reforms in 1913–1914," *Armenian Review* 39, 1 (Spring, 1986).

Einstein, L. "The Armenian Massacres," *Contemporary Review* 616 (April, 1917).

Falk, R. "Responding to Severe Violations." In *Enhancing Global Human Rights*, 207–57, J. Dominguez, R. Falk, N. Rodley, and B. Wood, eds. (1979).

Finch, G.A. "The Genocide Convention." *American Journal of International Law* 43 (1949).

Franck, T.M. and N.S. Rodley. "After Bangladesh: The Law of Humanitarian Intervention by Military Force." *American Journal of International Law* 67 (1973).

Herbert, A. "Talât Pasha," *Blackwood's Magazine* CCXIII (April, 1923).

Heywood, C. "Boundless Dreams of the Levant: Paul Wittek, the George-Kreis, and the Writing of Ottoman History," *Journal of the Royal Asiatic Society*, 1 (1989).

Housepian, M. "The Unremembered Genocide." *Commentary* 42, 3 (September, 1966).

Hovannisian, R. "The Armenian Question in the Ottoman Empire." *East European Quarterly* 6, 1 (1972).

Howard, W.W. "Horrors of Armenia," *Armenian Review* XVIII, 4 (Winter, 1965).

Hughes, C.E. "Recent Questions and Negotiations." *American Journal of International Law* 18 (1924).

Ismail Kemal Bey, "Armenia and the Armenians," *Fortnightly Review* DCX, New Series (October 1, 1917).

Jacoby, A. "Genocide." *Schweizerische Zeitschrift für Strafrecht* (Revue Pénale Suisse) 4 (1949).

Karpat, K.H. "The Transformation of the Ottoman State, 1789–1908," *International Journal of Middle East Studies* 3 (1972).

Kazarian, H. "How Turkey Prepared the Ground for Massacre." *Armenian Review* 18, 4–72 (Winter 1965).

Kuhn, A.K. "The Genocide Convention and State Rights." *American Journal of International Law* 43 (1948).

Kunz, J.L. "The United Nations Convention on Genocide." *American Journal of International Law* 43 (1948).

Kuper, L. "The Turkish Genocide of Armenians, 1915–1917." In *The Armenian Genocide in Perspective*, 43–59, R. Hovanissian, ed. New Brunswick, New Jersey, (1987).

Le Blanc, L. "The United Nations Genocide Convention and Political Groups: Should the United States Propose an Amendment." *Yale Journal of International Law* 13, 2 (Summer, 1988).

Lemkin, R. "Genocide: A New International Crime, Punishment and Prevention." *Revue Internationale de Droit Pénal* 10 (1946).

_____. "Genocide as a Crime Under International Law." *American Journal of International Law* 41 (1947).

Mardin, Ş.A. "Ideology and Religion in the Turkish Revolution." *International Journal of Middle East Studies* 2 (1971).

Matas, D. "Prosecuting Crimes Against Humanity: The Lessons of World War I." *Fordham International Law Journal*, 13, 86 (1989–1990).

Melson, R. "A Theoretical Inquiry Into the Armenian Massacres of 1894–1896." *Comparative Studies in Society and History*, 24, 3 (July 1982).

————. "Provocation or Nationalism: A Critical Inquiry Into The Armenian Genocide of 1915." In *The Armenian Genocide in Perspective*, 61–84 (R. Hovanissian, ed. New Brunswick, NJ, 1986).

Milton, S. "Armin T. Wegner: Polemicist for Armenian and Jewish Human Rights," *Armenian Review* 42, 4 (Winter 1989).

Morgenthau, H. "The Greatest Horror in History." *Red Cross Magazine* (March, 1918).

Nazarbek, A. "Zeitoun," *The Contemporary Review* LXIX, 364 (April, 1896).

Pears, Sir E. "Turkey, Islam and Turanianism." *Contemporary Review* 14 (October, 1918).

Perry, D.M. "The Macedonian Revolutionary Organization's Armenian Connection," *Armenian Review* 42, 1/165 (Spring, 1989).

Peterson, T. "Turkey and the Armenian Crisis." *Catholic World* 61, 43 (1895).

Reid, J. "The Concept of War and Genocidal Impulses in the Ottoman Empire." *Holocaust and Genocide Studies* 4 (1989).

————. "Total War, the Annihilation Ethic, and the Armenian Genocide, 1870–1918." In *The Armenian Genocide: History, Politics, Ethics*, 21–52, R. Hovannisian, ed. (New York, 1992).

Schwelb, E. "Crimes Against Humanity." *The British Year Book of International Law* 23 (1946).

Sonyel, S. "Armenian Deportations: A Reappraisal in the Light of New Documents." *Belletin* (January 1972).

Toriguian, S. "Armenian Insurance Claims Arising from the 1915 Massacres." *Klatzor* (Special Issue, 1989).

Turlington, E. "The Settlement of Lausanne." *American Journal of International Law* 18 (1924).

Wiseberg, L.S. "Humanitarian Intervention, Lessons from the Nigerian Civil War." *Revue des Droits de l'Homme. Human Rights Journal* 70, 1 (1974).

Wright, L. "Crimes Under International Law." *Law Quarterly Review* 62 (1946).

Wright, Q. "The Legal Liability of the Kaiser." *American Political Science Review* 13 (1919).

German

Baumgart, W. "Zur Ansprache Hitler's vor den Führern der Wehrmacht Am 22. August 1939. Eine quellenkritische Untersuchung," *Vierteljahreshefte für Zeitgeschichte* 12, 2 1968.

von der Goltz, "Stärke und Schwäche des türkischen Reiches" (The Strength and Weakness of the Turkish Empire) *Deutsche Rundschau* XXIV, (October 1, 1897).

Harden, M. "Zwischen Ost und West. Armenien in Moabit," *Die Zukunft*, 29, 37 (June 11, 1921).

Haupt, W. "Deutsche unter dem Halbmond," *Deutsches Soldatenjahrbuch* (1967).

Jäschke, G. "Beiträge zur Geschichte des Kampfes der Türkei um ihre Unabhängigkeit." *N.S. Die Welt des Islams* 5 (1958).

————. "Die Entwicklung des osmanischen Verfassungsstaates von den Anfängen bis zur Gegenwart." *Die Welt des Islams* 5, 1–2 (1917).

————. "Das Osmanische Reich vom Berlinger Kongress bis zu seinem Ende (1878–1920/22)." In *Handbuch der Europäischen Geschichte*, (1968).

Kraelitz-Greifenhorst, F. "Die Ungültigkeitserklärung des Pariser und Berliner Vertrages durch die osmanische Regierung." *Österreichische Monatsschrift für den Orient* 43 (1917).

Mandelstam, A. "Das armenische Problem im Lichte des Völker-und Menschenrechts." *Institut für Internationales Recht an der Universität Kiel* [lecture series and monographs] 12 (1931).

Mühlmann, C. "Deutschland und die Türkei 1913–1914." *Politische Wissenschaft* 7 (1929).

Paraquin, E. "Politik im Orient," *Berliner Tageblatt* (January 24, 28, 1920 installments). A synopsis of the series is filed in the German Foreign Ministry Archives. A.A. Türkei 158/24, A1373.

Stillschweig, K. "Das Abkommen zur Bekämpfung von Genocide." *Die Friedenswarte für Zwischenstaatliche Organisation* 3 (1949).

Werner, E. "Ökonomishce und Militärische Aspekte der Türkei-Politik Österreich-Ungarns 1915 bis 1918," *Jahrbuch für Geschichte* 10 (1974).

French

Hanotaux, G. "En Orient," *Revue de Paris* 6 (December 1, 1895).

Mandelstam, A. "La Société des Nations et les puissances devant le problème arménien."

Revue Générale de Droit International Public 29, 5 (September–October 1922): 301–84; 29, 6 (November–December 1922): 515–46; 30, 5 (September–October 1923): 414–506; 31, 6 (New Series) (1924).

Panzac, D. "L'enjeu du nombre. La population de la Turquie de 1914 à 1927." *Revue du Monde Musulman de la Méditarranée* 50, 4 (1988).

Pinon, R. "La liquidation de l'Empire Ottoman." *Revue des Deux Mondes* 53 (September 1919).

_____. "L'Offensive de l'Asie" *Revue des deux Mondes* (April 15, 1920).

Quillard, P. "Pour l'Arménie," *Memoire et Dossier* (19th issue of the series) (Paris, 1902).

Rio, C. "Étude sur l'article 175 du code pénal mexicain 'genocide.'" *Études Internationales de Psycho-Sociologie Criminelle* 16–17 (1969).

Armenian

Hayrabedian, H. "Hadoutzoum" (Settling Scores). *Sovetakan Haiasdan* 8 (1984).

Hovannissian, R. "Vanee 1896 Tuwee Eenknabashdbanoutiunu" (The Self-Defense of Van in 1896), *Lraper* (July, 1976).

"Kegham Der Garabedianee Vugayatounu" (The Testimony of K. D. G.). In *Badmoutiun Daronee Achkharee* (History of Daron), 838–54, G. Sassouni, ed. (1957).

Khoren S. "Hishoghutiunner" (Memories), In Teotig, *Amenoun Daretzouytzu* (Everyone's Almanac), 10–14: 132–36. (1916–1920).

Mugurditchian, H. "Kaghdniknerou Gudzigu" (The Thread of the Secrets), *Hairenik* (an Armenian daily published by the author during the Armistice for a very short period in Istanbul). Installments Nos. 1 and 2 (October 28/November 10; October 30/November 12, 1918).

Sirounee, H. "Yegern mu yev eer Badmutyunu" (A Genocide and its History). *Etchmiadzin* (February-March-April joint issue 1965).

Yayloian, A. "Medz Deroutiunneri Goğme Moratzuadz Jhogovourt" (A People Forsaken by the Great Powers). *Sovetakan Haiasdan*. 4 (1987).

NEWSPAPERS (mostly from Constantinople-Istanbul. 1908–1920 Period).

Turkish:
Alemdar; Cumhuriyet; Dünya; Hadisat; Hayat; Hürriyet; Minber; Sabah; Tanin; Tasviri Efkâr; Vakit

Armenian
Azadamard (Ariamard); Hairenik (Armistice Daily, Istanbul); Nayiri; Zhamanag

French
Le Courrier de Turquie; L'Entente; L'Epoque; Le Journal d'Orient; Renaissance; Spectateur d'Orient

German
Berliner Tageblatt; Die Zeit; Frankfurter Allgemeine Zeitung; Kölnische Zeitung

Russian
Bakinski Rabotichi

American
Boston Globe; New York Times and its weekly reviews: Current History

Great Britain
London Times

ANNOTATED BIBLIOGRAPHY OF SELECTED BOOKS USED IN THIS WORK

In Turkish

Akşin, Sina, 1980: A critical examination of the ideology of Ittihad and of the conditions under which original liberalism gave way to autocracy and anti-minority oppression.

Akşin, Sina, 1983: Describes the conditions under which the Sultan's government in Istanbul grew weak in the Armistice and got embroiled in a hopeless contest with the Kemalist insurgents in Anatolia.

Atay, F.R.: The personal contacts with top Ittihadist leaders are recounted with considerable candor by the author who, as a former Ittihadist and subsequently an ardent Kemalist, had access to the inner circles of both regimes, thus able to learn some secret details about the attitudes and actions of men persecuting the Armenians.

Avcıoğlu, D.: Chronicles the phases of the Turkish War of Independence with details, some of which are revealing as far as they relate to the secret aspects of the wartime Armenian deportations culminating in genocide.

Bayur, Y.H.: A systematic approach to the conduct of the Ittihadist authorities prosecuting the war and in the process resorting to the Armenian deportations as a wartime emergency measure. Written under the auspices of the Turkish Historical Society and strictly from a Turkish point of view.

Bleda, M.: The edited memoirs of the chief administrator of the Ittihadist party explaining, justifying and excusing many of the transgressions and excesses of some of the top party leaders.

Ertürk, H.: Provides certain disclosures about the inner workings of the Special Organization and its relationship to the Central Committee of the party.

Gürün, K.: An elaborate attempt to deny any Turkish design of extermination of the Armenians, whose wartime losses are entirely attributed to the poor management of "the relocation" scheme, to Kurdish excesses and Armenian provocations through insurgency.

Karabekir, K.: A massive compilation of official documents relating to the Turkish War of Independence and to the Kemalist invasion of the Republic of Armenia in 1920.

Orel, Ş. and S. Yuca: Like the other two books by Bayur and Gürün described above, this volume is also sponsored and supported by the Turkish Historical Society, thus representing directly and indirectly official governmental stances on very controversial subjects, such as the wartime treatment of the Armenians. The two authors through this book endeavor to discredit completely another volume described to contain official Turkish documents on the authorization and implementation of the Armenian genocide, by declaring these documents "forgeries." For the refutation of these charges see Dadrian below on Naim-Andonian Documents in Articles Section in English.

Refik, A.: This is perhaps the main, if not the only, Turkish work, produced right after the war, that unequivocally admits the exterminating thrust of the wartime Armenian deportations and the premeditated and organized character of the mass murder involved. The value of this book is enhanced by the fact that the author had a military background, was assigned to Department II of the War Office where the military details of the genocide are reported to have been mapped out, and he quotes the War Ministry officials trying to concoct false accusations against the Armenians in an attempt to justify the severity of the anti-Armenian measures. A part of the book relates also the revenge acts of Armenian volunteers attached to the Causasian Russian Army, which in 1916 had captured several provinces in eastern Turkey, whose Armenian population by then had already been destroyed.

Talât Paşanın Hatıraları: A fragment of the memoirs Talât reportedly prepared while living in Berlin as a fugitive of justice, edited by others. Essentially, it is an effort of self-justification and of shifting the blame to others for the disastrous war and the excesses committed in the course of it, including the Armenian massacres.

Uras, E.: A major undertaking by a former Turkish secret service agent to trace the evolution of the Armenian Question to its historical origins, to minimize the responsibility of the Abdul Hamit regime in the outbreak of the massacres of that period and altogether

blame the Armenian revolutionaries for the misfortunes befalling the Armenian population during the reign of Abdul Hamit and subsequently during World War I.

Vardar, G.: Another piece of inside story type of narration relating to the role of Special
Organization operatives in the creation and development of Kemalist insurgency in the
1918–1920 period from cells in Istanbul, right under the nose of the Sultan's government.

Yalman, A.E., 1970: The first 2 volumes of this 4-volume memoir contain a wealth of information on the Ittihadist chiefs who, along with the author, were interned in Malta for later
trials before an international court on charges of war crimes, including Armenian massacres.

Ahmad, F.: A compact account of the trials and tribulations of the Ittihadist Young
Turks endeavoring to govern the country in the aftermath of their successful revolution
without possessing, however, the requisite experience, competence or the administrative
personnel.

In English

Genocide. A Critical Bibliographic Review. A survey by R. Hovannisian of the more important works in several languages on the Armenian genocide through brief annotations
attached to the respective bibliography.

Hovannisian, R., 1967: This study describes the overall post-genocide conditions playing
out in the formation of the independent Republic of Armenia and at the same time aggravating the latter's plight economically and politically.

Hovannisian, R., 1980: A bibliography of source materials on the Armenian genocide in
terms of archive depositories, published documentary tomes, historical studies and eyewitness accounts.

Institut für Armenische Fragen: Two volumes comprising a large body of selected documents dealing with the history of Armenian persecution and massacres in the 19th and
20th centuries. The archives of Europe, Russia, the United States and eyewitness
accounts in several languages constitute the source-bases of the two tomes.

Kuper, L., 1981: A pioneering study in the comparative aspects of the crime of genocide and
the problems of conceptualization and theory construction.

Marriott, J.: One of the best analyses of the origin, rise and the violent explosion of the
Eastern Question in the Balkans.

Morgenthau, H.: The most detailed personal account, based mostly on regular diary entries,
of the processes of decision making, organization and execution relative to the wartime
Armenian massacres, narrated by an American Ambassador to Turkey.

Nansen, F.: Exposure of the dimensions of the impact upon the fate of the surviving Armenians of the World War I Armenian genocide by a Nobel Peace Prize winning humanitarian High Commissioner of Refugees.

Permanent Peoples' Tribunal: The summary description of the proceedings of the Permanent Peoples' Tribunal investigating at Sorbonne in Paris the World War I Armenian
massacres and reaching the verdict that these massacres involved genocide. The Panel of
judges included several experts on international law and three Nobel laureates.

Shaw and Shaw: A comprehensive survey of modern Ottoman history with a strong bias for
Turkish historiographic parochialism, which bias lapses into outright misrepresentation
in the treatment of the Armenian Question, especially with regard to the series of massacres in modern times, including World War I.

Stoddard, P.: The only English language study, in a rudimentary form, of the origins of the
Special Organization and its operational program respecting the Arabs. It utilizes some
authentic Turkish sources, including interviews with one of its chief leaders.

Trumpener, U.: One of the most thorough analyses of the Armenian genocide in the light of
German state archive documents and within the framework of the wartime political and
military alliance between Germany and Turkey.

Ussher, C.: A first hand American account of the Turkish method of initiating the genocide
in the easternmost province of Van and then accusing the Armenians of provocation.

Walker, C.: A survey of modern Armenian history within the perspective of the evolving
Turko-Armenian conflict and the resulting repressive measures of Ottoman-Turkish
authorities.

In French

Domergue, E.: A contemporary French narrative of the Turkish conspiracy to liquidate the Armenian population with the tacit support of the Germans. It has a historical frame of reference.

Engelhardt, E.: One of the most authoritative treatments of the history, purpose, difficulties, successes and failures of the 19th century Tanzimat reform initiative.

Mandelstam, A., 1917: An informed contribution, by the First Dragoman of Russian Embassy, to the understanding of the wartime conditions under which the Armenians of Turkey were expelled, deported and destroyed.

Mandelstam, A., 1926: The legal examination of the many phases of the Armenian Question from the point of view of international politics and international law.

Noradounghian, G.: A comprehensive compilation of the record of official transactions of the Ottoman Empire in relation to other states in the period indicated.

Schopoff, A.: A catalog of treaties and agreements dealing with the quest for safeguards for the Christian nationalities and minorities of the Ottoman Empire.

Ternon, Y.: A critical inquiry into the Turkish patterns of denial of the Armenian genocide.

In German

Jäckh, E.: Written by a confidential operative of the German Foreign Ministry, the book contains some revealing admissions on the 1894–96 and 1909 Adana massacres which foreshadowed the World War I genocide.

Künzler, J.: A rare, first-hand, eye-witness account of the genocide being enacted in Urfa and its environs.

Lepsius, J.: An expanded version of the wartime collection by Dr. Lepsius of documentary data about the Armenian genocide.

Pomiankowski, J.: An eyewitness account of that genocide by the Austrian Military Plenipotentiary who was attached to the Ottoman Military Headquarters—General Staff.

Stürmer, H.: An eyewitness account of the genocide by the wartime correspondent of the influential German newspaper *Kölnische Zeitung*.

Zurlinden, S.: A documentary exposure by the Swiss historian of the crimes associated with the wartime deportations of the Armenians.

SUBJECT AND NAMES INDEX